Building a Solid Future

Eric Joss
Partner
Columbia Law School
Class of 1976

Paul Hastings definitely is not just a collection of offices using the same letterhead; we are truly one firm linked together by our ability to share information using the latest technologies.

Building Business Success

Paul, Hastings, Janofsky & Walker LLP

www.paulhastings.com

Atlanta • Beijing • Hong Kong • London • Los Angeles • New York
Orange County • San Francisco • Stamford • Tokyo • Washington, DC

Paul Hastings

The media's watching Vault!
Here's a sampling of our coverage.

"With admirable directness, the [Vault 100] tries to measure prestige by prestige."
— *National Law Journal*

"With reviews and profiles of firms that one associate calls 'spot on,' [Vault's] guide has become a key reference for those who want to know what it takes to get hired by a law firm and what to expect once they get there."
— *New York Law Journal*

"The well-written profiles make Vault.com the next best thing to camping out in a company rest room."
—*Yahoo! Internet Life*

"For those hoping to climb the ladder of success, [Vault's] insights are priceless."
— *Money Magazine*

"Vault.com is indispensible for locating insider information."
— *Metropolitan Corporate Counsel*

"The granddaddy of worker sites."
— *US News and World Report*

"Vault.com is another killer app for the Internet."
— *New York Times*

VAULT GUIDE TO THE
TOP 100
LAW FIRMS

VAULT GUIDE TO THE
TOP 100
LAW FIRMS

BROOK MOSHAN, J.D., MARCY LERNER, TYYA N. TURNER,
DINA DIMAIO AND VERA DJORDJEVICH

For information about permission to reproduce selections from this book, contact Vault Inc., P.O. Box 1772, New York,
New York 10011-1772, (212) 366-4212.

Library of Congress CIP Data is available.

ISBN 1-58131-163-X

Printed in the United States of America

ACKNOWLEDGEMENTS

Vault would like to take the time to acknowledge Dina DiMaio and Vera Djordjevich for their extraordinary efforts. Many thanks to Doug Cantor, Daire Coco, Hal Levey, Derek Loosvelt, Chris Prior, Clay Risen, Val Hadjiyski, Elena Rigalovskaya and Kevin Salgado. Thanks to Rob Schipano for his artistry, Ed Shen for his vision and cool head and Todd Kuhlman for designing a survey that actually works and for providing technical support. Thanks also to Mike Baker, Gerry Ferrara, Danielle Koza, Thomas Nutt, Kristy Sisko and Dan Stanco for their support.

Special thanks to all of the law firm recruiting coordinators and hiring partners who helped with this book. Your patience and good cheer in the face of tight deadlines and repeated requests for information are greatly appreciated.

Thanks also to Matt Doull, Ahmad Al-Khaled, Lee Black, Eric Ober, Hollinger Ventures, Tekbanc, New York City Investment Fund, American Lawyer Media, Globix, Hoover's, Glenn Fischer, Mark Fernandez, Ravi Mhatre, Carter Weiss, Ken Cron, Ed Somekh, Isidore Mayrock, Zahi Khouri, Sana Sabbagh and other Vault investors. Many thanks to our loving families and friends.

This book is dedicated to the over 9,500 law firm associates who took time out of their busy schedules to complete our survey. Many thanks!

Use the most **targeted** job search
tools for lawyers on the Internet.

Vault's Law Job Board and VaultMatch™ Resume Database

FOCUSED ON IP

picture losing MILLIONS over the

differences in a few PIXELS.

The technology inside this half-inch square is so advanced it takes a degree in electrical engineering to understand precisely where one patent begins and another ends. That's why the most innovative companies turn to Finnegan Henderson. With unsurpassed technical expertise, nearly 50 PhDs, outstanding trial lawyers, jury specialists, and decades of experience litigating to federal and state juries across the U.S., Finnegan Henderson can handle the most complex IP disputes. As one of the nation's most renowned litigation practices, we know that the real drama is in the details.

FINNEGAN
HENDERSON
FARABOW
GARRETT &
DUNNER LLP

Yours for the asking.

Your first job may be the most important career decision you'll ever make. Here's everything you need to know about choosing the right law firm but didn't know to ask.

To get your copy, go to www.15questions.com.
For more information, visit www.pillsburywinthrop.com.

Ask well. Choose wisely.

Shape your own future.

BEST OF THE REST   609

LEGAL EMPLOYER DIRECTORY   635

LEGAL SEARCH FIRM DIRECTORY   655

Granted, there was a bit of confusion at our first employee football match.

The law firms of Mayer, Brown & Platt of the U.S.
and Rowe & Maw of the U.K.
are now one.

MAYER
BROWN
ROWE
& MAW

INTRODUCTION

Welcome to the fifth edition of the *Vault Guide to the Top 100 Law Firms*, the most comprehensive, candid, up-to-date guide to the most prestigious law firms. Last year the guide underwent some dramatic changes, and this year we're sticking with them. In years past, we've ranked the top 50 law firms. Now we offer a ranking of 100 of the nation's top firms, complete with 100 law firm profiles incorporating quotes and opinions from thousands of associates. The guide also has law firm stats with contact and salary information, office locations, notable perks, major practice areas and more, including the ever-popular "Buzz" section, in which associates offer observations about firms other than their own.

This year, more associates than ever before participated in the Vault associate survey — over 9,500! We surveyed associates at over 100 firms and asked them to rank 126 law firms. Associates were invited to tell us what they thought of their peer law firms and were asked to score each firm based on its prestige. (Associates were asked only to rank those firms with which they are familiar.) We took those scores and calculated the Vault Top 100. We also asked associates to comment on and rank their own firm on subjects such as satisfaction, hours, compensation, diversity, treatment by partners and selectivity in hiring.

We're at it year after year, surveying associates and bugging law firm recruiting directors, for one reason: to provide lawyers and law students with an insider's view of what it's like to work at the nation's most prestigious law firms. But why do we bother ranking the Top 100 firms? Why does law firm prestige matter? A job is a job, after all, and many law firms not profiled in this guide pay as well as any firm on our list. Still, prestige matters plenty. Working for a prestigious law firm means being exposed to a greater variety and volume of work, as well as more prominent and high-profile cases and deals. It can also mean working with some particularly gifted and accomplished lawyers from whom you can learn a great deal. Most importantly, working for a prestigious firm will give you instant credibility in the job market and will mark you as someone to be taken seriously throughout your career.

But prestige isn't everything. Choosing the right firm for you may mean looking beyond prestige to such issues as compensation, hours, perks, exciting work, diversity and corporate culture. Our Best 20 Firms to Work For is where we rank the firms that associates find are the most amenable to an enjoyable lawyerly existence.

Landing a position at the firm of your choice has never been more intimidating, with the nation in a recession and many firms drifting in and out of hiring freezes. And competition at law schools across the country has never been more daunting, with law school applications hitting record numbers as lawyers-to-be flee an inhospitable job market. Those looking to join one of the prestigious firms profiled in this guide have their work cut out for them.

So get ready for those interviews. Comb your hair, don your best navy blue suit and practice that firm handshake. With the *Vault Guide to the Top 100 Law Firms* at your side, we're confident that you have access to the best resource on the top law firms.

The Editors
Vault
New York, NY

Detailed and expanded rankings information is available with the Vault Law Firm Survey Corporate Research Report and the Vault Law Associate Database.

Get valuable information on both prestige and quality of life rankings by demographics such as law school attended, gender and ethnicity, practice area and more. Go to www.vault.com/lawsurvey or contact recruitingsales@staff.vault.com.

THE STATE OF THE LAW

What a difference a year makes. In last year's edition of the guide, we reported on the sky-high year-end bonuses awarded to law firm associates at the close of 2000. This year, the bonus saga followed another track entirely. Some firms tried every trick in the book to avoid paying bonuses, while other firms were praised for doling out bonuses half the size of those paid in 2000. It seems that everything is different this year — from the drastic drop in M&A action to the seemingly endless recession to law firm layoffs to the gaping hole in the New York skyline. Let's take a look.

That dreadful day

When the planes careened into the twin towers of the World Trade Center, and the towers crashed to the ground, the entire world seemed to change in a matter of minutes. Firefighters, police officers, construction workers and countless good Samaritans cooperated to put out the fires, clean up the wreckage, help those victims who could be helped and find the bodies of those who could not.

Lawyers played a different role. In record numbers, they offered their services, volunteering to aid the families of victims of the attack and help small businesses that suffered losses. New York lawyers and others from around the country helped family members wade through perplexing legal forms, manned legal services hotlines, and created legal handbooks to assist families. Law firms, too, stepped in, making large financial donations to various relief organizations and charities, opening up their offices to the many firms and businesses that were displaced after the attacks, and encouraging their ranks to get involved in September 11-related pro bono projects.

After September 11, 2001, New Yorkers needed as many heroes as they could get. As the ashes of those fallen towers fell around them, the legal community proved that lawyers can be heroes, too.

A lean year

The dismal state of the economy has altered the face of the legal community. As stock prices fell last year, start-ups stalled and transactional work dwindled. The number of IPOs, already down in 2000, plummeted in 2001. Both the volume and value of M&A deals dropped. Practices that relied heavily on IPOs and emerging growth companies lost a vital source of revenue, and once-busy corporate attorneys twiddled their thumbs and gazed at empty desks. Firms that had aggressively expanded during the dot-com boom found themselves overstaffed and overextended. After September 11, a bad situation got even worse.

Traditional and diversified practices have weathered the storm more successfully than those focused on technology industries. Transactional work may have slowed to a trickle, but litigation is booming, and other practice areas like bankruptcy, employment, intellectual property and regulatory work continue to provide a steady stream of revenue. This shift in the balance of practice is reflected in associate workloads. Litigators are stretched thin, while anxious corporate associates hope they won't be the next casualties of a slow economy. Lawyers everywhere feel an increasing pressure to bill.

Associate anxiety

Firms responded to the recession with expense-trimming measures — eliminating perks, scaling back social events and postponing start dates for incoming associates. By summer 2001, the belt tightening became a crash diet. The first major round of layoffs came in August, when Cooley Godward made headlines with a firm-wide layoff of 86 lawyers. Mass layoffs at several other Bay Area firms followed.

If tech-heavy firms on the West Coast were the hardest hit, the rest of the country has not been immune. When Shearman & Sterling dismissed 10 percent of its associates in October, it was clear that layoff fever had hit the East Coast. Boston firms were especially hard hit. A few firms pledged not to engage in mass layoffs, only to renege after September 11. Davis Polk & Wardwell kept its pledge but angered associates with an ill-fated effort to cancel bonuses entirely. The attempt backfired after other New York firms failed to follow suit and Davis Polk eventually awarded bonuses to embittered associates who resented their firm's attempt to lead the market in reducing associate compensation.

Although most major firms did award bonuses in 2001, the amounts were roughly half what they had been in 2000. Salaries have generally remained stagnant. Lateral hiring has slowed. Retention has increased; in this time of economic uncertainty, associates tend to stay put. Lower attrition has led to office space crunches and more aggressive performance reviews, as firms continue to try to reduce overhead.

Enron, everyone?

You may not remember where you were the first time you heard about the Enron scandal, but if you're the managing partner at a big law firm, you might. Law firms may turn out to be the only winners in this bigger-than-life scandal, which has already cost thousands of employees their jobs and retirement funds, countless shareholders and investors hundreds of millions of dollars, several high-profile managers their reputations, and the downfall of one Big Five professional services firm.

With deal work down, a volatile stock market and a general lack of investor confidence, this is not a great time to be a law firm. It sometimes seems as if Enron-related work is single-handedly keeping law firms afloat. (The market for other bankruptcy work, of course, is robust, too.) *The American Lawyer* reports that, as of May 2002, more than half of The AmLaw 200 firms have been drafted into the Enron fray, doing work from white-collar criminal defense to contract disputes to restructuring. The hours are long, the fees are huge and the stakes are high.

For some law firms, the stakes are even higher. Houston-based Vinson & Elkins and Chicago-based Kirkland & Ellis were named as defendants in class action lawsuits filed by Enron employees and investors. Both V&E and K&E deny any responsibility in the debacle, and several other parties were also named in the suits, including Enron's ill-fated auditor, Arthur Andersen, and various investment banks.

A GUIDE TO THIS GUIDE

If you're wondering how our entries are organized, read on. Here's a handy guide to the information you'll find packed into each entry of this book.

THE BUZZ

When it comes to other law firms, our respondents certainly like to dish! We asked them to detail their opinions and observations about firms other than their own. We've collected a sampling of these comments in "The Buzz."

When selecting The Buzz, we included quotes representative of the common outsiders' perceptions of the firms, even if (in our opinion) the quotes did not accurately describe the firm. Please keep in mind when reading The Buzz that it's often more fun for outsiders to trash than praise a competing law firm. Nonetheless, we have found The Buzz to be another valuable means of gauging a firm's reputation in the legal field, or at least to understand common misperceptions.

FIRM FACTS

- **Locations:** A listing of the firm's offices, with the headquarter bolded. You may see firms with no bolded location. This means that these are self-proclaimed decentralized firms without official headquarters.

- **Major Departments/Practices:** Practice areas that employ a significant portion of the firm's headquarters' attorneys as reported by the firms.

- **Base Salary:** The firm's base salary at its headquarters. Base salary at other offices is given when available. Pay is for 2002 except where noted.

- **Notable Perks:** A listing of perks and benefits outside the norm. For example, we do not list health care, as every firm we surveyed offers health care plans.

- **Uppers and Downers:** Good points and bad points about working at the firm, as gleaned from associate interviews and surveys. Uppers and downers are the impressionistic perceptions of insiders and are not based on statistics.

- **Employment Contact:** The person that the firm identifies as the primary contact to receive resumes or to answer questions about the recruitment process. More than one contact is sometimes given.

THE STATS

• **No. of attorneys:** The total number of attorneys at a firm in all offices as of May 2002.

• **No. of offices:** The firm's total number of offices worldwide.

• **Summer associate offers, 2001:** The firm-wide number of second-year law students offered full-time associate positions by the firm.

• **Chairman, Managing Partner, etc.:** The name and title of the leader of the firm. Sometimes more than one name may be provided.

QUALITY OF LIFE METERS

Our meters are based on our surveys of over 9,500 law firm respondents. Associates surveyed were asked to rate their firm in a variety of categories on a 1 to 10 scale. The firm's score in each category is simply the average (mean) of the scores its associates gave in that area. We have highlighted the following categories for our meters:

• **Satisfaction:** Associates rank their satisfaction with their firm on a scale from "unsatisfactory" to "entirely fulfilling."

• **Hours:** Associates rank how they feel about their hours on a scale from "overwhelming" to "very livable." Please note the hours score is based on the subjective perceptions of associates, not on the actual hours they work.

• **Training:** Associates rank the level of formal and informal training their firm provides.

• **Diversity:** Associates rank their considerations of all diversity issues, including the situations of minority group members, gays and lesbians, and women.

• **Associate/Partner Relations:** Associates rank how well they feel they're treated and mentored by the partners at their firm.

Please note that firms that did not participate in our survey were usually not rated by our quality of life meters. In some cases, Vault contacted associates independently at firms that did not participate in our survey. If a representative sampling of associates completed our survey, the firm was rated by our quality of life meters, even if the firm did not participate in the survey.

THE PROFILES

You'll notice two types of firm profiles — long ones and short ones. What's the deal? Firms ranked one to 50 received long profiles, and shorter profiles were reserved for firms ranked 51 to 100. Both the long and short profiles are divided into three sections:

The Scoop, Getting Hired and Our Survey Says.

• **The Scoop:** The firm's history, clients, recent deals, recent firm developments and other points of interest.

• **Getting Hired:** Qualifications the firm looks for in new associates, tips on getting hired and other notable aspects of the hiring process.

• **Our Survey Says:** Actual quotes from surveys and interviews with current associates of the firm on topics such as the firm's assignment system, feedback, partnership prospects, levels of responsibility, summer associate program, culture, hours, pay, training and much more.

BEST OF THE REST

In addition to the 50 long and 50 short profiles, we've also included information on additional law firms that did not make our Top 100 list this year, including The Buzz.

THE VAULT PRESTIGE RANKINGS

Visit the Vault Law Channel, the complete online resource for law careers, featuring firm profiles, message boards, the Vault Law Job Board, and more. www.law.vault.com

VAULT CAREER LIBRARY

11

Making the smart decision is always

WorthWeil

Weil, Gotshal & Manges is among the largest and most prestigious law firms in the world. We have assembled a remarkably talented and diverse group of professionals in the United States and around the world to build a uniquely balanced firm that serves a premier client base in matters that capture the world's attention.

"If you want a big firm in New York City with intelligent and open-minded people, this is a good place for you." - *2002 Vault Guide to the Top 100 Law Firms.*

To learn more about Weil Gotshal, please visit us at *www.weil.com*

WEIL, GOTSHAL & MANGES LLP

BRUSSELS   BUDAPEST   DALLAS   FRANKFURT   HOUSTON   LONDON   MIAMI   NEW YORK

PRAGUE   SILICON VALLEY   SINGAPORE   WARSAW   WASHINGTON, D.C.

THE RANKING METHODOLOGY

TOP 100

Movement at the top! Finally. We were starting to think that our top firms were going to stay the same forever. But now, after four years of immobility, there has been some significant movement at the very top of the Vault Top 100, signifying some dramatic changes and noteworthy events in the legal community. Following last year's bonus debacle (see The State of the Law), Davis Polk & Wardwell slipped one notch from the No. 4 position (where it had rested comfortably for four years) to the No. 5 position, with last year's No. 5, Skadden, Arps, Slate, Meagher & Flom, taking up the No. 4 slot. And what of last year's No. 8 firm? After a very public round of mass layoffs, Shearman & Sterling has been banished from the Top 10 and now takes up the No. 13 position. And Cravath, this year's No. 1 for the fifth straight year, fought off a vigorous challenge from No. 2 Wachtell.

How does Vault come up with its list of the Top 100 firms in the country? The first step is to compile a list of the most renowned law firms by reviewing the feedback we receive from previous surveys, consulting our previous lists, poring over legal newspapers and talking to lawyers in the field. This list, our initial list was made up of 126 very impressive law firms.

We asked these 126 law firms to distribute a password-protected online survey to their associates. In total, 9,580 attorneys returned anonymous surveys to Vault. Associates from all over the country and the world responded. We heard from lawyers in New York, Los Angeles, San Francisco, Palo Alto, Chicago, Boston, Philadelphia, Houston, Dallas, Washington, D.C., Miami, Cleveland, Seattle and Atlanta, among other locations, not to mention London, Paris, Tokyo and beyond. The online survey asked attorneys to score each of the 126 law firms on a scale of 1 to 10 based on its prestige. Associates were asked to ignore any firm with which they were unfamiliar and were not allowed to rank their own firm.

We collected all the surveys and averaged the score for each firm. The firms were then ranked in order, starting with the highest average prestige score as No. 1 on down to determine the Vault Top 100. Remember that in the Top 100, Vault is not assessing firms by profit, size, lifestyle or quality of service — we are ranking the most prestigious law firms based on the perceptions of currently practicing lawyers at peer firms.

Think it's easy getting 9,580 law firm associates to take our survey? Think again. Lawyers are busy people, and many are stressed out as it is without having to take 30 minutes out of their day to work on a non-billable project — especially with the increased emphasis on racking up billable hours. Despite it all, thousands upon thousands of associates came through for us and helped us produce the Vault Top 100. Associates, many thanks for your insight and patience.

The Vault 100

2003*

The 100 most prestigious law firms

2003 RANK	LAW FIRM	PRESTIGE SCORE	2002 RANK	2001 RANK	2000 RANK	LARGEST OFFICE/ HEADQUARTERS
1	Cravath, Swaine & Moore	8.928	1	1	1	New York, NY
2	Wachtell, Lipton, Rosen & Katz	8.925	2	2	2	New York, NY
3	Sullivan & Cromwell	8.447	3	3	3	New York, NY
4	Skadden, Arps, Slate, Meagher & Flom...**	8.161	5	5	5	New York, NY
5	Davis Polk & Wardwell	8.117	4	4	4	New York, NY
6	Simpson Thacher & Bartlett	7.783	6	6	6	New York, NY
7	Cleary, Gottlieb, Steen & Hamilton	7.692	7	7	7	New York, NY
8	Covington & Burling	7.513	10	14	14	Washington, DC
9	Latham & Watkins	7.447	9	9	9	Los Angeles, CA
10	Weil, Gotshal & Manges LLP	7.415	12	13	10	New York, NY
11	Williams & Connolly LLP	7.395	11	12	16	Washington, DC
12	Kirkland & Ellis	7.361	14	11	11	Chicago, IL
13	Shearman & Sterling	7.199	8	8	8	New York, NY
14	Paul, Weiss, Rifkind, Wharton & Garrison	7.105	15	15	13	New York, NY
15	Wilmer, Cutler & Pickering	7.071	18	23	23	Washington, DC
16	Sidley Austin Brown & Wood LLP	7.057	17	16	20(tie)	Chicago, IL
17	Debevoise & Plimpton	7.048	16	18	12	New York, NY
18	Gibson, Dunn & Crutcher LLP†	7.028	20	17	19	Los Angeles, CA
19	Arnold & Porter†	7.028	23	21	20(tie)	Washington, DC
20	White & Case LLP	6.782	19	20	18	New York, NY
21	Jones, Day, Reavis & Pogue	6.772	29	30	24	Cleveland, OH
22	O'Melveny & Myers LLP	6.756	21	19	17	Los Angeles, CA
23	Hale and Dorr LLP	6.754	22	27	31	Boston, MA
24	Morrison & Foerster LLP	6.670	24	22	25	San Francisco, CA
25	Clifford Chance Rogers & Wells LLP	6.651	28	33	46	New York, NY

NR = Not Ranked

* Vault rankings span two calendar years; they are dated as the second of these years. For example, our 2003 rankings are based on surveys completed in summer 2002 and apply to the 2002-2003 academic year.

** Skadden, Arps, Slate, Meagher & Flom LLP and Affiliates

† Gibson Dunn (7.0280) and Arnold & Porter (7.0276) are separated by a score difference not shown on the chart.

2003 RANK	LAW FIRM	PRESTIGE SCORE	2002 RANK	2001 RANK	2000 RANK	LARGEST OFFICE/ HEADQUARTERS
26	Fried, Frank, Harris, Shriver & Jacobson	6.619	30	29	27	New York, NY
27	Milbank, Tweed, Hadley & McCloy LLP	6.601	25	26	22	New York, NY
28	Ropes & Gray	6.576	27	28	30	Boston, MA
29	Dewey Ballantine LLP	6.462	34	31	28	New York, NY
30	Hogan & Hartson L.L.P.	6.450	35	39	42	Washington, DC
31	Wilson Sonsini Goodrich & Rosati	6.410	13	10	15	Palo Alto, CA
32	King & Spalding	6.304	36	35	39	Atlanta, GA
33	Boies, Schiller & Flexner LLP	6.298	47	NR	NR	Armonk, NY
34	Mayer, Brown, Rowe & Maw	6.282	31	25	26	Chicago, IL
35	Willkie Farr & Gallagher	6.249	32	36	29	New York, NY
36	Akin, Gump, Strauss, Hauer & Feld, L.L.P.	6.158	49	43	37	Washington, DC
37	Winston & Strawn	6.082	41	44	40	Chicago, IL
38	Munger, Tolles & Olson LLP	6.073	37	40	NR	Los Angeles, CA
39	Baker & McKenzie	6.039	44	45	36	Chicago, IL
40	Cadwalader, Wickersham & Taft	6.009	46	47	41	New York, NY
41	Orrick, Herrington & Sutcliffe LLP	6.001	39	42	33	San Francisco, CA
42	Paul, Hastings, Janofsky & Walker LLP	5.991	40	41	35	Los Angeles, CA
43	Cahill Gordon & Reindel	5.991	42	50	38	New York, NY
44	Brobeck, Phleger & Harrison LLP	5.985	26	24	NR	San Francisco, CA
45	Proskauer Rose LLP	5.961	48	48	43	New York, NY
46	Cooley Godward LLP	5.947	33	32	NR	Palo Alto, CA
47	Baker Botts L.L.P.	5.943	55	49	44	Houston, TX
48	Morgan, Lewis & Bockius LLP	5.933	38	34	34	Philadelphia, PA
49	Fulbright & Jaworski L.L.P.	5.880	45	NR	50	Houston, TX
50	McDermott, Will & Emery	5.845	51	NR	47	Chicago, IL

†† *Paul, Hastings, Janofsky, & Walker (5.9913) and Cahill Gordon & Reindel (5.9906) are separated by a score difference not shown on the chart.*

The 100 most prestigious law firms

2003 RANK	LAW FIRM	PRESTIGE SCORE	2002 RANK	2001 RANK	2000 RANK	LARGEST OFFICE/ HEADQUARTERS
51	Steptoe & Johnson LLP	5.707	50	NR	NR	Washington, DC
52	Chadbourne & Parke LLP	5.698	59	NR	49	New York, NY
53	LeBoeuf, Lamb, Greene & MacRae, L.L.P.	5.686	53	NR	48	New York, NY
54	Irell & Manella LLP	5.671	58	NR	NR	Los Angeles, CA
55	Pillsbury Winthrop LLP	5.666	64	NR	32	San Francisco, CA
56	Jenner & Block, LLC	5.657	56	NR	NR	Chicago, IL
57	Kaye Scholer LLP	5.564	60	NR	45	New York, NY
58	Goodwin Procter LLP	5.554	61	NR	NR	Boston, MA
59	Sonnenschein Nath & Rosenthal	5.550	67	NR	NR	Chicago, IL
60	Heller Ehrman White & McAuliffe LLP	5.518	65	NR	NR	San Francisco, CA
61	Coudert Brothers LLP	5.474	62	NR	NR	New York, NY
62	Dechert	5.432	68	NR	NR	Philadelphia, PA
63	Fish & Neave	5.397	66	NR	NR	New York, NY
64	Perkins Coie LLP	5.394	57	NR	NR	Seattle, WA
65	Howrey Simon Arnold & White, LLP	5.389	75	NR	NR	Washington, DC
66	Alston & Bird LLP	5.387	89	NR	NR	Atlanta, GA
67	Testa, Hurwitz & Thibeault, LLP	5.355	63	NR	NR	Boston, MA
68	Piper Rudnick LLP	5.316	69	NR	NR	Washington, DC
69	Holland & Knight LLP	5.315	76	NR	NR	Washington, DC
70	Hunton & Williams	5.250	82	NR	NR	Richmond, VA
71	Foley & Lardner	5.239	81	NR	NR	Milwaukee, WI
72	Crowell & Moring LLP	5.224	78	NR	NR	Washington, DC
73	Fenwick & West LLP	5.172	70	NR	NR	Palo Alto, CA
74	Kirkpatrick & Lockhart LLP	5.169	77	NR	NR	Pittsburgh, PA
75	Bingham Dana LLP†	5.145	100	NR	NR	Boston, MA

* Vault rankings span two calendar years; they are dated as the second of these years. For example, our 2003 rankings are based on surveys completed in summer 2002 and apply to the 2002-2003 academic year.
† Bingham Dana and McCutchen Doyle have announced a merger scheduled for July 2002

2003 RANK	LAW FIRM	PRESTIGE SCORE	2002 RANK	2001 RANK	2000 RANK	LARGEST OFFICE/ HEADQUARTERS
76	Stroock & Stroock & Lavan LLP	5.118	79	NR	NR	New York, NY
77	Patton Boggs LLP	5.103	72	NR	NR	Washington, DC
78	Gray Cary Ware & Freidenrich LLP	5.089	73	NR	NR	Palo Alto, CA
79	Baker & Hostetler LLP	5.087	93	NR	NR	Cleveland, OH
80	McCutchen, Doyle, Brown & Enersen, LLP†	5.075	71	NR	NR	San Francisco, CA
81	Schulte Roth & Zabel LLP	5.019	84	NR	NR	New York, NY
82	Bryan Cave LLP	4.997	91	NR	NR	St. Louis, MO
83	Pennie & Edmonds LLP	4.974	74	NR	NR	New York, NY
84	Shaw Pittman	4.971	80	NR	NR	Washington, DC
85	Dorsey & Whitney LLP	4.969	94	NR	NR	Minneapolis, MN
86	Vinson & Elkins L.L.P.	4.936	52	46	NR	Houston, TX
87	Choate, Hall & Stewart	4.921	83	NR	NR	Boston, MA
88	Arent Fox Kintner Plotkin & Kahn, PLLC	4.906	NR	NR	NR	Washington, DC
89	Greenberg Traurig, LLP	4.901	85	NR	NR	Miami, FL
90	Gunderson Dettmer Stough...**	4.869	43	38	NR	Menlo Park, CA
91	Finnegan, Henderson, Farabow...***	4.816	97	NR	NR	Washington, DC
92	Fish & Richardson P.C.	4.767	NR	NR	NR	Boston, MA
93	Hughes Hubbard & Reed LLP	4.731	87	NR	NR	New York, NY
94	Wiley Rein & Fielding LLP	4.723	96	NR	NR	Washington, DC
95	Kelley Drye & Warren LLP	4.697	90	NR	NR	New York, NY
96	Mintz Levin Cohn Ferris Glovsky...****	4.694	86	NR	NR	Boston, MA
97	Katten Muchin Zavis Rosenman	4.673	95	NR	NR	Chicago, IL
98	Foley Hoag LLP	4.654	92	NR	NR	Boston, MA
99	McGuireWoods LLP	4.629	98	NR	NR	Richmond, VA
100	Thelen Reid & Priest LLP	4.566	NR	NR	NR	New York, NY

** Gunderson Dettmer Stough Villeneuve Franklin & Hachigian, LLP
*** Finnegan, Henderson, Farabow, Garrett & Dunner, L.L.P.
**** Mintz Levin Cohn Ferris Glovsky and Popeo, P.C.

REGIONAL RANKINGS

Sometimes all you care about is how a firm stacks up against its peer firms in a particular region of the country. That's where our regional rankings come in. We asked associates in each regional area to rate the firms headquartered in their area. In most cases, firms that ranked well locally made the Vault 100 list, though the order of the firms in the regional ranking differs in some interesting ways from the order of the firms in the Top 100.

This year's regional categories are: Boston, Chicago, California, Texas, New York, Pennsylvania and Washington, D.C.

New York

RANK	FIRM	SCORE	2002 RANK
1	Wachtell, Lipton, Rosen & Katz	9.171	1
2	Cravath, Swaine & Moore	9.039	2
3	Sullivan & Cromwell	8.531	3
4	Davis Polk & Wardwell	8.294	4
5	Simpson Thacher & Bartlett	7.952	5
6	Skadden, Arps, Slate, Meagher & Flom...*	7.951	6
7	Cleary, Gottlieb, Steen & Hamilton	7.787	7
8	Debevoise & Plimpton	7.253	10
9	Paul, Weiss, Rifkind, Wharton & Garrison	7.189	9
10	Weil, Gotshal & Manges LLP	7.161	11
11	Shearman & Sterling	6.858	8
12	White & Case LLP	6.346	12
13	Willkie Farr & Gallagher	6.256	14
14	Milbank, Tweed, Hadley & McCloy LLP	6.248	15
15	Fried, Frank, Harris, Shriver & Jacobson	6.23	13
16	Boies, Schiller & Flexner LLP	6.211	19
17	Clifford Chance Rogers & Wells LLP	6.170	18
18	Dewey Ballantine LLP	6.164	17
19	Cahill Gordon & Reindel	6.049	16
20	Proskauer Rose LLP	5.868	20

*Skadden, Arps, Slate, Meagher & Flom LLP and Affiliates

REGIONAL RANKINGS (cont'd)

California*

RANK	FIRM	SCORE
1	Latham & Watkins	7.760
2	Gibson, Dunn & Crutcher LLP	7.314
3	O'Melveny & Myers LLP	7.222
4	Morrison & Foerster LLP	7.033
5	Munger, Tolles & Olson LLP	6.915
6	Irell & Manella LLP	6.616
7	Wilson Sonsini Goodrich & Rosati	6.591
8	Orrick, Herrington & Sutcliffe LLP	6.337
9	Cooley Godward LLP	6.252
10	Brobeck, Phleger & Harrison LLP	6.146
11	Heller Ehrman White & McAuliffe LLP	6.124
12	Paul, Hastings, Janofsky & Walker LLP	6.063
13	Pillsbury Winthrop LLP	6.055
14	Fenwick & West LLP	5.791
15	McCutchen, Doyle, Brown & Enersen, LLP†	5.619

* Unlike other regional rankings charts, there is no historical comparison for California because Vault previously published separate Northern California and Southern California rankings.

† Announced merger with Bingham Dana, scheduled for July 2002

Washington, DC

RANK	FIRM	SCORE	2002 RANK
1	Williams & Connolly LLP	8.451	1
2	Covington & Burling	8.312	2
3	Wilmer, Cutler & Pickering	8.049	4
4	Arnold & Porter	7.836	3
5	Hogan & Hartson L.L.P.	7.314	5
6	Akin, Gump, Strauss, Hauer & Feld, L.L.P.	6.372	6
7	Steptoe & Johnson LLP	6.347	8
8	Crowell & Moring LLP	5.894	13
9	Shaw Pittman LLP	5.889	10
10	Wiley Rein & Fielding LLP	5.846	12

REGIONAL RANKINGS (cont'd)

Chicago

RANK	FIRM	SCORE	2002 RANK
1	Kirkland & Ellis	8.287	1
2	Sidley Austin Brown & Wood LLP	8.010	2
3	Mayer, Brown, Rowe & Maw	7.785	3
4	Winston & Strawn	7.182	4
5	McDermott, Will & Emery	6.335	6
6	Jenner & Block, LLC	6.030	5
7	Baker & McKenzie	5.982	7
8	Sonnenschein Nath & Rosenthal	5.871	9
9	Katten Muchin Zavis Rosenman	5.365	8
10	Schiff Hardin & Waite	5.276	10

Boston

RANK	FIRM	SCORE	2002 RANK
1	Ropes & Gray	8.262	1
2	Hale and Dorr LLP	8.073	2
3	Goodwin Procter LLP	6.971	3
4	Testa, Hurwitz & Thibeault, LLP	6.578	4
5	Bingham Dana LLP†	5.987	7
6	Foley Hoag LLP	5.914	6
7	Mintz Levin Cohn Ferris Glovsky & Popeo...*	5.512	5
8	Choate, Hall & Stewart	5.456	8
9	Palmer & Dodge LLP	5.355	9
10	Fish & Richardson P.C.	5.082	NR

* Mintz Levin Cohn Ferris Glovsky and Popeo, P.C.
† Announced merger with McCutchen, Doyle, Brown & Enersen, LLP, scheduled for July 2002

REGIONAL RANKINGS (cont'd)

Texas

RANK	FIRM	SCORE	2002 RANK
1	Baker Botts L.L.P.	7.830	2
2	Vinson & Elkins L.L.P.	6.961	1
3	Fulbright & Jaworski L.L.P.	6.809	3
4	Andrews & Kurth L.L.P.	5.870	5
5	Bracewell & Patterson, L.L.P.	5.692	6

Pennsylvania

RANK	FIRM	SCORE	2002 RANK
1	Morgan, Lewis & Bockius LLP	7.759	1
2	Dechert	7.690	2
3	Ballard Spahr Andrews & Ingersoll, LLP	6.417	4
4	Drinker Biddle & Reath LLP	6.315	5
5	Blank Rome Comisky & McCauley LLP	5.567	6

DEPARTMENTAL RANKINGS

Associates were allowed to vote for up to three firms in their practice areas and were not permitted to vote for their own firm. Associates who identified themselves as corporate attorneys were allowed only to vote in corporate-related categories (securities, business finance, etc.); litigators were allowed only to vote in the litigation category, and so on. We indicate the top firms in each area, as well as the total percentage of votes cast in favor of the firm. (If each associate surveyed chose three firms, the maximum percentage of votes per firm would be 33.3 percent.)

Corporate

RANK	FIRM	% OF VOTES	2002 RANK
1	Cravath, Swaine & Moore	18.51	1
2	Skadden, Arps, Slate, Meagher & Flom LLP...*	14.03	2
3	Wachtell, Lipton, Rosen & Katz	13.87	4
4	Sullivan & Cromwell	12.18	3
5	Davis Polk & Wardwell	9.10	5
6	Simpson Thacher & Bartlett	5.15	6
7	Cleary, Gottlieb, Steen & Hamilton	3.33	9
8	Shearman & Sterling	2.77	8
9	Latham & Watkins	2.26	NR
10	Wilson Sonsini Goodrich & Rosati	1.31	7

*Skadden, Arps, Slate, Meagher & Flom LLP and Affiliates

Litigation

RANK	FIRM	% OF VOTES	2002 RANK
1	Cravath, Swaine & Moore	9.45	1
2	Williams & Connolly LLP	8.16	2
3	Kirkland & Ellis	7.85	3
4	Paul, Weiss, Rifkind, Wharton & Garrison	6.22	5
5	Davis Polk & Wardwell	5.19	7
6	Skadden, Arps, Slate, Meagher & Flom LLP...*	4.41	6
7	Boies, Schiller & Flexner LLP	4.39	4
8	Wachtell, Lipton, Rosen & Katz	3.70	10
9	Sullivan & Cromwell	3.34	9
10	Jones, Day, Reavis & Pogue	3.25	NR

*Skadden, Arps, Slate, Meagher & Flom LLP and Affiliates

DEPARTMENTAL RANKINGS (cont'd)

Labor & Employment

RANK	FIRM	% OF VOTES	2002 RANK
1(tie)	Littler Mendelson, P.C.	13.35	1
1(tie)	Paul, Hastings, Janofsky & Walker LLP	13.35	2
2	Seyfarth Shaw†	12.11	4
3	Proskauer Rose LLP	11.34	3
4	Morgan, Lewis & Bockius LLP	8.23	5
5	Jones, Day, Reavis & Pogue	3.11	7
6	Akin, Gump, Strauss, Hauer & Feld, L.L.P.	2.33	9
7(tie)	Gibson, Dunn & Crutcher LLP	2.17	8
7(tie)	O'Melveny & Myers LLP	2.17	6
8	Orrick, Herrington & Sutcliffe LLP	1.71	NR
9	Skadden, Arps, Slate, Meagher & Flom LLP...*	1.55	NR
10	McDermott, Will & Emery	1.40	8

Skadden, Arps, Slate, Meagher & Flom LLP and Affiliates
† No profile in this year's guide

Bankruptcy/Corporate Restructuring

RANK	FIRM	% OF VOTES	2002 RANK
1	Weil, Gotshal & Manges LLP	29.77	1
2	Skadden, Arps, Slate, Meagher & Flom LLP...*	19.55	2
3 (tie)	Kirkland & Ellis	7.27	4
3 (tie)	Milbank, Tweed, Hadley & McCloy LLP	7.27	NR
4	Wachtell, Lipton, Rosen & Katz	6.59	3
5	Willkie Farr & Gallagher	3.86	5
6	Jones, Day, Reavis & Pogue	3.64	7
7	Davis Polk & Wardwell	2.73	9
8	Akin, Gump, Strauss, Hauer & Feld, L.L.P.	2.27	6
9	Cadwalader, Wickersham & Taft	1.59	10
10	Latham & Watkins	1.14	NR

Skadden, Arps, Slate, Meagher & Flom LLP and Affiliates

DEPARTMENTAL RANKINGS (cont'd)

Intellectual Property

RANK	FIRM	% OF VOTES	2002 RANK
1	Finnegan, Henderson, Farabow, Garrett & Dunner...*	15.66	2
2	Fish & Neave	11.19	1
3(tie)	Pennie & Edmonds LLP	7.86	4
3(tie)	Fish & Richardson P.C.	7.86	NR
4	Cooley Godward LLP	4.75	6
5	Morrison & Foerster LLP	4.54	9
6	Wilson Sonsini Goodrich & Rosati	3.93	3
7	Kirkland & Ellis	3.66	NR
8	Brobeck, Phleger & Harrison LLP	3.39	5
9	Howrey Simon Arnold & White, LLP	2.85	10
10	Foley & Lardner	2.51	NR

* Finnegan, Henderson, Farabow, Garrett & Dunner, L.L.P.

Mergers & Acquisitions

RANK	FIRM	% OF VOTES	2002 RANK
1	Wachtell, Lipton, Rosen & Katz	25.55	1
2	Skadden, Arps, Slate, Meagher & Flom LLP...*	21.19	2
3	Cravath, Swaine & Moore	17.39	3
4	Sullivan & Cromwell	8.67	4
5	Davis Polk & Wardwell	5.25	6
6	Simpson Thacher & Bartlett	5.20	5
7	Shearman & Sterling	2.37	7
8	Cleary, Gottlieb, Steen & Hamilton	1.57	9
9	Weil, Gotshal & Manges LLP	1.18	10
10(tie)	Kirkland & Ellis	0.97	NR
10(tie)	Latham & Watkins	0.97	10

*Skadden, Arps, Slate, Meagher & Flom LLP and Affiliates

DEPARTMENTAL RANKINGS (cont'd)

Securities

RANK	FIRM	% OF VOTES	2002 RANK
1	Sullivan & Cromwell	14.36	3
2(tie)	Cravath, Swaine & Moore	13.78	1
2(tie)	Skadden, Arps, Slate, Meagher & Flom LLP...*	13.78	2
3	Davis Polk & Wardwell	11.36	4
4	Wachtell, Lipton, Rosen & Katz	6.41	5
5	Shearman & Sterling	5.42	8
6	Cleary, Gottlieb, Steen & Hamilton	5.07	9
7	Simpson Thacher & Bartlett	4.88	7
8	Wilson Sonsini Goodrich & Rosati	3.45	6
9	Latham & Watkins	2.23	NR
10	Sidley Austin Brown & Wood LLP	1.85	NR

Skadden, Arps, Slate, Meagher & Flom LLP and Affiliates

Technology/Internet/E-Commerce

RANK	FIRM	% OF VOTES	2002 RANK
1	Cooley Godward LLP	16.31	3
2	Brobeck, Phleger & Harrison LLP	15.60	2
3	Wilson Sonsini Goodrich & Rosati	12.77	1
4	Morrison & Foerster LLP	4.26	5
5(tie)	Fenwick & West LLP	3.55	7
5(tie)	Shaw Pittman LLP	3.55	NR
6(tie)	Alston & Bird LLP	2.84	NR
6(tie)	Fish & Neave	2.84	NR
6(tie)	Gunderson Dettmer Stough Villeneuve...*	2.84	6
6(tie)	Gray, Cary, Ware & Freidenrich, LLP	2.84	10
7(tie)	Skadden, Arps, Slate, Meagher & Flom...**	2.13	NR
7(tie)	Venture Law Group	2.13	4

* Gunderson Dettmer Stough Villeneuve Franklin & Hachigian, LLP
** Skadden, Arps, Slate, Meagher & Flom LLP and Affiliates

DEPARTMENTAL RANKINGS (cont'd)

Tax

RANK	FIRM	% OF VOTES	2002 RANK
1	Cravath, Swaine & Moore	12.48	1
2(tie)	Cleary, Gottlieb, Steen & Hamilton	9.95	3
2(tie)	Skadden, Arps, Slate, Meagher & Flom LLP...*	9.95	2
3	Davis Polk & Wardwell	8.69	4
4	Sullivan & Cromwell	6.79	5
5	Wachtell, Lipton, Rosen & Katz	6.16	6
6	McDermott, Will & Emery	5.53	8
7	Baker & McKenzie	3.95	7
8	Fenwick & West LLP	3.32	NR
9	Kirkland & Ellis	3.00	9
10	Shearman & Sterling	2.37	NR

*Skadden, Arps, Slate, Meagher & Flom LLP and Affiliates

Real Estate

RANK	FIRM	% OF VOTES	2002 RANK
1	Skadden, Arps, Slate, Meagher & Flom LLP...*	8.10	1
2(tie)	Fried, Frank, Harris, Shriver & Jacobson	5.53	4
2(tie)	Piper Rudnick LLP	5.53	2
3	Paul, Hastings, Janofsky & Walker LLP	4.94	5
4(tie)	Cadwalader, Wickersham & Taft	3.95	6
4(tie)	Holland & Knight LLP	3.95	10
5	Mayer, Brown, Rowe & Maw	3.56	3
6	Stroock & Stroock & Lavan LLP	3.36	8
7(tie)	Ballard Spahr Andrews & Ingersoll, LLP	2.96	NR
7(tie)	Latham & Watkins	2.96	7
8	Sullivan & Cromwell	2.57	NR
9(tie)	Orrick, Herrington & Sutcliffe LLP	2.37	NR
9(tie)	Shaw Pittman LLP	2.37	NR
10	Sidley Austin Brown & Wood LLP	2.17	NR

*Skadden, Arps, Slate, Meagher & Flom LLP and Affiliates

QUALITY OF
LIFE RANKINGS

Be a better lawyer faster.

Why take a job where you'll be a six-figure file clerk? At Sutherland, you'll have challenging projects from the start, working one-on-one with the firm's partners for top clients. Visit our Web site to find out more about us and our wide range of specialties, from M&A to IP. Or contact Victoria Tate at 404.853.8000 or vdtate@sablaw.com, or Melissa Wilson at 202.383.0100 or mwilson@sablaw.com.

Voted one of the "Best 20 Law Firms to Work for" the past two years.
— Vault Guide to the Top 100 Law Firms

Sutherland
▪ Asbill & ▪
Brennan LLP

ATTORNEYS AT LAW

www.sablaw.com
Atlanta • Austin • New York • Tallahassee • Washington

Quality of Life Rankings

METHODOLOGY

Associates were asked to rate their firm on a 1 to 10 scale for each of several quality of life categories. This year's categories are: satisfaction, hours, treatment by partners, training, pay, diversity, retention and offices. The firm's score in each category is simply the average of the scores its associates gave in that area. It is important to note that those firms without a high enough aggregate of associates completing the survey were ineligible to appear in these rankings.

In the following charts, please note that the average scores in each category reflect the entire population of firms, not just the firms listed on the chart (those that ranked in the top 10 or 20).

THE BEST 20 FIRMS TO WORK FOR

Which are the best firms to work for? For some, this is a far more important question than which firms are the most prestigious.

To determine our Best 20 firms, we analyzed our initial list of 126 firms using a formula that weighed the most relevant categories for an overall quality of life ranking. Each firm's overall score was calculated using the following formula:

40 percent satisfaction

10 percent hours

10 percent treatment by partners

10 percent training

10 percent pay

10 percent diversity (with respect to women, minorities, and gays and lesbians)

5 percent retention

5 percent offices

Like our Top 100 rankings, our Best 20 is meant to be the subjective opinion of associates. By its nature, the list is based on the perceptions of insiders — some of whom may be biased in favor (or against) their firm.

BEST 20 LAW FIRMS TO WORK FOR

Average score = 7.37*

RANK	FIRM	HEADQUARTERS/ MAIN OFFICE	SCORE
1	Morrison & Foerster LLP	San Francisco, CA	8.485
2	Winston & Strawn	Chicago, IL	8.239
3	Troutman Sanders LLP	Atlanta, GA	8.165
4	Alston & Bird LLP	Atlanta, GA	8.138
5	Hale and Dorr LLP	Boston, MA	8.112
6	Debevoise & Plimpton	New York, NY	8.086
7	McCutchen, Doyle, Brown & Enersen, LLP†	San Francisco, CA	7.922
8	Fish & Richardson P.C.	Boston, MA	7.913
9	Morgan, Lewis & Bockius LLP	Philadelphia, PA	7.896
10	Davis Wright Tremaine LLP	Seattle, WA	7.841
11	Testa, Hurwitz & Thibeault, LLP	Boston, MA	7.833
12	Arnold & Porter	Washington, DC	7.813
13	Baker Botts L.L.P.	Houston, TX	7.808
14	Jenner & Block, LLC	Chicago, IL	7.801
15	Gray Cary Ware & Freidenrich, LLP	Palo Alto, CA	7.784
16	Vinson & Elkins L.L.P.	Houston, TX	7.766
17	Sutherland Asbill & Brennan LLP	Atlanta/ DC	7.734
18	Sullivan & Cromwell	New York, NY	7.728
19	Hogan & Hartson L.L.P.	Washington, DC	7.709
20	Kirkland & Ellis	Chicago, IL	7.700

† Announced merger with Bingham Dana, scheduled for July 2002

* All average scores in Vault's Quality of Life Rankings reflect averages for ALL firms who took the survey (not just the top-ranking firms that are listed on each chart).

Top three firms to work for

1. Morrison & Foerster LLP

Kudos to MoFo! This San Francisco firm (which didn't make last year's Best 20) now ranks as the very best law firm to work for. Morrison & Foerster wins a blue or red ribbon in a remarkable six of our quality of life categories, including employee satisfaction, partner-associate relations, diversity and pro bono commitment. The numbers bolster the senior associate who confidently asserts that "MoFo is the best large firm to work for — bar none."

Whether it's cutting-edge corporate finance or high-profile litigation, MoFo associates enjoy "exciting work" in a "friendly, laid-back and liberal" environment. Insiders are effusive in their praise. "I love working here," gushes one lawyer. "The people are outstanding. The partners are completely approachable and always seem to be looking out for me. I am particularly pleased with the firm's commitment to pro bono." Laterals who compare prior experiences to their life at Morrison & Foerster maintain that "the people and the environment at MoFo leave the others in the dust."

What makes MoFo folks so happy? For one thing, "the work is always interesting." Also, the people are "communal and cooperative." It's not just that associates are laid back and social among themselves, but the firm culture as a whole is "open-minded — to suggestions and new ideas." "One of the things I value most," explains one attorney, "is that the firm stresses an absence of division between the attorneys and staff. We are all on the same team and treated with equal importance." This egalitarian attitude is reflected in the firm's outstanding record for diversity: ranking No. 1 for women and No. 2 in commitment to both minorities and gays and lesbians. "Well," sighs a contented MoFo associate, "since I can't work full time for a noble charity and earn money, this is the next best thing."

"We are proud that MoFo is viewed as both a good place to work and a firm where associates can find a great deal of satisfaction in their jobs. Our goal is to have a firm where an associate coming to the firm can expect to work on cutting-edge deals and cases in an environment of mutual trust and respect," says Pamela Reed, Managing Partner for Operations.

2. Winston & Strawn

Having climbed to second place last year, this year Winston & Strawn retains the No. 2 spot among the nation's top law firms to work for. Winston is such an inviting place that, for the second year in a row, this venerable Chicago institution also takes home the winning trophies for employee retention and office space. It even earns a white ribbon for associate compensation. Many things make Winston associates happy: the high "caliber of legal work," "friendly environment," "fantastic" salaries and opportunity to work with "a lot of top-notch attorneys." And those famously "gorgeous" offices undoubtedly help maintain the upbeat and "comfortable" atmosphere.

Don't be misled by rumors of formality and stuffiness. Beneath Winston's formal, well-heeled exterior, a "surprisingly casual and laid back" culture thrives. "The firm has a reputation for being a stodgy place, which could not be farther from the truth," insiders insist. "There is a great mix of people and personalities at the firm." The formality exists only "on the surface," and "once you get to know them, the vast majority of lawyers here are friendly and laid back." You'll find people "down to earth and fun to be around." Attorneys frequently socialize together and "partners care about associates' lifestyles."

Partners also exhibit a "high degree of respect" and many are "excellent teachers." "Working with very smart people who are great at what they do is inspiring," notes an eager young lawyer. "It makes you think, I hope I'm that good some day." This enthusiasm is also shared by more experienced colleagues. A mid-level associate declares, "Now several years out of law school and having seen numerous friends drop out of large firms, I am pleased beyond measure with my experiences at Winston. I don't believe that I could find a better fit at any other large firm in the United States."

Managing Partner Jim Neis says, "We are delighted to be known as one of the best firms to work for. We have a culture that values teamwork, collegiality and inclusivity and we believe this has made Winston an attractive place to build a career."

3. Troutman Sanders LLP

Our No. 3 firm may not have achieved the national prestige of the other top firms in this category, but associates at Atlanta's Troutman Sanders consider their firm just about the best "law firm working environment, in Atlanta or anywhere else." A real estate attorney tells us, "This is the best job I will ever have. I really love coming to work every day." Her colleagues voice similar enthusiasm: "I love the work that I do and the amount of responsibility I am allowed," gushes one associate. "I doubt I could find a better law firm," says another. Among the factors that most please associates are the "sophisticated practice" and absence of hierarchy amid a genuinely friendly, collegial culture. Lawyers "from partners to junior associates" work as a team and even first-year associates feel "comfortable with making suggestions, voicing any concerns, and so on about the project." Attorneys enjoy "substantial responsibility" on "very interesting work" and find the firm's 1,800-hour billable requirement "very reasonable." "Partners not only let you have a life outside the office," observes an associate, "they want you to."

"Firm culture is our strong suit," remarks one associate. "Lawyers enjoy spending time with one another and socializing outside of work." An attorney in Washington, D.C., happily reports, "I can truly say that I am friends with virtually everyone in this office, from partners to support staff." It helps that "no one takes themselves too seriously or loses perspective on the fact that, while we pride ourselves on good work and client service, there is more to life than just work." Managing Partner Bob Webb says, "We are very proud of our associates, the commitment they show to our firm, and the contributions they make day in and day out. Our firm is dedicated to providing our associates with a superior work environment, one that encourages and supports individual development on a professional as well as a personal level. While we will always stive to do more, we are gratified to receive survey results such as these which indicate that our efforts have been successful and are appreciated."

SATISFACTION

	Average score = 7.45	
RANK	**FIRM**	**SCORE**
1	Williams & Connolly LLP	8.742
2	Morrison & Foerster LLP	8.571
3	Alston & Bird LLP	8.302
4	Troutman Sanders LLP	8.264
5	Morgan, Lewis & Bockius LLP	8.241
6	Fish & Richardson P.C.	8.224
7	Debevoise & Plimpton	8.222
8	Winston & Strawn	8.097
9	Hale and Dorr LLP	8.080
10	Sutherland Asbill & Brennan LLP	8.066

Top three in satisfaction

1. Williams & Connolly LLP

For the most satisfied associates in our Vault survey, check out Williams & Connolly. The Washington, D.C., firm that ranked seventh in satisfaction for 2001 rises to the top this year. W&C is simply a "great place to be a lawyer." The "hard-driving" culture might not be for everyone, but those who thrive on a "high level of responsibility," an "extraordinary range of cases" and an "intense" desire to win seem to feel right at home. The firm is a hotbed for high-profile litigation, so if the atmosphere isn't exactly relaxed (it's "not laid-back, that is for sure!"), it is nevertheless "extraordinarily collegial." Explains one associate: "Although we have a frightening 'take no prisoners' reputation, the firm is actually astonishingly friendly. Attorneys, both associates and partners, regularly eat lunch together in the dining room, and associates often get together for drinks."

Approachable partners and absence of hierarchy contribute to "a spirit of camaraderie" in which "competition among associates is virtually non-existent." The "firm's lack of structure" allows "associates to assume as much responsibility" as they can handle, "which makes for a very interesting job." In the words of one satisfied attorney: "If you can't get excited about the work here, you don't have a pulse."

Hiring Partner F. Lane Heard III says, "For the 20+ years that I have been at the firm, lawyers have been attracted to the firm — and have stayed at the firm — because of the quality and excitement of the work, the amount of responsibility given to young lawyers, and the challenge of working with very talented colleagues. I am pleased to see from the survey results that those same factors still hold true."

2. Morrison & Foerster LLP

Associates consider themselves "very fortunate to work at MoFo." Indeed, they should. They get to "work with some of the best lawyers in the country doing exciting work. The pay is good and the hours aren't as bad as most other big firms." Moreover, the firm "promotes a friendly, team-oriented atmosphere." This egalitarian spirit seems to be a central component of associates' contentment. That partners keep politics and hierarchy "at a minimum" in a firm of such size amazes many insiders. Partners value associates' opinions, and socializing often occurs between partners and associates as well as among attorneys and staff.

Though never less than professional and always "serious when warranted," folks at MoFo are "friendly, supportive and enjoyable to work with." "Everyone is very bright and almost no one is mean," says a lawyer in D.C. Associates appreciate the "laid-back," "inclusive" culture which inspires collegiality while retaining respect for attorneys' personal commitments. Many associates "have been close friends for years and socialize frequently," and parents appreciate how "accommodating" the firm is toward their family schedules. MoFo lawyers are so happy in their home that few can even think of a downside to working there. Shrugs one lawyer, "I couldn't think of a reason to leave."

3. Alston & Bird LLP

Some of the happiest associates in this year's survey work at Alston & Bird. Not surprisingly, the third place firm in associate satisfaction also ranks among the top three for employee retention. According to insiders, the Atlanta-based firm "is a terrific place to work." One third-year associate goes so far as to declare that "Alston & Bird is simply the best firm in the State of Georgia and the Southeast, if not the nation." A major factor in associate contentment is the firm's successful blend of professionalism and collegiality. "Alston & Bird provides a wonderful combination of challenging work and a relaxing atmosphere," says one source. Another associate observes, "Things like the quality of your legal work matter, things like white shirts and ties don't — I like that."

Some insiders believe that "the best part about this firm's culture is that everyone gets along great." Associates emphasize the "feeling of teamwork and unity" and lack of "barriers between associates and partners." Everyone is friendly and Alston & Bird "encourages casual social interaction" at events like the firm-sponsored Friday happy hour. Given the "intellectually stimulating" work, "unbelievable culture of cooperation and mentoring" and "very good benefits," many associates simply "cannot imagine practicing law anywhere else."

Hiring Committee Chair Jonathan W. Lowe says, "Alston & Bird strives to create a working environment in which each individual — attorney and staff person alike — is valued for his or her contribution and is happy to be a part of the firm. We're extremely proud of our high rankings in this and other similar surveys."

PAY

RANK	FIRM	SCORE
1	Testa, Hurwitz & Thibeault, LLP	9.733
2	Wachtell, Lipton, Rosen & Katz	9.476
3	Winston & Strawn	9.269
4	Irell & Manella LLP	9.238
5	Gray Cary Ware & Freidenrich, LLP	9.170
6	Jenner & Block, LLC	9.083
7	Skadden, Arps, Slate, Meagher & Flom LLP...*	9.026
8	Fish & Richardson P.C.	8.800
9	Sullivan & Cromwell	8.787
10	Hale and Dorr LLP	8.722

Average score = 7.77

Skadden, Arps, Slate, Meagher & Flom LLP and Affiliates

Top three in pay

1. Testa, Hurwitz & Thibeault, LLP

This firm may not have made the Top 50 in our prestige rankings, but when it comes to associate pay, Testa, Hurwitz & Thibeault hits a resounding No. 1. "You can't compare TH&T's compensation," asserts an associate. "It's bar none the highest in Boston and competitive with major New York City firms." How does this mid-ranked Boston firm beat top compensation contenders like Wachtell and Skadden? Not by outbidding on bonuses — Testa Hurwitz refuses to engage in those bonus games. Instead, this high-tech firm remains above the fray by loading associate compensation up front in a generous salary structure that forgoes bonuses entirely.

"Just check the numbers!" gleefully boasts a junior associate evidently very happy with his salary. "I feel sorry for the attorneys who were depending on a bonus this year." Colleagues share his appreciation both for the high salaries and for avoiding the "premium on favoritism and billable hours" generated by other firms' bonus regimes. "I like that we don't have a bonus system," comments one attorney. "It eliminates competition among associates, and it's nice to know exactly what you'll be taking home for the year." Advises an insider, "Other firms should take notice!"

Managing Partner William B. Asher says, "Our culture, including our compensation system, is a reflection of our total commitment to team building. Every barrier to open communication and cooperation is avoided. Our associates benefit from the collegiality engendered by the absence of a bonus-based system. Our clients benefit from the firm's total focus on client service rather than individual incentives."

2. Wachtell, Lipton, Rosen & Katz

One firm that has managed quite well, thank you, with a bonus regime is Wachtell, Lipton, Rosen & Katz. Wachtell led the pack last year with the happiest-paid associates and this year slides into second place in our rankings. The world's richest law firm according to *The American Lawyer*, Wachtell distributes that wealth to associates in the form of top-of-the-market salaries and envy-inducing bonuses. Associates know they would "not be paid more at any other firm." Moreover, Wachtell keeps attorneys happy with lots of "non-compensation perks" like cell phones, laptops and Blackberries as well as car service, errand runners and "too much food."

Wachtell tries to ensure "that its associates are the best paid in the city." As one lawyer notes, "both the base salary and the bonuses are larger than other law firms." First-year associates currently start at $140,000, while fourth-years are pulling in a base salary of $180,000. Add to those sizeable paychecks bonuses that might amount to 50 percent of salary and Wachtell lawyers "certainly have nothing to complain about." On the other hand, associates hardly feel they are overpaid. They work "very, very long hours" on "incredibly important" cases. An attorney concludes, "I earn what I'm paid."

3. Winston & Strawn

After two years among the top ten firms, Winston & Strawn's "top-of-the-market" pay earns it the No. 3 spot this year. Associates are happy with both the multi-tiered salary system and the bonus opportunities. "Our salaries match market," says one Chicago insider, "and for those who work extraordinary hours, the bonuses are great." Another associate finds that "the compensation vs. the number of billable hours is hard to beat." Lawyers have some flexibility in this regard since the base compensation system "takes into account class, billable hours and evaluation grade. There are six evaluations grades and three billable hour tiers: 1,950 and above, 1,850 to 1,949, and below 1,850." Bonuses are based on a combination of hours and merit and provide "a very attractive incentive to work harder if you feel like going for it."

Associates are particularly pleased that their firm's "generosity has not flagged in the economic downturn," and Winston continued to pay top salaries and "outstanding" bonuses in 2001. "This," asserts one lawyer, "was a good indicator of the success the firm is enjoying, despite the down economy." Associates seem confident that "Winston will likely always pay top of market salary for very attainable hours goals."

Paul Hensel, Chair, Associate Programs, says, "Our competitive compensation package reflects the high level of importance Winston places on attracting and retaining top legal talent to help ensure the future success of our practice."

Base salary for firm HQ or main office*

FIRM	1ST YEAR	2ND YEAR	3RD YEAR	4TH YEAR	5TH YEAR	6TH YEAR	7TH YEAR	SUMMER (WEEKLY)
Akin, Gump, Strauss, Hauer & Feld, L.L.P.	125,000	135,000	150,000	160,000	170,000	185,000		2,400
Alston & Bird LLP	100,000	105,000	110,000	115,000	122,000	130,000	137,000	1,800
Andrews & Kurth L.L.P.	110,000							
Arent, Fox, Kintner, Plotkin & Kahn, PLLC	125,000							2,300
Arnold & Porter	125,000	135,000	145,000	155,000	165,000	175,000	185,000	2,400
Baker & McKenzie	125,000	130,000	140,000	150,000	170,000	180,000	185,000	
Baker Botts L.L.P.	110,000	114,000	121,000	130,000	140,000	145,000	155,000	2,100
Bingham Dana LLP†	125,000	130,000	135,000	160,000	180,000	190,000	200,000	2,400
Blank Rome Comisky & McCauley LLP	105,000							
Boies, Schiller & Flexner LLP	135,000							
Bracewell & Patterson, L.L.P.	119,800							2,100
Brobeck, Phleger & Harrison LLP	125,000	135,000	150,000	165,000	185,000	195,000	205,000	2,400
Brown Rudnick Berlack Israels LLP	125,000							2,404
Bryan Cave LLP	90,000							1,500
Cadwalader, Wickersham & Taft	125,000	135,000	150,000	170,000	190,000	205,000	220,000	2,400
Cahill Gordon & Reindel	125,000	135,000	150,000	170,000	190,000	210,000	220,000	2,400
Chadbourne & Parke LLP	125,000	135,000	150,000	170,000	190,000	205,000	210,000	2,403
Choate, Hall & Stewart	125,000							2,400
Cleary, Gottlieb, Steen & Hamilton	125,000	135,000	150,000	170,000	190,000	205,000	220,000	2,404
Clifford Chance Rogers & Wells LLP	125,000	135,000	150,000	170,000	190,000	205,000	220,000	2,404
Cooley Godward LLP	125,000	130,000	135,000	150,000	165,000	185,000	195,000	2,400
Coudert Brothers	125,000	135,000	150,000	170,000	190,000	200,000	205,000	2,400
Covington & Burling	125,000	135,000	150,000	155,000	165,000	175,000	185,000	2,400
Cravath, Swaine & Moore	125,000	135,000	150,000	170,000	190,000	205,000	220,000	2,500
Crowell & Moring LLP	125,000	135,000						2,400
Davis Polk & Wardwell	125,000	135,000	150,000	165,000				2,400
Davis Wright Tremaine LLP	95,000							
Debevoise & Plimpton	125,000	135,000	150,000	170,000	190,000	205,000	220,000	2,400
Dechert	105,000							2,000
Dewey Ballantine LLP	125,000	135,000	150,000	170,000	190,000	200,000	205,000	2,403
Dorsey & Whitney LLP	90,000	95,000	100,000	105,000	110,000	115,000	120,000	1,750
Drinker Biddle & Reath LLP	105,000							2,019
Duane Morris LLP	105,000							2,109
Fenwick & West LLP	125,000	135,000	145,000	160,000	180,000	195,000	205,000	2,400
Finnegan, Henderson, Farabow, Garrett & Dunner...**	125,000							2,400
Fish & Neave	125,000	135,000	150,000	165,000	185,000	200,000	215,000	2,400

*Does not include bonus **Finnegan, Henderson, Farabow, Garrett & Dunner L.L.P.   † Announced merger with McCutchen Doyle, scheduled for July 2002

Base salary for firm HQ or main office* (cont'd)

FIRM	1ST YEAR	2ND YEAR	3RD YEAR	4TH YEAR	5TH YEAR	6TH YEAR	7TH YEAR	SUMMER (WEEKLY)
Fish & Richardson P.C.	135,000	145,000	150,000	160,000	175,000	180,000	190,000	2,400
Foley & Lardner	115,000	120,000	125,000	130,000	140,000	150,000	185,000	2,100
Foley Hoag LLP	125,000	135,000	140,000	145,000	155,000			2,400
Foster Pepper & Shefelman PLLC	100,000	105,000						1,550
Fried, Frank, Harris, Shriver & Jacobson	125,000	135,000	150,000	168,000	190,000	205,000	215,000	
Fulbright & Jaworski L.L.P.	110,000	110,000	110,000	115,000	125,000	135,000	140,000	2,100
Gibson, Dunn & Crutcher LLP	125,000	135,000	150,000	165,000	185,000	195,000	205,000	2,404
Goodwin Procter LLP	125,000	135,000	135,000	145,000	155,000	165,000	180,000	2,400
Gray, Cary, Ware & Freidenrich, LLP	125,000	135,000	150,000	165,000	180,000	195,000	205,000	2,400
Greenberg, Traurig, LLP	85,000							
Gunderson Dettmer Stough Villeneuve Franklin...†	125,000	135,000	145,000	160,000	175,000	190,000	195,000	2,400
Hale and Dorr LLP	125,000	135,000	145,000	155,000	165,000			2,400
Haynes and Boone, LLP	110,000							2,100
Heller Ehrman White & McAuliffe LLP	125,000	130,000	140,000	150,000	165,000	175,000	185,000	2,400
Hogan & Hartson L.L.P.	125,000	135,000	150,000	165,000	180,000	190,000	200,000	2,400
Holland & Knight LLP	110,000							2,200
Howrey Simon Arnold & White, LLP	125,000	135,000	145,000	155,000	165,000	175,000	185,000	12,000
Hughes Hubbard & Reed LLP	125,000	135,000	150,000	165,000	175,000	180-185K	170-200K	2,403
Hunton & Williams	100,000							1,800
Irell & Manella LLP	130,000	135,000	150,000					2,400
Jenner & Block, LLC	125,000						205,000	2,403
Jones, Day, Reavis & Pogue	110,000							9,000/month
Katten Muchin Zavis Rosenman	125,000	130,000	142,500	157,500	170,000	180,000	190,000	2,403
Kaye, Scholer LLP	125,000	135,000	150,000	165,000	186,000	196,000	205,000	2,410
Kelley Drye & Warren LLP	125,000	135,000	150,000	165,000	180,000	195,000	205,000	2,403
Kilpatrick Stockton LLP	100,000						160,000	1,800
King & Spalding	100,000							1,750
Kirkland & Ellis	125,000	135,000	150,000	165,000	185,000	195,000		2,404
Kirkpatrick & Lockhart LLP	100,000							1,920
Latham & Watkins	125,000	135,000						2,400
LeBoeuf, Lamb, Greene & MacRae, L.L.P.	125,000	135,000	150,000	170,000	190,000	200,000	205,000	2,404
Littler Mendelson, P.C.	110,000							2,000
Lord Bissell & Brook	125,000							2,403
Mayer, Brown, Rowe & Maw	125,000	135,000	150,000	165,000	185,000	195,000	205,000	2,400
McCutchen, Doyle, Brown & Enersen, LLP††	125,000	135,000	150,000	160,000	180,000	190,000	200,000	2,400
McDermott, Will & Emery	125,000	135,000	150,000	165,000	175,000	180,000	185,000	2,400

*Does not include bonus †Gunderson Dettmer Stough Villeneuve Franklin & Hachigian, LLP
††*Bingham Dana and McCutchen Doyle have announced a merger scheduled for July 2002*

Base salary for firm HQ or main office* (cont'd)

FIRM	1ST YEAR	2ND YEAR	3RD YEAR	4TH YEAR	5TH YEAR	6TH YEAR	7TH YEAR	SUMMER (WEEKLY)
McGuireWoods LLP	95,000							1,800
Milbank, Tweed, Hadley & McCloy LLP	125,000	135,000	150,000	165,000	190,000	205,000	215,000	2,403
Miller Nash LLP	85,000							1,400
Mintz Levin Cohn Ferris Glovsky & Popeo, P.C.	125,000	135,000	145,000	155,000	170,000	175,000	180,000	2,400
Morgan, Lewis & Bockius LLP	105,000	110,000	112,500	120,000	122,500	130,000	132,500	22,000
Morrison & Foerster LLP	125,000							2,400
Munger, Tolles & Olson LLP	125,000	135,000	150,000	165,000	185,000	195,000		2,400
O'Melveny & Myers LLP	125,000	135,000	150,000	165,000	185,000	195,000	205,000	2,400
Orrick, Herrington & Sutcliffe LLP	125,000	135,000	150,000	165,000	185,000	195,000	205,000	10,400/month
Palmer & Dodge LLP	110,000	120,000	130,000	140,000	150,000	160,000	170,000	
Patton Boggs LLP	120,000	125,000	135,000	145,000	155,000	165,000	175,000	2,200
Paul, Hastings, Janofsky & Walker LLP	125,000							1,750-2,400
Paul, Weiss, Rifkind, Wharton & Garrison	125,000	135,000	150,000	170,000	195,000	210,000	220,000	2,400
Pennie & Edmonds LLP	125,000	135,000	150,000	165,000	185,000	200,000	210,000	2,400
Perkins Coie LLP	100,000	102,000+	105,000+	108,000+	111,000+	115,000+	120,000+	2,000
Pillsbury Winthrop LLP	125,000	135,000	150,000	170,000	190,000	195,000	195,000	2,400
Piper Rudnick LLP	115,000	117,500+	120,000+	125,000+	130,000+	138,000+	140,000+	2,200
Preston Gates & Ellis LLP	100,000	104,000						1,900
Proskauer Rose LLP	125,000	135,000	150,000	165,000	185,000	195,000	205,000	2,403
Ropes & Gray	125,000	135,000						2,400
Schiff Hardin & Waite	125,000	135,000	145,000					2,400
Schulte Roth & Zabel LLP	125,000	135,000	150,000	170,000	190,000	205,000	220,000	2,403
Shaw Pittman	125,000	135,000	145,000	155,000	175,000	185,000	195,000	2,400
Shearman & Sterling	125,000	135,000	150,000	165,000				2,538
Sidley Austin Brown & Wood LLP	125,000	135,000	150,000	165,000	185,000	195,000	205,000	2,400
Simpson Thacher & Bartlett	125,000	135,000	150,000	170,000	190,000	205,000	220,000	2,404
Skadden, Arps, Slate, Meagher & Flom LLP and...†	140,000	150,000	170,000	185,000	200,000	212,000	220,000	2,400
Sonnenschein Nath & Rosenthal	125,000							2,400
Steptoe & Johnson LLP	125,000	131,000	138,000	145,000	155,000	165,000	172,000	2,400
Stoel Rives LLP	80,000							
Stroock & Stroock & Lavan LLP	125,000	135,000	150,000	170,000	190,000	205,000	210,000	2,400
Sullivan & Cromwell	125,000	135,000	150,000	170,000	190,000	205,000	220,000	2,404
Sutherland Asbill & Brennan LLP	100,000	106,000	111,000	116,000				1,750
Swidler Berlin Shereff Friedman, LLP	125,000							2,400
Testa, Hurwitz & Thibeault, LLP	135,000	150,000	165,000	177,500	190,000	202,500	215,000	2,400
Thelen Reid & Priest LLP	125,000	125,000+	130,000+	135,000+	140,000+	145,000+	150,000+	2,400

*Does not include bonus   †Skadden, Arps, Slate, Meagher & Flom LLP and Affiliates

Base salary for firm HQ or main office* (cont'd)

FIRM	1ST YEAR	2ND YEAR	3RD YEAR	4TH YEAR	5TH YEAR	6TH YEAR	7TH YEAR	SUMMER (WEEKLY)
Troutman Sanders LLP	100,000							1,750
Venture Law Group	100,000	105,000	115,000	130,000				2,400
Vinson & Elkins L.L.P.	110,000	114,000	121,000	130,000	140,000	145,000	155,000	2,100
Wachtell, Lipton, Rosen & Katz	140,000	150,000	165,000	180,000	195,000			2,404
Weil, Gotshal & Manges LLP	125,000	135,000	150,000	165,000	190,000	205,000	215,000	2,400
White & Case LLP	125,000	135,000	150,000	170,000	190,000	200,000	205,000	2,403
Wiley Rein & Fielding LLP	110,000	120,000	130,000	140,000	150,000	160,000	170,000	2,400
Williams & Connolly LLP	140,000	150,000	170,000	180,000	190,000	200,000	210,000	2,400
Willkie Farr & Gallagher	125,000	135,000	150,000	170,000	190,000			2,404
Wilmer, Cutler & Pickering	125,000	135,000	158,000	168,000	191,000	201,000		2,400
Wilson Sonsini Goodrich & Rosati	125,000	135,000	150,000	165,000	up to 180K	up to 195K	up to 205K	2,400
Winston & Strawn	125,000	135,000	150,000					2,400
Wolf, Block, Schorr and Solis-Cohen LLP	107,000							2,050

*Does not include bonus

RETENTION

RANK	FIRM	SCORE
1	Winston & Strawn	8.427
2	Alston & Bird LLP	8.200
3	Troutman Sanders LLP	7.988
4	Davis Wright Tremaine LLP	7.806
5	Morrison & Foerster LLP	7.667
6	Hale and Dorr LLP	7.600
7(tie)	Arnold & Porter	7.500
7(tie)	Sutherland Asbill & Brennan LLP	7.500
8	Fish & Richardson P.C.	7.458
9	Vinson & Elkins L.L.P.	7.439
10	Preston Gates & Ellis LLP	7.414

Average score = 6.40

Top three in retention

1. Winston & Strawn

Winston & Strawn is doing something right. For the third year running, the Chicago firm ranks No. 1 in employee retention. Unlike some firms where low turnover is attributed more to the depressed economy than to attorney loyalty, Winston associates credit their firm with creating such a positive environment there is simply no reason to leave. "Winston is definitely a place where you can start as a first-year and make partner eight or nine years later," one lawyer asserts. "The firm values loyalty and dedication." Another contact agrees: "The firm works hard at making sure the attorneys are happy and have no desire to go to another firm, or elsewhere for that matter."

When people do leave, they "often go in-house to high-profile positions," "leave the city or move into another industry." Moreover, many who set off for greener pastures eventually decide they'd left richer fields behind. A junior associate notes, "Many attorneys who have left the firm actually return to Winston, which sort of speaks for itself." One lawyer shares her contentment: "I never thought I'd be in a large firm after eight years, but I haven't encountered anyone who likes their job more than me, so I don't expect to be leaving any time soon."

Paul Hensel, Chair, Associate Programs, says, "We've worked hard to develop a positive and energetic atmosphere where associates can get challenging work and shape their own careers. Our retention rate tells us we are on the right track."

2. Alston & Bird LLP

"Hardly anyone leaves this firm," observes an associate at Atlanta's Alston & Bird. Witness the firm's climb from sixth place last year to No. 2 in this year's retention ranking. "Our culture supports retention," say insiders. Since "people genuinely enjoy working here and believe they are treated well," why would they leave? Not to join other law firms, according to our sources. Lawyers "only seem to leave for unique opportunities in business, government or academia." And when people remain "past the first few years," they "tend to stay forever." A first-year notes that "there are people all over the place that have been here 20 to 40 years."

"There is a reason we are the top-rated law firm in the country according to *Fortune* magazine," one associate reminds us, referring to the firm's rank among the top ten companies in *Fortune's* list of the 100 Best Companies to Work For. Attorneys appreciate that Alston's high retention rate is unusual among large law firms. "Our associate turnover rate is about one-half of the average turnover rate of firms of comparable size," estimates one attorney. Another attributes the low attrition to "a sense of loyalty at this firm that probably does not exist at most other firms."

3. Troutman Sanders LLP

This year's dark horse, Troutman Sanders not only makes a surprise showing as one of the best firms to work for, but also makes it into the top three on our retention rankings. One associate believes the reason the "retention rate here is one of the best" is "because so much effort is put into making sure that each attorney is comfortable and happy in their surroundings." Contacts observe that this firm "rarely lose[s] associates to other firms even when lots of money is offered." Since associates are "satisfied with the work level and compensation," they are "not inclined to look elsewhere." The prospect of becoming partner offers additional incentive to remain. "If you come in as a summer associate," says one lawyer, "it is very likely that you will stay to make partner."

Naturally, people depart occasionally, but "those who do leave seem to move out of town, go in-house or quit practicing law altogether." Given the firm's supportive environment, however, Troutman Sanders not only "will view it as a positive for a lawyer to go in-house with a current client or potential client," but "in some instances may lobby for it, if it is in the best interest of the lawyer."

Says Managing Partner Bob Webb, "Nothing is more important to us than keeping the smart, well-rounded, motivated and hardworking associates who choose to join us. Retaining our lawyers — by providing them with opportunities for a rewarding long-term career — is a major factor in our success as a law firm."

TRAINING

Average score = 6.88

RANK	FIRM	SCORE
1	Testa, Hurwitz & Thibeault, LLP	9.033
2	Kirkland & Ellis	8.952
3	Ropes & Gray	8.542
4	Hale and Dorr LLP	8.522
5	Davis Polk & Wardwell	8.182
6	Morrison & Foerster LLP	8.160
7	McCutchen, Doyle, Brown & Enersen, LLP†	8.065
8	Jones, Day, Reavis & Pogue	8.036
9	Alston & Bird LLP	7.968
10	Sullivan & Cromwell	7.933

† Announced merger with Bingham Dana, scheduled for July 2002

Top three in training

1. Testa, Hurwitz & Thibeault, LLP

Testa, Hurwitz & Thibeault takes first prize in another of our quality of life rankings this year by scooping up top honors in training. Testa Hurwitz associates find more to gloat over than their salaries, as they praise the "first-rate" training provided by their firm. "I've heard of no firms that even come close to the training provided by TH&T," declares a first-year associate. Another maintains that "Testa's reputation speaks for itself in this department. I am willing to bet that we spend twice as much time in formal training [as] the runner-up."

A colleague agrees that "many hours" and much money are "spent in developing and conducting in-house seminars on legal topics tailored to our practice areas." Testa Hurwitz offers "tons of training," according to another associate. Opportunities include "weekly lunch seminars for junior associates and weekly lunch seminars on specific topics," as well as offsite and online CLE courses. The "delicious food" provided at the seminars especially pleases one young lawyer. Attorneys also receive billable hours credit for time spent preparing and presenting seminars. "Between the mentoring I get from the senior associates/partners in my department and the firm-sponsored seminar programs," says a third-year associate, "I couldn't ask for more opportunities for training."

Managing Partner William B. Asher says, "Our process of capturing day to day learning and sharing the best practices across all of our practice groups is the first step in deploying the intellectual capital of the firm to the best advantage of our clients. Every attorney in the firm actively participates in training and this commitment to lifelong learning serves as an important connective tissue for the entire firm."

2. Kirkland & Ellis

Kirkland & Ellis, tops in training for three years running, may have been nudged from first place this year, but that doesn't keep associates from insisting, "Training at Kirkland, particularly litigation training, is second to none." It's not only litigators who believe that the "training, real-life and in the classroom, is unparalleled." The firm also offers "exceptional training programs for corporate associates." According to an IP lawyer, the "amount of time, effort and money that K&E spends on training is unsurpassed by any firm."

Structured programs include KITA (Kirkland Institute of Trial Advocacy) for litigation associates and KICP (Kirkland Institute of Corporate Practice) for corporate lawyers. Both multi-week programs receive rave reviews, particularly KITA, which is called "amazing," "fantastic" and "unparalleled." "If you want to become a good trial attorney," argues one litigator, "you can either work for the government and get thrown into the fire or you can come work for Kirkland." Moreover, in "addition to excellent in-field and cross-field training programs that go year-round," associates report that "individual partners are fantastic and patient teachers." A bankruptcy lawyer "can't imagine any firm having a more fanatical training program," adding, "This firm will make you an excellent attorney."

Hiring Chairman of the Chicago office, John Donley says, "When you take a job at K&E, it's an unwritten part of the 'contract' that you will get direct, and intensive, training from the best in the business — whether in trial practice, intellectual property or structuring transactions. It's been a part of our culture for decades, and always will be."

3. Ropes & Gray

"Training is a big deal here," observes a junior associate at Ropes & Gray. That explains why this Boston firm wins the white ribbon in training for the fourth year in a row. "The training program is outstanding," maintains an R&G attorney, "and the firm takes it very seriously." Toward that end, Ropes & Gray provides associates with "many, many opportunities to learn and to become a better attorney." "In addition to formal, required training sessions," says a litigator, "there are tons of informal and optional training sessions on pretty much anything that might be of use to you in your practice." Ropes & Gray also "encourages associates to attend and/or teach outside seminars" and gives associates "a virtual blank check to attend Boston-area CLE courses."

The firm-wide and department-specific programs are reportedly "excellent." "But," according to a corporate associate, "that's not the reason R&G gets such a high score." The reason the firm's training is so highly rated is "because they staff matters so leanly and give you responsibility right from the start." It undoubtedly helps that "many of the lawyers love to teach associates." In the view of one young lawyer, her firm's training is simply "hands down the best."

Hiring Partner Doug Meal says, "Ropes & Gray recognizes that well-trained associates bring substantial benefits to the clients we serve, thereby ensuring the firm's future success. Our low partner-to-associate ratio allows for a great deal of partner-associate interaction, resulting in significant hands-on opportunities that might not be afforded at firms with higher ratios. Our firm-wide and department-specific training programs are designed to supplement the learning that occurs on the job. It is gratifying to know that our associates recognize and appreciate our commitment to providing quality training opportunities."

ASSOCIATE/PARTNER RELATIONS

Average score = 7.87

RANK	FIRM	SCORE
1	Morrison & Foerster LLP	9.107
2	Debevoise & Plimpton	8.919
3	Davis Wright Tremaine LLP	8.846
4	Wachtell, Lipton, Rosen & Katz	8.773
5	Morgan, Lewis & Bockius LLP	8.736
6	Troutman Sanders LLP	8.663
7	Winston & Strawn	8.657
8	Williams & Connolly LLP	8.567
9	Steptoe & Johnson LLP	8.565
10	Hale and Dorr LLP	8.536

Top three in associate/partner relations

1. Morrison & Foerster LLP

What's the most frequently cited benefit of working at Morrison & Foerster? "Bright, intelligent, kind colleagues who do not understand the meaning of the word hierarchy." These "terrific" partners who foster true team spirit contribute to associates' overall satisfaction and launch the firm to the top of this year's associate/partner relations rankings. "The relationship among partners and associates is very comfortable," declares one attorney. Perhaps this is because MoFo partners "are very accessible and genuinely welcome input from newer associates." Before making decisions which affect associates, management consults the associates." The firm holds "regular town hall meetings for both attorneys and staff, associate meetings, all-attorney meetings, and every Friday we have a happy hour together." Not only do partners actively promote the "non-hierarchical" camaraderie so valued by MoFo lawyers, they also take seriously their role as mentors. Associates enjoy "a lot of direct partner contact" and partners "try to make sure that an associate's first years are good learning experiences." Partner-associate interactions prove especially "healthy and productive" because many partners "see the value in taking each case as a chance to train younger associates — constantly pointing out little tips and lessons along the way."

Director of Professional Development Janet Stone Herman says, "We expect that MoFo attorneys treat each other with respect regardless of seniority. Our culture encourages and rewards collaboration of partners and associates across practice groups and offices. Associates know that they can pick up the phone and call a partner they've never met, in an office thousands of miles away, and get an answer to a pressing question."

2. Debevoise & Plimpton

Associates at our No. 2 firm rate their relations with partners very highly. A Debevoise & Plimpton associate says, "The partners are some of the best people I've ever worked with — brilliant but actually pleasant, and always, always kind to associates." Although relations naturally vary by partner, our sources are generally "impressed with the level of partner/associate contact." "Most partners are very respectful, even of very junior associates," reports a New York lawyer, "some exceptionally so." An attorney in the Washington office voices a similar sentiment: "Almost without exception, the partners here are extremely considerate of associates and treat them very well. Their doors are always open and they never, ever speak harshly." Beyond conveying civility and respect, partners exhibit a genuine interest in associates' progress. "There is a fairly serious mentoring culture" at Debevoise, notes one associate. Partners have "a real desire to teach and enjoy the intellectual aspects of the law," says another. They "are always accessible" and "eager to answer questions that arise during the course of a transaction."

"At the core of top quality service to clients lies a mutual professional respect for each other as lawyers. We are happy to see recognition in this important area," says Presiding Partner Martin Frederic Evans.

3. Davis Wright Tremaine LLP

Sliding into third place is the friendly, Seattle-based Davis Wright Tremaine. Even if this firm did not place in our prestige rankings, Davis Wright attorneys know they have a good thing going. Associates appreciate the "congenial culture" of their Northwest firm, a congeniality that owes quite a bit to the comfortable relations between partners and associates. "There is a fairly flat hierarchy here," many associates report, "and not a lot of formalities to distance associates from partners." A mid-level attorney finds the "working relationship between associates and partners is very collegial and productive" and includes none of those "games that I have seen elsewhere (e.g., 'hide the ball,' 'berate the associate')."

There is so little "stratification" that, according to one lawyer, "it is often difficult to tell who partners are and who associates are." With an open-door policy and everyone "on a first name basis," it seems that "partners are just as focused on keeping our environment pleasant" as associates. Moreover, "management is genuinely interested in developing associates to be partners as well as well-rounded citizens." With such a supportive environment, it's no wonder that a number of associates happily describe partners as "friends as well as colleagues."

Managing Partner Richard D. Ellingsen says, "We are very pleased to see our high ranking with respect to associate/partner relations. The culture at Davis Wright Tremaine is one of tremendous professional respect and courtesy throughout, and this ranking shows that our associates recognize, appreciate and value this culture."

OFFICES

Average score = 7.26

RANK	FIRM	SCORE
1	Winston & Strawn	9.200
2	Dewey Ballantine LLP	8.800
3	Arnold & Porter	8.600
4	Cleary, Gottlieb, Steen & Hamilton	8.596
5	McCutchen, Doyle, Brown & Enersen, LLP†	8.533
6	Hale and Dorr LLP	8.509
7	Wachtell, Lipton, Rosen & Katz	8.381
8	Troutman Sanders LLP	8.360
9	Crowell & Moring LLP	8.177
10	Baker Botts L.L.P.	8.165

† Announced merger with Bingham Dana, scheduled for July 2002

Top three in offices

1. Winston & Strawn

Working in "the best offices in the city" undoubtedly contributes to the overall satisfaction of Winston & Strawn associates. Those glorious views and spacious offices so "tastefully decorated" win top honors yet again for this Chicago powerhouse. The firm's headquarters are conveniently located in the city's downtown "Loop" and occupy the top 13 floors of the Leo Burnett Building. That "35th floor attorney dining room is a huge perk." There is no question in the minds of these associates that their firm deserves its No. 1 rank. "No firm in Chicago has nicer offices than

Winston," declares one lawyer. "Office décor, space and comfort cannot be topped by our competition in Chicago," agrees another.

Just what makes this "the best office space in town"? In addition to the "prime location," the firm "places a premium on décor," which is described as "refined," "very elegant and stylish." But the firm's design goes beyond mere aesthetics; associates appreciate space that is "comfortable" as well as "classy." Offices "are as nice as you will find without being ostentatious or off-putting to clients, but are supremely functional as well." Gushes one attorney, "If there was a higher number [than 10] on the scale, I would give it that."

Paul Hensel, Chief Administrative Partner, says, "We are proud of the high marks we have received over the last several years in this category. Providing a comfortable work environment is one of the ways we show our appreciation for our associates and the hard work they do."

2. Dewey Ballantine LLP

Jumping from the No. 6 spot last year, Dewey Ballantine's New York headquarters now rank as the second best law office space, according to Vault's insiders. Dewey associates exhibit their pride with typical New York attitude. "I defy someone to tell me who has better offices," dares one lawyer. Located in the heart of midtown Manhattan, Dewey's offices are "very nice and luxurious," according to an associate. Another attorney lingers over details of the firm's elegant décor: "Entire South American rain forests [were] decimated and Italian marble quarries were emptied to clad every surface in the offices in marble or tropical hardwoods. Expensive silk fabrics, fresh flowers and original art are on every floor and the conference rooms."

With "huge space, tons of storage and great lighting," associate offices "are large, attractive and well maintained." That every office has "a big window" also pleases Dewey lawyers. "These have to be among the best offices in the city for a business of our size," asserts a senior associate. Or, in the words of a junior litigator: "Our offices rock." And, if you don't want to take our word for it, "come on in," this lawyer urges, "we will be glad to show it off."

3. Arnold & Porter

One Arnold & Porter associate claims his firm has "the best offices in D.C. — bar none." Since A&P is the only one of this category's top three firms headquartered in Washington, this eager young attorney might well be right. His colleagues share his enthusiasm for the "gorgeous building" with "open and airy" offices. "It is quite a modern and dramatic building," reports another lawyer, "and the interior design is bright and refreshing." The well-lit space and combination of steel and light marble "meshes a contemporary look with a comfortable feel."

The "beautiful building" and "superb" common spaces draw special praise — and an invitation to visit. "For anyone who hasn't seen our firm's lobby," suggests an associate, "you should schedule a special trip to do so (even if you must travel from the West Coast just to check it out)." The "amazing art collection" alone might be worth the trip. And with onsite child care, an in-house gym, cafeteria and "Garden Room" where attorneys gather for a free happy hour every evening and pizza every Friday, A&P associates are pretty happy in their home. "Even after being here for four years," concludes one lawyer, "I feel good about coming into the building each morning."

"All lawyers spend a lot of time at work, and your physical surroundings have a lot to do with how you feel about being there. Providing nice office space is a way of showing respect for the people who work in an organization. We've tried to design our space to be comfortable, light and enjoyable for all of our colleagues," says Managing Partner James Sandman.

SELECTIVITY

Average score = 7.92

RANK	FIRM	SCORE
1	Williams & Connolly LLP	9.750
2	Wachtell, Lipton, Rosen & Katz	9.727
3	Munger, Tolles & Olson LLP	9.615
4	Davis Polk & Wardwell	9.333
5	Sullivan & Cromwell	9.264
6	Covington & Burling	9.215
7	Cravath, Swaine & Moore	9.147
8	Wilmer, Cutler & Pickering	9.013
9	Irell & Manella LLP	9.000
10	Boies, Schiller & Flexner LLP	8.941

Top three in selectivity

1. Williams & Connolly LLP

Jumping from fourth to first place, Washington, D.C.'s Williams & Connolly leads the field as the most selective law firm. If you're not sure you want to litigate at W&C, don't even bother applying, say associates. "The firm is only looking to hire candidates serious not only about litigating, but about litigating at W&C specifically," emphasizes a second-year. As another lawyer notes, "litigation isn't an afterthought here, it's the main focus, and the attorneys are some of the best in the country." In order to join them, candidates must be "intelligent" as well as "poised, self-confident" and prepared to "take the initiative." One associate describes the "key factors" in hiring: "credentials, personality, drive, genuine interest in the firm, team players, ability to thrive with a minimum of hand-holding."

Certainly, "grades and journal experience are significant," and "nearly all the associates have clerked." It's worth noting that among our contacts the law schools most heavily represented are Harvard and the University of Chicago. However, according to several lawyers, "credentials alone aren't enough." "Intellectual acumen is essential," but, after all, "this isn't an egghead firm." Since W&C attorneys "tend to be interesting" and "very sociable," another "important factor" for prospective associates "is a confident and engaging personality."

2. Wachtell, Lipton, Rosen & Katz

It's hardly surprising that one of the most highly respected — and high-paying — law firms in the country would be among the most difficult to get into. Wachtell retains its hold this year on the No. 2 spot in both prestige and selectivity. This M&A powerhouse "is extremely selective in its hiring," say associates. "The firm hires only the most accomplished law school graduates," sniffs one lawyer. Wachtell favors top-tier schools, "focusing its attention primarily on top students from Yale, Harvard, Columbia, Chicago and NYU," although it "also hires from Stanford and University of Pennsylvania."

One mid-level associate thinks no firm is "more selective" than Wachtell. "That's not to say that I'm anyone special," he adds with refreshing modesty. "The firm simply has fairly rigid criteria for prospective candidates that is based heavily on scholastic performance, professional experience and school prestige." But don't count on sliding into the firm on a shining résumé alone. You'll find interviews "extremely stressful." Hiring "attorneys want to make sure you'll be able to handle the work." Wachtell seeks "bright, motivated people who understand the challenges of working" for this top-notch firm. It also helps, suggests one associate, to "have a demonstrated interest in mergers and acquisitions."

3. Munger, Tolles & Olson LLP

The No. 1 firm for three years running has slipped a couple of notches, but Los Angeles-based Munger Tolles still remains among the nation's most selective law firms. A highly respected practice with something of an "egghead" reputation, Munger Tolles "usually takes only the most credentialed associates." "Brainiacs with stellar credentials" is how one associate describes the firm's ideal candidates. What does Munger Tolles consider "stellar credentials"? Oh, the usual: "top law school, Order of the Coif, law review, clerkship" and "high grades, high grades and more high grades." This "firm likes candidates with good grades and law review experience," confirms a contact. "Most of the associates have clerked for federal judges."

But "being an overachiever on paper is just the beginning," advises an attorney, who says you'd better "interview well," too. A colleague agrees, "Coming off well in the interviews is also a must." In fact, the entire hiring process is described as "intense." The firm can be "pretty tough on prospective hires" and will chase down your references. However, the lucky lawyers who prove to have that "something very special" can look forward to enjoying "a great reputation" and "the best quality of life among the top law firms."

PRO BONO

RANK	FIRM	SCORE
Average score = 7.30		
1	Morrison & Foerster LLP	9.692
2	Arnold & Porter	9.667
3	Debevoise & Plimpton	9.533
4	Crowell & Moring LLP	9.412
5	Paul, Weiss, Rifkind, Wharton & Garrison	9.371
6	Ballard Spahr Andrews & Ingersoll, LLP	9.310
7(tie)	Vinson & Elkins L.L.P.	9.250
7(tie)	Jenner & Block, LLC	9.250
8	Hunton & Williams	9.233
9	Wilmer, Cutler & Pickering	9.177
10	Simpson Thacher & Bartlett	9.023

Top three in pro bono

1. Morrison & Foerster LLP

In yet another category, Morrison & Foerster hits the top of the chart. Associates rave over their firm's "amazingly strong" pro bono program. The firm "donates tons of hours to pro bono" and every hour that associates put in counts "100 percent toward billables, bonuses and everything else." MoFo's "unbelievable commitment to pro bono work" begins with partners who actively encourage associates and staff "to take on pro bono matters," including regular projects as well as "high-profile cases." Moreover, "there is no limit on pro bono hours." One lawyer claims that she has "yet to know of the firm telling people not to take on pro bono projects, unless they spend more than 60 percent of their time on pro bono without prior consultation with their managing partners."

The firm makes great effort to see that associates "find pro bono work that is of interest to them." Each office has a pro bono committee and lawyers receive regular emails about opportunities. Should an associate report a low number of pro bono hours, partners will explore other projects in which the associate might want to participate. As one attorney proudly remarks, "Pro bono is one of the most important ways that MoFo distinguishes itself."

"As a firm, we are extremely proud of our pro bono efforts and our leadership in helping those who are denied equal access to justice because they cannot afford legal services. We have a deep and long-standing commitment to providing pro bono services and strongly encourage our lawyers to make contributions in a wide range of areas from children's rights to civil liberties," says Keith C. Wetmore, Chair of the Firm.

2. Arnold & Porter

Arnold & Porter's "wonderful commitment to pro bono" rates it a No. 2 slot in our pro bono category. "The accolades that we receive in this respect are well placed," contends one associate. "Among the best pro bono programs in the country," proclaims another. Lawyers across the board praise A&P's dedication, which is "deeply ingrained in the culture and actively encouraged." Associates report a "true, deep and long-standing commitment by the majority of partners." This commitment is supported by a policy that encourages attorneys "to devote up to 15 percent of their [billable] time to pro bono matters." "Pro bono is pushed very strongly," say insiders, and "opportunities abound in litigation as well as corporate and government-related projects."

Arnold & Porter's "excellent" commitment to pro bono is frequently cited as one of the best things about the firm. In fact, one associate claims that this devotion "is the main reason I joined this firm over its competitors. The passion for pro bono at the firm is incredible!" His own excitement is apparently widely shared, for he declares that "people clamor to be involved in pro bono." And when they are, associates find that A&P is "very supportive with firm resources."

"Our pro bono commitment is a critical part of who we are as a firm. If you ask people why they came to Arnold & Porter and why they've stayed here, pro bono is going to be among the top three reasons for almost everyone. That's true at all levels of the firm. It's sure true for me. And that will never change," says Managing Partner James Sandman.

3. Debevoise & Plimpton

Debevoise & Plimpton is "the best place, hands down, to do pro bono," declares an insider. Associates agree that Debevoise's "very strong" commitment is an integral part of firm culture. "The pro bono program is among the firm's highest priorities, the importance of which is stressed early and often," says one associate. "The result is one of the world's leading pro bono practices." A litigator notes, "Almost every litigation associate I know has a pro bono matter and the firm is very supportive." But it's not only litigators who get in on the act: "The firm encourages pro bono work for associates in all departments and has its own pro bono department." Pro bono involvement is so widespread that, one associate muses, "it seems that almost everyone does some."

Opportunities abound and pro bono work receives billable credit. "Hardly a day goes by without e-mails listing new pro bono opportunities," remarks a Debevoise attorney. The firm's pro bono practice is "strong and diverse" and "generally provides attorneys with many of their interesting cases," observes another associate. According to a first-year lawyer, "It's a very important part of the firm's ethic, which is why I came here."

"We work hard each year to build on a strong tradition of work for the public good. I am glad to see we continue to be viewed as a leader in this area," says Hiring Partner Michael J. Gillespie.

[they told him it was a "lifestyle" firm]

Vault Law Channel >
- Law Firm Profiles
- Message Boards
- Law Member Network
- Law Job Board
- Law Resume Database

VAULT
> the insider career network™

Visit www.law.vault.com

DIVERSITY RANKINGS

Visit the Vault Law Channel, the complete online resource for law careers, featuring firm profiles, message boards, the Vault Law Job Board, and more. www.law.vault.com

VAULT CAREER LIBRARY   59

WE ARE MANY.

WE ARE ONE.

Diversity means different things to different people. To us at Davis Wright Tremaine, it means the unique characteristics that make every individual distinctive.

Our firm and our clients are stronger because of our similarities *and* our differences. Our combined efforts and diverse perspective allow us to be innovative and progressive in resolving problems and serving clients. We are a team of many talents, working together as one to help clients succeed.

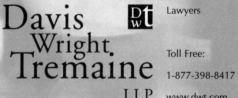

Davis Wright Tremaine LLP

DWt Lawyers

Toll Free:
1-877-398-8417
www.dwt.com

ANCHORAGE • BELLEVUE • HONOLULU • LOS ANGELES • NEW YORK
PORTLAND • SAN FRANCISCO • SEATTLE • SHANGHAI • WASHINGTON D.C.

BEST 20 LAW FIRMS FOR DIVERSITY

Lawyers and firm management place increasing value on a diverse working environment. That's why, for the first time, Vault has devoted a special section to associates' rankings on diversity issues. This year we've expanded the section to include separate categories for minorities, women, and gays and lesbians. To determine our Best 20 Law Firms for Diversity, we used a formula that weighed the three categories evenly for an overall diversity ranking.

It is important to remember that, like our other quality of life rankings, the diversity ranking reflects the opinions and perceptions of insiders.

Detailed and expanded rankings information is available with the Vault Law Firm Survey Corporate Research Report and the Vault Law Associate Database.

Get valuable information on both prestige and quality of life rankings by demographics such as law school attended, gender and ethnicity, practice area and more. Go to www.vault.com/lawsurvey or contact recruitingsales@staff.vault.com.

BEST 20 LAW FIRMS FOR DIVERSITY

Average score = 7.46

RANK	FIRM	HEADQUARTERS	SCORE
1	Morrison & Foerster LLP	San Francisco, CA	9.317
2	Arnold & Porter	Washington, DC	9.093
3	McCutchen, Doyle, Brown & Enersen, LLP†	San Francisco, CA	8.710
4	Arent Fox Kintner Plotkin & Kahn, PLLC	Washington, DC	8.515
5	Alston & Bird LLP	Atlanta, GA	8.432
6	Preston Gates & Ellis LLP	Seattle, WA	8.386
7	Littler Mendelson, P.C.	San Francisco, CA	8.328
8	Gray Cary Ware & Freidenrich, LLP	Palo Alto, CA	8.297
9	Davis Polk & Wardwell	New York, NY	8.286
10	Davis Wright Tremaine LLP	Seattle, WA	8.272
11	Jenner & Block, LLC	Chicago, IL	8.181
12	Winston & Strawn	Chicago, IL	8.117
13	Hogan & Hartson L.L.P.	Washington, DC	8.073
14	Schulte Roth & Zabel LLP	New York, NY	8.061
15	Skadden, Arps, Slate, Meagher & Flom*	New York, NY	8.060
16	Steptoe & Johnson LLP	Washington, DC	8.027
17	Hale and Dorr LLP	Boston, MA	8.015
18	Debevoise & Plimpton	New York, NY	7.946**
19	Heller Ehrman White & McAuliffe LLP	San Francisco, CA	7.946**
20	Vinson & Elkins L.L.P.	Houston, TX	7.931

*Skadden, Arps, Slate, Meagher & Flom LLP and Affiliates   † Announced merger with Bingham Dana, scheduled for July 2002
**Debevoise (7.9463) and Heller Ehrman (7.9459) are separated by a score difference not shown on the chart.

Top three firms for diversity

1. Morrison & Foerster LLP

At the top of our diversity rankings this year is California's Morrison & Foerster. The only firm to make it into the top three of each of the diversity categories (as well as four quality of life categories), MoFo's reputation for tolerance and respect is underscored by the opinions of insiders. This 1,000-lawyer firm inspires the sense of community one might expect from a smaller, more intimate boutique. With an environment that is "progressive" and "open," associates say the "firm culture promotes an informal, friendly, inclusive attitude."

Having an openly gay managing partner, Keith Wetmore, no doubt contributes to this attitude. "From what I can tell," a D.C. attorney remarks, "it appears this firm is very tolerant of all lifestyles." MoFo's embrace of diversity extends beyond sexual orientation to gender and race. The firm is "very proactive in wanting to retain women and other minorities," says a minority attorney. The firm has a standing diversity committee and, according to an Asian-American associate, "actively recruits minorities." Associates also find the firm surprisingly "family-oriented for a large firm" and "accommodating" of parents' needs — a quality reflected in Morrison & Foerster's place on *Working Mother* magazine's list of the 100 Best Companies for Working Mothers.

"Morrison & Foerster has been one of the most diverse large law firms for many years. We are proud of the firm's diversity and believe it makes us stronger as a firm," says Laurie Hane, Managing Partner for Operations.

2. Arnold & Porter

Arnold & Porter may have slipped a notch to second place in overall diversity, but some insiders consider their firm's commitment to this issue "unparalleled." According to associates, A&P is "very family/female friendly" and "very friendly" toward gays and lesbians, and it "works very hard to recruit and retain minorities." Contacts describe the environment as "open," "diverse and tolerant." "The firm culture is very decentralized, individualistic and very liberal," observes one lawyer, which makes it "comfortable for all types of personalities."

A&P just missed the top three ranking in diversity for women, but in the view of a female lateral, "A&P's approach to and respect for women is off the charts." A frequently cited perk is the "amazing in-house child care facility" in D.C., "now famous in the legal industry." In 2001, *Working Mother* magazine rated A&P one of the 100 Best Companies for Working Mothers. The firm's efforts to attract minorities are also praised. Associates of color say that the "firm is committed to diversity," and an Asian-American attorney notes, "The firm has made great strides in hiring minorities in the past few years." Insiders find the firm "very supportive" of gays and lesbians, a number of whom apparently "feel very comfortable being out."

"We have a culture that values individuality and differences among people. We're not a bunch of clones. We think an environment that values and encourages diversity and that allows people to be comfortable being themselves makes a firm not only a good place to work for everyone, but a higher quality organization," says Managing Partner James Sandman.

3. McCutchen, Doyle, Brown & Enersen, LLP

McCutchen Doyle's rank among the top three firms for diversity should come as little surprise to insiders. According to one associate, "We have a diverse group of people, and respect for differences is part of our culture." Another attorney mentions the firm's "four core values of integrity/ethics, diversity, public service and high work quality." McCutchen receives high marks for its commitment to minority hiring. The firm "actively reaches out to minorities" and "wants to see them thrive." "McCutchen," observes an Hispanic associate, "makes a big effort to hire people of color." The firm is also "very receptive" to gays and lesbians. "I can't think of many other firms that have had such an open and welcoming attitude towards members of all sexual orientations," comments an LA lawyer.

McCutchen holds the No. 3 spot for diversity with respect to women, and insiders widely praise the firm's efforts to hire, promote and retain women. A female litigator notes that "there are more women partners at McCutchen than most places," and a male associate claims, "We have had such a high percentage of women for such a long time at this firm that it hardly ever comes up as an issue."

DIVERSITY FOR WOMEN

Average score = 7.63

RANK	FIRM	SCORE
1	Morrison & Foerster LLP	9.458
2	Ballard Spahr Andrews & Ingersoll, LLP	9.091
3	McCutchen, Doyle, Brown & Enersen, LLP†	8.929
4	Arnold & Porter	8.895
5	Preston Gates & Ellis LLP	8.645
6	Davis Wright Tremaine LLP	8.611
7	Hogan & Hartson L.L.P.	8.600
8	Alston & Bird LLP	8.573
9	Davis Polk & Wardwell	8.462
10	Vinson & Elkins L.L.P	8.448

† Announced merger with Bingham Dana, scheduled for July 2002

Top three in diversity for women

1. Morrison & Foerster LLP

You'd think a firm that *Working Mother* magazine frequently cites as one of the top 100 companies to work for would score well in the category of diversity for women — and you'd be right. The law firm rated the most welcoming to women is San Francisco's Morrison & Foerster.

The firm's No. 1 ranking is reflected in the comments of insiders like the attorney in San Diego who boasts, "I have never seen or heard of any firm being more receptive to women than MoFo." According to another female associate, "the firm is on the cutting edge of these issues, and very proactive in wanting to retain women and other minorities." MoFo's efforts have resulted in a population numbering "lots of intelligent and diverse women," with "many women in leadership positions." A third-year lawyer reports that "our entire summer associate class last year was women, and the majority this year is women as well." At least one associate chose to work at Morrison & Foerster specifically "because of their reputation among women in the field," and, she declares, she has "not been disappointed."

2. Ballard Spahr Andrews & Ingersoll, LLP

The No. 2 firm on our list this year is Philly-based Ballard Spahr Andrews & Ingersoll. What it lacks in national prestige, Ballard Spahr makes up in quality of life for women. As noted by an associate who believes "the firm is extremely receptive to women in terms of hiring, promotion, and so on," the firm's main office in Philadelphia is led by a woman, managing partner Lynn R. Axelroth. "Being a woman, hiring women," that's simply "not a problem at Ballard," says a female associate.

Women in the Washington, D.C., office report that the office is "very receptive to female associates in hiring, promoting and mentoring." In fact, one lawyer says she "came to the D.C. office because of the number of senior female attorneys" who "are available for mentoring." She also notes that the firm has "started an all female partner dinner/meeting." An attorney in Denver agrees the firm "has done a good job to hire and promote women." Women comprise "probably half" of the lawyers in her department "and several large clients insist upon having women lawyers work on their matters." Associates also report that Ballard Spahr is "quite accommodating" about arranging flexible work schedules for parents.

3. McCutchen, Doyle, Brown & Enersen, LLP

"This firm is probably the best in the nation when it comes to having womEn attorneys," proclaims an associate at McCutchen, Doyle, Brown & Enersen. While McCutchen ranks third in diversity for women, insiders feel their firm "leads the pack on this issue." The California firm "consistently hires more women than men out of law school," notes one associate — and, more importantly, it keeps them. Another attorney boasts, "We have a large percentage of women not only in the associate ranks, but in the partnership, where I believe diversity is almost more important." According to a Los Angeles lawyer, the firm has "almost as many female partners as male, including a part-time female partner."

The firm's impressive record is reflected in its place on *Fortune* magazine's list of the 100 Best Companies to Work For, among which it was singled out as one of the Best Companies for Women. A part-timer applauds McCutchen's efforts to "ensure that the part-time schedule works" and praises "incredibly supportive" partners. "McCutchen realizes that there is a benefit to retaining attorneys who need to work part-time for childcare purposes. If more firms learned this," she maintains, "the practice of law would be a much happier place."

DIVERSITY FOR MINORITIES

Average score = 6.91

RANK	FIRM	SCORE
1	Arnold & Porter	9.000
2	Morrison & Foerster LLP	8.952
3	Winston & Strawn	8.549
4	McCutchen, Doyle, Brown & Enersen, LLP†	8.296
5	Alston & Bird LLP	8.182
6	Davis Polk & Wardwell	7.870
7	Troutman Sanders LLP	7.835
8	Littler Mendelson, P.C.	7.790
9	Gray Cary Ware & Freidenrich, LLP	7.759
10	Preston Gates & Ellis LLP	7.714

† Announced merger with Bingham Dana, scheduled for July 2002

Top three in diversity for minorities

1. Arnold & Porter

No. 1 last year in overall diversity, Arnold & Porter takes top place again this year in diversity for minorities. This honor should come as little surprise to A&P associates, one of whom notes, "It is no secret that the firm has the best reputation in the country with regard to minority recruitment and retention." Another boasts, "We are regularly honored and nationally recognized as one of the best (if not the best) place in terms of diversity." An Asian-American attorney believes that "A&P is constantly thinking about minorities and how to improve retention. It is easy to tell that this is an important issue to management."

As an example, a lawyer describes the creation of a group called Minorities at Arnold & Porter (MAP) which assists in attorney recruitment and "also provides a support network for minority attorneys at the firm." In addition, the firm welcomes minority candidates to whom it has extended offers by holding an annual cocktail party specifically for them. A&P's "unparalleled commitment to workplace diversity" makes associates proud. "All in all," concludes an African-American, "compared to other firms, ours is leaps and bounds ahead."

2. Morrison & Foerster LLP

Morrison & Foerster's achievements in diversity continue to win accolades, as well as a No. 2 ranking for its approach to minority issues. If MoFo doesn't yet house as many racial minorities as associates might like, it doesn't seem to be for lack of trying. Associates "know the firm wants diversity," in pursuit of which MoFo has established a standing diversity committee — and "that fact alone is great," exclaims an eager associate.

Relations among attorneys and staff are very friendly and open. Associates note with pride the firm's "progressive" and "tolerant" atmosphere. As a Southern California lawyer reports, "I've never detected even the slightest bigotry from anyone in our office." Associates say the firm's record of drawing a diverse body of lawyers is especially "good with respect to Asian minorities." According to an Asian-American attorney, "the firm is very aware and proactive on the issue [of diversity] and actively recruits minorities on campuses and otherwise."

3. Winston & Strawn

Making it into the top three for the first time is Chicago's Winston & Strawn. Many associates believe that "Winston is a leader in diversity in terms of hiring, promotion, mentoring and support" and one insider notes that the firm is "an award winner in Chicago in minority recruitment and retention." An African-American attorney asserts that "there is no firm with better diversity than Winston & Strawn." Insiders praise the firm for both minority recruitment and retention. One senior associate voices the opinion of many when she says, "I think Winston really cares about these issues and is trying to come up with ways in which to retain and promote minorities." According to another source, "Winston actively recruits minority associates and provides a support base to retain them."

Even if "the mix isn't quite where we want it yet," says a lawyer in D.C., "genuine strides are being made on this front." One Chicago associate declares, "I am a minority, and I find nothing but a comfortable work environment at Winston & Strawn and recognition for any additional things you can bring to the table as a minority, or otherwise."

Tom Poindexter, Chair, Diversity Committee, says, "We are pleased our associates recognize the firm's ongoing commitment to improving workforce diversity. We have a lot more to accomplish before we truly will be satisfied. Our goal is for a diverse workforce to naturally occur at Winston through implementation of day-to-day processes and programs that are a natural part of providing exceptional client service."

DIVERSITY FOR GAYS/LESBIANS

Average score = 7.82		
RANK	**FIRM**	**SCORE**
1	Arent Fox Kintner Plotkin & Kahn, PLLC	9.654
2	Morrison & Foerster LLP	9.542
3	Arnold & Porter	9.383
4	Irell & Manella LLP	9.200
5	Heller Ehrman White & McAuliffe LLP	9.127
6	McCutchen, Doyle, Brown & Enersen, LLP†	8.905
7	Jenner & Block, LLC	8.850
8	Littler Mendelson, P.C.	8.846
9	Preston Gates & Ellis LLP	8.800
10	Cleary, Gottlieb, Steen & Hamilton	8.787

† *Announced merger with Bingham Dana, scheduled for July 2002*

Top three in diversity for gays/lesbians

1. Arent Fox Kintner Plotkin & Kahn, PLLC

"This is the best firm in Washington for gays and lesbians," announces an associate at Arent Fox. This boast turns out to be an understatement, as Arent Fox Kintner Plotkin & Kahn captures the No. 1 title nationwide for providing the most receptive atmosphere for gays and lesbians. "If you are gay or lesbian at Arent, you are right at home," claims an associate. "The gay network is strong," she continues, noting that there "is a significant gay and lesbian population at Arent among attorneys and support staff." Another attorney agrees that Arent Fox provides "a great environment" in which "most gays and lesbians feel comfortable being 'out' at the firm — including a few partners."

This welcoming environment seems to stem from both a genuine appreciation for diversity and a meritocratic attitude in which "people are treated with respect for who they are." An associate declares that "Arent Fox celebrates its diversity." Evidence of that attitude includes the firm's provision of domestic partner benefits. At the same time, "Live and let live is basically the firm's policy. If you do good work, you will succeed."

The firm says, "We are delighted to learn that the prevalence of constructive professional relationships between attorneys of different orientations is recognized as a valuable element of our firm culture."

2. Morrison & Foerster LLP

Morrison & Foerster may rank second in our survey with respect to gays and lesbians, but it is "primo" among MoFo's own associates. A lawyer in the San Diego office explains the firm's attitude: "The firm has always been very open minded about hiring gays and lesbians; we follow the best features of the don't ask, don't tell policy insofar as it is of no moment what someone's sexual orientation is. If someone chooses to share it with the firm and be proud about it, the firm is supportive and generous, but otherwise, not intrusive at all."

The fact that Keith Wetmore, the managing partner, is openly gay "says a lot" to MoFo folks. So does the firm's willingness to provide domestic partner benefits and include the names of same-sex domestic partners in the firm directory. MoFo's welcoming reputation is well earned according to a gay associate, who declares that "diversity is not just tolerated but celebrated at MoFo."

3. Arnold & Porter

Arnold & Porter "is probably the leading big firm on being gay- and lesbian-friendly," declares an A&P associate. The firm that ranked No. 1 in overall diversity last year ranks among the top three firms this year for receptiveness to gays and lesbians. "Sexuality does not seem to be an issue as far as hiring, promotion and other programs," reports a lesbian attorney. Other lawyers cite the presence of "plenty of openly gay partners and associates" at Arnold & Porter. Gay and lesbian attorneys among Vault's contacts give the firm high marks in this category. "I am out at work and feel very comfortable being out," declares a litigator. The firm also welcomes domestic partners on its insurance plan.

A&P ranks No. 1 in diversity for minorities this year, and, according to one associate, the "friendly, open minded attitude towards gays and lesbians is mirrored with the attitude towards women and minorities." He congratulates the firm "for fostering such an environment. It comes from top management all the way down."

"Gays and lesbians are welcome at Arnold & Porter. We work hard to maintain an environment in which people are comfortable being out, because you can't enjoy your job or do your best work if for any reason you don't feel accepted for who you are," says Managing Partner James Sandman.

QUALITY MATTERS

Integrity. Quality.
Hard Work. Service.
Collegiality.

Since 1901,
Hunton & Williams attorneys
have adhered to these core
values. To learn more about
us, visit our website at
www.hunton.com.

**HUNTON&
WILLIAMS**

Atlanta · Austin · Bangkok · Brussels · Charlotte · Dallas · Hong Kong · Knoxville · London
McLean · Miami · New York · Norfolk · Raleigh · Richmond · Warsaw · Washington

THE VAULT 100:
FIRMS 1-50

Cravath, Swaine & Moore

Worldwide Plaza
825 Eighth Avenue
New York, NY 10019-7475
Phone: (212) 474-1000
www.cravath.com

LOCATIONS

New York, NY (HQ)
Hong Kong
London

MAJOR DEPARTMENTS/PRACTICES

Corporate
Litigation
Tax
Trusts & Estates

THE STATS

No. of attorneys: Approximately 450
No. of offices: 3
Summer associate offers: 83 out of 83 (2001)
Presiding Partner: Robert D. Joffe
Managing Partners: Richard W. Clary (Litigation) and
C. Allen Parker (Corporate)
Hiring Partners: Stephen L. Burns (Corporate) and
Julie A. North (Litigation)

BASE SALARY

New York, 2002
1st year: $125,000
2nd year: $135,000
3rd year: $150,000
4th year: $170,000
5th year: $190,000
6th year: $205,000
7th year: $220,000
Summer associate: $2,500/week

NOTABLE PERKS

- Half-price gym memberships and a discount at Tiffany's
- SeamlessWeb food-ordering service
- Back-up child care facility on premises
- Notebook computers and Blackberry pagers

THE BUZZ
WHAT ATTORNEYS AT OTHER FIRMS ARE SAYING ABOUT THIS FIRM

- "The gold standard"
- "I'll take 'Sweatshop' for $500, Alex"
- "M&A honchos"
- "Prestige with a price"
- "See 'laurels, resting on,' above"

UPPERS

- Cravath name carries significant weight
- Rotation system means variety of work
- "Great training, great cases, great responsibility"

DOWNERS

- "Hardly anyone makes partner"
- The hours are legendary
- "The work can be daunting and the pressure can get pretty high"

EMPLOYMENT CONTACT

Ms. Lisa A. Kalen
Associate Director of Legal Personnel and Recruiting
Phone: (212) 474-3216
Fax: (212) 474-3225
lkalen@cravath.com

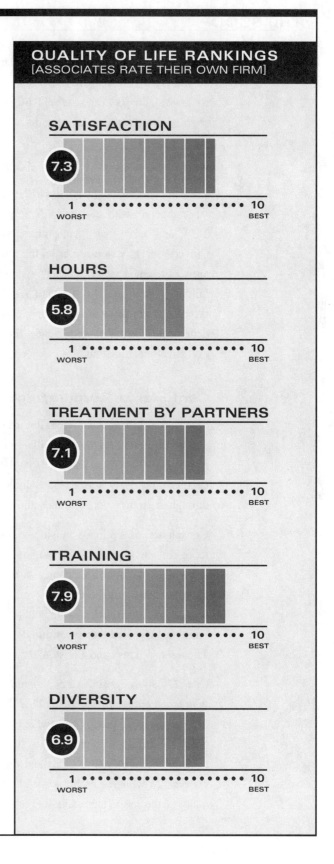

QUALITY OF LIFE RANKINGS
[ASSOCIATES RATE THEIR OWN FIRM]

SATISFACTION
7.3
1 WORST — 10 BEST

HOURS
5.8
1 WORST — 10 BEST

TREATMENT BY PARTNERS
7.1
1 WORST — 10 BEST

TRAINING
7.9
1 WORST — 10 BEST

DIVERSITY
6.9
1 WORST — 10 BEST

THE SCOOP

What's in a name? Plenty — if the name happens to be Cravath. While some firms follow the crowd, New York's Cravath, Swaine & Moore has been setting the trends for nearly 200 years. Renowned for its corporate and litigation practices, as well as its legion of hardworking and talented attorneys, Cravath remains a legend in the legal community.

A bastion of old New York

Cravath's roots extend back to 1819, when R.M. Blatchford founded a law firm in New York City. After a merger with an Auburn, N.Y., practice, the firm became Blatchford, Seward & Griswold in 1854, and, after many name changes, eventually Cravath, Swaine & Moore in 1944. Paul Cravath's early vision serves as the model for many of today's law firms: a practice built on an army of talented junior attorneys who strive to join a select partnership circle and, if their efforts fail, leave the firm. The "Cravath Way" continues to guide the firm's operation: Cravath offers no merit bonuses; associates regularly rotate to different partners or groups of partners within each department, acquiring experience through on-the-job training; and promotions come almost exclusively from within.

Centuries of corporate clout

Since the establishment of the railroads in the mid-19th century, the realization of many a corporate empire has rested on the twin pillars of Cravath's corporate and litigation departments. Industry giants like AOL Time Warner, Bristol-Myers Squibb, Georgia Pacific, IBM, J.P. Morgan Chase, Credit Suisse First Boston and Salomon Smith Barney regularly call on Cravath to guide them through the transactional hurdles and legal tussles of the corporate arena.

Cravath acts as a primary outside counsel for J.P. Morgan Chase and Credit Suisse and regularly represents those banks in arranging acquisition financing for leveraged buyouts, such as the acquisition of Laporte's chemical arm by KKR. Cravath showed its team spirit by helping J.P. Morgan Chase arrange the $190 million of financing for the construction of the San Francisco Giants' Pacific Bell Park. In addition, Cravath pitched in and assisted J.P. Morgan Chase in arranging the credit that permitted the acquisitions of the Texas Rangers, Cleveland Indians, Minnesota Vikings and Houston Texans.

Over 270 attorneys staff Cravath's mighty corporate department. In an effort to create generalists with broad corporate expertise rather than "narrow specialists," the firm rotates associates through different practice groups with which they spend 12 to 15 months. From commercial banking to M&A to securities offerings, Cravath attracts a premium corporate clientele and participates in some of the most visible deals and offerings on the market. Scroll through *The New York Law Journal*, *The American Lawyer* or *The Wall Street Journal* and you'll find Cravath's name next to many of the most impressive mergers and acquisitions reported. And despite Cravath's limited overseas presence (the firm's only offices outside New York are in London and Hong Kong), more than one-fourth of its largest clients are based outside the United States.

Merger magnates

The Wall Street Journal ranked Cravath seventh in a list of the top legal advisers for 2000, based on the firm's aggregate M&A deal value of $356.2 billion. Although the value of deals for all law firms fell by more than half in 2001, Cravath remained among the busiest of firms, even across the border. According to Canada's *Globe and Mail*, Cravath was also among the five most active firms on Canadian M&A deals. Two years ago, Cravath helped Time Warner make history with its landmark $165 billion merger with America Online, Inc., pocketing a healthy $35 million contingency fee in the process. Cravath also assisted at the birth of Vivendi Universal, the world's second-largest media company, when a team lead by partner Faiza Saeed represented Vivendi in the three-way merger with Seagram and Canal Plus. A Harvard Law grad whom *New York* magazine named one of ten up-and-coming young New York lawyers in February 2001, Saeed continues to score successes for Cravath. (Saeed is also handling Vivendi's $10.3 billion deal to acquire USA Networks, proposed in December 2001.)

In addition to making media moguls, Cravath works with leading companies in the energy, pharmaceutical and technology industries. Some celebrated deals from the firm's resume include Paine Webber's $12 billion merger with banker UBS, the $20 billion merger of Lucent Technologies and Ascend, and the creation of the world's second-largest oil company when ARCO joined forces with BP Amoco plc. Cravath recently counseled another energy client, Houston-based Conoco Inc., in its proposed merger with Phillips Petroleum Inc., a union that would create a company valued at a cool $35 billion. (The deal is scheduled to close in the second half of 2002.) And in 2001, Cravath represented the underwriters (led by Merrill Lynch, Credit Suisse First Boston and BOC International) of the massive IPO of CNOOC Limited, China's third-largest oil producer.

Cravath has assisted drug giant Bristol-Myers Squibb in its return to its pharmaceutical roots — first by shedding its Clairol line of hair products (purchased by Procter & Gamble in July 2001), then by acquiring E. I. Du Pont de Nemours and Company's pharmaceutical line for $7.8 billion, and most recently by negotiating a co-development and co-promotion agreement with ImClone Systems Inc. which will give Bristol-Myers a 19.9 percent equity stake in the company and licensing rights to the cancer treatment drug IMC-C225.

More than M&A

Cravath's prominence and reputation do not arise solely from success in the M&A arena. The firm's primary practice areas in corporate and tax are ranked at or near the top in virtually every ranking, including Vault's own. In this edition of the Vault guide, associates ranked Cravath No. 1 in litigation, corporate and tax, No. 2 in securities, No. 3 in M&A, and No. 2 overall in New York.

In last year's 4th edition, associates gushed similarly for Cravath, ranking the firm No. 1 in litigation, securities, tax and corporate, No. 3 in M&A, and No. 2 overall in New York.

White shoe warriors

A superior litigation department has made Cravath the firm of choice in cases ranging from antitrust to copyright and patent enforcement to securities fraud. Cravath's name frequently appears on the NLJ Client List, *The National Law Journal*'s "who's who" of firms defending corporate America. Cravath's current docket includes the defense of Campbell Soup Co. in a class-action securities fraud suit, representation of creditor Lucent Technologies against Winstar Communications in bankruptcy-related litigation, representation of Credit Suisse First Boston in connection with financings provided to Enron, and prosecution of a Napster-like copyright infringement case against the web site Aimster on behalf of clients including Warner Bros., AOL Time Warner and New Line Cinema Corp.

Not only does Cravath counsel corporate clients on mergers and acquisitions, but it ably defends them in efforts to thwart those deals. In 1998 Cravath represented WorldCom in GTE Communication's vain attempt to prevent the proposed merger of WorldCom and MCI Communications. Two years later, the firm successfully defended CBS against an action to enjoin its merger with Viacom Inc. Robert Joffe, the firm's presiding partner and long-time litigator on behalf of AOL Time Warner, recently negotiated a settlement with the FTC in The Three Tenors antitrust suit against The Warner Music Group and Universal Music Group. While former joint-venture partner Universal prepared for trial, Joffe's agreement enabled Warner to avoid both a trial and any admission of wrongdoing in exchange for a promise to refrain from future price-fixing. (Joffe termed the agreement a win-win situation, telling *The American Lawyer*, "Because our position was that we didn't break the law, we were more than happy to walk away.")

They're top of the heap

Payoffs for attorneys who meet Cravath's high standards are considerable: the New York firm consistently ranks at or near the top of national surveys based on prestige and profits. The Cravath System, which binds partners together in a lockstep compensation system, eschews merit-based bonuses for partners and associates alike. Partners receive no bonuses at all and associate bonuses are based on seniority, not merit or hours billed. This practice doesn't prevent Cravath's partners from taking home more money than their counterparts at almost every other firm. While *The American Lawyer*'s 2000 survey of the 100 top-grossing law firms ranked Cravath No. 25 in terms of gross revenue, the firm placed second in partner profits, with average partner compensation exceeding $2 million.

Cravath associates don't do so badly either. Since 1968, when Cravath nearly doubled its starting salary to $15,000, the firm has set the standard for salaries among top firms nationwide. In 1986 Cravath raised the bar by increasing first-year associate salaries from $53,000 to $65,000. In 2000

Cravath let California's Gunderson Dettmer Stough Villeneuve Franklin & Hachigian take the lead in base salary, while it upped the ante by awarding associates bonuses ranging from $40,000 to $100,000. Cravath also boosted summer associate salaries to a record $2,500 per week.

Setting the bonus trend ... again

Alas, all good things must come to an end. In 2001, Cravath slashed those generous bonuses in half. On November 21, 2001, Robert Joffe sent a memo to all Cravath lawyers explaining that the 2000 year-end bonuses, which were the result of "an extraordinary year," would not be matched (and even hinted that 2002 might leave attorneys without any bonuses at all). Some were disappointed that 2001 bonuses didn't match the spectacular bonuses of 2000. Many, however, were simply relieved that they were to receive any bonuses at all, considering the grim economic climate and Davis Polk & Wardwell's announcement earlier in the year that it would be dispensing no bonuses whatsoever to its associates. (Most associates interpreted Davis Polk's bold no-bonus announcement as an attempt by that firm to eliminate, by example, bonuses across all top firms that year.) Associates around the country held their breath and waited for an indication whether other firms would follow Davis Polk's lead. Cravath broke the tension by announcing its bonus structure, and other firms (including Davis Polk) dutifully fell in line. Looks like Cravath is once again the standard-setter for salaries.

Despite the smaller 2000 bonuses, first-year compensation for Cravath associates, between bonus and salary, nears the top of the chart at $145,000. Salaries for summer associates remain frozen at $2,500 per week, allowing Shearman & Sterling to inch ever-so-slightly ahead of Cravath with a weekly salary of $2,538.

GETTING HIRED

Only the best

"Cravath is, and hires, only the best." No false modesty here. You need "impeccable academic and extracurricular credentials" to be invited to join Team Cravath. "If you weren't at a big name school," advises an associate, "you'd better either have a connection or have been No. 1 in your class and editor-in-chief of the law review." (The firm notes, however, that it hired from over 20 law schools in 2001.) Although the "candidate needs to be smart, as demonstrated by proficiency in law school," she "must have a personality. You work a lot of hours here in small groups, so an associate must be able to get along and work well with others." The firm looks for "drive, genuine interest in legal issues, creativity, curiosity" and "stamina." "Quirks" or "eccentricities, if they indicate a passion for something and are not overly weird, can help."

Running the gauntlet

Candidates who successfully negotiate the initial interview face the gauntlet of the callback, a grueling affair in which interviewees spend a full day with partners and associates and have lunch with two associates. "Initial interviews are competitive," explains a lawyer, "and tend to weed out both weak resumes and transcripts and — usually — dud personalities. Callbacks are day-long and exhausting, but as good a way as any to get to know the firm. Most candidates see three or four partners during the interview day. The rest of the time, associates will answer questions and look for veto opportunities — for example, rudeness or stupidity." Offers are typically made the same day, and insiders suggest that "once you get an interview, chances are good that you will receive an offer."

OUR SURVEY SAYS

A serious place to practice law

"Cravath culture is 100 percent work-oriented." Associates enjoy early responsibility and work on "very high-level, newsworthy deals" with "partners who are at the top of their field." Satisfied sources "cannot imagine working anywhere else." "The work is top-notch and the experience second-to-none," claims one insider. Another believes that "no firm is doing more complex, more interesting or more rewarding work." That said, "all of this comes with a price: the hours can be grueling and the firm, the transactions and the clients are your life."

"This isn't the place to come for happy hours or firm socials," warns an associate. "Cravath is a serious place to practice law." Many lawyers praise the "performance-oriented" environment, but others call it "uptight." "Cravath culture is somewhere between perfectionist and neurotic, with each component fueling the other," according to one associate. At the same time, the atmosphere breeds a deep loyalty to this most traditional of firms. "The firm's culture is 100 percent focused on professional matters, paying client and pro bono alike," states one insider. "Against that backdrop, the atmosphere is informal though very serious. Lawyers are accessible, friendships develop and people make sacrifices for the good of the firm."

As far as socializing, sources tend to agree that "people are relatively friendly" and "cordial," but Cravath "is not a very social firm." Generally, "lawyers look outside the firm for opportunities to socialize." A certain amount of formality continues to reign; other than during the summer, when there is business casual dress on Fridays, lawyers are "still wearing suits five days a week."

Partners set the tone

Sources say that the degree of formality depends "upon which group and which partners you work with." "Each group between which associates periodically rotate has its own definite culture and personality. Partners definitely set the tone for their groups," opines one insider. Partners are said to range from "nasty" and "derogatory" to "exceptionally friendly and very generous with their time." Associates' experiences vary accordingly. It's all "very hit or miss. Whether an associate leaves within two years is almost entirely dependent on his partner," sources say. "There are a lot of A-type personalities among the partners," summarizes one associate, who concedes that "most associates fall within the same camp as well."

Cravath is well-known for its rotation system, where associates work with partners in shifts that range from 12 months to two years. After each shift is up, they rotate to the next partner group. Many associates believe that "the rotation system is a highlight of the firm," in that it "fosters a true team atmosphere" and "promotes mentoring and feedback from partners to associates." On a practical level, partners have a vested interest in helping their associates learn; because partners "are stuck with their associates for a year or two, slash and burn tactics don't serve the firm well." Even if not all associates agree that the firm has a "rigid hierarchy," many note a "gap between partners and junior associates."

Tremendous training

Some insiders report that the firm's rotation system may be behind Cravath's commitment to training its junior lawyers. "Because partners are stuck with their own associates," an insider says, "they train them or they don't get work done. In addition to the one-on-one mentoring from a partner, there are almost-weekly CLE seminars taught by partners on timely topics." A number of detractors find the system "overrated" and claim the firm has "taken the 'sink or swim' attitude to a new extreme. This results in needless worrying, lack of confidence and anxiety over asking what appear to be simple questions." But most associates gush over the "unparalleled" training — both formal and hands-on. The "independence required by young associates generally results in tremendous on-the-job training." This, sources say, is "surely one of the top reasons to come to Cravath."

The price of admission

Yes, Cravath associates work long and hard, but most seem resigned to, if not thrilled with, their schedules. "The long hours are an inherent part" of the Cravath experience, sighs one associate. "The hours are the price of admission, not an item that provides independent satisfaction or dissatisfaction," sniffs another. Many sources say their hours are "very long, but what I expected." "It's hard for me to legitimately complain," concedes a first-year. After all, "I read the Vault report." One lawyer claims the hours are "not as bad as I anticipated," while another finds herself working "many more hours than I reasonably expected." A litigator gripes that he works "too many hours for the same pay as associates at other firms."

Several associates comment on the "cyclical" or "erratic" nature of their workloads, but since "there is no face time," at least "when there is a lull, of which there were many this past year, no one will question you going home at an early hour." One lawyer advises prospective Cravathniks:

"The hours are so many that you really have to commit to giving up a lot of other things for the time that you're here. That's not a bad thing, as long as you know you've made that decision at the outset and remember it on the days when the hours start to get unbearable."

Entitled to the best

When you work at one of the top firms in the world, you expect to be paid top dollar. Indeed, according to associates, "Cravath makes sure it is not outpaid by peer firms." Nevertheless, many lawyers feel underpaid. "It's fine," one associate grudgingly concedes of his salary, "but a firm that prides itself on being the best should pay better than all of the other firms, and it does not." "Excluding Wachtell, Cravath should be at the very top of the market — period," insists another lawyer. "Cravath associates should be compensated commensurate with what is expected of them. With very few exceptions, if any, no other firm expects what Cravath expects from its associates and extracts what Cravath extracts from the lives of its associates." It's "hard to complain about a six-figure income," an associate acknowledges, "but the level at which I am asked to work on a consistent and daily basis is extraordinarily high."

One lone litigator would "take a pay cut in exchange for better hours or a better sense of what I'm doing. But," he notes, "I seem to be in the minority." Several associates mutter about greedy partners, and one lawyer suggests that "there will always be Wachtellian whispers of 'Why do the partners make twice as much as their competitors, but we do the work and make the same as every other associate in the city — with even lesser chances for partnership to boot?'" Sighs one contact, "It's the most money I've ever made, but given the long work hours, the cost of living in the city and the attending deprivations in terms of quality of life, the compensation seems barely adequate."

A springboard to success

Another gripe among Cravath New Yorkers is that they share offices until their third year. "Associates share offices for way too long" is a frequent lament. Lawyers like the "great views" from their West Side location but suggest that the "offices are showing their age" and could "use a facelift sometime soon." Associates hope that ongoing renovations will help relieve the cramped quarters.

The space crunch might be due in part to a falling attrition rate. Ordinarily, the firm maintains a notoriously "high turnover," an issue about which "Cravath doesn't seem overly concerned." An associate explains, "There is very limited space at the top — the partnership — and so even the best and brightest are not catered to by the firm." Moreover many associates regard "the firm's reputation as a springboard to something else." "Perhaps," a lawyer suggests, associates "come here committed to the idea of a short stint — to capture the real benefits of the training and prestige of the firm — before going to other places."

Room for improvement

Sources see room for greater diversity at Cravath. Even those who find Cravath "gender blind" note "the low ratio of female partners to male partners," and at least one woman believes there's "a bigger hurdle for women to overcome here in terms of partnership." Several associates complain about poor retention and lack of mentoring by female partners. A litigator reports that "Cravath has a generous maternity leave policy and does allow women associates to work part time." But another source complains, "There is no sense that part time could possibly lead to partnership and working part time frequently is regarded as a nuisance."

Minorities are even scarcer than women. "There is only one minority partner and there has not been another made during the last 15 years." Some insiders believe that "the firm does make a legitimate effort to hire minorities," but "not to the extent there should be." "This is not a progressive place," declares one associate. As far as sexual orientation, "personal lives and thus sexual preference are rarely if ever discussed at the office, so this sometimes appears to be a non-issue." Contacts note that Cravath has openly gay partners and associates, one of whom maintains that "this firm is probably better than average for gays and lesbians, believe it or not. Nobody cares about your social life here — they care about your work."

Still the one

Despite their griping, the majority of Cravath associates are pleased, even honored, to be working for the firm. Along with Blackberry pagers, Cravath associates consistently cite the level of responsibility, the training and the quality of work among the best things about the firm. Most understand that, if they ever choose to leave the firm, virtually any legal door will be open to them. "Working here gives me lots of options for when I decide what I want to do next — be it going in-house, working in the U.S. Attorney's Office, teaching or moving to a small boutique firm. Cravath people are well connected and are everywhere, thankfully," says one first-year associate.

So what is Cravath all about? In sum, says one insider, "Cravath is all about doing the best work possible and doing it as well as possible. People cooperate intensely on behalf of the firm and make serious sacrifices. Quality control has always been far more important than growth here. And seeing a satellite office of Arthur Andersen bring down the entire firm, one appreciates that philosophy. If one fits in here — which is not an unmitigated blessing given the level of commitment required — there is no better legal job around."

Wachtell, Lipton, Rosen & Katz

51 West 52nd Street
New York, NY 10019-6150
Phone: (212) 403-1000
www.wlrk.com

LOCATIONS

New York, NY (HQ)

MAJOR DEPARTMENTS/PRACTICES

Antitrust
Corporate
Creditors' Rights
Executive Compensation & Benefits
Litigation
Real Estate
Tax

THE STATS

No. of attorneys: 179
No. of offices: 1
Summer associate offers: 21 out of 21 (2001)
Chairman: Richard D. Katcher
Hiring Partner: By committee

BASE SALARY

New York, 2002

1st year: $140,000
2nd year: $150,000
3rd year: $165,000
4th year: $180,000
5th year: $195,000
Summer associate: $2,404/week

NOTABLE PERKS

• Free cookies, yogurt machine and other delectable foodstuffs
• Firm will represent associates buying property
• Errand-runners and other concierge services

THE BUZZ
WHAT ATTORNEYS AT OTHER FIRMS ARE SAYING ABOUT THIS FIRM

• "Still there at 3 a.m."
• "Total ninjas"
• "Show me the money"
• "Brilliant people but masochistic"
• "Ultra-prestigious and great quality of work"

UPPERS

- "Stupefyingly" high-profile cases
- Superior working relationships with partners
- Mo-nay mo-nay

DOWNERS

- Notoriously long hours
- "Ridiculously few" women
- Short on socializing

EMPLOYMENT CONTACT

Ms. Ruth Ivey
Recruiting Director
Phone: (212) 403-1374
Fax: (212) 403-2374
recruiting@wlrk.com

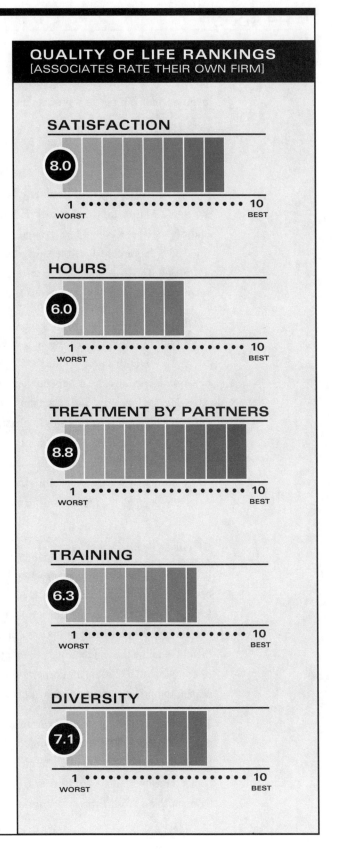

QUALITY OF LIFE RANKINGS
[ASSOCIATES RATE THEIR OWN FIRM]

SATISFACTION
8.0
1 WORST • • • • • • • • • • • • • • • • • • • 10 BEST

HOURS
6.0
1 WORST • • • • • • • • • • • • • • • • • • • 10 BEST

TREATMENT BY PARTNERS
8.8
1 WORST • • • • • • • • • • • • • • • • • • • 10 BEST

TRAINING
6.3
1 WORST • • • • • • • • • • • • • • • • • • • 10 BEST

DIVERSITY
7.1
1 WORST • • • • • • • • • • • • • • • • • • • 10 BEST

THE SCOOP

What a year for the prestigious Wachtell, Lipton, Rosen & Katz. The 36-year old New York firm pulled together the single biggest deal of the year, rewarded associates with record-breaking bonuses and paid partners profits that make it the wealthiest law firm in the world.

An innovative new firm

In 1965 four classmates from New York University Law School created a new law firm, unshackled by restrictive traditions common to more established firms. Founders Herbert Wachtell, Martin Lipton, Leonard Rosen and George Katz opened their doors to Jewish lawyers and others whose ethnic background rendered them persona non grata at some city firms. They rejected a hierarchical partnership structure in favor of softer lines between junior and senior attorneys. The firm's nearly one-to-one partner-to-associate ratio continues to foster close working relationships among lawyers and to enhance each associate's chance of making partner.

Wachtell does things its own way — because it can. Since its founding, the firm has taken on new work only through transactions and does not enter into retainer relationships or serve as general counsel. While this policy limits the potential for conflicts of interest, it also poses business risks because the firm has no steady clientele on which to rely. Unlike many firms who in recent years have invested heavily on expansion, Wachtell remains relatively small, with fewer than 200 attorneys operating out of a single office in midtown New York. The firm seems more interested in satisfying the lawyers it has than in acquiring more: Wachtell's compensation for both partners and associates is the highest in the nation (though the sky-high compensation numbers don't hurt when it comes to recruiting either). The firm does share some traditions with other top-rated practices, such as long hours, big-name clients and prestige.

"Poison pill" pioneer

In the 1970s, Wachtell made a name for itself in the M&A market, and by 1980 the firm had become expert in defending companies against hostile takeovers. In 1982, co-founder Marty Lipton developed a revolutionary strategy for companies to ward off unwanted suitors: the shareholders' rights plan, or "poison pill," would permit shareholders to buy stock at a discount, thereby making those assets unavailable to the would-be raider and raising the company's purchase price. More than 250 major corporations adopted Lipton's tactic, and versions of the "poison pill" remain the primary defense against hostile bids.

The heyday of the hostile takeover brought the young firm a flood of business — and a bundle of money. In the 1980s, Wachtell joined Skadden, Arps, Slate, Meagher & Flom in instituting a new fee system for M&A clients, charging a premium based on the value of the transaction and the firm's contribution to the ultimate result. This success-based billing system, which was adopted by many New York firms, often produced staggering fees. When Philip Morris Companies took over Kraft, Inc. in 1988, Wachtell's work on the deal not only upped the final price Kraft shareholders received but also netted the law firm a pretty $20 million fee.

Big deals are big business

Wachtell may not handle the most M&A transactions, but it often works on the biggest and most complex. The firm recorded 2001's largest merger when client AT&T Broadband and Comcast Corp. announced a $72 billion plan in December 2001. Wachtell also participated in Deutsche Telekom's purchase of VoiceStream Wireless for $55 billion and Warner-Lambert's $93.4 billion union with Pfizer Inc. in 1999. Last year Wachtell faced off with rival M&A master Cravath, Swaine & Moore to arrange a $35 billion marriage between Phillips Petroleum and Conoco Inc. Wachtell's acknowledged expertise in big-scale bank mergers is so impressive that sometimes both sides of a deal choose the firm as their counsel: in 1998, for example, Wachtell represented both Bank One and First Chicago in their $30 billion merger, and advised both Wells Fargo and Norwest Corp. in a $34 billion deal in the same year.

Wachtell stands at the top of the 2001 M&A chart for overall U.S. mergers, with a combined value exceeding $250 billion. And although the firm only logged 48 U.S. deals last year — a fraction of the 400 worldwide transactions announced by Jones, Day, Reavis & Pogue, for example — at $252.5 billion, the total value of Wachtell's activity amounted to more than double that of its more prolific colleagues. In fact, according to data compiled by Thompson Financial, the firm's average deal value for transactions announced in 2001 was $4.7 billion, the highest in the world.

More than mergers

Wachtell also boasts a first-rate creditors' rights department and litigation team, as well as top-quality departments in other areas like antitrust, tax and real estate that support the corporate practice. The firm's litigation matters often turn on transaction-related issues, like mega-merger antitrust concerns. Wachtell represented frequent client AT&T in the litigation challenging its $60.5 billion merger with Media One. The communications giant also turned to Wachtell for advice on restructuring when it divided into four companies in October 2000, and Wachtell's talents have served the new AT&T family members in their own recent mergers and acquisitions.

Wachtell has joined in the tobacco trials, as counsel for Philip Morris in several lawsuits. The firm recently won a notable victory for reinsurers when New York's highest court rejected an effort by Travelers Casualty to aggregate losses resulting from environmental contaminations at different sites. And after the destruction of the Twin Towers on September 11, 2001, Larry Silverstein, the developer who controlled the World Trade Center, retained Wachtell to represent him in suits against his insurance companies.

A controversial partner bids adieu

The 14-member creditors' rights group at Wachtell Lipton counsels major financial institutions around the world. In 2001 the firm represented creditors FINOVA Group Inc. and PSInet Inc. in two of the 10 largest public company bankruptcies of the year. Although the firm typically advises creditors, Wachtell switched sides to represent debtor W.R. Grace & Co., the multinational conglomerate that, deluged by asbestos-related claims, filed for Chapter 11 protection last year.

Wachtell's lean, mean creditors' rights team just got a little leaner — and maybe a little nicer. The sudden departure of long-time partner Chaim Fortgang in December 2001 deprives the firm of one of its most aggressive advocates. The brilliant bankruptcy lawyer, whose abrasive, pugnacious style made him a hero to clients and a headache to opponents, joined the firm in 1971. Neither the firm nor Fortgang have commented publicly on the reasons for his departure, but rumors suggest that Fortgang's antics (which reportedly included chucking a bagel at an adversary and threatening to rip out another lawyer's tongue) may have soured his relations with some important people — including his own partners. Then there's the fee factor: bankruptcy fees, which require court approval, tend to be far lower than the premium fees generated by Wachtell's litigation and corporate practices. But the firm compensates partners based on seniority and not the business they bring in. *The Wall Street Journal* reported resentment among some partners that Fortgang's practice didn't support his (very substantial) share of the pie.

The world's richest law firm

Wachtell Lipton is the wealthiest law firm in the world, according to the November 2001 Global 100 survey from *The American Lawyer* and London's *Legal Business*. Average profits per partner exceeded $3 million in 2000, almost half a million dollars higher than its nearest competitor, Robins, Kaplan, Miller & Ciresi of Minneapolis, and over $1 million more than New York rival Cravath, Swaine & Moore (whose partners pulled in a relatively paltry $2,245,000).

The firm's generous pay scale extends to associates. On top of a base salary that meets or exceeds those of rival firms (currently $140,000 for first-years), Wachtell often pays associates eye-popping bonuses. In 2001 bonuses ranged from $70,000 for first-years to $125,000 for senior associates. These bonuses weren't quite as high as 1999 and 2000 bonuses, which equaled 100 percent of associates' base salaries, but were enough to ensure that Wachtell remains at the top of the compensation charts.

Wachtell's largesse has also extended beyond the office. Soon after the September 11 terrorist attacks shook the city, Herbert Wachtell himself set up a $5 million scholarship fund at his alma mater, NYU, for dependents of firefighters, police officers and medical personnel.

GETTING HIRED

Picky picky

With its stellar reputation, small size and top-of-the-market pay, Wachtell can afford to be choosy. "It would be surprising for me to learn that there is any other law firm in New York City or, for that matter, the United States, that's more selective." One source advises that to land an offer from Wachtell, candidates must "graduate from a top 10 school and be in the top 10 percent of your class." Another associate raises the bar higher: "You need to be on law review, period, or have an extremely high GPA, above 3.8 at a top five law school. While the firm does hire and recruit students from a variety of law schools, out of 25 or 26 summer associates last year, about 20 of them were from just three schools: Harvard, Yale and Columbia." Students from New York University, Stanford, Chicago and Penn are also well-represented.

Beyond "demonstrated academic success," Wachtell looks for "evidence of a willingness to work hard and learn quickly." Candidates might find interviews "extremely stressful. The attorneys want to make sure you'll be able to handle the work." Similarly, students expecting to be wined and dined in a "cushy," "activity-filled" summer program should look elsewhere. Although "the firm does sponsor numerous events and outings for the summer associates," it pursues the more earnest goal of revealing "what young associate life is really like." This means that "the firm expects to, and does, get work from the summer associates."

OUR SURVEY SAYS

As good as it gets

Perhaps the success of Wachtell's rigorous hiring process is best measured by the degree of satisfaction associates express with their professional life. "As far as law firm legal work goes, this is about as good as it gets," raves one lawyer in a view shared by many colleagues. "I've been extremely satisfied with the work and responsibility that I've been given and the way the firm treats its associates." Another attorney reports that the "firm's reputation assures you will be working on high-profile complex matters, while the firm's size assures you of having greater responsibility than that of your peers at other firms." A third-year associate is pleased to find herself "negotiating with partners on the other side of deals."

Sources advise that such high-quality work does come at a price; you'd better decide which you prefer — "a social life or the practice of law." Suggests one associate, "If you come here for the practice of law, you'll find it very fulfilling. But, due to the hours, your social life will be very unfulfilling." Notwithstanding the social sacrifices, the insider concludes, "I wouldn't want to practice law at any other law firm." One emphatic first-year maintains that "if you want to practice corporate law, there is no better practice in the entire world."

But seriously

Wachtell attorneys are "very friendly," but the firm in general is "strictly business" and "not overly social." "The firm is laid back in the sense that it isn't a stickler for protocol. However, when it comes to serving clients, the firm prides itself on meeting clients' needs quickly and without errors." After-hours socializing appears limited; don't count on this as "a place to meet your next best friend," warns one lawyer. Associates note that "most attorneys, even junior associates, are married and have families, so they want to get their work done and go home." Partners and associates do gather over firm-sponsored dinners in the dining room, and despite the limited socializing the atmosphere is "not at all stuffy or segmented by seniority. The most senior partners and the lowliest of associates rub elbows routinely."

Although one reason for limited social contact is undoubtedly the volume of work, another factor may be the firm's generous office distribution. One lawyer writes that "the offices are generally quiet, with everyone working on his or her own matter. A part of this culture has to do with the fact that every associate, even the first-years, have their own offices." These offices, which associates rate highly, are described as "functional, but by no means posh and luxurious." One lawyer claims, "We're into Spartan Chic."

And then there's the money

If Wachtell doesn't lavish money on luxurious office space, it does spread the wealth where it counts. "You will not be paid more at any other firm," boasts a corporate attorney. Another associate notes, "My regular salary matches the top levels in New York City, and the firm is famous for its bonuses." Wachtell bonuses, which are not tied to a billable hours requirement, are calculated as a percentage of associates' base salaries. Even if last year's bonus didn't reach the dizzying heights of 2000, the bonus was, an insider reports, "substantially higher than other law firms."

"The firm makes an effort to make sure that its associates are the best paid in the city," asserts one insider. In addition, the firm employs a highly praised support staff "available at all hours" and generously supplies associates with laptops, cell phones, Blackberry pagers and "enough food to feed the Big Apple Circus." Wachtell lawyers "certainly have nothing to complain about," but one source maintains that the compensation isn't unreasonably high. "I think I do a good enough job that I earn what I'm paid."

No free lunch (so to speak)

"Challenging work," "brilliant attorneys," "unmatched" compensation. There has to be a catch, right? Alas, "the rumors are true," an associate confirms. "We do work harder and longer" than associates at other top firms. The firm has no billable hours minimum, and one lawyer says he has "never felt pressure to put in face time." Nevertheless most Wachtell respondents report billing at least 226 hours per month and working more than 60 hours per week, with several clocking more than 80. "The hours can be very, very long," sighs a third-year associate. One lawyer declares that "no one leaves the office before 8 p.m., period, even if you have no work." "The firm culture is goal-oriented and driven to the creation of a perfect work product," reminds one attorney. It shouldn't come as a surprise then that "the amount of responsibility that associates have will often require them to work long hours."

Respondents had little to say about the firm's pro bono efforts. "Pro what?" asks one wit. "The opportunity to do pro bono work is there if you are interested," one lawyer suggests, a bit tentatively. Another reports spending "hundreds of hours on bar association work" and claims that "classic pro bono for indigent clients is made available for all associates and many take part." The same attorney suggests that "in general, pro bono activities are treated like other matters and associates are expected to juggle them like they do anything else."

Rewards of a meritocracy

The mutual respect and close working relationships between partners and associates are considered among the firm's many assets. "Partners are approachable," and although they "may impose seemingly insurmountable demands, they treat you with respect. First-year associates often work closely with the name partners." Reports another lawyer, "If you do your job well, partners actively seek out your advice on matters." Wachtellians believe that "in many ways, the firm is a meritocracy" and that good work is rewarded with greater challenge and responsibility. "There is an assumption of competence that you are given the opportunity to prove or disprove. If you do well, you get more responsibility and your relationships will improve. The firm is small enough that there are informal policies regarding how senior someone needs to be before they can be assigned a particular task."

In view of the qualities Wachtell seeks in its candidates, the firm's "sink or swim" approach to training should come as little surprise. "There is not a lot of hand-holding. The people who come here and do well tend to learn on the fly and be comfortable with stretching to perform various tasks." Although the firm has begun instituting formal training classes, "there is a strong tendency to encourage associates to learn on their own." "It's all on-the-job training," writes one lawyer, "with varying levels of review, which makes it challenging and intimidating at the same time."

Little focus on diversity

Responses to Vault's diversity questions were both limited and varied. The firm's attitude toward gays and lesbians generally garnered more favorable ratings than its policies with respect to women and minorities. "Diversity is not really a firm focus," shrugs one associate. A minority attorney remarks, "It may be tough to find a mentor that looks like you, but it doesn't mean you will not find a mentor." A female lawyer believes "the firm is open to women and tries to recruit women." She says that "as a woman I haven't felt that I have been treated any differently than my male counterparts. Still," she adds, "there are ridiculously few women here, at both the partner and associate level."

Another lawyer suggests that the small number of women is a reflection of the firm's work ethic rather than discrimination. "Obviously, it takes a great deal of commitment regardless of sex to want to work here, so there may be some self-selection that may reduce the number of women who would want to work here. I know that in my interviews with potential candidates I focus on their capabilities irrespective of their sex, race or religion." The same insider feels that "the firm has always focused on hiring the best. I've always believed we'd hire little green men if they could do the job."

"The most senior partners and the lowliest of associates rub elbows routinely."

— *Wachtell associate*

Sullivan & Cromwell

125 Broad Street
New York, NY 10004
Phone: (212) 558-4000
www.sullcrom.com

LOCATIONS

New York, NY (HQ)
Los Angeles, CA
Palo Alto, CA
Washington, DC
Beijing
Frankfurt
Hong Kong
London
Melbourne
Paris
Sydney
Tokyo

MAJOR DEPARTMENTS/PRACTICES

Commercial Real Estate • Corporate & Finance • E-Business & Technology • Estates & Personal • Executive Compensation & Benefits • Financial Institutions • Litigation • Mergers & Acquisitions • Project Finance • Tax

THE STATS

No. of attorneys: 693
No. of offices: 12
Summer associate offers: 115 out of 115 (2001)
Chairman: H. Rodgin Cohen
Hiring Partners: Christopher L. Mann (NY); Robert H. Craft (DC); Michael H. Steinberg (LA); Scott D. Miller (Palo Alto)

BASE SALARY

All domestic offices, 2002
1st year: $125,000
2nd year: $135,000
3rd year: $150,000
4th year: $170,000
5th year: $190,000
6th year: $205,000
7th year: $220,000
8th year: $235,000
Summer associate: $2,404/week

NOTABLE PERKS

• Firm-sponsored yoga and pilates
• Monthly women's cocktail parties
• Blackberries
• Free soda — "even Cherry Coke!"

 ## THE BUZZ
WHAT ATTORNEYS AT OTHER FIRMS ARE SAYING ABOUT THIS FIRM

• "Epitome of a New York City firm"
• "George Washington's law firm"
• "Pretentious and cocky"
• "Shark tank"
• "First-rate all around"

UPPERS

- "Nice balance of formal and friendly"
- No billable hours requirement
- Salary leader

DOWNERS

- Downtown NYC location "is a drag"
- Shared offices for two years
- Punishing hours

EMPLOYMENT CONTACT

Ms. Sarah K. Cannady
Manager of Legal Recruiting
Phone: (212) 558-4847
cannadys@sullcrom.com

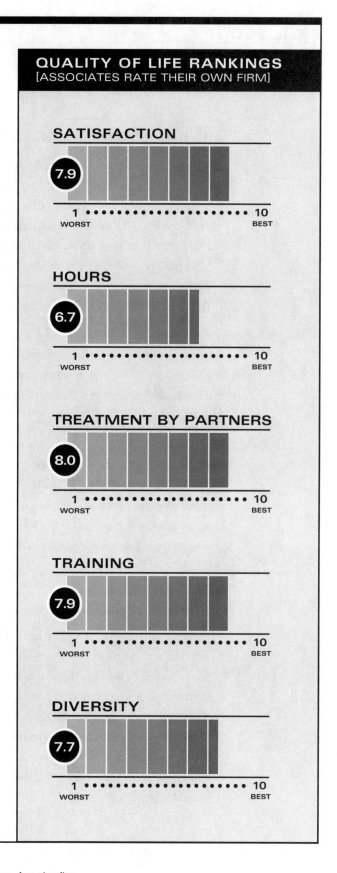

QUALITY OF LIFE RANKINGS
[ASSOCIATES RATE THEIR OWN FIRM]

SATISFACTION

7.9

1 WORST • • • • • • • • • • • • • • • • • • 10 BEST

HOURS

6.7

1 WORST • • • • • • • • • • • • • • • • • • 10 BEST

TREATMENT BY PARTNERS

8.0

1 WORST • • • • • • • • • • • • • • • • • • 10 BEST

TRAINING

7.9

1 WORST • • • • • • • • • • • • • • • • • • 10 BEST

DIVERSITY

7.7

1 WORST • • • • • • • • • • • • • • • • • • 10 BEST

THE SCOOP

One of the grand New York elite firms, Sullivan & Cromwell has a reputation for true excellence. The prestigious firm is all business and is repeatedly selected by top clients for its high-quality work.

History: blockbuster deals for over a century

Founded in 1879 by Algernon Sydney Sullivan and William Nelson Cromwell, Sullivan & Cromwell made a name for itself by being involved in some blockbuster deals in the industrial, commercial and financial areas of the late 19th and early 20th centuries. The firm was involved in the formation of Edison General Electric Company in 1882 and United States Steel Corporation in 1901. The firm represented European financiers who helped finance the nation's railroads and other projects, including the building of the Panama Canal. By 1928 S&C had offices in Berlin, Buenos Aires and Paris to meet the needs of the growing stream of capital across foreign borders. The Great Depression didn't stop the firm. From then on, it only grew, on the forefront of federal income tax law and antitrust and shareholder litigation law.

Partners John Foster Dulles and Arthur Dean gave the firm a foothold in politics and international affairs. With the growth of international capital flows and the European, Asian and Latin American markets, the firm opened offices in London in 1972, Washington, D.C. in 1977, Melbourne in 1983, Los Angeles in 1984, Tokyo in 1987, Hong Kong in 1992, Frankfurt in 1995, Beijing in 1999, Palo Alto in 2000 and Sydney in 2001.

S&C started the bonus war of 2000 by announcing a $35,000 bonus for first-years. Cravath upped the ante to $40,000 and S&C followed suit. Like most firms in 2001, Sullivan & Cromwell too pulled its purse strings a little. In 2001 S&C first-year associates received a $20,000 bonus while senior associates received bonuses higher than $50,000. Though the firm pinched bonuses a tad, it went ahead full steam by adding over 100 lawyers to the firm.

Public service pros

S&C is committed to excellence in all areas, and public service is no exception. In May 2001, Lawyers Alliance for New York handed out its third annual Cornerstone Awards to law firms and individuals in the New York area who set a high standard for volunteer service by business lawyers. S&C was one of the three firms that received the honor. In another award ceremony, S&C retired partner and current senior counsel Robert MacCrate, a former president of the American Bar Association, was awarded the ABA Medal in August 2001 for his dedication to public service. MacCrate was counsel to late Governor Nelson Rockefeller from 1959 to 1962. In 1969, he served as special counsel to the U.S. Army in its investigation of the My Lai incident, in which U.S. military personnel allegedly murdered Vietnamese civilians. The ABA Medal is the ABA's highest award for legal professionals.

Firm leadership and employees continued the spirit of public service after the events of September 11. To aid in the September 11 fund, a paralegal at the firm contributed his September 11 pay, and 500 other S&C employees followed, adding almost $1 million to the $1 million the firm had already donated. In addition S&C is lending a hand to small business owners in Manhattan's downtown area. The firm donated money to Seedco, a non-profit organization helping Mom and Pop get back on their feet, as well as to Wall Street Rising, dedicated to the revitalization of the Wall Street area.

Banking on banks

When it comes to fat financial mergers and acquisitions, S&C is tops. In the biggest acquisition in Mexican history, Citigroup Inc. bought Grupo Financiero Banamex-Accival SA, known as "Banacci," for $12.5 billion. The firm represented Grupo Financiero in the 2001 deal. In a stock and cash deal coming in at a little over $5 billion, Washington Mutual Inc., the Seattle financial services company, bought New York's Dime Bancorp Inc. in September 2001. S&C client Dime began in 1859, allowing its customers to open an account with just a dime; it now has more than $14 billion in deposits in New York.

Attorneys at S&C know what to do with a conflict of interest: let the clients decide. In a July 2001 deal, First Union Corporation acquired Wachovia Corporation for $13.4 billion in stock. S&C has ties to both First Union and Wachovia and asked the companies to decide which one would use the firm. A final deal involved Citizens Financial Group, the U.S. subsidiary of the Royal Bank of Scotland, in its acquisition of Mellon Financial Corp. for roughly $2.1 billion. This purchase helps the bank in its quest to expand in the U.S. market. Since 1988, it has made 17 acquisitions.

Never-ending Napster

Napster is in the news again. In June 2001, the nation's leading retailer of vintage radio show audio content and audio books, Mediabay Inc., sued the infamous web company for copyright infringement and unfair competition. The twist in this latest Napster net is that the radio shows are nonmusical, whereas the previous Napster conflicts all involved music. Mediabay was represented by lawyers from S&C's Los Angeles and Palo Alto office.

In other IP news, biotechnology companies Affymetrix Inc. and Hyseq Inc. were involved in a patent dispute over DNA sequencing technology. In November 2001, they quashed the kvetching and decided two heads were better than one. The pair entered into a joint venture called N-Mer Inc., which has access to both companies' DNA technology. Affymetrix was represented by lawyers in S&C's Palo Alto and Los Angeles offices.

Don't touch that dial

In a $25 billion dollar deal in November 2001, S&C represented Echostar Communications Corp., a direct broadcast satellite programming services and products provider, when it merged with

Hughes Electronics Corp., provider of DirecTV Inc., the largest direct broadcast satellite operator in the country.

GETTING HIRED

Grades, grades, grades

Without top grades, you'll find it awfully hard to get through the door at the "extremely grade conscious" Sullivan & Cromwell. "Grades are clearly the first factor," sources emphasize, "unless you are coming from Yale or Harvard." A candidate "has to be top 10 percent at a top-tier law school or top one or two students at another law school." "It really doesn't matter where you went to law school," an insider reports, "but you have to be in the top echelon of your class to be considered." Additional factors include "very good interviewing skills," "interesting experiences, additional degrees, multiple languages" and "a certain spark."

Getting that "first interview is key," say associates, but after that "the hiring process goes pretty smoothly." That said, "callbacks definitely matter." During the half-day callback, expect a "substantive rigorous series of interviews" in which "they might query you in depth about a legal point, a class you took, a paper you wrote, and so on, and not just one or two questions." Offers are often extended the same day.

OUR SURVEY SAYS

"A healthy respect for decorum"

S&C's historical reputation as a stuffy place to work clearly rankles many associates. The "firm's culture is more laid back than it is given credit for. It can be an intense place at times, but that is mostly the result of the level and novelty of some of the work we do." S&C has "a more formal workplace," but it "is not the least bit uptight." People are professional and "friendly when appropriate." Some associates appreciate "that it's not a free-for-all. There's a healthy respect for decorum, and there's nothing wrong with that." A New Yorker complains that "S&C unfairly gets tagged as old school. The culture is more accurately described as professional and courteous with regard to how employees conduct themselves at the workplace." The same attorney suggests that "if you want to play whiffle ball in the hallways, then go work at some 'friendly' or 'laid-back' firm and good riddance to you!"

Few associates miss the corridor antics. They value the professional but friendly environment and marvel over "the wide variety of work and the amount of responsibility," as well as "the character [and] quality of the people" with whom they work. "The practice is exciting, the clients amazing and the other lawyers are by and large top-notch," according to a New York associate. Those who want to socialize with colleagues can usually find plenty of opportunities, especially at the junior levels. One fourth-year associate notes that "as new people join," old labels become less apt. "While there are a few remnants of S&C's more formal days, it for the most part has become an associate-friendly firm." An LA litigator chimes in, "The people are supportive and are willing to help each other out. There is no sense of competition, which is nice."

Soothingly beige

Many associates feel the décor of the New York office is another area in which the firm is getting a bad rap. Yes, the headquarters are predominantly "beige," yes, there is a "plethora of Currier and Ives," and yes, "it's kind of the 1970s take on a gentleman's club," but a surprising number of associates like it just fine. They "find it soothing" and "a comfortable setting to spend the inevitable late nights." Many lawyers value the "traditional" surroundings. "This place feels like a law firm. It would make a perfect movie set." In addition, "every attorney has a window office with real walls," and there are "lots of amenities." What has associates grumbling more than the "drab" décor is the overcrowding. Because "the economy is preventing normal attrition," offices are "cramped" and "incoming juniors have to share offices for far too long." The firm points out that it is addressing the problem, and new office space on the 36th floor should be available in May 2003.

Perhaps because they haven't the weight of century-old traditions behind them, newer S&C offices in California and Washington, D.C., get high marks for comfort and design without provoking any defensiveness. Palo Alto offices are "both beautiful and functional," D.C. is "great," and an LA lawyer claims his offices are "just like *The West Wing*."

Trusting partners

On the whole, associates report that partners "treat associates at S&C with great respect and professionalism." Partners "have high standards," according to a New York associate, "but place trust in your abilities from day one." In LA there is said to be "a healthy give and take between associates and partners, especially as one gets more senior," and associates are pleased that partners "ask for our opinion and listen to what we have to say." One lawyer compares the office to an "academic atmosphere, where the partners are the professors and the associates are the students." A few lawyers have close relationships with mentoring partners, and most claim that at a minimum they are "treated with respect and their opinions valued." S&C "emphasizes civility," which doesn't mean that there aren't "some really bloody-minded partners who seem to enjoy tormenting associates," but such unpleasant folks seem to be in fairly short supply at S&C. Perhaps that's because "at a business level, the partners know the strong associate base is one of the great strengths of the firm in the eyes of clients and others, and treat associates accordingly."

Training expansion

Building that strong associate base requires effective training, a topic that continues to draw varied reviews from S&C sources. Lawyers note that the "in-house training program has expanded drastically in the last few years" and, according to some, "made tremendous strides." "Extensive formal training programs" include "breakfast seminars, lunch seminars, practice group seminars, and so on." Many associates find these programs "informative and relevant," while others say they are "inadequate training sources." One source describes S&C training as a "university within a firm" but where there is "still a focus on learning by doing." Because "some partners are much better than others," associates don't agree on the quality of informal training. "It's scary," according to one litigator, "the amount of experience young lawyers get here if they demonstrate any kind of willingness to do it." "Outstanding!" claims another attorney. But one lawyer believes that training is "the most disappointing aspect of S&C."

S&C-ers in sunny California consider their office's training program top-notch. A litigator in the LA office declares, "I find that the partners and especially the more senior associates provide excellent feedback and assistance, even on cases in which they are not involved. There is a more formal training program, but I think I learn more from doing." Another LA associate agrees: "The firm has a comprehensive training program for first- and second-year attorneys, with breakfast training sessions several times a month. The programs are informative and relevant."

Prepare for long hours

"If you are not prepared to put in the hours, don't bother coming here," advises one attorney. "The hours are long but no worse than others I know in large New York City law firms." Most S&C associates seem to agree. "The hours can be tiresome," sighs a mid-level associate, "but it's not like I didn't know what I was getting into." A litigator admits, "Very long hours on very interesting matters are still very long hours," and an LA associate says, "It still sucks to work hard." But one very practical attorney maintains that it is "just a part of our providing the best possible legal representation to our clients." At least "you're treated like a professional and no one says a word about billable hours here," which means that "when the work is done, there is little pressure to put in face time." A few senior associates assure newer colleagues that "it does get better" and those "crazy unpredictable hours that first year do pass." One attorney praises S&C for helping her set up an "alternative work schedule" under which she can "telecommute from home on a regular basis." One Los Angeleno sums it up: "We work hard — but it could be worse."

Always a market leader

With compensation "equal [to] or better" than "just about every other firm in the city — except Wachtell," few S&C associates are complaining about money. Confident that "S&C will always be a pay leader," most sources are quite happy. One incredulous first-year asks, "Are you kidding? When I started law school, if you had told me I would have made this much upon graduating, I would have laughed." Nevertheless a few insiders question "whether the compensation is appropriate for the time, energy and emotion spent." Even though it "was disappointing to make less money in 2001 than in 2000," a grateful New Yorker acknowledges that "we still got the largest bonus out there."

'A' for effort

As with many established, large law firms, "when you look at the partnership, you will see predominantly white men." A corporate associate in the firm's LA office says, "They do well on hiring and are making an effort on mentoring, but the small number of women who are partners and senior associates is discouraging." Despite the dearth of women and minorities at upper levels, S&C wins praise for its efforts in "trying to attract and retain" both women and minorities. "They are trying," maintains a litigator, "and I feel the effort is genuine." The firm's open-mindedness extends to sexual orientation. "S&C has a number of openly gay partners and associates," reports a gay attorney, "and overall is a very good place to work as a gay associate." However, the "lack of mentoring" and the long hours make it difficult to hang on to a truly diverse body of attorneys. Echoing the complaints of women lawyers everywhere, many S&C women find that the job "is difficult to balance with motherhood."

Proud of pro bono

S&C lawyers are proud of their firm's commitment to pro bono work. "The firm makes a lot of noise about pro bono, and most of it is true," according to one associate. A New Yorker says, "I don't think there's a firm in the city that can match our commitment to pro bono. It's extraordinary." Not only are there "lots of pro bono opportunities," but "they are given the same level of importance as work for paying clients." That means "you never have to say to yourself, 'If I just had more resources or more staffing or more time I could have made a difference.' Here, the firm's full resources are at your disposal." Sources are proud that S&C has "a pro bono fellowship for one associate to devote his or her full time to pro bono matters." The only problem associates report with pro bono work is, "We just usually don't have much time for it."

Skadden, Arps, Slate, Meagher & Flom LLP and Affiliates

4 Times Square
New York, NY 10036
Phone: (212) 735-3000
www.skadden.com

LOCATIONS

New York, NY (HQ)
Boston, MA
Chicago, IL
Houston, TX
Los Angeles, CA
Newark, NJ
Palo Alto, CA
Reston, VA
San Francisco, CA
Washington, DC
Wilmington, DE
Plus 12 more offices worldwide

MAJOR DEPARTMENTS/PRACTICES

Antitrust/Sports Law • Corporate Restructuring •
E-Commerce • Intellectual Property • Investment
Management • Litigation • M&A, Banking & Finance •
Mass Torts • Real Estate • Tax, Trusts & Estates •
White Collar Crime

THE STATS

No. of attorneys: 1,692 (781 in New York)
No. of offices: 23
Summer associate offers: 132 out of 135 (2001)
Managing Partner: Robert C. Sheehan
Hiring Partner: Wallace L. Schwartz (NY)

BASE SALARY

New York, Los Angeles, Palo Alto and San Francisco, 2002
1st year: $140,000
2nd year: $150,000
3rd year: $170,000
4th year: $185,000
5th year: $200,000
6th year: $212,000
7th year: $220,000
8th year: $225,000
Summer associate: $2,400/week

NOTABLE PERKS

- In-house gym with personal trainer and free juice
- $3,000 technology allowance and $1,000 allowance for upgrades
- Car home after 8:30 p.m.

THE BUZZ
WHAT ATTORNEYS AT OTHER FIRMS ARE SAYING ABOUT THIS FIRM

- "Well-paid bastards, great work"
- "Unnecessarily adversarial"
- "Great pro bono emphasis"
- "If I can make it there, I can make it anywhere"
- "Honeymoon cancelers"

UPPERS

- Lively social life for junior associates
- Highest-quality transactions

DOWNERS

- Space crunch (NY)
- Associate availability expected 24/7

EMPLOYMENT CONTACT

Ms. Carol Lee H. Sprague
Director of Legal Hiring
Phone: (212) 735-3815
Fax: (917) 777-3815
csprague@skadden.com

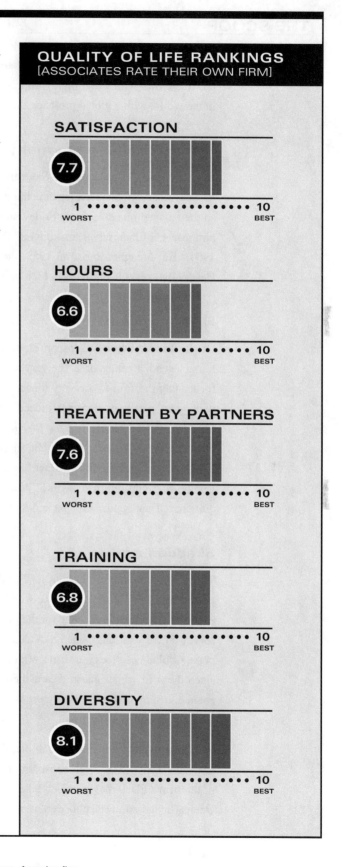

QUALITY OF LIFE RANKINGS
[ASSOCIATES RATE THEIR OWN FIRM]

SATISFACTION

7.7

1 WORST .... 10 BEST

HOURS

6.6

1 WORST .... 10 BEST

TREATMENT BY PARTNERS

7.6

1 WORST .... 10 BEST

TRAINING

6.8

1 WORST .... 10 BEST

DIVERSITY

8.1

1 WORST .... 10 BEST

THE SCOOP

No disputing it — Skadden, Arps, Slate, Meagher & Flom LLP and Affiliates is a big, highly profitable firm with a big, highly impressive name. It is one of the most widely recognized firms in the world, with a global presence thanks to offices from Boston to Brussels to Beijing.

History: from one to many

In 1948 Marshall Skadden, John Slate and Les Arps opened a law firm. Joseph Flom was the firm's first associate. A Skadden legend claims that the firm was not able to pay Flom when he started, so they played pinochle every Friday and gave him the pot. Another story says the partners paid him instead of themselves, making him the highest-paid lawyer in the firm. Flom made partner in 1954. Bill Meagher joined in 1959, the year the firm hired its first woman attorney, Elizabeth Head. Two years later, the firm took on its current (very long) name.

Flom, no flim-flam

Of all Skadden attorneys, Joseph Flom is probably held in highest regard at the firm. Many call him a legend, a genius or, at the very least, the best lawyer of his generation. Flom takes the cake for leading the firm to the very top in mergers and acquisitions. But great work like that comes with great personal sacrifice; indeed Flom's status as a true workaholic is indisputable. In *Skadden: Power, Money and the Rise of a Legal Empire*, Lincoln Caplan writes that before Flom proposed to his fiancée, he bought an engagement ring from his colleague Les Arps, who had bought that ring earlier for a former fiancée. Flom had his fiancée stop by the firm so he could give her the ring and return to work. When complimented on the ring, Flom's fiancée supposedly quipped, "Thanks, Les Arps picked it out for me."

Skadden's id

The firm makes money. Lots of it. For three years in a row (2000, 1999 and 1998), the firm was ranked No. 1 in the AmLaw 100, which ranks firms based on gross revenue. In 2001 Skadden exceeded $1 billion in revenue for the third year in a row, with $1.1 billion. Respondents to a 1996 survey on corporations named Skadden the most arrogant firm, with 11 percent of the vote. In his book, Caplan describes the firm's 40th anniversary black tie gala (the firm has celebrated its 50th since then) in which guests heard their names announced by herald and a trumpet when they entered. (Supposedly some partners were so delighted with the fanfare that they reentered to hear their names called again.)

Perhaps arrogant, though not infallible, the firm has seen its share of criticism concerning its web site. In January 2002, Web consultant Larry Bodine in *Law Technology News* cited the slowness of the firm's Flash movie, which takes more than two minutes to download using a 56K modem. One particular annoyance to web users is that visitors are unable to bookmark or forward specific pages of the site. In addition, the pages are difficult to print out. The firm reports that it is in the process of correcting some of these problems.

Raking in the dough

Joe Flom established Skadden's M&A practice, but it really grew in the 1980s, when the firm was involved in just about every major merger of that decade. The buck didn't stop there. In July 2001, Sara Lee Corp. acquired fresh-bakery and refrigerated-dough business Earthgrains Company for a sweet $2.8 billion. Skadden attorneys from the Chicago, New York, Palo Alto and Washington, D.C., offices represented Sara Lee Corp. Skadden also helped Cendant Corporation make two acquisitions. The New York-based travel and real estate consumer services provider bought Galileo International Inc., a travel reservation service, for a whopping $2.9 billion in June 2001. Two months later, Skadden lawyers lent their legal know-how again when Cendant bought Cheap Tickets, Inc., a discount ticket retailer, for $425 million.

Computer chaos

In a major computer merger, Hewlett-Packard Company announced in September 2001 that it would join forces with Compaq Computer Corp. The controversial merger faced difficulties in December 2001 when Hewlett-Packard Director Walter Hewlett and other members of the founding families expressed opposition to it. In February 2002, the European Union gave clearance for the merger, causing shares to go up. Since then, Hewlett has lost the proxy contest and the merger is going through. The $23.6 billion deal, when done, would bring in total revenues of $87.4 billion to the combined company. A multi-office force of Skadden attorneys stands behind client Compaq.

Biotech blast

The latest boom after the dot-com bust is the biotech industry. Skadden is in on the ground floor of some of the major biotech deals. In December 2001, the firm represented Immunex Corp., a biopharmaceutical company, in its merger with Amgen Inc., the world's largest biotech company, in the biggest biotech merger ever (worth $16 billion). The deal was a complex one, as it involved a third party, American Home Products, that owns 41 percent of Immunex. Partners Roger Aaron and Stephen Arcano headed the 10-attorney team in the matter. Months earlier, in June 2001, the firm advised another biotech company. A team of Skadden attorneys helped Medarex Inc. sell $175 million worth of notes, which are convertible to stock. These notes are popular now because they have both the security of bonds and the allure of stock.

Big names — and big fees

The fall of energy giant Enron Corp. has proved a lucrative source of business for many legal wranglers. Skadden's work on behalf of Enron has already generated fees in excess of $6 million, according to documents filed in bankruptcy court. Of course, it helps if those fees actually get paid. Skadden partner Robert Bennett (whose billing rate in the Enron matter neared $700 per hour) knows what it is to get stiffed by a client. The *New York Daily News* reports that Bill Clinton still owes the firm $1 million for Bennett's defense of the former Prez in the Paula Jones case. Meanwhile, fellow Enron laborer Jack Butler is also working hard to get the bankruptcy case of discount retailer Kmart Corp. wrapped up by July 2003.

In another high-profile matter, Skadden attorneys were on hand in May 2002 to help Merrill Lynch reach an agreement with New York Attorney General Eliot Spitzer, settling his investigation into alleged conflicts in Merrill Lynch's stock research. Under the terms of the agreement, Merrill Lynch makes no admission of liability but must pay $48 million to New York State and another $52 million to other states, both payments contingent on acceptance of the agreement by all 50 states.

GETTING HIRED

Beyond the obvious

Naturally Skadden looks for "top-notch people." However, "unlike comparable firms that only hire from law review, Skadden looks at whether you will be a good lawyer, which often has more to do with whether you have common sense and can work well in a team setting." Accordingly, Skadden casts "a wide net" and draws attorneys from "a lot more places than a lot of top firms." Many insiders praise the firm's "ability to recognize talent regardless of pedigree. It prefers the top student at an undistinguished law school to an undistinguished candidate from a top law school. There are no snobs here: the only thing that counts is ability."

Sources insist that "it would be difficult for someone with great grades but little in the way of personality to be hired here." "Personality is an absolute requirement," repeats another associate, who claims that it "doesn't really matter what type of personality, so long as you have one." A D.C. attorney has more specific qualities in mind; a successful candidate is someone "we can imagine not killing if we were stuck in an airport with them for an extended period of time. Funny, casual, laid back, genuine and not overly intellectual or self-impressed."

OUR SURVEY SAYS

Work hard, play hard

"To the extent there is a firm-wide culture" at Skadden, most associates call it "a mixture of friendly and formal." Skadden is "laid back and friendly," say several sources. The atmosphere is "business-like" yet "casual," and "dress is business casual year round." The firm is "focused on getting things done," but within that framework associates find room for making friends and engaging with colleagues. According to many Skaddenites, "close-knit groups of friends who socialize are common." At the same time, there is "no pressure to do so." Respondents in several cities agree that "the old 'work hard play hard' cliché is definitely true here."

Many associates are happy to work so hard. From California to Chicago to the East Coast, respondents gloat over "the best cases in the country" and "some of the most exciting deals of the past year." "In terms of type of work, level of responsibility, culture and most other measures, I find Skadden a terrific place to be." Such excitement isn't universally shared. Where some associates crow over the "challenging work and boundless responsibility," a few others (particularly in litigation) complain that they aren't rewarded with enough responsibility and sense a "ruthless undercurrent" beneath the surface of congeniality. The Boston office suffers from "very low" morale, as does the "directionless" IP department in New York. Skadden is a "total sweatshop," one attorney maintains. On the other hand, a Chicago lawyer believes he has "found out where Jeff Spicoli has been hiding all these years."

An absurd amount of money

Skadden's base salary is "higher than every other law firm except for Wachtell." It's "the gold standard." Appropriately enough, most associates are "very happy" with their compensation, sometimes sheepishly so. "I should not be paid the salary that I am making. It's that simple," confesses a Skaddenite. One first-year associate confesses of her $140,000 salary, "It's an absurd amount of money, since the majority of us have no idea what we're doing yet." "We are ridiculously well paid," agrees another lawyer, "and anyone who argues otherwise is out of touch with reality."

In that case, Skadden may house some delusional folks, because even with those "spectacular" salaries, a few lawyers find cause for complaint. Senior associates point out that "despite popular wisdom, after the fifth year Skadden lags [behind] most firms." And the topic of bonuses draws scattered grumbling, from New Yorkers because "Skadden chose not to match" the scale set by top New York firms, and from Skaddenites elsewhere since they received even less than the "paltry" sums awarded to lawyers in the home office. Most respondents, however, are content with Skadden's salary structure, preferring to be "guaranteed the money that other firms only give out in bonuses." One source says simply, "We get paid very, very well."

Expect long hours

"If you want the big bucks, you're going to work long hours," acknowledges one associate. It will surprise few to learn that Skadden lawyers work long hours but, according to several sources, "The sweatshop label is not really fair." "The hours are not even a fraction as bad as law students tend to believe about Skadden," asserts a first-year litigator. "Hours have been fine," says one associate, although another groans over "too many hours, too many all-nighters, too many weekends."

Even if the hours are long, many lawyers consider them a small price to pay for the quality of the work and training. "While there are times I have worked hard, I always feel that I am a part of something important and gaining useful experience." "Lots of hours," a D.C. attorney concedes, "but the caliber of cases, level of involvement and stake in matters keeps you motivated. Let's face it, President Clinton and Enron — two past or current clients — need more than 9 to 5 representation!" The absence of "pressure to bill a certain number of hours or put in face time" helps, as does knowing that "the partners work every bit as hard as the associates." But more than a few sources find that Skadden's client-driven focus leaves "little respect for an associate's personal time." "You are on call 24 hours a day, 365 days a year," a lawyer complains.

Part-time stretch

"The firm is very open to flex-time schedules," several Skadden sources report. "However there is no consistency between individuals' arrangements," and "the concept of part time is a bit of a stretch." Attorneys are "considered 'part-time' because [they] work only 40 hours per week," laments one associate. One frustrated lawyer points out that she has "to account for 48 hours per week as an 80 percent attorney, while full-time attorneys only account for 40 hours per week." (The firm disputes this.)

Home away from home

When attorneys spend so much time at work, their surroundings matter. Fortunately, most Skaddenites express satisfaction with their offices. The firm's New York headquarters in the Condé Nast building wins praise for "bright and airy" offices, a "good cafeteria," free in-house gym ("A major, major plus!"), "great views" and "top-notch" equipment. What disappoints New Yorkers is that "more junior people are stacked up in offices" than was promised. According to the firm, a newly renovated floor should help with the crowding. Chicago attorneys find their space "very new, streamlined and comfortable," and a D.C. lawyer notes that "Skadden isn't about luxurious appointments — but the facilities are fine."

Associates in the new Palo Alto building appreciate "modern décor, a great view and a high level of comfort and efficiency." Renovations in Los Angeles and Houston are less well received. Though one Los Angeles associate states, "We're in the middle of a remodel, which promises to be fantastic," another claims, "The new offices are very poorly designed," and a third calls them "horrible." A Texan describes her offices as "still pretty ugly despite a remodel. The art is so bad it hurts to look at." Boston views "are great. All else is plain to poor." On the other hand, the Wilmington office "is spacious, functional, well kept and provides an excellent environment."

The times they are a-changing

Doubled-up New Yorkers might blame the space crunch, at least in part, on the recession. "Lately," one associate writes, "the firm is having major trouble getting people to leave — there's not enough space for everyone who has chosen to stay." The "economy is terrible, so nobody is leaving now," reports another. "The times are a-changing. Retention is no longer a problem," notes a senior associate. Although most sources agree that fewer people have been leaving lately, they disagree whether Skadden's usual rate of attrition is "higher than other places" or whether "folks tend to stick around." One lawyer claims that "the Houston office has a problem keeping good people." (The firm maintains that its attrition rate is lower than comparable large firms.)

Several associates say that departing lawyers do not leave for other law firms but rather for in-house or non-legal opportunities. "There are constant opportunities for Skadden associates to go in-house or accept other offers," a phenomenon that "keeps turnover fairly constant." Others argue that "people don't stay very long and move to other law firms quite frequently." Regarding associates who remain for the long haul, a New Yorker complains, "Unfortunately some of the people who have been here for years are the ones you wish would leave." For those seeking greener (or just different) pastures, Skadden's "reputation really does go a long way," and "people leave to do incredible things."

Endless pro bono

In the pro bono arena, the firm's reputation as "a true leader" seems well earned. "More than any other firm," a New York associate asserts, "Skadden puts its money where its mouth is on pro bono and related public service law." Sources in other offices agree. A California lawyer says the firm's "commitment to pro bono is exceptional," and a Bostonian reports, "There is a real belief in such causes in the office and support from the partners." Skadden "has a partner-level attorney dedicated to pro bono work who oversees matters and provides training to interested associates" and a full-time coordinator who sends out "incessant" e-mails outlining pro bono projects. "The opportunities are endless," concludes an associate.

Room at the top

Skadden generally gets good marks for its diversity practices, especially in New York where associates praise the new diversity manager who "has done a solid job of increasing awareness." But many associates see "room for improvement." "While Skadden does a lot for hiring minority associates, there is little mentoring and promotion to partnership still is extremely rare." The Los Angeles office comes in for criticism. In contrast to one minority attorney who finds "the firm overwhelmingly welcoming," others complain that there are "few minorities and few stay very long." One associate claims, "The firm has done nothing to remedy the lack of diversity."

Many locations boast openly gay attorneys, several of whom responded to the survey with positive remarks. Although some women call the firm a "meritocracy," they also note a "disproportionately male partnership." (The firm, however, notes that the New York office has more women partners than peer firms.) Even those who think "the firm as a whole does an OK job" believe that more "work needs to be done to provide flexible options for women with children and to promote women to partnership."

Davis Polk & Wardwell

450 Lexington Avenue
New York, NY 10017
Phone: (212) 450-4000
www.dpw.com

LOCATIONS

New York, NY (HQ)
Menlo Park, CA
Washington, DC
Frankfurt
Hong Kong
London
Madrid
Paris
Tokyo

MAJOR DEPARTMENTS/PRACTICES

Corporate
Litigation
Taxation
Trusts & Estates

THE STATS

No. of attorneys: 648
No. of offices: 9
Summer associate offers: 100 out of 100 (2001)
Managing Partner: John Ettinger
Hiring Partner: Gail Flesher

BASE SALARY

New York, 2002
1st year: $125,000
2nd year: $135,000
3rd year: $150,000
4th year: $165,000
Summer associate: $2,400/week

NOTABLE PERKS

- Superb subsidized cafeteria on premises
- Monthly cocktail receptions
- Holiday party for children of lawyers and staff
- Summer softball game at Shea Stadium against the Mets organization

THE BUZZ
WHAT ATTORNEYS AT OTHER FIRMS ARE SAYING ABOUT THIS FIRM

- "Best all-around law firm in New York"
- "Sweatshop with a smile"
- "Ally McBeal wannabes"
- "Kinder, gentler Cravath"
- "Still good despite the bad buzz"

UPPERS

- Civil, polite culture
- Beautiful office space convenient to Grand Central Terminal (NY)
- "Working on front-page matters"

DOWNERS

- Associates share offices into their third or fourth year
- "Inexplicable penny-pinching"
- Increased tension between partners and associates

EMPLOYMENT CONTACT

Ms. Bonnie Hurry
Director of Recruiting
Phone: (212) 450-4144
Fax: (212) 450-5548
bonnie.hurry@dpw.com

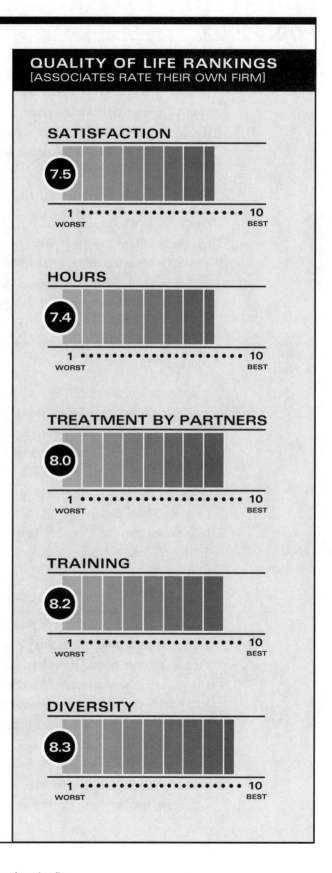

QUALITY OF LIFE RANKINGS
[ASSOCIATES RATE THEIR OWN FIRM]

SATISFACTION
7.5
1 WORST   10 BEST

HOURS
7.4
1 WORST   10 BEST

TREATMENT BY PARTNERS
8.0
1 WORST   10 BEST

TRAINING
8.2
1 WORST   10 BEST

DIVERSITY
8.3
1 WORST   10 BEST

THE SCOOP

Davis Polk & Wardwell has long been considered one of the nicest firms around, with a to-die-for securities practice, stellar litigation and corporate departments, and record revenues to boot. The year 2001, however, brought controversy to Davis Polk's door when the firm announced in October that its associates would not be receiving year-end bonuses (though neither would they face layoffs). The firm has since awarded generous bonuses to its associates.

History: the former Bangs & Stetson

Davis Polk & Wardwell was founded in 1849 under the delightful name of Bangs & Stetson, named after early partners Francis N. Bangs and Francis Lynde Stetson. Bangs was a litigator who made a name for himself battling William "Boss" Tweed and his corrupt Tweed Ring of Tammany Hall. Stetson succeeded Bangs, giving up litigation for corporate work. In 1887 J.P. Morgan made Stetson the chief legal counsel of his banking business. The keen-witted Stetson aided Morgan in creating General Electric by stringing together several electrical companies. Around this time, the firm also helped create corporate structures for huge corporations like U.S. Steel, International Paper and ITT.

When Stetson died in 1921, litigator John Davis took the helm. Once a Democratic presidential candidate, Davis argued before the U.S. Supreme Court 141 times. Corporate lawyer Frank Polk led the U.S. delegation to the Paris Peace Conference that created the ill-fated Treaty of Versailles. Alan Wardwell was a banking specialist who worked in Russia during its 1917 revolution. That wasn't the firm's first involvement in foreign affairs. In the 1890s, it worked on behalf of JPMorgan in Europe, Africa and Asia. Today Davis Polk remains one of JPMorgan's primary counsels. Other high-profile clients include Credit Suisse First Boston and Morgan Stanley and corporations such as Comcast, Emerson Electric, Verizon Wireless, Roche, Bertlesmann and Telefonica, S.A.

High-profile and high stakes

It seems that Davis Polk (as well as loads of other prestigious law firms) just can't get enough of Enron-related litigation. In January 2002, J.P. Morgan Chase sought legal assistance from DPW in the bank's Enron-related lawsuit against Federal Insurance Co., a subsidiary of Davis Polk client Chubb Corp. Due to a perceived conflict of interest based on the firm's existing client relationship with Chubb, Davis Polk was disqualified from the lawsuit. (New York's Kelley Drye & Warren has since taken over the case on behalf of J.P. Morgan Chase.) Davis Polk was also hired by accounting bigwig and Enron auditor Arthur Andersen to advise it in connection with a Securities and Exchange Commission investigation of Enron. Relatedly, DPW served as lead counsel in the high-profile Andersen criminal trial, in which Andersen was convicted of obstruction of justice in connection with the destruction of documents related to the energy giant.

Bonus uproar

Despite the economic recession in 2001, Davis Polk was one of three New York firms to pledge it would not resort to layoffs to save money. In October the firm sent a firm-wide memo promising not to lay off associates or rescind job offers to new associates. Instead, it announced that it did not anticipate paying discretionary associate bonuses. (The firm had awarded bonuses in 2000 ranging from the standard $40,000 for first-years to $100,000 for senior associates.) Davis Polk's no-bonus announcement was the first bonus announcement of the year from a top-tier firm, and most observers concluded that Davis Polk was trying to set a budget-saving no-bonus trend. But this was one fad that didn't catch on. In mid-December 2001, after several of its peer firms had announced substantial bonuses (albeit smaller than the previous year), Davis Polk reinstated its year-end bonus, matching the bonus scale set by firms like Cravath, Swaine & Moore. Despite the bonus controversy, 2001 was a record year for the firm in terms of employment offer acceptances; the full-time acceptance rate from both its summer 2001 class and summer 2002 class was unprecedented.

Have a heart

Even in the midst of tough economic times, the firm stepped up to the plate to help New York in its hour of need. Davis Polk donated $1 million to the relief efforts set up after the September 11 terrorist attacks (which included matching employee contributions to charitable organizations). Also in late 2001, former Whitewater prosecutor and celebrated litigation partner Robert B. Fiske Jr. donated $2 million to his alma mater, the University of Michigan Law School, earmarking his donation towards debt repayment for graduates who enter government service.

Media mogul

When it comes to big media deals, Davis Polk is plugged in. Comcast Corp., the nation's third-largest cable television provider and a DPW client, announced in December 2001 its plan to merge with AT&T Broadband, the country's largest broadband services provider, in a deal valued at $72 billion. The new company, AT&T Comcast Corp., will serve over 22 million customers and rake in revenues of over $19 billion.

In June 2001, the 169-year-old Houghton Mifflin, the U.S.'s fourth-largest publisher of educational materials, was gobbled up by Vivendi Universal, the second-largest publisher of educational materials in the world. Davis Polk represented J.P. Morgan Securities Inc., which served as the financial advisor for Houghton Mifflin board of directors in the transaction. In August 2001, Davis Polk attorneys also represented C-Mac in its the $2.7 billion acquisition by Solectron Corp., the world's largest electronics manufacturer.

Keeping cruise ships afloat

Ships ahoy! When London-based P&O Princess Cruises announced plans to merge with Royal Caribbean Cruises Ltd., headquartered in Miami, Fla., Davis Polk jumped aboard, representing its longstanding client. The new company will be the world's largest cruise vacation group, serving about three million customers and having revenues over $5 billion. Royal Caribbean sought counsel from attorneys in the London and New York offices of Davis Polk.

Slick moves

Davis Polk continues to make headlines in mergers and acquisitions. The two oil mammoths, Chevron Corp. and Texaco Corp., merged in October 2001, creating the second-largest oil company in the country and the fifth-largest in the world. Combined, the two giants earned revenues of $117 billion in 2000. The new company, called ChevronTexaco Corp., is headquartered in San Francisco. Pillsbury Winthrop represented Chevron in the deal, while Davis Polk offered its legal expertise to Texaco.

Davis Polk also cleans up when it comes to flashy financial acquisitions. In the biggest acquisition in Mexican history, Citigroup Inc. bought Grupo Financiero Banamex-Accival SA, known as "Banacci," for the not inconsiderable sum of $12.5 billion. Davis Polk represented Citigroup in the 2001 deal. Bristol-Myers Squibb Company bought a 19.9 percent stake in Davis Polk client ImClone Systems Inc., a biopharmaceutical company. The $2.5 billion deal includes an agreement by the two companies to co-develop the anti-cancer drug IMC-C225. The drug is designed to block the epidermal growth factor receptors on the surface of certain cancer calls.

GETTING HIRED

Personality counts

Davis Polk is one firm that can afford to be choosy. Davis Polk "is very selective, both for academic credentials and fit with the firm culture." According to one associate, "The vast majority of associates come from top 10 law schools, and probably a majority come from just Columbia, Harvard, Yale and New York University. At schools outside the top five, grades and law review become increasingly important. Outside the top 10, you just have to be incredibly brilliant and exceptionally lucky." However, "it is not enough to be intelligent. You must be interesting and personable too." Insiders emphasize, "Personality is important here and it shows in the people they hire."

What makes candidates interesting? One litigator believes that "the firm is looking for people who have many of the same qualities as Bob Fiske — the firm's most renowned litigator and reportedly one of the nicest individuals that you will ever meet — intelligence, intellect and, most important, modesty." Another associate advises, "Brash and obnoxious people will not find a job here, regardless of their academic credentials." Even if you get a callback, don't assume you are a shoo-in. "Callbacks are given to many more applicants than there are slots," and the process is "extremely competitive." Although a few sources "cannot figure out what they are looking for in an interviewee," most contacts offer a variation of the following opinion: "You must be extremely presentable, intelligent and articulate. If you are not enthusiastic and interesting, you will not be offered a job."

OUR SURVEY SAYS

A very nice place to work

Many insiders find Davis Polk an "ideal place to work." "I can't imagine being happier at a corporate law firm," boasts one lawyer. "The work is very interesting, the projects are challenging and my colleagues are extremely impressive." A litigator reports, "No job is ever perfect, but I don't know how an employer could do better than Davis Polk in terms of the combination of a collegial atmosphere and top-notch work." A colleague agrees: "The litigation department at Davis Polk is second to none. The partners open their doors to your ideas, regardless of your respective seniority. People are given a tremendous amount of responsibility whenever they are ready for it."

Not everyone is as content with the quality of work. "Work distribution is very unequal," claims one lawyer. There is "lots of grunt work to go around among junior associates," says another. A disappointed first-year concedes that "the people are incredibly smart and nice and you can't complain about the pay, but the work itself is just awful. It's boring, mindless, meaningless, repetitive, detail-oriented drudgery." Even dissenters nevertheless agree that "the people are the best part of being here. A rude or unfriendly person is the anomaly."

New Yorkers note that their offices are quite spectacular in appearance but bemoan the fact that "associates share offices into their fourth years." "The office space situation is a sore point for many associates." Despite décor almost uniformly described as "beautiful and tasteful," discontented adjectives like "cramped" and "tight" dot across survey responses.

More civil than social

"Courteous" and "professional," Davis Polk attorneys get high marks for civility. "The firm places a premium on civility," and "everybody is extremely respectful." In terms of sociability, responses are more varied. "Davis Polk only hires very friendly people," asserts a New Yorker who has "found very good friends" with whom she socializes regularly. Others agree that attorneys are "friendly and supportive" but see "limited social interaction outside of work." The atmosphere is "extremely professional and relaxed at the same time." Dress is business casual. Some sources call the culture "laid back," but the firm also retains a sense of formality. A few lawyers suggest that the firm is stuffier than its reputation. "The right pedigree definitely matters," remarks one associate. "With a few exceptions," another contends, "your role models are stuffy, over-brained, Ivy League types who share little in common with the average man." (The firm notes that its partners come from more than 35 law schools.)

Respectful partners

Civility starts at the top, and Davis Polk associates can expect to be treated with "a good deal of respect" by partners. A litigator claims that he "wouldn't work at another firm in New York City for this reason alone," adding that the "relationship between the partners and associates here is one of mutual respect and admiration." Others agree that partners are "very respectful and good to learn from," but "they have no interest in getting to know you." Amid such uniform politeness, the "occasional bad apple" tends to stand out. "Most partners are very pleasant to work with, which makes the exceptions all the more glaring," a source notes. Sometimes, one lawyer claims, the partners' respectful attitude toward associates "verges on the exaggerated." Another characterizes relations as "very formalized and stiff."

Bonus brouhaha

Despite good feelings toward individual partners, last year's "bonus fiasco" left a bad taste in the mouths of many associates toward the partnership as a whole. "Recanting on the bonus issue destroyed all credibility," one source bluntly writes of the firm's initial announcement that it would not pay bonuses, reversed only after other firms failed to follow suit. "A disgraceful performance," grumbles one frustrated associate. For some, the episode suggests the "firm ethos of respect" is deteriorating. "Last year's bonus debacle said a lot to associates. Partners value us as much as they value a good computer." One contact bitterly remarks, "The partners tried to be the grinches who stole Christmas, but the market didn't let it happen. Few of us will quickly forget their greed."

This bitterness taints many associates' satisfaction with their pay, although "Davis Polk's compensation is on a par with the highest compensation anywhere outside of Wachtell." Despite the fact that associates eventually received market-rate bonuses, resentment runs deep over the firm's obvious reluctance to ante up. "It took a lot of pain, suffering and public humiliation for them to admit what their associates are worth." "It is extremely irritating," fumes one lawyer, "that the partners are consistently in the top five in the world in profits per partner, and yet they are so miserly with the associates."

"Many associates here feel that Davis Polk should take a more proactive role in leading the market in pay," explains a source, "but in the end the firm does usually match the top end of the market." That the firm "only matched associate compensation kicking and screaming" suggests that "partners totally do not have the pulse of associates on this issue." Not all associates gripe about the firm's stinginess. One third-year measures satisfaction differently. "No one has been fired here, and our salaries are exactly the same as everyone else, so that puts us ahead in my book." Even those who complain that "this firm will never be first in raising salaries or giving bonuses" acknowledge that "as long as the market moves, they will eventually match." The firm points out, however, that DPW was the first New York firm to match the Silicon Valley starting salaries in February 2000.

Manageable hours

There's no doubt that Davis Polk lawyers work hard, but many claim that the hours are not brutal. They're "quite reasonable for a firm of this size and stature." "The hours fluctuate," according to several sources, but the "workload is usually manageable." A senior associate waxes philosophical: "As an associate practicing in New York, you have to anticipate periods during which long hours are spent at the office. It's the price you pay for the quality and importance of the work." Among the advantages associates report "no billable hour minimum or pressure" and partners who "are aware of associates' quality of life." "Vacations are encouraged and usually taken," and during busy periods, partners "are usually quite apologetic when you do have to work weekends."

Some part-time respondents report that Davis Polk partners are generally respectful of their schedules. Although one complains that she has "had to give up a lot in terms of the quality of the work to achieve those hours," another has "continued to do interesting work." A third-year associate contends that "in reality, most of the part-time associates work as many if not more hours than the full-time associates," though the firm maintains that its part-time associates work significantly fewer hours.

All you can eat pro bono

"The firm is very committed to pro bono," report Davis Polk associates. The firm offers "all you can eat pro bono." "Opportunities abound," and "many lawyers are involved in the entire spectrum of pro bono work." The full-time coordinator wins praise for "matching associates with opportunities of interest to them." A few attorneys suggest that litigators are more strongly encouraged (and rewarded) for participating than those in the corporate departments. One lawyer grumbles that "the firm is almost too committed — a few associates appear to spend the majority of their time on pro bono — thus leaving the rest of us with the less exciting billable matters."

Heading in the right direction

Sources praise Davis Polk for its hiring of women and minorities, but say the firm puts little effort into their retention. Several women report that gender is "not an issue here." A male attorney notes that "in the litigation department, many of the best senior associates are women who work part-time, and the firm will need to address the issue of part-time partners within the next few years." Despite the firm's support of its women attorneys, some associates express displeasure regarding the lack of mentoring or a discussion group for the firm's female attorneys.

"Very few African-Americans stay at the firm," sources report, and several minority associates suggest that despite "aggressive hiring," the firm "needs to take a hard look at what it's doing to retain associates of color." Respondents generally believe "the firm is receptive" to gays and lesbians, although one insider notes that Davis Polk "does not attract many gays and lesbians." Overall, "there is room for improvement," maintains one contact, "but the firm is heading in the right direction." The firm points out that it was the first large New York firm to be awarded the Minority Corporate Counsel Association's Thomas L. Sager Award (in 1999) for success in and commitment to the hiring, retention and promotion of minority attorneys. Moreover, the firm was ranked second overall in *The American Lawyer*'s Diversity Scorecard 2001.

"The partners tried to be the grinches who stole Christmas, but the market didn't let it happen. Few of us will quickly forget their greed."

— *Davis Polk associate*

6

Simpson Thacher & Bartlett

425 Lexington Avenue
New York, NY 10017
Phone: (212) 455-2000
www.simpsonthacher.com

LOCATIONS

New York, NY (HQ)
Los Angeles, CA
Palo Alto, CA
Hong Kong
London
Singapore
Tokyo

MAJOR DEPARTMENTS/PRACTICES

Bankruptcy
Corporate (M&A, Private Equity, Securities, Banking and
Project Finance)
Executive Compensation & Benefits
Exempt Organizations
Intellectual Property
Litigation (and Labor)
Personal Planning
Real Estate
Tax

THE STATS

No. of attorneys: 681
No. of offices: 7
Summer associate offers: 103 out of 107 (2001)
Chairman: Richard I. Beattie
Senior Administrative Partner: George R. Krouse
Hiring Partners: Paul Curnin and Marissa Wesely

BASE SALARY

New York, 2002
1st year: $125,000
2nd year: $135,000
3rd year: $150,000
4th year: $170,000
5th year: $190,000
6th year: $205,000
7th year: $220,000
8th year: $235,000
Summer associate: $2,404/week

NOTABLE PERKS

- Subsidized gym membership
- Firm resources available for personal legal matters
- Free-flowing Starbucks coffee and Poland
  Spring water
- Quarterly cocktail parties

THE BUZZ
WHAT ATTORNEYS AT OTHER FIRMS ARE SAYING ABOUT THIS FIRM

- "Corporate finance powerhouse"
- "Plain Janes"
- "Could be stronger internationally"
- "Coolest of the top NY firms"
- "Vanilla"

UPPERS

- Top-notch desktop technology
- "As nice as a big firm can be"
- Strong pro bono tradition

DOWNERS

- Overly formal partners
- Unpredictable bonuses
- Alas, no more cookie hour

EMPLOYMENT CONTACT

Ms. Dee Pifer
Director of Legal Employment
Phone: (212) 455-2687
Fax: (212) 455-2502
dpifer@stblaw.com

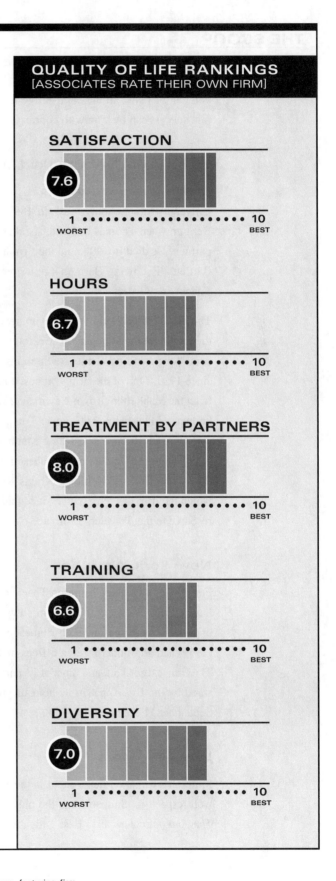

QUALITY OF LIFE RANKINGS
[ASSOCIATES RATE THEIR OWN FIRM]

SATISFACTION

7.6

1 • • • • • • • • • • • • • • • • • • 10
WORST   BEST

HOURS

6.7

1 • • • • • • • • • • • • • • • • • • 10
WORST   BEST

TREATMENT BY PARTNERS

8.0

1 • • • • • • • • • • • • • • • • • • 10
WORST   BEST

TRAINING

6.6

1 • • • • • • • • • • • • • • • • • • 10
WORST   BEST

DIVERSITY

7.0

1 • • • • • • • • • • • • • • • • • • 10
WORST   BEST

THE SCOOP

It's nice to be important, but it's more important to be nice. Simpson Thacher & Bartlett proves you can be both. In the competitive legal world, every firm strives to be No. 1. Simpson shows that success can be won with courtesy.

History: out with the old, in with the new

Simpson Thacher & Barnum was founded on New Year's Day in 1884 by three Columbia University Law School grads. In 1899 the firm changed its name to Reed, Simpson, Thacher & Barnum when Thomas B. Reed, speaker of the United States House of Representatives, became a partner. He died in 1902, and the firm had another name change to Simpson, Thacher, Barnum & Bartlett. Following Barnum's retirement in 1904, the firm adopted its present name, Simpson Thacher & Bartlett.

The decade after World War I saw many changes in the firm, as senior partners passed away or quit the firm, and the younger set was interested in new business and investments. The firm has had some long-standing clients, such as investment bank Lehman Brothers, which has been a client since 1930. One of the firm's biggest coups transpired in 1952, when the firm snatched 10 lawyers from the Manhattan firm of Newman & Brisco, which represented the company that would later be known as Manufacturers Hanover Trust. The firm has represented all of Manufacturers' successors including Chemical Bank, Chase Manhattan Bank and currently J.P. Morgan Chase in connection with lending and underwriting transactions and litigation. Other long-term representations include the buyout firms of Kohlberg Kravis Roberts & Co. (KKR) and The Blackstone Group, both of which the firm has represented since their inception. The firm has been the principal outside legal resource to the Travelers Insurance Co. for more than two decades.

New York, New York

For most of its history, Simpson Thacher has been known as a New York firm, though the firm does have offices elsewhere. The firm's London office opened in 1978. The 1990s were a period of expansion for Simpson, with domestic offices sprouting up in Los Angeles (1996), Palo Alto (1999) and additional foreign offices in Tokyo (1990), Hong Kong (1993) and Singapore (1997). The firm is tight-knit, and most of its partners started as associates with the firm. Simpson Thacher stood by the Big Apple in its hour of great need by donating $1 million to relief funds after the September 11 attacks.

Lotsa litigators

Simpson's litigation department is the largest in New York City, but it's not just big — it's also well-respected. Simpson was the only New York law firm listed among the top five finalists for *The American Lawyer*'s Best Litigation Department of the Year. Litigation partner Mary Kay

Vyskocil was recently identified by *The National Law Journal* as one of the 50 leading women litigators in America.

Currently, the firm represents Viacom, Paramount and Summer Redstone in antitrust actions brought by owners of independent video stores. The plaintiffs allege that the Viacom defendants, as well as Blockbuster (also owned by Viacom) and others, discriminated in their pricing in favor of Blockbuster and conspired among themselves to give preferential pricing terms to Blockbuster, putting independent video stores at a disadvantage. Potential damages, before trebling, run in the hundreds of millions of dollars.

Simpson Thacher's insurance litigation practice is top-notch. The firm's clients include many of the nation's largest insurers — AIG, American General, CNA, GE, Mitsui, St. Paul, State Farm, Sumitomo, Swiss Re and Travelers among them. The firm currently represents Swiss Re, the largest participant in the $3.5 billion property insurance program for the World Trade Center, in the coverage litigation arising out of the real estate developer's claim that the September 11 attack constitutes two occurrences, entitling him to double his insurance recovery.

Here's to your health

Simpson Thacher may be Mr. Nice Guy, but it's no pushover. The firm has become a top M&A advisor due in part to the extra push from head partner Richard Beattie and M&A leader Casey Cogut. Thomson Financial Securities Data ranked Simpson No. 2 in 2000 for U.S. mergers and acquisitions in terms of deal value, listing the firm as advising on 117 deals worth over $589 billion. According to American Lawyer Media, the firm was No. 1 in terms of deal value in its representation of principals.

The year 2001 proved a good one for Simpson's health care clients. In November 2001, Simpson helped its client, Wellpoint Health Networks, Inc., a health insurer, buy RightChoice Managed Care Inc., a health care provider. The deal was worth $1.3 billion.

In December, Amgen, Inc., the largest biotech company in the world, acquired Immunex Corp., a biopharmaceutical company. Amgen also acquired the 41 percent of Immunex owned by American Home Products Corporation, a pharmaceutical and consumer health care company. Simpson represented American Home Products in the $16 billion deal. In another Wellpoint deal that took place in December, the health insurer agreed to purchase CareFirst BlueCross/BlueShield for another $1.3 billion.

LBO ASAP

Simpson Thacher represents many of the most active leveraged buyout sponsors, money-center lenders and investment banks. In 2001, the firm represented Silver Lake Partners in its $20 billion LBO/acquisition of Seagate Technology, Kohlberg Kravis Roberts & Co. in its acquisitions of Shoppers Drug Mart and Wassall plc., Cypress Group and The Carlyle Group in their participation in the pending acquisition of Carter-Wallace's health care unit, and Vestar Capital Partners in its participation in the acquisition of Sunrise Medical Inc.

Fine in finance

A star in the financial services arena, Simpson represented Manufacturers Hanover in its merger with Chemical Bank, Chemical in its merger with Chase Manhattan Bank and Chase in its merger with JPMorgan. In a stock and cash deal coming in a bit over $5 billion, Simpson client Washington Mutual Inc., the Seattle financial services company, acquired New York's Dime Bancorp Inc. in September 2001. In another bank deal, Simpson represented Wachovia Corporation when it was acquired by First Union Corporation for $13.4 billion in stock.

Splendid securities

In 2001, the corporate department, headed by George Krouse, was ranked by Thomson Financial No. 1 in worldwide equity issuances by U.S. issuers, No. 1 in worldwide initial public offerings by U.S. issuers and No. 1 in U.S. equity and equity-related offerings (based on proceeds in engagements for issuers and underwriters).

For Kraft Foods, Simpson Thacher advised the underwriters in the global IPO that raised $8.7 billion in gross proceeds. Simpson Thacher represented Accenture in the United States and on a global basis in coordinating and implementing its IPO in 2001.

Making time for pro bono

The National Law Journal named Simpson Thacher winner of its Pro Bono Award in 2001 in recognition of its 2001 victory for New York City public school children. The firm represented the Campaign for Fiscal Equity in a constitutional challenge to New York State's system for allocating funds to public education. Simpson Thacher won a seven-month trial to ensure that the 1.1 million New York City public school children receive the sound basic education guaranteed by the New York State Constitution.

GETTING HIRED

Top tier

The door at Simpson isn't always open — unless, of course, you're a law grad of "Harvard, Yale, Columbia or NYU." As for the type of candidate the firm desires, a New York associate says, "They want an individual who is intelligent, personable and thinks outside of the box." The "very informal" callback arrangement consists of "one initial 30-minute interview followed by a subsequent 2.5-hour interview with a series of people."

Sensational summers

Criticism of the Simpson summer associate program is rare, which may be due to the fact that associates are offered heaps of choices in designing their summer experience. A New Yorker boasts, "I got to do both corporate and litigation and go to the firm's London office for three weeks." Another contented New York associate adds, "The firm even flew me to Asia for three weeks to work out of the Hong Kong office." One source maintains, "I was encouraged to try everything I had any interest in participating in, from white-collar to a pro bono asylum matter to corporate finance." Some say the summer program is "all about the lunches." One junior associate contends that "the summer associate program was quite lavish — choose your pick of the city's best restaurants." Though the summer was fun, a Big Apple associate does not think the program prepared him for life at the firm. "It was the calm before the storm."

OUR SURVEY SAYS

Formal yet friendly

The atmosphere at Simpson Thacher is an interesting combination of formality and friendliness, according to associates. One survey-taker notes, "Some groups of associates and partners socialize outside of the firm, but most interaction is very professional." Another source says that "wonderful people and a great administrative staff make the long hours bearable." There seems to be discrepancy among associates as to the amount of socializing occurring at the firm. One associate says, "People here tend to work during the day and go home to their families at night." Another remarks that associates socialize a lot, involving "dinner or drinks after work and on weekends." In the Tokyo office, "junior attorneys in particular do socialize with each other quite frequently."

A friendly atmosphere is important, but what about the work? A New York associate calls it "stimulating," adding, "I have a tremendous amount of responsibility, but also receive excellent feedback from the partners I work with. Almost all the work the firm does is cutting edge and is often written up in the papers. I have built strong personal and professional relationships with the clients I work with, and my work is not repetitive." Most associates want in on Simpson's big cases, but inevitably some are left doing work with which they are less than delighted. Recently, says one lawyer, "the partnership held a department-wide conference specifically designed to elicit feedback from the associates about satisfaction and development, so I believe they are aware of this and are trying to do something about it."

Following the herd

Simpson doesn't let another firm show it up. Though the firm "has a reputation for hanging back in the pack when it comes to making salary decisions," the firm "always matches other top firms." Palo Alto associates don't seem to be as riled up by the salary wars as associates in New York. A

Palo Alto associate says, "I don't really know how my compensation compares to my peers at other firms, and I don't care." He considers his compensation "adequate" and "fair." Associates in New York have mixed feelings about the pay they take home. A corporate associate maintains, "If you divide our base salary by the number of hours we spend in the office, we're all making peanuts." In the litigation department, some associates consider their salary acceptable in downtime but insufficient during a busy stretch.

While most Simpson associates agree that they are paid "top dollar," many think the firm dropped the ball during the 2001 bonus season. A New Yorker asserts, "Simpson was late in including first-years in 2001 year-end bonuses and paid perhaps a bit less than Cravath and Sullivan."

From reasonable to crushing

At Simpson, hours seem to vary according to practice group. A corporate attorney in the New York office reports, "Most mid-levels have no time to do anything outside the office Monday through Friday. I usually work at least one day of every weekend, or even worse, I'm on call babysitting a deal." A litigation associate says he hasn't "gotten home before 10 p.m. in a month." In the corporate department, "When we are busy, we are extremely busy, and when we are not, there is lots of downtime." In mergers and acquisitions, things are "leisurely" with "no face time." "I almost never work weekends," brags one M&A associate. In the tax department, associates hate the "constant feeling of being on call," though they admit the hours are reasonable. A Palo Alto associate sums it up: "Some months are quite reasonable. Others are crushing."

Despite the crazy hours, the firm has a positive attitude toward part-time work. A female associate remarks, "Everyone here has been wonderful about the arrangement. So long as you, as the part-time employee, recognize that there will be times when you are called upon to work late hours and/or weekends and/or change your hours or days of work at times, the arrangement can provide associates with a fulfilling balance of work and time at home with their families."

How do you spell diversity?

The firm does an "outstanding" job when it comes to hiring women attorneys. But, says one associate, "The firm generally has difficulty retaining women." The reason behind this difficulty may be a suspicious lack of mentoring and "the fact that the firm does not support alternative working situations to accommodate two working parent families." Another female associate says, "The problem is not so much promotion, as it is retention. Most women just don't stick around long enough to make partner." The firm's promotion, mentoring and part-time employment options are "beyond deplorable," according to one female associate. Another female attorney thinks things aren't so bad. "In terms of quality of work, there is no difference in assigning for men and women. In fact, some of the most respected associates at the firm tend to be women." In litigation, a female associate notes that she has "been mentored by male and female partners." She adds, "There are a number of women associates' events to foster a network among women."

While Simpson may be adept at hiring a racially diverse incoming class, some associates think the firm has a problem retaining a diverse body of associates. One source maintains, "I don't think there's much institutional commitment to mentoring or promoting minorities in particular." An African-American associate concurs: "I feel that the firm does make an effort to recruit qualified minority candidates, but I don't think they do enough to retain those employees." An Hispanic associate suggests that the firm is more welcoming towards Asians than African-Americans and Hispanics. He notes that the firm recently promoted three Asian attorneys to the partnership level.

As for gays and lesbians, one associate notes that there are about "six or seven openly gay partners" at the firm. Another lawyer mentions that the firm "is effectively neutral with respect to gays and lesbians," claiming, "I have never heard of any adverse employment action or harassment being taken due to sexual orientation, though I also do not sense that the firm is committed to increasing or welcoming gays and lesbians in particular." A heterosexual female associate notes, "There may be problems I am unaware of, but there are gay partners. We have domestic companion coverage, and many gay colleagues don't hide their orientation."

Sink or swim

Most associates at Simpson say the firm offers little formal training, though one insider notes, "This is an area the firm is trying to improve." The amount and quality of training may vary by practice group. A corporate associate remarks, "Training has been exceptional. While training materials are lackluster, hands-on experience and excellent supervision provide unmatched on-the-job training." Another corporate associate adds, "The formal training is OK, but I think that the partners and more senior associates do a terrific job training the more junior associates." Training is not taxing in the tax department. As one associate there maintains, "Our department does extensive and quality training. There are also some great training opportunities offered firm-wide, such as a step-by-step guide on how to form and qualify a nonprofit." Litigators insist that training in their department lags behind other areas. A litigation associate assesses the situation: "My understanding is that the corporate department has a much more extensive formal program than litigation. The litigation department's emphasis on informal training can be problematic for those associates who are assigned to cases that do not give them much opportunity to develop new skills. The department is aware that this is perceived as a significant problem and has recently solicited associate feedback on how training can be improved."

Cleary, Gottlieb, Steen & Hamilton

One Liberty Plaza
New York, NY 10006-1470
Phone: (212) 225-2000
www.cgsh.com

LOCATIONS

New York, NY (HQ)
Washington, DC
Brussels
Frankfurt
Hong Kong
London
Milan
Moscow
Paris
Rome
Tokyo

MAJOR DEPARTMENTS/PRACTICES

Antitrust • Capital Markets • Corporate, Finance &
Banking • Employee Benefits • Energy, Project Finance
& Infrastructure • International Sovereign Debt &
Privatization • Litigation • M&A • Real Estate • Tax •
Trusts & Estates • Workouts & Bankruptcy

THE STATS

No. of attorneys: 710
No. of offices: 11
Summer associate offers: 103 out of 103 (2001)
Managing Partner: Peter Karasz
Hiring Partner: Jeffrey S. Lewis

BASE SALARY

New York, 2002
1st year: $125,000
2nd year: $135,000
3rd year: $150,000
4th year: $170,000
5th year: $190,000
6th year: $205,000
7th year: $220,000
8th year: $235,000
Summer associate: $2,404/week

NOTABLE PERKS

- "Best corporate cafeteria in New York"
- Free gym membership
- Weekly wine and cheese parties
- "Late-start culture," with many associates beginning their day at 10 a.m.

THE BUZZ
WHAT ATTORNEYS AT OTHER FIRMS ARE SAYING ABOUT THIS FIRM

- "Amazing reputation in Europe"
- "Quirky but brilliant people"
- "Unjustifiably full of themselves"
- "Late, late nights"
- "The firm for lawyers who don't want to be lawyers"

UPPERS

- "Unbelievable international practice"
- Plush offices with great art work
- Opportunities for overseas work

DOWNERS

- Informal assignment structure causes disparity in associates' workload
- Grueling hours and high stress
- Lack of real guidance from partners

EMPLOYMENT CONTACT

Ms. Norma F. Cirincione
Director of Legal Personnel
Phone: (212) 225-3150
Nyrecruit@cgsh.com

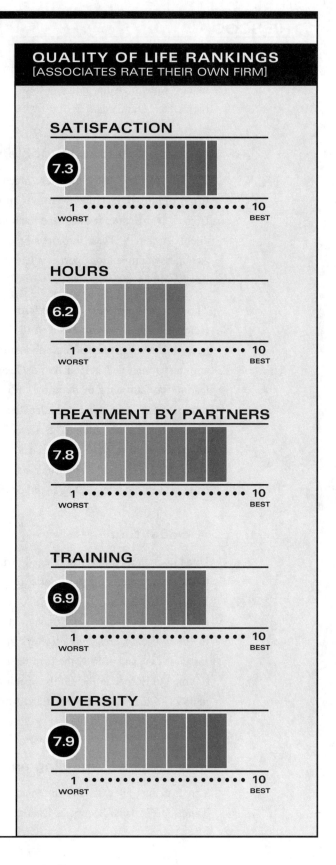

QUALITY OF LIFE RANKINGS
[ASSOCIATES RATE THEIR OWN FIRM]

SATISFACTION
7.3
1 WORST .... 10 BEST

HOURS
6.2
1 WORST .... 10 BEST

TREATMENT BY PARTNERS
7.8
1 WORST .... 10 BEST

TRAINING
6.9
1 WORST .... 10 BEST

DIVERSITY
7.9
1 WORST .... 10 BEST

THE SCOOP

Cleary isn't a traditional kind of law firm — and Cleary attorneys prefer it that way, thank you very much. Known as the "quirky" New York firm, Cleary commits itself to individuality along with high ethical standards.

History: founded by noble spirits

The founders of Cleary, Gottlieb, Steen & Hamilton were no mere tyros when they opened their firm in 1946. In fact, they were star attorneys at Root, Clark, Buckner & Ballantine who defected from their firm after it established an unfavorable compensation system based on hours billed and clients ensnared. These attorneys fancied themselves noble spirits and were loath to practice law as a messy competition sport. At Cleary Gottlieb, they decided, partners' compensation would be based only on seniority.

This idea was a success, and the founders themselves achieved continued success in their careers. Henry J. Friendly became one of the Second Circuit's most celebrated judges. George W. Ball became Undersecretary of State and ambassador to the United Nations in the Kennedy and Johnson administrations and helped found Cleary's European practice. George Cleary was one of the leading tax attorneys of his time. Fowler Hamilton served as director of the U.S. Agency for International Development under the Kennedy administration. Following in the founders' footsteps is partner Alan L. Beller of the New York office. In November 2001, Beller was appointed head of the Securities and Exchange Commission's corporation finance division. In April 2002, Giovanni Prezioso, a partner in the firm's Washington office, became SEC general counsel, and outgoing SEC general counsel David M. Becker became a Cleary partner in May.

A global tour

Upon its founding, the firm opened offices in New York and Washington, D.C. In no time at all, Cleary extended its reach to Paris, opening shop there in 1949. Offices followed in Brussels in 1960 and London in 1971. The 1980s became the Asian era of the firm, as it expanded its horizons eastward. Two offices were opened in that decade, one in Hong Kong in 1980 and one in Tokyo in 1987. Cleary's resident attorneys in Tokyo were the first foreign lawyers to be licensed under Japanese law, and in 1989 the firm was the first U.S. firm to promote Japanese attorneys. The firm returned to Europe in the 1990s, opening offices in Moscow and Frankfurt and an office in Rome in 1998. Cleary was only the third American law firm to open an office in Italy, and it now has two — in Rome and Milan.

International wheeling and dealing

The firm has an extensive international M&A practice in Asia, Europe and Latin America. Thomson Financial Securities Data ranked the firm No. 2 in global M&A in 2001, and according to the *New York Law Journal*, Cleary ranked eighth in the top ten U.S.-based law firms handling European M&As in 2001, with deals amounting to $82.3 billion. Not a bad showing — and Cleary can thank New York partner Victor Lewkow for making much of that merger magic happen. Lewkow landed two of the European deals, totaling $47.9 billion.

For Cleary, the green in the Emerald Isle signifies cash — and lots of it. Cleary advised on some of the largest M&As in economically reviving Ireland in 2000 and 2001. Other countries host Cleary clients as well. In January 2002, Cleary advised IMAX Corporation of Canada on the acquisition of its Digital Projection International Limited by Brandplain Limited. Currently, Cleary is in talks on a South Korean deal. Hynix Semiconductor Inc., a microchip maker, may merge with competitor Micron Technology Inc. — at least as of May 2002. (These things can take a while.)

Not only does the firm do global M&A work, it also helps unstable governments get back on their feet. The firm has counseled the governments of Indonesia, Mexico, Argentina, Chile, Colombia, Ecuador, Russia, Korea and the Philippines on debt management.

Capable capital markets

When it comes to capital markets, Cleary, a leader in domestic and international capital markets practice, has been there, done that. The firm represented Goldman Sachs in the $20 billion IPO of Prudential Insurance Company in December 2001 — one of the largest transfers of private wealth into the public markets ever. Cleary advised Salomon Smith Barney in the March 2002 $4.3 billion IPO of Travelers Property Casualty Corp., which was the largest U.S. insurance IPO and the fifth-largest U.S. IPO in history. Moreover, the firm is currently at work on the IPO of legendary sports car manufacturer Ferrari, having already taken a ride with motorcycle-maker Ducati.

Downtown on a horrifying morning

Few of us will ever forget September 11, 2001. Employees of Cleary's downtown Manhattan office were right in the thick of things. The firm's office at One Liberty Plaza, located across from where the two towers of the World Trade Center once stood, suffered broken windows on the floors below Cleary's offices after terrorists flew two planes into the towers. Well before the attacks, the smart planners at Cleary equipped its midtown conference center to serve as a second Manhattan office site in the event of an emergency, so the firm set up shop there to regroup after the attacks. Groups of lawyers also camped out at fellow law firms Debevoise & Plimpton and Paul, Weiss, Rifkind, Wharton & Garrison, with others taking temporary refuge at the offices of clients such as Instinet and Ziff Brothers. Despite the economic (and social) turmoil of the time, Cleary assured its associates that there would be no layoffs at Cleary. And indeed, there were none. In addition, the firm made its traditional contribution that year to the Legal Aid Society of New York, donating between $100,000 and $200,000, and paid associates bonuses for 2001 at the top of the scale. Happily, Cleary was able to return to its downtown office in December 2001.

Gas and cash flow

When Phillips Petroleum Company, a natural gas and petroleum producer, merged with Conoco, another gas and crude oil producer in November 2001, Conoco called on Cleary for legal aid. The Phillips/Conoco union created the third-largest oil company in the United States and the sixth-largest in the world. Advising attorneys for Conoco in the $35 billion deal were Cleary lawyers from the D.C. office.

In a big-bucks acquisition expected to close in the third quarter of 2002, Cleary lawyers advised Nationwide Financial Services, Inc. in its purchase of Provident Mutual Life Insurance Company for $1.56 billion in stock and cash. The deal, which took place in October 2001, will help Nationwide increase its presence in variable life insurance. In yet another billion-dollar deal, Tyco International Ltd. bought Sensormatic Electric Corp., a security systems developer and manufacturer, for $2.3 billion in stock and debt. Cleary represented Sensormatic in the August 2001 deal.

In still another moneymaker, Cleary advised BNP Paribas in its acquisition of United California Bank from UFJ Holdings, Inc., based in Tokyo. The $2.4 billion cash deal will help BNP Paribas gain ground in California.

GETTING HIRED

Grades are just the beginning

When it comes to hiring, Cleary doesn't mess around. For the most part, "stellar grades are a prerequisite for a callback interview," say Cleary associates. But brains alone aren't enough to get you in the door. "Once at the callback, grades are irrelevant — in fact, the callback interviewers do not even get to know your grades — and the real test is whether you will fit into the family." So what does it take to pass muster with the Cleary Gottlieb crowd? "Life experience and other useful skills, such as foreign language ability." "Summer associates often get to work six weeks abroad in one of the firm's foreign offices," explains one associate. If your German or French is a little rusty, start brushing up.

Summer in the city

The summer program receives mostly high marks from associates. "I had a very good time, and I got a real sense of what it was like to work at Cleary," says a sixth-year associate, who considered himself "fortunate" to work on a variety of cases while summering at the firm. But a second-year cautions that summer associates should actively seek assignments. "The amount and quality of work that each summer associate receives varies dramatically, from excessive and overwhelming to absolutely no work."

The firm recruits for its New York and Washington, D.C. summer associate programs at 26 U.S. law schools during the late summer and throughout the fall. Cleary also interviews at some Canadian law schools for the New York program. Suitably impressive applicants are cordially invited to the office for a full day of interviews.

OUR SURVEY SAYS

The quirky firm

Overall, Cleary attorneys say their firm is a cordial and friendly place to work. The firm, as one attorney puts it, is "generally laid back — or as laid back as any large New York City law firm can be." One insider terms it "officially informal." "There is no hierarchy — partners know the messengers by their names," claims a New York-based associate. On the other hand, one insider claims that the general amiability of the firm simply obscures the hierarchy. "It's still a large law firm." Several associates note that culture does differ by practice group.

But just because the folks at Cleary are congenial, don't think they spend their time gabbing by the water cooler. There are opportunities to socialize, but Cleary attorneys normally don't spend every night partying in a bar, like the noisome lawyer-characters of "Ally McBeal." "People are friendly, but generally not overly social with each other," explains one attorney. Cleary Gottlieb is "informal and friendly, for a bunch of workaholics," quips one associate. The weekly wine and cheese event is said to "draw a small showing." And adversity reportedly has brought the firm closer together. "Our mutual dislocation post-September 11 has brought us even closer together in a more personal way," says one associate. Another observes more "cross-socialization: lawyers doing things with non-legal staff" since that dark day.

One associate refers to the firm's reputation as a place for very bright but slightly eccentric attorneys: "The firm is generally full of laid-back but rather peculiar individuals." Because the attorneys at the firm come from very diverse backgrounds (many of them have lived abroad) this attorney says, "There's all sorts of quirky individuality, which you become more and more aware of as time goes by." Other insiders call their co-workers "loosey-goosey and somewhat nerdy — but in a good way" and possessed of "interesting and bizarre non-legal interests." Glad to hear it.

Time keeps on slippin' (slippin', slippin')

Cleary attorneys are in agreement that they put in long hours. Some, however, seem to deal with long days better than others. "The reward for good work is definitely more work and lots of it," complains one first-year associate. "It sucks having to tell your significant other every night, 'I have no idea when I am coming home.'"

Even lawyers who love the job don't care for the hours. While "the work is quite interesting and extremely challenging, the hours are long and the stress level very high," laments one second-year associate, who hastens to add that Cleary is "definitely not a 'lifestyle' firm." The long hours have other attorneys singing the burnout blues. "Although the work I do is often intellectually interesting, I do far too much of it, and my personal life suffers as a result." A typical complaint: the alleged lack of control associates have over setting their schedules. On the bright side, "there's no face time required," and associates often opt to put in long days during the week so that they can have weekends off.

Compensation contentment

When it comes to salary, Cleary is clearly a follower, not a leader, but most Clearyites say they're fine with that. "Cleary seems to be a cautious follower at the high end. We pay at the top of the market but will not lead in terms of declaring raises or bonuses," observes an associate in the corporate practice. "Only Wachtell is better paid," brags another associate. "Though Cleary never acts first in bonus wars, it always comes out at the top of the scale." And that's what matters.

While most associates seem pleased with their compensation package, a few rebels express discontent. Three percent of an associate's bonus is automatically transferred into a retirement account, a practice that one attorney describes as "sneaky." Still, attorneys give Cleary high marks for continuing to pay large bonuses in 2001, since the firm had to vacate its New York offices "for three months due to its proximity to the former World Trade Center." The firm "could have tried not to" give bonuses because of the tragedy and the recession, observes one grateful associate.

Wanna partake in pro bono?

There seems to be some confusion as to the role of pro bono work at the firm. Some associates say that pro bono work counts toward billable hours. Others contend that pro bono does not count, while still others express uncertainty as to exactly what the policy is. One associate attempts to clear up what may simply be an issue of semantics: "The firm does not have a billable hours requirement, so it doesn't matter that pro bono work does not count toward billable hours." This same associate goes on to praise the firm's policy, saying, "We were told up-front that the firm encourages strong involvement in pro bono work as early as possible in one's career." According to another insider, "Cleary does not explicitly discourage pro bono work, but it makes clear that pro bono work is the equivalent of vacation time and that billing work always comes first." The firm points out that its long-standing commitment to pro bono work is evidenced by its decision to have two associates participate in rotating three-month externships at full salary at MFY Legal Services and Lawyer Alliance for New York, as well as by the many other opportunities available for pro bono work.

Strong effort on diversity

Associates give the firm strong marks for its efforts to be inclusive — even as they also note that the firm is predominantly white and the partnership is mostly white and male. "As a senior female associate, I believe that I get fantastic work — just as high-quality and demanding as my male colleagues — and that I am treated with complete respect," reports one associate, who specifically lauds the firm's efforts to recruit and retain women.

Still, for all its efforts, some associates believe "the jury is still out, given the small number of women partners." "The firm hasn't made a woman partner in the New York office in ages," one associate confides. This same attorney says that even though firm management has created a new senior attorney position ("a step below special counsel, which is a step below partner"), it is viewed by "many women and parenting dads like an inferior 'mommy track,' not an equal option." Explains a litigation attorney, "I think the biggest problem at the end of the day is that the big firm legal profession is completely incompatible with having a family, or at least with having a family where both spouses or partners work."

After successful efforts to recruit more minority associates in the early 1990s, the firm has found itself criticized in later years because many of these associates — in particular, African-American associates — have left in large numbers. A lingering resentment of that criticism was brought to the surface in December 2001 by an article in *The American Lawyer*. A number of associates say the article, which chronicled Cleary's racial diversity efforts and potential reasons for the exodus of black attorneys, "was off-base." "Diversity is one of the defining hallmarks of this firm," according to one minority associate, and a lack of diversity "would be antithetical to the 'internationalism' of the firm." While some associates acknowledge that the firm has a way to go before becoming truly integrated, the prevailing belief is that the firm "will stay on the path." Indeed, the editor-in-chief of *The American Lawyer* published an apology for inaccurate reporting in connection with the article.

Cry for attention

Is a little guidance too much to ask for? Some Clearyites don't think so. A second-year associate describes having ongoing confidence issues as an attorney because of the lack of mentoring and interaction with partners at Cleary. "The worst part of my job is getting the attention of a partner," frets one insider. "The partners I work with seem so pressed for time that I no longer expect mentoring from them, and I would be happy — actually elated — if they simply reviewed my work to ensure I'm not screwing up a deal they assigned to me." Another junior associate gives the partners low marks. "The associates are generally friendly and very interesting, but the partners can be downright abusive in their treatment of associates."

The consensus, though, seems to be that the partners make an effort to treat associates with respect, and try to be available, even if they can't always give a lot of their time. "When people get really busy," says an understanding second-year associate, "you can't expect every e-mail to be returned." In fact, one first-year already seems to have a handle on dealing with the higher-ups: "Partners do respect the associates, and expect us to contribute from the very beginning, but it can vary from partner to partner and depends on how confident you are in your abilities."

VAULT TOP 100

8

PRESTIGE RANKING

Covington & Burling

1201 Pennsylvania Avenue, NW
Washington, DC 20004-2401
Phone: (202) 662-6000
www.cov.com

LOCATIONS

Washington, DC (HQ)
New York, NY
San Francisco, CA
Brussels
London

MAJOR DEPARTMENTS/PRACTICES

Antitrust • Arbitration/ADR • Communications •
Corporate, Securities, Insolvency & Real Estate •
Employee Benefits • Employment • Energy •
Environmental • Financial Services • Food & Drug •
Health Care • Information Technology, Privacy &
E-Commerce • Insurance • Intellectual Property •
International Legislative • Litigation (Trial & Appellate) •
M&A • Patent Advice & Litigation • Sports • Tax •
Transportation • White Collar Defense·

THE STATS

No. of attorney: 512
No. of offices: 5
Summer associate offers: 52 out of 55 (2001, DC)
Managing Partner: Stuart C. Stock
Hiring Partners: Mark E. Plotkin and Thomas L. Cubbage III

BASE SALARY

Washington, DC 2001*
1st year: $125,000
2nd year: $135,000
3rd year: $150,000
4th year: $155,000
5th year: $165,000
6th year: $175,000
7th year: $185,000
8th year: $195,000
Summer associate: $2,400/week
* Base salary includes pension contribution for
Washington associates who received offers prior to
January 2000

NOTABLE PERKS

• Six-month pro bono rotations
• Friday happy hours and beer and candy nights
• Tickets for sporting events
• Triennial firm retreat at a Virginia resort

 THE BUZZ
WHAT ATTORNEYS AT OTHER FIRMS ARE SAYING ABOUT THIS FIRM

• "Top dogs in Washington"
• "Can be a sweatshop"
• "Some of the smartest lawyers"
• "Cool pro bono work"
• "Stuffy, stuffy, stuffy. Did I say 'stuffy'?"

136 **VAULT** CAREER LIBRARY

© 2002 Vault Inc.

UPPERS

• High-profile cases and clients
• Emphasis on training and supporting junior associates

DOWNERS

• Increasing emphasis on billables
• Loss of close-knit, family feeling due to recent expansion

EMPLOYMENT CONTACT

Ms. Lorraine Brown
Director, Legal Personnel Recruiting
Phone: (202) 662-6200
legal.recruiting@cov.com

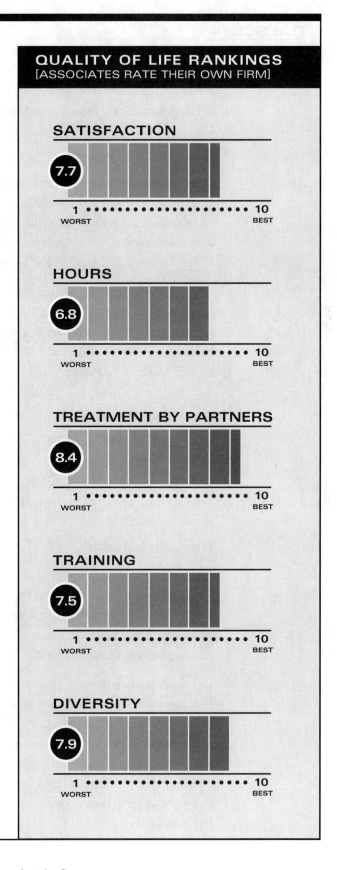

QUALITY OF LIFE RANKINGS
[ASSOCIATES RATE THEIR OWN FIRM]

SATISFACTION
7.7
1 WORST ••••••••••••••••••• 10 BEST

HOURS
6.8
1 WORST ••••••••••••••••••• 10 BEST

TREATMENT BY PARTNERS
8.4
1 WORST ••••••••••••••••••• 10 BEST

TRAINING
7.5
1 WORST ••••••••••••••••••• 10 BEST

DIVERSITY
7.9
1 WORST ••••••••••••••••••• 10 BEST

THE SCOOP

An old-line D.C. firm that exudes prestige, Covington & Burling prides itself on bringing unique solutions to cases involving local, federal and foreign law. Covington is happy to lend a legal hand to big tobacco clients, as well as to food and drink companies such as Bacardi.

First in federal law

When the firm opened its doors on January 1, 1919, its founders, J. Harry Covington and Edward Burling, were already well established in the legal field. Covington, having served in Congress, was a supporter of the legislation that created the Federal Trade Commission. Burling had already co-founded another firm, Bentley & Burling, in Chicago. But after meeting through mutual friends, the two men decided to join forces to create a new firm that would specialize in federal law.

After 70 years spent solely in the District, the firm began a rapid expansion first marked by the opening of its London office in 1988. (The firm now has over 50 attorneys in London and Brussels.) In March 1999, the firm opened an office specializing in intellectual property and technology in San Francisco, and in October 1999, it established a New York office by merging with the Manhattan corporate/white-collar criminal law boutique firm of Howard, Smith & Levin.

Room to grow

Tight quarters have forced the firm to triple the size of its San Francisco office. After locating to the city a mere two years ago, the firm moved to new offices in December 2001. The new space is needed in part to accommodate the office's over 20 lawyers and 18 staff, plus a large number of attorneys who drop by the office each week from other Covington offices while in the Bay Area.

No case is too big

The firm is one of many involved in the most high-profile case of the year — Enron. In January 2002, a team of Covington attorneys successfully represented investment bank UBS Warburg in its bid for the beleaguered energy firm's electricity and natural gas trading business. Covington had previously represented the bank in an October 2001 case that resulted in the overturning of a $5.6 million judgment against Warburg.

Covington has been keeping busy with a variety of cases for other well-known corporate clients. Just a month earlier, the firm represented Schering-Plough as it finalized a worldwide drug partnership with pharmaceutical firm Merck. Covington scored a victory against the Department of the Interior in October 2001 when a federal district court ruled that several major oil companies represented by Covington were being overcharged by the government for royalties related to offshore oil. In September 2001, Covington scored two victories in as many days, when the Federal Circuit reversed two earlier decisions in patent cases against Covington client ExxonMobil.

A girl's best friend

Celebrated jewelry design company Cartier turned to Covington when it needed help battling cybersquatters who had registered more than 100 domain names containing the Cartier name. In July 2001, a federal court ruled in favor of Cartier, ordering that the names be turned over to the company. And in May 2001, Covington secured a preliminary injunction against office supply megastore Staples in favor of its client Montblanc. It seems Staples was not only reselling the high-status writing implements at bargain prices, but also with the serial numbers and trademark symbols scratched off. Covington's other well-known intellectual property clients include the Smithsonian Institution, Microsoft, USA Networks and Computer Associates.

Sportin' life

Covington lawyers are good sports. The firm represents big-name athletic organizations like the National Hockey League, National Basketball Association and National Football League. For more than 40 years, Covington has been the firm of choice for the NFL, representing the league on matters from antitrust to labor disputes to copyright infringement. In July 2001, the firm represented the NFL in a complex four-way deal with CBS, America Online and SportsLine.com. The agreement calls for the three media outlets to feature content provided by the NFL.

Promoting pro bono

One of the firm's more unusual recent cases was a pro bono matter involving the governments of the United States and Belize. Stuart Irvin and David Orlin of Covington acted as counsel to The Nature Conservancy, a U.S.-based environmental rights group that facilitated an agreement between the two governments whereby the United States would forgive Belize $8.58 million in debt if Belize paid the money to its local rainforest conservation organizations.

In February 2001, the firm scored another major pro bono victory, this one a matter of life and death. Covington partner Timothy C. Hester represented convicted murderer and death row inmate Jerry Rogers on a pro bono basis with assistance from a team of associates. In a unanimous opinion, the Florida State Supreme Court overturned the murder conviction of Rogers on the basis that evidence was withheld that identified another individual as a suspect. Covington, which has represented Rogers since 1995, secured a new trial for Rogers, who was sentenced to death in 1984 after representing himself at trial.

Although the firm has long prided itself on its pro bono achievements, Covington has only recently instituted a formal program to recognize the efforts of its attorneys. The firm held its first pro bono recognition reception in August 2001. The ceremony honored attorneys who had performed more than 50 hours of pro bono work during the previous year, and special merit awards were given to a partner and associate for their commitment to pro bono service during the year. Covington's pro bono program focuses on civil rights/civil liberties, child welfare initiatives, criminal and court-appointed cases, environment, historic preservation and intellectual property matters.

GETTING HIRED

A great summer

While a Covington summer is "full of activities and lunches," it also provides associates with the opportunity to do some "good work." One D.C. associate says, "It was a great summer — the social events were varied and plentiful, and for the most part, I received assignments on subjects I had professed an interest in working on." "The summer experience is well-regulated, with assignments given one at a time with good follow-up from senior lawyers. The social schedule was certainly not wild, but very pleasant," chirps an associate currently in the firm's Brussels office. The road to Covington is paved with summer success. A D.C. associate maintains, "They still rely a lot on the summer program as a means of hiring and less so on laterals. If you were ever in the summer program, you will always find a place here."

High standards

The D.C.-based firm puts high emphasis on candidates who are "smart, engaging and able to handle challenging work." A New York associate mentions that "clerkships and top schools" help. A D.C. associate says grades aren't the end-all: "We also consider an applicant's personality, attitude, oral skills and desire to remain in private practice. We have declined to give offers to many people who had good paper records but who were not impressive during the interview." And be sure to give good references. One associate remarks, "I gave them four references. No other firm called my references; they called all four." The partners at Covington get personal. Says one associate, "They gave me comments on my writing sample!"

OUR SURVEY SAYS

"Collegial" Covington

Associates agree: "Above all, there is a sense that we're all in this together. [There is] very little competition among associates." This perception of life at Covington appears consistent firm-wide, though a Brussels associate notices, "The smaller offices, such as Brussels and San Francisco, tend to be more informal than the larger offices." A New York associate notes, "There is a very intellectual culture, and people come together often, both formally and informally, to discuss cases and ideas. Most importantly, the environment is friendly and supportive and there is a strong emphasis placed on teaching." A corporate associate maintains, "This is the best place to be for experience and training. I'm already running deals as a second-year, thanks to many, many hours as a first-year behind the scenes." A New Yorker notes, "Most all of the partners here treat associates with respect. Many take time to help younger associates with their skills development and other mentoring." While the atmosphere at Covington is cordial, there is not a lot of socializing outside of the office, according to a D.C. associate. "People come in and get their work done," remarks another.

Consistent Covington

When it comes to compensation, "Covington keeps itself in line with its competitors," says one associate, "though they are not price-setters." In New York, associates are pleased that their firm "matches the top of the market." A D.C. associate notes, "It is not off the charts, but it is competitive." While associates are happy with their base salary, they are anything but pleased with the bonus system, which associates describe as "confusing." "I am not a big fan," grumbles a D.C. associate. Another D.C. insider sighs, "Without bonuses, we barely keep up with other large D.C. firms." (The firm says it has implemented a new bonus system that takes into account a wide range of contributions, including not only billable work, but also pro bono work and activities contributing to the operation of the firm.) Another aspect of the firm's pay structure that makes associates antsy is the firm's abandonment of the "long-standing policy of matching associates' contributions to their 401(k) plans," though the firm points out that it never "matched" associate contributions and continues to make retirement contributions for associates who received job offers prior to December 31, 1999.

No face time

Though Covington associates work hours comparable to the hours logged by their counterparts at peer firms in New York and D.C., many associates at Covington don't feel "chained to the desk." "I'm not required to put in any face time and other lawyers are very understanding when I have prior commitments that I have to keep," says one D.C. associate. Many associates say they work very little or not at all on weekends, "unless a big case or project demands extra time." According to a D.C. associate, "The firm has begun to join others in stressing billable hours." However another insider mentions that billable hours aren't "pushed excessively." A New York associate sums it up: "Although Covington is a great firm in many respects, it is not a lifestyle firm. We are glad that we have continued to be extremely busy during difficult economic times. However, as a result of our being busy and this being a relatively small office, the hours can be rough." Though hours are long, the treatment from higher-ups is "humane." A London associate remarks, "Sometimes the hours are long — in excess of 70 chargeable hours a week. However the work is interesting and you are appreciated for the extra hours you put in."

Does Covington have a part-time program? "I've heard there is [one]," says a female associate, "but I worry about using it." Another female associate explains, "The part-time program, while good in theory, is not necessarily good in practice. Some people are able to make it work. My impression is that the success of a part-time arrangement varies from group to group. In some cases, part-time lawyers are simply getting paid less for full-time work." On the other hand, "Covington is extremely accommodating with respect to part-time work," says one associate. The firm points out that several associates who have worked true part-time schedules have been promoted to partnership.

Opening doors for diversity

Diversity for minorities and gays and lesbians seems to be a priority at the firm. According to a black associate, "This firm pulls out all the stops and really tries to encourage diversity. The firm's best selling point, I think, is that four of the five African-American partners started here as first-year associates and came up through the ranks. I looked at that when I was in law school, and it's hugely different than other firms that may have more black and Latino associates but the minority partners are lateral hires. The opportunity is truly there." A lesbian associate notes, "The firm as an institution is very favorable to gay and lesbian associates. There are also a few partners who are genuinely thoughtful and concerned about the environment for gay, lesbian and bisexual attorneys." A gay associate is delighted that the firm performs "significant pro bono work for the gay and lesbian community." One insider points out that the firm was one of the first D.C. firms to offer domestic partner benefits.

Things don't look as sunny for women at the firm. "There are not that many women partners here." One insider offers some distressing evidence: "There are few mid- to senior-level female litigation associates. We have 19 female partners in the D.C. office, with over 110 male partners." The firm notes, however, that fully one-third of the firm's mid-level and senior litigation associates are women, and one associate maintains, "The firm is very welcoming in terms of flex-time policies, maternity leave and other policies." A female associate disagrees, adding, "As a woman, I worry about what will happen when I start a family."

Tops in training

Most associates at Covington agree that the firm trains associates well. "The firm offers a wide range of training programs that are available for the taking, such as oral advocacy skills and writing workshops." A litigation associate notes that "the firm provides in-house training programs for writing, deposition skills and trial skills" and deems the programs useful. Litigators also have monthly "nuts and bolts" lessons. A corporate associate maintains, "The corporate group has recently instituted a lunchtime training program which is quite helpful and deals with a variety of issues. Personally, however, most of my training has come from the partners with whom I work, on a project-by-project basis, rather than any formal training programs." An associate in the mergers and acquisitions area agrees that on-the-job training is best. He says, "There is a general lack of a formal training program but the 'in the trenches' training is superb. As soon as you have the ability to take charge, you are given significant responsibility." A banking associate notes the availability of in-house CLE courses, adding, "And they've paid to send me to two outside conferences in my first year here. They take training very seriously." Insiders in the tax department appear less thrilled with their training opportunities. An associate there remarks, "Associates are expected to learn what they need to know to do their work on their own."

Pro bono pioneers

"The firm historically has been one of the leading firms in terms of commitment to pro bono," notes one D.C. associate. However, "that commitment has waned somewhat but is still very strong in comparison to other firms." The firm offers full-time and half-time pro bono rotations along with a wide variety of pro bono projects. Another associate mentions, "There is a very active pro bono coordinator and everybody seems to be doing some form of pro bono work or another." Though there is plenty of pro bono work to go around and it is encouraged, a litigation associate sees a new trend: "It's become clear that pro bono work comes after billable work." This sentiment was echoed by the several respondents who expressed dismay that pro bono hours are not counted towards billable hours. The firm points out that Covington's new bonus system takes into account pro bono work as well as billable hours, among other things.

9
PRESTIGE RANKING

Latham & Watkins

633 West Fifth Street
Suite 4000
Los Angeles, CA 90071-2007
Phone: (213) 485-1234
www.lw.com

LOCATIONS

Boston, MA • Costa Mesa, CA • Chicago, IL • Los Angeles, CA • Newark, NJ • New York, NY • Reston, VA • San Diego, CA • San Francisco, CA • Silicon Valley, CA • Washington, DC • Brussels • Frankfurt • Hamburg • Hong Kong • London • Milan • Moscow • Paris • Singapore • Tokyo

MAJOR DEPARTMENTS/PRACTICES

Corporate (including Health Care, Venture & Technology & Communications)
Environmental
Finance/Real Estate
Litigation
Tax

THE STATS

No. of attorneys: 1,430
No. of offices: 21
Summer associate offers: 187 out of 199 (2001)
Managing Partner: Robert Dell
Hiring Partner: Christopher Lueking

BASE SALARY

All domestic offices, 2002
1st year: $125,000
2nd year: $135,000
Summer associate: $2,400/week

NOTABLE PERKS

- Annual office retreat and firm meeting
- Brand new laptops for associates
- International Office Exchange Program for associates

THE BUZZ
WHAT ATTORNEYS AT OTHER FIRMS ARE SAYING ABOUT THIS FIRM

- "Transparent management style"
- "Associates never see the light of day"
- "Fraternity atmosphere, cultish"
- "Rising international profile"
- "Best in the West"

UPPERS

- National prestige
- Relaxed social atmosphere
- Outstanding pro bono commitment

DOWNERS

- Unassigned status for first 2½ years can mean work in ill-favored practice groups
- Bonus disgruntlement
- "Spirit-crushing" hours and emphasis on billables

EMPLOYMENT CONTACT

Ms. Debra Perry Clarkson
National Recruiting Administrator
Phone: (619) 236-1234
Fax: (619) 696-7419
debra.clarkson@lw.com

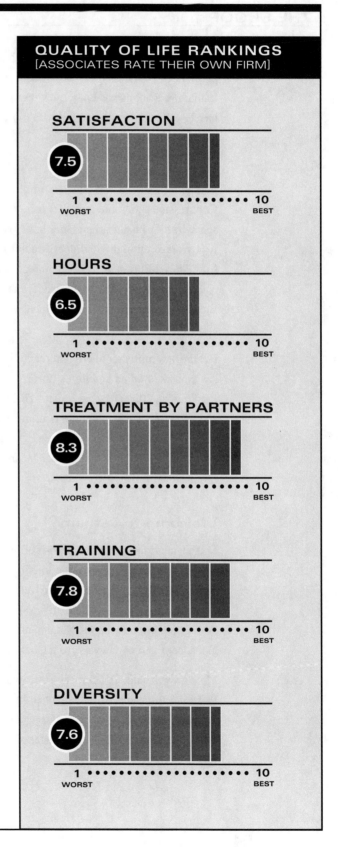

QUALITY OF LIFE RANKINGS
[ASSOCIATES RATE THEIR OWN FIRM]

SATISFACTION

7.5

1 WORST — 10 BEST

HOURS

6.5

1 WORST — 10 BEST

TREATMENT BY PARTNERS

8.3

1 WORST — 10 BEST

TRAINING

7.8

1 WORST — 10 BEST

DIVERSITY

7.6

1 WORST — 10 BEST

THE SCOOP

Latham & Watkins or Watkins & Latham? The California-born firm claims that its founding partners chose the name order by tossing a coin. With such chancy beginnings, it's apparent that Latham & Watkins has Lady Luck on its side. The prestigious firm is the largest in California and has 21 offices, globally staffed with more than 1,400 attorneys.

Big boom

Latham & Watkins was founded in 1934 by Dana Latham, a tax law expert who later served as Commissioner of Internal Revenue under President Eisenhower, and Paul Watkins, who specialized in business and labor law. By 1987 the firm had tripled in size. During the 1980s, the firm worked on high-yield debt structuring for infamous junk bond king Michael Milken and his firm, Drexel Burnham Lambert, and advised on Kohlberg Kravis Robert's (KKR) takeover of RJR Nabisco in 1988. The next decade, the firm rolled sixes, losing major clients like GM Hughes Electronics Corp. and Drexel, which went bankrupt. In response, the firm laid off 41 associates and cut partner bonuses.

But the new millennium brought renewed growth to the firm on a global scale. Since 2001, Latham has embarked on an ambitious European expansion, opening offices in Brussels, Paris, Hamburg, Frankfurt and (the latest) in Milan. These new offices, combined with Latham's successful London and Moscow offices, give the firm more than 250 lawyers in Europe and establish the firm as a major player in the European arena. In addition, Latham's Tokyo office has grown from two to nine lawyers and now offers local Japanese law capability through a joint venture with Kyobashi International Law Office.

Welcome to Latham

Latham continues to recruit high-profile lateral partners for its U.S. offices. The firm hired Bruce Babbitt, former Secretary of the Interior, and David Hayes, former Deputy Secretary of the Interior and former Latham partner who returned to the firm and is now leading the firm's global environmental practice. Latham's M&A practice got a makeover with the addition of prominent Wall Street lawyer Charles Nathan, and its antitrust practice was beefed up with a group of three global competition lawyers from Coca-Cola, led by Abbott "Tad" Lipsky.

More growth came in February 2002, when Latham snatched four partners from Wilmer, Cutler & Pickering to launch its first practice in Brussels. Despite the wilting economic climate of 2001, Latham opened offices in Hamburg and Frankfurt that year and added 39 lawyers to its New York office. The firm is also on the roster in the Enron case, representing a number of Enron creditors.

Pro bono progress

Latham & Watkins' pro bono commitment has come a long way since 1994. Back then, *The American Lawyer* ranked the firm in the bottom third of firms in terms of dedication to pro bono work, with a little over 15,000 hours, or 29.5 pro bono hours per attorney. Two years later, under managing partner Robert Dell, the firm began the mission of beefing up its pro bono hours. Efforts paid off in 2000 when the firm soared to *The American Lawyer*'s top 10 with over 63,000 hours, or 70.7 per attorney. In December 2001, it was the recipient of the Bar Association of San Francisco's Outstanding Law Firm in Public Service Award. It received similar accolades from the D.C. Bar Association. Public Counsel, the largest provider of pro bono legal services in the country, named Latham its Pro Bono Law Firm of the Year in 2000. (Latham has been awarded this title twice.) In 2002, the firm won the Public Law Center's law firm of the year accolade, and D.C. associate Andrew Morton was the D.C. Bar's Lawyer of the Year. The firm soared to over 90,000 pro bono hours in 2001.

After the devastation of the September 11 attacks, the firm raised $200,000 in one day, and in total contributed over $500,000 to the Latham & Watkins Disaster Relief Fund. Los Angeles-based partner Ursula Hyman, experienced in disaster relief legal issues, helped out by developing an outreach plan for the New York City Bar.

Runaway monk

In January 2002, the firm represented a Tibetan monk seeking asylum after escaping from the custody of Chinese police. Lortsel Gyamtso was arrested for protesting human rights violations and fled the country after authorities found his pictures of environmental devastation. Lortsel was granted asylum in January and is now living in the United States. Attorneys in the New York office worked on Gyamtso's case.

Biotech boom

In 2001 Latham was involved in several notable biotech transactions. One of the biggest deals was the multibillion-dollar merger of Amgen Inc. and Immunex Corp. in December. Amgen, the largest biotech company worldwide, bought its Seattle rival Immunex, including a 41 percent share that was owned by American Home Products Corporation (now called Wyeth), a pharmaceutical and health care product company. A 20-attorney Latham team represented Amgen in the $16 billion deal. That year, Latham lawyers also represented Aviron in its $1.5 billion acquisition by MedImmune and have represented other biotech players, such as Genentech, Aclara Biosciences, Geron Corp., Axyx Pharmaceuticals, CV Therapeutics and Signature Biosciences.

Fighting fraud

A team of nine Latham partners and 15 associates is representing HCA Inc., a health care service provider, against the federal government's allegations of Medicare and Medicaid fraud. The federal government claims HCA violated the False Claims Act and other laws by paying kickbacks to physicians for patient referrals and overbilling the government for Medicare reimbursements. HCA has already paid $745 million settling similar claims.

Beam me up

In a billion-dollar deal in November 2001, Echostar Communications Corp., a direct broadcast satellite programming services and products provider, merged with Hughes Electronics Corp., provider of DirecTV Inc., the largest direct broadcast satellite operator in the country. Representing the management and the board of directors of Hughes in the $25 billion merger was a 30-attorney team comprised of lawyers in Latham's New York, Washington, D.C., San Francisco, Los Angeles, Hong Kong, Singapore and San Diego offices. Another November deal included IBM Corp.'s acquisition of CrossWorlds Software Inc. for $129 million. Latham lawyers from San Francisco and Los Angeles represented CrossWorlds' principal shareholders. In June 2001, IBM and Informix completed their $1 billion cash deal for the database assets of Informix Corp. In keeping with its team approach to matters, the legal team for Informix included lawyers from San Francisco, Silicon Valley, Los Angeles, Orange County and San Diego.

GETTING HIRED

Summers in the sun

For the most part, Latham associates give their firm's summer associate program high marks. An associate now located in the Singapore office calls Latham summers "life in heaven." A New York associate remarks, "There are the usual bells and whistles: baseball games, cooking classes, limos and dinners." But he speculates that, due to the slumping economy, "there probably will be a mellower scene [in 2002]." Another New Yorker, not satisfied with mere frivolity, believes there is "enough serious training exercises to make [the summer program] worthwhile."

Getting over the hurdle

Because the firm has high standards, the interview process is a real challenge. "Candidates meet with many lawyers before being offered a spot," says a New York associate. "I came through three rounds of interviews." A San Francisco associate notes, "I am impressed with the amount of time, money and energy Latham invests in recruiting — [it is] definitely looking for more than just good grades and a good school." In New York, the firm is said to be seeking "intelligent and articulate people who fit into the culture — friendly, capable and hardworking, without the aggressiveness and competitiveness better suited for other firms."

A Chicago lateral explains, "The more senior you are, the more people you have to meet to ensure you are a good fit for the firm. Maintaining the firm's culture is a priority. Many partner and associate lateral candidates may make it through a first or second round of interviews, yet offers are not automatic after getting an initial or second interview."

OUR SURVEY SAYS

Here's the brief, dude!

Looking for proof that Latham has a laid-back corporate culture? One happy Latham associate tells Vault that he commonly refers to some Latham partners as "dude." While this extraordinary lack of formality may be an anomaly, many Lathamites proclaim that the vibe at Latham is relaxed. A San Francisco associate describes the culture as "suburban and mainstream." In D.C., things are no different. "Partners on the whole are very approachable." A lateral cheerfully remarks, "Partners here are prone to giving compliments and expressing appreciation for a job well done. The firm emphasizes the importance of treating others well, and the partners seem to lead by example. I find the culture to be friendly, respectful and not overly formal — but definitely hard-working and serious about quality." Praise for partners permeates the Midwest as well. A Chicago associate remarks, "The partners consistently provide encouragement and recommendations on how to better complete the tasks before us. They manage client expectations quite well so that a life outside work is possible. If you'd like more responsibility they're more than happy to give you more, and if you're overwhelmed they can quickly reallocate parts of [the] workload." An associate in the firm's Singapore office sums it up: "The most open-door, partner-accessible, positive-cultured big firm on the block — any block."

Not only is the firm a great place to work, it's also a great place to socialize. "Partners, associates and staff both work and socialize together," says a Los Angeles associate. In New York, "junior lawyers tend to socialize together; the more senior associates tend to place a premium on family time." In D.C., "the single attorneys are very social and do many things together." In Singapore, "associates and partners really are friends and socialize after hours together." Hey, it could happen, dude.

Where's the love?

According to one associate in D.C., "Associates felt betrayed (or misled) about their bonuses for 2001, which were around half of the previous year's, when the firm's profits increased by more than 15 percent." A San Francisco associate shares the pain. "Salaries are excellent, though the bonus pool seems to suffer while partner take-home pay remains at record levels."

A patient Chicago associate explains the bonus situation: "We are paid the standard base salary plus a bonus that for the past two years has been at about the 75th percentile of top-tier firms. The bonus is primarily based on hours worked and merit. Prior to 1999, the bonus policy was tied to firm profitability — it no longer is — and so those associates who put in extra hours are disincentivized from doing so under the current system. Bonuses used to be tied much more closely to individual profitability, but they now appear to be capped for no explanation other than 'sticker shock.'"

Those Latham hours

It's no secret that associates at Latham put in a fair amount of hours. But, as one litigation associate says, "You work long hours, but you're rewarded for them." One San Diego associate sees the silver lining, remarking, "Coming in with the expectation that Latham is a sweat shop, I have been pleasantly surprised… [T]here really isn't pressure to work above the minimum. Combine that with the base salary and opportunity to live in San Diego and you have a pretty nice employment situation." A corporate associate reminds others of the bottom line: "Sure you work hard, but who doesn't? You really drive your own ship in determining how hard you want to work here, with no doubts that the harder and better the work, the better the chances at making partner." A securities associate gives some insight into hours. "The firm has a heavy emphasis on billable hours. Every month there are reports generated and distributed to show everyone's 'pace.' You are expected to work long hours, and other priorities are not really manageable with such a heavy emphasis on billable hours."

Diversity disagreement

While Latham may not be perfect when it comes to recruiting and promoting minorities, most agree that the firm scores points for effort. As one minority associate puts it, "I get a very strong sense that we are judged on merit alone." An Hispanic associate adds, "The firm is making an effort to recruit the most talented minority students throughout the United States." An Asian associate agrees: "The office does make an effort to hire minorities and support events for people of color, and tries very hard to provide mentoring to the minorities as well." Gays and lesbians seem to be faring even better. One associate mentions there are "lots of gay attorneys who seem to fit seamlessly into the firm culture." A gay associate agrees: "No one goes around inquiring into people's personal lives. People are free to be who they are and are mainly judged by their work product." Another gay associate applauds the firm's efforts: "There are several openly gay male partners and associates. It is a very welcoming place for gays. During the summer recruiting process, the gay partners and associates make a special effort to reach out to gays and lesbians." Another lawyer maintains, "I'm openly gay and feel totally comfortable here. My boyfriend comes frequently to firm events, both informal and formal, and is always totally welcome. There aren't many [other] gay (and no lesbian) attorneys in the office, but the atmosphere is still completely welcoming. The domestic partner benefits are good as well."

Women are divided on how the firm meets their needs. One female associate says, "We do a great job recruiting women and have created a part-time program that offers some flexibility to young mothers. I have found mentoring to be more than adequate. However, this is due to the firm's culture and not due to my office's formal mentoring program." While another female lawyer agrees that the firm is doing a good job when it comes to hiring women attorneys, she points out that "women don't seem to succeed past the mid-level associate stage, especially in corporate and health care groups." The firm points out, however, that the managing partners in the Los Angeles, Moscow and Orange County offices are women, as is the department chair of the firm's global finance and real estate department. Moreover, two local corporate department chairs are women, as is one local tax department chair and 12 practice group chairs/co-chairs firm-wide. "While the entire legal field can improve in this department," remarks a Latham woman, "Latham does its best to support women at the firm and certainly doesn't treat us any differently. Latham's female partners are an inspiration to young associates."

Three cheers for pro bono

Latham's pro bono achievements have received accolades. "The firm's pro bono program is outstanding," says one satisfied source. A D.C. associate states, "They encourage you to do the work that you want to do and it counts towards billable hours." The Los Angeles office seems to house pro bono go-getters. "Every hour of pro bono work counts as a billable hour, with no limit. I do a lot of work pro bono, and I enjoy it! The firm supports me every step of the way." A Chicago associate notes, "We have an active pro bono practice and a committee of attorneys coordinating the pro bono effort." At Latham, pro bono cases have equal billing with client cases. In New York, an associate adds, "The firm treats every pro bono hour the same as any client-billable hour, and a pro bono success is as valued as a client success."

Weil, Gotshal & Manges LLP

767 Fifth Avenue
New York, NY 10153
Phone: (212) 310-8000
www.weil.com

LOCATIONS

New York, NY (HQ)

Dallas, TX • Houston, TX • Miami, FL • Silicon Valley,
CA • Washington, DC • Brussels • Budapest • Frankfurt •
London • Prague • Singapore • Warsaw

MAJOR DEPARTMENTS/PRACTICES

Advertising • Antitrust/Competition Law • Business
Finance & Restructuring • Business & Securities
Litigation • Capital Markets • Consumer Finance •
Corporate • Criminal/White Collar • First Amendment •
Institutional Finance • Intellectual Property • Labor &
Employment • Litigation & Arbitration • Media &
Technology • Mergers & Acquisitions • Private Equity •
Product Liability • Real Estate • Sports • Structured
Finance & Derivatives • Tax • Trade Practices &
Regulatory Law

THE STATS

No. of attorneys: 950+
No. of offices: 13
Summer associate offers: 71 out of 71 (2001)
Executive Partner: Stephen J. Dannhauser
Hiring Chairs: Debra J. Pearlstein, Jeffrey E. Tabak and
Jeffrey L. Tanenbaum

BASE SALARY

New York and Silicon Valley, 2002
1st year: $125,000
2nd year: $135,000
3rd year: $150,000
4th year: $165,000
5th year: $190,000
6th year: $205,000
7th year: $215,000
Summer associate: $2,400/week

Dallas, 2002
1st year: $125,000
2nd year: $135,000
3rd year: $150,000
4th year: $165,000
5th year: $190,000
6th year: $205,000
7th year: $215,000
Summer associate: $1,750/week

Washington, DC, 2002
1st year: $115,000
2nd year: $130,000
3rd year: $145,00
4th year: $155,000
5th year: $165,000
6th year: $185,000
7th year: $200,000
Summer associate: $2,212/week

Houston, 2002
1st year: $115,000
2nd year: $130,000
3rd year: $140,000
4th year: $150,000
5th year: $165,000
6th year: $180,000
7th year: $190,000
Summer associate: $1,750/week

THE BUZZ
WHAT ATTORNEYS AT OTHER FIRMS ARE SAYING ABOUT THIS FIRM

- "Best in bankruptcy"
- "Plush and progressive"
- "Tough as nails"
- "Hourly expectations unreasonable"
- "The place to be in a down economy"

NOTABLE PERKS

- Retention bonuses for long-term associates
- One month paid paternity leave
- $2,000 technology stipend for first- and second-year associates
- Generous ticket giveaways

UPPERS

- "High-quality deals in both good times and bad"
- Excellent training
- Gorgeous views of Central Park (NY)

DOWNERS

- "Hours can be daunting"
- Insufficient office space
- "Pressure of working with overachievers"

EMPLOYMENT CONTACT

Ms. Donna J. Lang
Manager of Legal Recruiting
Fax: (212) 735-4502
donna.lang@weil.com

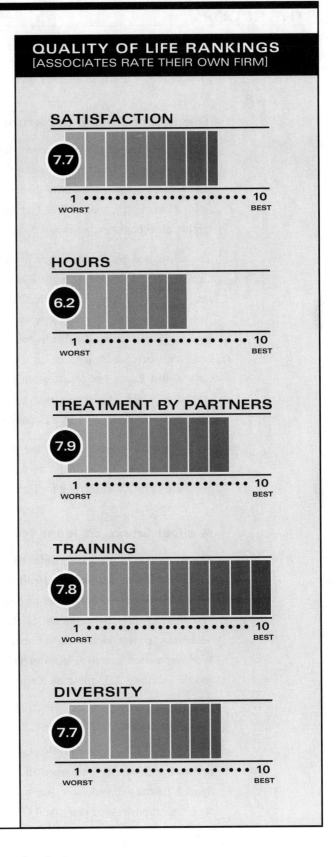

QUALITY OF LIFE RANKINGS
[ASSOCIATES RATE THEIR OWN FIRM]

SATISFACTION
7.7
1 WORST ... 10 BEST

HOURS
6.2
1 WORST ... 10 BEST

TREATMENT BY PARTNERS
7.9
1 WORST ... 10 BEST

TRAINING
7.8
1 WORST ... 10 BEST

DIVERSITY
7.7
1 WORST ... 10 BEST

THE SCOOP

Formed in 1931 by a group of lawyers who faced discrimination at other firms, Weil, Gotshal & Manges is now a very large, very diverse and very prestigious New York-based firm.

The mother of all bankruptcy cases

Weil Gotshal is probably best known for its bankruptcy practice, which is considered one of the best in the world. The firm's list of bankruptcy clients spans the spectrum of business and industry, and includes both companies in distress and their creditors. Despite its illustrious history in the field of bankruptcy, none of Weil Gotshal's past cases compares to its current darling — Enron, the mother of all bankruptcy cases.

The convoluted history of Enron's financial failure is too well-documented to reiterate here. Weil Gotshal entered the picture when it was hired by the embattled energy trader in October 2001 to assist Vinson & Elkins, Enron's then regular counsel, in representing Enron in its proposed merger with Dynegy, another large energy trader. At the time, Weil Gotshal was brought on for its know-how in M&A; Enron had hardly worked with the firm before. The situation soon changed, however, when the Dynegy/Enron merger fell through in November 2001. It was clear to Weil Gotshal that Enron had to act quickly to avoid the seizure of its assets by creditors. Working around the clock, Weil completed a petition for Chapter 11 and filed it electronically with the bankruptcy court at 5 a.m. on a Sunday morning.

As of April 2002, Weil Gotshal had at least 30 attorneys dedicated to helping Enron through its bankruptcy woes. The attorneys have pulled frequent all-nighters for the case, including a 24-hour-plus auction for those bidding for Enron's assets.

A silver lining, at least for Weil

The misfortune of other companies has brought business and recognition to Weil. In November 2001, Weil Gotshal assisted Sun Healthcare Group in drafting a reorganization plan, and in October 2001, the firm served as counsel to movie theater chain Regal Cinemas in its bankruptcy filing. The firm continues to represent Sunbeam in its ongoing efforts to restructure. Other recent bankruptcy clients include Bethlehem Steel Corporation, Safety-Kleen, PG&E and Armstrong World Industries, as well as telecom provider Global Crossing in its January 2002 Chapter 11 filing and the February 2002 filing by Kasper A.S.L., owner of the Anne Klein clothing label.

For the love of art

Weil, Gotshal & Manges is firmly planted in the glamorous world of arts, media and entertainment. In October 2001, Weil represented television network NBC in its $1.98 billion purchase of Spanish-language broadcaster Telemundo Communications Group. That same month, in another communications-related deal, Weil Gotshal represented DirecTV owner Hughes Electronics in its pending $26 billion acquisition by EchoStar Communications. The firm is also involved on a regular basis with other major media and entertainment companies, such as Disney/ABC, Viacom/CBS and AOL Time Warner.

At Weil Gotshal, art is serious business. Its most newsworthy art-related case has to be its representation of New York auction house Sotheby's, which pleaded guilty to charges of conspiring with rival auction house Christie's to fix art prices. Weil, Gotshal & Manges has also represented several prestigious museums, including the Guggenheim, the Museum of Modern Art and the Museum of Fine Arts, as well as the American Association of Museums, the Association of Art Museum Directors and various art dealers and galleries. The firm provides pro bono services on an ongoing basis to Volunteer Lawyers for the Arts, an organization that represents the New York City arts community on a pro bono basis.

Are those Bugle Boy Jeans you're representing?

Weil Gotshal was ranked third in the M&A league tables for a number of announced deals in 2001 and consistently ranks among the world's top M&A firms. In July 2001, Weil Gotshal represented GE Capital in its $5.3 billion acquisition of Heller Financial. That same month, the firm also represented the British Internet company Scoot.com in its sale to the French-owned entertainment and telecom firm Vivendi. Bugle Boy Jeans got a fresh start in August 2001 thanks to the firm, which represented Schottenstein Stores Corp. in its $68.8 million acquisition of the bankrupt clothing retailer. Gasoline giant Texaco sought the firm's help in its October 2001 swap of oil assets with Shell. American Airlines was represented by Weil in its $3 billion purchase of TWA. Other regular M&A clients include Leucadia, Reuters, Estee Lauder, L'Oreal, Pirelli, Texas Instruments and Hicks Muse. The firm also counts financial giants Lehman Brothers, Merrill Lynch, Citigroup, Solomon Smith Barney, DLJ Merchant Bank and Credit Suisse First Boston among its regular clients.

Frequent passport use

Business is also booming internationally. The firm is continuing to expand in its established overseas offices. Fifteen new attorneys joined the firm's Frankfurt office at the beginning of 2002, doubling the number of lawyers in the German outpost. In addition, the firm opened an office in Singapore in early 2002.

Good sports

Weil Gotshal is a player in one of the biggest football dramas of the past year. As counsel to the NFL Players Association, the firm is working on behalf of Terry Glenn, a receiver for the New England Patriots who was suspended on drug-related charges. The firm is arguing that the basis for Glenn's suspension is nonexistent under the National Football League's collective bargaining agreement with the players. The firm is no stranger to controversial client-athletes. It represented the NBA Players Association on behalf of Latrell Sprewell when Sprewell was suspended for assaulting the coach of his team, the Golden State Warriors. Other sports clients include Giants second baseman Jeff Kent, Baseball Hall of Famer Dave Winfield and the players' associations of the NFL, the National Basketball Association and Major League Soccer.

Trustworthy antitrust

IP and antitrust fans will be happy to learn that Weil Gotshal prides itself on its trade regulation, intellectual property and patent litigation practices. Clients include Matsushita, Intel, Cisco, Micron Technology, National Semiconductor, Texas Instruments and Samsung. The firm counsels and litigates in the antitrust area for clients like American Airlines, retailing behemoth Wal-Mart and Matsushita Electric.

Crisis managers

Although its offices overlooking Central Park are miles away from the site of the World Trade Center disaster, Weil, Gotshal & Manges dug deep to lend a hand in the wake of the tragedy of September 11. For many years, executive partner Stephen Dannhauser has been the president of a fund that serves the widows and children of New York police officers and firefighters. Since the attacks, the fund has raised over $100 million. Attorneys and staff at the firm donated approximately $1.3 million for relief efforts and provided legal assistance to families by drawing up death certificates and other documents. Secretaries have traveled downtown to pitch in at the fire department headquarters, and the firm opened its offices to over 200 personnel from clients who were displaced because of the destruction.

GETTING HIRED

More than book smart

Weil Gotshal, sniffs one associate, "will not take just anybody." Like other large New York firms, Weil "looks for the best law students." More specifically, according to one associate, that means "either attendance at a highly ranked school in the top 25 percent of your class or top 10 percent at a lesser school." And, as always, "law review helps." The firm is willing to look "beyond the typical first-tier law schools," and a wide variety of schools are represented among survey respondents. One associate says that's what she likes about Weil: "They're not so wrapped up in pedigree. They give a lot of local students a second look, when other top firms won't give them the time of day. I think we get a lot of smart, down-to-earth people that way."

A senior associate suggests that "the firm seems to recruit actively for outgoing, unique personalities," adding "Interviewers want to hear about unusual special interests and accomplishments." Another attorney agrees that "personality and social abilities" matter. "They are looking for a candidate that is more than just book smart and can handle the dynamic atmosphere." Weil's summer program gets rave reviews: "Amazing," "outstanding," "excellent." The firm offers a "good balance of work and play," with "a perfect combination of top-notch, fulfilling assignments and socializing."

OUR SURVEY SAYS

A healthy balance

Most Weil insiders are happy with the "excellent" quality of their work — and they like their colleagues, too. "This is a great firm," gushes one associate. "If you want a big firm in New York City with intelligent and open-minded people, for the most part, this is a good place for you." Another attorney agrees that "as far as large New York law firms are concerned, I think that Weil is a great place to work." Most of the "bad things about Weil are things that are bad about big New York law firms in general." The good points include "high-quality deals both in good times and in bad times (due to our great, counter-cyclical bankruptcy practice), superb training and a general tolerance for individual personalities."

Apart from a few gloomy lawyers, most associates say the firm's culture provides "a healthy balance. People are demanding and hardworking, yet personable and earnest." "Everyone gets along pretty well," shrugs a banking associate. Though the atmosphere is termed "dynamic" and "intense," the "general culture is informal" and "the open door policy is a real one, with most senior attorneys and partners participating." Associates emphasize that the firm is "encouraging of diversity and self-expression" and people are "very respectful" of associates' private lives. A third-year associate happily concludes, "I learn something new every day and really enjoy coming to work."

An unparalleled location

New Yorkers rave about Weil's "unparalleled" location in the GM building with "gorgeous" views overlooking Central Park. The only issue that really has associates grumbling (aside from the occasional attorney who mutters about "scrappy-looking furniture") is overcrowding. The space crunch varies widely by department; some first-year attorneys have their own offices, others share into their fourth year. Naturally this discrepancy colors associate responses. "You should see my view of Central Park!" boasts one happy litigator. Meanwhile, a colleague carps, "The offices are tiny and lots of associates get stuck sharing for years. The partners may like their Central Park views, but the rest of us could use a little more room to work in." The firm says it recently acquired the entire 22nd floor of the GM building and is negotiating for additional space.

In addition to the "spectacular" views, sources say offices are "clean, comfortable and very functional." One associate adds, "You have to take into account the art with which Weil covers all walls — it's really great. They also take pains to rotate the pieces every year or so, and it's a nice aspect of the space." Another lawyer proudly observes, "My office is more like home than home."

Turning down the volume

Most associates say that partners treat them "with a tremendous amount of respect, both personally and professionally." "Every firm has its anomaly, but nearly all Weil partners treat you like equals," claims a second-year lawyer. Sources are grateful that the firm has "made a concerted effort to weed out the screamers and encourage respectful treatment of associates." "Several senior partners who treated associates with little respect have departed in recent years, greatly alleviating problems that did exist here," notes a senior associate. "Younger partners tend to be homegrown and very respectful of the associate population." Some lawyers note that there remain "a few exceptions, though even the exceptions are not egregious." One sympathetic associate notes that any misbehavior "is generally unfortunate as even these partners (at least in most cases) are genuinely good people and they lose touch with their good side due to the pressures of the job."

Excellent training

Insiders believe "the firm does a very good job of training in an informal setting." Although this informal training is partner-dependent, associates report that "more partners than not are very good, and very patient, with associates who are interested in learning." An attorney claims "the daily on-the-job training is tremendous." "We work on the biggest cases with the best clients," says one lawyer. "I am getting an unbelievable diversity of work," declares another.

Weil's formal training programs also draw good reviews. "Excellent CLE training and programs," says one associate. "Although the formal training can get really boring," according to a litigator, "I have found it to be extremely helpful." A colleague is less appreciative. "The amount of mandatory training goes up every year, but it's all just a weak effort to make up for the fact that junior associates just do grunt work."

Overworked and overpaid

Weil Gotshal associates are "overworked and overpaid." "The hours are long, but I suppose that is to be expected," sighs a bankruptcy attorney. Other sources agree. "I do still feel like a slave, but it would be like that at any firm on this level." Just because long hours are expected doesn't make them easy to endure. "The hours here are no different than at any other large law firm, but brutal at times nonetheless." Many "wish the hours were more predictable" and allowed "more time to spend with friends and family." Yet most lawyers acknowledge that they work in a rarified world. A sixth-year associate notes, "I spend too many hours in the office for a normal person. For a normal associate, my hours are tolerable almost all the time and reasonable a lot of the time." And one lawyer reminds colleagues, "We don't make all this money for nothing." According to the firm, average billable hours for associates in 2001 were 1,861.

And just how much is all this money? Associates tell us that "Weil keeps up with the big guys." The firm may never lead the market, but it's "pretty good about following along." In addition to "the base/winter bonus compensation package offered by most firms," Weil "pays a pretty substantial retention bonus during the key mid-level and senior associate years" and "provides first- and second-year associates with a $2,000 technology stipend." Although most associates are quite pleased with their compensation, one lawyer believes that "the bonuses this year could have been better, considering that the firm did as well [as] if not better than the year before." Another associate surprisingly — and refreshingly — would like to redistribute some of that "obscene" amount of money: "I sometimes wish they would pay me less and support staff, particularly secretarial, more."

Supportive of pro bono

Many associates report that Weil Gotshal "has a very strong commitment to pro bono work." A few grumble that it is just "lip service," and one disappointed lawyer warns, "Do not come here if your interest in pro bono is an interest in doing something good. Only pro bono which advances the firm image is acceptable." However more associates seem to agree that "there will always be some partners who think it is a drain on the firm, but overall, the firm is really supportive of the lawyers' pro bono efforts."

Half of our survey respondents were unable to tell us whether pro bono matters count toward billable hours. According to one source, "it's still a gray area among associates whether billables count for pro bono or not. I believe they must, since so many respected associates take on big pro bono cases." The firm states that pro bono hours are considered equal to hours spent on billable matters.

A third-year litigator asserts that the firm "encourages its attorneys to work a minimum of 50 hours a year towards pro bono matters, and significantly, counts the pro bono hours as billable hours." Weil also "has an externship program where junior associates can work at a pro bono site for up to three months at Weil Gotshal salary."

Diversity hiring better than retention

What strikes many associates is that despite active recruitment of women and minorities, "few stick around long enough to be promoted." A litigator claims that "women don't make it past the third year in my department." (The firm says its data does not support this statement.) Female respondents are not "aware of any committees or mentoring programs for women" and note that "there are only a handful of women partners at Weil." The firm does have a part-time policy, but some attorneys complain that it "does not allow for a work schedule in which women can comfortably have a family and fulfill the business requirements of the firm." Associates believe "the firm is sensitive to the issue but hasn't really taken major steps to correct it." The firm indicates that it has recently formed several committees to address associate issues, including the recruitment and retention of women.

Respondents report similar problems with respect to minority attorneys. "Although I believe [the firm] makes a legitimate and sincere effort to hire and retain minorities, it just doesn't seem to be working." "There are still very, very few minority partners," notes an associate. But Weil has recently hired a professional diversity manager "specifically to address minority hiring and retention." One minority attorney believes the firm is "very responsive to diversity issues" and praises the firm for its "Martin Luther King Jr. Day celebration which was simulcast to all domestic offices. This was a very positive experience for all employees but made minority employees feel especially at home." According to associates, Weil was one of the first firms to offer domestic partner benefits, and sources contend that Weil is welcoming to gays and lesbians.

"I spend too many hours in the office for a normal person. For a normal associate, my hours are tolerable almost all the time and reasonable a lot of the time."

— Weil Gotshal associate

Williams & Connolly LLP

The Edward Bennett Williams Building
725 12th Street, NW
Washington, DC 20005
Phone: (202) 434-5000

LOCATIONS

Washington, DC (HQ)

MAJOR DEPARTMENTS/PRACTICES

Corporate
Litigation
Tax

THE STATS

No. of attorneys: 175
No. of offices: 1
Summer associate offers: Because most summers have judicial clerkships, formal offers are not extended until they have begun their clerkship and received authorization from their judges to apply.
Hiring Partners: F. Lane Heard III and Heidi Hubbard

BASE SALARY

Washington, DC, 2002
1st year: $140,000
2nd year: $150,000
3rd year: $170,000
4th year: $180,000
5th year: $190,000
6th year: $200,000
7th year: $210,000
8th year: $220,000
Summer associate: $2,400/week

NOTABLE PERKS

- "The best seats in Camden Yards" (home to the Orioles)
- Free, tasty lunch
- Rooftop garden

THE BUZZ
WHAT ATTORNEYS AT OTHER FIRMS ARE SAYING ABOUT THIS FIRM

- "Only for the thick-skinned"
- "Some of the best litigators in the U.S."
- "The lawyers I'd want to represent me"
- "Not so good for women"
- "No web site"

UPPERS

- Extremely approachable partners
- Minimal bureaucracy
- Early court and trial opportunities

DOWNERS

- No formal training
- Minimal support staff after 5 p.m.
- No reimbursement for late-night meals

EMPLOYMENT CONTACT

Ms. Donna M. Downing
Recruiting Coordinator
Phone: (202) 434-5605
ddowning@wc.com

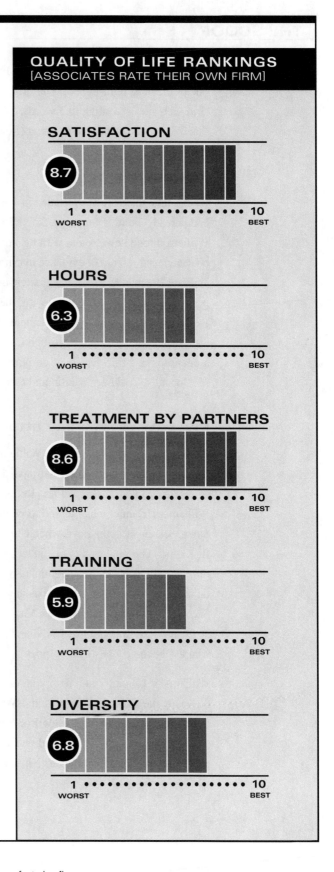

QUALITY OF LIFE RANKINGS
[ASSOCIATES RATE THEIR OWN FIRM]

SATISFACTION
8.7
1 WORST — 10 BEST

HOURS
6.3
1 WORST — 10 BEST

TREATMENT BY PARTNERS
8.6
1 WORST — 10 BEST

TRAINING
5.9
1 WORST — 10 BEST

DIVERSITY
6.8
1 WORST — 10 BEST

THE SCOOP

Washington, D.C.'s Williams & Connolly is one of the most prestigious firms in the country — and one of the most tight-lipped. The firm rarely speaks about its cases. While the late 1990s saw law firm web sites sprouting like weeds, W&C chose to maintain a low profile. It was only in 2002 that W&C announced that it would (finally!) launch its own web site.

Power brokers

By the time the firm was founded in 1967, founders Edward Bennett Williams and Paul Connolly had already built reputations defending clients such as alleged mob associate Jimmy Hoffa. Williams broke new ground with his successful argument before the Supreme Court for limitation on search and seizure of evidence in criminal cases. He was once lauded by Supreme Court Justice William Brennan as one of the greatest litigators that ever appeared before the Court and associated personally and professionally with the likes of Ben Bradlee and Katherine Graham of *The Washington Post*. As the firm's sphere of influence throughout Washington grew, it attracted other top-notch attorneys, such as Joseph Califano, who brought the Democratic National Committee as a client to the firm. Its list of corporate clients is nothing to sneeze at, either. Among them are McDonald's, Lockheed Martin and General Electric.

Celebrity clients, shy attorneys

Despite its camera-shy image, Williams & Connolly's client list often places the firm at the forefront of cases that receive national, and even international, attention. The firm's star clients are New York State Senator Hillary Rodham Clinton and former President Bill Clinton, for whom Williams & Connolly has served as counsel since 1992. In August 2001, the firm made one of its rare appearances in the news when Clinton signed a contract for his memoirs with publisher Alfred A. Knopf. The deal, said to be the largest book deal ever, reportedly earned Clinton more than $12 million. The contract was negotiated by W&C attorney Robert B. Barnett, whose practice focuses on the literary works of Beltway insiders and top news personalities. Other Barnett clients include Second Lady Lynn Cheney, West Virginia Senator Robert Byrd, anchors Andrea Mitchell of ABC and Christine Amanpour of CNN, and Mattie Stepanek, an 11-year-old with muscular dystrophy, who has become a best-selling poet.

Williams & Connolly is a firm with deep roots in the sports world. Founder Williams was once owner of the Baltimore Orioles and Washington Redskins, and former partner, Larry Lucchino, became part owner of the Boston Red Sox in 2001. The firm has a thriving sports law practice that caters to professional athletes and outstanding college athletes who are poised to turn pro. Current clients include basketball players Nikki McCray, Tim Duncan, Christian Laettner and Shane Battier.

Defenders and defendants

Sometimes law firms find themselves the subject of a legal investigation. When they do, they often turn to W&C. So it's no surprise that Houston-based Vinson & Elkins, which has received more than its share of media attention for its involvement in the Enron bankruptcy scandal, tapped Williams & Connolly to defend it. Enron officials are pointing fingers at V&E, saying the firm provided bad legal advice to the company regarding its infamous partnerships. In another twist on the Enron mess, Williams & Connolly is also representing Milberg Weiss Bershad Hynes & Lerach. Milberg, the country's leading firm specializing in shareholder lawsuits, is seeking to be named the lead counsel in shareholder litigation against Enron. Milberg, however, has turned to W&C to defend it in a federal grand jury investigation of its client recruitment practices.

Kings of all media

Even though its Beltway digs are far removed from the glamour of New York or Hollywood, Williams has its share of big-name media and entertainment clients. The firm has been advising the Warner Music Group in the music industry's suit against Napster. In similar cases, the firm is also representing a group of eight movie studios and 20 record labels suing three file-sharing services for copyright infringement and the Motion Picture Association of America against Aimster, a fifth file-sharing company. Other clients of the firm's First Amendment/media practice include *The Washington Post*, *Newsweek*, ABC, NBC, CBS, Paramount and CNN.

Who ya gon' call?

When the writing on the wall indicated that a settlement would soon be reached between Microsoft and the federal government in its long-running antitrust suit against the software giant, a group of state attorneys general who were dissatisfied with the agreement turned to Williams & Connolly. Partner Brendan Sullivan (who many remember as the lawyer who defended Oliver North) signed on in October 2001 as the lead attorney of a team that includes Steven Kuney, the head of the firm's antitrust practice. When the chairman of travel and financial services company Cendant was indicted on charges of fraud and conspiracy in February 2001 in connection with huge company losses, he too sought out Williams & Connolly to defend him.

GETTING HIRED

Hard to get

"Williams & Connolly was regarded at my school as probably the most difficult firm from which to secure an offer," says one Harvard grad. "I believe the firm is looking for people who really want to do litigation and who will fit in well with the aggressive, can-do culture here." Another associate recommends that W&C hopefuls get their academic profiles into shape. "Grades and

journal experience are significant and are scrutinized," he cautions. Another W&C lawyer stresses the importance of the interview: "The interview process is fairly formal. You meet with four or so attorneys, and then are taken to lunch in the firm's dining room by two other associates." He adds, "Arrogant candidates or people who make clear that they're only going to stay until they land that perfect government job are not hired."

Summer business

The "no-frills" summer associate program at Williams & Connolly is actually appreciated by many associates. One comments, "This firm feels, correctly, that it can sell itself on the basis of the quality of its work and the quality of its people, rather than engaging in the bait-and-switch that is so common at top firms." Another associate sums it up: "Summer associates are treated like full-time hires. They're assigned to one or two matters, sometimes working only with a partner or two, and given meaningful projects that would otherwise have been completed by a full-time associate. W&C doesn't have a 'wining-and-dining' summer program, but there's plenty of informal socializing, such as softball and happy hours, with W&C attorneys. When I finished my summer at W&C, I knew what it would be like to work here full time."

OUR SURVEY SAYS

Williams wins

W&C is "just a bunch of attorneys focused on a single goal — winning," boasts one associate. "That attitude forges an esprit-de-corps among attorneys here that has spawned life-long friendships, and even a few marriages!" According to our sources, "associates often socialize together after work," and "the relations between partners and associates are very collegial." Disagreeing with his colleagues, a W&C-er describes the firm as "not extremely social outside the office." Most don't care one way or the other. Socializing isn't what brings them to Williams. "The work here is first-rate and the experience associates get is excellent," brags one lawyer. Another remarks, "Williams & Connolly entrusts even junior associates with great levels of responsibility on all cases; that most of the cases Williams has are exciting, high-profile litigations makes the work all that more fulfilling. It's nice to be treated as an equal and to have your opinion and work valued." Williams has it all: "high-profile cases, cutting-edge legal issues and innovative approaches to cases." Why wouldn't associates be happy?

Long, lovely hours

Associates at Williams & Connolly are blasé about the hours they work. One associate says, "The firm gets some extraordinary cases and working on those cases provides an amazing experience but usually requires a great deal of hours." Another associate adds, "This is not a firm that is driven by billable hours. However, the work is interesting and challenging, which often leads associates to work harder than they would otherwise." Yet another associate confirms the firm-wide feeling: "There's no fluff time here. Nobody's padding their hours to earn a bonus. You do your work and you go home. Unfortunately, there's a lot of work. The consolation is that the work tends to be very, very interesting." Some perks Williams' associates enjoy: "There's no minimum billable target, hours-based bonus or face-time at W&C." A litigator explains, "In litigation, hours are totally determined by the case schedule. Some weeks are 40-hour (or less) weeks. On the other hand, on the eve of trial, you might as well be living at the office. There is no face time at the firm. So long as the work gets done, no one cares if you are at the office."

No bonus, no problem

Frankly, Scarlett, the associates at Williams & Connolly don't give a damn. As one contented Williamsite insists, "The firm does not award year-end or hours-based bonuses, but frankly that's fine with me. Williams & Connolly pays top dollar for its associates." Another associate thinks his salary is "obscene for someone who just graduated from bar review." Though Williams & Connolly associates are not rewarded with year-end bonuses, they do earn a high salary and, as one associate puts it, "do not get laid off or pushed out during rough times." 'Nuff said.

Does diversity exist?

According to many associates at Williams & Connolly, diversity "is an area where the firm falls regrettably flat." A female associate notes, "The firm is great about hiring women, and women seem to get great experience here, but women are not yet a significant portion of the partnership." Another female adds, "It will take a few more years to see how retention pans out." One female associate offers a reason why the firm does not have any formal mentoring program for women: "I think principally because the firm is small enough and ad hoc enough that you could always just bring problems up informally with a partner you feel comfortable with." Associates think the firm could broaden its diversity efforts. One associate notes, "The firm has recruited a lot of African-Americans in recent years but has apparently overlooked the fact that there are other minorities as well." While W&C management would like to make the firm even more diversified, it points out that minorities comprise 12 percent of the firm as a whole and 19 percent of associates. Women, 14 of whom are partners, make up 17 percent of the firm. The firm says it does not inquire about sexual preference, which it considers a private matter.

On your own

When it comes to pro bono, most associates are on their own. As one associate puts it, "As a firm, there is very little commitment to pro bono. Associates are free to do pro bono work on top of their regular work if they so choose." Another associate thinks, "There has been improvement since my summer here, but they still need more." In an effort to improve, an associate mentions one of the firm's new pro bono efforts: "The firm has made a substantial commitment to providing criminal defense services to low-income individuals in partnership with the Montgomery County Public

Defender's Office. Many of the attorneys at the firm attended two full days of training for the program and are currently handling cases. The firm handles a variety of other pro bono matters as well." One good thing: "There is no limit as to the type or amount of pro bono work that attorneys can take on. The firm encourages it."

Training? Heck, no!

"If you learned how to swim by being thrown into the deep end of the pool, this is the place for you," says one associate. At Williams & Connolly, there is no formal training program. "Training tends to be through experience rather than seminars," notes another associate. "We have periodic seminars on different lawyering skills, but they are strictly optional." The firm does offer CLE courses on a variety of legal topics. But as far as formal training goes, it's strictly on-the-job. "You're simply assigned to take the deposition or argue the motion," says one eager associate. "A partner might accompany you to your first court appearance, but otherwise you get your training by doing the work." One associate does add, "There have been notable efforts spearheaded by senior associates to host more formal lunch session trainings this year."

One of the herd

When it comes to partner-associate relations, there's no better place to work than Williams & Connolly. "Partners at Williams & Connolly treat associates like junior colleagues rather than employees and actively solicit associates' opinions on everything from client relations to firm life," notes one satisfied associate. Another associate adds, "The relationships are genuine — no artificial hierarchy." While the firm employs the occasional bad apple, most associates have had "very positive" experiences with partners.

"They expect a lot from associates, but no more than they are willing to put in themselves. Generally, there is mutual respect between partners and associates," explains an associate. That respect goes a long way: "The most senior partners tend to solicit, and value, the opinions of junior associates."

Once you go Williams, you never go back

Why work anywhere else? "If [associates] do leave, it's to work in an administration or U.S. Attorney's Office," says one happy camper. Another notes, "A few people leave, but more because of family issues or a desire to pursue teaching or public service. Almost nobody leaves because they hate the job here." One associate sums it up: "People generally don't lateral to other firms in D.C. They leave to move back home, to teach, to go into government, change careers, and so on." Another lawyer adds, "I haven't seen anyone leave to switch firms, unless it's in a different geographic location."

Why do so many associates choose to stay? One associate explains, "W&C has an exceptional record of retaining associates, probably because we handle interesting cases, get meaningful opportunities to handle depositions, hearings and trials, and have a good chance of making partner." A newbie notes, "I've only been here a few months, but I am amazed at the retention rate of associates here."

Kirkland & Ellis

Aon Center
200 East Randolph Drive
Chicago, IL 60601
Phone: (312) 861-2000
www.kirkland.com

LOCATIONS

Chicago, IL (HQ)
Los Angeles, CA
New York, NY
Washington, DC
London

MAJOR DEPARTMENTS/PRACTICES

Bankruptcy
Intellectual Property
Litigation
Tax & Planning
Transactional

THE STATS

No. of attorneys: 795
No. of offices: 5
Summer associate offers: 163 out of 170 (2001)
Firm Administrator: Douglas O. McLemore
Hiring Attorney: John Donley

BASE SALARY

All domestic offices, 2002
1st year: $125,000
2nd year: $135,000
3rd year: $150,000
4th year: $165,000
5th year: $185,000
6th year: $195,000
Summer associate: $2,404/week

NOTABLE PERKS

- Ice cream socials
- Annual $5,000 training budget for each attorney, including travel
- Free breakfast each morning
- Dinner and a ride home after 7 p.m.

THE BUZZ
WHAT ATTORNEYS AT OTHER FIRMS ARE SAYING ABOUT THIS FIRM

- "Brilliant litigation practice"
- "Will eat your young, slowly"
- "National reputation"
- "Excellent training and lawyers"
- "Right-wing stronghold"

UPPERS

- Free market assignment system
- Midwest star with national reputation

DOWNERS

- Associate disgruntlement regarding compensation
- Emphasis on billable hours

EMPLOYMENT CONTACT

Ms. Kimberley J. Klein
Attorney Recruiting Manager
Phone: (312) 861-8785
kimberley_klein@chicago.kirkland.com
(See firm web site for employment contacts at other offices)

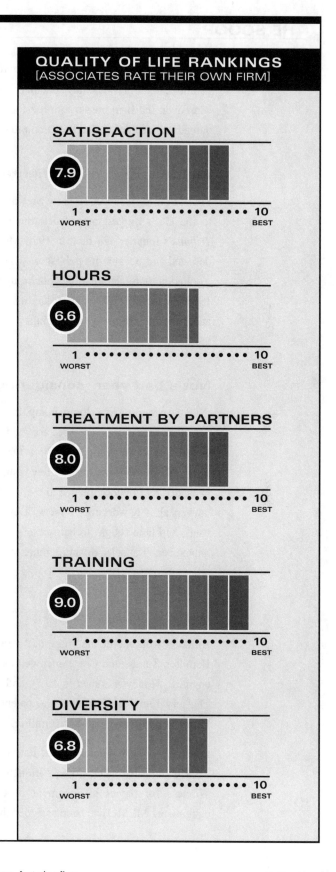

QUALITY OF LIFE RANKINGS
[ASSOCIATES RATE THEIR OWN FIRM]

SATISFACTION

7.9

1 WORST   10 BEST

HOURS

6.6

1 WORST   10 BEST

TREATMENT BY PARTNERS

8.0

1 WORST   10 BEST

TRAINING

9.0

1 WORST   10 BEST

DIVERSITY

6.8

1 WORST   10 BEST

THE SCOOP

Kirkland & Ellis is considered by many to be the star of the Midwest legal scene. With a top-notch venture capital/private equity practice, the firm has represented over 40 private investment groups. Moreover, the firm boasts a to-die-for litigation department that *The American Lawyer* recently named one of the top five in the country.

History: free speech fighters

Founded in Chicago in 1908 by Stewart G. Shepard and Robert R. McCormick, the firm had ties to the city's biggest newspaper, the *Chicago Tribune*. McCormick was the grandson of the *Tribune*'s founder. In fact, in 1920 McCormick got so involved in the *Tribune*'s affairs that he defected and became its publisher. Under McCormick, the newspaper had a candid tone, which resulted in many defamation suits brought against it. Weymouth Kirkland, who joined the firm in 1915, defended the *Tribune* in landmark cases. Howard Ellis, who also joined the firm in 1915, aided Kirkland in many of the trials. Together, they made a winning team and became the stars of the firm.

Not a bad year, considering

With the economy in a slump, many firms are cutting corners anywhere they can. While most firms cut back, Kirkland has pressed forward. In June 2001, it hired 170 summer associates, 54 more than the previous year. In addition the firm acquired the LA-based bankruptcy boutique Wynne Spiegel Itkin, boosting the attorney count at the firm's Los Angeles office to 85. The firm has also expanded its London practice to include English and German lawyers in addition to the American lawyers already working overseas. Demonstrating its heart at a time when the firm was doing well itself, Kirkland sought to help others in need. Kirkland contributed to recovery efforts after the September 11 attacks, donating more than half a million dollars to New York and Washington, D.C. relief efforts.

IP hype

Kirkland won one of the biggest IP verdicts in 2001. Honeywell International Inc. claimed that Hamilton Sundstrand Corp. infringed its patent for an auxiliary power unit in commercial aircraft engines. Honeywell sued in 1999, and Sundstrand claimed the Honeywell patents were invalid. The jury found in 2001 that the patents were both valid and infringed upon. Kirkland client Honeywell was awarded $46.6 million.

In another win, Kirkland helped its client avoid a $271 million claim and injunction. In 1999, MLMC Ltd. sued Alltel Corp., Airtouch Corp., GTE Wireless, PrimeCo and, subsequently, Verizon Wireless for patent infringement of two patents related to cellular telephone infrastructure equipment. MLMC had been assigned these patents from their original owner, Harris Corporation, in 1995. In November 2001, the defendants were granted summary judgment of noninfringement of one of the patents and in December 2001, a jury found no infringement by the defendants of the remaining patent. In addition, the jury found the remaining patent invalid.

Major M&As

When it comes to handling major deals, the attorneys at Kirkland & Ellis know what to do. When Net2Phone Inc. formed Adir Technologies Inc. in partnership with Cisco Systems, Inc. and Softbank to develop long-distance telephone software for the Internet, Net2Phone turned to K&E to get the deal done. In October 2001, K&E represented Gaylord Container Corp., a manufacturer of paper products when Temple-Inland Inc. acquired it for $850 million.

In a billion-dollar deal, Echostar Communications Corp., a direct broadcast satellite programming services provider, agreed in October 2001 to merge with Hughes Electronics Corp., a subsidiary of General Motors Corp. and the provider of DirecTV Inc., for about $25 billion. K&E represented General Motors in the deal. In another billion-dollar bang, National Broadcasting Company, Inc. bought Telemundo Communications Group, Inc. for $1.98 billion. K&E represented one of the stockholders of Telemundo, which ranks second in the Spanish television market, in the December 2001 deal.

Boasting of Bernick

K&E is proud to have Chicago litigator David Bernick on its team. Bernick has been singled out by numerous publications as one of the top trial lawyers in the nation and has a reputation for excellence when it comes to trying complex mass tort cases — such as silicone breast implants, cigarettes and asbestos. Most recently, Bernick and his team in 2001 obtained a voluntary dismissal of the Manville Trusts' suit against the tobacco industry after an eight-week trial in federal court in Brooklyn. He also won a $600 million fraudulent transfer trial in federal court in New Orleans in February 2002 in connection with the asbestos-related Babcock & Wilcox bankruptcy.

Dandy defense

When *The National Law Journal* choose the top defense verdicts of 2001, Kirkland was on the list. The firm represented Motorola Inc. in an environmental contamination class action suit brought in 1992. Motorola used a degreasing agent called trichlorethylene (TCE) to clean electronics parts at its Scottsdale, Ariz., plant from 1957 through 1975. Because of reports that TCE could be a carcinogen, the company discontinued using it in 1975. However local property owners sought actual damages in the amount of $260 million plus punitive damages for contamination of the groundwater. In May 2001, a jury in Phoenix rejected the claim. Motorola then settled for $15 million with the property owners and two other groups of plaintiffs making claims for personal injuries and medical monitoring.

Starr is a star

Most of us know Kenneth Starr as the man who played Javert to Bill Clinton's Jean Valjean. The former independent prosecutor's investigation of Clinton led to the former president's impeachment. But Starr is also a Kirkland & Ellis partner. In August 2001, Starr, who served as solicitor general of the United States in the first Bush administration, battled for big tobacco and won an impressive reduction in punitive damages. The year before, Richard Boeken, a Marlboro smoker since 1957, sued Philip Morris Inc., alleging product defects, negligence and fraud after he was diagnosed with lung cancer and had surgery, radiation and chemotherapy treatments. On June 6, 2001, a Los Angeles jury awarded him $2.29 million in economic damages, $3.25 million in non-economic damages and $3 billion in punitive damages. Philip Morris sought to reduce the verdict and hired Starr to do it. Starr's argument that the verdict was grossly excessive persuaded the judge, who knocked punitive damages to $100 million in August.

GETTING HIRED

Wined and dined

Summer associates at Kirkland get the royal treatment, with "fancy lunches, parties and events." After the special treats are gone, one associate says, "The summer program does prepare you for life in the firm." A Chicago associate notes, "I drafted pleadings and researched memos. [I] also had some client contact." A New York associate had real trial experience. Another advises summer associates not to be shrinking violets: "The best and most interesting projects go to those who seek them out." In Los Angeles, things are no different. "You really get to know the attorneys. There's a high quality of work assignments that actually mean something."

Ahead of the pack

Hiring at Kirkland is competitive. A D.C. associate says, "Kirkland generally hires only those from the top law schools, and those who have completed judicial clerkships." The firm notes, however, that it is not focused on whether or not the candidate clerks, but rather on whether the individual has the drive, intellectual firepower and personal skills to be a first-rate lawyer. In Chicago, "Interviews are fairly intense." A New York associate explains that candidates in the Big Apple should expect an "initial screening interview with two people followed by a callback interview with four or maybe five people." According to one associate, "Once you have a callback, its seems quite likely that an offer will follow." No rush, though. A D.C. associate notes, "Once the offer is extended, they do a great job of recruiting, giving you access to more people and information and giving you plenty of time."

OUR SURVEY SAYS

We're Kirkland. Got a problem with that?

In Kirkland's litigation practice, attorneys are geared up and ready for a fight. "We are confident and we want to win. And our attitude is come and beat us. We don't understand why people seem to have such a problem with that. In fact, I would say that any lawyer who doesn't have that attitude is not fulfilling his or her ethical duty to his or her client," boasts one eager associate in the Chicago office. In D.C., associates are just as voracious. One notes, "It is true that when it comes to nitty gritty litigation, a certain degree of measured aggressiveness doesn't hurt." This firm is not for the weak of heart. Another associate cautions, "You need to be highly motivated and strong willed. No one is going to hold your hand. If people want that, they should go somewhere else."

Kirkland manages to balance aggression and civility. "The associates for the most part do not battle one another. The freedom of the (mostly) free market system is noteworthy and contrary to many big firms where you either must choose or are told your practice area and even the partners who will be using you, all right upon coming in the door," says an IP associate. "Socially, the work environment is very friendly and laid back. People genuinely seem to like each other. And as for lifestyle, there are no limitations. You can work however you want here. (In fact, many associates and partners work at home quite a bit.) We do also tend to socialize together, usually after work for dinner if we are staying late or on Friday nights," maintains one happy associate in the firm's Chicago office.

Follow the leader

That's what most associates say Kirkland does when it comes to compensation. "K&E has fallen from grace here. They clearly aren't leading the market in terms of compensation as used to be the K&E mantra. In fact, they are lagging behind," says one unhappy Chicago associate. New York associates feel the pain of their Chicago counterparts. "Too low for a premier firm in New York City — it's not fair for K&E's New York lawyers to make the same as its Chicago, D.C. and LA lawyers." But the firm is doing something right by its D.C. lawyers. An associate there remarks that the K&E "salary is comparable with other top firms." In Los Angeles, the salary is tops, too. "My base salary is top of the market for big law firms," says one associate there. But he mentions that "bonuses last year left a little to be desired." In fact, bonuses are on the minds of many Kirkland associates. "Kirkland touts that their bonuses are above market average. But the process is steeped in mystery and far more people are unhappy than are satisfied," states a Chicagoan. The firm notes that it rewards its associates and partners by compensating them at or above the market and that at the equity partner level, the AmLaw 100 data report that K&E has $1.4 million profit per partner (compared to $410,000-850,000 for its principal competitors in Chicago). The firm also states that it has monitored the market carefully and is paying its people at or above the top in all cities.

No life? No way!

Associates think the firm's free market system leads to a better quality of life. A D.C. associate explains that associate hours from 1998 to 2001 "can only be described as oppressive," due mostly to "tremendous growth in business and not enough bodies to meet demand — particularly in a tight associate market." According to this associate, the firm made a conscious effort to correct the problem by recruiting more quality associates and partners to alleviate the pressure. "The oppressive hours were probably one of my biggest complaints about Kirkland," the associate explains. "If the firm continues to show a commitment to allowing associates and partners to enjoy a life outside of the office, I think that will go a long way in solidifying this firm as one of the best."

While things are better firm-wide, there is some variation between the different practice groups. As one tax associate notes, "I have plenty of time to have a life. [T]his is a feature of my practice group, and varies widely across practice groups at the firm." An IP associate says, "K&E doesn't really care where you bill the hours, so long as they get billed. At other firms, face time has been an important element of success. Here, the focus is on getting the work done regardless of where. Also, I haven't felt any pressure to really bill more hours than I am [actually billing]." A corporate associate is not as satisfied. "It's been either all or nothing since I started here," he begins. "I had months where I struggled to bill 100 hours, followed by 200+ hour months. I'm left wondering whether there has been a 'snag' in the free market system, for example whether it might be better to have a central assigning partner who could ensure that the junior associates are getting roughly the same amount of work."

What matters most

That's the focus of attorneys at Kirkland & Ellis when it comes to issues of diversity. "No one has the time to waste worrying about color. It only matters if you are a good lawyer. No one has the time to waste worrying about sexual orientation. It only matters if you are a good lawyer," asserts one associate. A female associate notes, "Since I was in law school, I have heard rumors that Kirkland is a boys club and is not a good place for women. In my experience, these rumors are totally unfounded. Kirkland has given me fantastic opportunities, and the partners treat me with respect." Another woman adds, "Maybe the culture of long hours eventually disadvantages women who want to have kids. But you know what you're getting into when you sign on."

At Kirkland, diversity issues do not take precedence. An Asian associate notes, "In my experience, the partners here don't care what sex, race or religion you are — they're only concerned with whether you get the work done and get it done well." One hopeful associate chimes in, "The firm is trying to be more receptive to various diversity issues as evidenced by the organization of a diversity committee which is served with the task of increasing diversity at the firm." An Hispanic associate remarks, "As to how the firm treats minorities, the bottom line is that Kirkland is a meritocracy — if your work is good, you will be rewarded without regard to your gender, race, ethnicity, religion, sexual orientation or political views." An Asian associate points out, "Kirkland also has been active in minority recruiting and development." The firm notes that it was named a winner of the Minority Corporate Counsel Association's 2001 Thomas L. Sager Award for the Midwest Region, which recognizes law firms that have demonstrated a sustained commitment to improve the hiring, retention and promotion of minority attorneys.

Pro bono? OK.

A D.C. associate best explains the firm's commitment to pro bono: "The firm probably doesn't actively push associates to do pro bono work as much as it should. But that said, once an associate takes it upon him- or herself to do pro bono work, the firm provides almost unlimited support for this work." A Chicago associate shares his experience: "I've done a great deal of pro bono work, and the firm has been very supportive. I am a third-year associate, and I brought in a large pro bono case which will cost the firm a lot of money and attorney time. The K&E pro bono committee agreed to take and fund the case with no reservation. I doubt many other firms would have made that sort of commitment to such a young associate. It was quite impressive." An LA associate went through a similar situation. She explains: "I have spent hundreds of hours this year on a civil rights pro bono case, and the firm has stood fully behind me."

Another Chicago associate notes, "I think the firm's pro bono program, while not widely publicized, is one of its strongest points. I have been involved in one pro bono case since my first week of work, and it makes up about a quarter of my billable hours so far. Unlike other firms, there is no cap on how many pro bono hours you can work or how many pro bono cases you can take. The partners respect that pro bono work is important and don't try to place paying clients first. The firm also supports the Public Interest Law Initiative program in Chicago, and last summer 10 or 11 incoming associates split their time between studying for the bar and working at pro bono agencies." In London, associates participate in pro bono activities through a variety of community development projects sponsored by K&E and other U.S. law firms.

Shearman & Sterling

599 Lexington Avenue
New York, NY 10022
Phone: (212) 848-4000
www.shearman.com

LOCATIONS

New York, NY (HQ)
San Francisco/Menlo Park, CA • Washington, DC • Abu
Dhabi • Beijing • Brussels • Dusseldorf • Frankfurt •
Hong Kong • London • Mannheim • Munich • Paris •
Rome • Singapore • Tokyo • Toronto

MAJOR DEPARTMENTS/PRACTICES

Antitrust • Bank Finance & Bankruptcy • Capital
Markets • Corporate Finance & Investment • Executive
Compensation & Employee Benefits • Private Clients •
Intellectual Property • Litigation • Leasing • Mergers &
Acquisitions • Project Development & Finance •
Property • Tax

THE STATS

No. of attorneys: 1,025
No. of offices: 18
Summer associate offers: 111 out of 113 (2001)
Senior Partner: David W. Heleniak
Hiring Partner: Stephen Fishbein

BASE SALARY

New York, 2002
1st year: $125,000
2nd year: $135,000
3rd year: $150,000
4th year: $165,000
Summer associate: $2,538/week

NOTABLE PERKS

• Longevity bonuses
• Use of skybox at Madison Square Garden
• Subsidized in-house dining room
• Sabbatical program

THE BUZZ
WHAT ATTORNEYS AT OTHER FIRMS ARE SAYING ABOUT THIS FIRM

• "Good securities"
• "Resting on its past laurels"
• "Prestigious, but you earn your stripes in blood"
• "Laid off people in NY = bad move!"
• "Classic NY with good rep in Europe"

UPPERS

- First-class international practice
- Flexible transfers to domestic and foreign offices
- Prestigious, high-profile deals

DOWNERS

- Slump in morale due to layoffs
- Headquarters in need of renovation
- Increased billable hours pressure

EMPLOYMENT CONTACT

Ms. Suzanne Ryan
Manager, Professional Recruiting
Phone: (212) 848-4592
Fax: (212) 848-7179
sryan@shearman.com

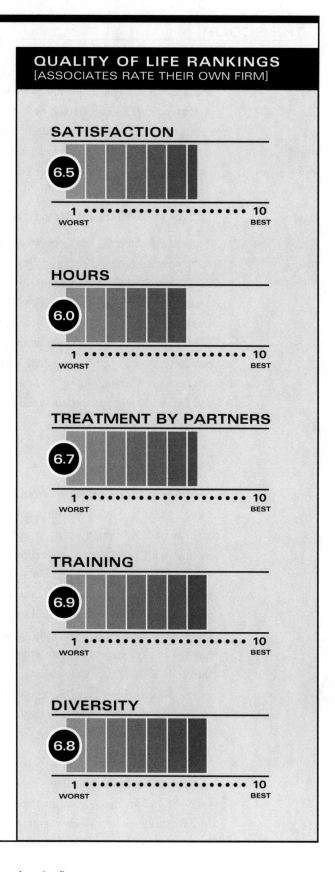

QUALITY OF LIFE RANKINGS
[ASSOCIATES RATE THEIR OWN FIRM]

SATISFACTION

6.5

1 WORST .... 10 BEST

HOURS

6.0

1 WORST .... 10 BEST

TREATMENT BY PARTNERS

6.7

1 WORST .... 10 BEST

TRAINING

6.9

1 WORST .... 10 BEST

DIVERSITY

6.8

1 WORST .... 10 BEST

THE SCOOP

One of the oldest law firms in the world, Shearman & Sterling is tops when it comes to mergers and acquisitions and its prestigious international presence. The firm name carries tremendous weight in the legal community, even though laying off about 10 percent of its associates in 2001 didn't do wonders for the morale of its associates. Admirably, the firm acknowledges that the layoffs were economically driven, not due to supposed "underperformance." Fortunately, the future looks bright for this top-tier law firm.

History: a firm on the forefront

Shearman & Sterling was born way back in 1873, when Thomas Shearman and John Sterling started a law practice together in New York. Shearman, a former law reporter for *The New York Times*, and Sterling, a lawyer who was No. 1 in his graduating class at Columbia Law School, opened shop together in New York's Fourth National Bank Building after having both worked for David Dudley Field, head of the New York Bar. The young firm's principal client was industrialist Jay Gould, whom the firm aided in his 1875 takeover of the Union Pacific Railroad. Other high-profile 19th century clients included Jonathan Thome, a wealthy Quaker merchant; Charles Osborn of Osborn & Chapin, one of the largest Wall Street brokerage houses; railway magnates George and Donald Smith; and the Rockefellers. This is a firm with a very clear sense of its place in our country's history.

Going global

Many firms these days have overseas offices and style themselves "international." Shearman, though, is the real deal. The firm has been committed to its non-U.S. offices for nearly 40 years and has built its foreign offices over time, avoiding the cultural friction that often accompanies mergers with established foreign firms. The middle of the 20th century saw the beginning of the firm's international expansion. In 1963 it opened its first foreign office in Paris. More offices followed in the years to come: London in 1972, Abu Dhabi in 1976 and Hong Kong in 1978. More than 100 years after the opening of its New York office, the firm expanded back home, opening a San Francisco office in 1979, with Washington, D.C., following in 1987. From then on, the firm has had an explosion of new outposts. In fall 1998, the firm opened up in Menlo Park to cater to the needs of its Silicon Valley clients. The opening was considered to be very late in the game by certain Shearman partners. Several of these partners wanted Shearman to be more aggressive in seeking out its tech business, so they defected to firms who were doing just that. (With the latest bust in the tech industry, Shearman's cautious stance may have proved the right one.)

The firm's growth didn't stop in Silicon Valley. In 1987 the firm opened its Tokyo office. It also set up space in Toronto in 1989, Frankfurt and Dusseldorf in 1991, Beijing in 1993 and Singapore in 1995. In May 2000, Shearman acquired most of the German firm Schilling, Zutt & Anschutz. In 2001 it entered into a joint venture with Singaporean firm Stamford LLC. The firm headed back to Europe again and opened a Brussels office in July 2001, a Munich office in September and a Rome office in March 2002.

Roll out the red carpet, but try not to trip

Shearman is known for giving its attorneys the royal VIP treatment. In 1999 the firm announced a new set of perks for its lawyers. First, the firm set aside a minimum of $2 million a year for an associate benefit fund in which associates accrue bonus shares during their first three years of practice and receive a payout in their fourth. Second, any associate who has spent at least two years at Shearman is permitted to shift to a part-time or flex-time schedule without hurting his or her partnership chances. Third, Shearman gives all senior associates a comprehensive review and appraisal of their partnership prospects as a way to demystify the partnership process. (The firm also provides a $50,000 bonus as an extra incentive to stick around for any associate that shows a reasonable likelihood of a long-term career with the firm as partner or counsel.) Finally, associates in their fifth or sixth year are asked to choose between taking a one-month sabbatical devoted to career development or spending three months in another practice group or office.

But in 2001, Shearman felt the sting of a sagging economy. In October 2001, the firm announced that it would lay off about 80 associates. (The associates received three months pay and outplacement assistance.) Though the layoffs were certainly an unpleasant chapter in the Shearman story, the firm earned respect by acknowledging openly that the layoffs were economically driven, as opposed to blaming them on associate underperformance. To help combat the effects of the plummeting economy, the firm also shifted some associates to areas of the firm's practice with the highest activity levels.

M&A magic

Despite the shaky economy of fall 2001, the firm saw clients through many sizeable transactions during that bleak autumn. In August the firm represented Corning Inc., a telecommunications and information display company, in its joint purchase of Lucent Technologies Inc.'s Optical Fiber Solutions business with Tokyo's Furukawa Electric Company for $2.75 billion. The next month, a team of Shearman attorneys helped Barrick Gold Corporation acquire Homestake Mining Company, founded during the gold rush in the late 1800s, for $3.2 billion.

Not only did the firm mine for gold, it also drilled for dollars. In September 2001, Shearman represented Santa Fe International, an offshore drilling company, in its $3 billion merger with Global Marine Inc., another offshore driller. Another major fall deal was the acquisition of Zurich Scudder Investments Inc., the U.S. affiliate of the Zurich-based insurance group Zurich Financial Services AG, by Shearman client Deutsche Bank AG for $2.5 billion. Finally, in another transaction of note, S&S represented a consortium that purchased the Boston Red Sox baseball franchise for $660 million.

Globe-trotting litigators

Shearman's litigation practice handles trial and appellate work throughout the United States, England, France and Germany. The group has also argued cases before a wide range of arbitration panels and tribunals worldwide, including the International Chamber of Commerce, the London Court of International Arbitration and the Iran-U.S. Claims Tribunal at the Hague.

Shearman has also developed a strong litigation practice representing U.S. media companies, helping clear the legal hurdles for client Viacom's $40 billion acquisition of CBS and, more recently, representing NBC in its dispute with Paxson Communications concerning NBC's $3 billion acquisition of the Telemundo Group. The firm's white-collar criminal defense practice is active as well and has been center stage in several recent high-profile criminal cases involving allegations of price fixing by foreign cartels — some of the biggest criminal cases ever brought by the Justice Department.

Rescuing Rwanda

After the brutal 1994 genocide in this African nation, the U.N. Security Council created the Office of the Prosecutor of the International Criminal Tribunal for Rwanda. Shearman attorneys have helped with legal research on issues of international criminal law on a variety of substantive and procedural issues, many of first impression. In December 2001, the firm sent lawyers to Arusha, Tanzania — along with senior prosecutors from the Yugoslavia tribunal and leading American former prosecutors and jurists — to conduct a trial-practices seminar for members of the Rwanda prosecutor's office. Moreover, a number of S&S associates have spent their sabbaticals working for the Rwanda tribunal at its Tanzania headquarters.

GETTING HIRED

A time of flux

Although Shearman & Sterling is competitive in hiring, associates report few "inflexible benchmarks." To be sure, grades matter, but the firm is "not snobbish about schools." "What I like about this firm," declares an insider, "is that it will hire someone 'hungry' from a less well-known law school if grades and experience meet their criteria. And not only that — they will make them partner. There is no culture of 'you have to be from Harvard to succeed.'" Beyond an impressive class rank, Shearman "looks for very smart, hard-working people," and language skills help get your foot in the door of this international firm. Says an associate in an office overseas, "One of the most important things to have in your favor is something that shows your interest in the global nature of the firm's practice."

Several lawyers warn, however, that things are changing at Shearman. One associate finds it "is now becoming less of a Wall Street firm and more like a multi-local firm and hiring local lawyers."

OUR SURVEY SAYS

More than lawyers lost in layoffs

When Shearman & Sterling laid off some 80 lawyers last fall, it lost not only a good number of associates, but also much of the good will of some of those who remained. Our sources' satisfaction with their firm and its partners dropped markedly from last year. "Well," one associate dryly responds, "after they fired [10 percent] of associates and just as many secretaries, and partners started to yell and scream and generally act nasty and totally selfish, it is difficult to feel 'satisfied.'" While not universal, the bitterness and tension are deeply felt. A lawyer writes, "The firm f——-ed up big time this past year — first by over-hiring in a down year, then by mismanaging the layoffs." The layoffs "really soured the mood around here," sighs a New Yorker, and insiders report an "air of suspicion between partners and associates." Even some lawyers who praise the firm's normally "friendly culture" note that Shearman has not "been the easiest place to work recently."

The excitement of front page deals

Still, many associates seem happy with their firm and mention neither layoffs, nor partner distrust nor "terrible" management. "I am surrounded by brilliant, kind and interesting people," declares an enthusiastic first-year, "which creates a challenging, supportive and fun work environment — and the high-profile matters we work on keep the adrenaline pumping." Insiders generally agree that the "associates are a great group." Several rave about the "cutting-edge work" and "tremendous responsibility." A fifth-year finds Shearman "an ideal work environment." Lawyers appreciate the "good training" and "huge transactions," as well as the firm's "great reputation." And many even insist that they "are treated with a lot of respect" by partners who are "generally nice to associates and are top-notch lawyers." At least one attorney gets a thrill out of seeing the deals he is working on in "the front pages of *The Wall Street Journal* and the *Financial Times* every day."

Ups and downs

Relationships have their peaks and their valleys — and the relationships between partners and associates are no different. Some insiders seem wary of partners who had been widely praised for their respectful treatment of associates. Though several sources describe a "breach in trust" between associates and partners, at least one New York lawyer disputes this grim view of partner-associate relations: "Despite other tensions between partners and associates in 2001, partners continue to respect those associates that they work with." Others continue to describe the firm as "collegial and friendly."

The consensus seems to be that relations among associates are friendly and cordial but that "partners and associates can be a little 'cool' towards one another." Some lawyers report "lots of socializing" in their offices; others say it's usually junior associates who socialize together and it really "depends upon the practice group." Certain European offices seem to be quite sociable, while real estate lawyers in New York complain about the unfriendly, "competitive" spirit within their department. Although the firm's overall atmosphere is described as "somewhere between laid back and formal," there are hints that Shearman wants to reestablish more formality.

Time for a facelift

Something has to be done about the firm's headquarters, according to many New York insiders. Sources describe an office that is overcrowded, with some first-years using spare conference rooms as temporary offices. Moreover, "they have to do something about décor," which is "showing signs of age." The old brown carpet is hit with particularly vicious criticism: "Weekly shampooing isn't quite doing the trick." And, pleads one associate, "please, please, somebody, anybody, put that lobby art out of its misery!"

Despite the common request for a "facelift," a couple of lawyers "don't know why people complain about our offices." A first-year associate contends it's a "lovely office, [with] lots of space and sunlight." At least Bay Area associates are happy. An ecstatic lawyer gloats over the space: "Brand spankin' new! Dark wood, huge offices, lots of windows! All of my friends at other offices are envious."

Keeping pace on compensation

Shearman pay is "always at or near top market rate." Yet it frustrates many insiders that their firm is a follower rather than a leader when it comes to setting compensation. Shearman waits for "peer firms to set salaries and bonuses." And then "the firm keeps the pace," but "grudgingly." An associate voices respondents' most frequent complaint: "I feel my compensation is OK. But I do get upset about the fact that we are generally the last firm to announce bonuses." Some lawyers fear this delay reveals a "weakening commitment to pay market." Other associates charge that bonuses are actually "behind market, vis-à-vis the firms they compare themselves with." "You have to stay at least three years and receive the longevity bonuses to make up the shortfall in bonus pay," claims one source. "In addition to boom-year bonuses," a lawyer explains, "the firm pays out a retention bonus to fourth-year associates and an incentive bonus to seventh-year associates."

Attorneys in overseas offices report that their "base salary is comparable to other firms," but complain that bonuses had to be "practically forced out of partners" and that the firm "slashed their ex-pat packages." For some Shearman lawyers, however, the firm's slower payment of bonuses doesn't alter the fact that "associates' gross pay here is staggering." And one attorney assures colleagues that Shearman always "matches the top-paying firms in the city. You don't have to worry about getting your money."

The price you pay

When asked about insiders' satisfaction with their hours, one lawyer retorts, "This is not a fair question. No one is happy about working long hours, but this is the price you pay to work at a top-tier global law firm." Other respondents share this view. "Do I work the hours I think are reasonable for the experience/remuneration I receive? Yes. Would I like to spend more time at home? Yes. Do I contradict myself? Yes." That said, many attorneys report a more palpable pressure to bill long hours since last year's layoffs. According to one anxious associate, "Hours never seemed to worry anyone before the layoffs, but now everyone seems to worry about face time and getting enough work." Some sources wish they "could spend less time at work," while others whose departments are feeling the slump long for "a bit more work" so that they "could actually learn something." Still, some hard-working Shearmanites are philosophical about their full schedules. "What can you say? That is the tradeoff for a decent job working with decent people for a decent salary."

A pro bono commitment

Insiders believe the "firm overall is generally committed" to pro bono work. Several lawyers praise the firm's "first-rate pro bono manager," although they note that it's "hard to tap into the pro bono thing" outside of the New York office. An attorney finds "endless opportunities, but not always enough time," and some report apprehension about taking on a large amount of non-billable work in these uncertain times. Those associates who overcome their trepidation can choose from a wide range of pro bono projects, such as advising on the legality of the recent Zimbabwe elections, rescuing women from honor killings in Pakistan, advising low-income and minority business owners in New York and assisting on a wide range of projects stemming from the events of September 11.

An effort to improve diversity

Many associates agree that there are "too few women partners" and that more could be done to make Shearman welcoming to women. "It is very difficult," complains one source, "to focus on the promotion, mentoring and advancing of women when there are so few role-models and those that have achieved some level of status, respect and knowledge leave for 'better opportunities.'" Several female associates report being treated fairly, but according to one attorney, "some of the women definitely feel like we have a male-dominated culture. The softball team and playing golf and football are emphasized a little too much." Sources speak of a "glass ceiling" in the foreign offices, where the attitude of some partners is cause for "genuine embarrassment."

Insiders would also like to see more minority partners and associates outside of the New York office. "Although there are lots of minorities among the junior associates, those numbers dwindle drastically as you look at the upper associate classes and among partners," laments an insider. But some lawyers highlight the presence of a firm diversity management attorney as evidence of "a concerted effort" to improve the situation.

Paul, Weiss, Rifkind, Wharton & Garrison

1285 Avenue of the Americas
New York, NY 10019
Phone: (212) 373-3000
www.paulweiss.com

LOCATIONS

New York, NY (HQ)
Washington, DC
Beijing
Hong Kong
London
Paris
Tokyo

MAJOR DEPARTMENTS/PRACTICES

Bankruptcy
Corporate
Employee Benefits & Executive Compensation
Entertainment
Environmental
Litigation
Personal Representation
Real Estate
Tax

THE STATS

No. of attorneys: 495
No. of offices: 7
Summer associate offers: 101 out of 101 (2001)
Chairman of Management Committee: Alfred D. Youngwood

BASE SALARY

New York and Washington, DC, 2002
1st year: $125,000
2nd year: $135,000
3rd year: $150,000
4th year: $170,000
5th year: $195,000
6th year: $210,000
7th year: $220,000
8th year: $235,000
Summer associate: $2,400/week

NOTABLE PERKS

- Well-attended Friday evening cocktail parties
- Subsidized gym memberships
- Personal printers for every associate
- "Free tickets to most everything"

THE BUZZ
WHAT ATTORNEYS AT OTHER FIRMS ARE SAYING ABOUT THIS FIRM

- "Fabulous litigators"
- "Zero quality of life"
- "Feisty"
- "Not as strong outside of litigation"
- "My smartest friend went there"

UPPERS

• Superior litigation practice
• "Clearly number one" in the pro bono department

DOWNERS

• "It ain't 9 to 5"
• Bonus disgruntlement

EMPLOYMENT CONTACT

Ms. Patricia J. Morrissy
Legal Recruitment Director
Phone: (212) 373-2548
Fax: (212) 373-2205
pmorrissy@paulweiss.com

Ms. Joanne Ollman
Legal Personnel Director
jollman@paulweiss.com

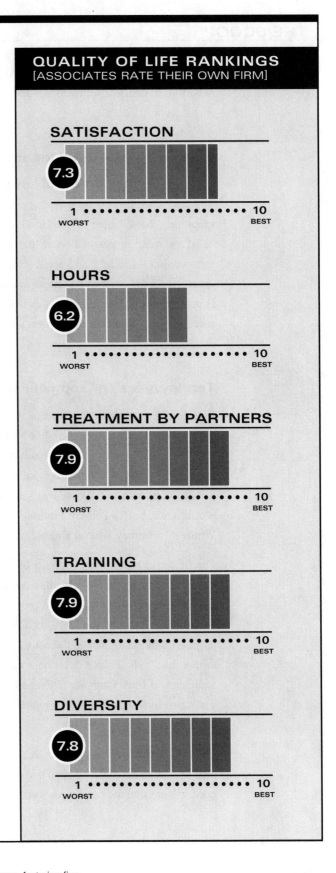

QUALITY OF LIFE RANKINGS
[ASSOCIATES RATE THEIR OWN FIRM]

SATISFACTION

7.3

1 WORST .... 10 BEST

HOURS

6.2

1 WORST .... 10 BEST

TREATMENT BY PARTNERS

7.9

1 WORST .... 10 BEST

TRAINING

7.9

1 WORST .... 10 BEST

DIVERSITY

7.8

1 WORST .... 10 BEST

THE SCOOP

Old doesn't always mean old school. Although it's more than 127 years old, Paul, Weiss, Rifkind, Wharton & Garrison remains a super-star New York firm known primarily for its top-notch litigation practice.

Continuing the legal legacy

Since its founding in New York City in 1875, Paul Weiss has been a litigation leader. While litigation continues to be a primary focus for Paul Weiss, the firm has expanded far beyond litigation. Today some of the firm's major cases are in the areas of entertainment law, M&A, bankruptcy and representation of high-profile individuals. The expansion hasn't been limited to the addition of a few additional practice areas. The continuing growth of the firm's five international offices provides opportunities to associates looking to gain international experience. In Asia alone, the firm has offices in Beijing, Hong Kong and Tokyo. The firm has seen significant success among Japanese companies with business interests in Tokyo, and the firm recently opened an office in London.

Top lawyers for top clients

High-profile litigation? You betcha. How about Napster, Enron and the California energy crisis? With respect to Napster, the firm has put its entertainment and litigation practices to work in a battle with the music download site. Paul Weiss filed a suit against the Internet music distributor on behalf of a group of songwriters and music publishers on the grounds that Napster infringed on existing copyrights. The case was settled for $36 million in September 2001. Napster is a high-profile name, but the firm isn't intimidated; its roster of celebrity clients includes the likes of Oprah Winfrey, Sigourney Weaver and Spike Lee.

The firm also represents Citigroup in the series of litigations and proceedings arising out of the Enron bankruptcy. In another high-profile case, Paul Weiss is representing the California Public Utilities Commission in the bankruptcy proceeding filed by Pacific Gas and Electric Co. in the U.S. Bankruptcy Court for the Northern District of California. The PG&E bankruptcy is one of the largest and most complex in the country. In February 2002, the firm achieved a significant victory in this case. The court's decision accepted the Paul Weiss arguments and rejected the contrary arguments of Prof. Laurence Tribe and held that PG&E's proposed bankruptcy plan could not be confirmed as it would have preempted state law. This decision was praised in a lead editorial of the *San Francisco Chronicle*.

The firm is also working to clear Johnson & Johnson of allegations of discrimination. The suit, filed in November 2001 by Hispanic and African-American employees of the healthcare product giant, alleges that the employees were denied promotions and raises because of their race.

Michael Milken and beyond

Defending individuals involved in newsworthy white-collar criminal cases is a long-standing tradition at Paul Weiss. Past clients include the now-pardoned king of insider trading, Michael Milken. The firm is currently defending another financier, Wall Street money manager Alan Bond. He's been accused of fraud and redirecting profitable stock trades that totaled more than $56 million from client accounts into his personal account. Another Paul Weiss client is Senator Robert Torricelli of New Jersey. Paul Weiss is one of several prestigious firms defending Torricelli against charges by the U.S. Attorney's office that the legislator accepted illegal contributions during his 1996 Senate campaign. The firm's representation of Torricelli successfully concluded on January 3, 2002, with the four-year investigation terminated without the filing of any criminal charges. The outcome of the case had great political implications, as the senator's exoneration allowed the Democratic Party to maintain control of the U.S. Senate.

Helping hands

When Paul Weiss attorneys aren't busy using their legal skills to defend their wealthy clients, they're likely to be found fighting the good fight to help those who are less privileged. Paul Weiss has received plenty of awards for its commitment to pro bono work. Recent firm recognition includes honors from *The American Lawyer* in December 1999 and December 2001 and from *The National Law Journal* and the American Bar Association in January 2002.

New York City's 2012 Olympic Bid Committee and former death row inmate Johnny Paul Penry are among the firm's current pro bono clients. In June 2001, the firm was successful before the U.S. Supreme Court in securing a new sentencing hearing for Penry based on his assertion that he is mentally challenged. Attorneys at Paul Weiss have been just as generous when it comes to lending a hand to fellow JDs in need. After the Twin Towers of the World Trade Center were destroyed by terrorists on September 11, Paul Weiss donated nearly an entire floor to fellow firm Cleary, Gottlieb, Steen & Hamilton, which lost its offices in the attacks. Currently, Paul Weiss attorneys are advising over 30 individuals, families and small businesses who were victims of the events of 9/11 on a myriad of issues, including surrogate, tax, worker's compensation, social security and insurance issues. Paul Weiss attorneys also counsel their clients on issues relating to the Victim's Compensation Fund.

The firm represents micro-entrepreneurs and small business owners in upper Manhattan through an arrangement with the Business Resource & Investment Service Center (BRISC) in Harlem. In 2001, 79 Paul Weiss attorneys, 19 summer associates and 10 paralegals advised 49 BRISC clients, including 31 new clients. In March 2001, the firm received the ABA Business Law Section's 2001 National Public Service Award for its work on this project. In February 1999, a federal jury in Portland, Ore., awarded Paul Weiss clients, Planned Parenthood and four doctors targeted by anti-abortion extremists who were threatening doctors with violence through "wanted" posters and an anti-abortion web site, $107 million in compensatory and punitive damages. A panel of the Ninth Circuit reversed the verdict and the firm successfully obtained an en banc review. In May 2002, the en banc panel of the Ninth Circuit agreed with the arguments by Paul Weiss and affirmed the jury and district court findings of true threats.

Measured growth

Paul Weiss officials say the firm isn't feeling the pinch of the slowing economy to the extent that other firms have in the past year because the firm expanded only minimally (from 450 to 500 attorneys) during the freewheeling 1990s. The firm appears to have learned from its mistakes. In the late 1980s, Paul Weiss expanded rapidly. But when stocks slumped and a recession hit the country, the firm was forced to lay off 41 associates in 1991. Since then firm leaders have adopted a more cautious approach to growth. That's not to say that growth is viewed as a bad thing at Paul Weiss. In 2001 the firm played host to 101 summer associates and extended full-time employment offers to each and every one.

All's well that ends well

Never give up. That's the lesson that one Paul Weiss associate learned after receiving his New York bar exam score. When the associate received the alarming news that he failed the bar exam, he did not give up. His score was so low that he felt certain he was the victim of a terrible blunder on the part of the bar examiners. Thanks to the associate's persistence and some diligent work by the legal personnel director on his behalf, the associate learned that a mix-up had indeed occurred; the bar examiners had mixed up his seat number with that of another bar-taker who had failed "spectacularly," according to *New York Lawyer*. The associate, who was one of 189 bar-takers wrongly informed that they failed the exam, was correctly notified that he passed the exam. Now that, folks, is a happy ending.

GETTING HIRED

Offers for everybody

Attorneys report that summer associates can look forward to a relaxing summer at Paul Weiss. "The summer is very laid back," a first-year associate tells us. "Some people go out to lunch every day and do zero work. Others take on interesting projects and get to know as many senior people as possible. Of course, everybody gets an offer." That doesn't mean you should view the summer program as an opportunity for endless fun in the sun. "Many people treat it as a big party but, if you treat it as a job, the rewards during the summer and when you return can be great," says a fourth-year lawyer.

As for the selection criteria, the firm is known for being "quite pedigree conscious," but often "turns down lots of honor students from the top schools. Hitting it off with the interviewers" is just as important as having an astronomically high GPA. "In recent years," says another associate, "the firm has become a little more open to schools from which it did not traditionally hire."

OUR SURVEY SAYS

A group of individuals

Paul Weiss is the type of firm where "partners will seek out your sentiments, and your opinions are respected," associates say. "Though people are friendly, it's a lot like school," remarks one first-year source. "You find your crowd, usually the group that comes in with you," and pretty much stick with those people. Finding a group to hang with shouldn't be a problem, as "there are all kinds of lawyers at Paul Weiss. We have geeks and jocks, alpha-people and wallflowers, and super-serious people and class clowns." All those personality types in such close proximity make for an environment that can be "either uptight or laid back, depending with whom you are working."

That's not to say that the firm is ruled by groups of self-contained cliques. "Socializing is encouraged through traditions like the weekly cocktail party, recruiting events and holiday parties." The London office is considered "friendly and informal. We socialize some together at least weekly."

The power of money

"I think I'm overpaid for what I do," admits one happily compensated sixth-year associate. Attorneys of all ranks agree that Paul Weiss isn't stingy. Still they've got some strong opinions about how the firm handles compensation issues, and don't mind letting them be known. Some lawyers express disappointment that the firm "slavishly follows the lead of other comparable New York firms." Instead of waiting to match what other firms pay, "it could probably risk being a leader in this field once — not in amount, just in timing," gripes a corporate attorney. But those associates are just whiners, according to one M&A attorney. Paul Weiss "associates are just as well paid as the really good firms, but they feel — unjustifiably, in my opinion — shortchanged by the firm."

Even more of a sore spot are bonuses, which, according to one New York attorney, "were cut in foreign offices last year — so that they did not match New York scale — to the surprise and consternation of some overseas associates who did not expect their acceptance of an overseas assignment would mean getting out of lockstep with other members of their class." Others say that the 2001 bonuses were "too low, below market or certainly below those firms that Paul Weiss considers its peers."

Of course, there are those who say they're happy, not just with what they're making, but also because they're employed during a time when other firms have let associates go. "Associates always want more, but I feel fortunate to have a job in a place like this in this economy," says a contented fifth-year associate. The unsteady economy and the rise in attorney salaries have combined to create an "up or out" environment that has produced an uneasiness among some of the attorneys at Paul Weiss.

Doin' time

Depending on who you ask, the hours at Paul Weiss are either long, yet manageable, or all-consuming. "I have accepted these hours, but I can't exactly be enthusiastic about them," explains a fifth-year associate. Like-minded colleagues consider "the overall effect of the workload" to be "softened by the fact that the work is fun and the people are great." Topping the list of complaints about hours are feelings of being under-appreciated and the lack of time for a personal life. One fourth-year who finds the "workload is unevenly distributed," resents that "many associates of my level do not work nearly as hard as I do." Another grouses, "At other firms people applaud when you bill 2,500 hours a year. At Paul Weiss, you feel like you should be billing more." For another burnout candidate, the hours make it "virtually impossible to have any kind of social life outside of the firm.

On the other side of the equation are attorneys who say their "hours at Paul Weiss are in line with those at other large firms, probably even less" and don't feel that partners take advantage of their time. "I've had partners apologize to me because I had to go into the office for four hours on a Saturday," says an attorney who had expected to work longer hours but has so far been pleasantly surprised. "People need not bill 2,400 hours a year to be recognized," says a third-year associate. Those who do good work can rest assured that "quality, not quantity, of work is what is rewarded," although this source admits the reward is generally more work.

A few associates praise the firm's part-time program for allowing them to work a reduced schedule and still bring home a hefty paycheck. The downside? For one senior associate, "there is no one that I'm aware of who has been made partner while working a flex-time schedule. So I don't really have any role models in terms of how I might advance."

Boomerang

Even in the slowing economy, "people seem to leave [the firm] regularly," although "not any more than at other large firms." Word is, people generally leave "when they realize that they are not on the partner track." While one associate describes the turnover rate at Paul Weiss as "typical of big New York City law firms," another believes the partnership would be relieved if more associates would leave, thereby reducing the head count. The D.C. office seems to do "a great job of retaining staff and partners, but seems to have a problem holding onto associates," reports an attorney from that office. The problem may be that the office "is possibly too small to offer long-term career satisfaction for associates."

An associate in the tax department reports a different experience: "One thing that may set this firm apart is the fact that a lot of people who leave here end up coming back here. This firm welcomed them back."

Partner highs and lows

For the most part, Paul Weiss associates say they're a lucky bunch to work with "some terrific partners who treat associates as valued members of the team and are genuinely concerned about our professional development." Most partners "have been considerate and solicitous of my opinion, especially as I become more senior," says one litigator. But there is "substantial variance between partners," associates warn. One source cautions that there are "a number of partners and senior associates who are so appallingly nasty and abusive as to make life here, at times, absolutely unbearable for the associates who work under them." According to one of the firm's M&A attorneys, "some are great teachers, mentors, sources of inspiration, and so on, while others are evidently only one prescription away from a very different type of institution." The firm points out that associates have a voice in firm management, elect their own Associates Committee, sit on firm committees and upwardly review partners.

Diversity: good, could be better

"The firm is welcoming" of female associates, say women attorneys at Paul Weiss. Some female associates cite the firm's efforts to recruit and retain women, such as its Women's Issues Committee, as examples of the firm's commitment to keeping its female attorneys happy. Although "it certainly feels like the firm is dominated by women at the associate level," associates say there are still inroads to be made for women at Paul Weiss, especially when it comes to partnership. There are "very few women partners, and male associates in general seem to receive slightly preferential treatment," observes an M&A attorney.

Some suggest that attitudes may have to change before there is a significant increase in the number of women partners. The female partners "seem to have absolutely no interest in mentoring the female associates," laments one attorney. Says another, "In general, if there are two juniors of the same class rank, identical skills and different gender on a deal, the man will get the more advanced junior assignments and client contact and the woman will always get assigned the scut work 'to avoid discouraging' her male colleague." A first-year associate cites an example of a long-time female associate who "has watched men in classes below her become partner. I think you just can't become partner if you are married and have kids." The firm, however, disputes this characterization and remarks that its women partners have diverse lifestyles, and most of them are married with children. Indeed, there is room for optimism. "There are a lot of senior women associates coming up for partner in the next few years, so we all are hopeful that the numbers could improve soon." Moreover, another woman partner was elected in December. And the firm notes that the Women's Issues Committee hosts breakfast meetings regularly and the annual women's networking event, whose past speakers have included Hillary Clinton, is one of the most anticipated events of the year.

And while associates also give the firm credit for recruiting minorities, they say the firm could make improvements, "especially in the areas of retention of minorities and development of minority partners." "The minority senior associates and partners here really go out of their way to serve as mentors and resources," a minority associate tells us. "I suspect the firm feels that responsibility should fall substantially on them alone."

The firm notes that its Diversity Committee works to improve and enhance diversity at the firm. Committee projects include creating a diversity calendar so that the goal of promoting diversity becomes a regular part of firm life, developing a mentoring program for minority associates, and participating in and sponsoring more than 20 diversity-related organizations.

"We have geeks and jocks,
alpha-people and wallflowers,
and super-serious people and
class clowns."

— *Paul Weiss associate*

15

Wilmer, Cutler & Pickering

2445 M Street, NW
Washington, DC 20037-1420
Phone: (202) 663-6000
www.wilmer.com

LOCATIONS

Washington, DC (HQ)
Baltimore, MD
New York, NY
Tysons Corner, VA
Berlin
Brussels
London

MAJOR DEPARTMENTS/PRACTICES

Antitrust & Competition
Communications & Electronic Commerce
Corporate
Financial Institutions
International Aviation, Defense & Aerospace
Litigation
Securities
Tax
Trade

THE STATS

No. of attorneys: 504
No. of offices: 7
Summer associate offers: 33 out of 35 (2001)
Chairman: William J. Perlstein
Hiring Attorney: David P. Donovan

BASE SALARY

**Washington, DC, Baltimore and
Tysons Corner, 2002**
1st year: $125,000
2nd year: $135,000
3rd year: $158,000
4th year: $168,000
5th year: $191,000
6th year: $201,000
Summer associate: $2,400/week
[These figures include a $15,000 bonus guaranteed
in an associate's first year]

New York, 2002
1st year: $125,000
2nd year: $135,000
3rd year: $158,000
4th year: $168,000
5th year: $191,000
6th year: $205,000

NOTABLE PERKS

- Annual sailing trip
- Emergency child care
- In-house gym
- Sabbatical program

THE BUZZ
WHAT ATTORNEYS AT OTHER FIRMS ARE SAYING ABOUT THIS FIRM

- "Top heavy in big names"
- "Most prestigious DC law firm"
- "Modern, bright, efficient"
- "Wonk-ish"

UPPERS

- Decidedly woman-friendly atmosphere and policies
- Reasonable hours
- Superior commitment to training

DOWNERS

- Cramped DC offices
- "Endless talk about budget cuts"
- Corporate culture in flux

EMPLOYMENT CONTACT

Ms. Mary W. Kiley
Lawyer Recruitment Administrator
JoinWCPLawyers@wilmer.com

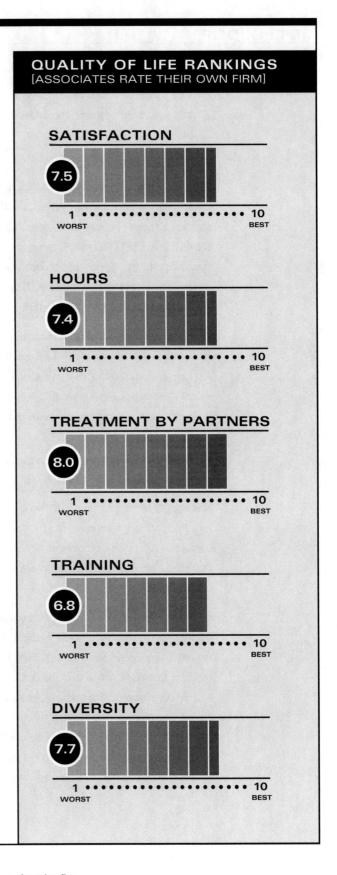

QUALITY OF LIFE RANKINGS
[ASSOCIATES RATE THEIR OWN FIRM]

SATISFACTION

7.5

1 WORST   10 BEST

HOURS

7.4

1 WORST   10 BEST

TREATMENT BY PARTNERS

8.0

1 WORST   10 BEST

TRAINING

6.8

1 WORST   10 BEST

DIVERSITY

7.7

1 WORST   10 BEST

THE SCOOP

Founded in Washington, D.C., in 1962, Wilmer, Cutler & Pickering has established itself as one of the city's foremost legal experts. While the firm has no shortage of prestigious paying clients, it is equally dedicated to the plights of its nonpaying clients.

Hiring power

Wilmer, Cutler & Pickering has a knack for bringing former government officials into its ranks. As the Bill Clinton era drew to a close, the firm made it a mission to woo some of the administration's senior attorneys. In July 2001 alone, Charlene Barshefsky and Robert Novick, both formerly with the Office of the U.S. Trade Representative, and former Solicitor General Seth Waxman, joined the firm as partners. Later that month, the firm announced it was losing one of its partners to an international government position. The head of the firm's Latin American practice group, Roberto Danino, was named Prime Minister of Peru.

As the Enron scandal began to heat up, the company's outside directors retained Wilmer, Cutler & Pickering in October 2001. Led by William McLucas, (former Director of the Securities and Exchange Commission's Division of Enforcement), the firm drafted what *The Washington Post* called "a scathing investigative report into Enron's collapse" that detailed the company's transactions with partnerships managed by Enron employees.

Location, location, location

Capitalizing on its location in the nation's capital, the firm has developed a strong regulatory practice to serve its clients in the United States and abroad. This practice, comprised of five groups, includes: antitrust and competition; international aviation, defense and aerospace; communications and electronic commerce; financial institutions; and trade. Wilmer, Cutler & Pickering also counsels companies in a variety of other industries, including energy and pharmaceuticals.

One of the firm's most vibrant practices is class-action litigation. Several large banks and financial institutions have sought out Wilmer, Cutler & Pickering's expertise in class-action defense. Among these clients are Citibank, First USA, Salomon Smith Barney and Merrill Lynch. Recently, the firm defended investment bank Credit Suisse First Boston. Along with several other banks, CSFB was charged with extracting overly high commissions and promises of future business from clients in exchange for the opportunity to purchase shares of IPOs offered through the bank. In January 2002, CSFB agreed to pay a $100 million settlement to end its involvement in the case. But considering that more than 600 suits were filed against CSFB in connection with the class action, the firm is likely to be busy wrapping this one up for some time to come.

Practices make perfect

The firm's most recent major trial success came when it won a $505 million verdict in favor of its client IGEN after a 10-week jury trial in federal district court in Virginia. Other rising stars within the firm include the media/communications and litigation practices. The growth of the technology industry, both nationally and within D.C., fueled the firm's media practice. Some of its clients include Internet services provider PSINet, which Wilmer, Cutler & Pickering is advising in bankruptcy proceedings in both the United States and Canada, DirecTV, CBS and Fox Broadcasting. The firm is frequently called upon to advise these clients on both financial and litigation issues. Wilmer, Cutler & Pickering's cases have covered domain name registration, copyright, access and digital signature disputes.

Another major client is AOL Time Warner, which the firm has advised on cases ranging from defamation lawsuits regarding messages written by third parties and transmitted over the AOL network, to charges that the Internet provider used its Netscape browser to invade the privacy of its users. The firm has been defending AOL on these and other cases by claiming that the company should not be subject to class-action suits because it is incorporated in Virginia, a state that doesn't allow such suits. However, the firm's request to settle the privacy case in arbitration on that basis was denied in a July 2001 ruling.

Corporate litigation clients include Lufthansa, Bristol-Myers Squibb, Fannie Mae, Sallie Mae and MCI. Wilmer, Cutler & Pickering also counts several sports teams on its client roster, including the Dallas Cowboys, Carolina Hurricanes, Washington Redskins and the Washington Capitals. Securities lawyers find themselves working for clients that include Salomon Smith Barney, Merrill Lynch and Goldman Sachs, among other high-profile clients.

Courting success

Wilmer, Cutler & Pickering endeavors to use its legal experience to influence laws throughout the country. That spirit motivated the firm to argue two cases on behalf of the University of Michigan before the Sixth Circuit Court of Appeals in December 2001. The cases involve the University of Michigan's affirmative action policies for admitting students. Recently, the firm has been retained to defend the McCain-Feingold campaign finance reform legislation in the courts. Wilmer, Cutler & Pickering has also been known to file an amicus brief or two in support of Supreme Court cases it strongly believes in.

All it's Quack-ed up to be

They may have just missed Oktoberfest, but that didn't stop the lawyers at Wilmer, Cutler & Pickering from celebrating when it announced its merger with Berlin-based Quack Rechtsanwalte in November 2001. The size of the firm's Berlin office more than doubled post-merger, which was completed in January 2002. The office, known as Wilmer, Cutler & Pickering-Quack in Germany, now employs more than 40 attorneys in the country.

Committees that care

Making the grade at a top firm like Wilmer, Cutler & Pickering requires hard work and often grueling hours. The firm has established a number of committees that attempt to make the transition from law student to lawyer a bit easier. Mid-level associates, counsel and partners oversee the New Associate Working Group, which develops training and manages assignments and feedback for junior associates. It has recently established a Career Development Committee to expand the New Associate Working Group's work to support the development of mid-level and senior associates. The Women's Forum is an informal group that allows the firm's female attorneys to network with and serve as mentors to each other.

The firm also manages a part-time program, which is coordinated by a partner who synchronizes schedules between attorneys wishing to work part time and their practice groups. Another partner serves as a pro bono coordinator. Dedicating a partner exclusively to find and assign pro bono cases has gotten the firm noticed. In 2001, *The American Lawyer* named Wilmer, Cutler & Pickering the No. 1 firm for pro bono in its ranking of the top 200 law firm pro bono programs.

GETTING HIRED

Pretty classy

Wilmer, Cutler & Pickering associates have few negative things to say about the hiring process at their firm. "They're pretty classy about interviewing here," notes one approving associate. The firm is so sensitive that it "gave on-campus offers in the wake of September 11, so that people who were afraid to fly to D.C. for a callback wouldn't have to do so. I think it was a very humane thing to do and typical of the firm's approach." The interviews themselves are "casual," with friendly, if sometimes inexperienced, interviewers — one associate commented that "often the interviewer seemed more nervous than I was." It's tough, say insiders, to get a callback from an on-campus interview, but "if you get a callback, the deck is stacked in your favor." How to get an interview in the first place? Be "brainy" and able to "write very well." Though Wilmer, Cutler & Pickering is said to crave grads from top schools, it's less snobby about lower-tiered schools "if you have excellent grades." Several associates note that Wilmer, Cutler & Pickering gets "back to you quickly with an answer" on hiring decisions.

Clerks welcomed

Since Wilmer, Cutler & Pickering is a D.C.-based firm, many hires have done clerkships. One associate hired from a clerkship volunteers that his hiring process involved "one interview lasting about four hours, including lunch. A lot of people have clerked for federal appeals courts and we have around 35 former U.S. Supreme Court clerks here, and many former bigwigs from the government." "Wilmer, Cutler & Pickering has had a lot of recent success hiring Supreme Court clerks," concurs one insider, "and I believe the hiring process has become increasingly more competitive as a result." Lateral hires involve "an initial screening interview followed by a half day of interviews."

Wilmer, Cutler & Pickering's New York office is said to be similarly selective. "Wilmer, Cutler & Pickering's New York office is a small office that has had the luxury of cherry-picking its attorneys from an impressive list of candidates. The firm tends to screen candidates on two axes: traditional academic/clerkship credential and likeability/maturity/life experience. Failure to impress on either axis usually spells doom to an applicant's candidacy," notes one New York-based associate.

Lawyers seem to love the firm's summer program, which offers "lovely, interesting work, and not too much of it" as well as "great social events." While "summers are expected to do real work on real projects to find out how the firm works," "everyone encourages you to take two-hour lunches on the firm and attend all the summer functions." The "amazing sailing trip" comes in for special praise.

OUR SURVEY SAYS

Changes afoot

While most associates seem to enjoy their time at Wilmer Cutler, there's a sense of change in the air — and many aren't happy about it. One of the things associates grumble about is the recent growth at the firm. "Now that the firm has grown beyond 500 lawyers," intones one insider dramatically, "the firm suffers from a loss of humanity." Other insiders seem antsy about new hires at the partner level, especially "recent additions from the Clinton administration." "The firm has hired several former Supreme Court clerks and associates whom these new partners knew from the government," claims one associate, leading to a situation where "a clique has infected the firm." Other associates note that a new concentration on billables and larger cases has decreased the variety of work given to them. "The cases are getting bigger, with tons of document production," laments one associate.

At the same time, many associates say they've gotten interesting work merely by asking for it. States one new hire, "The firm does a lot of interesting work. I have had to do some document review but when I asked to get more challenging, interesting work the assigning partner responded immediately." The partners do seem open to input. "I have no qualms telling a senior partner I think he or she is wrong and having a vigorous and frank discussion of the issue presented. We are all colleagues here, not boxes on an organization chart," says one associate.

The firm is a work-minded but cordial place, say insiders. "People here are serious and focused on their work," says one D.C. associate. "We welcome the socially challenged," says another. "The work's the key, not schmoozing. It's OK to go home after work." Peers are said to be "very kind"; several insiders rush to say that "Wilmer has the reputation of being stuffy. It really isn't." Some associates cherish hearing of the olden days of D.C. political life from veteran and name partners. Office socialization seems civil and relatively frequent — one New Yorker reports "an extraordinary number of cake and champagne parties to celebrate the most minor events." Still, associates don't spend their entire existence at the firm. At this "laid-back, live-and-let-live place," "some of the younger lawyers hit happy hours or play basketball or poker together, but most folks head off to their own lives when the working day is over."

The hours: "As good as you could ever hope for"

Insiders rush to praise the firm for its "benign" hours. "The hours are very reasonable," commends one D.C. associate. "Projects with short deadlines do come up, but that's inevitable in a big law firm. But several times I've had partners tell me to go home when it was only 8:30 at night, which never would have happened in New York. The hours here are as good as you could ever hope for at a big firm." The hours in New York are said to be "perfectly sane" as well. While "the pressure to bill hours has increased somewhat over the last few years," the firm's leadership remains highly conscious of quality of life, and is said to be "understanding of family obligations and planned vacations."

Are there exceptions? Sure. Some associates say they "choose to work hard." Says one insider: "The most interesting assignments often come with heavy work demands." Choosing pro bono assignments can also pump up the hours. On the whole, though, say lawyers, "the partners generally manage their time well. It almost never happens that you get the Friday afternoon phone call and have to work all weekend. When we are asked to work late, there is very clearly a need for it, and usually the partners are there with us." Summarizes one D.C. associate, "I don't know of another law firm that's as reasonable as Wilmer in terms of its demands on associates."

Well-trained associates

The firm takes pains to make sure its associates are well-trained and well-supported, and Vault contacts express their appreciation for the firm's efforts. "The firm offers plenty of internal and external training opportunities, and participation is strongly encouraged. I find the training very helpful to my practice, especially because it involves an area with which I'm not very familiar." Another insider raves that "the training program is excellent. All incoming associates have weekly training sessions on a variety of topics for the first two to three months at the firm. There are separate writing workshops, negotiation workshops, and so on." Associates with prior legal experience tend to get less training — not that they mind necessarily. The firm "tends to hire associates who have done one or more clerkships or who have other interesting legal experience and then throws them into the water with little additional training," contends one lateral hire. The result? "Always exciting, usually beneficial and only occasionally frightening." Partners earn praise for "explaining things and leading you in the right direction to research new concepts."

Not quite top of the market

While Wilmer, Cutler & Pickering is doing most things right when it comes to training and scheduling, associates are far less lavish with their praise when it comes to cash. "Compensation is very good," says one associate, "but it's no longer at the top of the D.C. salary scale." (The firm states that only Williams & Connolly offers its D.C.-area associates higher compensation.) Another fellow Washingtonian is harsher. "[Wilmer] has several problems with compensation right now. It thinks it's above market compared to its peers, even though it's not. There is a holdback of salary that you don't get until the end of the year and only if you make the minimum billables that makes the monthly take home less." The firm also earns criticism for "dramatically increased employee contributions to health insurance." (The firm points out that, while co-payments for the PPO plan increased slightly, the employee costs for the HMO remained at zero.)

Other associates show more equanimity about their compensation. "The firm's compensation structure rewards people above market for reaching a relatively low number of billable hours — 1,850," maintains one associate, who also indicates that Wilmer, Cutler & Pickering "does not provide huge rewards for billing large numbers of hours." One philosopher shrugs: "I get paid an obscene amount of money to work here. If it is incrementally less or more obscene than other firms, I really don't care."

Go to the government or stick around

Wilmer, Cutler & Pickering has something of a revolving door when it comes to associates — and that's a good thing. "People leave and come back to Wilmer all the time," claims one insider. "The firm prides itself on allowing people to leave, go to the government and try out new things and come back if it doesn't work. It's very satisfying to know that it's an option." Note the important distinction between moving to a government position and going to another firm. It's "rare for people to leave for another firm," but apparently somewhat common to head out to a government position. For those not interested in a life working for Uncle Sam, Wilmer, Cutler & Pickering seems to be more of a destination rather than a stepping stone. "I haven't seen too many people leave since I started," says one mid-level associate. "Generally, I believe retention is above average." The situation is similar in New York. While the office is new, says one New Yorker, "it appears to have the same come-and-make-a-life-here feel of the D.C. office. The only people who tend to leave are the people who candidly indicated their intention to stay only for a short time."

Torn between two offices

While D.C. offices are "nice and comfortable," there just aren't enough of them. "The firm has outgrown its offices and is split between two buildings," complains one insider. "This is not a good situation." However, Wilmer, Cutler & Pickering is "looking for new offices and a move to bigger and better offices is expected." The office crunch means conference rooms are tough to come by, according to associates. The Georgetown location is generally liked; a "lot of people find it's easier to commute to this location." Offices themselves are "fairly spacious" if "plain." But if the firm's looking to save some money, it might consider divesting itself of its art collection. There's "plenty of expensive art that no one enjoys or even notices," sneers one insider, while another confides, "There is an extensive art collection all over the public areas that receives mixed reviews. Personally I think we could do without the art because no one really admires [it]." New York is said to be "functional," though "the décor is stuck in the 1980s."

Faboo pro bono

This firm doesn't just talk the pro bono talk, it walks the pro bono walk. Many pro bono projects are "groundbreaking in some way — Supreme Court cases or immigration cases. Right now the firm is defending the McCain-Feingold campaign finance regulations against constitutional challenges." The firm is "well connected within the pro bono network," and for those who choose to partake, the firm "counts 150 pro bono hours towards the billable hours requirement." The high value Wilmer, Cutler & Pickering puts on pro bono starts at the very top of the firm. "The two remaining founders of the firm, Mr. Cutler and Mr. Pickering, have referred to their pro bono work as the most important thing they have done and make it clear that that's a very important part of their legacy," praises one associate. Indeed, insiders say they are highly encouraged to undertake pro bono assignments. "We get told very often about our responsibility to the community, and how important pro bono work is." Most concur that "the firm is extremely committed on all levels" to pro bono work.

Doors open to everyone

Wilmer, Cutler & Pickering appears to be making a concerted effort to ensure that all of its associates, regardless of race or gender, are comfortable at the firm. Wilmer, Cutler & Pickering earns particular praise for its support of women lawyers. "In contrast to some of my previous work experiences, female attorneys are treated no differently from their male counterparts. If anything, the partners are very concerned with how we are treated by clients — and try to make sure that we don't have to deal with a client's sexist attitudes." The firm has "an emergency day care center and good female role models." One new associate recounts, "In my first week, two female partners in my group took all the new female associates out for lunch and offered themselves as friends and sounding boards. Our class is about 50-50 male-female. I've seen male and female associates and partners with their children at the office from time to time." The firm is so woman-friendly that one male associate jokes, "Women are so well-represented that there are periodic grumblings by guys that the place is too pro-woman."

Wilmer, Cutler & Pickering is plugging away at the issue of minority representation as well. The firm is said to be "very welcoming to minorities," though one Asian associate says, "I don't know of any specific programs designed for minority development." Another minority associate is less pleased with the firm's efforts. "Although the firm deserves credit for hiring a good number of minorities, there is very little done to help minorities once they are within the firm. Few minority partners make an effort to reach out to minority associates or to monitor the professional development of minority associates," claims that associate. Still, says another insider, "there is a new diversity committee" being formed to address these issues.

As for gays and lesbians, the firm is said to be downright hospitable. "There are many gay lawyers here, and there seems to be absolutely no problem. The firm recently helped one partner who is gay adopt a child with his life partner," states one associate. A New York-based lawyer confirms: "There are multiple gay and lesbian lawyers in this small office, and they seem comfortable in this environment."

Sidley Austin Brown & Wood LLP

Bank One Plaza
10 South Dearborn Street
Chicago, IL 60603
Phone: (312) 853-7000

787 Seventh Avenue
New York, NY 10019
Phone: (212) 839-5300
www.sidley.com

LOCATIONS

Chicago, IL • Dallas, TX • Los Angeles, CA • New York, NY • San Francisco, CA • Washington, DC • Beijing • Geneva • Hong Kong • London • Shanghai Singapore • Tokyo

MAJOR DEPARTMENTS/PRACTICES

Bankruptcy • Business & Banking Transactions • Corporate/Securities • Employee Benefits • Employment & Labor • Environmental • Intellectual Property • Litigation • Real Estate • Tax • Trusts & Estates

THE STATS

No of attorneys: 1,431
No. of offices: 13
Summer associate offers: 181 out of 189 (2001)
Managing Partners: Tom Cole, Chuck Douglas and Tom Smith
Hiring Partner: John Levi

BASE SALARY

All domestic offices, 2002*
1st year: $125,000
2nd year: $135,000
3rd year: $150,000
4th year: $165,000
5th year: Up to $185,000
6th year: Up to $195,000
7th year: Up to $205,000
8th year: Up to $210,000
Summer associate: $2,400/week
*Associate salaries in the New York office range $5,000–$10,000 higher.

NOTABLE PERKS

• New gym with satellite TV (DC)
• Cheap movie tickets
• Three months paid maternity leave

THE BUZZ
WHAT ATTORNEYS AT OTHER FIRMS ARE SAYING ABOUT THIS FIRM

• "Great Supreme Court work"
• "First-rate Wall Street practice"
• "Pigeonholes associates into one particular transaction"
• "Good merger — Brown & Wood married up"

UPPERS

- Terrific brand-new offices (DC)
- Prestigious securities practice
- Quick and impressive recovery after September 11 disaster

DOWNERS

- Continuing culture clashes
- Bonus disgruntlement
- Exasperating bureaucratic obstacles

EMPLOYMENT CONTACT

Chicago
Ms. Jennifer C. Hernandez
Recruiting Manager
Phone: (312) 853-7495
Fax: (312) 853-7036
jherna01@sidley.com

New York
Ms. Shana Kassoff
Recruiting Manager
Phone: (212) 839-8600
Fax: (212) 839-5599
skassoff@sidley.com

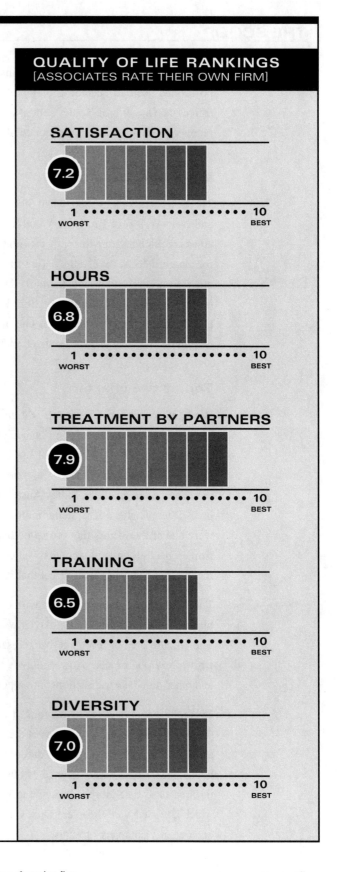

QUALITY OF LIFE RANKINGS
[ASSOCIATES RATE THEIR OWN FIRM]

SATISFACTION
7.2
1 WORST — 10 BEST

HOURS
6.8
1 WORST — 10 BEST

TREATMENT BY PARTNERS
7.9
1 WORST — 10 BEST

TRAINING
6.5
1 WORST — 10 BEST

DIVERSITY
7.0
1 WORST — 10 BEST

THE SCOOP

Although still feeling the growing pains of its 2001 merger, Sidley Austin Brown & Wood has positioned itself to become a major player in New York and Chicago. When Sidley's former offices at One World Trade Center were destroyed on September 11, the firm made a rapid recovery, moving into permanent new digs in 2002.

Whirlwind courtship

The firm dates back to 1866, when Sidley & Austin was founded in Chicago. Both Sidley & Austin and New York firm Brown & Wood had carved comfortable niches for themselves, but in some areas lacked the stature to compete with the very top firms. Separately, each firm had been longing for a partner for several years before finding each other. Each began promising relationships with other firms, only to watch them fizzle. It wasn't until a consultant employed by both firms introduced them that everything clicked. Firm managers first met in October 2000 to discuss the possibility of a merger, and by the end of the year they were already sure they wanted to complete the union. The merger was finalized in May 2001.

Top of the charts

While other firms may have suffered during the slump of 2001, Sidley's securities practice had a banner year. When Thompson Financial released its legal league tables at the start of 2002, it was Sidley that topped the list as No.1 legal advisor for debt, equity and other transactions. The firm also placed in the top 10 in several other categories. And in *The American Lawyer*'s 2001 survey of top corporate practices, Sidley Austin Brown & Wood ranked second overall with top 10 listings in 13 different categories. Stellar multi-billion-dollar deals with Morgan Stanley and Merrill Lynch were one of the factors that propelled the firm to the top. But the success was largely due to the firm's tenacious pursuit of clients — it completed more than 1,000 deals — than its ability to attract the big spenders from Wall Street that gave them the edge over competing firms.

The firm has had modest success with corporate clients, although it's not considered a big-league player on the level with firms like Cravath, Swaine & Moore or Wachtell, Lipton, Rosen & Katz. The obscure area of mortgage-backed securities is another financial area in which Sidley Austin Brown & Wood excels. Now, Sidley is looking to parlay its success with mortgage-backed deals and other mundane transactions into a position of strength — brokering large-scale M&A deals.

On the litigation side, the firm ranked third in *The National Law Journal*'s 2001 Who Defends Corporate America survey. Some of the nervous accountants at Andersen have called on SAB&W, among other firms, to assist in its defense against charges that the company helped Enron cook their books. (Andersen was convicted of obstruction of justice in June 2002.) There's another Enron-inspired case on Sidley's docket: the firm is also representing the General Accounting Office, which has sued Vice President Dick Cheney for access to records of his meetings with Enron and other energy company officials.

Supreme justice

Making history comes as naturally to some firms as taking a deposition. In what may be the first instance of a father and sons arguing before the U.S. Supreme Court, Sidley associate Michael Lee went before the court on behalf of the state of Utah. Lee and his brother Thomas, a Brigham Young University law professor, along with prominent D.C. partners Carter Phillips and Gene Schaerr, argued in March 2002 that Mormon missionaries who were out of the country at the time of the Census should be counted. (Their father, Rex Lee, was the former Solicitor General and a Sidley partner and argued many cases before the court.) If the court sides with Sidley, Utah will gain another seat in the House of Representatives, resulting in the loss of a seat for North Carolina. The highly anticipated Utah case comes on the heels of another victory in the high court. A January 2002 6-2 decision in favor of Sidley's client, the National Cable & Telecommunications Association, is expected to lead to major changes in the way Internet services are delivered to consumers.

D.C. litigation partner George Jones has been named to one of the most prestigious positions of the Beltway legal community. Jones, whose practice handles a variety of corporate cases, including product liability and bankruptcy, was voted in for a three-year term on the board of the D.C. Bar. Jones, who began his term as president-elect in June 2001, will then become president of the legal association in 2002, and serve the final year of his term as immediate past president.

Trying times

Even law firms sometimes run into difficulties when interpreting the law. The Equal Employment Opportunity Commission has launched an ongoing investigation of the firm. According to the agency, Sidley & Austin may have violated the Age Discrimination in Employment Act prior to the merger because it lowered its expectation for partners to retire from 65 to a range between 60 and 65. Sources also alerted the agency after Sidley & Austin demoted 32 partners to senior counsel and of counsel in 1999 that more than half the demotions may have been based on the age of the partners. Generally, partners would not be subject to such scrutiny by the EEOC, but the agency says the partners in question are really employees because they have no voting power in the firm. A district court judge ordered Sidley Austin Brown & Wood to turn over documents about the partnership to the EEOC, but the firm is appealing the ruling.

With the completion of the merger, Sidley had succeeded in attracting the attention of the national legal community. But a few months later, the firm found itself receiving attention for reasons it never imagined. The New York office of the new firm resided in One World Trade Center, taking up most of the space on the 54th to 59th floors. When those offices, along with those of many other companies, were destroyed in the September 11th terrorist attacks, the firm was placed in the unenviable position of having to quickly set up temporary offices and reconstruct paper and electronic files for its many clients. Incredibly, only one employee (switchboard operator Rosemary Smith) out of the office's 600 attorneys and staff failed to make it out of the building safely.

New moves

In spite of their losses, Sidley Austin Brown & Wood has made a rapid recovery. In December 2001, the firm found a permanent space in the Equitable building in Manhattan and announced plans to move into the new space in 2002. That same month, Nancy Karen, the firm's chief information officer, was named a Chief of the Year by *InformationWeek* magazine. Karen's infrastructure and data recovery plan had the firm up and running less than a week after the attacks.

Moving and expansion were a theme for the firm in 2001 and early 2002. New office space near the White House was leased in August 2001 for the Washington, D.C. attorneys and staff. At 190,000 square feet, the D.C. digs have room for the current 395 attorneys and staff, plus room for more as the firm grows. The firm expanded its practice focused on Korean business in November 2001 by adding attorneys to its Hong Kong and New York offices. And in May 2002 a 33-lawyer group specializing in international trade law, policy and WTO dispute resolution joined the firm. There was even talk that the firm was in negotiations for yet another merger—this time with a Munich-based firm. So far, no agreement has been reached.

GETTING HIRED

Sidley Austin Brown & Wood recruits associates from top schools around the country. "The on-campus interview is conducted by two attorneys in half-hour segments," explains a fifth-year associate in Chicago. If you make the grade in the initial on-campus interview, you'll be invited to Sidley's office for a full day of interviews. This same source says, "The callbacks are fairly intensive, consisting of six or seven half-hour interviews and lunch with two associates." The firm notes that callback interviews vary by office and says candidates will typically meet with several attorneys and may dine with a couple of junior associates.

"I'm not sure what we're looking for after the merger" in terms of candidates, a second-year admits. Colleagues say the firm's current outlook on hiring remains unclear. "It was not easy to be hired by Sidley New York, but who knows how hard it will be to be hired by the combined firm," says a sixth-year associate. Notes another, "At Brown & Wood they hired good people. They didn't care where they went to school — if you were smart and worked hard, you were hired. Sidley only likes to look at top-tier schools."

Associates highly recommend Sidley's summer program. "Summer associates are not simply resigned to research and writing memos." "Everyone knows they're going to get an offer, so there's no pressure at all" to be a star performer, remarks a litigator. According to the firm, it is not unusual in most years for a few summer associates to not receive an offer. However, the majority do. It's not nearly as easy for lateral hires. But for those who meet expectations, offers are often made "on the spot" or within hours of the interviews.

OUR SURVEY SAYS

The many moods of Sidley

Sidley is many things to many associates; it all just depends on whom you ask. Although the merger of Sidley & Austin and Brown & Wood is more than a year old, associates say, "the firm culture remains quite schizoid." "Working for the merged firm has become like working for a large corporation or government bureaucracy," a mid-level associate confides, because "there are now all sorts of approvals one needs to get to undertake some of the most simple tasks. For every action there is at least one form to fill out." Some blame the problems on a now-fragmented culture. "The firm seems to lack overall direction, and there are definitely two competing cultures at play in the New York office. In addition, communication between management and associates is not very good," says a corporate attorney. One miffed associate had this to say: "The people from Brown & Wood are great — very eager to integrate you into their practice, good mentors to junior lawyers, actually friendly. Can't say the same about the Sidley people in D.C. They are more prima donnas. And if you weren't a Supreme Court clerk, you're not even worth saying 'hello' to in the hallways and elevators."

Still, there are plenty of associates who would consider their peers' opinions exaggerated. "Attorneys are very respectful of each other and willing to help each other at a moment's notice," says a junior associate. According to an attorney in the D.C. office, "The atmosphere is generally more laid back and there is an emphasis on life outside of the office as time permits. There is a Midwestern feel to the office, which is unusual in D.C." "Sidley is as kind, gentle and civil as a large firm can be," says a Chicago associate.

Others say the firm culture is just fine, but express dissatisfaction with the job itself. "If you enjoy working long hours performing tedious and repetitive work and are not interested in ever participating in any trials or appearing in court, this is the job for you," says a fifth-year. "The people are great, but the work can be boring and repetitive. The variety is lacking," a third-year informs us. Other associates enjoy the professional experience at Sidley. "The work is surprisingly substantive and challenging," says a third year.

For the love of money

"While salaries are top level, the New York office clearly paid below market bonuses," a corporate associate gripes. A colleague echoes this frustration: "The bonus situation is a constant source of tension between management and associates." "Brown & Wood was considered a lifestyle firm, and our compensation was generally under market. However, we are no longer a lifestyle firm, and compensation remains low," according to a New York attorney. Associates say they received low bonuses in 2001 because of the losses the firm suffered in the September 11th attack. However, some say that the low bonuses given do "not reconcile with the insurance settlement touted."

One $200,000-a-year attorney beseeches his colleagues, "Stop complaining about money, already! Sure, the firm can't decide sometimes if it wants to pay top dollar for top hours or not, but we're hardly starving here." Then there are those who consider the lower pay a fair tradeoff, saying, "Some other New York firms pay more, but they are much more demanding places to work." A fifth-year associate who thinks the firm is perceived as paying less than it actually does says the firm should be tooting its own horn more. "Sidley pays top of the market in Chicago."

Hours: a numbers game

As is typical at many firms, "the hours worked differ greatly" among the various Sidley practice groups. Flexibility seems to be a hallmark, with a number of associates feeling that "everyone at Sidley is very respectful of my time." "I arrive at and leave the office at virtually the same time every day. I make every effort to get all of my work done during that time," says one senior associate. Some sources report taking advantage of a remote connection to the office for getting work done at home. Another associate shares that she has "been extremely successful keeping my at-work hours between 9:30 a.m. and 5 p.m. and doing some additional work at home at night and on weekends." The firm's part-time program is "great for family-oriented people." While "the firm tries to be very accommodating to lawyers who want to work part-time," a sixth-year warns that associates "who expect to work only a certain set number of days per week often are disappointed" because the nature of the work can't be restricted to a regular schedule.

"I guess when compared to Cravath or Skadden, the combined Sidley Austin Brown & Wood is a lifestyle firm. But compared to the old Brown & Wood, where lifestyle still meant something, the new firm" doesn't compete, grumbles a litigator. Lawyers who spend more time at the office than they'd like say the hours are "very inconsistent" and that the workload could be managed more efficiently. An attorney in the New York office believes that "the number of manufactured crises created by the work style at the firm has made the word 'emergency' meaningless." The inconsistent hours mean that "in between busy times, it is hard to bill a respectable number of hours in the day." This can cause high levels of frustration, says a junior associate, because "there is pressure to hit 2,000 hours." A third-year describes this pressure as "palpable," adding, "Many are rumored to have been let go for 'performance' reasons for not billing an acceptable" number of hours. The firm, though, tells us that this is not the case.

A philosophical eighth-year sums up the reality of big-firm hours: "Show me a large firm where people are totally happy with their hours, and I'll show you a firm that hasn't been invented yet."

Retention: high, but why?

When it comes to retention, Sidley can happily report that its attorneys are going nowhere fast. A D.C. attorney considers the firm's attitude toward retention to be "one of the best attributes of the firm." This lawyer adds, "The firm's goal when one is hired is to retain that person throughout his or her entire career." "Retention over the last year has been extremely high; over the last five years, it has been significantly above that of comparable firms," a Chicago associate offers. Others say that "attorneys tend to stay here for their entire careers."

While most agree that retention at Sidley is high, there are varying opinions as to why. A few are of the mind that "people just don't leave this firm," but most seem to believe the slow economy is a major factor in the low number of defections. "Almost no one is leaving. I strongly suspect that this is due to the economic environment," says a seventh-year. Overall, it's hard to tell how many attorneys have left the firm "because there's no firm-wide process to announce that someone is leaving."

That doesn't mean everyone's staying put. "People leave because they find better work elsewhere and those places pay a good deal more. Can you blame them?" asks a first-year. "Uncertainty post-merger and perceived cheapness regarding compensation are major factors." Although concerns about the firm's direction and the hard feelings many express about bonuses may be spurring some to move on, few associates blame their colleagues' departures on negative feelings about the firm. "It is usually not due to the desire to practice at another firm." Teaching posts at prestigious law schools and positions with high-profile government agencies are cited as reasons attorneys leave Sidley. "Personal reasons — marriage, baby or relocation" — are also common explanations.

Moving day

When it comes to office space, attorneys in D.C. are a pretty happy bunch. "We just moved into a gorgeous new building with a great cafeteria and gym," raves a first-year associate. The new building features "all new amenities and a killer atrium," and is "quite impressive, especially if you ever saw our last offices," says a third-year. The strongest complaints center on the furniture, which one lawyer describes as "70-ish looking — in style, not necessarily age. Desks and bookcases are not real wood." Attorneys in Chicago and LA say they can't complain much. Chicago associates have "serviceable, but not particularly flashy" offices and "everyone has his/her own office." In LA, associates have "beautiful, bright offices," "but the individual office setups are sub par."

Naturally, the office situation in New York, between the World Trade Center collapse and the move to new permanent space, has left a lot to be desired. "Former Sidley folks remain in singles, while former World Trade Center Brown & Wood people are squashed into temp space." (Former Brown & Wood associates were temporarily moved into Sidley & Austin's building after the World Trade Center was destroyed.) While the New York attorneys grumble quite a bit about "the cramped, crappy, character-less temporary office space that we currently occupy," many are optimistic about the new offices they'll occupy come summer 2002. A sixth-year looks at it this way: "The firm has done the best it could do with a bad situation."

Debevoise & Plimpton

919 Third Avenue
New York, NY 10022
Phone: (212) 909-6000
www.debevoise.com

LOCATIONS

New York, NY (HQ)
Washington, DC
Frankfurt
Hong Kong
London
Moscow
Paris

MAJOR DEPARTMENTS/PRACTICES

Corporate
Litigation
Tax
Trusts & Estates

THE STATS

No. of attorneys: 521
No. of offices: 7
Summer associate offers: 93 out 93 (2001)
Presiding Partner: Martin Frederic Evans
Hiring Partner: Michael J. Gillespie

BASE SALARY

New York and Washington, DC, 2001
1st year: $125,000
2nd year: $135,000
3rd year: $150,000
4th year: $170,000
5th year: $190,000
6th year: $205,000
7th year: $220,000
8th year: $235,000
Summer associate: $2,400/week

NOTABLE PERKS

- Car service after 8 p.m.
- Discount memberships at Equinox gym
- Biweekly lawyers' tea with food and drinks
- Krispy Kreme doughnuts and Starbucks coffee

THE BUZZ
WHAT ATTORNEYS AT OTHER FIRMS ARE SAYING ABOUT THIS FIRM

- "Not the highest prestige in NY but a nicer place to work"
- "Smart, geeky"
- "Solid internationally"
- "Artsy types who work on toxic torts"

UPPERS

- Impressive pro bono commitment
- Respectful and civil corporate culture
- First-rate M&A practice

DOWNERS

- "I just want to go home"
- Associates share offices for too long
- Uneven support services

EMPLOYMENT CONTACT

Ms. Ethel F. Leichti
Manager of Associate Recruitment
Phone: (212) 909-6657
Fax: (212) 909-6836
recruit@debevoise.com

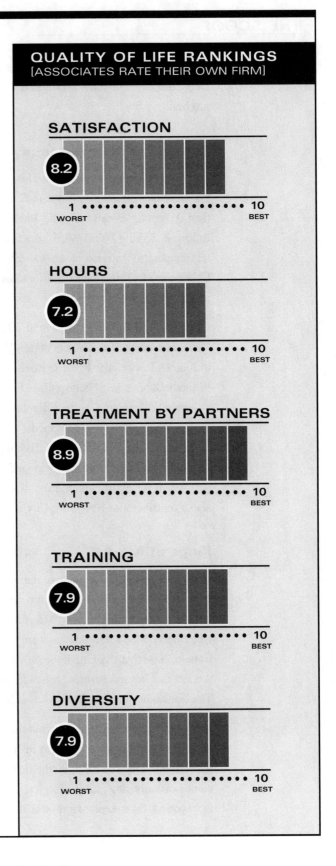

QUALITY OF LIFE RANKINGS
[ASSOCIATES RATE THEIR OWN FIRM]

SATISFACTION

8.2

1 WORST •••••••••••••••••••• 10 BEST

HOURS

7.2

1 WORST •••••••••••••••••••• 10 BEST

TREATMENT BY PARTNERS

8.9

1 WORST •••••••••••••••••••• 10 BEST

TRAINING

7.9

1 WORST •••••••••••••••••••• 10 BEST

DIVERSITY

7.9

1 WORST •••••••••••••••••••• 10 BEST

THE SCOOP

Although its name has changed several times, a few things that have remained constant are Debevoise & Plimpton's prestigious corporate and litigation departments and its commitment to pro bono service.

Brushes with greatness

The firm was founded in 1931 as Debevoise & Stevenson when Eli Whitney Debevoise convinced Oxford-educated attorney William E. Stevenson to go into practice with him. Early success with then-illustrious clients such as Phelps Dodge Corporation and Consolidated Coal Company followed. During World War II, the firm faced its first major crisis when a number of its attorneys left temporarily to assist in the war effort. Merging with Hatch, McLean, Root and Hinch solved Debevoise & Plimpton's problem, as the other firm was experiencing a similar wartime personnel shortage.

Debevoise & Plimpton has several connections to historical and well-known figures. Founder Debevoise was a descendant of cotton gin inventor Eli Whitney. Debevoise's father was an advisor to John D. Rockefeller Jr. (The Rockefeller Foundation now houses the professional papers of Eli Whitney Debevoise.) Name partner Francis T.P. Plimpton was the father of writer, editor, actor and all-around dilettante George Plimpton. At the 1924 Olympic Games, founder and former name partner Stevenson won a gold medal for the U.S. in 1,600-meter relay. That's not the firm's only tie to the games. Partner David Rivkin pursued his Olympic dream in Salt Lake City in 2002 — but not as an athlete. Rivkin was one of two Americans to serve on the nine-member Court of Arbitration for Sport, which decided all legal disputes arising from the competition. The firm is also a contributor to New York City's committee to bring the 2012 Olympics to the Big Apple.

Kings of M&A

With 51 deals, Debevoise was the seventh-ranked legal adviser for M&A deals in 2001, as compiled by web site TheDeal.com. SNL Securities ranked the firm first in both deal value and number of deals for insurance M&A transactions with a U.S. party announced in 2001. At a time when fewer M&A transactions were being completed, the value of Debevoise's 2001 deals rose from its 2000 total, making it the only top-10 firm to show an increase over the previous year. No wonder that several partners got together to pen *Takeovers*, a guide to constructing M&A deals. The lead author on the tome? Meredith Brown, an M&A partner at Debevoise.

Summer 2001 was an especially hot time for Debevoise attorneys in M&A. Montreal-based paper maker Dotmar called on the firm in June 2001 to close its $1.65 billion acquisition of four U.S. paper mills. That same month, the firm signed on as legal to counsel Merrill Lynch. The financial giant was advising pharmaceutical firm Alza Corp on a potential acquisition and needed Debevoise's legal expertise to seal the deal. In July 2001, the firm represented England-based software maker Misys during its purchase of an Arizona data management company. Provident Mutual Life Insurance turned to Debevoise for advice during its acquisition by Nationwide Financial Services in August 2001.

Are you insured?

Insurers not only look to Debevoise as corporate attorneys who can close big deals, but also as litigators who defend them in liability and discrimination cases. Debevoise has counseled MetLife Insurance for several years and is defending the insurer from a suit alleging that the company systematically denied proper coverage to African-American clients. The firm has had some success in this arena before: in August 2000, Debevoise settled a similar case for American General Life and Accident Insurance Company. The firm's reputation in the insurance industry likely influenced Principal Financial Group to tap Debevoise as advisor on the company's October 2001 IPO. Tom Kelly, co-chair of the firm's insurance industry practice, was one of 10 attorneys named as a Dealmaker of the Year in the April 2002 issue of *The American Lawyer*.

Prominent prosecutor rejoins firm

Former U.S. Attorney Mary Jo White, one of the nation's leading prosecutors, has returned to Debevoise to head its litigation department. White had been a partner at the firm for several years before she led the U.S. Attorney's office in Manhattan. During her nearly nine-year tenure, White prosecuted high-profile organized crime, racketeering and terrorism cases, including the trial of those responsible for the 1993 bombing of the World Trade Center. Back at Debevoise, her practice will concentrate on white-collar crime.

In addition to the firm's work in the insurance industry, international arbitration is a large component of the firm's litigation practice. Other major areas within the firm's litigation department include antitrust, bankruptcy, intellectual property and media, product liability and white-collar crime. Some of the firm's other gold-plated clients include Global Crossing, American Airlines, Compaq Computer, Goldman Sachs, Lever Brothers, the National Football League, Owens Corning, Oxygen Media and John Hancock Mutual Life Insurance.

They can't all be winners

Debevoise found itself involved in one of the biggest media cases of 2001. It didn't involve a sale or an IPO, but generated a great deal of attention because of its potential to change copyright law in the Internet and database worlds. Together with Prof. Laurence Tribe, Debevoise acted as outside counsel for *The New York Times*, *Time* and *Newsday* in June 2001 when N.Y. Times Co., et al. v. Tasini went to the Supreme Court. Unfortunately, the case didn't go Debevoise's way. The high court ruled that when publishers put their print editions into online or electronic formats, the Copyright Act does not authorize them to include freelancers' contributions without separate permission from (and, presumably, compensation for) the writers. The case was remanded to the district court for further proceedings.

The tobacco cash cow

Long-standing suits between consumers and big tobacco firms have kept many prestigious firms busy for years, and Debevoise is no different. The firm has served as counsel on a number of cases for the Council for Tobacco Research USA, a group that provides research in support of tobacco firms.

The softer side of Debevoise

Working on the cases that don't bring financial rewards or make headlines is just as much a part of life at Debevoise as closing big deals. Some of the firm's pro bono clients include the Song Tsen Tibetan Community Outreach group, an organization that helps Tibetan political refugees, and a group of minority citizens who have filed a complaint against the New York City Police Department, alleging the force unfairly profiles suspects based on race. The firm also successfully litigated a case on behalf of a class of mentally ill inmates in New York City in which a trial court judge ordered the city to begin "discharge planning" for these inmates.

The firm strives to cultivate an interest in, and a commitment to, pro bono work in all attorneys at the firm. Each year, some of the New York summer associates are allowed to spend a few weeks working at a legal services organization. And all new litigators are required to work on a pro bono case as one of their initial assignments. Individual attorneys have also won awards from community organizations for working on behalf of the mentally ill and abused women.

As a wave of layoffs sloshed over firms on both coasts in 2001 and 2002, attorneys and law students took notice of Debevoise's bold announcement that it would not lay off associates. As of June 2002, the firm has kept that promise. Debevoise's outreach efforts includes comrades in need. After the September 11th attacks, Debevoise provided temporary office space to 75 displaced attorneys from Cleary, Gottlieb, Steen & Hamilton.

GETTING HIRED

Associates say the summer experience at Debevoise is unparalleled. Summering at the firm is "fun but not indulgent," and some say the firm manages to provide "a pretty close approximation to actual working life." There are the requisite social events featuring well-stocked buffets, but the firm also emphasizes opportunities to learn new skills such as taking depositions or developing negotiation abilities.

But be warned: When selecting law students for the summer associate class, management is "very picky." To even score an interview, candidates must boast stellar grades. From there, personality and fit are the dominating criteria. "Many law review students from elite schools have been rejected," confides a first-year associate, because they were not viewed as a good fit for the firm. "Particularly in this uncertain economy, I think it has gotten a lot more difficult to get hired here than it once was, and it wasn't very easy to start out with," says a litigation attorney.

Newly hired associates are generally given the option of choosing which practice group they'd like to work with. Those who are undecided can rotate through departments for about a year before making a final decision. Some associates inform us that the firm has been known to send associates on overseas assignments that can last from a few months to two to three years.

OUR SURVEY SAYS

Pleasantville

Debevoise is "more academic and less hierarchical than other peer New York firms," says a second-year associate. Colleagues describe the firm as being "friendly and generally laid back," but say Debevoisians tend to be a less boisterous group than attorneys at other firms. "People here tend to be quiet, intelligent, funny and frequently quirky. People are quite friendly and socialize somewhat during the business day, but there is relatively little socializing outside the office," according to an associate in the tax department. "The lawyers are very friendly in a quiet, laid-back way," says another attorney. "You have a good feeling about coming to work each day to be around people who are as warm and funny as they are smart and accomplished."

In general, "younger lawyers tend to have lunch together frequently and occasionally socialize after work," says a D.C. associate. But on a whole, don't expect to find a very active social scene at this "family-oriented" firm. "There is generally not a lot of socializing among lawyers outside of the firm's biweekly lawyers' tea." Associates say they're fine with that, because "most people have families they want to get home to, so they are never here if they don't need to be."

Early responsibility is an aspect of life at Debevoise & Plimpton that the attorneys enjoy. "I have had the opportunity to work on important deals that were featured in the news often and, more importantly, interact closely with the partners and senior associates," boasts one junior associate. Another first-year lawyer reports being pleased that "since the first week, I have been given significant responsibility in a supportive and reasonably laid-back environment." Of course, there's usually a downside to every good thing. "The work is interesting, but there's too much of it," says one tired senior associate.

Big pay, no big deal

Associate are content, if somewhat blasé, about their vast salaries since, "like all other big firms, we match what everyone else is paying. No more, no less." Attorneys are a bit more animated when it comes to the firm's bonus structure. A few associates note that bonuses are not tied to billable hours. Says one, "I am happy that bonuses and raises are not based on billable hours since we associates have little control over how much work the firm has at any given time versus the number of associates who are available."

"Compensation is high. However there is a sense that the firm is a follower rather than a leader in salary increases among its peer group," confides a third-year associate. A colleague agrees that "D&P always does what it takes to be competitive with all the big firms — they just do it last." This attorney adds that she is not complaining because "I think we're all overpaid." Not everyone would agree with that assessment. "I am being paid market-rate compensation, but for the number of hours we put in, I feel it's too low," says one attorney who earns $190,000 a year.

No screamers

Associates think highly of the partners at Debevoise. The "partners are fairly approachable and very nurturing," says a bankruptcy attorney. In fact the firm is the very essence of civility. "No one really yells or is rude or hostile." "Partners seem to treat associates very much as colleagues rather than as employees," says a lawyer in the trusts and estates department. A colleague echoes this sentiment: "Most partners I work with make a real effort to ask for the input and judgment of associates and try to get them involved in the strategy of the case as well as the more mundane tasks."

While outright abuse is infrequent, some associates see a "frustrating 'indirectness' at the core of the firm culture that engenders a psychological and emotional distance between partners and associates that can drive more senior associates literally crazy if they take it too seriously." Even though most of the partners receive high marks, "there are a few who bring the curve down with the complete inability to socialize and speak with young people in an intelligent manner."

Hours: all over the map

The amount of time that associates at Debevoise & Plimpton spend in the office varies widely. "I tend to work more than I would like; however, it varies quite a bit, and I have a reasonable amount of control over how busy I am," shares a litigator. "In M&A, hours generally tend to be very volatile, so there are times when you work long nights and weekends." This contact downplays the weekend work: "I rarely lose a whole weekend, and usually I lose only one or half a day." "My hours are high," says an eighth-year associate, "but I enjoy the work and find that I perform better and learn more when I am very busy. I'd much rather be busy than not." The firm's part-time program has provided some of these hard workers with extra flexibility. "There are weeks when I get no sleep, and I work from home a lot, but I almost never have to come in on the days when I am not supposed to work, including weekends," says one part-timer. Another part-timer reports sometimes having to work a full week but sighs, "It's required at a firm like this." Part-time associates commit to working a certain number of hours a year and are paid extra if they exceed their annual commitment.

"My work has been somewhat slow as of late, but I still feel like I'm expected to be here for 'appearance's sake,'" says a member of the not-so-busy camp. "I work hard when necessary but feel no pressure to work long hours if there is no client emergency. I have the impression that other associates might work more than me, but I really do not care, because I know that I and my work are very appreciated by the partners I work for," reports a fifth-year associate, who, on average, bills 150 to 175 hours a month.

Little retention tension

"D&P seems to do better than most of its peers in New York City" when it comes to retaining attorneys. "The retention problem is more of a lifestyle problem that is shared by all big New York firms" than an issue that affects Debevoise specifically. It's not uncommon to hear of major law firms that ask associates to leave after deciding they're not partner material. But Debevoise associates say, "If you make it past year four or five, you're very likely to stick around at least until you've been told you won't make partner, or are asked to leave." The firm has had retention committees in the past. "Three years ago, a retention committee was formed in response to the feeling that a lot more associates than usual were leaving," confides a fifth-year associate. This source adds, "I think that the committee was recently dissolved." According to the firm, the committee wasn't dissolved but its roles and responsibilities were merged with the liaison committee, which addresses concerns of associates and counsel.

New digs

Debevoise's New York associates have happily settled into their new offices — well, some of them are happy, anyway. The new offices have "more space, a large and welcoming cafeteria with delicious food and larger conference rooms," says a junior associate. "The new offices are bright, comfortable, very tasteful and incredibly functional, including lots of high-tech improvements over the old offices." However some feel they lack a certain "'Davis Polk-like splendor." A labor attorney elaborates: "Our new offices are functional but do not reflect our firm's reputation and caliber. I feel that the décor could be much more luxurious." Another widely heard complaint: "Associates are asked to share offices for too long and do not get a single office with a window until at least their third year." The firm's D.C. office, where "even paralegals have their own offices," are "great."

Gibson, Dunn & Crutcher LLP

333 South Grand Avenue
Los Angeles, CA 90071-3197
Phone: (213) 229-7000
www.gibsondunn.com

LOCATIONS

Los Angeles, CA (HQ)
Century City, CA
Dallas, TX
Denver, CO
Irvine, CA
New York, NY
Palo Alto, CA
San Francisco, CA
Washington, DC
London
Munich
Paris

MAJOR DEPARTMENTS/PRACTICES

Antitrust
Appellate
Corporations
Entertainment/Media
Environmental
Labor
Litigation
Real Estate
Tax/Probate

THE STATS

No. of attorneys: 750
No. of offices: 12
Summer associate offers: 165 out of 174 (2001)
Chairman: Kenneth M. Doren
Chairman, Hiring Committee: Kevin S. Rosen

 ## THE BUZZ
WHAT ATTORNEYS AT OTHER FIRMS ARE SAYING ABOUT THIS FIRM

- "Best West Coast firm"
- "Not as prestigious as they think they are"
- "Excellent SEC practice"
- "Republican stronghold"
- "Man, can these guys bill"

BASE SALARY

All domestic offices, 2002
1st year: $125,000
2nd year: $135,000
3rd year: $150,000
4th year: $165,000 ($170,000 - NY)
5th year: $185,000 ($190,000 - NY)
6th year: $195,000 ($205,000 - NY)
7th year: $205,000 ($220,000 - NY)
8th year: $210,000 ($235,000 - NY)
Summer associate: $2,404/week

NOTABLE PERKS

- Retreats at lavish resorts
- $1,000 per associate for "client development," "which is to be used to entertain friends"
- Blackberries for all associates
- Firm pays when associates take new associates to lunch

UPPERS

- Prestigious litigation and M&A departments
- Helpful telecommuting technology
- Free market assignment policy means work flexibility

DOWNERS

- Bonus disgruntlement
- Billable hours pressure despite less work to go around
- Few female or minority partners

EMPLOYMENT CONTACT

Ms. Leslie Ripley
Director, Professional Development & Recruiting
Phone: (213) 229-7273
Fax: (213) 229-7520
lripley@gibsondunn.com

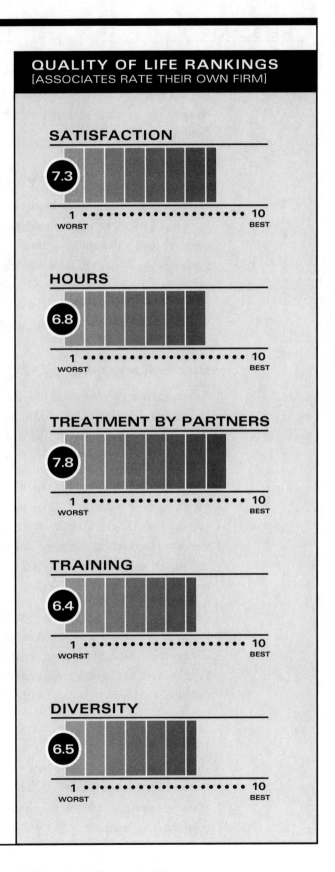

QUALITY OF LIFE RANKINGS
[ASSOCIATES RATE THEIR OWN FIRM]

SATISFACTION

7.3

1 WORST   10 BEST

HOURS

6.8

1 WORST   10 BEST

TREATMENT BY PARTNERS

7.8

1 WORST   10 BEST

TRAINING

6.4

1 WORST   10 BEST

DIVERSITY

6.5

1 WORST   10 BEST

THE SCOOP

Founded in 1890 in Los Angeles, Gibson, Dunn & Crutcher is one of LA's "Big Three." The firm has a prestigious litigation and M&A practice, but it may be most infamous for hiring the top Stanford law graduate as a legal secretary in 1952. That grad was U.S. Supreme Court Justice Sandra Day O'Connor.

History: same old story, unique response

Unlike similar firms, Gibson has had a labor practice since the 1930s. Since 1967, the firm has been a player on the international stage. In the early 1990s, California firms suffered as the economy took a downturn. Gibson wasn't immune to this dip. However, it was unique in its response. Unlike other firms, it didn't lay off associates. Instead, Gibson closed its smaller offices in San Jose, Brussels, Moscow and Seattle. The economic boom of 1999–2000 saw the firm both closing an office in San Diego and expanding its London and Paris offices significantly. In July 2001, the firm opened a new office in Munich, Germany.

Buy, sell and hold

Gibson has quickly risen to the top ranks of M&A advisors. In the first quarter of 2002, it ranked second in completed M&A transactions, according to the Thomson Financial Securities Data Company. A month later, Gibson ranked first in Mergerstat's ranking of firms with announced deals year-to-date. The firm web site boasts 128 completed transactions worth over $49 billion.

Last October, the firm handled the successful $170 million acquisition of PeopleFirst.com Inc., the nation's largest online provider of direct motor vehicle loans, by Capital One Financial Corp. Gibson client U.S. Foodservice was acquired by Royal Ahold, a Dutch multinational corporation who owns food-related merchandisers around the world. Another transaction of note is the global investment group Investcorp's 2002 acquisition of Executive Conference Inc. of Wayne, N.J., a provider of audio and Internet conferencing services. Gibson represented Investcorp.

A high-profile deal in which Gibson had its hand was the takeover of Indigo NV by Hewlett-Packard Co. Gibson represented Indigo in the $882 million acquisition. WebMD Corp. bought Gibson client MedicaLogic/Medscape Inc. for $10 million. The firm also represented Casden Properties Inc., a California real estate manager, as it was acquired by Aimco, the largest apartment owner in the country, in a deal worth $1.5 billion.

Comings and goings

Gibson Dunn welcomed some new colleagues and said goodbye to others in 2001. In that year, former Congressman Richard A. Zimmer (R-NJ) joined the D.C. office, providing his clients with advice on strategic government affairs as well as taxation, international trade, health care and environmental issues.

As one joins up, so others bid adieu. Chairman Ronald S. Beard said so long after 11 years at the helm, retiring last December. The son of Antonin Scalia, Eugene Scalia, worked in the D.C. branch until recently. While at Gibson, he co-authored an opinion piece with partner Thomas Hungar on prompting lawyers to challenge violations of the Americans with Disabilities Act by the Equal Employment Opportunity Commission. Now, Scalia's taken his observations to the office of Labor Secretary Elaine Chao where he works as a consultant. But perhaps the most notable departure is that of Theodore B. Olson, who was chosen by President George W. Bush to serve as the forty-second solicitor general of the United States. Previously, Olson served as assistant attorney general in the Reagan administration.

Other stars of the Gibson stage

Gibson is a powerhouse of legal skill. John Olson, a respected securities partner, has served on the legal advisory committee of the National Association of Securities Dealers and now serves on the legal advisory board for the New York Stock Exchange. Mel Levine (D-CA), who served in Congress, now chairs the firm's public policy practice group. Joseph Kattan, a D.C. partner, represented Intel during an antitrust investigation by the Federal Trade Commission. Robert Cooper, senior litigation partner in Los Angeles, successfully defended American Airlines in the government's latest antitrust attack on the airline industry.

Theodore J. Boutrous Jr., another LA partner, co-chairs the firm's appellate and constitutional law and its media law practice groups. He's stellar at winning the reduction of damage awards. To date, he's gotten $1 billion in reductions, including $200 million against *The Wall Street Journal*. In October 2001, he led a team of attorneys, including fellow Gibson attorneys Theodore B. Olson and Thomas H. Dupree, in the reversal of a $259 million verdict, including $250 million in punitive damages, against DaimlerChrysler Corp. Thomas G. Hungar, a D.C. partner, also co-chairs the appellate and constitutional law practice group. He served as assistant to the solicitor general of the United States. He's also been involved in appellate matters such as Supreme Court cases regarding the presidential election of 2000 and the scope of the Americans with Disabilities Act.

Take one daily

Do you believe that if every person with coronary heart disease began taking vitamin B-12 and folate 310,000 lives would be saved in 10 years? A study published in the August 2001 issue of the *Journal of the American Medical Association* thinks so, and the attorneys at Gibson Dunn have faith in that suggestion. In November, the firm won $4.6 million (plus several times that in future royalties and an amount of punitive damages yet to be determined by the court) in a case involving a patent on a highly sensitive indicator of certain vitamin deficiencies in humans. Two University of Colorado professors, Dr. Robert H. Allen and Dr. Sally P. Stabler, and the late Dr. John Lindenbaum of Columbia University discovered the indicator.

GETTING HIRED

Tough nut

Associates say Gibson, Dunn & Crutcher is a tough nut to crack. The firm recruits at more than 30 schools and "solicit[s] resumes from another 20 law schools." When it comes to grades, "Gibson is generally not flexible at all in deviating from its minimum grade guidelines at each law school." Once all the tangibles (grades, law school, and so on) have been taken into account, the deciding criteria "seems to be 'will this person fit in at our office?'" While it's "tough to get in the door," associates say, "once you're in the summer program, it's smooth sailing." Those who make the cut should expect to be "very, very busy" as the summer is "full of activities and events." Not everyone thinks the firm's hiring criteria is all that stringent. "I have seen what I consider to be top candidates rejected by my firm," a lateral hire reveals. "Sometimes it makes me wonder how I slipped through the interview process."

A lateral hire explains the hiring process thusly: "I had a morning interview in the San Francisco office with four to five lawyers and then an afternoon interview in the Palo Alto office with three to four lawyers. I felt like they were interested in knowing what I was like to work with, not in testing me in any way."

OUR SURVEY SAYS

The wide world of Gibson

It's hard to generalize about the corporate culture at Gibson, say insiders. A fourth-year associate elaborates: "A candidate considering my law firm should not assume that a good match with a particular office will mean a good match at all offices." Conversely, "a bad match at a particular office does not mean a bad match at all of the other offices." San Francisco "has a laid-back, somewhat nerdy culture, with a subtype of sociable people," reports a mid-level associate. The Los Angeles area offices "tend to be somewhat friendly, with the Century City office being a great place for lawyers to socialize and work as a team," opines an associate in the LA office. "The firm's culture epitomizes business casual," gushes a very contented Los Angeleno. This associate adds, "The firm is professional in its dealings with associates and partners yet is casual. And many attorneys socialize outside of the office."

One D.C. source characterizes his office as having "a good mix of formal and friendly" atmosphere, while another Washingtonian says the firm on a whole is "definitely uptight — especially, the D.C. office." Go figure. According to one associate, "Gibson Dunn's New York office is a friendly" and relatively "informal place." Some New Yorkers insist that social opportunities are there if you want them, but socializing "is not necessary for success at the firm." Others, however, report that "there is a formal work relationship and little socializing during work hours." Insiders report that work in the London office has been very slow, reflecting the listless economy. Although the pace of the work has begun to pick up, "I had a couple of months of sheer boredom," reveals an associate in that office.

Be responsible

Just as the cultures vary from office to office, associates in different offices report variations in the amount of responsibility they receive. In the D.C. office, associates report being given "a lot of responsibility on the most interesting and challenging cases." And a colleague says, "The work is great — cutting-edge and lots of responsibility."

But some Californians disagree. "The level of responsibility for young attorneys is not great," says a junior associate in the San Francisco office, "and it seems new attorneys have difficulty breaking into the work flow from partners." A colleague concurs, saying, "I think the firm handles some challenging cases, but my experience so far is that anything interesting is handled by more senior attorneys or partners."

Money isn't everything

Gibson Dunn associates can't believe their good fortune when it comes to salary. Associates' compensation is "too high" according to an eighth-year associate. Instead, "the firm and its clients would be better off if we lowered billing rates and pay and focused on work instead of where we rank on the national 'profits per partner' scale." "If Gibson paid more for my services, I'd question their sanity," a seventh-year raves. According to one third-year associate, "any associate complaining about salary needs mental health care."

Of course, crazy can be in the eye of the beholder — especially when it comes to bonuses. One New Yorker tells us, "The firm's commitment to keeping salaries at market levels in New York is dismal." This associate went on to say that when associates met with the partners to discuss pay disparities between Gibson and other firms, "the partners acknowledged the base salary disparity and stated they would do nothing about it." An attorney in LA explains why some associates feel Gibson Dunn hasn't lived up to its standing as one of the country's top firms. "The vast majority of associates billed around 2,100 hours and received bonuses which they feel are 25 to 50 percent of the size of their peers at New York firms who billed comparable hours."

Hours: hot and cold

One of the consistencies of life at Gibson Dunn is the inconsistency of the hours, associates say. "Did I really go to law school so that I could organize, copy and staple thousands of pages of documents?" asks a first-year litigator rhetorically, whose days are either spent "scrounging for work and sitting around bored" or "stuck here around the clock and all weekend" due to a suddenly heavy workload. "In the last year, hours have been hard to come by," laments a corporate associate. This has meant fewer "nights in the office, but it also means sitting around not billing — and therefore, not getting any credit — in order to be available if and when something arises." "With the downturn in the economy, hours have dried up. Nevertheless, the pressure to bill continues," says an exasperated LA lawyer.

Some associates also express discontent about the pressure to bill more hours. "The firm is very hours-conscious. Attorneys are very mindful of the minimum billable hours requirement," a corporate associate tells us. Others say, "The informal minimum has moved from 1,850 to 1,950, and probably now stands somewhere north of 2,000." But the majority of Gibson Dunn associates believe "the firm is generally up-front about the hours required, and while they are not low, they are pretty reasonable." "Not making 1,950 in corporate was common at the end of last billable year, and it didn't seem as if anyone was punished for it." A fifth-year waxes philosophical: "Choosing to work for a large, prominent law firm is itself a choice to work more than the average person."

Some associates seem better able to cope with these issues than others, with the most common method of managing the hours crunch being to work from home. "I find I can do a lot of work at home with my laptop," says a labor attorney. But, adds this associate, "I don't think this is at all true for all departments or offices of the firm." Still, "there is a good amount of flexibility, telecommuting technology and no face-time requirements." A small number of associates say they work parttime, but "it is generally understood that asking for part-time or flex-time work arrangements is a step out the door."

Approachable partners

Although "associate/partner relations will always differ based on personalities," partners are said to be "generally very approachable and go out of their way to be friendly and welcoming." The firm is free of "screamers" and has a non-hierarchical atmosphere that's conducive to good associate/partner relationships. Associates give kudos to Gibson's "free market policy that permits associates to decline work from partners." This means "the partners have to be nice" if they want their cases staffed. While an LA lawyer raves, "I have never heard of a firm that puts more effort into treating associates well," an associate in the London office says, "The bulk of the partners are very good — a few need to learn some more people skills." A New York associate warns of "a growing mistrust between the associates generally and the partnership generally, based on recent financial decisions and recent partnership decisions." "In my view, the less contact with partners, the better. Always have a senior associate as a buffer zone, if you can," says a suspicious first-year.

Diversity catch-22

Gibsonites acknowledge that the firm is "making a concerted effort to hire and retain minority lawyers," as well as female and gay and lesbian attorneys, but say the efforts are slow to make an impact on the partnership ranks. Several attorneys describe a catch-22 in hiring minority attorneys. "Minorities may be turned off from coming to Gibson because there are so few minorities. I think we need a critical mass of minorities in order to make them feel more welcome, despite the best efforts of non-minorities in the meantime." "With the exception of the LA office, there is little or no racial diversity among attorneys in the firm's offices. As a result, it is difficult for recruiters to convince minority applicants that Gibson Dunn is the right place for them," says a sixth-year associate.

"We are very receptive to hiring women, but seem to have a lot of trouble retaining them and making them partner," says an associate in the Dallas office. An attorney in the D.C. office describes some of the obstacles that may be keeping women from moving up in the firm. "A non-existent part-time policy combined with a lack of mentoring makes for a distinct lack of diversity with respect to women. Gibson is not a family-friendly place." "There is an all-women-attorney lunch once a month to discuss these issues," a first-year lawyer reports, "but they often turn into a rather depressing discussion." "There's plenty of female associates," says a junior female attorney, but "very few female partners." Not everyone thinks women lawyers at Gibson lack the firm's full support. "There are several female partners in this office, and I believe that a majority of associates are women. I have little doubt that women will make up about 50 percent of partners in this office within five to 10 years," enthuses an associate in the San Francisco office. "There is a very strong group of female associates that are well respected and moving up through the ranks," adds a colleague from the same office.

When it comes to diversity issues regarding gays and lesbians, Gibson attorneys seem to think everything is A-OK. "I am not aware of any gay or lesbian lawyers at our office or the D.C. office," admits an attorney in the Denver office, "though they may very well be there. I have never once heard any negative comments or perceived any negative attitude toward homosexuality at this firm." A New Yorker remarks, "Although there are a number of individuals at the firm who seem uncomfortable with the issue, there are a few openly gay and lesbian associates and at least one partner who is gay." Though an LA associate thinks the firm treats the small number of openly gay associates fairly, she insists, "I wouldn't go so far as to say that we actively recruit gays or lesbians." A junior associate in LA sniffs, "Sorry, but I don't ask people about their sex lives. There's enough work to do around here."

Arnold & Porter

555 12th Street, NW
Washington, DC 20004
Phone: (202) 942-5000
www.arnoldporter.com

LOCATIONS

Washington, DC (HQ)
Century City, CA
Denver, CO
Los Angeles, CA
McLean, VA
New York, NY
London

MAJOR DEPARTMENTS/PRACTICES

Antitrust • Banking • Bankruptcy • Benefits •
Corporate & Securities • Environmental • Food & Drug •
Governmental Contracts • Intellectual Property •
Legislation/Public Policy • Life Sciences • Litigation •
Real Estate • Tax & Estates • Telecommunications •
Trusts

THE STATS

No. of attorneys: 687
No. of offices: 7
Summer associate offers: 102 out of 106 (2001)
Managing Partner: James Sandman
Hiring Partner: Claire Reade

BASE SALARY

Washington, DC, 2002
1st year: $125,000
2nd year: $135,000
3rd year: $145,000
4th year: $155,000
5th year: $165,000
6th year: $175,000
7th year: $185,000
8th year: $195,000
Summer associate: $2,400/week

NOTABLE PERKS

• Nightly cocktails, soft drinks and hors d'oeuvres
• On-site child care and back-up care
• Mentor/mentee lunch program

THE BUZZ
WHAT ATTORNEYS AT OTHER FIRMS ARE SAYING ABOUT THIS FIRM

• "Litigation powerhouse"
• "Fading prestige"
• "Fabulous place to be an attorney"
• "Great on diversity"
• "Tobacco-tainted"

UPPERS

- "Jim Sandman, the best managing partner in the world"
- Close ties to many government agencies
- Impressive client list

DOWNERS

- "The firm sees no problem shipping people off to do document review for months at a time"
- Politically homogeneous
- Dissatisfaction with bonus structure

EMPLOYMENT CONTACT

Ms. Lisa Pavia
Manager of Attorney Recruitment
Phone: (202) 942-5059
Fax: (202) 450-4500
Lisa_Pavia@aporter.com

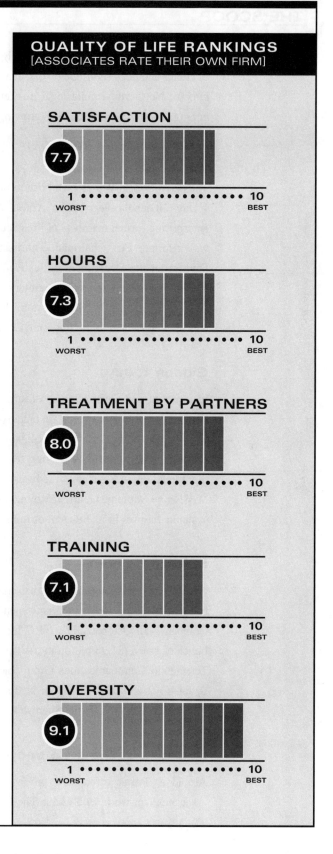

QUALITY OF LIFE RANKINGS
[ASSOCIATES RATE THEIR OWN FIRM]

SATISFACTION
7.7
1 WORST · · · · · · · · · · · · · · · 10 BEST

HOURS
7.3
1 WORST · · · · · · · · · · · · · · · 10 BEST

TREATMENT BY PARTNERS
8.0
1 WORST · · · · · · · · · · · · · · · 10 BEST

TRAINING
7.1
1 WORST · · · · · · · · · · · · · · · 10 BEST

DIVERSITY
9.1
1 WORST · · · · · · · · · · · · · · · 10 BEST

THE SCOOP

As one of the vaunted "Washington Big Three," Arnold & Porter represents an impressive group of clients and does significant work in a diverse range of practice areas. The firm recently plunged into the Northern Virginia legal market with a new office that opened in the summer of 2001, hoping to prosper from the ever-growing need for legal representation in the technology field.

FDR's boys

The end of World War II gave birth to more than just sailors kissing nurses in Times Square on V-J Day. It also gave birth to Arnold & Porter, which was formed just after WWII by three enterprising former members of President Franklin Delano Roosevelt's administration. Paul Porter was a former FCC chairman, Thurman Arnold was assistant attorney general in the Antitrust Division of the Department of Justice and then a judge on the U.S. Court of Appeals, and Abe Fortas was Roosevelt's undersecretary of the interior. In 1963 Fortas argued the landmark case Gideon v. Wainwright, which established the right to an attorney for all criminal defendants; he was later appointed to the Supreme Court.

Gideon today

In a current and novel effort to ensure the right established by Gideon v. Wainwright, Arnold & Porter is representing three financially-strapped rural counties in litigation against the State of Mississippi for breaching its obligation to provide an adequate criminal defense to indigent persons. The Arnold & Porter team developed this legal theory to challenge ineffective representation on a system-wide basis. The theory was validated last October by a decision of the Mississippi Supreme Court, affirming the right of A&P's clients to sue the State of Mississippi for systemic failures in its indigent criminal defense system.

Spicy TV dinner

Arnold & Porter, longtime antitrust counsel to General Electric, has once again helped the we-bring-good-things-to-life company spend money, this time on behalf of The National Broadcasting Company. In October 2001, NBC Inc., a division of General Electric Company, spent a whole bunch of green ($1.98 billion in cash and stock and $700 million in assumed debt) in order to buy Telemundo Communications Group Inc. The Spanish-language broadcaster is the number two Spanish network and owns ten stations serving 86 American markets, behind only Univision Communications Inc. in the Spanish television market.

Helping out the little people

Arnold & Porter offers two pro bono rotation options for associates. Lucky, high-minded associates can work with either The Legal Aid Society in Washington, D.C. or the Washington

Lawyers' Committee for Civil Rights and Urban Affairs. At the Washington Lawyers' Committee, which the firm began to offer as a second pro bono rotation option in 2001, associates work in the civil rights, equal employment and housing arenas. The firm has a history of stepping up to fight injustice. Way back in the 1950s, the firm's own Paul Porter was crucial in the fight against McCarthyism, and Abe Fortas, as noted above, argued Gideon v. Wainright in the early 1960s. In 2002, Arnold & Porter was named Pro Bono Law Firm of the Year by the District of Columbia bar, an honor the firm also won in 1999.

Webcasting for dollars

Arnold & Porter partners Robert Garrett and Hadrian Katz and more than 18 of their colleagues are currently representing the Recording Industry Association of America (RIAA) against an array of Internet-based music providers. The battle is before an arbitration panel of the U.S. Copyright Office and concerns song royalties potentially owed to song writers and performers. The parties are fighting over what amounts to significantly less than one penny per song play. It sounds minor, but considering how many thousands of times some songs are played on the air, a mere fraction of a cent can, over time, add up to an impressive sum of money. The RIAA counts Sony Corp., AOL Time Warner and Bertelsmann AG among its supporters. Oddly enough, a service owned by AOL Time Warner is one of the RIAA's opponents, which means that one piece of the media giant is pitted against another. Other webcasters opposing RIAA before the arbitration panel include MTV and Listen.com.

The talented Mr. Dodds-Smith

In early 2002, Arnold & Porter coaxed Ian Dodds-Smith, a renowned pharmaceutical and product liability litigator, from London's CMS Cameron McKenna. Along with Dodds-Smith came two partners and six associates from his old firm, enlarging Arnold & Porter's London office, where Dodds-Smith will lead the firm's product liability practice. Dodds-Smith will also co-head the firm's food and drug practice along with D.C. partner William Vodra. Dodds-Smith has extensive experience in all aspects of the law relating to pharmaceuticals, medical and biotech products. He is also a specialist in licensing and related regulatory affairs and in the field of product liability.

Europeans want a piece of tobacco, too

Tobacco litigation fever has stretched across the pond, and A&P is smack in the middle of it. In August 2001, several European Union members initiated lawsuits against the two largest U.S. tobacco companies, R.J. Reynolds and longtime Arnold & Porter client Philip Morris. The charges against these tobacco goliaths allege violations of the Racketeer Influenced and Corrupt Organizations (RICO) Act, including money laundering and wire and mail fraud, as well as unjust enrichment, public nuisance and conspiracy in the illegal smuggling of cigarettes into Europe in violation of U.S. law. The plaintiffs include Belgium, Finland, France, Greece, Germany, Italy, Luxembourg, the Netherlands, Portugal and Spain.

GETTING HIRED

Summer fun

No associate doubts the summer program at Arnold & Porter is fun. "Like summer camp," says one lawyer, "except you get paid." "This translates into spoiled and lazy summer associates," tut-tuts another associate. Other associates disagree, feeling the firm has a "good balance" between social activities and work. One second-year associate recalls fondly that "the firm made a lot of effort to get us assignments we wanted."

Cream of the crop

Like most top firms, Arnold & Porter has an "unspoken bias" towards recruits from the "most selective and prestigious" schools, though it's said not to be "as concerned with pedigree" as other top firms. One associate says a "top performer" from a lower-ranked school has got "a shot" while "a little birdie" told another associate that candidates from lower-ranking schools have "an awful lot of praying" to do.

Clear-cut callbacks and lightning laterals

Most of Arnold and Porter's hiring is through on-campus interviews. In most instances, there is a callback interview before an offer is made. One associate says offers are plentiful, resulting in "a whole lot of associates sitting around with little to do." Another says the callback process, lunch with "getting-to-know-you" questions, is a "joke." But a good joke.

Laterals, too, find the process of moving to Arnold & Porter "easy" — or at least they used to. One used a headhunter and another "had a friend" who worked there. Another lateral describes the process as "painless and frighteningly quick." A more senior lateral says the firm hasn't hired a lateral in "months" unless they have a "scientific or engineering background" to do "patent law." Another insider agrees that laterals are not currently being hired.

OUR SURVEY SAYS

Laid back and lovin' it

Most associates agree that Arnold & Porter has a "relaxed attitude" in relation to other "big" firms. People find the firm "informal" with everyone being on a "first-name basis." There seem to be conflicting views about socializing. Some associates say few attorneys socialize outside the office while others think there is a great deal of mingling. One associate notes, "I know more people here, at all levels, than I expected to know in a career." According to one associate, the firm has nightly happy hours that "pretty much summarize" the firm's atmosphere.

The firm is said to have a "liberal political" culture. A male associate notes: "I have a sense that you can be whoever you want to be around here as long as you fit into a particular political ideology in every conceivable way." Others construe liberalism more broadly, noting that "the firm culture is very decentralized and individualistic."

Though Arnold & Porter is "open" and "friendly," the livin' isn't necessarily easy at the firm. There is an "intense commitment to quality work," and one associate finds that the firm is obsessed with the bottom line. He goes on to say, "There seems to be an emphasis on getting it done, rather than getting it done well." One associate feels that his access to substantive and challenging work has been greater than he anticipated. Another says the firm "works hard" to make sure associates are happy and treats them as adults. According to a litigation associate, the work is "very demanding" and an associate's outside life "always takes a back seat." Another associate agrees, noting a growing emphasis on billable hours.

Bonus blues

Associates at A&P, for the most part, are happy with their base pay but not thrilled with the firm's bonus structure. The firm has two kinds of bonuses: one based on the overall financial performance of the firm, and one based on hours worked. The firm notes that in 2001, every associate in the firm received a financial performance bonus. The firm also has a bonus for associates who bill at least 2,400 hours during a one-year period (360 hours can be pro bono hours). Many associates consider this hours-based bonus beyond their reach. Because of the high threshold for the hours-based bonus, says one associate, "A&P does not compensate its associates as well as its peer firms in the current market."

Not all associates dislike the bonus system. A second-year associate remarks, "I like that bonuses are not based on hours worked." One associate points out that though compensation is not up to par with comparable firms, "most people are extremely satisfied that there were no large scale layoffs like at other firms, and are willing to be paid slightly less in bonuses in return for greater job security."

Happy hours

The hours at Arnold & Porter are "reasonable," "typical for big firms" and "vary substantially based on deal flow." Associates are expected to bill 2,000 hours, not "an unreasonably high expectation," though this number is not a requirement. Although hours are comparable to other big firms, partners are "flexible" and understanding of "familial demands." A first-year associate says, "Everyone is very respectful of your schedule and preferred working hours. It's not when you get the work done that matters, but rather the quality of your work." In fact, associates say that they rarely find themselves stuck in the office once Saturday rolls around.

While the full-timers are enjoying hours at Arnold & Porter, part-timers seem conflicted. One female associate is "thrilled" with the part-time program because it gives her "challenging work and significant interaction with partners and clients." In addition, she adds, "I can accommodate my family needs and my professional needs, which is very satisfying." Another associate says, "I work 80 percent time, better than fulltime but still longer than I'd like." One associate sees part-time work as having a "negative impact" on advancement prospects.

A&P's respect for women "off the charts"

It is no secret that Arnold & Porter has the "best reputation in the country" with regards to its efforts to diversify. One associate maintains the firm is "leaps and bounds ahead" of the competition. A male associate notes that the firm is one of two mentioned in *Working Woman* magazine's Top 100 Places to Work. It has the only full-time child care center in a firm in the country. One female associate remarks, "I use [the center] for all four of my children." Many associates agree hiring efforts for women, minorities and openly gay and lesbian associates are "very good."

The firm has many openly gay and lesbian attorneys, according to one lesbian associate. Another lesbian associate says the firm is "very supportive." A gay associate says that he feels "welcomed, accepted and supported." The firm offers insurance for domestic partners. A female associate mentions the firm allowed a gay associate to take paid paternity leave when he and his partner adopted a child. Another gay associate would like to see an "official" group for gays and lesbians like the ones minorities and women have voluntarily organized at the firm. (The firm notes that there is an informal group for gay and lesbian attorneys and that the firm pays for lunches and meetings for all such groups.) The group Women at Arnold & Porter, or WAP, provides "some support," according to a female associate. An Asian associate notes the group Minorities at Arnold & Porter (MAP) "provides a support network" for minorities. Though one associate remarks that the diversity issue is stressed a little too much, he also says, "Kudos to the firm for fostering such an environment." One associate notes that the firm is diverse "demographically" but doesn't have "diversity of thought." "There are almost no conservatives," he adds.

A few bad apples...

... don't ruin the bunch. Most associates agree that associate-partner relations are "generally good." As one associate puts it, "There are a few yellers and bad actors, but in general that conduct is frowned upon here." One associate says relations have "improved dramatically" due to the efforts of the firm's managing partner, Jim Sandman. He notes, "Partners take an interest in associates, and there is a good formal mentoring program." Beyond a "few exceptions," partners treat associates with respect and have "great confidence" in their associates. One says, "They always encourage me to speak up with questions or comments." Two associates mention a change in relations during the economic downturn. One grumbles that partners were more patient and easygoing before the economic slowdown. Yet another associate mentions that he likes being treated like a professional but finds it hard to make a "true mentor" at the firm. He notes the firm's formal mentoring program but wishes partners "did this more on their own."

Teach a man to fish...

Associates at Arnold & Porter differ when it comes to the level of training they receive once employed. Some say there is little or no formal training while others think there are "many opportunities." A Washington associate notes, "Training received varies by practice group." A member of the litigation group says, "Litigation associates routinely receive training regarding most major aspects of litigation, for example depositions, pleadings and so on." Another litigation associate mentions that partners "volunteer as faculty members" and "are willing to answer questions and give feedback." A Washington associate who came from another firm particularly values the seminar on organizing files, saying, "I wish they'd had this at the firm I was at before. It took me a year to develop a system I like."

White & Case LLP

1155 Avenue of the Americas
New York, NY 10036-2787
Phone: (212) 819-8200
www.whitecase.com

LOCATIONS

New York, NY (HQ)
Los Angeles, CA
Miami, FL
Palo Alto, CA
San Francisco, CA
Washington, DC
34 other offices worldwide

MAJOR DEPARTMENTS/PRACTICES

Antitrust
Banking
Equipment Leasing
Intellectual Property
Litigation
Mergers & Acquisitions
Project Finance
Securities
Tax

THE STATS

No. of attorneys: 1,530
No. of offices: 40
Summer associate offers: 52 offers out of 54 (2001)
Managing Partner: Duane Wall
Hiring Partner: M. Elaine Johnston

BASE SALARY

New York, Los Angeles, Palo Alto and Washington, DC, 2002
1st year: $125,000
2nd year: $135,000
3rd year: $150,000
4th year: $170,000
5th year: $190,000
6th year: $200,000
7th year: $205,000
8th year: $210,000
Summer associate (NY, LA and Palo Alto): $2,403/week
Summer associate (DC): $2,400/week

Miami, 2002
1st year: $105,000
2nd year: $110,000
3rd year: $120,000
4th year: $140,000
5th year: $155,000
6th year: $165,000
7th year: $170,000
8th year: $175,000
Summer associate: $2,019/week

NOTABLE PERKS

• Foozball table
• "Great cafeteria"
• Free in-house gym

 THE BUZZ
WHAT ATTORNEYS AT OTHER FIRMS ARE SAYING ABOUT THIS FIRM

• "Outstanding, but they will own you"
• "*The* international law firm"
• "Tend to think highly of themselves"
• "A bit too big for its own good"
• "Great arbitration"

UPPERS

- "International flavor" with opportunities to work in foreign offices
- Prestigious antitrust, banking and corporate litigation practices
- "Strong and sincere commitment to pro bono"

DOWNERS

- "Forget about having a child while working here"
- Bonuses tied to hours, so many in certain departments are shut out
- Headquarter office in need of renovation

EMPLOYMENT CONTACT

Ms. Dana E. Stephenson
Director of Attorney Recruiting & Employment
Phone: (212) 819-8200
recruit@whitecase.com

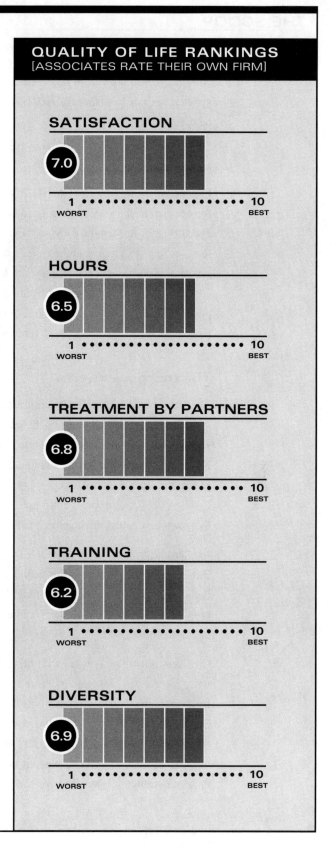

QUALITY OF LIFE RANKINGS
[ASSOCIATES RATE THEIR OWN FIRM]

SATISFACTION
7.0
1 WORST • • • • • • • • • • • • • • • • • • 10 BEST

HOURS
6.5
1 WORST • • • • • • • • • • • • • • • • • • 10 BEST

TREATMENT BY PARTNERS
6.8
1 WORST • • • • • • • • • • • • • • • • • • 10 BEST

TRAINING
6.2
1 WORST • • • • • • • • • • • • • • • • • • 10 BEST

DIVERSITY
6.9
1 WORST • • • • • • • • • • • • • • • • • • 10 BEST

THE SCOOP

These days, lots of law firms claim to have a global presence. But White & Case is the real deal, with over 1,500 lawyers in 40 offices spanning the globe. Want to practice law in Almaty? How about Jeddah or Bratislava or Ankara? If you've even heard of these places, White & Case may be the law firm for you.

Lofty origins

Founded in New York City in 1901 by J. DuPratt White and George B. Case, White & Case was fortunate from the very beginning to have the support of Henry Davison, a powerful J.P. Morgan executive. Not only did Davison encourage the founding of the firm, but he also retained its services for J.P. Morgan and swayed other companies to hire White & Case as well. The firm's association with the powerful Davison had another positive effect on the young founders, as they and the firm quickly became an influential part of the Wall Street community. In 1903 the firm played a vital role in the creation of Bankers Trust and served as its legal counsel for 96 years, until its acquisition by Deutsche Bank (another White & Case client).

The merger experts

The firm is best known for its antitrust, banking and corporate litigation practices. Recent cases include successfully arguing on behalf of financial news web site TheStreet.com for access to sealed testimony involving a dispute between the Securities and Exchange Commission and the New York Stock Exchange. That same month, the firm nabbed a piece of the Echostar/Hughes Electronics merger when it represented Echostar's financial advisor, Deutsche Bank, on the deal. In August 2001, an appeals court upheld an earlier White & Case victory for agricultural company Syngenta in a patent infringement suit.

Intellectual property is an area of growth for the firm. White & Case represented the Baltimore Ravens and the National Football League against a claim that the team illegally used an individual's sketches when designing the team's logo. This wasn't the firm's first sports-related case. The Green Bay Packers came to White & Case when it was accused of trademark infringement in 2000.

Conducting its own mergers with other firms has given White & Case a fair amount of expertise when it comes to brokering mergers and acquisitions. In September 2001, the firm advised Dutch food company Royal Ahold on its $2.7 billion acquisition of Alliant Exchange and Bruno's Supermarkets. The firm negotiated a $3.2 billion deal on behalf of its client Amerada Hess to purchase Triton Energy in July 2001. Earlier that month, White & Case snagged $12.5 billion for its client Bannamex-Accival when it was purchased by Citigroup. The firm continues to build on its M&A strength. When *The Wall Street Journal* published a list of "Legal Eagles" in April 2002, featuring preliminary first-quarter rankings for legal advisers on global deals, White & Case ranked ninth, with an aggregate deal value of $13.46 billion.

Case of the millennium

But even with all the money changing hands in those high-priced deals, the cases detailed above pale in comparison to the century's most controversial and high-stakes lawsuit, in which power, not money, was on the line and democracy, not business, was the playing field. When the 2000 presidential election was deemed too close to call, George Bush called on White & Case to block Al Gore's petition to recount the Florida votes. Although Gore was granted a recount, the Supreme Court intervened and, based in part on work by White & Case partner George Terwilliger, held that the recount was unconstitutional.

Globe trotters

Since the opening of its Paris office in 1926, White & Case has been on an almost uninterrupted drive to expand internationally. It now has 40 offices in 29 countries. In January 2001, the firm formed joint ventures with Varrenti e Associati in Rome and Milan and with Colin Ng & Partners in Singapore. Having previously decided against a merger with London-based Rowe & Maw, White & Case reportedly attempted to revive merger negotiations in summer 2001 after the U.K. firm received overtures from elsewhere. Alas White & Case missed its opportunity, and Rowe & Maw joined up with Chicago's Mayer, Brown & Platt. But don't feel too badly for White & Case. In March 2002, *Legal Week* reported that W&C was pursuing Araoz & Rueda, a Madrid-based firm specializing in corporate and tax-related matters.

The firm's international expansion combined with the addition of laterals and newly minted associates led to a whopping 22 percent growth in the size of the firm from October 2000 to September 2001.

Charity begins at the office

White & Case's tradition of pro bono work dates back to its efforts to assist the Red Cross during World War I. In keeping with its global firm strategy, today's White & Case attorneys participate in a variety of pro bono matters around the world. In 2001 the firm named an attorney in its London office as coordinator of pro bono efforts, becoming the first U.S.-based firm in London to create a position dedicated to pro bono work. Using the London office as a base, the firm is also working to increase the availability of pro bono assistance in other countries where it is not provided widely. In May 2002, James Stillwaggon, head of White & Case's corporate immigration law practice, took over the helm as full-time chair of the firm's pro bono committee, in which role he hopes to expand pro bono representation by lawyers in the New York office and enlist more corporate attorneys in pro bono activities.

The firm has earned awards for its pro bono program in legal circles and from local community agencies, including a special recognition award from the New York State Bar Association in May 2001 for its commitment to pro bono activities over the years. Volunteer Lawyers for the Arts, The Legal Aid Society and inMotion (formerly Network for Women's Services) are just some of the organizations that honored White & Case in 2001. In addition, the firm has two full-time externships with pro bono organizations, one with the Lawyers Alliance for New York and the other with inMotion; one associate is seconded on a full-time basis to each organization, each rotation being three or four months.

White & Case was among the many firms that provided assistance to the families of victims of the attacks on the World Trade Center and the Pentagon. In addition to settling estates and assisting those who have been displaced from their homes and businesses, the firm also established a $500,000 relief fund to aid the families and survivors of the tragedies. The firm also plans to match up to $500,000 in donations from its employees.

GETTING HIRED

Variety is the key

White & Case may be choosy about its attorneys, but "no one thing will make or break a candidate because White & Case LLP emphasizes diversity." Another lawyer clarifies, "Variety is the key word here, not necessarily ethnic diversity." Grades matter to White & Case, as does personality. "And yes," one associate assures W&C wannabes, "offers are given to students at the lower-tier schools." In fact, according to one associate, "the law school you attend is not nearly as important as your grades, personality and life experience. They particularly favor candidates who have spent substantial time abroad and speak several languages." W&C looks for "socially adept," "well-rounded" applicants. Keep in mind that "interview reports are every bit as important as a candidate's resume in the process," and applicants "must receive positive evaluations from all six interviewers on the callback."

Several insiders highlight the value of an international background. "Unique experiences and language capabilities are always an asset," suggests one source. "It definitely helps to have an international background," says another. "The firm is looking for a diverse class of associates to reflect the global culture of the firm." According to some attorneys, "coming in as a lateral is easy if there is an urgent need, but almost impossible if a practice area is not actively recruiting you." On the other hand, at least one lateral believes that "if you get the interview you are almost guaranteed the job."

OUR SURVEY SAYS

A fragmented culture

Insiders find it difficult to generalize about the environment at White & Case. A D.C. lawyer says that the "office does not have a uniform culture because it is fragmented, primarily by practice groups." A New Yorker agrees: "One's view of 'firm culture' depends on the partners and senior associates with whom one interacts." Responses vary from "formal and uptight" to "very friendly and social." The IP department in New York appears to be "one of the more laid back and social groups here." Lawyers value the "quality of the work, the opportunities for professional development and the camaraderie." Similarly, litigators enjoy their work and praise the group, including the partners, as "young, smart and approachable."

Sources in corporate departments give the firm more mixed reviews. "Collegial and chatty," says one lawyer. "Uptight and dishonest," asserts another. A junior associate in corporate finance raves, "The firm culture is fantastic. I have been so surprised with the kindness and civility that I have found with most everyone with whom I have worked." Quite a contrast with the M&A attorney who advises, "Avoidance is the key. Avoid work, avoid peers, avoid the office." Perhaps some of the low ratings are attributable to the slowdown in corporate work. "Normally," reports one associate, "this is a very friendly firm. However, it is a little tense these days."

As social as you want

Even some associates who find their own group relaxed report that "the firm's culture as a whole is a bit stiff." Any inter-office socializing appears to be independently organized rather than "formally encouraged" by the firm. W&C "rarely has events to facilitate people (including families) getting to know each other." Some attorneys claim that "lawyers do not typically socialize together" or that "socialization [is] limited to cliques." And yet many associates form "long-term friendships" with colleagues and "socialize together often." In addition to lunch and after-work drinks, "we go to ballgames, we celebrate births, weddings, departures, victories, and so on." A few sources offer a somewhat cryptic description of the firm environment. It is "quite cool, but one must be careful," advises an associate. According to another insider, "Lawyers tend to socialize together at the firm. However, you must mind your Ps and Qs at all times." One lawyer in the D.C. office suggests that the "litigation associates definitely socialize. Corporate associates socialize less but are still friendly."

The Ritz it's not

New Yorkers rate their office space only "slightly above average. It has not changed at all in seven years and is beginning to show. Beige, beige and beige." Although one lone associate thinks the offices are "decorated with tasteful conservatism," most respondents agree with the lawyer who pleads, "The office needs some updating!" The more diplomatic express their opinions in measured tones. "Our space is very nice and well maintained, but the style is a bit dated. We are working on some new ideas right now." Others are more emphatic: "The interior is UGLY! UGLY! I can't say that enough." One lawyer dryly remarks, "The Ritz it's not." Aside from the "drab, dreary colors," many associates also grumble about doubling up for too long. "Traditionally, associates have to share offices until the end of their second year. However, the high retention rate has forced many third-year associates to share." Lawyers in the Washington, D.C. office appear happier with space said to be "nice, but certainly not luxurious." They also appreciate the window offices and "good secretarial support."

Grudgingly competitive compensation

Though most sources agree that "White & Case always meets market compensation for top firms," many associates express dissatisfaction with their 2001 bonuses. The firm "initially announced below-market bonus amounts," but then "grudgingly" increased the bonuses to match the going rates. And because "the bonus structure was exclusively linked to billable hours (over 2,000 to obtain the minimum bonus and then a higher bonus for over 2,400)," many associates — particularly in the corporate department "where billable work was hard to get" — did not receive bonuses at all. This episode "hurt morale" and colors associates' satisfaction with compensation that might otherwise be considered "excellent."

Some mid-level and senior associates also claim that the firm lags behind the market for senior associates. According to one lawyer, compensation for the first five years is the "same as all New York firms," while "years six to eight [are] lower than average." Another associate interprets, "In other words, they pay their least profitable associates at market rates and their most profitable at below market rates." Notwithstanding the litany of complaints, some W&C associates appreciate taking home "lots and lots of dough."

Feast or famine

"Like all New York firms, the hours are long," sighs a W&C associate, "but there is no face time required." Many insiders are resigned to long hours. "Of course I would like to work less but 9 to 5 just isn't part of the deal in any large firm and you know that going in." One glass-half-full type in D.C. says, "The partners do not tend to give busy work just to fill hours. They understand and allow you to do other things, so long as the work gets done right and on time." Like lawyers around the country, associates object more to the unpredictability of their schedules than to the hours themselves. "It is difficult to never have the ability to plan a weekend or an evening with friends without the proverbial sword of Damocles hanging over your head," complains one attorney. The "feast or famine" nature of the practice creates other stresses: "When it's the former, I feel like a robot sometimes, operating on auto-pilot and worried about not having enough time to think. When it's famine, I worry I am not meeting the hours requirements."

In a slow economy, many attorneys worry about meeting the hours requirements. "I wish I was busier," rues a tax attorney. A corporate lawyer reports, "I have a lot of free time these days, but that is not necessarily a good thing." A colleague agrees, "There isn't enough work. I didn't go to (and pay for!) law school to surf the Net." Moreover, some sources report "preferential treatment" in the distribution of work. The "workload is not balanced well by the partners," according to more than one attorney. This imbalance extends across practice groups. "Certain departments work all the time at the expense of attorneys' private lives, others hardly work at all."

A sincere commitment

White & Case "has a very strong and sincere commitment to pro bono and has always actively encouraged it," according to many insiders. "On this one, the firm's in great shape," maintains one lawyer. "Pro bono opportunities abound and are taken seriously by management." The firm also sponsors two externships and has an annual pro bono awards dinner. "Best pro bono work in the planet," insists an associate.

Nevertheless, the firm's method of recording pro bono time draws mixed reactions. While "100 percent of pro bono used to count towards billable" hours, now "rumors abound regarding limits on pro bono hours as billables." "Pro bono hours count," associates report, "as long as it is not 'too much' — but there is no official word as to how much is too much." Pro bono counts "up to a reasonable level," says one source. An associate notes that despite the firm's commitment, "this change in policy makes it practically difficult for associates to do much pro bono."

Bringing diversity home

W&C is not immune to diversity issues facing most large law firms. It's the "usual program," says a male associate: "heavy participation in early classes that dwindles as partnership decisions approach." "They try," claims another lawyer, "but this is definitely a white male firm." One attorney reports that some female colleagues "feel they have to work harder to gain recognition and respect," and another claims that a few "touchy-feely" partners "make women uncomfortable." A female associate finds the firm "good at hiring an almost even number of women for each incoming class but terrible at mentoring." "Forget about having a child while working here," advises one woman.

Many associates note that W&C's global reach means "the firm as a whole is fairly diverse." "The firm dining room looks and sounds like a United Nations luncheon," exclaims one associate. And yet "the New York City office is predominantly white [and] male." A lawyer explains, "The firm has a misplaced emphasis on the fact that we have over 30 foreign offices and over half the associates worldwide are persons of color. But it doesn't help that those persons of color are in other countries and not here in New York. The firm needs to bring 'em in and keep 'em in." A D.C. lawyer points out that there is not "a single minority partner in the office." One New Yorker gives the firm higher marks: "I am a minority and my experience has been great, but there could always be greater representation." Respondents don't see "any problems" for gays and lesbians at W&C. According to one lawyer, although sexual preference "is not generally discussed, it isn't hidden either."

"Avoidance is the key.
Avoid work, avoid peers,
avoid the office."

— White & Case associate

Jones, Day, Reavis & Pogue

North Point
901 Lakeside Avenue
Cleveland, OH 44114-1190
Phone: (216) 586-3939
www.jonesday.com

LOCATIONS

Atlanta, GA • Chicago, IL • Cleveland, OH
Columbus, OH • Dallas, TX • Houston, TX
Irvine, CA • Los Angeles, CA • Menlo Park, CA
New York, NY • Pittsburgh, PA • Washington, DC
Brussels • Frankfurt • Hong Kong • London • Madrid •
Milan • Paris • Shanghai • Singapore • Sydney • Taipei •
Tokyo

MAJOR DEPARTMENTS/PRACTICES

Business Practice
Government Regulation
Litigation
Tax

THE STATS

No. of attorneys: 1,670
No. of offices: 24
Summer associate offers: 148 out of 157 (2001)
Managing Partner: Patrick F. McCartan
Hiring Partner: James C. Hagy

BASE SALARY

Atlanta, Cleveland, Columbus and Pittsburgh, 2002
1st year: $110,000

Dallas and Houston, 2002
1st year: $115,000

Chicago, Irvine, Los Angeles, Menlo Park, New York and Washington, DC, 2002
1st year: $125,000

Atlanta, Dallas and Houston, 2002
Summer associate: $8,500/month

Cleveland, Columbus and Pittsburgh, 2002
Summer associate: $9,000/month

Chicago, Irvine, Los Angeles, Menlo Park and Washington, DC, 2002
Summer associate: $10,400/month

New York, 2002
Summer associate: $10,417/month

NOTABLE PERKS

• Annual associate retreat in a different resort each year
• Home loan program
• In-house gyms
• Excellent paternity and maternity leave policy

THE BUZZ
WHAT ATTORNEYS AT OTHER FIRMS ARE SAYING ABOUT THIS FIRM

• "Good full-service firm"
• "Tobacco boys"
• "Jones, Day, Nights, Weekends ..."
• "Outstanding litigation"
• "The Starbucks of law firms"

UPPERS

- Ample travel opportunities
- First-rate training
- First-year associates have a year to decide on a practice group

DOWNERS

- "Everyone snickers when they hear" Cleveland
- Can easily get lost in the shuffle
- Mysterious bonus structure

EMPLOYMENT CONTACT

Ms. Jolie A. Blanchard
Firm Director of Recruiting
Phone: (202) 879-3939
Fax: (202) 626-1700
jablanchard@jonesday.com

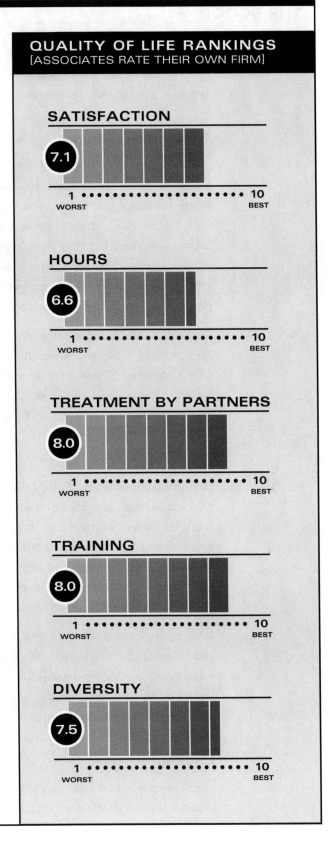

QUALITY OF LIFE RANKINGS
[ASSOCIATES RATE THEIR OWN FIRM]

SATISFACTION
7.1

1 WORST • • • • • • • • • • • • • • • • • • 10 BEST

HOURS
6.6

1 WORST • • • • • • • • • • • • • • • • • • 10 BEST

TREATMENT BY PARTNERS
8.0

1 WORST • • • • • • • • • • • • • • • • • • 10 BEST

TRAINING
8.0

1 WORST • • • • • • • • • • • • • • • • • • 10 BEST

DIVERSITY
7.5

1 WORST • • • • • • • • • • • • • • • • • • 10 BEST

THE SCOOP

Jones, Day, Reavis & Pogue is a multinational law firm with 1,670 attorneys at its disposal. It is not only one of the world's largest law firms in terms of number of attorneys but is one of the largest in terms of gross revenue as well.

Size does matter

Jones Day was established in 1893 by building up alliances with Cleveland-area manufacturing, transportation and industrial clients. In the 1940s, the firm expanded and established a Washington office, and then in the 1980s opened 13 more offices to become the gargantuan legal presence it is today. Although Cleveland is the largest office, the firm has six other domestic offices with 100 attorneys or more, including New York, Los Angeles, Chicago, Dallas, Washington, D.C. and Atlanta, as well as five other offices of considerable size in Irvine, Houston, Menlo Park, Columbus and Pittsburgh. In addition, Jones Day has over 230 attorneys practicing in its offices in Europe (including its newly opened firm in Milan) and more than 80 in Asia.

The firm's client list is growing, too. Its top five clients are Bridgestone/Firestone, Inc., RJR Nabisco, IBM, General Motors and Texas Instruments. The firm also represents Amazon.com, CBS Corporation, Citigroup, Coors Brewing Company, the County of Los Angeles, Eastman Kodak Company, Goldman Sachs, J.C. Penney, Johnson & Johnson, PepsiCo, Pfizer, Procter & Gamble, the San Jose Sharks, The Tribune Company and *The Washington Post*, among others.

Oil in the family

San Antonio-based Valero Energy Corporation agreed to buy out its neighbor, Jones Day client Ultramar Diamond Shamrock Corporation, in May 2001. The purchase price is nothing to scoff at, nearly $6 billion, which breaks down to approximately $4 billion in cash and stock and an assumption of approximately $2 billion of debt. The deal will create the largest independent oil refiner in the United States. In addition, the new company will have a refining capacity of just under 2 million barrels per day, second only to ExxonMobil Corporation. It took the collective energy of several attorneys from several different offices and departments to make this deal happen.

In other oil-related news, Jones Day helped Texas lawyers put together a deal that will combine two Dallas oil and gas companies in a stock and debt transaction worth a cool 40 and a half million smackaroos. In a deal announced on October 4, 2001, Toreador Resources Corp. will acquire Jones Day client Madison Oil Company and create a new company that will keep the name Toreador. The new company will have proven oil and natural gas reserves valued at $90 million.

Casting the dye

Most women won't trust their hair to just anyone. That's why a trusted hair coloring company like Clairol is such a valuable prize. Summer 2001 saw a victory by longtime Jones Day client Procter

& Gamble Company when P&G won a bidding war against Japan's Kao Corporation to purchase the Clairol line of hair coloring products. Bristol-Myers Squibb Company, the former owner of the famous Clairol hair color line, watched as P&G and Kao went at it neck and neck until the eleventh hour, when P&G upped its bid to $4.95 billion. The purchase was the biggest acquisition ever for P&G, the consumer products giant that offers everything from diapers to deodorant to paper towels.

Do you have that in a medium?

Think Macy's and you think department store giant (you may even think *Miracle on 34th Street*!). Jones Day, though, thinks litigation client. When Macy's West Inc., operator of Macy's department stores in California, faced a class of plaintiffs comprised of disabled shoppers alleging discrimination, the department store called on Jones Day for some legal assistance. The plaintiffs alleged that Macy's crowded aisles and small restrooms and fitting rooms made it difficult for disabled shoppers to enjoy the store. The parties settled in December 2001, with Macy's West paying $3 million in damages. Besides coughing up the cash, Macy's West will enhance entrances, restrooms, fitting rooms and cash register stands to make them more easily accessible to customers with physical disabilities. The settlement covers 72 Macy's stores in California.

Have corporation, will travel

While everyone loves to travel, few actually enjoy planning a trip, even though computers and the Internet have made planning easier than ever. Cendant Corporation, the New York-based provider of travel and real estate consumer services and owner of hotel chains such as Days Inn, Ramada and Super 8, as well as rental car company Avis, announced in June 2001 that it was ready, willing and able to acquire Rosemont, Ill.-based Jones Day client Galileo International Inc., the second-largest computerized travel reservations company. The deal was for stock and was valued at about $2.9 billion, with Cendant assuming $600 million in Galileo's debt.

Winning awards and doing good

Jones, Day, Reavis & Pogue won a number of awards in 2001. It ranked first in The BTI Consulting Group's Client Service A-Team list, in which survey respondents identified 17 key client-service areas and rated firms according to those behaviors and skills. The firm was also ranked No. 4 by *Corporate Board Member* magazine in its America's Best Corporate Lawyers survey. Jones Day's litigation group was named Litigation Department of the Year by *The American Lawyer* magazine. But that's not all. The firm took top honors on Thomson Financial's list of legal advisors on worldwide M&A deals and was ranked No. 8 for the aggregate value of completed worldwide deals in 2001.

In the wake of September 11, Jones Day joined numerous other law firms and companies around the country in making charitable donations to assist victims of the terrorist attacks. Jones Day contributed $200,000 to benefit funds in New York and Washington, with $100,000 to the New

York City Police and Fire Widows and Children's Benefit Fund, $25,000 to the Twin Towers Fund and $75,000 to the newly created Survivors' Fund of the Community Foundation for the National Capital Region.

GETTING HIRED

Challenging summer

Associates agree that a Jones Day summer is "meaningful." In LA, one associate notes, "The summer is typical of big firms, except you will likely work more than you might expect. The firm wants to see work product they can use for evaluation." Though there is work to be done, the summer is still an enjoyable one. Another LA associate mentions, "The summer program also provided a great mix of social and work opportunities, and I felt like we truly got to see what it meant to be a Jones Day lawyer." A Chicago associate adds, "We spend a lot of time with our summer associates in both social and work settings."

Good fit

An LA associate notes that "grades do matter" in the interviewing process. But he adds, "Someone who falls a little below our grade guidelines has a good chance of getting in if they exhibit attributes like being hardworking." A Cleveland associate adds, "It all depends on the law school. If you're from the Ivy League, you'll probably get a job. If you go to a local state school, you better be on law review." Some suggest that in New York, it's a tad easier to get an offer from Jones Day. Says an associate in the Big Apple, "I think of the New York office as a hidden gem of sorts in that it is relatively easy to get a job here even though the caliber of work done and the quality of the attorneys is high. I think the firm does a great job of seeking relatively well-rounded individuals who offer more than a high GPA."

OUR SURVEY SAYS

Conflicting culture

"Each office has its own flavor," remarks one Jones Day associate regarding the firm's culture. "For the number of brilliant, talented people, there is almost no ego, and people from partner down to paralegal are friendly, supportive and unselfish. The everyday atmosphere is fun, friendly and fosters creativity and excellence without requiring outdated formalities," says an associate in the firm's LA office. In Cleveland, things are a bit different, with associates describing the atmosphere as formal and lamenting the Friday-only business casual dress policy. Though Cleveland associates do socialize together after hours ("whether at happy hours or at houses"), sources admit that the culture is "uptight, in the sense that it often feels like crisis-mode. But what big law firm isn't like that?" The D.C. office lies somewhere in between. "Intensely academic and intellectual, but with a fun side — occasionally."

Dallas associates describe their colleagues as "helpful" and "cooperative," and an associate there notes, "Lawyers definitely socialize together outside of the office." In Chicago, people are friendly but prefer to go home as soon as the work day is over. Maintains a lawyer in the Windy City, "The attorneys do socialize to a certain extent. Typically classes stick together and attorneys within the same group stick together. However, many of the attorneys have lives outside the firm, and when faced with the option of going home to be with family and friends or going out with fellow attorneys, understandably many attorneys decide to go home."

Slackers beware

When it comes to compensation, Jones Day associates have some advice: "Hard work and good work is rewarded. We do not have lockstep increases, so slackers beware." Despite the jitters that a merit-based system of raises naturally causes, most Jones Day associates appear satisfied with their paychecks. An associate located in one of the firm's California offices offers insight into the compensation system: "Our salaries are competitive and at the top of the market. After your third year, each associate's salary is different and no one knows what each other is making. I like this, as it keeps competition and backstabbing down, and the differential in your salary is merit-based. That merit-based raise is determined through a very extensive review process that I believe produces fair results."

Contented New Yorkers tell Vault that they "have no basis to complain" when it comes to their salaries, while in Atlanta, salaries are "right on pace with the market." But in Cleveland, the subject of compensation leads to some grumbling. An associate there explains, "The firm compensates very well for Cleveland, but less than the national firms we compete against." Another Clevelander asserts, "They'll always be able to get regional and local grads becase they pay more than any other Cleveland firm. But if they want to realistically compete with Skadden, Kirkland and so on … on a consistent basis, they must pay competitively." In Dallas, associates think their base salary is just fine, but the bonus structure is another story. A Texan sighs, "The lack of a defined bonus structure sometimes results in working lots of hours for little or no bonus." This frustration with the bonus system is echoed throughout the offices. "The mysterious bonus structure could be improved with some clearer definitions," insists an LA associate.

Hours vary

"The hours spent in the office seem to vary depending on your practice group and what cases you happen to be on. Overall, my hours have been exceptionally manageable," notes a D.C. associate. While hours may be long, some associates are grateful to have them. A Cleveland associate mentions, "There is a lot of work that needs to be done. Today, that must be considered a good thing." And if there is too much to do, "people are willing to help out in a crunch and keep a good sense of humor while doing it." Another Dallas associate notes, "Hours are long when necessary; however, there is no requirement of 'face time' on the weekends or otherwise."

A Houston associate isn't surprised by the long hours: "I have found that the required billable hours are comparable to the number of hours I work and I am expected to work. There is no expectation that you will work more than you need to work. There's no need to keep a jacket hanging on the back of your door with your computer running when you leave for the day. You're expected to get your work done. In my experience, no one cares when you do it, as long as you do a good job." Things are just as good on the West Coast. An associate in one of the California offices remarks, "People take their vacations, they take days off after a particularly hard stretch, and nobody is cracking the whip, constantly reminding you about your hours." A New Yorker adds, "As a general rule if I need time off I can take it, including four weeks of vacation each year. And that's really all I can ask." Besides, notes a Chicago associate, there is "down time" that allows attorneys to "relax." He adds, "If anything, the hours are cyclical in nature, but rarely have I had to cancel a trip or engagement due to work."

Great for women

Though Jones Day could do with a bit more mentoring, associates are impressed with the firm's hiring and promoting of women. A female associate states, "I have never felt that gender was an issue one way or the other." "There are several women partners and countless women associates," adds a male associate. Several associates praised the firm for its "great maternity and paternity leave benefits." One woman explains, "I feel comfortable in the knowledge that when the time comes, I will have paths to choose here that will allow me to raise a family and keep practicing. Jones Day has a part-time track and will allow me to make the decision if necessary. Also, I have seen a number of women decide to keep working full time, raise children and make partner." When it comes to minorities, insiders admit "the numbers aren't where they should be." The firm reports that 12 percent of its lawyers are minorities. Associates commend the firm for its reception to gays and lesbians. "No one asks, no one tells. Even if they did, no one would really care one way or the other. It's a non-issue." Another associate commends the firm for its "very open atmosphere" and the fact that it offers domestic partner benefits.

Pro bono — seek and ye shall find

Self-motivated Jones Dayers should have no problem finding interesting pro bono projects on which to toil. Passive types, however, may have a more difficult time. As a Los Angeles associate notes, "Although the firm will support almost any type of pro bono work we want to do, you have to be fairly self-motivated to seek out and develop the opportunities outside of whatever the long-standing program of the office has been." A Cleveland associate explains the firm's pro bono policy: "The firm lets you bill up to 200 hours a year on pro bono, and it will count towards your hours requirement. I don't know that many people who take advantage of this, but the opportunity is always there." Some associates seem confused about what the real pro bono policy is, suggesting that perhaps the firm message regarding pro bono isn't sinking in. "There are contradicting reports as to whether it really counts towards billable hours," confesses one associate, while another insists, "It is not clear to me that it really does count." A New York associate maintains that the firm has been "making more of an effort lately" and is "in the midst of developing a corporate pro bono program." Jones Day has a firm-wide pro bono partner who manages and promotes pro bono matters within the firm. The firm reports that pro bono work does count as billable hours and wants attorneys to report all time they spend on pro bono work.

Training a real strong point

Most associates agree that Jones Day excels in its training. An LA associate notes, "Jones Day provides countless quality formal training opportunities for associates at all levels. But, more importantly, partners seem to recognize the importance [of training associates] and take the time to provide invaluable informal training through mentoring, feedback and providing new experiences. Sometimes you have to ask for the feedback, but it is freely given." A Clevelander is similarly pleased with the training she is receiving. "They have extensive training programs. If there's any CLE program you want to take, they will pay for it. Extensive in-house programs on writing, depositions, motion and trial practice, and evidence [are available]. A real strong point." The in-house programs are offered through the firm's associate training program, which focuses on areas such as negotiating and time management, and practice-specific trainings given by each group.

O'Melveny & Myers LLP

400 South Hope Street
Los Angeles, CA 90071-2899
Phone: (213) 430-6000
www.omm.com

LOCATIONS

Los Angeles, CA (HQ)
Century City, CA
Irvine, CA
New York, NY
Newport Beach, CA
San Francisco, CA
Silicon Valley, CA
Tysons Corner, VA
Washington, DC
Beijing (est. opening 2002)
Hong Kong
London
Shanghai
Tokyo

MAJOR DEPARTMENTS/PRACTICES

Intellectual Property & Technology • Labor &
Employment • Litigation • Tax • Transactions

THE STATS

No. of attorneys: 777
No. of offices: 13
Summer associate offers: 89 out of 92 (2001)
Chairman: Arthur B. Culvahouse
Hiring Attorney: David Enzminger

BASE SALARY

Los Angeles, 2002
1st year: $125,000
2nd year: $135,000
3rd year: $150,000
4th year: $165,000
5th year: $185,000
6th year: $195,000
7th year: $205,000
8th year: $210,000
Summer associate: $2,400/week

NOTABLE PERKS

• Choice of home computer, laptop or Palm Pilot for
  all associates and counsel
• Free parking
• Tickets for local sporting events
• Reimbursed dinners when you work two or more
  hours over standard workday

THE BUZZ
WHAT ATTORNEYS AT OTHER FIRMS ARE SAYING ABOUT THIS FIRM

• "Warren Christopher"
• "Good quality litigation"
• "Partners only care about money, money"
• "Macho"
• "Stellar work"

UPPERS

- Even first-years get their own offices
- High-quality, sophisticated work
- Pro bono hours are given full billable credit

DOWNERS

- Increased emphasis on billable hours
- Few minority or female partners
- Punishing hours — or not enough work

EMPLOYMENT CONTACT

Ms. Michele Marinaro
Recruiting Manager
Phone: (213) 430-6677
Fax: (213) 430-8064
mmarinaro@omm.com

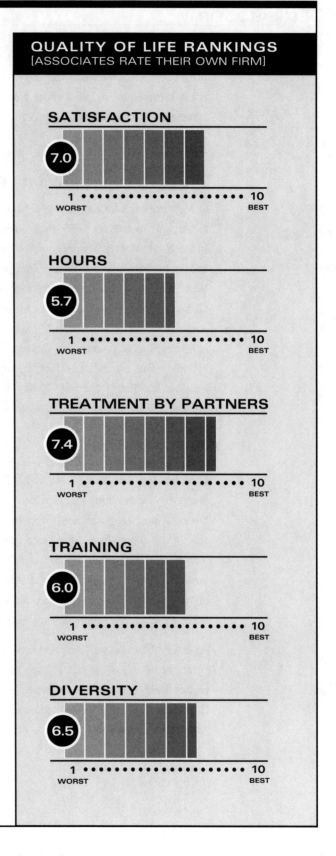

QUALITY OF LIFE RANKINGS
[ASSOCIATES RATE THEIR OWN FIRM]

SATISFACTION

7.0

1 WORST .... 10 BEST

HOURS

5.7

1 WORST .... 10 BEST

TREATMENT BY PARTNERS

7.4

1 WORST .... 10 BEST

TRAINING

6.0

1 WORST .... 10 BEST

DIVERSITY

6.5

1 WORST .... 10 BEST

THE SCOOP

Founded in 1885, O'Melveny & Myers is the oldest law firm in Los Angeles. Despite its age, the firm is able to cater to the needs of cutting-edge corporate clients, while continuing to provide top-notch representation to its more traditional clientele. During its 117 years, O'Melveny has expanded far beyond its California roots. In fact, the firm's second and third largest offices are in Washington, D.C. and New York.

Welcome to the law firm California

O'Melveny has a long and colorful history. The firm was founded by Jackson A. Graves and Henry O'Melveny in January 1885, back when Los Angeles had a population of approximately 15,000. In those days the big business out West was land speculation, a "profession" in which lawyers were needed to legitimize shadily acquired property. The firm remains dedicated to preserving its Wild West past. It retains a curator to oversee its artwork (an impressive collection that rotates among all the firm's offices) as well as historical archives in the nearby O'Melveny Museum in Los Angeles (tours are available by appointment). It's no surprise that this LA-based firm has represented more than its fair share of movie stars and film studios. The firm's high-profile and historic client list includes Jack Benny, Gary Cooper, Bing Crosby, silent film heroine Mary Pickford and Jimmy Stewart. Today the firm counts industry powerhouses CBS, Paramount and Sony Pictures Entertainment as clients.

Vive la Yahoo!

O'Melveny client Yahoo! Inc. won a significant victory in federal court in a case that has potentially far-reaching ramifications on the scope of U.S. law and its control on the Internet. U.S. District Court Judge Jeremy Fogel ruled that Yahoo!'s First Amendment rights trump a French court order compelling Yahoo! to prevent French users from viewing Nazi memorabilia and other Nazi-related expression on the U.S. site. The sale of memorabilia, which consisted of Nazi medallions, swastika-emblazoned battle flags and other Third Reich paraphernalia, and the display of other Nazi-related expression were protested by two French anti-hate groups who sued Yahoo! under a French law that makes it illegal to display Nazi symbols and emblems.

At stake: the idea that foreign courts cannot impose their laws on a web site just because their citizens can access the site in their country. Reacting to the federal court's ruling, O'Melveny partner Bob Vanderet, who handled the case along with associates Neil Jahss and Kerry Lyon-Grossman, stated that the decision was "a great victory, not just for Yahoo! and its users, but for all American citizens in its protection of our important constitutional rights."

Mickey Mouse buys new house

O'Melveny & Myers is all in the family — Fox Family, that is. The firm represented Fox Family Worldwide Chairman and CEO Haim Saban when The Walt Disney Company purchased the network for $5.3 billion. (The purchase does not include the immensely popular Fox Kids Network.) Experts say that the deal will benefit both corporate parties in the transaction — Disney because it has added 81 million viewers to help with its notoriously poor distribution capability, and News Corp. because it is making out with a huge sum of money. O'Melveny client Saban owned a 49.5 percent share in Fox Family.

Fun and gaming

Lawyers in O'Melveny's transactional practice represented IGT in connection with its agreement to acquire Anchor Gaming in a stock for stock transaction valued at $1.365 billion, based on IGT's July 6, 2001 closing price of $59.20 and the assumption of indebtedness of $430 million in March 2001. The combination creates a company with total combined annual revenues in excess of $2 billion. The firm has represented International Gaming for more than 15 years on various gaming-related deals, including the acquisition of Sodak Gaming in 1999, as well as helping the company raise $1 billion through a note offering that same year. International Game Technology is best known for its manufacture of slot machines, but it is involved in many facets of the gaming industry.

Enron, anyone?

As energy titan Enron tumbles spectacularly into bankruptcy, many top firms have been called upon to offer some legal aid — and O'Melveny is no exception. The firm's own Bruce Hiler, the same man who served in the SEC's Enforcement Division (where he helped to prosecute insider trader Ivan Boesky), has been retained by Enron's ex-CEO Jeffrey Skilling. Hiler will help Skilling respond to the request for information sent to him by House Energy and Commerce Committee Chairman Billy Tauzin (R-La.) and Oversight and Investigations Subcommittee Chairman James Greenwood as part of an ongoing investigation into the financial collapse of Enron Corporation. In addition, Hiler was retained by Skilling to represent him in connection with a related SEC investigation, and other related civil litigation and government investigations. Hiler may have quite a fight ahead of him: Skilling resigned just before the Enron collapse and rid himself of 500,000 Enron shares the day the markets reopened after the September 11 attacks. Also assisting on the case are O'Melveny partners Ira Raphaelson, former U.S. Attorney in Chicago, and Jeff Kilduff, head of the firm's Tysons Corner office.

Stepping into the fray

O'Melveny & Myers doesn't shy from the tough cases. The firm represented Ford Motor Company in a suit by Holocaust victims who had been forced to work at Ford's German subsidiary, Ford-Werke, during World War II. The case was dismissed, and although Ford denies any responsibility for use of forced labor, the company has contributed several million dollars to the $5 billion fund set up by the German government and industry to compensate victims. In November 2001, O'Melveny convinced the Ninth Circuit Court of Appeals that the $5 billion punitive damages awarded against ExxonMobil in a civil suit resulting from the Exxon Valdez oil spill was excessive. The court vacated the award and remanded the case to the district court to come up with a lower figure.

Expanding pro bono

O'Melveny takes its commitment to community work seriously. In 2001, O'Melveny launched its Ninth Circuit Pro Bono Program, which provides counsel on Ninth Circuit appeals that judges identify as needing an attorney. Last year the program scored many victories including a habeas corpus case that raised an important issue of federal law regarding the application of a tolling rule to a federal statute of limitation for prisoners challenging their convictions in federal court.

Moreover, O'Melveny continues its long-standing Christopher and O'Melveny scholarship awards programs, providing scholarships of up to $16,000 to disadvantaged college-bound high school students who otherwise might not have had the opportunity to attend college. O'Melveny's Shanghai office provides scholarships to law students at Shanghai's leading law schools, and attorneys in the Shanghai office also provide mentoring with respect to the students' careers.

GETTING HIRED

Top grades are the key

Insiders agree that "academic performance is probably the most important criterion" in landing a job at O'Melveny & Myers. O'Melveny "is very serious about the traditional credentials: top law school, high GPA, law review and clerkships…. Personal qualities may get you hired once you've gotten an interview, but they won't get you through the door if you've got the wrong resume." The firm reportedly has "strict hiring guidelines regarding class rank." According to one lawyer, "There is a minimum grade cutoff of about A-." At least one associate acknowledges that the "grade cutoff probably eliminates a lot of good lawyers, but no one can say we hire low-quality people."

After the stringent academic requisites, the firm looks for "personable" people with "good communications skills" and "outside interests." Those too hung up on their own credentials better stifle that self-importance, since "displays of arrogance or attitude in an interview will get you a rejection letter." A mid-level associate involved in recruiting says, "The test I use is 'How would I feel spending two weeks in a warehouse in Cleveland looking through documents with this associate?'" Some lawyers suggest that laterals "with excellent specialized experience" might overcome the rigid grade requirement. Our survey respondents include many laterals in the litigation department who were drawn to the firm's "reputation for having some of the nation's finest, sharpest and most dedicated attorneys."

OUR SURVEY SAYS

Exceptional attorneys and spectacular work

Insiders at O'Melveny & Myers clearly value the "variety and complexity of the cases" and think very highly of their colleagues. "The quality of the work is spectacular, and the lawyers are equally impressive," exclaims a litigator. According to another lawyer, O'Melveny "attorneys are exceptional people — very smart, very dedicated, very professional." They are "generally friendly, approachable, down-to-earth and tend to enjoy each other's company."

The D.C. office provides a "nice mix of professionalism with friendliness." "Some attorneys socialize together," but many "tend to have their own lives outside the firm." While New Yorkers admire their colleagues, many report that "firm morale is very low right now" as a result of an "extremely high number of partner and associate departures in [the] past few years." The firm's Southern California offices are considered congenial and laid back, and the "variety and quality of work is unquestionably fantastic." But an increasing emphasis on billable hours has many attorneys alarmed. The firm "is certainly becoming more focused on partner profits and losing some of its collegiality."

Increasing emphasis on the bottom line

The perceived pressure to bill is causing "increasing concern and tension within the associate ranks." A senior associate is "alarmed at how [the firm] is changing for the worse." The same associate says, "It used to be a place where I enjoyed coming to work every day — great people, great work, great talent. It is now focused almost exclusively on profits, billables and more profits." Another lawyer agrees: "We used to be a much friendlier firm. New management has made us more focused on billing and bringing in new business."

Not everyone sees the change in such stark terms. "Although it is becoming more profit-oriented, O'Melveny's culture remains friendly, laid back and supportive," says an insider. Many lawyers still describe their firm as "friendly and supportive." And a mid-level associate finds the firm "an excellent place to practice." He goes on to say, "The work is engaging, and the people are of the highest quality. I can't imagine that I would be happier at any other large law firm."

Many, many hours — or not enough

Several O'Melveny associates say they work too hard and too long. One attorney mourns "too many lonely evenings and weekends in the office while my family drifts away." Associates enjoy the nature of their work — just not the volume. "I love this job, but there's just too much of it at times." The firm expects an annual minimum of 1,950 hours. Reaching the billable hours target is easier in some departments than in others. "The workload disproportionately impacts litigation associates," say litigators. "Whereas the firm-wide official minimum is 1,950, it's common knowledge that last year the O'Melveny litigation department averaged at least 2,400 hours per associate, with several associates nearing or reaching the 3,000-hour range." This makes for "many unhappy junior associates."

Stress for lawyers in less busy departments may be just as intense. Says one such associate, "I never thought I'd be saying this as a first-year associate, but I want more hours! I feel pressure to bill a certain number of hours, but the work is just not there." Some attorneys worry about the long-term effect of this pressure. The "tremendous emphasis on billables," uneven distribution of work and linking of bonuses to hours create "an incentive for associates to pad their hours," argues one source. "The system sends the wrong message: 'All we care about is billable hours.'"

Nevertheless, many lawyers maintain the hours are "typical for a large law firm." "I work a lot, but I get paid a lot. It goes with the territory." "Look," responds one associate, "I wish there wasn't the pressure on keeping hours up, but it's a big firm and that's the way it goes." "At least it is good work," several folks add. One lawyer sees the billable-bonus relationship not as a stick but as a carrot. "The hours can be long, but they are rewarding. Plus, with the new bonus structure, there is no longer a disincentive to work long hours; people are rewarded for their hard work."

Part-time program could be better

Several associates note that even if long hours are expected, O'Melveny is "very flexible as to where those hours are spent." Several attorneys report working reduced hours, although they say "the part-time program is poor." It is "not a realistic option," since part-timers are "not eligible for partnership or for an annual bonus." And their "pay scale includes a significant pay cut, which increases exponentially as you sign up for fewer hours." According to one attorney, "I work 75 percent but only get paid 65 percent." Moreover, "it seems that the only people who will really be permitted to work part time without incurring any stigma as a slacker or not being a team player are those with children."

A lot of dough

When it comes to compensation, few associates complain. "The partners treat us well," asserts an O'Melveny insider. "They want the best attorneys, so they pay top dollar." The "salary is near the top tier of law firms," and Los Angeles lawyers enjoyed "the highest bonuses in LA last year." But attorneys in Manhattan mutter that the firm's "New York bonuses do not keep pace with the market." Others complain that the bonus structure unfairly deprives associates "who have not met 1,950 billable hours — regardless of how much non-billable work they have done." In response to those who feel underpaid, one senior associate offers this perspective: "Many lawyers have never worked outside of the law and have a bizarre view of their worth. I have had many other working experiences — we are grossly overpaid relative to our societal value." And despite the grumbling, the majority of survey respondents acknowledge, "We get paid a lot of dough."

Sardine cans and dated décor, but the best view in Manhattan

If New Yorkers aren't thrilled with their bonuses, they at least enjoy their offices. All associates, including first-years, have their own "spacious" offices in an "absolutely fabulous" space with the "best views in Manhattan." By contrast, lawyers in D.C. "are in a terrible space crunch." "While the space is very nice, we are squeezed together like sardines. Plans, however, are being made to change that." Within the next two years, the firm is expected to move to a "stellar" new D.C. space. Los Angelenos would like to see their downtown office get a makeover, "especially in the associate offices, where nothing has changed since the office was opened in the early 1980s."

Commitment to community

Pro bono is "one area where the firm does well," opine several sources. An associate boasts, "We're one of the highest-hour pro bono firms in the country." The Los Angeles office has a "program with the Redondo Beach City Attorney's office which lets associates prosecute misdemeanor cases." Pro bono work counts toward billable hours and there is no cap — as long as the project is "approved." An insider explains that the hours "are given full billable credit, but there is also a committee that screens every case to make sure it is worthy of having the firm take it. That's the fly in the ointment — they won't take just any pro bono case." A few attorneys express concern over the firm's selection criteria. One lawyer has "the impression that the firm's real interest is in the publicity that certain pro bono matters generate or in training associates."

A self-perpetuating problem

When asked about their firm's diversity policies, the consensus among O'Melveny associates is that "something's not working." The firm has "very few female partners" and even fewer minority partners. "Hiring is fine," but the firm is "terrible at promoting and retaining" women, which leaves "fewer role models and mentors for women." Some sources fault a weak reduced hours program. Others note that "client development programs tend to be sports oriented" and are "allocated disproportionately to men."

With respect to minorities, sources can't pinpoint the cause but agree that a dearth exists. One associate says, "The firm can't seem to recruit and retain minorities. There is nothing identifiably unwelcoming to minorities about the firm. It seems at this point to be a self-perpetuating situation. There are virtually no minority attorneys, so minority students don't come here." The firm is more representative of some communities than others. "We are unacceptable with regard to African-Americans, but genuinely reaching out. We are better with Latinos and best with Asian-Americans," admits an OMM-er. Several insiders "still see an awful lot of white men." The firm is generally "tolerant and accepting" of gays and lesbians. More than one gay attorney reports that the San Francisco office is "very receptive" and notably "more diverse and accepting than other offices."

Hale and Dorr LLP

60 State Street
Boston, MA 02109-1816
Phone: (617) 526-6000
www.haledorr.com

LOCATIONS

Boston, MA (HQ)
New York, NY • Princeton, NJ • Reston, VA •
Waltham, MA • Washington, DC • London (Brobeck
Hale and Dorr) • Munich (Brobeck Hale and Dorr) •
Oxford (Brobeck Hale and Dorr)

MAJOR DEPARTMENTS/PRACTICES

Commercial
Corporate
Environmental
Government & Regulatory Affairs
Intellectual Property
Labor & Employment
Litigation
Private Client
Real Estate
Tax

THE STATS

No. of attorneys: 479
No. of offices: 6
Summer associate offers: 52 out of 55 (2001)
Managing Partner: William F. Lee
Hiring Partner: Daniel W. Halston

THE BUZZ
WHAT ATTORNEYS AT OTHER FIRMS ARE SAYING ABOUT THIS FIRM

- "Boston's best"
- "Competitive environment"
- "Dedicated to public service"
- "The bad guys in *A Civil Action*"
- "So blue-blooded you'll freeze"

BASE SALARY

Boston and Washington, DC, 2002
1st year: $125,000
2nd year: $135,000
3rd year: $145,000
4th year: $155,000
5th year: $165,000
1st yr. jr. partner: $180,000
2nd yr. jr. partner: $190,000
3rd yr. jr. partner: $200,000
Summer associate: $2,400/week

New York, 2002
1st year: $125,000
2nd year: $135,000
3rd year: $150,000
4th year: $160,000
5th year: $175,000
1st yr. jr. partner: $195,000
2nd yr. jr. partner: $205,000
3rd yr. jr. partner: $215,000
Summer associate: $2,400/week

Princeton, 2002
1st year: $115,000
2nd year: $135,000
3rd year: $145,000
4th year: $155,000
5th year: $165,000
1st yr. jr. partner: $180,000
2nd yr. jr. partner: $190,000
3rd yr. jr. partner: $200,000
Summer associate: $2,200/week

NOTABLE PERKS

- Twenty-dollar bills handed out at each firm meeting
- Superior home technology assistance
- In-house gym (Boston)
- Weekly happy hours and biweekly attorney lunches

UPPERS

• Superb training
• Notable commitment to pro bono work
• Posh digs

DOWNERS

• Salary freezes and reduced bonuses
• Volatile hours
• Uneven allocation of work

EMPLOYMENT CONTACT

Ms. Evelyn M. Scoville
Director of Legal Personnel
Phone: (617) 526-6590
Fax: (617) 526-5000
evelyn.scoville@haledorr.com

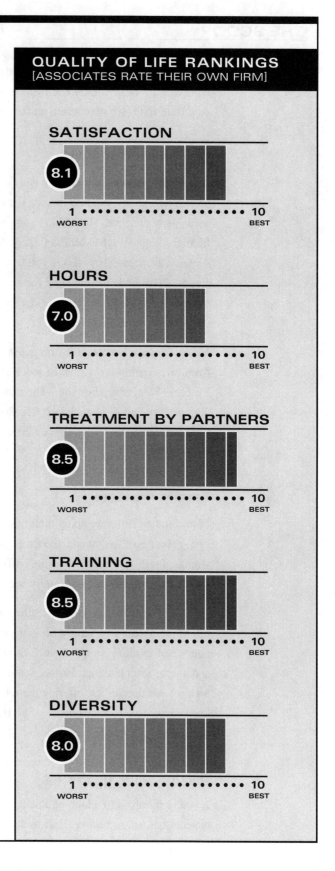

QUALITY OF LIFE RANKINGS
[ASSOCIATES RATE THEIR OWN FIRM]

SATISFACTION
8.1
1 WORST — 10 BEST

HOURS
7.0
1 WORST — 10 BEST

TREATMENT BY PARTNERS
8.5
1 WORST — 10 BEST

TRAINING
8.5
1 WORST — 10 BEST

DIVERSITY
8.0
1 WORST — 10 BEST

THE SCOOP

There's more to Boston than beans and baseball. It's also the home of Hale and Dorr. Hale and Dorr was one of the first major firms to dedicate a department just to intellectual property. To this day, Hale and Dorr's corporate practice is built around the high-tech industry.

A firm of influence

When Richard Hale and Dudley Dorr established their Boston law firm in 1918, they must have known technology would influence society in extraordinary ways. Since its founding, the firm has seen many changes. In 1954, it represented the U.S. Army in the Army-McCarthy hearings. Partner Joseph Welch asked McCarthy the famous question at the hearings: "Have you no sense of decency, sir, at long last? Have you left no sense of decency?" Twenty years later, in 1974, partner Jim St. Clair made the cover of *Time* when he became the special counsel to the President of the United States, Richard Nixon. The firm branched out from Beantown in 1981, opening a new office in Washington, D.C.

Nine years later, in 1990, the firm made history by co-founding the first independent law firm made from two existing law firms, Brobeck Hale and Dorr in London, along with San-Francisco-based Brobeck, Phleger & Harrison. The new independent firm opened more offices, one in Oxford in 2000 and another in Munich in 2001. However, Brobeck Hale and Dorr felt the effects of the year's poor economy, and in November 2001 laid off seven corporate associates from its London and Oxford offices.

Family matters

Many top law firms are doing their best to offer a family-friendly environment, and Hale and Dorr is no exception. To that end, the firm opened an in-house day care facility in the Boston office and similar facilities near its other offices, to help employees juggle the often-competing responsibilities of work and family life.

Hale and Dorr cares about the families of its clients, too. The firm is one of the few law firms to offer the services of a family office to its high net-worth clients. A family office advises a small number of families on topics such as tax planning, wealth management planning, tax consulting and investment planning. Partner Jennifer Snyder of the Boston office is known for her work with high net-worth families, offering them her know-how on everything the well-to-do client needs to know to manage her personal wealth. If a client has a family office, Snyder collaborates with that office in providing her expertise.

Billion-dollar business

If you're involved in a high-end deal, you might want to call Hale and Dorr. In one of the largest biotech mergers in history, Hale and Dorr represented Millennium Pharmaceuticals, Inc. when it acquired COR Therapeutics, Inc. in December of 2001 for $2 billion. In June 2001, the State of Wisconsin Investment Board of Madison, Wis., bought 1.82 million shares of Princeton's Cytogen Corp., a biopharmaceutical company, for $8.19 million. The firm represented medical device manufacturer NMT Medical Inc. when it was acquired by competitor C.R. Bard Inc. for $34 million in November 2001.

Hale and Dorr represented Raytheon Co. when L-3 Communications Holdings Inc., a supplier of secure communications systems and communication products, acquired Aircraft Integration Systems, a Texas aircraft modification and integration business and part of Raytheon Co. The January 2002 deal was valued at a cool $1.13 billion.

Make yourself at home at Hale

Every summer associate's dream: a corner office with a stellar view of the expansive, exciting city below. Well, at the D.C. office of Hale and Dorr, that dream was at least partially realized for a few summer associates in 2001. Managing partner James Quarles, senior partner William McElwain and office manager Judi Weltmann generously turned their offices, which overlook the Washington Monument, over to six lucky summer associates. The firm was building new offices a couple of floors below, and Quarles and McElwain didn't want the associates to be cooped up in uncompleted, shabby offices. The six summer associates got the partner treatment as they spent the summer gazing at one of the most photographed and beloved symbols of our country.

Namaste, namaste very much

Who says lawyers can't relax? With longer hours at work and higher stress levels, lawyers are trying various methods to pare the pressure. One of the best and most popular ways of taming the tension is yoga. Some very Zen lawyers at Hale and Dorr's Boston office are jumping on the yoga bandwagon, meeting informally each week to try their hands at the ancient practice. They are finding that serenity doesn't have to impede a lawyer's ability to be tough when necessary. If the informal yoga meetings gain enough support, attorneys at Hale and Dorr may find themselves doing backbends down the hallways.

GETTING HIRED

Looking for that "something special"

Like most top law firms, Hale and Dorr seeks the "brightest and most well-rounded applicants." Candidates need "top credentials." According to several sources, "Harvard students have an easier time getting hired than other people." However, associates agree that "good numbers are not enough." "Though a stellar academic record is important, the firm seems to look for candidates with personality." "Being smart, hardworking and responsible is just a prerequisite," explains an attorney, since "the firm is looking for people who are not only great attorneys but great individuals." Or, as another lawyer puts it: "Candidates definitely must have that 'something special' that sets them apart from the group — it's not enough to have good grades and a nice resume."

That something special could include "ties to the city of Boston," a technology background, a "type A personality" or "valuable career/business/government experience in addition to law school achievement." Candidates should exude confidence and demonstrate enthusiasm for the legal profession. Insiders describe the interview process as standard but "very efficient." Applicants endure one initial on-campus interview that lasts approximately 20 minutes with a representative of the firm. Next comes a longer callback interview at the firm with three or four attorneys, often including lunch. Try not to sleepwalk your way through the initial interview. One lawyer advises, "It's usually partners on the hiring committee that go on screening interviews, so it's definitely important to make a good first impression."

OUR SURVEY SAYS

A culture of cooperation

"The people make this place," claims a third-year Hale and Dorr associate. Many of her colleagues agree. "The firm is full of intelligent, friendly people who are focused on doing the best possible job for the client while maintaining a comfortable, approachable atmosphere." The firm is "focused on quality work," but lawyers are "informal," "fairly laid back and collegial." First names are used, and "the open-door policy truly is an open-door policy." Several insiders praise the firm's "culture of cooperation" and "ethic of teaching younger associates." "The partners and senior associates are great to work with and take a lot of time to help train the young associates," says an insider. Associates are quick to point out, however, that the friendly culture doesn't signify a lazy approach to the work at hand. It's a "great place to practice law, but it's still a large law firm, meaning first-year work is somewhat menial, clients are demanding and the work ethic is firm first, family and life later."

Though Hale and Dorr attorneys are friendly to each other, many associates insist that "socializing seems limited to classmates," and "in general, attorneys keep their private and professional lives separate." "If you want to socialize," say associates, "there are plenty of opportunities to do so," including a happy hour every Friday and biweekly firm-sponsored attorney lunches. The Boston office is home to the "Thursday Night Club," a "group of attorneys who go out practically every Thursday night." Some associates find the firm's atmosphere cliquish. "Each group tends to socialize only with each other," asserts a third-year associate, "even though people are, for the most part, civil."

"Pretty darn posh"

Boston associates love their Hale and Dorr digs. "The most convenient office space in Boston" has "a gym and a cafeteria," it is located "near the waterfront, next to a giant food court," with a "subway station right out the door." But best of all, "There is no office sharing and at least half of the associate offices have spectacular views of the waterfront." Even those offices that don't overlook the harbor have large, floor to ceiling windows. Insiders praise the furniture and facilities and report that, "with the exception of some hideous art here and there, this place is pretty darn posh." Associates in D.C. also give their space high marks. "The overall office space is lovely and impressive with intriguing art and fabulous views of the Washington Mall and the Potomac." Even New Yorkers are pleased with space that is "nice, comfortable and very efficient."

Praise for partners

"The partners are one of the best reasons for working here," says a fourth-year associate. Hale and Dorr respondents lavish praise on partners who "treat associates with great respect" and "take their role as teachers extremely seriously." "It still amazes me," declares a junior litigator, "how much time partners are willing to spend with associates explaining to them the intricacies of the case, even if it is not necessary to complete the assignment." Of course, "as in any firm, some partners are excellent to work with and some are simply socially inept." One lawyer finds "the partners are fantastic people one-on-one, but they collectively have a bottom-line economic approach to the business of law that makes me feel very insecure." Respect for associates is also reflected in the upward evaluation process. This "process is helpful in giving partners feedback about their interactions with associates," and the "evaluations are then taken into account during the partner review process."

The Boston salary freeze

Generally, Hale and Dorr "maintains a competitive compensation rate" by which it will "match the highest salary in town." Many insiders believe the firm's "compensation package is as good as any in the country." However, in keeping with "the economic realities" and following the lead of other Boston firms, Hale and Dorr froze attorney salaries and reduced bonuses for 2002. "Extremely disappointing," grumble associates who claim the firm is "no longer a leader in compensation in Boston." Others argue that the firm's ability "to maintain salaries and continue to pay bonuses in an environment where other firms are laying off attorneys or imposing pay cuts" attests to the firm's smart management.

Despite praise for partners' communication with associates as to the firm's fiscal goals and budget situation, few respondents seem to know how bonuses are calculated. "The firm says bonuses aren't strictly tied to hours," reports one puzzled lawyer, but "it's not clear to us how bonuses are determined." According to another associate, "Bonuses were based on four criteria, of which one was hours worked." Some New Yorkers complain of being underpaid relative to other top firms in Manhattan, although at least one New York lawyer maintains that the firm is still "at the top of the pay scale." A few associates seem almost embarrassed by their income. "We are ridiculously overpaid," admits a corporate attorney. "What can I say?" adds a first-year lawyer. "It's a lot of money."

No escaping the billables

On the whole, associates are relatively resigned to their immense workload. "There's no escaping billable hours at any big firm," says an insider, "but Hale and Dorr does place an emphasis on looking out for associates' quality of life." Associates explain that the firm sets a target of 2,000 billable hours, but "you don't get in trouble if you don't meet that target." That said, many sources do spend more time in the office than they'd like. "At times," one lawyer sighs, "the workload is so heavy that I could spend all my time at the office and never be done." Yet other attorneys report that a "9 to 7 weekday schedule, with rare weekend appearances, is definitely possible here." Moreover, the firm is reportedly "excellent in working with those who need flexibility in their work schedules."

Some glass-half-full types recognize that the hours are "not bad at all considering how much they pay us." "The redeeming factor" for one lawyer "is that I really enjoy my colleagues and I have access to exciting projects that I would not otherwise have." A third-year associate acknowledges the "eternal conflict between quality of life and the opportunity to participate in the interesting, fast-paced complexity of big-firm litigation."

Giving diversity a try

Associates give Hale and Dorr high marks for its commitment to diversity, especially the efforts of the firm's Asian-American managing partner. "Bill Lee has a great attitude about diversity and respect for everyone. His tone has carried through the ranks and has made a difference," remarks an associate. And yet most insiders acknowledge that these efforts have not necessarily altered the makeup of a predominantly white male leadership. One litigator voices a common view: "I think the firm does well in terms of hiring, but the lack of women in the partnership leaves much to be desired." (The firm points out that four women were elected to senior partnership and 13 were elected to junior partnership in May 2002.) Similarly, "the racial composition of the lawyers here suggests that this is not the most diverse place." The firm does employ "quite a few" Asian-Americans, but "the truth of the matter is that there are only a handful of African-American lawyers." A few lawyers suggest that this "could be more a reflection of Boston than of Hale and Dorr itself." Other attorneys note that "although the issue is apparent, there does not seem to be a consensus on how to address it."

Sources believe "the firm is actually fairly progressive in its attitudes and policies toward gays and lesbians." Hale and Dorr offers same-sex partner benefits and, an attorney reports, "I am gay myself and I find the firm very positive in terms of benefits that it is willing to provide its gay associates."

One of the best in Boston

"Hale and Dorr has one of the best pro bono records in Boston," a respondent claims. It "has taken on litigation in areas from death penalty post-conviction review to IOLTA funding." Other lawyers agree that the firm has "an enthusiastic commitment to pro bono." "I don't do it," admits a corporate lawyer, "but I'm glad everyone else does." Most associates maintain that pro bono work counts toward billable hours, but a few insiders claim that it really falls "somewhere between billable and office hours." One lawyer notes that under "a new billing computer system, ... pro bono hours are clearly separated from billable hours and grouped with 'meetings' and 'interviewing candidates' hours — not with the real hours." A source calls the firm's commitment "outstanding, even in tough economic times." And more than one associate maintains that the firm's "excellent record in this area" was one of the firm's attractions.

Morrison & Foerster LLP

425 Market Street
San Francisco, CA 94105-2482
Phone: (415) 268-7000
www.mofo.com

LOCATIONS

San Francisco, CA (HQ)
Century City, CA • Denver, CO • Los Angeles, CA •
New York, NY • Northern Virginia, VA • Orange
County, CA • Palo Alto, CA • Sacramento, CA • San
Diego, CA • Walnut Creek, CA • Washington, DC •
Beijing • Brussels • Hong Kong • London • Singapore •
Tokyo

MAJOR DEPARTMENTS/PRACTICES

Corporate Finance
Financial Services
Intellectual Property & Patent
International
Labor & Employment Law
Land Use, Environmental & Energy
Litigation
Real Estate
Tax & Estates

THE STATS

No. of attorneys: 1,015 (As of February/March 2002)
No. of offices: 18
Summer associate offers: 117 out of 130 (2001)
(Includes offers of associate employment as well as
offers to return for summer of 2002 given to first-
years)
Managing Partner: Keith C. Wetmore
Hiring Partner: James E. Hough

BASE SALARY

**New York, Washington, DC, Tokyo and California ,
2002**
1st year: $125,000
Summer associate (New York, Tokyo and
California): $2,400/week

Denver, 2002
1st year: $110,000
Summer associate: $2,000/week

NOTABLE PERKS

• Lots of free cookies
• Weekly happy hours
• Friday morning breakfasts
• Occasional gift certificates as spot bonuses

 ## THE BUZZ
WHAT ATTORNEYS AT OTHER FIRMS ARE SAYING ABOUT THIS FIRM

• "Epitome of prestigious California law firm"
• "Best work environment"
• "Skillful attorneys"
• "Not as touchy-feely as they pretend to be"
• "Suffering from delusions of grandeur"

UPPERS

- Much-adored partnership
- "Unbelievable" commitment to pro bono work
- Stellar diversity record

DOWNERS

- "No sense of job security"
- Bonuses tied to hours worked

EMPLOYMENT CONTACT

Ms. Jane Cooperman
Senior Recruiting Manager (Firm-wide information)
Phone: (415) 268-7665
Fax: (415) 268-7522
jcooperman@mofo.com

To apply to the firm, applicants should contact the Attorney Recruiting Department in the appropriate office (see MoFo web site at www.mofo.com for office addresses).

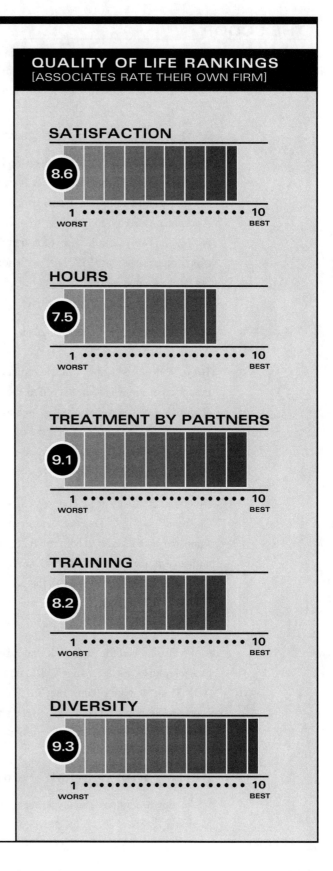

QUALITY OF LIFE RANKINGS
[ASSOCIATES RATE THEIR OWN FIRM]

SATISFACTION
8.6
1 WORST · · · · · · · · · · · · · · · 10 BEST

HOURS
7.5
1 WORST · · · · · · · · · · · · · · · 10 BEST

TREATMENT BY PARTNERS
9.1
1 WORST · · · · · · · · · · · · · · · 10 BEST

TRAINING
8.2
1 WORST · · · · · · · · · · · · · · · 10 BEST

DIVERSITY
9.3
1 WORST · · · · · · · · · · · · · · · 10 BEST

THE SCOOP

It's easy to tell from its vaguely racy nickname ("MoFo") that San Francisco-based Morrison & Foerster is a law firm that's not afraid to take risks.

MoFo plays the name game

The San Francisco-based Morrison & Foerster has long embraced its once-facetious nickname "MoFo," and now proudly uses it for its URL address. As a matter of fact, MoFo has had 14 different names in its 118-year history. The firm was born in 1883, when Thomas O'Brien and Alexander Morrison founded O'Brien & Morrison. Seven years later, Constantine Foerster joined on. Within two years, the firm took on its current name. But when Foerster died in 1898, it became Morrison & Cope. In 1918, Foerster's son, Ronald, joined the firm and, like any good son, restored his father's name in 1925. In the next 50 years, the firm played the name game until it was once again known as Morrison & Foerster, officially.

MoFo has undergone many changes unrelated to nomenclature. The firm now boasts offices in Los Angeles, Washington, D.C., Denver and New York, as well as international offices in London, Tokyo and Hong Kong. In November 2000, the firm plucked Keith Wetmore from the San Francisco office, where he served as the managing partner of that office, to head the whole firm as chairman. Wetmore is only the second openly gay man to head up a major law firm. (Often, Wetmore can be spotted around the office sporting a nifty "Homo at MoFo" cap.)

Going full throttle

Does your company need a boost? Consider calling MoFo for help. In 1953 the Indian Motorcycle Co. went bankrupt. Decades later, a pair of venture capital companies wanted to get it running again and asked MoFo to help rev things up. In July 2001, Morrison & Foerster aided the company with a cash infusion of about $45 million. In the mid-1990s, Indian Motorcycle Co. went head to head over trademark rights with the person who received the original motorcycle company's estate after it went bankrupt in 1953. Lawyers in the Denver office helped the company settle the suit and also won them the Indian trademark rights.

MoFo also helped the high-tech magazine *Business 2.0*, published by The Future Network, boost its declining profits. In June 2001, Future Network sold the magazine to The Fortune Group of AOL Time Warner's Time Inc. for $68 million. Future Network is based in England and the magazine is based in San Francisco, and the publisher chose Morrison & Foerster because it wanted a firm that could handle a cross-border purchase.

Dealing with debt differently

In the down economy, many companies have been selling debt notes to raise money. With Morrison & Foerster's help, Novellus Systems Inc. is doing the same — but with a difference.

Because debt notes typically pay a low interest rate, they offer a guaranteed return of bonds. They can also be converted to stock at a premium on the stock's present value, so as long as a company's shares trade above the premium, debt notes are like stock. Novellus sold its 30-year notes at a 52 percent premium paying no interest; therefore, its stock needs to trade higher than $76.36 in order for buyers to make money.

A shaker-full of deals

The attorneys at Morrison & Foerster make a deal like a good bartender makes a dry martini. That's comforting to Campari Group. In December 2001, Morrison & Foerster helped the Italian beverage company acquire an additional 50 percent of Skyy Spirits LLC. This acquisition brings Campari's stake up to 58.9 percent, giving it control of the company. The deal was worth $207.5 million.

Also in December 2001, MoFo helped turn the channel to Spanish-language TV. Its client, the National Broadcasting Company, Inc., bought Telemundo Communications Group, Inc., the second largest Spanish network, for a whopping $1.98 billion (also assuming $700 million of the network's debt). This deal links the No. 1 English-language network with the No. 2 Spanish network, which owns 10 stations.

In October 2001, MoFo had a hand in two notable acquisitions. Phonextra bought Wire One Technologies, Inc.'s voice communications business for about $2 million. MoFo client Sage Inc., a digital processor developer, swapped stock with Genesis Microchip Inc., a manufacturer of integrated circuits and video display products.

MoFo no no

Like many firms dealing with the angst of a lackluster economy, MoFo was forced to make cutbacks in personnel in 2001. The firm claims the undisclosed number of cuts were performance-based — not layoffs. The firm admits that the number of associates at the firm has declined of late but maintains that the decline is primarily due to normal attrition.

A lawyer for Walker

One of the curiosities of the American military assaults on the Al Qaeda organization in Afghanistan was the apprehension of John Walker Lindh, an American citizen and Taliban warrior. Seasoned MoFo partner James Brosnahan has agreed to represent John Walker Lindh. Brosnahan is used to being in the political limelight; he was the lead trial attorney in the Iran-Contra case against Caspar Weinberger, and testified against the appointment of William Rehnquist as Chief Justice of the U.S. Supreme Court.

None of your business

With the rising importance of legal privacy issues, MoFo sees an opportunity. The firm wants to be a big player on privacy issues for corporate clients. It's taken on board Peter Swire and Lauren Steinfeld, a pair who worked on the federal government's medical privacy regulations. Swire was the chief counselor for privacy under the Clinton administration. In December 2001, Barbara Wellbery joined the D.C. office. Wellbery worked in the U.S. Department of Commerce and crafted the Safe Harbor Data Privacy Accord with the European Union. In all, MoFo has nearly 50 attorneys in their privacy practice group.

GETTING HIRED

Be yourself

If you're looking to join the MoFo team, you have your work cut out for you. "This is such a great firm that many law students and lateral attorneys want to join. As such, there is a lot of competition." According to some insiders, MoFo "has gotten more difficult to get into in the last year or so." "We are very picky," warns an associate. Certainly an applicant must have "excellent credentials" — namely, "good grades, good school and helpful work experience." Says one source, "A candidate must generally go to a first-tier law school and be near the top of their class." Several sources agree that the "firm looks for top notch credentials, but [personality] fit is even more important." "So in the interview process," advises an associate, "it is important to be yourself." What makes a good fit? Appreciation for the firm's "laid-back attitude," for starters. Also, someone who is "smart, mature, professional and easy to get along with — a team player." The self-important should be forewarned: "Prima donnas and those with an overdeveloped sense of entitlement generally don't do well in the interview process." One associate claims that the firm has turned down qualified candidates in "busy periods" due to poor personality fit.

OUR SURVEY SAYS

Shiny, happy people

Clearly, this firm is doing something right. When it comes to measuring overall job satisfaction, most insiders feel "very fortunate to work at MoFo." Comments are almost universally positive. Associates describe the firm environment as "friendly," "laid back and progressive." "People work hard," but the firm as a whole remains "quite laid back and sociable." There is "very little hierarchy" and "politics are at a minimum."

Associates appreciate the "intellectual challenge of the work" and enjoy working alongside colleagues who are "unbelievably intelligent, hardworking, kind and mentoring." One lawyer describes the firm in less sentimental terms: "Generally friendly and collegial, but sort of like the Island of Misfit Toys — people are quirky and often odd." While some lawyers delight in after-hours socializing with their colleagues, others prefer to "run home to be with their families." A senior associate reports, "Many of us have been close friends for years and socialize frequently," while a working parent finds the firm "very family friendly." (Morrison & Foerster provides access to emergency child care services in most of its offices.) One happy litigator declares, "Although I would prefer to be working for a noble cause and changing the world, this is the next best thing."

Top of the scale

Sure, MoFo lawyers love their firm's high-caliber work, respected colleagues and friendly, open-minded atmosphere — but it doesn't hurt that a healthy paycheck is included in the package. Compensation at Morrison & Foerster is "very competitive." "We're at the top of the pay scale," says an associate. In addition to a "generous market rate salary," the firm awards both hour-based and merit bonuses, which some associates believe "could be higher." Several associates express a longing for bonuses not tied to hours worked, though others appreciate the firm's pay structure. "Associates are very lucky," admits a litigator. One experienced associate "still find[s] it almost embarrassing how much lawyers make."

Mostly manageable hours

For a large firm, many associates find that "the hours are extraordinarily manageable" at Morrison & Foerster. That doesn't mean MoFo lawyers don't work hard; most sources report billing between 176 and 200 hours per month. But the "hours aren't bad, relative to our competition," according to associates. And some attribute those long hours more to the nature of the work than to the culture of the firm. "In general, people work hard," says a lawyer based in D.C., "but not just to impress the partners." The firm maintains a two-tier compensation structure, whereby associates who bill over 1,950 hours per year earn more than their lesser-billing colleagues. "As in all firms," explains another attorney, "the billable hour requirement is the least pleasant of all responsibilities." He adds, "By having two tiers for our base compensation and additional hour requirements for bonuses, the firm reduces the onerousness of these requirements as much as possible."

At least one associate finds the distinction between billable and non-billable time irksome. "Since the Internet bubble burst, there has been a lot of pressure to work long hours whether or not those hours include billable work. If I am going to work that hard," she argues, "I should not have to worry about whether or not those hours generate revenue." Others "would like to work less," but acknowledge that the hours are "commensurate with the position and the salary." Attorneys also appreciate that MoFo "is very flexible in accommodating requested schedules."

Genuine team spirit

Partners at Morrison & Foerster could hardly have drawn higher praise from our survey respondents. Raves one insider, "The partners I work with are, in a word, terrific." "The best I've seen or heard of," exclaims one lawyer. Another maintains, "All the partners, to a person, are bright, intelligent, thoughtful and accessible. While some have management styles that make them easier to work with than others, no one here is a person I would not work with without hesitation." Such sentiments extend across the country. Lawyers in D.C. appreciate the sense of "team effort." Partners "have an open-door policy and are good teachers." A New York attorney reports that "overall the interactions between partners and associates are healthy and productive." Associates in Southern California find that "partners generally treat associates very well and try to give strong one-on-one training." Bravo, partners!

A diversity celebration

Having a managing partner who is openly gay says a lot about MoFo's welcoming attitude toward gay and lesbian lawyers. A gay lawyer claims that "diversity is not just tolerated, but celebrated at MoFo." Another associate notes that the "firm provides domestic partner benefits, and even lists same-sex domestic partners in the firm directory." Most associates say the firm also has an excellent record with respect to women. Female respondents note, "There are lots of intelligent and diverse women here, including partners." But "more importantly," explains a litigator, "the firm is on the cutting edge of these issues and very proactive in wanting to retain women and other minorities." An associate cites the firm's frequent ranking among *Working Mother* magazine's list of the top 100 companies to work for. One lawyer agrees that MoFo "is better than most," but adds that "most of the women partners do not have children, and the women associates are definitely afraid to take time off." The firm, however, points out that roughly half of the firm's female partners have children, and that the many partners and associates who are regularly out on family care leave are fully supported by the firm.

The firm's efforts in recruiting minority attorneys are praised, although many associates see little evidence of the fruits of these efforts. "I know the firm wants diversity," an attorney writes, "but it has been difficult to achieve." Several sources note that the firm has had less success retaining African-American or Hispanic attorneys than Asian-Americans. "At least in the San Diego demographic community, it is unbelievable that we do not have Hispanic or black associates and partners." The firm points out that the San Diego office has a Latino partner who has been with the firm since 2000, one Latino of counsel and a Latino associate, as well as six Asian-American associates. Attorneys in Orange County and Washington, D.C., note a similar problem. (The firm notes that the Orange County office employs several Asian-American associates and one African-American partner, and the D.C. office employs two African-American associates and one of counsel, one Latino associate, several Asian-American associates and one Asian-American partner.) Associates are pleased that the firm has a standing diversity committee, and according to one lawyer, "the firm is very aware and proactive on the issue, and actively recruits minorities on campuses and otherwise."

An impressive commitment

According to many associates, MoFo has an "unbelievable commitment to pro bono work." Each of the firm's offices has a pro bono committee dedicated to helping associates find appropriate pro bono work. According to a San Francisco lawyer, pro bono work is not only encouraged, it's required for junior associates. The majority of respondents find the firm very supportive and encouraging. They note happily that "pro bono hours count 100 percent toward billable hours, bonuses and everything else." A senior associate adds, "There is no limit on pro bono hours. The only time you hear anything about your pro bono hours is when they are low. Even then the message is not 'You're not doing enough pro bono,' it's 'Are there any pro bono projects you'd like to do or any projects you'd like us to find for you?'"

One attorney in the D.C. office reports an experience notably different from her colleagues: "Partners tend to discourage associates from working on pro bono projects in order to beef up on revenue-generating billable work."

Keeping people satisfied

"MoFo makes a real effort to keep people satisfied," which keeps the firm's attrition rate fairly low. "Although there is some natural attrition," explains one associate, "people stay here longer than at other places." A lawyer in D.C. explains that MoFo "is good at retaining lawyers who want to continue practicing law." She adds, "Most of the people who have left have left to pursue other careers or to work for the government." Other sources agree that when "people do leave, more tend to either go to another office of the firm in a different geographic region" or "switch careers entirely, so their leaving is not for another firm."

Clifford Chance Rogers & Wells LLP

200 Park Avenue
New York, NY 10166
Phone: (212) 878-8000
www.cliffordchance.com

LOCATIONS

New York, NY • Palo Alto • San Francisco •
Washington, DC • Amsterdam • Bangkok • Barcelona •
Beijing • Berlin • Brussels • Budapest • Dubai •
Dusseldorf • Frankfurt • Hong Kong • London •
Luxembourg • Madrid • Milan • Moscow • Munich •
Padua • Paris • Prague • Rome • Sao Paulo • Shanghai •
Singapore • Tokyo • Warsaw

MAJOR DEPARTMENTS/PRACTICES

Antitrust • Banking • Corporate Finance/Securities •
Cross-Border Finance • Debt & Equity Capital Markets •
Derivatives & Structured Products • E-Commerce •
Financial Restructuring & Insolvency • Intellectual
Property • Litigation & Dispute Resolution • Media/First
Amendment • Mergers & Acquisitions • Private Equity •
Project Finance • Real Estate • Securities Litigation •
Tax, Trusts & Estates • Technology • White Collar
Crime

THE STATS

No. of attorneys: 2,908
No. of offices: 30
Summer associate offers: 50 out of 52 (2001)
Managing Partner: James N. Benedict (The Americas
Region)
Hiring Attorney: David L. Taub

BASE SALARY

New York and Washington, DC, 2002
1st year: $125,000
2nd year: $135,000
3rd year: $150,000
4th year: $170,000
5th year: $190,000
6th year: $205,000
7th year: $220,000
8th year: $235,000
Summer associate: $2,404/week

NOTABLE PERKS

• One-time $2,000 technology grant
• Use of firm's two condos in Florida
• Subsidized gym memberships

THE BUZZ
WHAT ATTORNEYS AT OTHER FIRMS ARE SAYING ABOUT THIS FIRM

• "One of the biggest and best"
• "Frankenstein's monster"
• "Work product varies among offices"
• "International powerhouse"
• "Massive sweatshop"

UPPERS

- Impressive international work
- Worldwide prestige
- "Atmosphere of cordiality"

DOWNERS

- "Naïve obsession with billable hour targets"
- Not enough work to go around
- Windowless interior offices for mid-level associates

EMPLOYMENT CONTACT

Ms. Carolyn S. Older
Manager of Legal Recruiting
Phone: (212) 878-8252
Fax: (212) 878-8375
carolyn.older@cliffordchance.com

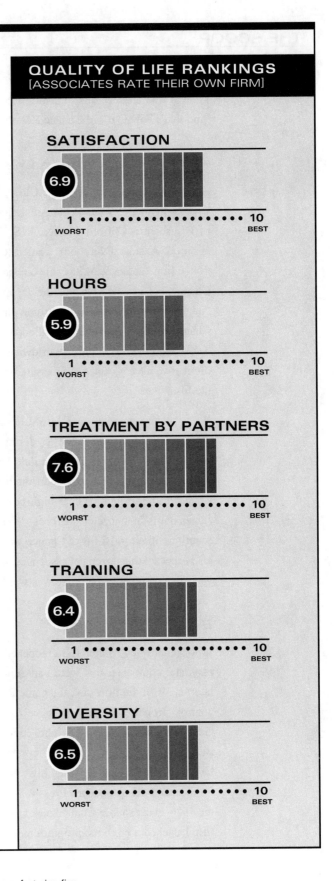

QUALITY OF LIFE RANKINGS
[ASSOCIATES RATE THEIR OWN FIRM]

SATISFACTION
6.9
1 WORST   10 BEST

HOURS
5.9
1 WORST   10 BEST

TREATMENT BY PARTNERS
7.6
1 WORST   10 BEST

TRAINING
6.4
1 WORST   10 BEST

DIVERSITY
6.5
1 WORST   10 BEST

THE SCOOP

The late 1990s brought an increasingly competitive legal market. U.S. law firm Rogers & Wells knew it would either sink or swim in the new economy. It had to do something bold to stand out. And that's how Clifford Chance Rogers & Wells was born.

A firm by any other name

A series of global mergers made Clifford Chance LLP the largest international law firm. Clifford Chance Rogers & Wells is the American name of the firm formed in January 2000 by the merger of British firm Clifford Chance, U.S. firm Rogers & Wells and German firm Punder, Volhard Weber & Axster. Everybody wanted to get into the Clifford Chance act. In February 2001, the Tokyo firm Tanaka & Akita came on board. In most parts of the globe the firm is known as Clifford Chance, but in some places, like Japan, the firm is known as Clifford Chance Tanaka Akita & Nakagawa, or in Germany and some places in Eastern Europe the firm goes by the name Clifford Chance Punder. Whatever it's called, it is the largest international law firm in the world with about 3,000 attorneys in 30 cities worldwide. The firm continues to bring in lateral candidates at an impressive pace — since the merger, 64 lateral partners, including 18 M&A partners, have joined the firm.

With its latest acquisition, Clifford Chance gains a secure foothold on the West Coast. In May 2002, the firm made headlines by luring 17 partners from Brobeck, Phleger & Harrison to set up new offices in San Francisco and Palo Alto. The group includes former Brobeck chairman Tower Snow Jr., who had been expelled from the firm after his plans to take partners with him to Clifford Chance came to light. Other high-profile defectors include former firm-wide managing partner James Burns Jr. and Michael Torpey, head of the securities litigation practice group. In addition to securities litigators, Clifford Chance will acquire several IP litigators and corporate attorneys. It is also expected that dozens of associates, including many Brobeck attorneys, will join the firm's new Bay Area outposts. The move westward creates the nation's largest securities practice.

Big time beginnings

In 1871 attorney Walter Carter opened an office in the New York Life Building to represent insurance companies that went bankrupt due to the Great Chicago Fire. Over one hundred years later, in 1973, the firm took the name Rogers & Wells when William Rogers and Jack Wells took control. Rogers was an impressive figure in the world of politics and law, serving as Attorney General under President Dwight Eisenhower and as Secretary of State under Richard Nixon. Between those positions, he was appointed by Lyndon Johnson to be the U.S. representative to the United Nations General Assembly. He also argued two landmark cases, New York Times v. Sullivan and The Associated Press v. Walker, and served as chair of the committee that investigated the 1986 space shuttle Challenger explosion. In January 2001, he died at age 87. This year, the firm launched a pro bono program in his name.

The other half of the firm, Clifford Chance, was established in 1802. In 1987 Clifford-Turner merged with Coward Chance, joining the group of choice British firms known as the Magic Circle. In 1992 it became the first major non-U.S. firm to practice U.S. law outside the United States.

The integration of Clifford Chance and Rogers & Wells was not without its challenges. One problem was client conflicts. Clifford Chance represented client Microsoft Corp. but had to cut the cord with the computer giant because Rogers & Wells' partner Kevin Arquit is involved in the antitrust case against the company. One of the firm's top priorities when it announced its merger was to build a conflicts clearing network worldwide. All new matters pass through this system. As evidence of Clifford Chance's commitment to being one firm globally, the firm instituted a unified global lockstep partnership compensation system.

Financing to rebuild post-September 11

Given the scope of Clifford Chance's practice and its Wall Street client base, it's not surprising that the firm is entrenched in post-September 11 and Enron-related work. In addition to acting for the underwriters Bear Stearns in the New York City Transitional Finance Authority's $1 billion note issuance to fund recovery for downtown Manhattan, the firm is advising insurers and reinsurers such as SCOR SA and the insurance companies of the GE Group in claims arising from the World Trade Center diaster. Clifford Chance also is defending Alliance Capital and Merrill Lynch in connection with Enron-related claims.

Drop your weapons

Four Clifford Chance attorneys want to combat the illicit trade in small arms and light weapons. With the goal of eliminating dangerous weapons brokers, Clifford Chance drafted a model convention that was presented to the United Nations delegations at a two-week conference in August 2001. This presentation was on behalf of their pro bono client, the Fund for Peace. The U.N. estimates that between 40 and 60 percent of these weapons are illegal, and trafficking them is worth $1 billion. Most weapons brokers are not regulated under the majority of jurisdictions. The United States is one of eleven nations that does have laws against unregistered brokers.

M&A, A-OK

You'd think with such a complex merger itself, Clifford Chance would not have time to deal with other mergers. Au contraire. Among recent M&A transactions, CCR&W represented Swedish corporation AB Volvo in its $1.8 billion acquisition of French automaker Renault V.I. and counseled Italian catering company Autogrill S.p.A. for its $1 billion acquisition of Host Marriott Services Corporation. When online trading company E*Trade bought the electronic broker-dealer and related technology subsidiaries of Tradescape Corp. in 2002, Clifford Chance was on hand to smooth the $100 million sale. Another high stakes deal is the $2.1 billion acquisition of Avon

Energy Partners Holdings, the holding company of GPU Inc.-owned U.K. electric utility Midlands Electricity PLC, by Aquila, a Missouri-based gas and electric utility.

Experts on antitrust

Clifford Chance boasts a thriving antitrust litigation and merger review practice. With more than 200 lawyers, the firm's antitrust group is one of the largest in the world. CCR&W attorneys obtained clearance for the marriage of soda and cereal giants, PepsiCo and Quaker Oats, and for Johnson & Johnson's merger with pharmaceutical company, ALZA Corp. On the litigation side, Sun Microsystems, Inc. has retained the firm as co-counsel in an antitrust action filed in March 2002 by Sun against Microsoft Corp. alleging anti-competitive behavior directed at Sun's Java platform.

In other recent litigation, Clifford Chance joins the list of law firms counseling clients on claims arising from the collapse of Enron. The firm also successfully defended Citigroup, Merrill Lynch, Prudential, SunAmerica and Dreyfus in a class action lawsuit, the largest suit ever brought against the mutual fund industry challenging director independence and investment advisory and distribution fees. (In March 2002 the plaintiffs voluntarily dismissed the action.) In a notable IP win in 2001, the firm obtained a unanimous jury verdict for biotech client Genentech in a patent infringement suit brought by GlaxoSmithKline. The firm also has a thriving white collar criminal practice that includes former federal prosecutors and SEC attorneys.

GETTING HIRED

Going for grades

School, grades and character all factor into Clifford Chance's hiring process, although many associates report that since the merger the firm has become "increasingly credentials-conscious." One lawyer asserts that the firm "is relying almost entirely on grades. If you don't have at least a 3.3 from a top 15 school, too bad." The flip side is that "if you have good grades, you are a shoe-in." Some sources believe that Clifford Chance "sets very high standards," but strains to meet them. The firm "tries its best to pretend it can compete with the Skaddens, Sullivans, Davis Polks, Simpsons and so on in terms of high-quality associates, but in reality anyone with really good grades and a personality gets an offer from one of those firms and goes there. Therefore, almost anyone with the grades — say 3.3 and above — gets an offer here." The firm responds that it uses many factors, including grades, to evaluate candidates.

Deprecating remarks aside, insiders say the firm is "looking for sharp kids interested in working hard and able to take on responsibility." A fourth-year associate maintains that the firm "commits tremendous resources to locating and hiring candidates that are intelligent, personable, have excellent communications skills and are committed to developing as quickly as possible." Clifford Chance values "varied backgrounds" and "credentials outside the classroom," especially those with "an international angle." The firm welcomes summer associates with a "very lavish" program, including "ridiculously expensive lunches," "extensive social events" and even some "real legal work."

OUR SURVEY SAYS

Competing cultures

In a firm of this size, it is perhaps not surprising that no clear culture governs at Clifford Chance. If one insider believes the firm offers "an exceptionally friendly and laid-back environment" where "lawyers constantly socialize together," another describes a "stiff," "hierarchical" and "uptight" atmosphere in which "lawyers do not tend to socialize together after work." The majority of respondents suggest "socialization is easy for those who want it," although one practical New Yorker notes that "the layout of the firm, which divides lawyers into suites of offices, tends to stifle any social interaction during the day." As to the effect of the merger, a few find the expanded firm's international flavor "enriching" and attribute a "laid-back" atmosphere to "the influence of the Brits." Others insist that "the culture has shifted dramatically," becoming "increasingly less social and more competitive for work and billable hours."

Opinions also vary as to the quality of work and professional development. One associate appreciates the "great, challenging work," and a litigator fairly gushes, "The high quality of clients and matters, coupled with the exceedingly helpful mid- to upper-level associates, have fostered a working environment where I am actually excited each morning about the day ahead." On the other hand, a senior associate contends that "this firm is interested in one thing and one thing only: making money. There is little regard given to the development of their attorneys or doing what is best for their clients." The firm disputes this view, highlighting opportunities for both in-house and offsite training, including the Lawyers Development Course, a three-day program focusing on negotiation, presentation and meeting skills. Another advantage associates have is the ability to control their work schedules. Associates can "turn down work from a senior associate or partner they do not wish to work for, and this adds to a sort of mutual market system, where senior attorneys who by nature are difficult to work for are incentivized to change (to get good junior associates) as much as junior associates are incentivized to do well (to get good work with good senior attorneys)."

While one contact reports that his "work schedule can be described in no other way than 'grueling,'" a corporate lawyer sees colleagues "struggling to find work." Many insiders maintain that billable "hours are definitely an obsession" and "the 2,200-hour requirement is oppressive, especially since the firm does not have enough business to support this kind of workload."

Quantity over quality?

"If you like to work long hours and learn in the process," Clifford Chance may be the firm for you. "The hours are long, as with any big New York City firm," according to a senior associate. "It is not great but it goes with the territory." With an annual requirement of 2,200 hours in "hard billables" and "an additional 220 hours worth of general office time," many sources report that "billing expectations are high and foremost on everyone's mind." (According to the firm, the 2,200-hour benchmark is for bonus eligibility, adding that many associates who billed less received a bonus.) "The hours worked are not that difficult," complains one lawyer, "but the relentless emphasis on billable hours is ridiculous." Others agree that billing requirements are "excessive" and "counterproductive, producing a bad atmosphere emphasizing quantity not quality." However, a number of attorneys remind colleagues that "that's what we get paid for" and "you can always work less hours and take less money elsewhere."

Few associates report working part time. Those who do suggest that you must make "your schedule clear and reassert it from time to time, which as an associate is difficult to do." One lawyer claims that "the part-time program is dead-end as far as advancement is concerned." The firm asserts that this is untrue, noting that CCR&W has recently added two part-time female counsel.

Pro bono could use more attention

The emphasis on billable hours also colors the approach to pro bono work. Until last year, "pro bono hours used to count towards billable hours." Now they only count towards the "220 additional non-billable hours that come on top of the 2,200 billables requirement." This change "has not gone over well." "Disgraceful," one litigator calls it. "Weekly case load reports" outline the potential for "lots of interesting pro bono work." However associates agree that there is actually "very little incentive or support" to take on projects, and "the fact that pro bono hours are not included as billable hours speaks for itself as to the firm's priorities." A few sources praise the firm's "strong commitment to pro bono work," highlighting the "tremendous resources" devoted to pro bono efforts following the World Trade Center attacks. But many more insiders believe that if the firm "were really serious, at least some pro bono hours would count towards the hours requirement."

Salary satisfaction but bonus envy

"I never thought I'd be making this much money at my age," announces a fourth-year associate. Most associates agree that Clifford Chance's salary scale is the same as the other top Big Apple law firms. "There aren't many that pay more," notes a litigator. Happy lawyers tout the high salaries and other perks "such as the technology allowance." Yet a slight frustration with the billable hours requirement also affects lawyers' satisfaction with their pay.

"I am not dissatisfied with my compensation per se," writes a corporate associate. "I am unhappy, however, that the only way for me to get market bonus is to bill over 2,200 billable hours." Only first-year associates are exempt from the billing requirement. The "2,200 billable hour expectation for bonuses is not market practice," several sources assert, "at least with regard to our supposed peer firms." A "repugnant" policy, one attorney sniffs. Another lawyer warns that "the firm needs to clarify its bonus policy if it wants to remain competitive in recruiting top candidates."

Could use more color, but international

Although "the firm tries," most sources agree that with respect to minority hiring and promotion, "the numbers are awful." One attorney finds Clifford Chance "a terrible firm for minorities. The retention rate is poor. There is no mentoring process and, because of the subjectivity at the firm, I don't think minorities are afforded work opportunities that would allow them to grow and succeed as their non-minority counterparts." Lawyers do mention "a nascent but operational diversity committee." The firm notes that, among other activities, the committee has instituted firm-wide diversity training for all lawyers. One New Yorker reports "an increasing amount of minorities here, which is very welcome, but the change somehow seems cosmetic — the dominant feel of the firm is still defined by straight white men. Also," she adds, "I can't imagine them hiring a black man in dreads or an Arab woman in a headscarf. Conformity's the key." However, the firm is said to be diverse in terms of country of origin. One associate calls his firm "very diversified with a mix of backgrounds and cultures," which "leads to a very enriching firm culture."

Women generally fare better, at least among associate ranks, but "as you start to look higher up, there are fewer and fewer women, especially as partners." Some women suggest that the "environment is more receptive to men" and note that there are "no mentoring or other programs specifically targeted to women." On the other hand, "strong and well-publicized anti-discrimination (including anti-harassment) policies are in place," and some sources believe that the firm takes the issue "very seriously — not just for show or perception." The consensus seems to be that sexual orientation is "not an issue here," and lawyers say there are "several openly gay associates."

Nice view if you can get it

New York lawyers appreciate the commuting convenience of working "above Grand Central — and its food court" and praise the "terrific views" from the MetLife building, but the limited availability of such views is a real sore spot. One fourth-year associate laments, "I'm currently in a windowless, inside office. What's the point of having the best skyline in the country if I can't enjoy it?" "For the first two years associates share window offices," a contact explains, and "in the third year associates can choose to spend another year in a shared office." Those who opt for privacy move into an interior office, or, as one lawyer dolefully describes it, they "are banished to interior prison cells for a few years until a window office opens up." Many associates find the prospect "depressing." "I dread the day I have to move into the drab, dark, cold and small coat closet that they call an inner office." One regulation-minded attorney declares that "working without any access to sunlight is illegal in most countries — and for good reason."

Other complaints include "ugly," windowless, "low, low tech" conference rooms and "god-awful faux-country club décor." Some sources attribute the office situation to "massive growing pains" and refer hopefully to the firm's "plans to move soon." Such plans might disappoint one fifth-year associate who "finally got a window — after four years! But now that I have it, I have one of the best views in the world."

"The hours worked are not that difficult, but the relentless emphasis on billable hours is ridiculous."

— *Clifford Chance associate*

Fried, Frank, Harris, Shriver & Jacobson

One New York Plaza
New York, NY 10004
Phone: (212) 859-8000
www.friedfrank.com

LOCATIONS

New York, NY (HQ)
Los Angeles, CA
Washington, DC
Frankfurt
London
Paris

MAJOR DEPARTMENTS/PRACTICES

Antitrust
Bankruptcy & Restructuring
Benefits & Compensation
Corporate
Litigation
Real Estate
Securities Regulation, Compliance & Enforcement
Tax
Technology & Intellectual Property
Trusts & Estates

THE STATS

No. of attorneys: 560
No. of offices: 6
Summer associate offers: 53 out of 54 (2001)
Co-Managing Partners: Peter v.Z. Cobb and Michael H. Rauch
Hiring Attorneys: Howard B. Adler, David I. Shapiro and Janice MacAvoy (NY); Elliot E. Polebaum and Vasiliki B. Tsaganos (DC); Ray La Soya (LA)

BASE SALARY

New York and Washington, DC, 2002
1st year: $125,000
2nd year: $135,000
3rd year: $150,000
4th year: $168,000
5th year: $190,000
6th year: $205,000
7th year: $215,000
8th year: $220,000
Summer associate: $2,400/week

Los Angeles, 2002
1st year: $125,000
2nd year: $135,000
3rd year: $150,000
4th year: $165,000
5th year: $185,000
6th year: $195,000
7th year: $205,000
8th year: $215,000
Summer associate: $2,400/week

NOTABLE PERKS

• Subsidized membership to New York Health & Racquet Club
• Paid monthly meals with associate advisors
• Friday cocktail parties
• Cappuccino breaks

THE BUZZ
WHAT ATTORNEYS AT OTHER FIRMS ARE SAYING ABOUT THIS FIRM

• "Top-notch corporate firm"
• "Boisterous"
• "Go Harvey Pitt!"
• "Terrible hours"
• "The people you disliked in law school"

UPPERS

- No billable hour requirements
- Serious political connections
- Top-notch in M&A

DOWNERS

- "There are many days when I wonder why they don't just give me the title of secretary"
- Uneven hours
- Retention and promotion of women and minorities need improvement

EMPLOYMENT CONTACT

New York
Elizabeth M. McDonald, Esq.
Director of Recruiting
Phone: (212) 859-8621
Fax: (212) 859-4000
mcdonel@friedfrank.com

Los Angeles
Ms. Marian Wilk
Recruiting Administrator
Phone: (213) 473-2049
Fax: (213) 473-2222
wilkma@friedfrank.com

Washington, DC
Leslie R. Rubenfeld, Esq.
Director of Recruiting
Phone: (202) 639-7133
Fax: (202) 639-7003
rubenle@friedfrank.com

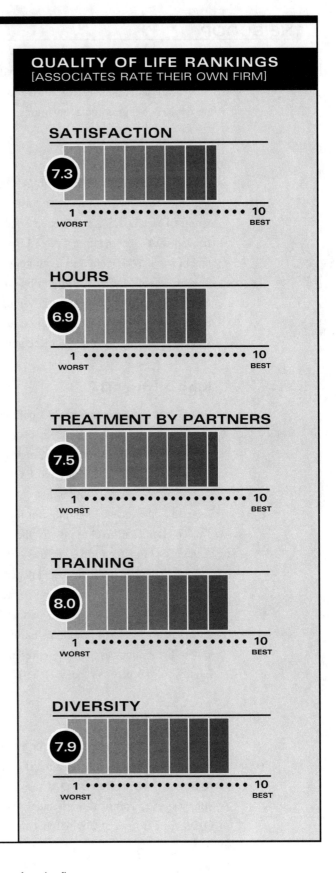

QUALITY OF LIFE RANKINGS
[ASSOCIATES RATE THEIR OWN FIRM]

SATISFACTION
7.3
1 WORST •••••••••••••••• 10 BEST

HOURS
6.9
1 WORST •••••••••••••••• 10 BEST

TREATMENT BY PARTNERS
7.5
1 WORST •••••••••••••••• 10 BEST

TRAINING
8.0
1 WORST •••••••••••••••• 10 BEST

DIVERSITY
7.9
1 WORST •••••••••••••••• 10 BEST

THE SCOOP

You can't make it to the top without dedication, as the attorneys at Fried Frank know. In the past 30 years, Fried, Frank, Harris, Shriver & Jacobson has become a major player in corporate practice, particularly mergers and acquisitions.

Branching out

Like the mighty sequoia, Fried Frank's limbs have grown slowly. Founded in the late 19th century, the New York-based firm opened a D.C. office in 1949. Approximately 20 years later, the firm ventured east, opening an office in London in 1970, and approximately 15 years after that, the firm headed west, opening an office in Los Angeles in 1986. In 1993, the firm's Paris office opened, and in April 2000, it embraced our neighbor to the north and formalized a 20-year relationship with Toronto-based McCarthy Tétrault by creating the McCarthy/Fried Frank Alliance, a collaboration on individual matters — primarily cross-border corporate transactions. (The two firms remain entirely independent.) In addition to its two foreign offices in London and Paris, the firm opened shop in Frankfurt, Germany, in December 2001.

King of the hill

Fried Frank has a plethora of D.C. political connections. One of the firm's name partners is Sargent Shriver, a member of the Kennedy clan. Partner Thomas Christopher is the son of former Secretary of State Warren Christopher. In August 2001, former corporate partner Harvey Pitt was sworn in as chairman of the Securities and Exchange Commission. Litigation partner Michael Bromwich served from 1994 to 1999 as inspector general for the Department of Justice and was recently selected as the independent monitor for the District of Columbia Metropolitan Police Department. Tax counsel Martin Ginsburg is the hubby of Supreme Court Justice Ruth Bader Ginsburg. Andrew Cuomo, the former secretary of the Department of Housing and Urban Development, was counsel to the firm until his recent departure to devote his full time to running for governor of New York. Partner Carmen Lawrence was the former regional director of the SEC's Northeast Regional Office. Former D.C. partner William Howard Taft IV, former ambassador to NATO during George Bush Sr.'s administration, is a legal advisor to the Department of State. D.C. partner David Birenbaum was the U.S. representative to the United Nations for U.N. Management Reform. Finally, former partners Jed S. Rakoff and Robert E. Gerber serve as judges on the federal bench.

Adept at antitrust

The year 2001 was a good year for Fried Frank's antitrust department, which successfully wooed several high-profile recruits. First the firm recruited Charles "Rick" Rule from D.C.'s Covington & Burling, where Rule headed the antitrust practice after serving as the Justice Department's youngest ever antitrust chief under Presidents Ronald Reagan and George Bush Sr. Deborah Garza, former head of Covington's antitrust practice after Rule's departure, joined the Fried Frank family in March 2001, and Anthony Nanni, a top antitrust official at the Department of Justice, was recruited as counsel at the close of 2001.

Fried Frank's newly buff antitrust group has already handled at least one impressive antitrust case involving the attempted sale of Newport News Shipbuilding, Inc., one of two suppliers of nuclear submarines to the U.S. Navy, to General Dynamics, the other supplier of nuclear subs. On behalf of Northrop Grumman Corporation, Fried Frank argued that a monopoly would be formed with a General Dynamics and Newport News fusion. The Justice Department agreed, forcing General Dynamics to drop out of the running and easing the way for Northrop Grumman to purchase Newport News Shipbuilding. This dramatic outcome, an excellent one for Fried Frank's client, means that Fried Frank has a good chance of being considered for lucrative large-scale antitrust cases.

Billion dollar bids

In 2001 Fried Frank also helped several other clients with deals reaching into the billions. The firm represented the Rouse Company in a joint acquisition with Westfield America Trust and Simon Property Group, Inc. of substantially all the assets of Rodamco North America NV for $5.3 billion. Fried Frank also helped add some color to Procter & Gamble Company when the consumer products giant purchased Bristol-Myers Squibb Company's Clairol line of hair coloring products. Japan's Kao Corporation bid $4.5 billion but lost to P&G's $4.95 billion bid.

Moreover, Fried Frank played a starring role in *Investment Dealer Digest*'s Technology Deal of the Year for 2001. The firm represented CommScope, Inc. which, together with Furukawa Electric Company, purchased Lucent Technology's fiber optic cable division in a transaction valued at approximately $2.3 billion.

Pro bono: definitely not a no-no

Though the September 11 attacks hurt downtown New York City's economy significantly, it doesn't mean the rest of the city should be neglected. Attorneys at Fried Frank have turned their focus uptown for their latest pro bono effort, after assisting the families of the victims of the September 11 attacks in administering their loved ones' estates and obtaining benefits. In October 2001, the firm instituted a new program with the Community Development Project of the Legal Aid Society of New York for mid-level associates to provide services to micro-entrepreneurs and not-for-profit entities in upper Manhattan. One associate will work on projects full time on a four-month rotating basis. The firm has a longstanding relationship with the Legal Aid Society. Under the leadership of corporate partner Lois Herzeca, the firm has undertaken a number of cases and received recognition for its representation of Harlem RBI (Reviving Baseball in Inner Cities) and a number of other projects. In addition, Fried Frank has seconded a litigation associate to the Office of the Corporation Counsel of the City of New York for six months. The Corporation Counsel had appealed to the private bar to assist it in trying cases and overcoming the backlog that resulted from September 11. Moreover, corporate partner Joseph A. Stern was recently named chairman of the board of MALDEF (the Mexican American Legal Defense and Educational Fund).

Don't get your panties in a jumble

In October 2001, undergarment manufacturer Fruit of the Loom settled with Fried Frank in a malpractice suit brought against the firm in the 1990s. Fruit of the Loom was asking for more than $80 million in damages for the firm's alleged negligence in its handling of a 1994 case that resulted in a $96 million judgment against the undergarment company. Fruit of the Loom alleged that Fried Frank failed to inform it of risks and settlement opportunities. Partner Sheldon Raab, designated by Fried Frank as the spokesman on the case, would not comment on the outcome. The amount Fried Frank agreed to pay Fruit of the Loom was undisclosed.

Lock 'em up, but don't throw away the key

Parole in the D.C. area needs a closer look, according to a September 2001 opinion in Long v. Gaines by Judge Emmet Sullivan of the U.S. District Court for the District of Columbia. Since paroled D.C. offenders came under the U.S. Parole Commission's jurisdiction in August 2000, "hundreds of alleged parole violators have been arrested and kept in custody for months, while the Commission has failed to provide due process through timely and adequate probable cause determinations and revocation hearings." As it is now, parolees wait on average four months for a hearing, though delays as long as six months are not uncommon. Attorneys at Fried Frank along with the D.C. Public Defender want to shorten the wait, and they signed on as co-counsel for pleadings and argued on behalf of the parolees. In November 2001, the Court ordered the Commission to implement a new plan that would address problems with the system.

GETTING HIRED

Head of the class

Word at Fried Frank is if you're not from an Ivy League school, then you must be at the top of your class to get in the door. The firm wants people who are "motivated and extremely bright but who also have a personality." One associate describes her interview experience: "I was interviewed for about 20 minutes by a third- or fourth-year associate. On the callback, I was scheduled to meet with four attorneys varying in seniority. When the first partner, who was a member of the corporate department, discovered I was interested in litigation, he made sure that the rest of my schedule was changed so that I could meet with people in the litigation department." Lateral candidates can expect to endure "two rounds of interviews within the department" for which they are applying, and many receive an offer "very shortly after the second interview."

High-powered summers

Summer associates at Fried Frank aren't just wined and dined — they're getting their feet wet. "I had a chance to meet many partners and associates and do interesting and meaningful work, such as work on a pro bono case before the Supreme Court," says one associate. Another D.C. summer associate notes, "It's a great program: quality work, meeting a large number of the attorneys who will remember you when you come back as a permanent associate, fantastic events — for example wine tasting and meeting Justice Ruth Bader Ginsburg." A New Yorker adds, "I was able to be a part of a huge IPO, a billion-dollar merger, a multi-billion dollar international arbitration and a white-collar criminal trial — all in six weeks." *The American Lawyer* thinks Fried Frank is doing something right; the publication has consistently ranked the firm's summer program as one of New York's best.

OUR SURVEY SAYS

"Anything goes"

At the firm's London office, that is, according to one associate. "With respect to dress and personal styles," explains an associate in London, the culture is "very diverse — and this is encouraged — and associates get along very well and in general socialize together, many times outside of the context of work." In New York, things are said to be just as freewheeling, though one New Yorker maintains that the atmosphere is "conservative to some extent." Plenty of others disagree. Says one associate, "The culture here is one of the things I like best about Fried Frank. The firm really goes out of its way to be laid back and social. There are weekly cocktail parties for all attorneys on Fridays and the Office of Associate Affairs always has social events planned." Another New York associate has a similar view: "For a large Wall Street law firm, the culture is exceptional. People are friendly, laid back and liberal. The firm's emphasis on diversity and willingness to pay attention to constructive criticism is wonderful — and a far cry from the experiences of my friends at other prestigious large New York firms."

What about the nation's capital? In D.C., "there's a fair amount of collegiality within each class. Not much mingling between partners and associates." But the office there has what counts: "The partners are really interested in exposing the first-year associates to diverse and challenging projects. Senior associates and partners feel comfortable letting you do your job without micromanagement. However, help is never too far if you need it." The firm notes that the Office of Associate Development is available to address Washington associates' concerns. Associates in the LA office seem a bit more sullen by comparison. One notes, "Most of the corporate partners are pretty unpredictable; that is, they are very moody. Overall, there is an unpleasant culture."

Skipping along behind the leader

When it comes to compensation, Fried Frank is not a trendsetter. A New York associate says, "Compensation, including bonus, at Fried Frank matches that of peer firms. However, during bonus time the firm tends to drag its feet when deciding to match the bonuses at peer firms." Another insider agrees: "We pretty much pay the going rate — our firm is definitely more likely to

follow than lead, though." Though the firm may not be a salary leader, associates aren't complaining. "The compensation here is competitive and is not hours-based, which makes it even better!" exclaims a Fried Franker. Another insider notes, "I like the fact that your bonus is not tied to the amount of hours you bill. It keeps you from having to pad your time, which we all know happens at firms with billing requirements." A practical first-year associate warns, "If you are coming from outside the New York City area, you should note that the firm does not reimburse for moving costs and brokers' fees, thus making the move here quite expensive." However, the firm notes, Fried Frank does provide a transition bonus and an optional salary advance to incoming associates.

Too much and too little

It's not just long hours that get Fried Frank associates down; it's not enough hours, too. A corporate associate says, "Some weeks I work till 5 a.m. three nights in a row and then I will go for three or four weeks and bill 20 hours total." Another associate notes, "Things have been slow for certain periods through the last year. At such times, the hours have been reasonable. However, at other times I have been staffed [for large active deals], and the hours have been tough."

There is a positive side to the long hours. Notes one associate, "When I was working crazy hours, it was on projects I really enjoyed so it wasn't so bad." Litigators seem to have it easier. A litigation associate mentions, "Litigation seems a little more flexible than corporate in terms of managing your workload and working from home." According to insiders, the tax department is dreamy, at least as far as schedules go. "I work from home one day a week, which is a wonderful arrangement and minimizes my very long commute," remarks an associate there. Real estate seems similarly ducky. "This is definitely not a 'face time' firm. Partners recognize when you have worked hard and clearly do not expect you to be here all hours all the time. Working very late and on weekends has been more the exception than the rule," says a real estate associate. All around, "The firm generally respects holiday plans and most partners themselves take their vacation."

Same old same old

"The firm hires minorities but keeping minorities here is another thing," a black associate notes. "It could just be that this is a hard job or people want to leave due to that. Maybe efforts could be made to develop programs to help the firm retain minorities." An Asian associate adds, "The firm apparently has become much more focused on recruiting and retaining its attorneys of color. The hiring rate is very good, the lateral hiring could be improved and the retention needs to be worked on." Another associate commends the firm for its "monthly associates of color lunches as well as a staff dedicated solely to the needs of associates of color in our firm."

Associates disagree about the firm's success with respect to diversity for women. One female associate sighs, "There are no female partners in my department." Another female associate is impressed with the firm's promotion of women. She remarks, "My understanding is that my firm has a higher percentage of female partners than any other firm of our size. At the very least the presence and power of women in this firm are equal to that of the men here." And, the firm notes, virtually all departments have female partners and several practice groups are headed by women. One associate suggests that "more women partners would be nice to see, but I think the lack thereof is due to personal decisions rather than firm-related politics." Another insider adds, "Generally, if a person is competent at his or her job here, his or her gender, race or sexual preference are completely irrelevant. The firm provides a very open, tolerant workplace."

Pro bono pros

Ask any associate at Fried Frank, and they'll tell you the firm is "extremely" committed to pro bono. "A great deal of my work here has been pro bono, both criminal and World Trade Center disaster relief," says a New York associate. Another Fried Franker mentions, "We have started a huge effort post-September 11 to assist victim's families in administering their loved ones' estates and obtain benefits." A plus: "Not only does [pro bono] work count toward billables, but it is strongly encouraged and integrated into the firm." In addition, the New York office has a "pro-bono special counsel who devotes half time to coordinating [the pro bono program] and half time to litigation." The D.C. office is equally as devoted to all things pro bono. Special Counsel Karen Grisez's sole responsibilty is managing the D.C. pro bono program, which has been recognized in the past by the D.C. Bar as the Pro Bono Law Firm of the Year. The office expects all attorneys to meet the fifty-hour pro bono minimum as set forth in the D.C. Rules of Professional Responsibility. An associate there says, "The firm has won awards for its work with regard to immigration law. They have [also] argued before the Supreme Court — and won." The Supreme Court victory involved a challenge to an error in criminal sentencing.

Exceptional training

Training at Fried Frank is "exceptional." Raves a New Yorker, "Not only are there weekly or bi-weekly seminars, but partners really take the time to train you and give you good advice." A litigation associate praises the firm's CLE-related weekly training sessions: "They have proven to be invaluable. The written materials are a great resource!" Another associate remarks, "There are so many training programs, it is hard to attend them all. I expressed interest in a PLI program and was able to attend for free." A fourth-year associate mentions, "I just got back from an intense four-day training conference in White Plains. The firm offers lots of other interactive programs and readily encourages and sponsors CLE outside the office." Other associates have nice things to say about the firm's first-year orientation program, known as Fried Frank University, and the year-long practice-specific training programs for new associates. This comment sums it up: "The firm trains you on everything law school never did."

Milbank, Tweed, Hadley & McCloy LLP

One Chase Manhattan Plaza
New York, NY 10005
Phone: (212) 530-5000
www.milbank.com

LOCATIONS

New York, NY (HQ)
Los Angeles, CA
Palo Alto, CA
Washington, DC
Frankfurt
Hong Kong
London
Singapore
Tokyo

MAJOR DEPARTMENTS/PRACTICES

Banking • Capital Markets • Communications & Space •
Corporate • Employee Benefits • Environmental •
Financial Restructing • High Yield & Acquisition Finance •
Intellectual Property • Litigation • Mergers &
Acquisitions • Power & Energy • Project Finance •
Public Interest Law • Real Estate • Securitization • Tax •
Technology • Transportation Finance • Trusts & Estates

THE STATS

No. of attorneys: 475
No. of offices: 9
Summer associate offers: 64 out of 66 (2001)
Chairman: Mel Immergut
Hiring Partners: Arnold Peinado, Drew Fine and
Jay Grushkin

BASE SALARY

New York, 2002
1st year: $125,000
2nd year: $135,000
3rd year: $150,000
4th year: $165,000
5th year: $190,000
6th year: $205,000
7th year: $215,000
8th year: $225,000
Summer associate: $2,403/week

NOTABLE PERKS

• $2,000 tech allowance for first-years
• Web-based system for ordering dinners
• Pro bono sabbaticals for senior associates
• Optional three-month rotation to overseas office

THE BUZZ
WHAT ATTORNEYS AT OTHER FIRMS ARE SAYING ABOUT THIS FIRM

• "Top project finance"
• "Brutal standards for partners"
• "Old-time Wall Street powerhouse"
• "Nice in a gloomy way"
• "Hard-working and hard-driving firm"

UPPERS

- World-class project finance practice
- Very lucrative involvement in Enron litigation
- Warmly hospitable to gays and lesbians

DOWNERS

- "Cost-cutting is so rampant that there aren't even water coolers on my floor!"
- Failure to give pro-rated bonuses to first-year associates
- Promotion and retention of women and minorities need improvement

EMPLOYMENT CONTACT

Ms. Joanne DeZego
Manager of Legal Recruiting
Phone: (212) 530-5966
Fax: (212) 530-5219
Jdezego@milbank.com

QUALITY OF LIFE RANKINGS
[ASSOCIATES RATE THEIR OWN FIRM]

SATISFACTION

7.0

1 WORST · · · · · · · · · · · · · · · · · · 10 BEST

HOURS

6.6

1 WORST · · · · · · · · · · · · · · · · · · 10 BEST

TREATMENT BY PARTNERS

7.4

1 WORST · · · · · · · · · · · · · · · · · · 10 BEST

TRAINING

6.7

1 WORST · · · · · · · · · · · · · · · · · · 10 BEST

DIVERSITY

6.9

1 WORST · · · · · · · · · · · · · · · · · · 10 BEST

THE SCOOP

Milbank has been a major player on Wall Street since its inception in the mid-19th century — 1866 to be exact. In its early days, Milbank provided counsel and advice to both John D. Rockefeller Junior and Senior. These days the firm is known best for a top-notch project finance practice and a welcoming attitude towards gays and lesbians.

Harvesting the Fruit of the Loom

Bankrupt underwear giant and Milbank client Fruit of the Loom was acquired in April 2002 by Berkshire Hathaway. Renowned investor Warren Buffett's Berkshire Hathaway Inc. has created the new FOL Inc., a subsidiary of the $34 billion Berkshire, which acquired substantially all of Fruit of the Loom's basic apparel business operations. Fruit of the Loom, which filed for Chapter 11 bankruptcy protection in 1999, controls as much as a third of the men's underwear market. The acquisition of the underwear company cost Berkshire $835 million in cash. Now that's a lot of tighty-whities.

Let there be light

Milbank lawyers proved to be essential in what was named the Best Project Finance Deal in 2000 by *Finance Asia*. That's no surprise, considering the firm's first-rate project finance practice. CBK power project (named after the three hydroelectric plants involved in the project — Caliraya, Botocan and Kalayaan I) involves the construction of a new hydroelectric plant and the rehabilitation of three existing ones in the Philippines. Gary Wigmore, managing partner of Milbank's Singapore office and head of its Asian project finance team, and others provided the international legal advice for this deal, representing BNP Paribas, DKB, IBJ and Soc Gen Asia. The $383 million transaction is believed to be the first completed project finance-based deal in Asia based predominantly on extended political risk coverage from the private insurance market. Bolstered by their success in the Asian market, firm leaders say they are considering opening an office in mainland China, most likely in 2004.

Flying to the rescue

Milbank's transportation finance group structured and closed the first U.S. government bailout of an airline. America West Airlines was reported to be on the brink of filing for bankruptcy when Milbank lawyers assisted America West in successfully obtaining the first government-backed loan under the government loan guarantee program put in place in the aftermath of the September 11 terrorist attacks. In exchange for guaranteeing the loans, the government received an option to obtain 33 percent of America West at a favorable price. The deal was sealed in January 2002. Since the success of the America West bailout, several other airlines have sought Milbank's assistance with their own financial woes.

Alguien tiene oil?

Milbank acted as counsel for the lead lenders in negotiating, structuring and completing the largest limited recourse financing of an offshore oil field in Latin America to date. The $2.5 billion Petrobas financing project, which was completed in December 2000, involved the construction, startup, ownership and operation of deep-sea production facilities for the Barracuda and Caratinga fields. The fields are located in the central part of the Campos Basin, Brazil's largest proven offshore oil and gas reserve, near Rio de Janeiro.

Milbank represented the commercial bank syndicate and the Banco Nacional de Desenvolvimento Economico e Social in the transaction. The deal's serious cash load ($500 million) sets a new benchmark for term bank loans in Brazil.

Sticking up for Venezuela

Milbank Tweed corporate finance lawyers represented CANTV (the leading Venezuelan telecommunications and Internet services provider) in connection with the unsolicited $1.37 billion cash tender offer for 43.2 percent of CANTV by the AES Corporation. Concluding that the offer was not in the best interests of CANTV or its shareholders, CANTV, with the advice of Milbank, developed a defensive plan, which resulted in AES withdrawing its unsolicited bid. The defensive plan consisted of an extraordinary dividend payment and share buyback program. CANTV made a tender offer in the U.S. and in Venezuela to repurchase 15 percent of its stock traded on the New York Stock Exchange and common shares traded on the Venezuelan Caracas Exchange, at prices significantly higher than those offered by AES. Verizon Communications Inc., which indirectly owns 28.5 percent of CANTV, supported CANTV in its buyback plan. Shareholders approved the buyback in a shareholder vote, which was subject to a counter solicitation by AES, in October 2001.

High profile and high-priced

Milbank Tweed is no stranger to high-profile cases. The firm is one of many law firms involved in the infamous Enron bankruptcy case, which is proving to be not only high profile for Milbank, but also exceptionally lucrative. According to *Legal Times,* the firm billed an astonishing $660,000 in fees and $52,000 in expenses in its first 20 days representing the doomed company's unsecured creditors. Leading Milbank into the Enron litigation battle is intrepid partner Luc Despins.

Milbank makes money, but it doesn't hoard it. After the World Trade Center was attacked by terrorists on September 11, Milbank stepped up to the plate by pledging $1 million to the Twin Towers Fund and The New York Times 9/11 Neediest Fund.

GETTING HIRED

One name spells Milbank summer

And that name is Joanne DeZego. Associates can't sing enough praise for their recruiting coordinator. She "is incredibly positive and enthusiastic about Milbank," says one. "She's wonderful," says another. Yet another lawyer observes, "The recruiting coordinator and staff have lots of energy and are accommodating to summer associate suggestions." With such a well-loved recruiting coordinator at the helm, it's no wonder that summer associates are happy at Milbank. Milbank's system lets associates "spend two to four weeks in three to four departments." In New York and LA, summers are "extravagant" and give "a good sense of the firm." In the smaller D.C. office, summers have "fewer activities and are slightly more real-world."

If you're got personality ...

... then you're a step ahead. At Milbank, New York associates say personality goes a long way to landing a job. No "arrogant" or "obnoxious" folks need apply. So you didn't make straight As? No problem. "The firm generally takes those with a B+ average or better from [the] top 10 to 15 schools. It will always take law review (top 10 percent) from top 40 schools," notes a New Yorker. "The interview and callback process is friendly and well-organized," says a New York associate. Another lateral associate says he "went through a headhunter, two rounds of interviews with four partners or senior associates each time." It "didn't take more than three weeks" for him to get an offer. Laterals have "an initial screening interview with one of the partners and an associate, which is followed by a half day of interviews with an additional six attorneys." Firm lawyers say that Milbank hires about five lateral partners a year. The hot spot for Milbank lateral hiring? Palo Alto. Economic setbacks in Silicon Valley mean that Milbank's had an easier time hiring top talent to staff its new Palo Alto office.

OUR SURVEY SAYS

Professional but not stodgy

While Milbank may have a rather reserved reputation, many associates find the firm's culture to be "laid back" and "easygoing." Younger attorneys seem to socialize together, but most people "prefer to do their work and go home." A New Yorker says, "The culture is friendly and cordial. Lawyers in the department tend to eat lunch together, and occasionally lawyers socialize with each other after work. My department has a definite open-door policy, and I have never thought twice about popping in to ask anyone, even senior partners, questions. Overall I think it is pretty friendly, and getting more so. We maintain a high level of professionalism but are pretty laid back." "The people in the LA office are just as friendly, though some are troubled by the lack of hand-holding new associates receive. An associate there notes, "Overall it is a great working environment, consisting of a great group of young attorneys who are fun and down to earth. Work-wise, however, the mentality is pretty much 'sink or swim' in that you are given a lot of responsibility early on and very little hand-holding or formal training."

Bonus bust

While Milbank meets the market for base salary, it "lags behind in salary increase per associate level." Associates point out that the firm failed to give year-end bonuses to first-year associates in 2001. An eighth-year associate notes, "The pay is great but I feel the firm made a very poor decision when they did not match bonuses for the first-year class." A second-year associate agrees: "Milbank needs to work on its bonus compensation structure. This year, it was not consistent with the market for some of the class years." One thing is for sure, associates at Milbank have a "very high potential payoff" if they make partner.

Long hours — got a problem with that?

Hours at Milbank are typical of a big firm. "Long but not terrible," says one litigation associate. "They vary a lot depending on the nature and status of your cases, so there is usually down time following very busy periods." An associate in Los Angeles says, "My department is consistently busy, which is good, considering the slow economy. Hours can be erratic and often long, but the group of people I work with is so great I don't really mind the long hours." Another LA associate remarks, "Look, it's a big firm. You work a lot of hours. Any firm that tells you they don't is lying to you. Still, the hours are flexible and the work and atmosphere are top-notch. Furthermore, when I needed time off for a family crisis, everybody was very understanding." Though there are long hours, "Nobody cares about face time. As long as you actively seek work, do your work and do it well, nobody cares whether you do it at the office or on the train or at home." How about weekends? One associate claims, "Some of the weekend work is attributable to partners just being demanding; the work really could wait until Monday. In addition, the message from the partners is that they had to work long hours, so today's associates should have to also."

Tales of diversity

When it comes to diversity, Milbank falls prey to an old problem — hiring is good, retention is bad. "The firm has hired many women in my year," says a first-year associate. "There are actually a large majority of first-year women in litigation compared to first-year men in this department." The problem, as this associate sees it, is not with hiring but with retention. The firm "needs a lot of help in retaining women. We only have one female partner in litigation," says another litigator. She adds, "Very few women stay in this department." An LA associate explains: "The firm markets itself as family friendly because it allows a few women to work part time. However, this is a Mommy-track. Several partners have acknowledged that the only candidates for partner are those that fit the male ideal worker stereotype — bill in excess of 2,100 hours, engage in substantial marketing activities and other non-billable firm work, and have a spouse to take care of family responsibilities." The firm does have a very generous maternity leave — "three to four months with full pay."

When it comes to minorities, there's also room to grow. "Milbank has some room for improvement when it comes to recruiting and retaining minorities, particularly African-Americans," says a black associate. An Hispanic associate notes, "I think the firm is welcoming to minorities and there is a very diverse group of associates, but that diversity is not reflected in our partner numbers."

The firm excels when it comes to diversity issues affecting gays and lesbians. "Milbank is very proud of its reputation for being the first firm to allow same sex partner benefits. There are a number of openly gay people working here at all levels," says a Milbanker. Another agrees that the firm is "very gay-friendly." A gay associate chimes in: "Sexuality is not an issue — which is exactly how it should be."

Trial by fire

Associates at Milbank agree the real training here is mostly hands-on. Before an associate starts working, she participates in a formal training program. A New Yorker notes, "We had extensive training at the Tarrytown retreat at the beginning of our employment. There were a number of more specific training programs once we got back to the firm." After that, it's "sink or swim." An LA associate sees the silver lining: "The upside is that we are given a lot of responsibility up front, so you can get great experience here if you are driven and hardworking and not shy about seeking out help from senior associates when you need it." Some associates mention that partners and senior associates are helpful. "How well an associate is trained largely depends upon the partners she works with and the types of deals she is staffed on," says a Milbanker. Corporate associates have mentors. "Mine is great," notes one insider, "and provides me training at all levels about every aspect of what is needed to be part of the firm, including client relations and marketing to some extent." Milbank also sponsors weekly CLE lectures.

Pro bono's great

At Milbank, 60 hours of pro bono work count toward billable hours per year. The problem? Finding time for it. "Although I've only worked on two pro bono matters, my sense is that Milbank has one of the better pro bono programs of the top-tier New York law firms," says an associate in that office. An LA associate agrees: "The firm's commitment to pro bono is top notch." But in D.C., "we are all too focused on billable hours to be willing to sacrifice time for pro bono." The firm offers many programs to interested associates. One is an externship opportunity that allows first-year associates to spend two months between the bar exam and the beginning of their rotations working full time on pro bono matters and being paid an associate salary. An LA associate adds, "We have a great eight-week-long first-year pro bono internship." According to a New York associate, the firm has a partner "dedicated solely to pro bono matters as well as a pro bono coordinator who is very active." But, mentions another, "outside of the litigation group you'll have to hunt for pro bono [work], and partners are less than understanding about pro bono requiring time." Speculates another insider, "Nobody will make partner doing a lot of pro bono work."

One International Place
Boston, MA 02110-2624
Phone: (617) 951-7000
www.ropesgray.com

LOCATIONS

Boston, MA (HQ)
New York, NY
San Francisco, CA
Washington, DC

MAJOR DEPARTMENTS/PRACTICES

Corporate
Creditors' Rights
Labor & Employment
Litigation
Private Client Group
Tax & Benefits

THE STATS

No. of attorneys: 470
No. of offices: 4
Summer associate offers: 73 out of 73 (2001)
Chairman and Managing Partner: Douglass N. Ellis Jr.
Hiring Partner: Douglas H. Meal

BASE SALARY

All offices, 2002
1st year: $125,000
2nd year: $135,000
Summer associate: $2,400/week

NOTABLE PERKS

• Technology allowance and home DSL access
• Associate investment plan
• 20 hours free backup day care per child per year
• Domestic partnership benefits

THE BUZZ
WHAT ATTORNEYS AT OTHER FIRMS ARE SAYING ABOUT THIS FIRM

• "Harvard alumni club"
• "Boston Brahmans"
• "Best of the best in Boston"
• "Intelligent and competent."
• "Corporate, yes; litigation, no"

UPPERS

- Boston big shot
- Little billable hours pressure
- Emphasis on teamwork and camaraderie

DOWNERS

- Few minority partners
- Member of the Boston salary freeze club
- Management is "on the secretive side"

EMPLOYMENT CONTACT

Mr. Thomas A. Grewe
Director of Legal Recruiting
Phone (local): (617) 951-7239
Phone (long distance): (800) 951-4888, ext. 7239
Fax: (617) 951-7050
legalhiring@ropesgray.com

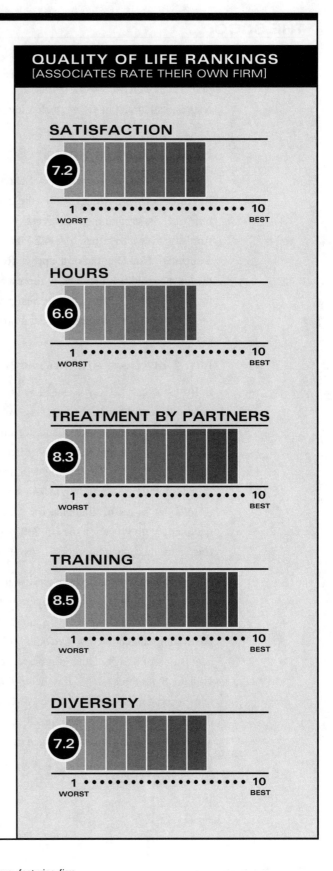

QUALITY OF LIFE RANKINGS
[ASSOCIATES RATE THEIR OWN FIRM]

SATISFACTION
7.2
1 WORST ·························· 10 BEST

HOURS
6.6
1 WORST ·························· 10 BEST

TREATMENT BY PARTNERS
8.3
1 WORST ·························· 10 BEST

TRAINING
8.5
1 WORST ·························· 10 BEST

DIVERSITY
7.2
1 WORST ·························· 10 BEST

THE SCOOP

Considered to be one of the best firms in Beantown, Ropes & Gray is known best for its corporate practice, as well as its work in trust and estates and health care. But Ropes & Gray isn't a firm that rests on its laurels; its IP and technology management groups are gaining in prominence.

History: it started at HLS

Founded in 1865 by Harvard Law School grads John Codman Ropes and John Chipman Gray Jr., Ropes & Gray grew quickly. By the 20th century, the firm was representing banks, utilities and railroads. Its commitment to diversity started early when in 1930, it hired Abram Berkowitz, the firm's first Jewish partner. In 1942 Mary Lennon and Blanche Quaid became the firm's first female associates. Not a big fan of the press, Ropes & Gray nevertheless got involved in the imbroglio of the Chappaquiddick incident by representing Senator Ted Kennedy. In 1974 Elliot Richardson, a former Ropes & Gray attorney, resigned as Attorney General when President Richard Nixon ordered him to fire Watergate special prosecutor and fellow Ropes alum Archibald Cox.

No. 1 in town and known all around

In Boston Ropes & Gray is considered the preeminent firm. Its national reputation isn't too shoddy either. In recent years, the firm has built up a strong leveraged buyout practice in addition to its impressive financial services and securities practices. The firm's LBO client list includes Bain Capital, Berkshire Partners, Fenway Partners, Monitor Clipper Equity Partners and Saunders Karp & Margue. Ropes & Gray works with Putnam, Scudder, Colonial and other groups in the financial services industry. According to *The American Lawyer*, Ropes & Gray ranks No. 1 when it comes to total net assets of all funds for which the firm acts as counsel, and Ropes took fifth place nationally with 40 new issues in 2001. (The firm itself also manages money — Ropes serves as trustee for more than $4 billion in assets under management.)

Additional areas of corporate expertise include acting as issuer's counsel in securities offerings and structuring IPOs, for which Ropes & Gray represents underwriters like powerhouse I-banks Goldman Sachs and Morgan Stanley. On the M&A front, in 2001 the firm represented the controlling shareholder of Odwalla when it was swallowed by Coca Cola and KB Toys in its acquisition of eToys. Other top-drawer clients include Fleet Financial Group, American Express, Gillette, State Street Bank, Raytheon, John Hancock, Timberland, Cabletron, EMC, Genuity, TJX and Reebok International. Ropes & Gray's health care practice, formally part of the corporate department, is nationally recognized. Clients have included hospitals in downtown Boston as well as physician organizations, managed care groups and academic medical centers around the country.

New focus on IP

In the past year Ropes & Gray has dramatically expanded its practice in the areas of intellectual property and technology management. The IP practice group has grown to over 40 attorneys, including 20 registered patent attorneys. Clients seeking Ropes' assistance in this area include top labs from Stanford, Harvard and MIT and tech-oriented businesses like Biogen and CMGI.

Order in the court

Picture it. A full-scale moot courtroom in the middle of a leading law firm equipped with the latest in cutting-edge technology so lawyers can perfect their skills in an ideal atmosphere. It sounds too good to be true, and for Ropes & Gray, it was. The firm built such a courtroom in its Boston office in 1995. The courtroom was supposed to emulate Courtroom 21 at the College of William and Mary Marshall Wythe School of Law in Virginia, one of the most technologically advanced moot courtrooms in the country. But the price wasn't worth the profit. In October 2001, the firm converted the courtroom into office space and built a smaller courtroom in the firm's former library. While the new courtroom is significantly smaller than its predecessor (the 14-person jury box has been cut, for instance), the technology is still top notch. The firm uses litigation support software and Elmo, a video monitor that magnifies evidence and can display 3-D images.

Stellar pro bono work

Ropes & Gray cares about its community. And it gets rewarded for the effort. The Boston-based nonprofit group, the Political Asylum/Immigration Representation Project, chose associate Mark C. Fleming as Pro Bono Attorney of the Year for 2001. The Project promotes the rights of political refugees. Fleming was honored because he helped a Chinese woman and a Somali woman secure asylum due to threat of persecution in their native countries. Not only are associates at Ropes & Gray doing star pro bono work, so are summer associates. Eighteen Boston-based summer associates, including a number of Ropes & Gray summers, worked for the city's chapter of the Anti-Defamation League. The associates spent time researching legal trends and preparing memoranda on such topics as Internet hate sites that are discriminatory or criminal. The Anti-Defamation League plans to compile the research into a database to be used in advising future clients.

The secret census

The census has been regarded as being somewhat illusive because of its tendency to have inaccurate information. Undercounting can be a problem for some communities in the amount of aid federal programs give to the undercounted areas. To alleviate the problem of undercounting, the Census Bureau devises an adjusted count from a statistical sampling that is then compared to the unadjusted data. It's the job of the secretary of commerce to find out which count is more reliable. Boston's Ropes & Gray wants to make sure all heads are counted. That's why the firm represented two Oregon legislators against the secretary of commerce after that department rejected their Freedom of Information Act (FOIA) request for the adjusted data. The federal government argued against disclosure of the information based on Exemption Five of the FOIA, the "deliberative process" privilege, which protects the process by which agencies make decisions. In December 2001, a federal judge found that the data was not protected under this privilege because it was not part of the process of the secretary's decision but the subject of the decision. It was a win for Oregon (and Ropes & Gray), though partner David O. Stewart expects the government to appeal.

Mixed ruling in an odd case

Who says law is boring? Ropes & Gray played a part in a recent case that involved everything from fraud to defamation to forgeries to the Kennedys. The firm represented investigative reporter Seymour Hersh, who was writing a book on the Kennedy clan in the late 1990s. After Lawrence Cusack Jr. told Hersh he had papers signed by the Kennedys that had belonged to his late father, Hersh and other journalists concluded that the materials were forged. Cusack was later arrested and convicted for fraud in connection with the papers. In 1997 the sellers of the documents sued Hersh, claiming defamation due to Hersh and others' public pronouncement that the Cusack papers were forgeries. Hersh counterclaimed that the plaintiffs had used his name in promotional materials to sell the documents. In December 2001, a federal judge made a two-fold finding: one, that Hersh failed to state a claim for unauthorized use in advertising under New York Civil Rights Law, and two, that Hersh had a cause of action against the sellers for publishing advertising materials that suggested Hersh was involved. Ropes & Gray partners Michael Nussbaum and J. Steven Baughman represented Hersh in his partially successful claim.

GETTING HIRED

Fun summer

"I had a great summer experience," one associate muses, echoing many of his colleagues' sentiments about their firm's summer program. "I received interesting work assignments in my specified areas of interest. The firm sponsored many (but not too many) summer social events, but I did not feel pressured to attend all of the events." Insiders at Ropes & Gray say the summer program is "well-designed for us to sample the different practice areas in the firm." And associates appreciate that the summer involved more than just cocktail parties and other events. "I worked on complex transactions and was given work to do that was important to those transactions. The partners and associates spent time explaining transactions and issues to me. Everyone was very nice and concerned that the summer associates get a good exposure to the kind of work we do at the firm."

Boston buffs

Like many Boston firms, Ropes & Gray exhibits a weakness for home-grown associates. "Connections to the area matter," remarks an insider. However, as another associate explains, "The firm seems to have shifted its focus and become less of a Boston-centered place. Students coming from schools outside of Boston appear to get greater consideration than they previously did." Hiring partner Doug Meal notes that the firm's 2002 summer class "is drawn from 25 different law schools, with 60 percent of the students coming from non-Boston-area law schools." What other qualities impress those in charge at Ropes? Insiders say that "generally, great grades are a given, and outside accomplishments are given serious weight." Coming from a top school helps, as well as being "intelligent, self-motivated and hardworking." The interview process is "low-key," and "nobody grills you on the law." Inside tip: "They also like people who had another career before law school."

OUR SURVEY SAYS

Not a gregarious bunch

Though the culture at Ropes & Gray may not be "as formal as these books historically have led people to believe," insiders report that "the people at this place are pretty uptight. For example, too many people stand together in the elevator every day and don't say a word to each other. Not even 'hello.' 'Gregarious' is not a word that describes most lawyers at R&G." If gregarious isn't the right word, what is? "Laid back and intellectual," offers one associate. "The firm is very friendly, with an open-door environment," says another. "There is occasional socializing outside of the office, but it is minimal." An associate suggests there may be a rational explanation for the lack of socializing: "Many associates are married."

Got your back

If Ropes & Gray is lacking in social activity, it wants for nothing when it comes to teamwork. A real estate associate explains, "The atmosphere among lawyers is extremely professional and respectful, and it has been my experience that lawyers and support staff see their roles as members of a team." He adds, "I have never asked a question of a colleague here at Ropes & Gray and been turned away or even told to come back later. I find that those with more experience consider it their obligation to pass on that experience to other lawyers, and they treat other lawyers with all of the respect of a client." A corporate associate confirms this camaraderie: "Partners will certainly roll up their sleeves and help associates with projects. Moreover, most attorneys at all levels take the time to sit down and explain things to you."

Joining the Boston salary freeze

Ropes & Gray associates agree they are well compensated — though not as well paid as they used to be. The year 2001 saw Ropes & Gray (as well as other Boston firms) institute salary freezes (equalizing second-year and first-year base salaries), as well as "significantly" reduce senior associate pay. In addition, the firm altered its bonus structure, which now disregards billable hours.

Amazingly, Ropes & Gray associates remain fairly satisfied with their compensation, despite these changes. Remarks an insider, "For a firm that has no billable requirement or billable pressure whatsoever, I am extremely satisfied with my compensation." However, a perceived disparity between their compensation and those of their counterparts at peer Boston firms irks many. An associate explains, "The level of compensation is great. The firm, however, seems fixated on claiming that it is a compensation leader in Boston, which is odd given the fact that the firm is neither a salary leader nor a total compensation leader." He adds, "It is absurd and juvenile for the firm to claim to be a compensation leader. We are well compensated, and that is enough." Not everyone thinks he is being left out in the cold. One senior associate notes, "I have always been very pleased with the compensation Ropes offers. I am sure that no lawyers in my class at other Boston firms made as much as I did last year. Year after year, they tell us to trust that they will not be topped when the dust settles at the end of the year, and I've never been disappointed."

Peaks and valleys

Hours at Ropes & Gray vary by practice group. Litigators report "pretty long" hours and claim that partners are unforgiving if you take some time off. One associate says, "Most people expect you to have dinner here, and the offices generally fill up for at least part of the weekend. I find that it is assumed that you will give up weekends and vacations, but you are not penalized if you can convince the partner of a legitimate family-related excuse. Even then, some partners appear to regard such excuses as weakness." An associate in the health care department, however, has it made. He notes, "Hours are very good. [There is] no pressure to bill, and I work very few weekends." A corporate associate maintains, "As with all transactional practices, there are many peaks of intense days and nights coupled with valleys of short days." However, another corporate associate explains the recent change. "The hours spent in the office in recent months do not reflect ordinary work habits of R&G junior lawyers," he says. "When things are busy, work can be overwhelming. Although work as a whole had slowed down, when a transaction you are working on is going, the hours can stack up." A labor associate says face time is a new emphasis. He remarks, "I find myself being less efficient during the day just to make sure I'm hanging around late at night when the partners 'take attendance.'"

While face time may be more important these days, the firm still has a good part-time program for those who want it. A female notes, "The part-time program is very flexible. Attorneys can create a schedule that works for them and their clients, whether that be a certain number of days a week or a limited number of hours a day." Another woman agrees but questions the future of part-timers.

"It is unclear whether people — women — who work part time, no matter how good they are, have any future at the firm," she says.

Diversity: making an effort

When it comes to diversity, Ropes & Gray is trying, some say without much success. An Hispanic associate says, "They're making a genuine effort, and seriously pursuing minority candidates." (The firm notes that over 20 percent of Ropes & Gray's 2002 summer class are students of color.) Another associate believes "the firm does a great job of making an added effort to hire, welcome and mentor minorities." But this associate also adds, "When it comes to partnership, however, the firm for better of worse makes no such added effort to promote minorities. In general, minority associates are treated no differently than majority associates. The place is color-blind." An Asian associate notices, "Overall, I think the firm has tried to reach out to attorneys of color. That said, there are very few partners at Ropes that are black, Latino or Asian." Some say "there seems to be a genuine commitment towards making the firm more diverse," but they "don't know what kind of specific support and encouragement minorities get once they are here." Lawyers appreciate the fact that there is a diversity committee and a "lawyers of color" group, which are wonderful initiatives, but lament that "we don't get a ton of minority applicants in general."

Though most agree that Ropes & Gray "is very committed to hiring women," many lament that the firm appears reluctant "to make the necessary changes in order to retain them." One woman sighs, "If you do not want to take maternity leave or work part time because you have kids, you are treated the same regardless of your gender. Women with children and husbands … do not make partner here, because they understandably tend to want more flexible hours, so they either leave for a more reasonable job, or the firm does not make them partner because they do not have an interest in having part-time partners." Some associates report satisfaction with the part-time program, regardless of whether it feeds into the partnership. One associate notes, "The part-time program is very attractive in terms of allowing women to continue working at a competitive level while having children. Most attorneys are very positive about the part-time program and try to be accommodating with people who are working part-time."

A number of insiders maintain that the problems women face at Ropes & Gray are the same faced by female lawyers around the country. "Women can and do succeed at this firm," asserts one associate. "Women who dedicate more time to family needs than client demands probably do not succeed — neither would men. I have never felt left out of a deal, a conference call, a negotiating session or any part of the process because I am a woman, nor have I ever felt that I wasn't getting the 'good work' due to my gender."

Dewey Ballantine LLP

1301 Avenue of the Americas
New York, NY 10019
Phone: (212) 259-8000
www.deweyballantine.com

LOCATIONS

New York, NY (HQ)
Houston, TX
Los Angeles, CA
Menlo Park, CA
Washington, DC
Budapest
Hong Kong
London
Prague
Warsaw

MAJOR DEPARTMENTS/PRACTICES

Bankruptcy
Corporate
Environmental
ERISA
International Trade
Litigation
Real Estate
Tax & Private Clients

THE STATS

No. of attorneys: 500+
No. of offices: 10
Summer associate offers: 76 out of 79 (2001)
Chairman: Everett L. Jassy
Hiring Partner: James A. FitzPatrick Jr.

THE BUZZ
WHAT ATTORNEYS AT OTHER FIRMS ARE SAYING ABOUT THIS FIRM

- "Great reputation, but high stress and hours"
- "Fantastic tax practice"
- "Poorly managed"
- "Trade policy experts"
- "Good job if you can keep it ..."

BASE SALARY

All domestic offices, 2002
1st year: $125,000
2nd year: $135,000
3rd year: $150,000
4th year: $170,000
5th year: $190,000
6th year: $200,000
7th year: $205,000
8th year: $210,000
Summer associate: $2,403/week

NOTABLE PERKS

- Annual dinner at the Plaza "ain't too shabby"
- In-house shoe shines
- "Beer hours" on alternating Friday evenings
- Laptop computers or Blackberries for home use

UPPERS

- Social, friendly atmosphere
- Beautiful office space
- Impressive M&A practice

DOWNERS

- Not enough work to go around
- Layoffs
- Discretionary bonus structure causes grumbling

EMPLOYMENT CONTACT

Mr. William H. Davis
Legal Personnel & Recruiting Manager
Phone: (212) 259-7328
Fax: (212) 259-6333
nyrecruiting@deweyballantine.com

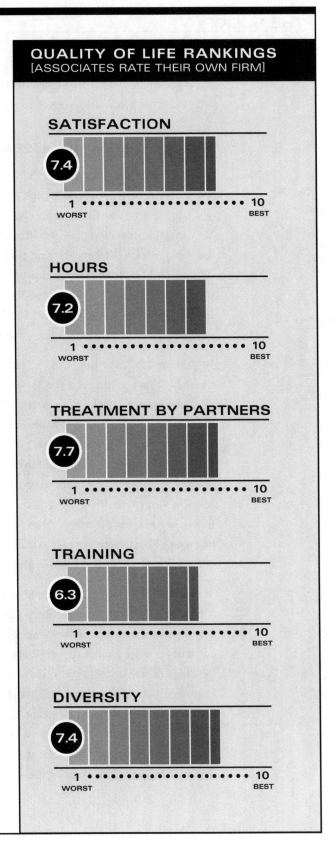

QUALITY OF LIFE RANKINGS
[ASSOCIATES RATE THEIR OWN FIRM]

SATISFACTION
7.4
1 WORST • • • • • • • • • • • • • • • • • • • 10 BEST

HOURS
7.2
1 WORST • • • • • • • • • • • • • • • • • • • 10 BEST

TREATMENT BY PARTNERS
7.7
1 WORST • • • • • • • • • • • • • • • • • • • 10 BEST

TRAINING
6.3
1 WORST • • • • • • • • • • • • • • • • • • • 10 BEST

DIVERSITY
7.4
1 WORST • • • • • • • • • • • • • • • • • • • 10 BEST

THE SCOOP

Dewey Ballantine is a star on the New York legal walk of fame. In a leap of faith in the city's management, it was the first tenant in 1984 to buy and occupy 250,000 square feet of one of the four towers of a new Times Square development in its pre-Disney days.

History: roaring in the '20s and beyond

Three friends from Harvard Law School decided to open a firm together in lower Manhattan in 1909. The firm, Root, Clark & Bird, expanded four years later when two more law school friends got into the act. The firm's name changed to Root, Clark, Buckner and Howland. In the 1920s, the firm grew steadily. For clients like AT&T, Beneficial, the Andrew Carnegie estate, Dillon Read and Guggenheim Brothers, the firm performed securities, corporate and estate work. The addition of the elder Elihu Root to the firm as counsel brought it great prestige. Root had served as secretary of state, secretary of war, senator of New York and also had won the Nobel Peace Prize. Ahead of its time in diversity, Dewey hired its first female attorney in 1925, Dorothy N. Cook, though comparable law firms would still refuse to hire women in years to come.

In October 1997, the firm took on its current name, Dewey Ballantine LLP, after having gone through 12 name changes. The Dewey belongs to Thomas Dewey, who ran in the presidential elections against Franklin Roosevelt in 1944 and Harry Truman in 1948. Arthur A. Ballantine had been the first Solicitor of Internal Revenue before he joined the firm. In the 1980s and 1990s, the firm strengthened its partner base by taking attorneys from other firms. Sixteen lawyers were added in 1988 from the leveraged buyout firm Lane & Edson, which helped expand Dewey's M&A practice. The next year, three corporate insurance specialists from LeBoeuf, Lamb, Greene & MacRae joined. In 1994, 10 securities lawyers from Winston & Strawn came onboard. In the following year, eight partners from White & Case joined, including that firm's former head of litigation. Six lawyers from the late Donovan Leisure joined the M&A practice in 1998. In June of the next year, the firm snatched leading tech and Internet attorney, John Keitt, from Rogers & Wells.

The year 2001 proved to be a remarkable one for the firm. In February Michael Sage joined the firm from Cadwalader's bankruptcy department. Later that year, Sanford Litvack, former vice chairman of the board of the Walt Disney Company, joined Dewey as of counsel (and also continues in a non-exclusive part-time executive role at Disney). In October 2001, Dewey opened the doors of its new Houston office. The office is headed by Alan Gover, a co-founder of the Houston office of Weil, Gotshal & Manges. Gover is lead counsel to PG&E in connection with its reorganization. Despite all its stellar accomplishments in 2001, the bad economy forced the firm to lay off 10 to 15 associates in New York with three months' pay and outplacement assistance. However, the firm notes that "total attrition in 2001 was less than in any of the last three years, and the firm's transition policy has remained consistent with our past practices."

Coping in the wake of tragedy

Many companies in New York were thrown into turmoil after the September 11 attacks. A few days after the attacks, Dewey Ballantine was one of two firms that received bomb threats. The firm temporarily evacuated personnel while police searched the building. In 2002, for insurance purposes, a lawyer for World Trade Center leaseholder Larry Silverstein debated whether or not the September 11 attacks on the Twin Towers were one or two separate attacks and called for an early hearing. Dewey Ballantine partner Harvey Kurzweil represented Travelers Indemnity Co. Kurzweil argued that engineering evidence would show that the collapse of one tower would have brought the second one down because of the common infrastructure they shared, making the attack a single one. In this case, Travelers and other insurers would owe $3.5 billion. Silverstein sought $7.1 billion on the argument that the attack on each tower counted as a separate event. The case is currently pending.

Quick (but not so easy) M&A

Dewey Ballantine was ranked No. 5 in Thomson Financial's July 2001 ranking of the highest value M&A deals, raking in a cool $56.9 billion for the first half of 2001. Dewey partners know how to make deals, though they aren't always easy ones. Partner Frederick Kanner of Dewey Ballantine's New York office led the team that advised health care product maker MedImmune Inc. on its $1.5 billion acquisition of Aviron, a biopharmaceutical company, in December 2001. MedImmune wanted to acquire a flu vaccine that required government approval, and Aviron didn't want the delay to dull the deal. Both companies settled on an exchange offer where MedImmune issued 1.075 shares for each share of Aviron.

Smoking out big tobacco

Dewey Ballantine is one of the few prominent firms not to seek out big tobacco clients. The firm has a no smoking commitment since former co-Chairperson Joseph Califano Jr. campaigned against puffing. In March 1998, Dewey took on as clients Blue Cross/Blue Shield insurers who wanted to recover health care costs in the area of $800 million from cigarette makers. The firm fixed its hourly rate for a cut of the damages, which have come up short. The lawsuit survived a motion to dismiss in February 1999. In June 2001, a federal jury rejected racketeering and civil fraud claims against the tobacco companies but found that tobacco firms had violated the New York State Consumer Protection Act and awarded Blue Cross/Blue Shield $17.8 million for the cost of treating New York smokers. Vincent FitzPatrick, a partner at Dewey Ballantine, represented Blue Cross/Blue Shield. While the outcome was only a partial victory for his client, he said, "This is a landmark, the first time that any insurer or third-party payer has prevailed in any of these suits against the tobacco industry." Judge Jack B. Weinstein also emphasized the significance of the victory when he awarded nearly $38 million in legal fees — more than twice the jury verdict — to Dewey Ballantine for its work on the case.

No kidding around

If you make a claim, make sure you can support it with facts. That seems elementary enough to anyone pursuing a career in law, but surprisingly, some lawyers do make frivolous claims. Dewey Ballantine helped catch some of these culprits. The firm represented a few insurance companies in a lawsuit against two law firms, New York's Schoengold & Sporn and Philadelphia's Berger & Montague. In July 2001, the Second Circuit Court of Appeals upheld the district court's finding that the firms should be sanctioned $84,153 for violating Rule 11 of the Federal Rule of Civil Procedure and the Private Litigation Reform Act of 1995 (PSLRA). The federal judge's decision was based on the fact that under Schoengold & Sporn's settlement, the plaintiffs would have received nothing while the firm received $200,000. Scheindlin suspected the firm was pursuing meritless claims to obtain attorneys' fees.

GETTING HIRED

"Better than summer camp"

Most associates we heard from have only good things to say about the firm's summer associate program. "Amazing," sighs one associate. "There are no words ... there is no other summer program that can even come close." Why is that? "Our HR and recruiting departments are unique. The group running the program makes sure that your experience is an enjoyable one; they add that personal touch lacking in so many other firms." However, it's not all fun and games. Says an associate, "My summer work experience was varied — some of it was 'make work,' but the vast majority of it was real and interesting." Another source agrees: "The life of a full-time associate at Dewey does not at all resemble the life of a Dewey summer associate. Oh, how great life would be if that were true."

Easy for top grads

"If you're from a top-10 school, being in the upper-middle of the pack is fine. From other schools, law review and high grades are necessary," advises one associate. Another insider explains the hiring process: "Potential summer associates will meet with one partner or senior associate in their initial interview. That attorney will determine whether to invite the candidate back, and if they are asked to return, they will meet with four or five other lawyers, ranging from second- or third-year associates through senior partners and will possibly have lunch with a junior associate. Those attorneys then review the candidate and a legal recruiting committee that is made up of partners, associates and recruiting department staff then determines on the basis of those reviews whether to extend an offer to the candidate." Once a candidate gets through the screening interview, grades become less important. "Once you have been given a callback, it's all about personality."

OUR SURVEY SAYS

"Dewey's best asset"

That's what one first-year associate calls the firm's culture. "Lawyers tend to have good, laid-back working relationships with their peers because the same group of lawyers usually works together. The lawyers are serious about their work but not uptight." Another insider raves, "The people at Dewey are fantastic. Recruiting has done a great job creating a diverse and friendly atmosphere." Yet another associate notes, "Dewey's firm culture is friendly and very collegial. Office doors are always open and people smile to each other in the hallways and elevators." What about quality of work? A second-year associate remarks, "The level of the work that I'm being asked to do as a second-year is much higher than I had any right to expect. I've been working directly with a partner since I got here and functioning as a mid-level for almost a year." A first-year associate doesn't feel the same. "The work I am often asked to perform consists of tasks that could be handled by a paralegal, a secretary or even the copy room staff," he sighs. "On the positive side, this menial work sometimes gives me an insight into the details of the deal that I am working on that those senior to me do not get."

When it comes to socializing, Dewey associates have many choices. One second-year associate notes, "I play on the firm's softball and hockey teams regularly and go out with friends from here often. I think firm-wide that there is a tendency for people to go their own ways when the day is over, but among my circle of colleagues and friends, we spend a fair amount of time together after work." A first-year attorney notes, "The lawyers here tend to socialize together, [though] I can't really discern a firm culture. The culture seems to vary by group and department."

A lateral notes, "As a lateral associate, I have found it difficult to meet people I don't work with directly." The firm does sponsor many socializing events, so there should be something for everyone, including a well-attended Friday happy hour in the New York office at which beer, wine and appetizers are served.

Pay matches similar firms

People at Dewey have little to say regarding salary. "Right for the market," notes one associate. "Quite sufficient and the extra perks throughout the year are more than enough," says another insider. The only dissatisfaction voiced concerns the handling of bonuses, which associates view as unfair and cheap. A New York associate explains, "A discretionary bonus means that the powers that be can give a bonus to, or withhold a bonus from, whomever they choose. Also, don't believe the hype when an announcement is made that might indicate that bonuses at a certain level are being paid to everyone. The firm always finds ways to cut considerably the number of people who actually receive a bonus, and the number given is always 'up to' a certain amount. Few people actually get the number quoted, if they get any bonus at all."

Dealing with a dry spell

Associates work a lot of hours. But many expected nothing less when they signed up for big firm life. What they didn't expect is how the "peaks and valleys" of the legal market would affect them. A corporate associate says, "You're either working for 70 hours or struggling to bill 15 hours in a week." A litigation associate complains, "Sometimes not enough work, sometimes not enough hours in the day for the work. It would be so wonderful if they actually cared about how this affects our lives and did something to try and stabilize this." Another criticism is that work isn't evenly distributed. A corporate associate notes, "Equal distribution of work is not even attempted." Another corporate associate agrees: "The number of hours is not the issue. The manner in which those hours are distributed throughout the year is the key to an associate's satisfaction or dissatisfaction in this area. It is not unusual to go for several days or even a week without having a single billable hour. This dry spell is often followed by many long days, if not nights, in the office with little rest. There is no predictability in my schedule and no way to plan ahead for life outside the office." There are some positive aspects of hours at Dewey. A corporate associate remarks, "There is no dumping of work on lower associates on late Friday afternoons. No one wants to work the weekends, and we do everything we can to get the work done well before that is necessary." A litigation associate adds, "Lawyers are understanding about non-work obligations and face time is unnecessary."

Diversity needs work

How successful is Dewey at promoting and retaining its women lawyers? Associates disagree. One associate notes, "There are a lot of female partners in comparison to other large New York law firms. No female partners that I know of worked part time or took time off to have children other than maternity leave." Another woman says, "I came to Dewey partly because it had an excellent reputation of promoting women. While I'm definitely not planning partner track, I don't think my female gender would in any way impede me." Another woman sees some obstacles: "There is no ability for women to advance if they have a family and cannot make an enormous time commitment to the firm and thus be on the standard partnership track. Things that would help would be a non-equity partnership track and/or a counsel program. The counsel position is not defined and its availability varies depending on the partner asked." Another female agrees, "I think that the firm as a whole is pretty good, but there needs to be more women partners. And if you work part time because you have a child, your chances of becoming partner shouldn't be so drastically lower."

"The recruiting staff is always eager to hire more minorities," maintains an associate. And while Dewey's summer class is usually diverse, an Hispanic associate notes that "its associate pool is less so." The associate continues: "I can only think of three African-American associates in the New York office. There are a few Asian-Americans and Hispanics. There are no African-American partners."

Pro bono?

Dewey is a "for-profit business," says one associate, "but you can do whatever pro bono that you want as long as you do your billable work." Some associates aren't sure how pro bono works. One lawyer notes, "Pro bono is a black box. I know the firm is involved in several pro bono projects, and I have seen people working on pro bono matters, but I have no idea who gives pro bono assignments, how they are treated with regard to hours, and even who to ask for information." Another associate maintains that "the pro bono commitment seems to vary greatly by department." A litigator remarks, "I have been doing a great deal of pro bono work. When associates are not busy, they are strongly encouraged to take on pro bono work." Another insider tells it like it is: "Pro bono work counts, but they would rather you bill. At the same time they love that pro bono work is great experience for junior associates who can get trial experience. [The firm is] very, very open to anyone taking on pro bono as long as it doesn't interfere with other work." One associate is particularly impressed with the firm's commitment to pro bono work. He maintains, "[The] head of one of the departments took time out of his vacation to help me with a pro bono criminal appeal. I know that is not happening at firms where my friends are working."

Hogan & Hartson L.L.P.

555 Thirteenth Street, NW
Washington, DC 20004
Phone: (202) 637-5600
www.hhlaw.com

LOCATIONS

Washington, DC (HQ)

Baltimore, MD • Boulder, CO • Colorado Springs, CO •
Denver, CO • Los Angeles, CA • McLean, VA • Miami,
FL • New York, NY • Berlin • Brussels • Budapest •
London • Moscow • Paris • Prague • Tokyo • Warsaw

MAJOR DEPARTMENTS/PRACTICES

Antitrust, Competition & Consumer Protection •
Business & Finance • Capital Markets •
Communications • Community Services • Education •
Energy • Environmental • Financial Transactions • FDA •
Government Contracts • Health • Intellectual Property •
International Trade • Labor & Employment • Legislative •
Life Sciences • Litigation (Trial & Appellate) • Mergers
& Acquisitions • Privacy • Private Equity/Venture
Capital • Project Finance • Public Finance • Real Estate •
Tax • Technology • Transportation

THE STATS

No. of attorneys: 900 +
No. of offices: 18
Summer associate offers: 62 out of 64 (2001)
Chairman: Warren Gorrell
Hiring Chair: Robert B. Duncan

BASE SALARY

Washington, DC, 2002
1st year: $125,000
2nd year: $135,000
3rd year: $150,000
4th year: $165,000
5th year: $180,000
6th year: $190,000
7th year: $200,000
8th year: $210,000
Summer associate: $2,400/week

NOTABLE PERKS

• Technology allowance of $1,000 per year, plus
  $2,000 laptop allowance
• Frequent associate lunches
• Bi-monthly evening cocktail hours
• In-house subsidized cafeteria (Chez Hogan)
• On-site daycare

THE BUZZ

WHAT ATTORNEYS AT OTHER FIRMS ARE SAYING ABOUT THIS FIRM

• "Great DC firm"
• "Cutting edge in terms of benefits, diversity"
• "Bloated"
• "Gentle giant"
• "Middle of the pack"

UPPERS

- Prestigious legislative practice group
- Enhanced emphasis on training

DOWNERS

- Bonus disgruntlement
- "The offices stink!"

EMPLOYMENT CONTACT

Ms. Ellen M. Swank
Associate Recruitment and Professional Development
Director
Phone: (202) 637-8601
Fax: (202) 637-5910
emswank@hhlaw.com

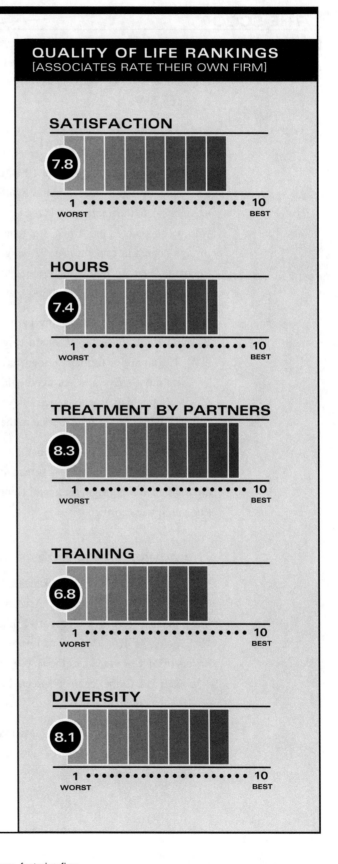

QUALITY OF LIFE RANKINGS
[ASSOCIATES RATE THEIR OWN FIRM]

SATISFACTION

7.8

1 WORST .... 10 BEST

HOURS

7.4

1 WORST .... 10 BEST

TREATMENT BY PARTNERS

8.3

1 WORST .... 10 BEST

TRAINING

6.8

1 WORST .... 10 BEST

DIVERSITY

8.1

1 WORST .... 10 BEST

THE SCOOP

Hogan & Hartson, the largest firm in our nation's capital, has just grown even larger, with the acquisition of New York's Squadron Ellenoff Plesent & Sheinfeld. The merger became effective in March 2002.

The globe and beyond

Founded nearly a century ago in 1904, the Washington, D.C.-based Hogan & Hartson has grown to include over 900 attorneys in 18 offices around the world. Hogan's relatively recent, rapid expansion into the international arena can largely be traced to the work of one man, Bob Glen Odle, who was appointed the firm's first managing partner in 1989. Within a year of opening its first foreign branch in London in 1990, Hogan had established offices in Brussels, Paris, Warsaw and Prague. Then, in quick succession, the firm saw the opening of offices in Moscow (1994), Budapest (1996), Tokyo (April 2000) and Berlin (August 2000).

Odle stepped down as managing partner at the end of 2000, but it's clear that his successor, J. Warren Gorrell, means to maintain Hogan's status as a leading international firm. In December 2001, Hogan added former LeBoeuf lawyers Garry Pegg and Hywel Jones to its London office. The next month, five new partners with a high-profile Latin American practice joined the Miami office. Hogan's international activities include both transactional work and litigation and extend beyond Europe and Latin America to the Pacific Rim, the Middle East and Africa.

Indeed Hogan's work is so international in scope as to be almost cosmic; this past year, Peter J. Pettibone, managing partner of Hogan's Moscow office, successfully negotiated with NASA and the Russian space program to send Dennis A. Tito and Mark Shuttleworth into space on board a Russian Soyuz capsule.

The power of the lobby

Not surprising for a D.C. powerhouse, Hogan has made a name — and substantial profit — for itself in the world of lobbying. According to Hogan, lobbying work brings in $8 million for the firm annually. The firm's legislative practice group includes four former Congressmen — Robert Michel (former House Majority Leader), John Porter (former Congressman from Illinois), Paul Rogers (a 24-year veteran of the House), and David Skaggs (former Representative from Colorado) — as well as a former cabinet officer, Clayton Yeutter, and Robert Kyle, who served in the Office of Management and Budget.

Hogan's legislative group represents manufacturers and trade associations in a wide variety of areas, including agriculture, automotive safety, health care, environment, tax and telecommunications.

Can't get enough of a good thing

Hogan opened its New York office in November 1998, with an emphasis on corporate and securities work, communications, energy, health care, tax and litigation. In April 2000, Hogan expanded its New York and Florida bases when the firm joined practices with Davis, Weber & Edwards, a 35-lawyer litigation firm with offices in New York and Miami.

Now Hogan has brought another firm to the fold — this time New York-based Squadron Ellenoff. The merger, which took effect in March 2002, added more than 100 attorneys to the Hogan family, tripling the size of Hogan's New York office and bringing the Los Angeles office to more than 40 attorneys. Squadron has a broad client base that includes a number of Fortune 500 companies. Among other benefits, the absorption of Squadron will likely make Hogan the primary outside counsel to News Corp., the media conglomerate controlled by Rupert Murdoch with whom Squadron has worked for nearly 30 years.

Courtroom command

Hogan's own litigation practice includes top trial and appellate lawyers with a record of wins in some high-profile cases. Should John G. Roberts Jr.'s pending nomination to the U.S. Court of Appeals for the D.C. Circuit go forward, Hogan might soon lose one of the brightest stars in its litigation team. Roberts currently leads the Appellate Practice Group and was named by *The National Law Journal* as one of Washington's top 10 civil litigators in 1999. More recently, Roberts won a resounding victory for Toyota Motors in the Supreme Court's January 2002 ruling in Toyota Motor Manufacturing, Kentucky, Inc. v. Williams, which held that a Kentucky assembly line worker with carpal tunnel syndrome was not a disabled worker under the Americans With Disabilities Act.

Roberts appeared before the Supreme Court again in January to argue another closely watched case. In Rush Prudential HMO Inc. v. Moran, the high court decided whether federal law, in the form of ERISA, preempts state laws requiring independent medical review of health benefit denials. Roberts represented Rush in its argument in favor of preemption and the uniformity of ERISA law. In June 2002, the Supreme Court held that ERISA does not preempt the Illinois HMO Act. The case, which touched on such thorny issues as patients' rights, states' rights and insurance law, is expected to have far-reaching effects in the health care industry. Roberts also argued the high-profile Tahoe-Sierra Preservation Council v. Tahoe Regional Planning Agency in January 2002. The Supreme Court, which issued its opinion in April, agreed with the firm's position on behalf of the agency that a temporary moratorium on development around Lake Tahoe to protect the lake's clarity from the consequences of development did not constitute a "taking" of private property.

A sense of community

Hogan takes justifiable pride in its devotion to community service. In 1970 Hogan became the first major American firm to create a separate practice group devoted exclusively to pro bono legal services. Since then the firm has worked with individuals and prominent public interest groups including the ACLU, the Lawyers Committee for Human Rights and the Washington Legal Clinic for the Homeless, in matters ranging from environmental protection to the death penalty to the First Amendment and the protection of human rights. It was Hogan & Hartson, together with the Washington Lawyers' Committee, that filed the 1993 class action lawsuit alleging race discrimination by Denny's, which resulted in the largest public accommodations settlement distribution in U.S. history.

While Hogan has a community services department that consists of a rotating group of attorneys and paralegals who work full time on pro bono projects, the firm emphasizes that most of its pro bono work is actually done by lawyers outside the department. Hogan lawyers are encouraged to view pro bono activity as a means not only to serve the public interest but also to gain valuable training and experience.

Making strides

Hogan has proved to be a comfortable home for women attorneys. Hogan's relatively large number of women attorneys includes respected litigators like former U.S. Attorney Loretta E. Lynch, who joined the New York office in February 2002, and Janet McDavid, a specialist in antitrust and trade litigation, who appeared on *The National Law Journal*'s 2001 list of the Top 50 Women Litigators. Moreover, the firm was ranked No. 1 in *Legal Times*' survey, "Women Lawyers at the D.C. Metro Areas 25 Largest Law Offices," with women comprising over 25 percent of the office's 201 partners.

In the area of minority diversity, the data is conflicting. On the one hand, *The National Law Journal* recently placed Hogan on what New York Lawyer calls a list of the "whitest law firms," those firms among the NLJ's 250 largest law firms with the smallest percentage of minority attorneys, with minority lawyers representing only 6.6 percent of Hogan's 767 attorneys. On the other hand, the firm also was ranked No. 1 in *Legal Times*' survey, "Minority Lawyers at the D.C. Metro Areas 25 Largest Law Offices." Despite the conflicting data, it's clear that the firm is making a concerted effort to recruit minorities. Between 1999 and 2001, the firm added six minority attorneys as partners or counsel through outside hiring and internal promotion, and added six more in early 2002. Also, the firm rose 35 points between 2000 and 2001 in the *Minority Law Journal*'s Diversity Scorecard (from No. 129 to No. 94).

GETTING HIRED

Serious business

If you want to participate in Hogan's summer associate program, you better get down to business. "Interviewers look for evidence that someone wants to actually practice law and is not hoping to just spend a summer or year or two in D.C.," advises an associate in the D.C. office. The firm looks for dedicated attorneys from the top schools, including Harvard and the University of Virginia. But the firm also likes seasoned attorneys. One associate notes, "The firm seems to favor candidates who took a couple of years off before law school and worked in finance, law or [another] professional capacity." Regarding the interview process, one associate remarks, "There was an intense one-day interview process, after which an offer was extended." Lateral hiring "has all but ceased for the corporate group, although litigation and some of the government groups continue to hire."

Real summer

Spend a summer at Hogan and you'll get a realistic picture of what life at the firm is really like. According to one associate, "My summer experience was able to replicate what it would be like to work at the firm as an associate quite well. The summers are able to choose what projects to work on which allows them to become as involved as they wish in projects." Another associate adds, "They had a very efficient system of assigning work, which provided a web site listing all [of] the potential projects and allowed students to choose among them." Mentions an insider, "The upshot is that summer associates could conceivably do some work in nearly every area of the firm's practice." Summer associates looking for a full-time employment offer from Hogan should relax. "Offers are always given to the entire class," notes one associate, "unless there is a serious problem."

OUR SURVEY SAYS

Best all around

"As far as law firms go, Hogan is as good as it gets," says one happy associate. "I would consider in-house and government opportunities, but I would never leave Hogan for another law firm." Another associate agrees: "Working at Hogan is about the best I can imagine working at a firm can be." What is so satisfying about life at Hogan? An associate answers, "A friendly yet professional atmosphere. Doors tend to remain open. The conventional wisdom about Hogan people is that they are nice, and the conventional wisdom is right in this case." Notes an insider, "Everyone I work with treats everyone else with respect and people are laid back. People I work for make extra effort to minimize interruptions to personal life such as vacations and personal events. Everyone has been nice to work with. The firm is large enough that there are many attorneys who go out and

socialize together and there are others who tend to go home after work to be with their families."
A New York associate isn't quite so enamored with the Hogan scene: "The lawyers are cordial
and respectful but distant. In general, few lawyers, from the associates up to the senior partners,
are personable."

Hogan gives choices

Some folks find choices liberating; others find them exasperating. A happy Hogan camper notes,
"I believe the pay scale is at the top of the market and I really like the flexibility of the two-track
system which allows associates to choose their hours and compensation." Another associate insists
that "the firm's two-tiered 'voluntary' compensation structure is a double-edged sword. In a down
market, those associates who had historically worked on the firm's 1,950 hour scale and would like
to continue to do so are forcibly dropped to the lower 1,800 hour scale. Even if an associate is in
good standing and advances with her compensation class, a drop in scale can mean as much as a
$15,000 decline in income." When it comes to bonuses, many associates are less than thrilled.
"Bonuses are very much tied to hours," a D.C. associate explains, "and if you do not exceed 1,950
hours, you are not likely to get any kind of bonus."

Associates have control

When it comes to hours, Hogan is like many other firms; the hours are "long" and sometimes
"erratic," but associate do have some control over them. A D.C. litigation associate notes,
"Associates at Hogan have a choice of trading hours for salary. Specifically, we can choose either
an 1,800 or 1,950 hour track. The latter comes with a salary on par with the highest-paying big
firms in D.C., while the former involves a slightly reduced salary. Although some groups at the
firm have embraced a high-billable culture, associates here generally have a lot of control over how
much time they are in the office." A New Yorker agrees: "There is a sense that you can make your
own hours. I have not had to work late evenings very often, and no weekends thus far. There does
not seem to be a face time requirement." Another litigator enjoys the flexibility: "Hogan &
Hartson is flexible enough to allow me to work long hours when it fits my schedule. I tend to work
very hard, but there is never a problem with taking an unscheduled slow week to recoup." Does
billing the minimum amount of hours affect an associate in the long run? Several associates say
no. "I know numerous associates who just meet the minimum billable and are progressing in the
firm and building their careers."

Where's the glass ceiling?

"Hogan has always been a great place for women," says a contented female associate. "We have a
significant number of women partners and have more part-time women lawyers than any other
D.C. law firm." The firm also recognizes the needs of working moms. "The firm has been very
supportive of me and my maternity leave. I have been able to balance the demands of a working
mother only because the firm has been so supportive of my need for flexibility." Another woman

concurs: "They have a wonderful maternity policy, and they are willing to work with women who would like to go part time. I do not perceive that there is any sort of glass ceiling at the firm at all."

There may be no glass ceiling for women at Hogan, but there seems to be a "revolving door for minorities," despite the efforts the firm has made in recent years in this area. A black associate mentions, "To its credit, the firm has made special efforts in recent years to attract and hire strong minority candidates into its summer program. Once hired, however, the age-old problems of poor mentoring, training and career guidance that affect many associates in large firms seem to have a disparate impact on minority attorneys. The firm has an abysmal record for hiring minority attorneys from the firm's summer program and subsequently promoting such attorneys to partnership." The firm points out that the 2001 summer associate program for the Washington office was composed of 67 second-year students, of which 17 were minorities, and that all but one of those 17 participants received offers for 2002 or 2003. The firm further notes that the 2002 summer associate program for the Washington office will be composed of 42 participants, of which 10 are minorities.

An Asian associate takes it all in stride: "Race is simply not an issue. If you went to a good school, did well and work hard, that is what they care about. I haven't seen the firm go out of its way to recruit minorities, nor do I think such a push is merited."

Diversity with respect to gays and lesbians gets mixed reviews. One gay associate notices, "You can be comfortably out at H&H and do gay and lesbian-related pro bono work. Still, for a firm of H&H's size, we have very few gay or lesbian associates or partners."

The heroes of Hogan

"Hogan has the best pro bono department in D.C., and perhaps the best in the country," brags an associate. Another maintains, "I know associates who have been allowed to clear their billable work for several weeks in order to take a pro bono case to trial. The community services department, staffed by one full-time partner, a full-time senior associate, three full-time junior associates and appropriate support staff, does a fantastic job of not only handling numerous cases but bringing potential work to the attention of other attorneys and then supporting them in their pro bono work." One hundred hours of pro bono work count toward billable hours. An associate explains, "Once you bill 1,800 hours you can count up to 100 hours of pro bono."

Back to school

Associates have long complained of Hogan's spiritless approach to training. Now the firm is doing something about it. To aid associates, the firm has instituted a program called H&H Academy. According to associates, "The H&H Academy was established recently to provide a more formal structure for the Hogan training process." Pam Winthrop, a Hogan & Hartson partner, is exclusively devoted to running the academy. But wait ... there's more! Hogan's library (otherwise known as the information resource center) also provides monthly "training on locating relevant information or using new software or applications. There are regular talks and seminars that are offered throughout the year on a variety of topics as well."

Any criticisms of the newly revitalized training initiative? Hogan associates say they wish their firm would be more proactive about pairing associates with mentors. "The bottom line is, whether a firm has good formal programs on legal training or law firm economics, what each associate needs is a mentor who will make sure the associate is developing the skills he or she needs by providing them with the right opportunities, the right projects and the right contacts. This, probably as in any other firm, is very much an individual-specific experience. I am starting to feel that I have a few mentors who are helping me to develop as an attorney, but it's still very much a work in progress."

"The firm seems to favor candidates who took a couple of years off before law school and worked in finance, law or [another] professional capacity."

— *Hogan & Hartson associate*

Wilson Sonsini Goodrich & Rosati

650 Page Mill Road
Palo Alto, CA 94304-1050
Phone: (650) 493-9300
www.wsgr.com

LOCATIONS

Palo Alto, CA (HQ)
Austin, TX
Kirkland, WA
McLean, VA
New York, NY
Salt Lake City, UT
San Francisco, CA

MAJOR DEPARTMENTS/PRACTICES

Antitrust • Corporate & Securities • Employee Benefits
& Executive Compensation • Employment Litigation •
Environmental & Real Estate • Intellectual Property •
Internal Investigations • Life Sciences • Litigation •
Mergers & Acquisitions • Patent Prosecution/Litigation •
Securities Litigation • Tax • Technology Transactions •
Trademark & Advertising • Venture Capital •
Venture/Investment Funds • Wealth Management •
White Collar Criminal Defense

THE STATS

No. of attorneys: 696
No. of offices: 7
Summer associate offers: 56 out of 71 (2001)
Chairman: Larry Sonsini
Hiring Partners: Kathleen Bloch, Leo Cunningham and
Matthew Sonsini

BASE SALARY

Palo Alto, 2002
1st year: $125,000
2nd year: $135,000
3rd year: $150,000
4th year: $165,000
5th year: Merit-based up to $180,000
6th year: Merit-based up to $195,000
7th year: Merit-based up to $205,000
8th year: Merit-based up to $215,000
Summer associate: $2,400/week

NOTABLE PERKS

• Casual dress
• On-site gym and sushi cafe

THE BUZZ
WHAT ATTORNEYS AT OTHER FIRMS ARE SAYING ABOUT THIS FIRM

• "'The Evil Empire' is their own nickname"
• "Its bubble popped"
• "Still the Valley leader"
• "Tech wreck"
• "Cutting edge"

UPPERS

- "Fascinating, cutting-edge" clients
- Entrepreneurial spirit
- Emphasis on training

DOWNERS

- Economic downturn means less fulfilling work to go around
- Strict scrutiny of associates' billable time

EMPLOYMENT CONTACT

Attorney Recruiting Department
1 (888) GO2-WSGR
attorneyrecruiting@wsgr.com

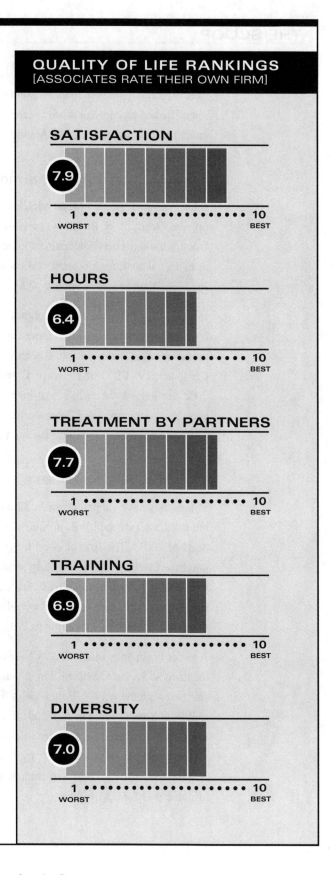

QUALITY OF LIFE RANKINGS
[ASSOCIATES RATE THEIR OWN FIRM]

SATISFACTION

7.9

1 WORST • • • • • • • • • • • • • • • • • 10 BEST

HOURS

6.4

1 WORST • • • • • • • • • • • • • • • • • 10 BEST

TREATMENT BY PARTNERS

7.7

1 WORST • • • • • • • • • • • • • • • • • 10 BEST

TRAINING

6.9

1 WORST • • • • • • • • • • • • • • • • • 10 BEST

DIVERSITY

7.0

1 WORST • • • • • • • • • • • • • • • • • 10 BEST

THE SCOOP

While most people think of the tech boom as a 1990s phenomenon, Wilson Sonsini Goodrich & Rosati founding partner John Wilson recognized the potential of the Silicon Valley as a center of scientific and technological advancement decades before the masses. This young firm has made a name for itself in the IPO, M&A and venture capital arenas.

History: California dreamin'

John Wilson helped co-found McCloskey, Wilson, Mosher & Martin — now known as Wilson Sonsini Goodrich & Rosati — in 1961 in Palo Alto, Calif. Name partners Larry Sonsini, John Goodrich and Mario Rosati came aboard in 1966, 1970 and 1971, respectively. John Wilson retired in 1983, but continued to serve as an advisor to the firm until a short time before his death in 1999. John Goodrich retired in January 2002, after more than 31 years of service to the firm.

Initially, the firm acted as a matchmaker by connecting clients long on ideas and technical know-how but short on cash with venture capitalists. Later, the firm began counseling clients on initial public offerings, mergers and acquisitions, and other transactions. The 1980 IPO of Apple Computer, 1994 IPO of Netscape Communications and the HP/Compaq merger and litigation in 2002 are among the firm's best-known successes. Today more than 3,300 companies in the computer, semiconductor, Internet, life sciences and investment banking industries regularly call upon Wilson Sonsini to advise them on legal and business matters.

Taking care of business

Things may have quieted down in Silicon Valley since the market fell and the dot-coms went bust, but that hasn't stopped Wilson Sonsini from taking part in one of the most high-profile technology deals of 2001. The firm advised longtime client Hewlett-Packard on its September 2001 bid to purchase Compaq Computer Corp., including leading Hewlett-Packard's winning defense of the high-profile lawsuit brought by director and stockholder Walter Hewlett. Although some investors and analysts have labeled the proposed merger a bad fit, a successful union of the two computing titans will prove very profitable to Wilson.

Another big-money client is SS8 Networks, a maker of high-speed Internet products. Thanks to the firm, SS8 secured $62 million in venture capital in November 2001. GoTo.com was apparently satisfied with the way Wilson Sonsini handled its 1999 IPO. The search engine company turned to Wilson Sonsini again in July 2001 to manage its $58.6 million follow-on offering. On the M&A front, the firm started the summer small and ended it with a super-sized deal. First up was the $15.2 million purchase of Wireless Inc. by Wilson's client Interwave Communications in June 2001. In August the firm advised electronics maker Solectron when it acquired another electronics manufacturer for $2.7 billion.

In addition, Wilson Sonsini won a huge defense verdict for client Broadcom Corp. in a patent infringement lawsuit filed by Intel Corp.

Batting for Boeing and beyond

Wilson also helps its clients when disgruntled shareholders sue. One such client was the aircraft manufacturer Boeing. Wilson represented the company and its executives when shareholders sued because unmet production deadlines allegedly caused the stock price to fall sharply. While Boeing's accusers charged that executives had covered up its ability to meet its production deadlines and lied about the company's financial health, Boeing officials maintained their innocence. Wilson helped orchestrate a settlement along the lines of $92.5 million in October 2001. From planes to eye surgery — medical laser manufacturer Visx sought Wilson Sonsini's counsel when a group of ophthalmologists accused the company of conspiring with another manufacturer to fix prices of equipment used in laser eye surgery. The firm helped Visx settle out of court for $30 million.

Weathering the storm

Unlike some firms that froze associate salaries at their 2001 levels, Wilson Sonsini pledged in January 2002 to grant annual increases and continue to avoid the need to lay off associates and other employees. Such an announcement is welcome news, though Wilson Sonsini hasn't been immune to the slide in the economy, as the number of M&A deals and IPOs handled by Silicon Valley firms dipped perilously in 2001. Still, Wilson closed as many as 170 M&A deals and 12 IPOs in 2001.

Because the firm has a sizeable number of corporate and securities associates, it has had to find some creative ways of utilizing their time now that there is less M&A and IPO work to go around. All attorneys have been asked to contribute to the firm's "knowledge management" systems. These projects include setting up a database of important court decisions. Though the firm expects associates to return to billable lawyering full time once business picks up, Wilson has hedged its bets on a quick economic rebound by extending offers to only 80 percent of its 2001 summer associate class and promoting just five new partners in November 2001.

Back to the fold

For a couple of Wilson attorneys, the saying "You can't go home again" has proven false. Partner Dave Segre rejoined the firm in October 2001 after having left 17 months before to work for FusionOne, an Internet startup that was a client of Segre's while he was at Wilson. His return followed that of partner Jonathan Axelrad, who rejoined the firm in January 2001, also after working for an Internet company. While their partner status undoubtedly influenced their ability to return during a downturn, the firm seems to consider retaining talent and maintaining its reputation with attorneys in these tough economic times top priorities.

Big-hearted lawyers

Attorneys at the firm were looking forward to celebrating the opening of its two newest offices in New York and Salt Lake City, Utah (home of the 2002 Winter Olympic Games). Locations for the celebrations were selected and the menus planned, but after the tragedies of September 11, firm leaders had a change of heart. The festivities were cancelled, and Wilson Sonsini donated the cost of the parties — more than $100,000 — to the relief efforts.

As California endured its energy crisis, the lawyers at Wilson Sonsini did their part to help out. The firm decided to deactivate some of its landscape lighting and shut off equipment and personal appliances, like fans and radios, that were deemed unnecessary. According to the firm's estimates, the plan saved enough electricity to power 4,500 homes for 24 hours. The firm has earned accolades for its energy programs and environmental efforts in the local community.

GETTING HIRED

Good grades and an interest in the industry

Several sources suggest that the current economic climate makes getting hired by Wilson Sonsini more difficult than in the past. "During the boom, it was much easier to get hired. Nowadays, the firm is only considering people with exceptional pedigrees." "We hire mostly from top-tier law schools," says a corporate attorney. She adds, however, that "grades are not everything — personality goes a long way. No one wants to be stuck at the printer for 24 hours with someone who is bright but has no social skills." Law students, suggests one lawyer, "need good grades and an interest in the industry." Demonstrate knowledge of and enthusiasm for the firm's business, since Wilson "likes people who really understand what it is about."

If it is "pretty difficult to get hired" out of law school, some say that "it has become impossible to get hired as a lateral unless you practice in a field that is busy, such as patent litigation." Those with "particular skills," such as admission to the patent bar or a technical background, have a good chance. According to a litigator, "the firm is always looking for qualified IP litigators, particularly people with a technical background."

OUR SURVEY SAYS

Friendly, hardworking and entrepreneurial

Insiders say there is no uniform culture at Wilson Sonsini "because the firm is so large and because of the individual groups within the firm, which tend to have distinct personalities." Overall, however, respondents agree that the firm is casual about things like attire but intense with regard to work. The environment is "friendly but hardworking" according to many associates. "My perception," says one lawyer, "is that the firm's culture is relatively laid back as long as you are performing to expectations. I wear jeans most days (unless meeting with clients or going to court) and I feel I am judged on my skills and abilities rather than my wardrobe." Another finds it "a very flexible place where nearly anything is accepted as long as you do your job well." A number of sources refer to the firm's "entrepreneurial spirit."

A few associates suggest that recently, as "work got a little slower, some of the associates became less collegial and more competitive." In addition, partners now "scrutinize associates' billable hours and huddle behind closed doors all day, which can lead to rumors and conjecture." One associate calls the firm "very laissez faire" and "casual." "It's very individualized," she says, "but as a result, the morale of the group is relatively low while individual happiness is relatively high."

Don't sweat the small stuff

The degree to which lawyers socialize varies widely — some sources claim that "attorneys regularly socialize together" while others report that "there isn't much socializing outside the office." The suburban setting of Silicon Valley lends itself to "maximizing family time" and more than half of the survey respondents are married. The Austin office is "laid back," and associates in Salt Lake City are "having a blast" breaking in the firm's new branch. "Bringing the Wilson brand to a young market like Salt Lake City is huge," raves one lawyer. Another says, "The office (and all of us) are so young, though, that we are developing our own mountain-casual strain of Wilson culture."

That mountain-casual culture extends to the firm's location, which Utah respondents praise for its "terrific view, nice space, free parking and [location] 15 minutes from the ski slopes!" The firm's headquarters in Palo Alto also gets high marks as "a pleasant work environment." "The firm really strives to make the workplace comfortable so that the lawyers can just focus on their jobs at hand and not sweat the small stuff." This means all attorneys have window offices, with free parking and a café in the building. The "only complaint is WSGR's insane and tacky decision to use purple as a major decorating motif." D.C. lawyers are slated to move to the Reston Town Center this summer, where the "space is supposed to be really nice with great views."

Fascinating clients

Job satisfaction among Wilsonians remains fairly high, although the economic downturn has adversely affected the quality and quantity of some lawyers' work. "With the deal flow lessening over the last year the amount of interesting work has declined," reports an attorney in corporate finance. However, other lawyers continue to be excited by "work with start-up companies which rely on us to provide both business and legal advice." Working at Wilson Sonsini "is very fulfilling in that it is interesting and the clients are fascinating," says an employment attorney. Several associates praise the firm for using the down time "to dramatically improve the training it offers associates at all levels." At least one corporate attorney is delighted with his experience. "This is hands down the best job I have ever had. I have worked in different industries, in university settings and in government. Other jobs have been close, but this job wins."

Associates sometimes find the firm's clients so fascinating that they can't resist joining them. Especially at "the height of the dot-com bubble," lawyers "were constantly being tempted by really sexy opportunities from our clients." Most insiders attribute the firm's high rate of attrition less to "dissatisfaction with Wilson than that people continue to be presented with attractive opportunities, many of them non-law related." With the slump in the economy, such opportunities have shrunk and retention is accordingly higher. Not all departures are for in-house positions, however. Over the last year, there have been a few partner defections to other firms.

Still a generous package

Bonus bitterness also prompted at least a few departures. Year-end bonuses were "down significantly from last year." One source gripes that her "1999 bonus was higher than my 2001 bonus … even though 2001 was the second-best year ever, after 2000, in terms of profits per partner. And they tried to spin it. So people were a little bitter — including, I must confess, me." But another associate maintains that Wilson associates "are very fortunate to be even getting such bonuses or increases in base. Many of our competitors received no such increases or bonuses, and in fact laid off attorneys and staff." Overall, associates seem pretty happy with their compensation, a package of base salary, year-end bonus and quarterly productivity bonuses, that puts them "on the higher side compared to other firms." A fifth-year associate contends, "You can't argue with getting paid this much. I earn it back for the firm and then some, but it is still a generous salary and bonus."

Slower business means fewer hours

One upside to the denouement of the dot-com scene may be a more manageable workload for some associates. Several attorneys report that the firm "is known as a hardworking firm, but the past year has been very balanced. Most associates probably bill between 1,900 and 2,100 hours." One source claims that "since tech work has been slow, the average hours billed is under 1,800." While a first-year associate says these "hours are a breeze!" not all lawyers regard the slowdown as a plus. "Sometimes it is difficult to find work," reports a corporate attorney, "but the firm expects you to bill a certain number of hours." And still others, particularly in litigation, complain about "too many hours." One associate calls it "a feast or famine situation," but she values the flexibility. "I love the way it balances out. I love the flexibility the firm gives me — I go horseback riding in the mornings and rarely show up before 11 a.m., and then just make up those hours when it's dark and I don't mind being inside."

Mixed feelings about pro bono

Just as the firm's culture "varies from practice group to practice group," the firm's attitude toward pro bono work "varies dramatically from group to group." According to one associate in the technology practice, "There are factions within the firm that care deeply about pro bono and factions within the firm that don't give a damn. My group happens to see it as a negative." Others feel more encouraged. There is no mandatory pro bono requirement, but a partner acts as pro bono counsel, and the firm "regularly solicits associate involvement in a number of pro bono matters."

Not hugely diverse

The fact that Wilson Sonsini's managing partner is a woman "speaks pretty highly about the treatment of women," say several associates. The firm is "very egalitarian," according to sources who claim that women "are not treated any differently" from men. Others note that "far too few women make partner" and find "isolated pockets" of a "good-old-boy culture." The firm's maternity leave and part-time programs are criticized as insufficiently "family friendly" and, according to one woman, "it's also widely believed that having a baby will take you out of the running for partnership." The firm notes, however, that it has signed on to the Bar Association of San Francisco's "no glass ceiling" commitments, including consideration of part-time attorneys' roles and flexible work schedules.

"What minorities?" responds a litigator when asked about Wilson's diversity program. One associate remarks, rather confusingly, "I don't think we're hugely diverse, but I think (or hope) that's just a reflection of the pool of people who pick us, not any action on the part of WSGR." A corporate attorney is dismayed that "to [her] knowledge, there was not one African-American summer associate in the 2001 summer associate class, and the firm had one of the largest summer associate classes in California." At least one lawyer, however, believes in "the genuineness of this firm's commitment to diversity." He cites the example of Issac Vaughn, an African-American and "one of the partners I most respect at this firm." The firm says it is proud of its record on minority partners and associates and values diversity.

Associates note that "there are no openly gay or lesbian partners" at the firm, but one lawyer maintains, "As a gay attorney, I feel perfectly welcome, respected and accepted." Another attorney suggests that any discrimination on the part of the firm is prompted less by sexual identity than by particular political leanings. "Let me put it this way: a gay or lesbian with 'fiscally conservative' politics would probably feel more comfortable than a straight person with 'left of Democrat' politics."

King & Spalding

191 Peachtree Street
Suite 4900
Atlanta, GA 30303-1763
Phone: (404) 572-4600
www.kslaw.com

LOCATIONS

Atlanta, GA
Houston, TX
New York, NY
Washington, DC

MAJOR DEPARTMENTS/PRACTICES

Business Litigation • Construction & Procurement •
Corporate Finance • Employee Benefits & Executive
Compensation • Environmental • Financial Restructuring •
Financial Transactions • Food & Drug • Global Projects •
Health Care • Intellectual Property • Labor &
Employment • Litigation - Special Matters • Litigation &
Trade • Mergers & Acquisitions • Private Equity • Public
Finance • Real Estate • Tax • Tort Litigation

THE STATS

No. of attorneys: 600+
No. of offices: 4
Summer associate offers (2001): 60 out of 63
(Atlanta); 9 out of 10 (Houston); 9 out of 9 (New
York); 14 out of 19 (Washington, DC)
Chairman: Walter W. Driver Jr.
Hiring Partners: Peter J. Genz (Atlanta); Kenneth S.
Culotta (Houston); Douglas A. Bird (New York); Mark S.
Brown (Washington, DC)

BASE SALARY

Atlanta, 2002
1st year: $100,000
Summer associate: $1,750/week

Houston, 2002
1st year: $110,000
Summer associate: $2,100/week

New York, 2002
1st year: $125,000
Summer associate: $2,400/week

Washington, DC, 2002
1st year: $125,000
Summer associate: $2,150/week

NOTABLE PERKS

• "Free fountain Coca-Cola — big client"
• Subsidized dining room (Atlanta)
• Tickets to local sports events
• On-site gym (DC) and discounted gym
  memberships (NY)

THE BUZZ
WHAT ATTORNEYS AT OTHER FIRMS ARE SAYING ABOUT THIS FIRM

• "The South's best firm"
• "New York hours, Atlanta wages"
• "Great clients"
• "Coke, Coke and more Coke"
• "Stuffy times ten"

UPPERS

- "Brand name in Atlanta"
- Prestigious M&A practice
- Professional and civil firm culture

DOWNERS

- Slim partnership prospects
- Bonuses tied to billable hours
- "Friday only" casual dress policy

EMPLOYMENT CONTACT

Atlanta
Ms. Patty Blitch Harris
Recruiting Manager
Phone: (404) 572-4990
Fax: (404) 572-5100
pbharris@kslaw.com

New York
Ms. Abigail B. Golden
Recruiting Coordinator
Phone: (212) 556-2200
Fax: (212) 556-2222
agolden@kslaw.com

Houston
Ms. Ann E. Harris
Recruiting Manager
Phone: (713) 276-7319
Fax: (713) 751-3290
aharris@kslaw.com

Washington, DC
Ms. Kara K. O'Connor
Recruiting Manager
Phone: (202) 626-2387
Fax: (202) 626-3737
koconnor@kslaw.com

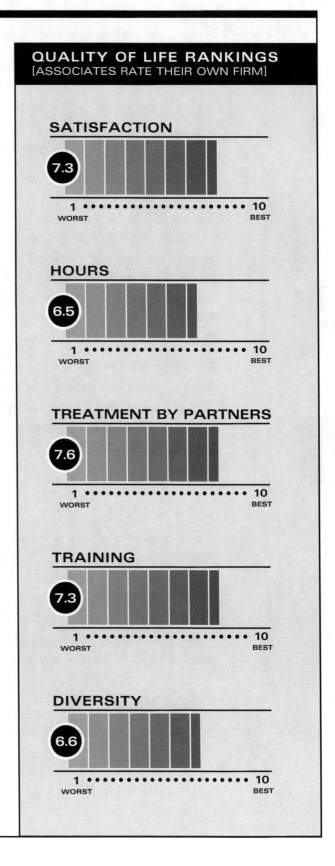

QUALITY OF LIFE RANKINGS
[ASSOCIATES RATE THEIR OWN FIRM]

SATISFACTION
7.3
1 WORST — 10 BEST

HOURS
6.5
1 WORST — 10 BEST

TREATMENT BY PARTNERS
7.6
1 WORST — 10 BEST

TRAINING
7.3
1 WORST — 10 BEST

DIVERSITY
6.6
1 WORST — 10 BEST

THE SCOOP

Founded in 1885, King & Spalding rose from the ashes left over from Sherman's March to the Sea and, over a century later, is tops in the South. Steeped in true Southern gentility, this isn't a place for khakis and T-shirts, but it is a place for highly regarded legal work.

History: some noteworthy folks

One of King & Spalding's founding fathers was Alex C. King, who would later become Solicitor General of the United States as well as a judge on the United States Court of Appeals for the Fifth Circuit. In 1979 the firm headed north to Washington, D.C., opening its second office. That year Griffin B. Bell rejoined the firm after stints as the Attorney General of the United States and as a judge on the Court of Appeals for the Fifth Circuit. In 1990 the firm opened a New York office specializing in corporate issues. Five years later, an office in Houston followed. In 1997 Sam Nunn joined the firm after 24 years in the U.S. Senate. Partner William S. Duffey Jr. left to become U.S. Attorney in Georgia's Northern District, and former partner Larry D. Thompson currently serves as Deputy Attorney General of the United States.

The National Law Journal named partner Chilton Davis Varner one of the nation's top 10 women litigators. When Varner joined the firm in 1976, she was the first woman in litigation. She was also the second to make partner and the first to be elected to the firm's management committee. Varner specializes in product liability defense, representing GlaxoSmithKline, Purdue Pharma, General Motors Corp., 3M, BASF Corp., General Electric Co., Coca-Cola Co., United Parcel Service Inc. and Nissan.

Getting a head

King & Spalding created the position of chairman in November 2001. Walter W. Driver Jr., an Atlanta partner who worked extensively on financing transactions, was named head. Driver served as firm-wide managing partner, a position now defunct with the creation of chairman. Along with the chairman, four managing partners for each of the national offices will lead the firm. Managing partners will focus on issues specific to their offices. The new managing partners are as follows: Mason W. Stephenson in Atlanta, J. Sedwick "Wick" Sollers in Washington, D.C., Mark Zvonkovic in New York, and Randolph C. "Randy" Coley in Houston.

King of the tabloids

King & Spalding found its name speckled in the tabloids in July 2001 after one of its associates sustained injuries when New York society girl Lizzie Grubman rammed her SUV into clubbers at a Southampton, N.Y., hotspot. The associate and another injured attorney are seeking several million dollars in total damages. In the highly publicized story, which became the obsession du jour of many a New Yorker in the summer of 2001, Grubman says she did not intentionally back into the crowd after an altercation with club security. The case is pending.

In another celebrity case, the former manager of the band Collective Soul claims the firm mismanaged the settlement of his 1995 dispute with the band's founder. In October 2001, the manager, William H. Richardson, and his wife claimed that they lost $1.5 million in royalties from the sale of Collective Soul records due to King & Spalding's negligently drafted settlement agreement. They claim that partner Bruce W. Baber lacked expertise in entertainment law and wasn't prepared for trial. The Richardsons' attorney said they got a raw deal in the confidential settlement while King & Spalding said the Richardsons have yet to pay their attorneys' fees.

Have no worries, Ken

BPS Billy won't be around much longer. At least that's United Parcel Service's wish for the anatomically correct doll dressed in a brown uniform with a package-shaped logo. UPS says this logo infringes on its trademark. In January 2002, its attorneys at King & Spalding requested the seller of the doll, which is marketed to gay men, get Billy off the shelves. The doll is sold on BeProud.com, a web site purveying goods geared toward gays and lesbians and manufactured by Totem International Ltd. Totem agreed to stop making the dolls, but BeProud posted a message on its web site that it will continue selling Billy despite the threats of a lawsuit.

In other IP news, King & Spalding client Scientific-Atlanta is defending its right to develop interactive program guide software. Gemstar-TV Guide International Inc., the maker of interactive TV program guides, claims it holds the patent on interactive program guide technology. This technology selects, records and sorts programs offered on premium cable packages with 100-plus channels. Within the cable industry, this technology is indispensable when dealing with 50 or more channels and can be likened to the Internet browser for the World Wide Web. Scientific-Atlanta says its interactive program guide software does not infringe on any existing patents. Furthermore, it claims Gemstar's patents are invalid and violate antitrust laws. The case is pending.

Crossing the border

King & Spalding is one of the top firms when it comes to international M&A work. According to an August 2001 ranking by Thomson Financial, the firm's Latin American Practice Group is one of the top five legal advisors for Mexican companies by the value of its M&A deals. One deal in particular helped King & Spalding make the list: its representation of Sprint Corp. in its $200 million investment in Pegaso Telecomunicaciones, S.A. de C.V. This is the first 100 percent digital wireless communications network in Mexico that provides nationwide service covering nearly 100 million potential customers. Continuing in its excellent advisement south of the United States, in November 2001, the firm helped The Home Depot sell its five stores in Chile to its joint venture partner, Falabella, and its four stores in Argentina to Hipermercados Jumbo.

Not the "NORM"

December 26, 2001, was a winning day for King & Spalding client ChevronTexaco. The oil and gas production company was taken to court for allegations of soil and groundwater contamination, including naturally occurring radioactive materials (NORM). The judge found that the plaintiffs, four couples owning property in the oilfield, did not have enough evidence to show Chevron had acted wrongfully. The plaintiffs were not awarded anything for mental anguish claims. They were awarded $88,500 for property damage, a fraction of the property's value. The litigation involved about 20 lawsuits with over 1,000 plaintiffs in several Mississippi counties. Bobby Meadows of King & Spalding's Houston office led the trial team for Chevron.

GETTING HIRED

Fab summer

King & Spalding associates have nothing but fond memories about their summer associate days. "It was a great time socially and attorneys showed genuine interest in my work product," reports one K&S real estate associate. "You are wined and dined and have the opportunity to meet lots of great people," notes another associate. "The program works on a rotation system so you actually rotate through a particular team for one, two or three weeks…. During the summer, you get real work not just something to occupy your time," says an Atlanta associate. Despite the praise for the summer program, some insist that the program is "lots of fun, but not a true reflection of the firm."

An associate fit for the King

"This firm is very selective on who is hired," says a New York associate. "Not only does someone have to meet the academic criteria, but the person must also be a good fit for the firm's culture." An associate in D.C. notes, "We look for people we'll be happy to have around the office, not just people with impressive resumes." A member of the hiring committee maintains, "If you are from a top school, it is pretty easy. Grades are very important, probably more so than the school because we don't have very many partners that went to top schools so they don't credit that as much as some places. We do hire from 2nd- and 3rd-tier schools if the grades are in the top 5-10 percent of the class but might pass on someone from Harvard in the bottom half of the class."

OUR SURVEY SAYS

"Collegial" King

According to associates, the culture in the firm's Atlanta office is "Southern," "professional" and "collegial." An associate there says, "Many of my friends are other lawyers in the firm. The firm provides a good mix of opportunity to socialize and interact without exerting a pressure that your work life is supposed to be your social life." Another insider offers, "The work is hard, the hours are long and the expectations are extremely high, but work done well is rewarded and if you're good at what you do, you receive ample recognition. The work culture is formal and intense. Among younger attorneys, however, socialization is prevalent."

In our nation's capital, one associate notes, "We socialize a lot. [There are] very collegial relationships among associates and between associates and partners." Over in the Big Apple, associates describe a slightly tamer firm experience built on respect. "King & Spalding has cultivated a culture of respect. Partners treat associates decently, and the firm does a good job of trying to create opportunities for lawyers to socialize," states an associate there. Another New Yorker insists that "lawyers tend to socialize. The culture is a good mix of being laid back yet hardworking when necessary. Outside and family life is encouraged and supported." An associate in Houston remarks, "The culture at K&S is exceptional considering its size. The associates spend a significant amount of time with each other outside of the firm. The culture is truly one of a partnership, not one in which everyone watches only his or her own back."

Compensation envy

When it comes to compensation, Atlanta associates are hoppin' mad. One such associate complains, "We work the same hours as New York and D.C. firms and the cost of living in Atlanta is not that low to warrant our salaries. My law school friends started working in September for New York firms and they received a year-end bonus. Our firm only gives out bonuses for billable hours or pro bono work." Another concurs: "There is some resentment among associates here because of discrepancies between the pay scale at the Atlanta office and other offices. For example, the cost of living in Houston is actually lower than it is in Atlanta, but Houston associates are paid more. K&S could set the market for associate salaries in Atlanta if it wanted to, but that might cut into profits per partner, which is the sacred cow around here." Another Atlanta associate sees things very differently: "The firm is at the top of the city and has a bonus structure unmatched in this market."

Says an associate based in Houston, "The bonus system is very equitable. Base pay is competitive with the other large firms in town." New Yorkers seem equally as pleased, noting that they'd rather have a smaller bonus and manageable hours. One notes, "We get paid New York salaries. There is not a large bonus, though. But we don't have to kill ourselves, so it's fair." Another New Yorker explains, "Our annual bonuses aren't very much, but that's because they're not hours-driven. I'd rather have a high base salary than high bonuses that require me to bill a lot of hours."

King no "gulag"

K&S associates generally are pleased with the amount of hours they work. A litigation associate says, "Considering how much they're paying me and how well they treat me, I can't complain about the occasional busy periods. And the hours overall are not bad." When the hours pile up, it's because a job needs to get done — not because partners demand face time. Notes an IP associate, "The hours I work are the direct result of my responsibilities to clients and the type of cases I am involved in. There is no busy work and no artificial deadlines that create unnecessary hours." In the New York office, an associate remarks, "Any job based on billing time tends to make you work more than usual. As far as big law firms go, however, I think K&S takes the right approach — focusing on getting work done rather than putting in face time." A labor and employment associate agrees, "The needs of the clients drive the hours, not the firm culture."

Promotion of women varies

It's the same old diversity story at King & Spalding — women are hired in large numbers, but only a few are retained and promoted to partner. "Most of the female partners are in regulatory groups and few hold positions of leadership," sighs an associate. "In fact, there's only one female litigation partner in the entire office. There is a lack of mentoring in general of younger associates, despite the existence of a formal mentoring program." Several associates hope that the women's groups that have formed in some of the firm's offices will be instrumental in improving the situation. But, insist others, "it is still a big problem. Women do not make partner — especially not equity partner — except in exceptional circumstances and usually when they do not have children. Women who have children generally end up back-benched when it comes to good work, upward mobility and respect." In the New York office, associates mention that the head of the firm's largest practice group (financial transactions) is a woman, and she is also a member of the policy committee that governs the firm.

Associates have similar complaints regarding the situation of minorities at King & Spalding. "As with women, the firm pretends that it cares about minority recruiting and retention," opines an Asian associate. "However, the lack of any official diversity committee belies that stated commitment." One associate feels the firm is "fairly diverse," noting that there are "German, African-American, Indian, Filipino, Arab, French, Belgian and other ethnicities" represented at the firm.

Pro bono gets better

When it comes to pro bono work, things are looking up. "The office just started a pro bono committee to coordinate more formally pro bono activities," notes a New York associate. In Washington, another associate says, "The D.C. office has recently accepted a 'pro bono challenge' by the D.C. Bar, committing to 60 hours of pro bono work per attorney. Since then, the office has affiliated with several organizations who have trained attorneys for certain types of work." She adds, "We're all hoping to see a vast improvement over the next year." A lawyer in the Atlanta office agrees, "The firm provides numerous opportunities to participate in pro bono work and provides training in connection with each opportunity." One K&S associate gloats, "King & Spalding was one of the first firms to allow summer associates to split [their summer] and compensate summer associates for the half of their summer they spend doing public interest work. In addition, this year the firm has created a pro bono rotation where summer associates will do solely pro bono work that is supervised by different partners."

Though the firm is making strides to strengthen its pro bono commitment, some associates see areas in which the firm could improve: "The firm could strengthen its commitment to pro bono work by counting those hours toward billable hours, with a reasonable cap on the hours per month that would count toward billable hours." The associate explains, "That would incentivize lawyers to do pro bono work as associates, and with luck create a habit that would carry over into partnership, when such an incentive is no longer necessary." Another source clarifies, "While pro bono work does not technically count towards billable hours, it does count towards a separate bonus for non-billable contributions."

Boies, Schiller & Flexner LLP

80 Business Park Drive
Suite 110
Armonk, NY 10504-1710
Phone: (914) 273-9800
www.bsfllp.com

LOCATIONS

Armonk, NY (HQ)
Albany, NY • Fort Lauderdale, FL • Hanover, NH •
Hollywood, FL • Miami, FL • New York, NY • Oakland,
CA • Orlando, FL • Palm Beach Gardens, FL •
Washington, DC

MAJOR DEPARTMENTS/PRACTICES

Antitrust • Appellate • Arbitration • Business Crimes •
Class Actions • Corporate • Employment/FLSA •
Environmental • First Amendment • Health Care •
Intellectual Property • International Arbitration • Product
Liability • Reorganization/Work-outs • Securities

THE STATS

No. of attorneys: 151
No. of offices: 11
Managing Partners: David Boies, Donald L. Flexner and
Jonathan D. Schiller
Hiring Partners: Robin Henry (Armonk); William Isaacson
(Washington, DC); Alan Vickery (New York); George
Carpinello (Albany); Richard Drubel (Hanover); Stuart
Singer (Hollywood); Stephen Zack (Miami)

BASE SALARY

Armonk, 2002
1st year: $135,000

NOTABLE PERKS

• Annual firm retreat to Disney World
• Laptops
• Ultra-casual dress

THE BUZZ
WHAT ATTORNEYS AT OTHER FIRMS ARE SAYING ABOUT THIS FIRM

• "Brilliant litigators"
• "Would be nothing without Boies"
• "Do they ever actually win?"
• "Insane hours, insane compensation"
• "Would die to work there"

UPPERS

- Tremendous responsibility early on
- Accessible partners
- Lively atmosphere of creativity and intensity

DOWNERS

- Poor administrative support
- Outrageous hours expectations
- No formal training at all

EMPLOYMENT CONTACT

Ms. Christine Schopen
Legal Recruiting Coordinator
Phone: (914) 273-9800
Fax: (914) 273-9810
cschopen@bsfllp.com
(See www.bsfllp.com for employment contacts in other offices)

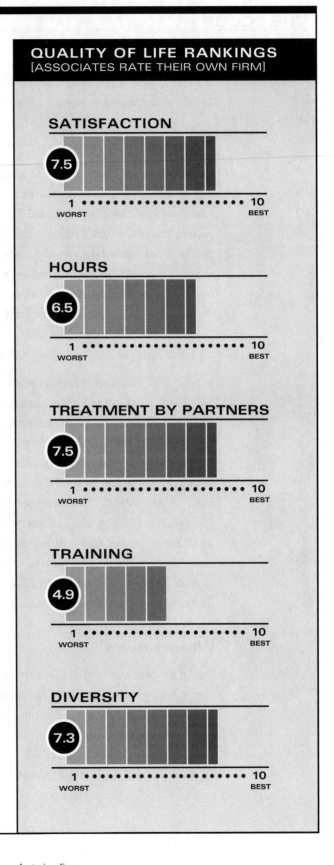

QUALITY OF LIFE RANKINGS
[ASSOCIATES RATE THEIR OWN FIRM]

SATISFACTION
7.5
1 WORST — 10 BEST

HOURS
6.5
1 WORST — 10 BEST

TREATMENT BY PARTNERS
7.5
1 WORST — 10 BEST

TRAINING
4.9
1 WORST — 10 BEST

DIVERSITY
7.3
1 WORST — 10 BEST

THE SCOOP

For class-action lawsuits and complex commercial litigation, you can hardly beat the credentials of the boutique firm of Boies, Schiller & Flexner LLP. The young firm's stellar reputation rests largely on the laurels of founder and superstar litigator, David Boies.

Hotshot's hot new firm

Boies, Schiller & Flexner LLP has inherited and built upon the legacy of one of the best-known and most sought-after attorneys in the country. After graduating from Yale Law School magna cum laude in 1966, David Boies joined New York's Cravath, Swaine & Moore and six years later became one of the firm's youngest partners. Boies soon distinguished himself by handling high-profile cases, including the successful defense of IBM in a 13-year long antitrust case, representation of CBS and 60 Minutes' Mike Wallace in General Westmoreland's libel suit, a $200 million victory for Continental Airlines in a RICO suit against United and American Airlines, and the recovery of $1 billion from junk bond king Michael Milken and Drexel Burnham Lambert as counsel to the FDIC during the savings and loan crisis. In 1986 *The New York Times Magazine* identified Boies as "the Wall Street lawyer everyone wants."

In June 1997, Boies left Cravath, where he had been a partner for 25 years, and invited his friend Jonathan Schiller to join him in starting a new law firm. The two attorneys set up shop in Armonk, N.Y., not far from Boies' Westchester County home. Schiller has tried cases nationally and internationally and prior to joining the firm had won a $100 million jury verdict in D.C. district court for a class of shareholders. Within a few weeks, they had acquired seven partners and eight associates, and by the end of 1998 the firm housed 35 attorneys. Over the next two years, Boies Schiller grew steadily. In December 1999, antitrust attorney Donald Flexner became the third name partner, bringing along clients Northwest Airlines, Southwestern Bell and DuPont. In June 2000, Boies Schiller added 20 lawyers when Barrett Gravante Carpinello & Stern, another firm started by former Cravath attorneys, became part of the firm. More recently, the firm gained 30 more lawyers when Miami-based Zack Kosnitzky also became part of the family in April 2002. Boies, Schiller & Flexner now boasts over 151 attorneys in 11 offices around the country.

Wonder Boies

One of the best-known civil litigators in the country, David Boies has frequently made magazine covers and headlines. In 1999, *The National Law Journal* named him Lawyer of the Year, and in 2000, he won the title again, this time as part of Al Gore's post-presidential election legal team, which was selected along with the Bush team as Lawyers of the Year. Like its namesake, Boies Schiller is best known for litigation — especially complex commercial litigation and high-risk class-action suits. Only a few months after hanging out his shingle, Boies began his stint as lead trial attorney for the government in United States v. Microsoft. His firm has since served as counsel in several of the most complex and significant antitrust cases in history, including suits against AT&T, Northwest and Continental Airlines, ADM and RJR Nabisco.

Boies Schiller has also built a formidable First Amendment practice. Boies and fellow partners have represented such major media as CBS and *The New York Times* in defamation cases including Westmoreland v. CBS, Inc., Herbert v. Lando and Brown & Williamson Tobacco Co. v. Wigand. The firm currently represents Court TV in a suit filed in September 2001 against New York State seeking to have the state's per se ban on cameras in the courtroom declared unconstitutional. When record companies sought to shut down Napster's music-sharing service, Napster called on Boies, who managed to postpone (but not prevent) the record companies' injunction. Boies suffered another loss in 2000 when the lifelong Democrat agreed to represent then-Vice President Al Gore pro bono in his ultimately unsuccessful fight for a recount of the presidential votes in Florida. Other notable firm clients have included Arthur Andersen (now embroiled in the Enron debacle), Columbia University, DuPont, EchoStar, Florida Power & Light, the French government, Miller Brewing, Gary Shandling, Siemens Westinghouse and the New York Yankees.

Arbitration sensation

The arbitration practice led by Jonathan Schiller has won notable victories, including a $261 million award following a trial in Paris over a cancelled power project, $50 million in damages following a trial of a fraud and breach of fiduciary case in London, and an award recognizing a Kuwait oil company's equity percentage in a binding consortium for billion barrel oil fields following a trial in London.

A class act

Boies Schiller claims to enjoy "one of the most selective and successful class-action practices in the country" — no idle boast. The firm handles clients on both sides of the courtroom aisle, although the firm may be better known for its high-profile — and highly profitable — plaintiff wins. In the 2000 antitrust case against auction houses Christie's and Sotheby's, the firm's confident bid that it would obtain at least a $405 million settlement in the price-fixing suit won it the role of lead counsel and — after the court approved a settlement of $512 million — a staggering $26.75 million in fees. In 1999 Boies Schiller's prosecution of a class-action price-fixing suit against vitamin makers resulted in a $1.1 billion settlement. In another health-related case, the firm is currently co-lead counsel in a class-action suit against seven HMOs on behalf of 80 million members who claim that the managed care companies failed to disclose practices used to limit care to participants.

Drivers of Ford Explorers are drawing on the firm's expertise in the ongoing federal litigation based on alleged cover-up of defects in Ford Explorers and Firestone tires. Boies Schiller currently serves as co-lead counsel in a case seeking more than $900 million in damages, making In re Alcatel Alsthom Securities Litigation one of the largest pending securities class actions in the country. A win would add to the firm's history of success in securities class actions. In 1989 Richard Drubel of the firm's Hanover, N.H., office won a $72 million jury verdict in a securities class action suit that *The National Law Journal* called one of the most significant cases of the year.

Suburban success story

Partner and co-founder Jonathan Schiller stated that his firm's original aim was "to have 10 lawyers and take on interesting and difficult cases." With a record of representing premium clients in diverse, complex cases and over 100 attorneys on staff, Boies Schiller has clearly exceeded its goal. And the media has responded. *The National Law Journal* called Boies, Schiller & Flexner the "new model of a national litigation boutique." Offices in towns like Armonk, N.Y., and Hanover, N.H. (often chosen for their proximity to lawyers' homes), offer attorneys a stimulating combination of casualness and intensity. In summer 2002, the firm is moving into its new Armonk headquarters, a 38,000 square-foot, brick neo-Georgian Colonial, with state-of-the-art offices, conference rooms, library and a small gym.

Litigators may be far removed from the glitz and glamour of the big city, but that doesn't mean they don't work as hard as, or harder than, their counterparts at more established urban law firms. Substantial profits demonstrate that the formula is clearly a winner: revenues in 2000 were reportedly between 50 and 75 million dollars. In addition to competitive salaries, Boies Schiller's small size offers eager associates an unusual measure of responsibility, the opportunity to work closely with partners (including Boies) and the possibility of a shorter partnership track.

Boies settles bias suit

But all is not rainbows and sunshine at Boies Schiller. The fairness of the firm's compensation and partnership policies has recently come under fire. In April 2002, the firm settled a discrimination suit with two female former attorneys who sued the firm for wage and sex discrimination, claiming that men at the firm received preferential treatment and that the firm's non-partnership track did not provide all that had been promised. The suit also named partners David Boies, Robert Silver and Philip Korologos personally. Both women joined the firm in 2000 and left within a year, claiming they were constructively discharged as a result of the firm's "discriminatory policies and practices."

Inter alia, the women claimed they received salaries and bonuses lower than their male counterparts. Managing partner Jonathan Schiller countered that the claims have "absolutely no merit" and that each plaintiff "was paid as much, or more, than other persons at the firm with comparable qualifications and productivity." According to *The New York Times,* although the plaintiffs sought $1 million when they filed suit, the parties recently settled the suit for $37,500 each with no admission of wrongdoing on the part of the firm. According to the *New York Law Journal*, the firm has made important changes, including raising the salaries of three female associates in the Armonk office and placing them on a partnership track, but the firm denies that these changes are in any way related to the lawsuit. The firm stated that it has never discriminated based on gender or other irrelevant criteria — and it never will.

GETTING HIRED

Esprit de corps

As a boutique firm handling premier, high quality cases, Boies Schiller & Flexner seeks candidates "who can hit the ground running." It's not easy to get in the door: "You have to pass through fine wire mesh intact." Some associates insist on "top-notch" credentials — "top law school, law review," clerkship. But, according to one lawyer, "there are also opportunities for less 'qualified' individuals who can prove their merit with their work product." In the end, the firm "doesn't care about much else … besides getting the job done." The schools attended by survey respondents seem to bear this out. Among these associates, schools such as the University of Miami, Vermont Law School and North Carolina Central University are as well represented as Yale, Harvard and Georgetown.

In addition to ability, it "helps to have a connection to the firm." Lawyers in the D.C. office note that it is "a fairly intimate place" and attorneys "want to find people with whom we would enjoy working." In the course of interviewing, candidates could meet "up to 30 percent of the attorneys who work here." At that point, "it's about the esprit de corps, baby." Boies Schiller seeks "extremely intelligent people who will fit into the environment the firm is trying to create — creative, intelligent, fun." One comfort for prospective candidates: "The process is very inclusive and assures that any new candidate has a vote of confidence from the general population if she receives an offer letter."

OUR SURVEY SAYS

Not your father's law firm

Boies Schiller has deliberately moved away from certain trappings of big law firm practice: where some firms have grudgingly slipped from formal business attire into khakis and button-down shirts, Boies Schiller attorneys show up for work in jeans, shorts and T-shirts. Instead of luxurious space and twinkling city lights, associates enjoy views of suburban parking lots. Not all these measures have proved entirely successful yet; the firm continues to experience "growing pains." Associates in the Armonk, N.Y., headquarters complain that the "suburban spaces [are] not well thought out." One lawyer reports, "Right now our offices are a disaster." There's " not enough room" while the firm "continues to hire." However, new headquarters are under construction and lawyers will soon be moving into a "state-of-the-art" building, which should prove a welcome change.

The firm's office in Washington, D.C., may be in a more conventional location, but it still disdains "the coffee-and-cream scheme in 80 percent of D.C. offices" in favor of a more "unique décor" which seems designed as much for effect as for comfort. Sources describe the space as "funky and modern." One lawyer proclaims, "Our office screams 'This is not your father's law firm,' which serves as a wake-up call to prospective clients that we are a different place here." Although it evokes an "initial moment of horror," associates have "come to love" the space. After all, they suggest, this firm is not really the place for a "colonial, rustic-art-and-carpets kind of" person.

Informal but intense

This litigation boutique cultivates a "very informal" environment. "The firm atmosphere is extremely laid back — from lack of administrative structure to casual clothing every day." The "ultra-casual" attire is not limited to junior attorneys. "Associates and partners alike wear jeans." Lawyers at Boies Schiller are "friendly, casual" and "irreverent." Moreover, "face time is unknown to the firm — people arrive at all hours of the morning and work as late as necessary to do their job well, often working from home."

While the "firm culture is very friendly," it is also fast paced. Sources emphasize that attorneys are "extremely hardworking" and the atmosphere is "professionally intense." Many lawyers complain of being "severely overworked." And the informality can border on disorder, according to some associates who call the firm "disorganized and chaotic." "The quality of work and exposure that the firm gives you is unparalleled," notes one lawyer. "However, it is a fly by the seat of your pants operation and, as with most litigation shops, the hours are often unpredictable and long." Several associates say "the administrative infrastructure is still woeful." A first-year associate enjoys "good cases and interesting law, but no structure, poor support, inefficient means of communication and too much time spent on, or worrying about, administrative concerns."

Still, the opportunity "to work closely with some of the best litigators in the nation on some of the biggest cases in the country" thrills many of our respondents. When asked to name the best things about his firm, one Boies Schiller lawyer responds: "The associates, followed by the partners, followed by the work, followed by the money, followed by the short commute (for me), followed by the experience you get. I'm actually a happy lawyer. And that is a cool and apparently rare thing."

No need to look for work — it's always there

Even though insiders don't decry the "sweatshop mentality" reported in last year's Vault Guide, they agree that at Boies Schiller the "hours are long." A second-year associate insists that the sweatshop label is "a relic of the days when the firm was trying to handle full-blown litigation with only eight lawyers in the office." Now, he says, "The hours are long, don't get me wrong, but you're getting such an incredible amount of responsibility, and the partners are working as hard as the associates, that you really can't — and have no desire to — complain." True, many attorneys share their colleague's appreciation for "cutting edge" work and "incredible responsibility." One lawyer declares, "The fact that the work is challenging and interesting makes the long hours pass much more quickly than billables for billables' sake."

Nevertheless, long hours is the most common complaint among respondents. Most associates report billing over 200 hours per month and spending an average of at least 60 hours in the office during the week. Annual billing of 2,500 hours is the norm, claims an associate. Another complains, "The expectation is that everyone will work 3,000 hours a year, an absurd target." However, one attorney voices a different perspective: "There is always work — and good work!" he exclaims. "Nobody needs work or even has to look for it." Still, even he admits, "Sometimes, the hours are too long."

A unique compensation scheme

Most respondents are happy with their "supra-competitive pay." The "base is the top of the market rate and pegged to New York scale," reports a contented lawyer in the D.C. office. On top of the base salary, Boies Schiller uses a complicated bonus system to reward associates based on the nature and volume of their work. One attorney explains: "The firm's bonus structure is based on a complex formula that depends on a combination of hours billed and the amount of money earned by the firm for those hours — for example, the firm's billing rate for those hours or the size of a contingency fee award in that matter." Many associates find this "unique" compensation system "very generous" in that it "really rewards hard work." Others believe the "system is unfair and does not entirely provide the right incentive." And a New York attorney claims that an "informal comparison with my friends in other firms and occasionally less senior positions indicates that the pay here is lower than in most other firms we compete with."

Free-form training

One of the best things about Boies Schiller, say associates, is the "enormous responsibility" with which they are entrusted. They enjoy being "treated as real lawyers, not merely drones." Junior associates are "attending depositions, writing briefs and pleadings, sitting in on phone calls" and they "work intimately with partners at every level." An attorney in the D.C. office believes "this is one of the few major firms where junior associates have a great deal of contact with senior and named partners who truly listen to and respect them and their opinions."

The flip side of so much early responsibility is very little hand-holding. The firm offers no formal training at all; associates must "learn by doing." "This firm is not into coddling associates," says one source. It's a "sink or swim atmosphere" in which some attorneys thrive. Associates "receive hands-on training, which is the best kind," insists one respondent. Others express frustration with the lack of "professional development" in which "there is no feedback system to establish where you are and where you are going."

No bonus for pro bono

The firm's pro bono program gets low marks from associates. Since "associates are not credited in their bonuses for work done on pro bono matters," they have "little time and no incentive" to participate. It's not that the firm won't "allow you to take on pro bono work," but "generally you'll be too busy to want the additional work, and your bonus will probably wind up being smaller if you do." One associate points out the lack of a pro bono committee but sees signs of improvement for an "abysmal" situation: "To the firm's credit, the firm is beginning to make a conscious effort to change this trend."

"Our office screams 'This is not your father's law firm," which serves as a wake-up call to prospective clients that we are a different place here."

— *Boies Schiller associate*

Mayer, Brown, Rowe & Maw

190 South LaSalle Street
Chicago, IL 60603-3441
Phone: (312) 701-7002
www.mayerbrownrowe.com

LOCATIONS

Charlotte, NC • Chicago, IL • Houston, TX • Los
Angeles, CA • New York, NY • Palo Alto, CA • Santa
Fe, NM • Washington, DC • Beijing (representative
office) • Brussels • Cologne • Frankfurt • London •
Manchester • Paris • Shanghai (representative office)

MAJOR DEPARTMENTS/PRACTICES

Bankruptcy & Reorganization • Corporate & Securities •
Employee Benefits • Environmental • Finance •
Government Relations • Health Care • Information
Technology • Intellectual Property • Litigation • Real
Estate • Regulated Industries • Tax Controversy • Tax
Transactions • Trust, Estates & Foundations

THE STATS

No. of attorneys: 1,300
No. of offices: 16
Summer associate offers (2001): 56 out of 58
(Chicago); 14 out of 14 (Houston); 9 out of 10 (Los
Angeles); 28 out of 28 (New York)
Managing Partner: Debora de Hoyos
Hiring Partners: Robert L. Mendenhall (Charlotte); J.
Thomas Mullen (Chicago); Terry OteroVilardo (Houston);
Michael F. Kerr (LA); Dennis P. Orr (NY); John J.
Sullivan (DC)

BASE SALARY

Chicago, 2002
1st year: $125,000
2nd year: $135,000
3rd year: $150,000
4th year: $165,000
5th year: $185,000
6th year: $195,000
7th year: $205,000
Summer associate: $2,400/week

New York, 2002
1st year: $125,000
2nd year: $135,000
3rd year: $150,000
4th year: $170,000
5th year: $190,000
6th year: $205,000
7th year: $215,000
8th year: $225,000
9th year: $235,000
Summer associate: $2,400/week

NOTABLE PERKS

• Gourmet coffee machines on every floor
• Annual associate party
• Free breakfast
• Subsidized health club memberships

THE BUZZ
WHAT ATTORNEYS AT OTHER FIRMS ARE SAYING ABOUT THIS FIRM

• "Merger makes it one of the tops"
• "Eggheads of Chicago"
• "Great appellate practice"
• "Miserable hours"
• "Too big and unfocused"

UPPERS

- Impressive big-wig clients and sophisticated high-quality work
- High-profile merger put firm in national spotlight
- Free market assignment system permits career flexibility

DOWNERS

- Perplexing discretionary bonus system
- Minimum billable hours requirement of 2,000 hours
- Poor diversity record

EMPLOYMENT CONTACT

Chicago
Ms. Laura L. Kanter, Legal Recruiting Coordinator
Phone: (312) 701-7003
Fax: (312) 701-7711
lkanter@mayerbrownrowe.com

Houston
Ms. Anne Thomas, Legal Recruiting Manager
Phone: (713) 546-0593
Fax: (713) 224-6410
amthomas@mayerbrownrowe.com

Los Angeles
Ms. Laryl Garcia, Legal Recruiting Manager
Phone: (213) 229-9575
Fax: (213) 576-8115
llgarcia@mayerbrownrowe.com

New York
Ms. Francie Vaughn, Associate Recruitment Manager
Phone: (212) 506-2799
Fax: (212) 262-1910
fvaughn@mayerbrownrowe.com

Washington, DC
Ms. Ann Pelizzari, Legal Recruiting Manager
Phone: (202) 263-3312
Fax: (202) 263-5312
apelizzari@mayerbrownrowe.com

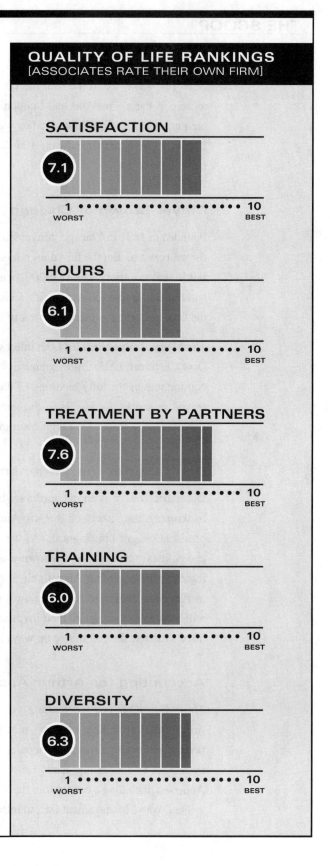

QUALITY OF LIFE RANKINGS
[ASSOCIATES RATE THEIR OWN FIRM]

SATISFACTION
7.1
1 WORST .... 10 BEST

HOURS
6.1
1 WORST .... 10 BEST

TREATMENT BY PARTNERS
7.6
1 WORST .... 10 BEST

TRAINING
6.0
1 WORST .... 10 BEST

DIVERSITY
6.3
1 WORST .... 10 BEST

THE SCOOP

The former Mayer, Brown & Platt is large and old and proud of it. And it continues to grow. Since New Year's Day 2001, the firm has completed three mergers with three different European firms located in Paris, Frankfurt and London and opened new offices in Palo Alto and Shanghai. The merger with U.K. firm Rowe & Maw was one of the largest trans-Atlantic mergers to date. Mayer, Brown, Rowe & Maw is now the 10th-largest law firm in the world in terms of number of attorneys and total revenue.

Mayer Brown of Chicago

Founded in 1881 in Chicago, Mayer Brown has been one of the big-time players in the legal game for many years. But the firm does not rest on its laurels. It continues to expand and move into new fields and countries. The year 2001 was the first year in its illustrious history that Mayer Brown had more attorneys located outside Chicago than inside and nearly as many attorneys working for the firm in Europe as there are back in Illinois.

The Mayer Brown client list is an impressive one, including Bank of America, BASF, Bertelsmann, Dow Chemical, EMI, Unilever and United Airlines, just to name a few. Firm attorneys feel rather comfortable in the lofty environs of the Supreme Court; as many as 13 Mayer Brown attorneys served as clerks for the U.S. Supreme Court and the firm has racked up an impressive 19 appearances in front of the high court in the past seven years, more than any other firm.

Don't cry for me, Argentina

December 2001 was an extraordinary time for Argentina as the country teetered on the brink of bankruptcy, the streets of Buenos Aires filled with looters and protesters, and president after president resigned in disgrace. As the country embarked on the long road to economic recovery and political stability, Mayer Brown was hired by the Argentine Bondholder Committee to provide legal counsel regarding Argentina's planned global debt restructuring. The bondholders fear that, as Argentina moves to reduct its unsustainable $132 billion public-sector debt burden, investors will be unable to safeguard their investments. That is where Mayer Brown comes in. The firm was hired to advise the committee on ways its members can safeguard their investments.

Accounting for Arthur Andersen

These days, it ain't easy defending Arthur Andersen. But for many, Mayer Brown is the go-to law firm for the accounting industry. It helped write the Securities Fraud Litigation Act of 1995 that favored accounting firms and discouraged "frivolous" shareholder lawsuits. And it has long served as counsel to accounting giants Ernst & Young, Deloitte & Touche, Grant Thornton and Arthur Andersen, including a case before the SEC last year in which Andersen was charged with allowing a client, Waste Management Inc., to inflate reported earnings. In the end, Andersen paid $7 million to settle, without admitting guilt. When the Enron scandal landed Andersen in the hot seat again, Mayer Brown played a roled in defending the accounting giant against obstruction of justice charges stemming from Andersen's destruction of Enron-related documents. In June 2002, a jury convicted Andersen after 10 days of deliberation.

What's good for big business

Mayer Brown's renowned appellate practice broke new ground two years ago when it wrote an amicus brief on behalf of General Motors supporting the University of Michigan Law School's affirmative action policy. GM argued that time has proved affirmative action — in particular, the diverse worldview such a policy encourages — is just what big business needs in a global economy. Twenty other blue chip companies followed with their own friend-of-the-court briefs endorsing the policy. In the latest decision, handed down on May 14, 2002, in what has been an up-and-down battle through the appellate process, the Sixth Circuit agreed with GM and the University.

Mayer Brown is also doing battle for big business in the U.S. Supreme Court, in a case that pits paternalism against protection in interpreting the Americans with Disabilities Act. In February 2002, the high court heard the firm's argument that Chevron could reject a job applicant whose medical condition would make the position he seeks dangerous to his health or life. Chevron had refused to hire the plaintiff who has Hepatitis C, because the job he applied for would expose him to liver-toxic chemicals, although the plaintiff had performed similar duties for many years in the same unit, as a worker for contractors hired by Chevron. While the Ninth Circuit sided with the plaintiff, in June 2002, the U.S. Supreme Court ruled in favor of Chevron in a 9-0 decision, landing a big win for Mayer Brown.

Altruism and chocolate

Mayer Brown has a heart — and sometimes it uses it for altruistic pro bono endeavors. One such endeavor involved the king of all chocolate. In 1909 Milton S. Hershey established the Milton Hershey School (MHS) Trust. To the trust he donated his entire fortune — $60 million in shares of the chocolate company he founded — for the operation of a school for orphans and disadvantaged youth. The school's endowment has today swelled to $5 billion, which places the school among the half dozen wealthiest educational institutions in the United States.

But all is not well in Chocolateville. Claiming that the trust has partially failed because it cannot prudently spend all of the income in support of the school, the school board recently sought broad discretion to divert the funds toward several projects in and around Hershey, Pa. Chief among these projects was a proposed think tank to study the education of underprivileged youth, which would cost $25 million to establish and an additional $25 million per year to operate.

In stepped the MHS Alumni Association, which filed briefs, under the direction of Mayer Brown, arguing that Milton Hershey's original intent was to help disadvantaged youth directly, "not build think tanks." The court agreed, holding that "the vision of Milton and Catherine Hershey was to relieve poor children from all of the conditions of poverty" and that "the proposed Institute does not approximate the Hersheys' express intention and would do violence to it." Mayer Brown attorneys provided, on a pro bono basis, all research, briefing and legal work for the Alumni Association, led by partner John F. Halbleib, who graduated from the Milton Hershey School in 1971.

GETTING HIRED

Shedding the egghead image

"You better have a very good grade point average," advises an associate, if you want to work at Mayer Brown in Chicago. This firm "is focused on credentials to a fault." Mayer "likes to hire from top-tier law schools," says one lawyer, "and the crème-de-la-crème of the second-tier law schools." According to an insider, that means "top 20-25 percent from national schools, top 10 percent from regional schools with law review, top 2-5 percent from lower-tier schools." Although "grades are very important," some attorneys report that personality is becoming more of a factor. "The firm seems to be making some effort to hire more well-rounded candidates, having had a reputation as a firm of eggheads in the past." One associate suggests that candidates run a nerd check before interviewing: "We are looking for those students that we can present to our clients without having to do a makeover on their hair, clothes and personality. In other words, you have to be smart but not geeky-looking."

Badly dressed brainiacs need not despair, however; according to associates, the D.C. office of Mayer Brown welcomes "nerdy people ... as long as they have the requisite intellect." Insiders report that the office "relies on letters of inquiry rather than on-campus interviews." In addition to "top grades, Ivy League law schools are preferred, and clerkships are highly valued, especially circuit and Supreme Court clerkships." Other office locations are reportedly less "stuffy." A New Yorker finds that "common sense, a personality and a good work ethic go a long way."

OUR SURVEY SAYS

An eclectic culture

Mayer Brown attorneys find it difficult to generalize about their firm's eclectic culture. "Each practice area is almost like a mini-firm within the firm," according to insiders. "The firm is so large that there are people to work with no matter what your personality is like. You can work for uptight, anal people if you like, or more laid-back people. Ultimately, the objective is to get the job done right for the client." This emphasis on professionalism and hard work is one aspect of the firm about which sources agree. "The firm is a straightforward, hardworking kind of place." With "everyday casual attire" and "no face time requirements," the goal is simply to get the work done. While some insiders report socializing with their colleagues after business hours, "there doesn't seem to be any firm pressure to do so."

In fact, one of the criticisms voiced by respondents regarding their fellow Mayerites is a lack of basic social skills, particularly among partners. "A disproportionately large percentage of lawyers tend to be introverted," explains an associate. Hallway hellos and "spontaneous elevator conversations are rare." This may be in keeping with the firm's "egghead" reputation, but not everyone is troubled by the absence of excessive chumminess. One lawyer fondly describes colleagues as "oddball characters — uniformly bright and funny." Others are disappointed by what they perceive as an "uptight" atmosphere. "Think of the top of your law school class," reflects one associate. "Now put them all in one firm."

Billables for bonuses

When it comes to money, most Mayer Brown associates think their base salaries are superior. Insiders are less happy about the discretionary bonus structure, which one lawyer claims "is almost impossible to figure out." Many believe the firm applies "a rigid formula that looks solely to hours," but others are just not sure how it all works. When the firm increased salaries, it "became more serious about billable hour targets," reports an associate. "Now, if you don't meet them, you don't get the full salary, let alone bonuses." A few attorneys shrug their shoulders: "Bonuses are hard to attain, but we get paid so much, who needs them?" A lawyer in Washington resents the fact that "there are people at other big firms in town who are making the same money for significantly fewer billable hours." Several associates "would prefer less pay for fewer hours requirements." And then there are the Zen types who conclude, "Let's face it — they pay us an obscene amount of money."

All about hours

Some attorneys at Mayer Brown are just as unruffled about their hours as they are about their paychecks. "Considering the outrageous salary increases we have enjoyed," declares an attorney, "I can't complain about my hours." But for many Mayer Brown associates, money and quality of work are not enough to compensate for the long hours. A litigator asserts, "Bad hours trump quality any day." Some sources find the firm's minimum requirement of 2,100 hours, including 2,000 billable hours and 100 creditable hours, "a high threshold," and "because bonuses are directly tied to client billable hours, there is a real tension in the office to maximize billing." "It is all about hours at Mayer Brown," complains a senior associate. Moreover, the "unspoken rule is that in order to be even considered to be on the partner track, associates must bill at the very least 2,250 hours." One math-minded lawyer calculates that in order to reach that threshold, "you'd have to bill six hours a day every day of the year — weekends and holidays. He adds, "Work a 12-hour day, take New Year's off. Work another, take a Sunday off," and so on.

Still, some lawyers don't mind the hours because they enjoy the work. Others insist that the free market assignment system allows associates "flexibility to control their hours within reasonable limits." They just "need to learn to say no to avoid getting crushed." The firm's part-time program gets somewhat mixed reviews. According to one attorney, "The firm allows part-time arrangements only begrudgingly and makes clear that it views part-time associates as less profitable and less valuable." But others report that "colleagues are extremely respectful" of reduced schedules. The real problem is that, "given the nature of the service we are providing, it is extremely difficult to limit the number of billable hours."

Complicated billing and pro bono

Many insiders are critical of Mayer Brown's pro bono program. Despite a commitment to pro bono work "on paper," in reality "the hours pressure and the bonus incentives make substantial pro bono projects unrealistic." Few lawyers are clear about the firm's manner of crediting pro bono time. Some associates claim, "Approved pro bono up to 100 hours counts towards the creditable hour requirement," with "creditable" hours worth "something less than billable hours in our very complex minimum hours and bonus calculations." Another lawyer says that the first 100 hours of a pro bono project count toward billable hours and the next 100 are creditable. In any event, most respondents agree that "the way in which pro bono hours count toward billable hours is confusing and not well thought out" and effectively "makes it impossible to do pro bono meaningfully." The firm tells Vault that it is meeting with associates to revise the bonus structure to address these issues.

Nevertheless, some associates contend that Mayer Brown is "remarkably supportive of pro bono work." They note that the firm "has a full-time pro bono coordinator," and quarterly newsletters inform associates of new opportunities. Sources particularly praise the Chicago office's "wonderful project with the Seventh Circuit," in which associates get to brief and argue cases on appeal.

Baptism by fire

Training at Mayer Brown is still, for the most part, on the job, which suits most survey respondents just fine. It's "baptism by fire. Of course, once you get used to it, it's far more valuable than a structured system." A tax attorney considers, "I can see how a new associate in my group might feel as if she had been thrown in the deep end of the pool without her water-wings. But that's the best training to get in our practice area." He adds, "Other more formal training, including various NITA programs, is available for those with that kind of time." To some associates, however, "this is Mayer Brown's weakest area." They claim "in-house training isn't great" and most "training comes from getting good work and feedback from partners, but the problem is that both are rare." Admits one Chicagoan, "I was hoping to find a partnership of inspiring mentors, people I could follow into battle. I wouldn't follow these guys to a picnic." However, several associates note that "the firm is making more of an effort to provide training this year." The firm reports that it has hired seasoned attorneys to assist in training and named a senior associate "dean of associates" with responsibility for training incoming associates.

A plea for greater diversity

Mayer Brown's diversity record has some room to improve. Many are "proud that our managing partner [Debora de Hoyos] is a woman," and some lawyers say the firm has an impressive record when it comes to hiring women. But there are still "very few women at the partnership level" and "no formal mentoring or other programs specifically for women at Mayer Brown." (The firm notes that six of the firm's major practice areas are under the direction or co-direction of women.) Moreover, several sources in Chicago report traces of an "old boys club" attitude.

Minority representation at the firm is poor, according to most associates. A lawyer in Chicago notes, "There are so few minorities here, it is impossible to believe that the place is very welcoming." The D.C. office is particularly criticized for a "dismal minority hiring record." One source admits, "Out of about 120 lawyers, there is not a single African-American in the office, not a single Hispanic and only about four Asians." Associates believe Mayer Brown is making a sincere effort, but acknowledge that "without at least one and preferably a few big minority partners, we will have trouble attracting minority associates." Firm management recounts efforts to chip away at the disparity, noting that two minority attorneys were made partner in the last year and that minorities make up more than 20 percent of the incoming class of associates.

Insiders note that there are "not a lot of openly gay people at the firm" and many believe that with respect to sexual orientation, "discretion is the wiser course of conduct." One lawyer in Chicago doubts sexual orientation "would be an issue, but," he adds, "nobody is flamboyant here in any way, so think twice about that."

Not 'wow' — but certainly 'fine'

Respondents don't have a lot to say about their firm's offices, which are generally described as "fine," "comfortable" or "completely average." A New Yorker reports that her "offices are spacious and comfortable if not the grandest things you've ever seen." A lawyer in Washington, D.C., is similarly satisfied but unimpressed: "We have new space that is fine. As decorated and managed, the space does not invoke 'wow' but it is comfortable." Associates at Mayer Brown's Chicago headquarters appreciate having their own offices, which are of "ample size and comfort." Some lawyers think they should "lose the Emerald City green carpeted look in the hallways." A few complain that the "technology infrastructure needs some work." Overall, sources find the space "fine," if "nothing spectacular." Ally McBeal fans should know that Mayer Brown offices are "not like the lawyers' offices you see on TV."

Willkie Farr & Gallagher

The Equitable Center
787 Seventh Avenue
New York, NY 10019-6099
Phone: (212) 728-8000
www.willkie.com

LOCATIONS

New York, NY (HQ)
Washington, DC
Brussels
Frankfurt
London
Milan
Paris
Rome

MAJOR DEPARTMENTS/PRACTICES

Business Restructuring & Reorganization
Corporate/Finance
Employee Benefits & Relations
Intellectual Property
Litigation
Real Estate
Tax
Trusts & Estates

THE STATS

No. of attorneys: 529
No. of offices: 8
Summer associate offers: 52 out of 52 (2001)
Chairman: Jack H. Nusbaum
Hiring Attorneys: Jeffrey R. Poss, Thomas H. Golden and William H. Gump

BASE SALARY

New York, 2002
1st year: $125,000
2nd year: $135,000
3rd year: $150,000
4th year: $170,000
5th year: $190,000
Summer associate: $2,404/week

NOTABLE PERKS

• Back-up day care
• Health club discount
• Free tickets to museums and sporting events
• Attorney lounge with flat-screen TV

THE BUZZ
WHAT ATTORNEYS AT OTHER FIRMS ARE SAYING ABOUT THIS FIRM

• "Family friendly"
• "Prestigious New York firm"
• "Sweatshop"
• "Layoffs hurt"

UPPERS

• No minimum billable requirements
• Lively social scene
• Early responsibility

DOWNERS

• Long, unpredictable hours
• Poor evaluation/feedback on assignments
• Current space crunch in headquarters

EMPLOYMENT CONTACT

Ms. Patricia Langlade
Recruiting Coordinator
Phone: (212) 728-8469
Fax: (212) 728-8111
planglade@willkie.com

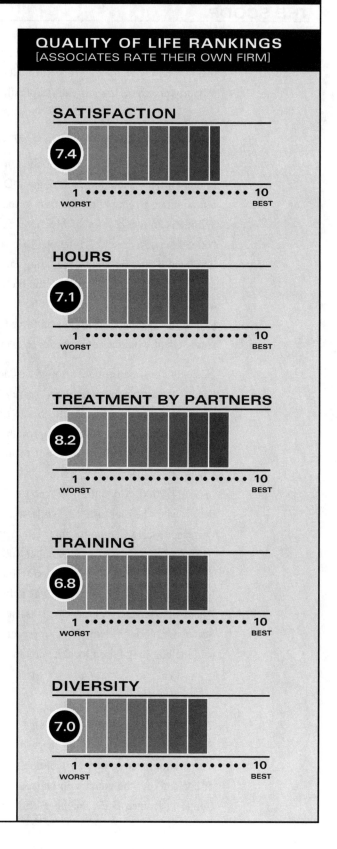

QUALITY OF LIFE RANKINGS
[ASSOCIATES RATE THEIR OWN FIRM]

SATISFACTION
7.4
1 · 10
WORST   BEST

HOURS
7.1
1 · 10
WORST   BEST

TREATMENT BY PARTNERS
8.2
1 · 10
WORST   BEST

TRAINING
6.8
1 · 10
WORST   BEST

DIVERSITY
7.0
1 · 10
WORST   BEST

THE SCOOP

Where does "The Donald" go when he needs reliable legal advice? To Willkie Farr & Gallagher, that's where. The New York firm, known best for its bankruptcy, corporate and intellectual property practices, has a rapidly expanding European presence.

History: business sense and political prowess

Willkie Farr & Gallagher was founded in 1889 in New York. Now it has more than 500 attorneys in eight offices, including Washington, D.C., Paris and London. In the year 2000, Willkie opened a new office in Frankfurt and two in the new European legal hot spot, Italy (Rome and Milan). Willkie is known best for its M&A work, and many in the firm think its bankruptcy department is "one of the best around." It helped Donald Trump, the New York real estate tycoon, restructure his hotel and casino buildings, including the Trump Plaza Hotel and Casino, Plaza Hotel, Taj Mahal and Trump Castle. In the 1980s, the broker Shearson Lehman was a Willkie client, accounting for as much as one-third of the firm's business. When it was sold in 1993, the firm suffered from the loss of that business. Willkie was forced to lay off 20 associates but from then on decided that no single client would account for more than 5 percent of the firm's business.

Not only does the firm have sound business sense, but it has also forayed into the political arena. One of the firm's name partners is Wendell Willkie, the 1940 Republican presidential candidate who lost to Franklin Roosevelt. Some former Willkie lawyers left the firm for political pursuits. Former partner Chester Straub, a prominent Willkie lawyer, has been named to the Second Circuit Court of Appeals. Former associate in bankruptcy, Craig Johnson, was elected to the Nassau County (N.Y.) Legislature in May 2000. He took the place of his mother, who died of breast cancer in March 2000. Good thing he knows his bankruptcy stuff, as Nassau County had a $178 million deficit when he took office. While some left Willkie for different aspirations, former New York Governor Mario Cuomo had his sights set on the firm after he left office in 1995. In an interview with *New York Lawyer* in December 2001, he said, "I never even considered any firm other than Willkie." In July 2001, he traveled to Puerto Rico to help defend Robert F. Kennedy Jr. and labor leader Dennis Rivera. The pair was jailed for protesting the U.S. Navy's practice bombing on the island of Vieques. Cuomo will assist partner Benito Romano, former U.S. Attorney for the Southern District of New York, representing protesters. The pair was among 180 protestors who said the bombing raised local health and environment issues.

Just say yes

That's what Manhattan federal judge John F. Keenan ruled in the case of accused cocaine dealer Salvatore Arena. Arena is charged with using his importing company, Mott Street Banana Corporation, as a front for a Colombian narcotics trafficking venture with plans to ship 450 kilos of cocaine into the country in banana crates. After a court order, doctors at the Federal Medical Center in Butner, N.C., diagnosed him with "delusional disorder." He was ordered to take anti-psychotic medication to get prepared for trial even though his attorneys, Martin B. Klotz and Emily Stein of Willkie Farr, intend to offer an insanity defense. Judge Keenan held that U.S. Supreme Court case law dictates the forcible administration of anti-psychotic medication when deemed "medically appropriate."

Offering help

Many companies and organizations reached out to the victims of the September 11 attacks. Law firms were no exception. Many with offices in New York offered office space to displaced downtown firms. Some are making charitable contributions. Willkie Farr & Gallagher created a $500,000 fund for donations to the families of victims. The fund gave $100,000 to the New York Police & Fire Widows' & Children's Benefit Fund and $25,000 to a charity for Pentagon attack victims.

Bogus calls alert attorneys

A Florida man was indicted for wire fraud in September 2001 for calling law firms, posing as a partner and asking firms to make retainer payments to accounts he set up in Florida for services by a firm he called "Dixon Stokes." If convicted, Jonathan David Ghertler could get five years in prison and a fine of $250,000. Willkie Farr was one of the firms he defrauded.

Show them the way

Over 20 years ago, the New York office of Willkie Farr & Gallagher started the MENTOR program. Lawyers from the firm are paired with a student from an area high school. Together, they participate in a variety of law-related activities, such as a Mock Trial and Moot Court Competition. Students visit the firm twice a week for three-hour periods to work with attorneys in group and individual sessions. Attorneys also teach law classes to junior and senior students. Adlai Stevenson High School, which has a high African-American and Latino population, sponsors a Law Day with a panel of distinguished judges. Each year, the students have lunch with former Governor Mario Cuomo. The purpose of the program is to build the confidence of students so that they can compete with private and advantaged public schools.

A win for Bloomberg

A case against the financial news service, Bloomberg L.P., was dismissed in June 2001 following the failure of the plaintiff to state a cognizable claim for fraud under securities laws. To his detriment, Mark Simeon Jakob decided to short sell 3,000 shares of Emulex. Emulex stock went up instead of down, leaving Jakob with a $97,000 loss. He then wrote a press release containing false information about problems in the company. Internet Wire Inc. published the hoax and Bloomberg republished it. Within 45 minutes of the release, Emulex's stock price dropped $60 per share to around $43. Nasdaq stopped Emulex trading, and within a half hour, Bloomberg announced the release was fake. By the end of the day, shares rebounded to $105.75 per share. The judge said that there was no allegation of intent to defraud on the part of Bloomberg and Internet Wire. Partners Richard L. Klein and Thomas H. Golden of Willkie Farr represented Bloomberg. In the past, the firm represented Bloomberg in establishing a network for broadcasting and publishing.

GETTING HIRED

More than grades

"The callback interviews generally last a half day and involve meeting partners and associates. On-campus interviews are with one partner," reveals a fifth-year associate. Though "Willkie is fairly competitive," getting hired "does not seem to be entirely dependent on grades or what school a candidate has attended, though the top grades or schools never hurt," says another attorney. According to a third-year Willkie-ite, "When I interviewed, it was not the hardest place to get a job." However, this attorney says the firm has "definitely gotten more competitive" since then. Candidates should be "assertive, and at the same time, pleasant to be around." What Willkie looks for are "personable candidates, from top-tier law schools with above-average grades, but not necessarily top of their class or law review. Personality and maturity really count." "I think the firm looks for non-boat-rockers, and people with whom it would be the least painless to work at midnight," says a second-year insider.

Associates explain that Willkie ensures that its summer associates are exposed to the breadth of the firm's practices. "The unique rotation system in which summer associates shadow at least three different partners during the summer allows one to get a real impression of how the various departments work from top to bottom." Also, "activities such as the mock negotiation exercise and the mock arbitration exercise help summers to try to determine what practice areas they are most interested in." Summer program participants receive "meaningful, substantive work and even a fair amount of client contact."

OUR SURVEY SAYS

A friendly clique

Being "a first-year associate isn't always an easy job," one young attorney tells us. "But liking the people with whom you work and the atmosphere in which you work makes it infinitely better. Willkie provides both of these elements in abundance." Many say the "open-door policy" among both partners and associates facilitates a more cordial working environment and enables attorneys to discuss client matters easily." The friendly office culture is considered "one of the best attributes" of the firm. Willkie is, "by and large, friendly and laid back, although work is taken very seriously," says an associate in the Milan office.

"Socializing occurs on different levels for different people. There are a number of associates who hang out together regularly, and others who mingle less frequently are always welcome." But this isn't a group of homebodies. After-hours socializing is common, associates say. While many praise the firm for promoting a social atmosphere, several associates complain of a "fraternity" feel and "a boys club culture that permeates the atmosphere" of the firm. "The 'cool' male partners often go out drinking with the 'cool' male associates, and then call them directly with work instead of going through the assigning system," complains one associate. "While most people would agree that they like the people at the firm," a third-year insider reports, "I am not sure that many of the associates would say that they feel as though they are a part of the firm's social milieu. This is particularly true for minority associates, who can sometimes find themselves excluded from frat boy-type activities — though the exclusion is not intentional." Another associate describes the atmosphere as "friendly, but cliquish — like high school with teeth."

Can you handle it?

As for the quality of the work itself, "associates are given as much responsibility as they are able to handle. So it is not uncommon to find yourself negotiating against more senior attorneys at other firms and taking on a fair amount of responsibility at an early stage in your career." Some associates get their first heady taste of responsibility and interesting work by taking on a pro bono case. Associates say that "pro bono tends to depend on individual initiative, but there are great opportunities once one takes the initiative." "Pro bono work that you take on is treated like any other matter, and the fact that it counts towards your billables is a huge plus," says a fourth-year associate.

Money matters

While many of the associates gave Willkie high marks for compensation, you wouldn't necessarily know it from their comments. According to associates, the firm generally "follows the New York trends slavishly" but recently instituted a salary freeze for long-timers. A "salary of over $200,000 is not something that is easy to complain about," admits an eighth-year insider, "although a salary freeze for senior associates while their billing rates continue to go up is somewhat maddening." The firm's "philosophy is to do the bare minimum not to be considered a second-tier firm," complains a fourth-year Willkie-ite. Another associate gripes, "The firm had a great year, yet the maximum bonus was still half what it was last year."

The root of associates' compensation woes may be the fact that "the firm adjusted its 2001 year-end bonus to match the market, after initially low-balling more senior associates." And Willkie associates don't easily forget such odious conduct. But not everyone thinks the firm needs to improve its compensation policy. "People who gripe that the salaries should be higher to account for the higher cost of living in New York aren't being realistic. There is only so much they can pay junior associates and remain profitable. We're getting the market rate, and I think it's adequate to live reasonably in New York," says a satisfied junior associate. "Everyone pays about the same in New York City, but Willkie is never on top, always in the middle of the top New York City firms," shrugs a second-year associate who is nonetheless satisfied.

Time for work and play

The number of hours associates spend in the office "ebbs and flows." One associate describes the hours as being "significantly more humane than I anticipated." Willkie Farr "prides itself on not having minimum billable requirements." A sixth-year associate explains the firm's philosophy on hours: "Long hours are viewed as a sometimes unavoidable consequence of the type of work that we do. When there is no work to be done, you don't find Willkie lawyers sticking around pretending they have work to do just to keep the appearance that they are working long hours." Associates express great appreciation for the fact that there is no minimum billable hours target. "In the years I have been here, I have never heard of specific minimum billables goal," says one happy Willkie-ite. But the lack of a billable target doesn't mean you should expect a light workload. "You are expected to keep a full plate commensurate with any large New York City firm."

Cramped quarters

Some of the folks at Willkie Farr's New York office say they're feeling the pinch — for space, that is. The firm got new offices in the Big Apple in 1998, but it's already outgrown that space. So, while it may seem hard to complain about working in a "building that is gorgeous," with offices that "are light, airy, sunny, clean, spacious, modern" and have incredible views "on all four sides of the building," attorneys aren't too happy about having to "share an office well into your third year." Associates are counting on getting some breathing room soon. "Rumor has it the firm is getting another floor in the fall." The firm confirms that it will occupy the entire 46th floor by September 1, 2002, which should alleviate the cramping. When they do make the move, attorneys are likely to find the new space just as aesthetically pleasing as the rest of the offices. At least one lawyer found the offices so striking that "the space and décor was, believe it or not, a factor in my decision to come to Willkie. None of that old dark wood crap — light, open and almost airy."

Trial by fire

Willkie may be a friendly place, but don't expect a lot of hand-holding when it comes to assignments. "There is more 'training by doing.' Formal training could be improved, especially after the first two years," says a fourth-year associate. Although some associates agree that "Willkie could use a stronger, firm-wide training program," several respondents consider the informal training they receive to be just fine. "I'm getting great training and mentoring and exposure to very interesting work. Partners and associates take time out of their day to explain deals and assignments and try to make themselves available for questions," says a junior corporate attorney. Remarks a colleague, "The most valuable training I have received is from the senior associates. Most of them take the time to mark up a draft and discuss their suggested changes. They often take the time to compliment, instruct and drop pearls of wisdom" based on their own experiences. Several lawyers also speak highly of the firm's "great access to CLEs, both inside and outside the firm."

According to some insiders, getting familiar with all things Willkie is a "sink or swim" process. Sighs a second-year associate, "They throw you into the corporate pond and expect you to figure out how to swim. The training for junior associates is pretty bad." "You learn from being thrown into the mix, and sometimes this can be overwhelming to junior associates," agrees a third-year associate. This attorney elaborates: "It is not unheard of for people to hand in assignments without receiving any subsequent follow up or feedback from partners or senior associates."

Akin, Gump, Strauss, Hauer & Feld, L.L.P.

Robert S. Strauss Building
1333 New Hampshire Avenue, NW
Washington, DC 20036
Phone: (202) 887-4000
www.akingump.com

LOCATIONS

Austin, TX • Dallas, TX • Denver, CO • Houston, TX •
Los Angeles, CA • McLean, VA • New York, NY •
Philadelphia, PA • San Antonio, TX • Washington, DC •
Brussels • London • Moscow

MAJOR DEPARTMENTS/PRACTICES

Antitrust
Corporate & Securities
Energy, Land Use & Environment
Financial Restructuring
International
Labor & Employment
Litigation
Public Law & Policy
Real Estate
Tax

THE STATS

No. of attorneys: 1,050
No. of offices: 13
Summer associate offers: 90 out of 127 (2001)
Chairman: R. Bruce McLean
Hiring Partner: Dennis M. Race

BASE SALARY

Washington, DC, 2002
1st year: $125,000
2nd year: $135,000
3rd year: $150,000
4th year: $160,000
5th year: $170,000
6th year: $185,000
[Salaries based on 2,000 hours]
Summer associate: $2,400/week

New York, 2002
1st year: $125,000
2nd year: $135,000
3rd year: $150,000
4th year: $170,000
5th year: $190,000
6th year: $195,000
Summer associate: $2,400/week

NOTABLE PERKS*

• Laptops for associates
• Weekly happy hours and coffee hours
• $500 communications stipend
• $60,000 longevity bonus after 6th year and
  counsel promotion
• Monthly breakfasts

* Perks vary by office

THE BUZZ
WHAT ATTORNEYS AT OTHER FIRMS ARE SAYING ABOUT THIS FIRM

• "Politically plugged in"
• "Texas firm thinks it's a DC firm"
• "Fun, laid back and outgoing"
• "Old boys' network"
• "Vernon!"

UPPERS

• Early responsibility
• High-profile litigation cases

DOWNERS

• Bonuses tied to billable hours
• Deferred salary system

EMPLOYMENT CONTACT

Ms. Erin L. Springer
Recruitment Manager (Firm-wide)
Phone: (202) 887-4184
Fax: (202) 887-4288
springer@akingump.com

Ms. Mary G. Beal
Director of Recruitment
Phone: (202) 887-4181
Fax: (202) 887-4288
mbeal@akingump.com

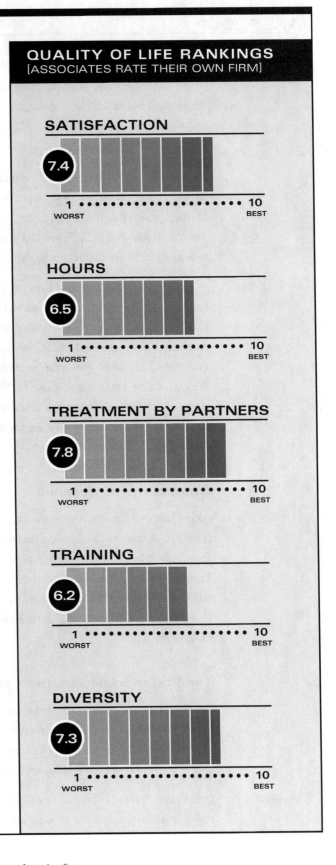

QUALITY OF LIFE RANKINGS
[ASSOCIATES RATE THEIR OWN FIRM]

SATISFACTION
7.4
1 WORST ... 10 BEST

HOURS
6.5
1 WORST ... 10 BEST

TREATMENT BY PARTNERS
7.8
1 WORST ... 10 BEST

TRAINING
6.2
1 WORST ... 10 BEST

DIVERSITY
7.3
1 WORST ... 10 BEST

THE SCOOP

One of the largest firms in the country, D.C. powerhouse Akin, Gump, Strauss, Hauer & Feld LLP offers both domestic and international clients a formidable litigation team, solid corporate department and rapidly developing technology practice.

History: G-men's giant

In 1945 FBI agents Richard A. Gump and Robert S. Strauss left government service to start a law firm in Dallas. Between 1945 and 1966, Gump and Strauss added five partners and, when Henry D. Akin joined the practice that year, the 20-lawyer firm acquired its current name: Akin, Gump, Strauss, Hauer & Feld. From that two-man Texas office, Akin Gump has grown into a legal behemoth, with approximately 1,000 attorneys in 13 offices around the world.

Although rooted in Texas, the firm showed hints of its future influence in the nation's capital from early on. In 1971 the same year partner Robert Strauss was appointed treasurer of the Democratic Party, Akin Gump opened its office in Washington, D.C. Strauss' service in the Democratic National Committee and, later, in the Carter Administration led to his being awarded the Presidential Medal of Freedom, the nation's highest civilian award, in 1981. In the last 30 years, the D.C. office has acquired close to 300 lawyers and is the firm's largest office. Its ranks have attracted prominent Washington insiders, including Vernon Jordan Jr., former U.S. Representative Bill Paxon, former Secretary of Agriculture Dan Glickman, and former Speaker of the House and Ambassador to Japan Tom Foley.

Champions of defense

Akin Gump's litigation team is the largest of the firm's practice groups, and its work ranges from commercial matters to white-collar crime to toxic tort and product liability defense. The firm frequently takes on high-profile cases. In 2000 Akin Gump won a victory for The Coca-Cola Company when a federal court dismissed PepsiCo's suit challenging Coke's exclusivity contracts with food vendors. More recently, the firm successfully defended Cinemark USA Inc. against charges by the Department of Justice that its stadium-style theaters violated the Americans with Disabilities Act.

The litigation department roars

On the plaintiffs' side, the firm scored an initial win, later overturned on appeal, for the supermarket chain Food Lion in its suit against ABC News for a hidden-camera exposé broadcast on PrimeTime Live. In the well-known case, Food Lion sued two ABC reporters who went undercover as Food Lion employees to record alleged sanitary violations at the food retailer.

Defendants facing Congressional inquiries, internal investigations, RICO charges and environmental crimes have also drawn on the firm's considerable expertise in the area of white-collar crime. The white-collar defense group includes William Hundley, former chief of the Justice Department's organized crime and racketeering section, and John Dowd, best known for representing baseball in the Pete Rose investigation. Akin Gump has also counseled defendants in the Iran-Contra scandal, the Whitewater investigation, Watergate and Koreagate.

The appellate practice is also growing, and is headed by Rex Heinke, a noted media law and First Amendment expert, and William A. Norris, a former Judge on the Ninth Circuit Court of Appeals. Both are in the Los Angeles office.

Big deals and tech developments

Akin Gump's work in the corporate arena has proved profitable. Major deals in which the firm participated in 2001 include The Walt Disney Company's $5.2 billion purchase of Fox Family Worldwide from Akin Gump client Haim Saban and Rupert Murdoch's News Corp. The firm was among counsel for Clear Channel Communications Inc., a San Antonio-based media company, in its $777 million stock deal to purchase The Ackerley Group Inc., a media and entertainment company. At the end of 2001, Akin Gump helped unite the No. 1 English-language network with the No. 2 Spanish-language network in an agreement for NBC to acquire Telemundo Communications Group Inc. And in November 2001, the firm acted as counsel for Houston-based Dynegy Inc. in a $7.8 billion deal to buy the now-notorious energy giant, Enron. (The deal fell through after further accounting irregularities at Enron were revealed.)

Joining in the nation's technology wave, Akin Gump has made efforts to expand its intellectual property resources. The firm created "Akin Gump Technology Ventures," a 200-lawyer multi-disciplinary tech team. In 1999 the firm merged with IP boutiques in Houston and Philadelphia and also opened an office in Northern Virginia, the new hotbed for technology companies, and one in Denver. *Intellectual Property Today* ranked the firm second in the number of trademarks registered in 1999. Akin Gump has also been recognized for its own use of technology in the sophisticated case studies featured on the firm's web site.

The Russia house

Akin Gump has established a thriving international practice, with particular concentrations on trade, energy and arbitration. The Texas firm counts a number of natural gas, crude oil and other energy companies among its clients. Many of their transactions are international in scope: in 2001, the firm represented an Indian oil and gas company in a sale of oil fields to Russia's national company. The firm has developed close ties with Russian interests; Akin Gump maintains a 13-lawyer office in Moscow and represents both Western and Russian clients in energy, restructuring and other transactions. In the 1990s, partner Robert Strauss served as Ambassador to the Soviet Union and, after the dissolution of the USSR, to the Russian Federation. In another oil-slicked region of the planet, Akin Gump maintains an affiliate office in Riyadh, Saudi Arabia.

In January 2002, another former ambassador to the Russian Federation, James Franklin Collins, joined the firm's D.C. office where he acts as senior international advisor to AG Global Solutions, the firm's recently formed joint venture with First International Resources, a strategic communications and political consulting group.

Akin's rakin' it in

The year 2001 turned out to be a very good year for the Texas giant. Although the firm was forced to institute a few cost-cutting measures (like substituting videoconferencing for some travel between offices), the slowdown was apparently more than made up for by increases in other areas of Akin Gump's practice, particularly financial restructuring and litigation. Between 1999 and 2001, the firm presciently beefed up its financial restructuring practice by adding 13 attorneys. The investment in restructuring paid off: the firm's litigation and financial restructuring practices posted 15 percent increases in billables in 2001.

In December 2001, the firm projected overall revenues 20 percent higher than 2000, while profits in the D.C. office alone rose nearly 30 percent. The firm is passing on some of those profits to its hardworking attorneys. In February it announced generous bonuses for New York associates, though the bonuses were tied to number of hours billed: first-year associates who billed 2,400 hours or more received $23,000, while fourth-years and above took home over $62,000. Associates who missed the 2,400-hour mark but worked at least 2,100 hours received bonuses between $20,000 and $50,000.

GETTING HIRED

The usual cha-cha

Insiders agree that in Akin Gump's "extremely competitive" hiring process, an "excellent educational background is a must." Akin Gump seeks "the smartest people we can find." "Grades, top schools, law review, the usual cha-cha," one lawyer recites. Another notes, "We interview only the top candidates from top-tier schools." This selectivity might be countered by "an outgoing personality and a genuine willingness to work hard," suggests one associate who adds, "I've never met an attorney who went to anything other than a first-tier school, and only met a handful who attended schools traditionally ranked below the top 20."

Finding the right fit

While academic credentials "are of primary importance," the firm also wants a "well-rounded" individual "who will fit into the firm culture." "Once you make the cut on grades, education and so on, a premium is placed on personality and compatibility. Being a team player is key." Lateral candidates might bypass the rigorous academic criteria in a "friendly and relatively gentle" hiring process. Notes one third-year, "The firm is very picky about grades, except when they need laterals from a particular practice area. I don't think they ever even looked at my transcripts." The firm notes that transcripts are reviewed, as are writing samples.

Contacts applaud Akin Gump's summer associate program. Some gush over activities — "Phenomenal! The summer program is like summer camp, but with lots of beer and free T-shirts" — while others compliment the "variety of work" and "litigation training program." Akin Gump notes that it tries to simulate a real world experience for the summer associates.

OUR SURVEY SAYS

Happy to be here

Akin Gump scores high marks for its "laid-back" culture and "friendly and open" atmosphere in which "lawyers socialize together frequently." One fifth-year associate comments, "The firm is laid back but also very professional. An oxymoron? No, because it works." Another lawyer comments, "I am a young associate who does high-caliber work with high-caliber people — I couldn't be happier." New York litigators are especially effusive: "This is an amazing department," raves one; another claims that "Akin Gump New York's prize feature is its people, especially in the litigation department." Although one corporate attorney finds the firm "cold and unfriendly," a colleague sighs contentedly, "The end result here is that I feel attached, interested and pretty goddamned happy."

Several attorneys in the D.C. office complain that the "supposedly laid-back" environment is "very negative and hostile" for women and that "morale is very low." (The firm points out that the Washington office has begun a Women's Professional Development Forum, which will include training, networking and social events.) Others suggest that "an increasing emphasis on the 'bottom line'" results in a "decidedly more uptight" atmosphere. One attorney describes the Washington office as a "solid group of friendly, motivated and intelligent people in a large, bureaucratic and sometimes cold and increasingly corporate environment." Virginia respondents find their workplace "far more laid back and less hierarchical than the D.C. office."

Partners part of the package

"On the whole," a New York associate writes, "I think the partners are terrific. Not a lot of 'screamers' here, if any." Most Manhattan contacts find partners "friendly, helpful and approachable." "It's instilled from top to bottom that you treat everyone with respect," claims a bankruptcy associate. Several sources attribute the good relations to the partners' relative youth. "Akin Gump New York is definitely a young office as far as things in the city go. Having the partner base close in age to the associates is definitely a plus in terms of having quality of life issues better understood." An insider reports that one leading partner insists that "associates do not work 'for' partners, but 'with' them — a mentality that's well received."

D.C. lawyers report personal experiences with partners who treat them "with respect and are very considerate and kind." However many mention "other partners" who are "confrontational" and whose treatment of associates is not "reined in" despite "the repeated assurances of firm management that this behavior is unacceptable." The firm, however, remarks that this type of behavior is not acceptable and is not tolerated by the partnership or other firm management. One fifth-year associate suggests that the disparate treatment is less the consequence of "a few bad seeds" than the result of associates' shoddy work: "People who do not perform well are often not treated well. People who perform well and understand the importance of teamwork and commitment to client needs are treated very well." And a Houston contact reminds attorneys that "this place is a business, plain and simple. They treat us as well as most business owners treat employees — really well when they need you and when they are happy and somewhat poorly when they don't need you."

Long hours but no face time

Akin Gump lawyers work long hours, but they "expected that going in." Describing the work as "client-driven" or "case-related," many express relief that "there is no such thing as face time here." Some associates take relative comfort: "The hours suck, but they're still not comparable to those of the schmucks on the East Coast." At least one New Yorker finds the long hours "offset by the fact that you are guaranteed a tremendous amount of experience earlier in your career." A few sources note that "work has actually been very slow lately," and one Dallas lawyer longs for "more billable hours."

This anxiety may be related to the firm's compensation system, which makes a portion of associate salaries in some cities contingent on billable hours. "There is pressure to bill at least 175 hours a month," complains a D.C. attorney. "I don't mind putting in the hours to produce high-quality legal services and to receive what I consider to be very good compensation," another writes, "but sometimes it feels as if the entire focus has become just how many hours you bill during the year." More than one lawyer disdainfully reminds the grumblers that "this profession is not, and will never be, a 9 to 5 job." A first-year lawyer in Virginia lays the blame squarely on the lawyers themselves: "Although associates work some weekends, it often is because they blew off work during the week to go to an extended lunch or play racquetball."

As far as flexible schedules, several sources praise partners for sensitivity to "personal commitments" and "responsiveness to requests for part-time schedules." In addition, the firm recently adopted a formal part-time policy of which many attorneys are taking advantage.

Deferred salary system is a drag

"We work hard, no doubt, but we're paid for it," says one source. Although official compensation is called "competitive" and "at or above market," there is widespread displeasure with the firm's deferred salary system, by which "a certain portion of an associate's salary [about 10 percent] is withheld until the next calendar year" when it is "paid out only if the associate bills 2,000 hours." The firm makes clear that this hours requirement does not apply in all offices; for instance, in New York and Los Angeles, salaries are not based on billable hours. Still, even associates who consider their salaries "extremely high" complain about the back-end pay system.

Insiders say that, because "it is difficult for many associates to bill 2,000 hours during the year," many associates — particularly junior associates — do not receive the deferred compensation. The system is "a horrible excuse for stiffing associates," one attorney angrily declares, though the firm notes that the two-tier track promotes fairness in pay. A few sources suggest more benign motives: "The deferred compensation system has allowed the firm to avoid associate layoffs when the economy takes a downturn." And a Houston philosopher concludes, "The deferred compensation piece is unfortunate, but that's simply how the firm works."

Not a big push for pro bono

The emphasis on billable hours limits work on pro bono matters, according to many associates — a common complaint among associates this year. Though some Akin Gumpers report that up to 100 hours of pro bono work count toward the billable requirement only after 2,000 non-pro bono hours have been billed, the firm says that all approved pro bono hours count against the 2,000 billable hours. Indeed, the firm provides "many opportunities…to do pro bono work," but some associates find that "there is not a big push for it." Others note that "the firm as a whole is committed to pro bono," but individual opportunity "depends on the partners you work for." However, several offices have pro bono committees and encourage attorneys and summer associates to participate in a wide variety of cases. A New York attorney praises the firm for a "donation drive to assist victims of September 11," for which "partners donated very generously."

Workspace: functional, not fancy

The New York office space evoked mixed reactions from associates, especially from litigators who say their floor is "aesthetically unappealing." Several lawyers bemoan the "soiled and worn" carpet. But other associates are grateful for the "amazing views of Central Park" from offices they don't have to share. On balance, most respondents find the space "comfortable and nice looking," even if not "posh and luxurious," which, one corporate attorney scolds, "is not appropriate for most law firms." Associates may appreciate the new office space that the firm recently took over on additional floors, which has relieved the space crunch. The firm notes that those floors have not yet been refurbished.

Renovations in D.C. have resulted in a "new and comfortable" space, although one lawyer laments the lack of "character" and condemns the artwork as "atrocious crap. They even hung an ampersand on the wall and called it art." Associates should enjoy, however, the new built-in office furniture with plenty of storage and work space. Texas digs are "functional" and "plain," even "drab." But a San Antonio associate suggests that the state-of-the-art equipment offsets the drabness of the décor: "We don't waste money on an art collection that clients would look at and wonder how much extra they are paying per hour to cover the cost. We do invest money in computer technology and office equipment to make the lawyers' work more efficient."

Room for greater diversity

In terms of hiring women, most sources suggest that "the firm has made excellent strides," but see a struggle "to retain more senior level women associates and partners." A corporate attorney notes that the "low number of female partners means that there is not a lot of mentoring." But a D.C. lawyer adds, "As recently as this month, there has been a new effort to form a professional development forum for women. It will start in April and I'm looking forward to experiencing the outcome of this overdue effort." The New York office has also begun what they call a Women's Initiative. Both programs are designed to provide opportunities for women attorneys to have specific training classes, networking opportunities, special speakers and social events. The firm notes that over 15 percent of the partnership is women and nearly 40 percent of the associate ranks are women.

Associates also give good marks to the firm's reception of gays and lesbians. Several note that "the firm is well represented by a number of openly gay partners and associates," although a few suggest room for "definite improvement."

One area in which sources tend to agree the firm should improve is the recruitment of minorities. "In terms of recruiting and hiring, I believe the firm takes a somewhat passive approach," states one attorney. A New Yorker also urges greater effort: "There is a disturbing lack of African-American and Latino attorneys in our office. The firm has made extensive recruiting efforts, but obviously they have not been enough. We should ascertain why so few minorities choose our firm over others, and work to correct the problem." The firm notes that it was a recipient of the 2001 and 2002 Sager Award, given by the MCCA to recognize firm efforts in minority hiring and retention, and that 9 percent of the partners and 14 percent of the associates are minorities.

VAULT CAREER LIBRARY

"I feel attached, interested and pretty goddamned happy."

— *Akin Gump associate*

Winston & Strawn

35 West Wacker Drive
Chicago, IL 60601-9703
Phone: (312) 558-5600
www.winston.com

LOCATIONS

Chicago, IL (HQ)
Los Angeles, CA
New York, NY
Washington, DC
Geneva
Paris

MAJOR DEPARTMENTS/PRACTICES

Contracts
Corporate & Financial
Employee Benefits & Executive Compensation
Employment & Labor
Energy
Environmental
Government Relations
Intellectual Property & Technology
Litigation
Real Estate
Tax

THE STATS

No. of attorneys: 875
No. of offices: 6
Summer associate offers: 79 out of 85 (2001)
Managing Partner: James M. Neis
Hiring Chair: Julie A. Bauer

BASE SALARY

Chicago, 2002
1st year: $125,000
2nd year: $135,000
3rd year: $150,000
Summer associate: $2,400/week

- Attorneys-only dining room
- Bi-monthly ice cream socials
- Impressive brass nameplates on office doors
- Free bagels and donuts on pay day (Chicago)

THE BUZZ
WHAT ATTORNEYS AT OTHER FIRMS ARE SAYING ABOUT THIS FIRM

- "Blue blood and old school"
- "Too many tobacco cases"
- "Good litigators"
- "Strong corporate department"
- "Better dressed than compensated"

UPPERS

- First-rate litigation practice
- "Subtly elegant" headquarters
- Top-notch support staff

DOWNERS

- Minimum billable hours requirement for top base salaries
- How about an associates committee?
- Air of secrecy regarding management decisions

EMPLOYMENT CONTACT

Ms. Paulette R. Kuttig
Senior Legal Recruiting Manager
Phone: (312) 558-5600
Fax: (312) 558-5700
pkuttig@winston.com

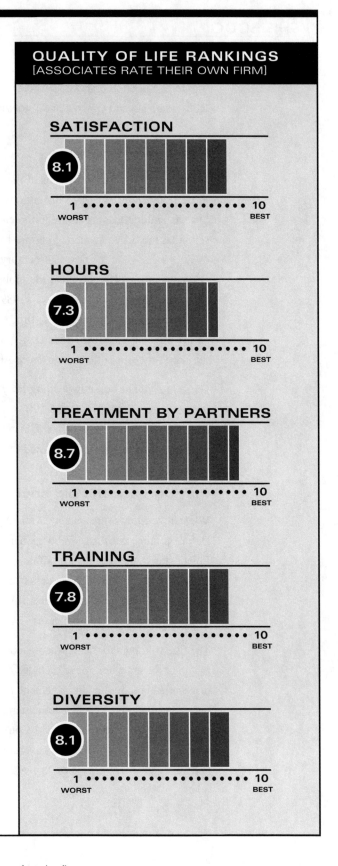

QUALITY OF LIFE RANKINGS
[ASSOCIATES RATE THEIR OWN FIRM]

SATISFACTION
8.1
1 WORST .... 10 BEST

HOURS
7.3
1 WORST .... 10 BEST

TREATMENT BY PARTNERS
8.7
1 WORST .... 10 BEST

TRAINING
7.8
1 WORST .... 10 BEST

DIVERSITY
8.1
1 WORST .... 10 BEST

THE SCOOP

One of the oldest and largest law firms in the country, Chicago-based Winston & Strawn boasts a top-notch litigation practice as well as an impressive corporate resume. Associates regularly have their breath stolen by Winston & Strawn offices, among the most stunning in the country.

Midwestern roots

Frederick H. Winston, a prominent member of the Democratic Party who served as a delegate to three Democratic national conventions, founded Winston & Strawn in Chicago in 1853. Silas Strawn, another leading figure in the city's legal and political circles, joined the firm in 1894 and served as the firm's managing partner for 40 years. By 1953 the Chicago firm was home to about 40 attorneys. Over the next half-century, in a series of fits and starts, Winston swelled to over 800 attorneys in six offices around the globe. Most of the firm's growth has been achieved through mergers in the last two decades. In 1989 Winston merged with New York-based Cole & Deitz; the next year, it joined with the D.C. firm Bishop Cook Purcell & Reynolds. In 1999 Winston added 15 lawyers from the firm of Hertzog, Calamari & Gleason, and in September 2000, a merger with the New York office of Whitman Breed Abbott & Morgan added 80 new attorneys to the Winston fold.

Winston continues to draw leading lawyers with ties to government. In 1991 James Thompson, a former governor of Illinois and U.S. Attorney, joined the firm as a partner and currently holds the post of chairman. Litigation head, Dan Webb, is a former federal prosecutor. The firm also boasts a former governor of New York and two former U.S. congressmen.

Playing with the big boys

Winston & Strawn presents a formidable litigation team led by veteran trial lawyer Dan Webb. Before joining the firm, Webb garnered national attention for his prosecution of General John Poindexter in the Iran-Contra affair. As a member of Winston, he has represented tobacco giant Philip Morris in several class action lawsuits and served as lead courtroom counsel on common issues for all tobacco defendants. In September 2001, he joined Microsoft's trial team in the company's ongoing antitrust cases.

The firm is known for taking on big, controversial clients (tobacco, anyone?), but its practice is far-ranging. Recent clients have included the Major League Umpires Association in a dispute between disgruntled umpires and management, the Chicago Board of Education in a lawsuit against the state over contributions to teacher retirement, pharmaceutical companies Abbott Laboratories and Barr Laboratories in patent cases, and Commonwealth Edison in an unsuccessful Fifth Amendment takings case against the federal government. (The dismissal of Edison's complaint by the Court of Federal Claims was upheld on appeal in November 2001.)

Hamburger helper

Winston's strengths don't lie only in the courtroom. The firm's corporate and finance attorneys, most of whom are based in New York and Chicago, provide a wide range of transaction-related services to clients that include General Electric, Goldman Sachs, Long Island Power Authority, Motorola Inc. and UBS PaineWebber Inc. On the securities front, Winston served as counsel for the Houston-based utility contractor Quanta Services Inc. in its efforts to defeat Utilitcorp's bid for control of the company. The firm also offers an impressive M&A record. Winston represented Keebler Foods when Kellogg Company swallowed up the cookie maker for $3.86 billion in November 2000. And, according to London's *World Law Business*, the firm ranked No. 9 in a 2001 listing of top global project finance practices based on dollar volume of deals.

Even Ronald McDonald has drawn on the special talents of the Chicago firm. After the FBI uncovered a criminal ring suspected of stealing high-level McDonald's game prizes, the fast-food giant tapped Chicago lawyer Dan Webb to chair a new, independent task force to ensure the integrity of future fast-food promotions.

Hot project lands firm in hot water

While Winston may be proud of its record, representing unpopular clients hasn't always been a smooth ride for the firm. Winston's dual role as government adviser on licensing for a nuclear waste dump and lobbyist for the nuclear industry has recently put the firm on the defensive. Winston was hired by the Department of Energy in a $16.5 million contract to help evaluate Yucca Mountain as the site for a nuclear waste dump in Nevada; meanwhile, the firm was also working for the Nuclear Energy Institute, a lobbying firm that supports the Yucca Mountain project. In November 2001, DOE Inspector General Gregory Friedman found that Winston had failed to disclose to the government its relationship with the lobbying firm. Friedman did not characterize the relationship as a conflict of interest, nor did he find that Winston's work resulted in an improper bias in the evaluation of the site.

Nevertheless, critics of the Yucca Mountain project, including Nevada Governor Kenny Guinn and Senators Harry Reid and John Ensign, argue that the firm's actions have contaminated the study. Winston has denied any conflict of interest but withdrew its legal services from the Department of Energy. Congressional investigators have since recommended that the Bush administration indefinitely postpone a decision on the nuclear dump. The recommendation in favor of the site has passed the House and is now in front of the Senate.

Chances are, however, that Winston will weather this episode as successfully as it has other unpleasant incidents in its long history. Witness the firm's quick rebound after then-managing partner Gary Fairchild pleaded guilty in 1994 to embezzling nearly $800,000 from the firm and five clients. Winston is now led by DePaul Law graduate James Neis as managing partner and former Illinois Governor James Thompson as chairman.

Promoting public service

Winston & Strawn encourages staff and attorneys to participate in pro bono activities, and in December 1999, the firm announced the appointment of a full-time director of public interest law. Through the Winston & Strawn Foundation, the firm has awarded more than $1 million in cash grants on an annual basis to a range of civic and charitable organizations. The firm has also instituted a matching program to support the charitable and volunteer work of its employees.

Like many law firms, Winston offered its resources in the aftermath of the September 11 World Trade Center attacks. The firm was also one of the supporting sponsors of Scientific American's 2002 "Summit on Privacy, Security and Safety: Preserving an Open Society in an Age of Terrorism" in New York.

GETTING HIRED

Looking for the esquires next door

When it comes to hiring, Winston & Strawn seems to seek out the well-rounded type — the esquire next door, so to speak. Most Vault contacts state that Winston's primarily "looking for well-rounded individuals who will fit in and have solid law grades." Winston is no label snob — the firm is "concerned about what school you attend, but does not place nearly as much stock in it as do other firms of the same size and stature." Indeed, it seems like fit is the overriding factor behind Winston's hiring decisions. "The firm hires and retains well-rounded individuals who demonstrate a good attitude and work ethic, as opposed to hiring difficult personalities who are superstars on paper. The firm does a great job of sifting through the quantitative data and hiring solid people who are enjoyable to work with."

Winston is said to be informal and efficient in its interview process; the firm hires many laterals through recruiters and headhunters. One lateral commends the firm for its efficiency: "It took less than a week to interview and get an offer." New associates are recruited "on campus and at various job fairs. Successful candidates are then asked back for more extensive interviews in the domestic office of their choice."

Social summer

Winston associates have nothing but good things to say about the summer program. We hear it's "fun and well-balanced. You are expected to do real work, but the expectations are easy to manage. Summer social functions are well-attended by lawyers and are focused primarily on summer associates getting to know the lawyers." A Chicago associate "can't say enough great things about the Chicago summer program," but tries anyway. "What a fabulous way," that associate continues, "to begin your career with a network of friendships and business associates already built in." Despite the economic downturn of 2001, Winston hasn't stinted on summer associate comforts.

"Essentially, I spent June through August lolling in the sun while they fed me grapes. Well, maybe it wasn't quite like that, but it wasn't far off," one associate wistfully recalls.

OUR SURVEY SAYS

Sophisticated and satisfied

Winston's one of those law firms that has, say insiders, an unjustified rap as a stuffy law firm. "Although [Winston] has a reputation as formal, it truly is a friendly and social place. People are far friendlier than I first thought," remarks one associate. Other associates concur that Chicago is a friendly place for Winstonians. "It is not uncommon to have lunch or socialize with other associates or partners in various practice areas," volunteers a Vault contact. One associate reminisces about "a baby shower that included approximately forty partners and associates." Most friendships are said to stem from the summer program.

Perhaps the reputation for stuffiness comes from the intensity of the work at Winston. "Everyone knows that when it comes to business — it's all business," contends an insider. "Everything gets done the right way and expectations are very high. That breeds a certain air of propriety and formality that detracts somewhat from the friendly, social aspects of working here at this firm."

Not too many hours (but you need them for the bonus)

Winston isn't one of those firms where associates need to beg for work — there's enough available, say insiders. At the same time, Winstonians don't seem work-obsessed. "There's always plenty of work here," says one insider, who goes on to advise that it's "up to the individual lawyer to control their own 'docket.' If you want to spend 70-80 hours a week here, you easily can." At the same time, Winston is "definitely not a sweatshop," at least according to one unhurried associate. "Although there are times that I've worked from 7 a.m. until 3 a.m., there are far more days that I've worked from 8:30 a.m. until noon." When there's work to be done, Winstonians work, but "nine times out of 10 you have your weekend to yourself."

Of course, there's a downside to such a leisurely a pace. "The lack of emphasis on billable hours or time spent in the office," observes one Winston lawyer, "causes a problem when you realize you just can't make the 2,100 billable hours required to make a bonus." There is a minimum billable hours requirement for top base salaries; it's 1,950. If you make the hours, you make the salary and bonus. Winston, say insiders, didn't "do anything sneaky this year like try to defer a portion of our raises."

Oh, behave (partners)!

Winstonians credit partners for being "civil" and "professional," for the most part. In fact, insiders imply that Winston partners respect associates so much that they can be a bit too hands-off.

Partners, comments one associate, "expect you to make sure your assignments are being handled, or as a senior associate, they expect you to make sure the case is being run properly, without unnecessary oversight unless you raise questions or concerns with them. As long as you do your part, they are very appreciative and professional." Concurs one senior associate, "Civility is a very important value at this firm and it goes both ways; partners are extremely respectful toward associates — almost to a fault."

Some associates cite cuddlier relationships with partners. "Partners often socialize with younger associates as if the associates were peers rather than employees. I have had countless experiences of reporting to a partner on a legal matter for five minutes and not leaving the office for half an hour after discussing non-related matters."

The associate/partner dynamic at Winston is not completely tension-free. There's sometimes competition for associates. One associate, while he says he's had "very few problems" with partners, admits that those problems he has had "have related to partners not respecting the fact that other partners have assigned projects to me." A new associate thinks that "every partner wants their work to get done and has a different approach to ensuring that you have their case as your first priority. Some partners use positive reinforcement, while others unfortunately find that negative reinforcement works best." Still, though there are a few "bad apples" in every firm, "most partners [at Winston] are professional and respectful."

Cranking up the training

Winston makes real efforts in training. Still, say insiders, training is somewhat dependent on department. In the corporate department, "early on, there is a lot of formal training in broad areas in the form of weekly corporate training meetings. After the first year, the formal corporate training meetings end, but the training still exists in more informal ways through interaction with partners." Litigation associates say that "both deposition and trial practice is mandatory"; they're also encouraged to attend seminars run by the National Institute for Trial Advocacy (NITA).

Smaller departments have less formal training. A real estate associate says, "There is no formal training program in my department, but several of the partners are excellent teachers and don't hesitate to take time out to explain things. Some partners aren't the best at this, though, especially when a deal needs to close quickly." When not rushed, however, partners and senior associates are said to "dedicate a large portion of their time to tutoring and mentoring younger associates." A senior litigation associate reports, "I just completed a well-run five-week trial training program for fifth- through eighth-years."

Everyone stays at Winston

After years of hearing tales of turnover, it's refreshing to learn that Winston associates are staying at the firm because they like it. One senior associate states, "I'm an eighth-year in litigation, and everyone from my incoming litigation class is still with the firm. Many who leave end up returning." Marvels another senior associate, "There are actually people at this firm with whom I attended law school — not so at most other big law firms."

Why the top-notch retention? Let's hear a theory from another senior-level associate: "Among the firms I considered and interviewed with, Winston really stood out in the area of associate retention. Very few people leave the firm either voluntarily or involuntarily. In fact, many who have left the firm for another firm have returned to Winston, presumably because they found that it doesn't get any better than this. As a result, minimal lateral hiring is necessary and the firm can afford to keep its summer classes small relative to peer firms. Since Winston keeps summer classes small, the firm invests more time and money in developing its younger associates with the expectation that they will stay and make partner." Summarizes another insider, "Bottom line, the firm keeps the people it wants to keep." And it looks like Winston wants to keep most everyone.

I have seen true beauty, and it is Winston & Strawn's Chicago office

Winston is perhaps most renowned for the great beauty of its Chicago headquarters. "No one's Chicago offices beat ours," boasts one associate, "and everyone knows it." "Subdued elegance is the best way to describe" the offices, coos one associate, while another gushes that "the décor is always maintained beautifully. Flowers on every floor add a great touch." Another adored office feature: the attorney dining room, catered by "Pierre," who "makes the best food." "Where else," wonders one gourmand, "can I get prime rib, salad bar, beverage and dessert for under $8?"

Describes another associate, "Winston's offices are the best I've seen, period, and I've seen a few. They are gorgeous, with rich, dark red wood and marble everywhere. Office furniture is of very high quality, even for the lowest associate. The firm obviously takes pride in its surroundings." That associate speculates on another reason for the gorgeous décor besides pure aesthetics, saying, "I wouldn't be surprised if the offices, particularly the upper floor conference rooms and reception area, overlooking Lake Michigan and loaded with marble, give us a 'home field advantage' and add an intimidation factor against opposing counsel and clients in certain situations."

Winston's New York offices, needless to say, don't reach the high standards set by the firm's Chicago headquarters. Carps one New Yorker, "The New York offices are not up to Winston's standards. They have two beautiful floors and three old floors (from the merger) that look like my grandmother's apartment. The floors are also split between elevator banks, so we spend a lot of time in the lobby of the MetLife building (aka Grand Central) fighting with the other tenants and passersby just to see a partner or another associate for a meeting or to deliver a document."

Talk to me

If there's anything Winston associates don't like about their firm, it's the lack of "openness on the part of upper management." "Very little important information comes down from the partners through normal channels. You have to be good friends with partners to learn things," laments one insider. Another lawyer contends, "Associates at Winston genuinely feel that they too have a stake in the performance of the firm and its general well-being. However, we generally are given no information regarding the firm's future plans or its performance."

Yet another insider makes this plaintive plea to Winston partners: "Quite often associates find out about major firm policy changes or developments after the fact. It would be nice to have a voice through an associates committee. We're not looking to 'unionize' or get militant. We just care about the firm and would like to have some input on firm happenings, whether we are actually listened to or not. "

"Very little important information comes down from the partners through normal channels. You have to be good friends with partners to learn things."

— *Winston & Strawn associate*

Munger, Tolles & Olson LLP

355 South Grand Avenue
35th Floor
Los Angeles, CA 90071-1560
Phone: (213) 683-9100
www.mto.com

LOCATIONS

Los Angeles, CA (HQ)
San Francisco, CA

MAJOR DEPARTMENTS/PRACTICES

Bankruptcy & Restructuring
Corporate
Environmental
Labor
Litigation
Real Estate
Tax

THE STATS

No. of attorneys: 150
No. of offices: 2
Summer associate offers: 25 out of 27 (2001)
Co-Managing Partners: Ruth E. Fisher and
Robert K. Johnson
Recruiting Chairs: Lisa J. Demsky and Kelly M. Klaus

BASE SALARY

Los Angeles, 2002
1st year: $125,000
2nd year: $135,000
3rd year: $150,000
4th year: $165,000
5th year: $185,000
6th year: $195,000
Summer associate: $2,400/week

NOTABLE PERKS

- In-house CLE luncheons with free food three times a week
- Free parking
- 401(k) plan in which firm contributes 3% of each associate's annual compensation up to a maximum of $5,100

THE BUZZ
WHAT ATTORNEYS AT OTHER FIRMS ARE SAYING ABOUT THIS FIRM

- "Prestigious corporate powerhouse boutique"
- "Superb lawyers who are real community leaders in LA"
- "Full of eggheads"
- "One of the best for complex litigation matters"

UPPERS

- Flexible hours
- Intense, intellectual community
- Participation in firm decision-making

DOWNERS

- Offices in need of renovation
- Limited after-hours socialization
- Sometimes inadequate guidance

EMPLOYMENT CONTACT

Ms. Kevinn Villard
Director of Legal Recruiting
Phone: (213) 683-9242
Fax: (213) 687-3702
villardkc@mto.com

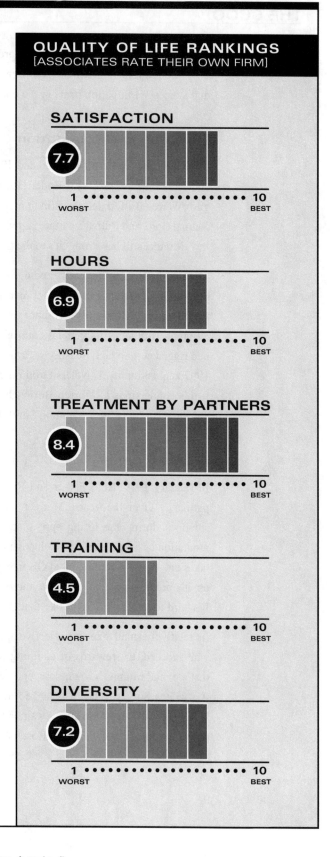

QUALITY OF LIFE RANKINGS
[ASSOCIATES RATE THEIR OWN FIRM]

SATISFACTION

7.7

1 WORST .... 10 BEST

HOURS

6.9

1 WORST .... 10 BEST

TREATMENT BY PARTNERS

8.4

1 WORST .... 10 BEST

TRAINING

4.5

1 WORST .... 10 BEST

DIVERSITY

7.2

1 WORST .... 10 BEST

THE SCOOP

Size isn't everything, as the stellar record of California firm Munger, Tolles & Olson proves. With only 150 lawyers in its two offices, Munger has established a reputation as one of the most selective and successful litigation firms in the country.

Firm financial foundation

Munger, Tolles & Olson was founded 40 years ago by seven lawyers, including Charles T. Munger and Harvard Law professor Roderick Hills. Munger, a longtime friend of billionaire investment guru Warren Buffett, left the firm to make his mark in the business world, as chairman of The Daily Journal Corp. and Buffett's partner and vice chairman of the investment company, Berkshire Hathaway Inc. Munger still has strong ties to the firm and maintains an office at the Los Angeles headquarters.

The firm boasts another partner who made a splash in the investment community. Robert Denham, one of Hills' Harvard law student recruits, joined the firm in 1971. After working with the firm for 20 years, including five as managing partner, he moved over to Buffett's management team at Salomon Brothers. As general counsel, Denham helped rescue Salomon from allegations that it had rigged certain U.S. treasury securities markets, and later, as CEO, he negotiated the company's 1997 acquisition by Travelers Group Inc. In 1998 Denham returned to Munger as a partner. The firm's connections to Warren Buffett have proved profitable. Munger has handled litigation for Salomon Brothers (now Salomon Smith Barney) and names Berkshire Hathaway among its clients.

A select circle

In January 1999, Ruth Fisher and Robert Johnson were named as the firm's first co-managing partners. Over the years, Munger has steadfastly remained a mid-sized firm, staying on the sidelines during the hiring sprees and law-firm mergers of the last decade. Munger has a reputation as an elite shop — selective not only for the attorneys it hires, but also for the clients it takes on. Name partner Ronald Olson explained the firm philosophy to *The Recorder* in 1999: "For us, it's pretty simple. We believe the best people will get the best results, hence the best clients." It's hard to argue with logic like that.

Its relatively small size and selective approach make joining Munger a difficult feat, but for those who succeed, the rewards of claiming membership among Munger elite can be great. Certainly that's what Munger's own lawyers believe. In American Lawyer Media's 2001 "Midlevel Associates Survey", the firm ranked at the top of a self-scoring prestige survey, alongside such legal stalwarts as Cravath, Swaine & Moore, Sullivan & Cromwell and fellow youthful powerhouses Wachtell, Lipton, Rosen & Katz and Williams & Connolly.

Leading litigators

In keeping with its reputation as a high-end litigation firm, more than two-thirds of Munger attorneys are litigators. The litigation practice covers a broad field, with matters ranging from media and communications, to product liability, to white-collar crime, to energy and the environment.

Ronald Olson, who leads the department with big-name clients like Edison International, Shell Oil and Merrill Lynch, reportedly brings in more than $10 million a year. Olson's talent and influence are widely recognized. In a 1997 poll conducted by *California Business Review*, 200 attorneys voted Olson California's most influential lawyer. Proving that settlement can be the better part of valor, Olson whittled down a $2 billion bankruptcy suit by Orange County against Merrill Lynch to a $400 million settlement. Olson also helped Alyeska Pipeline Service Co. settle for $98 million in disputes related to the Exxon Valdez spill, while Exxon, who opted to fight, got hit with $5 billion in punitive damages.

Munger makes headlines

Munger has played a role in a number of high-profile (and often controversial) cases. The firm is among counsel retained by Philip Morris to defend the class-action lawsuits against the tobacco industry, including a $4.6 billion suit filed in 1997 by the Republic of the Marshall Islands. The firm has defended Shell Oil in a statewide California antitrust action, represented Unocal Corp. against claims of human rights abuses, and helped develop a plan to rescue the financially troubled Southern California Edison Co., the state's second-largest electrical utility.

The firm's Los Angeles base also gives it a leg up in the entertainment field. Michael Ovitz, ABC, Universal Studios, MGM and Warner Bros. have all tapped Munger's litigation team. In August 2001, in a case cited by *The National Law Journal* as one of the top defense wins of 2001, the firm successfully defended MGM against an invasion of privacy claim by a couple who were informed of their son's death on the air of a Los Angeles-based reality TV show. Munger magic landed another big First Amendment win that summer, when the Ninth Circuit Court of Appeals reversed a trial court decision that had awarded actor Dustin Hoffman $3 million against *Los Angeles Magazine* for printing a digitally altered image of Hoffman in a red sequined dress from the 1982 film "Tootsie."

Munger's non-litigation practices, while smaller, bring their share of visibility to the firm. The firm's transactional work includes its representation of Berkshire Hathaway in all of its acquisitions, the restructuring of Edison International in connection with the deregulation of the California power industry, and longstanding relationships with local marquee clients such as KB Homes, Inc., City National Bank, Countrywide Savings and Universal Studios, Inc. Labor partner Terry Sanchez heads up an active employment law practice which includes such clients as Merrill Lynch and Delta Air Lines and recent high-profile cases such as the representation of multiple studios in connection with the television writers age discrimination lawsuit.

Committed to the community

In addition to its high-profile, high-paying clientele, Munger maintains a substantial pro bono practice. The firm reports that it devotes more than 3 percent of all attorney time to pro bono work, and Munger has been honored by the State Bar of California and the American Bar Association for its service to the community.

The firm has devoted substantial efforts on behalf of the homeless in Los Angeles. Other pro bono projects include work with AIDS Project LA, the Alliance For Children's Rights, the American Civil Liberties Union, Lambda Legal Defense and Education Fund, Inc., migrant workers from Mexico, Planned Parenthood, and the Yugoslav War Crimes Tribunal. In a move that highlights the firm's strong commitment to public service, two years ago a group of Munger associates created a fund to which they contribute a percentage of their salaries and from which donations are made to a variety of charitable organizations.

In the wake of the September 11 tragedy, Munger demonstrated its commitment to the public interest once again. The firm stepped forward as one of several California law firms to join with the state government in a public-private partnership aimed at providing pro bono legal services for families of victims of the terrorist attacks.

GETTING HIRED

A clerkship or two helps

If you've got top grades at a top school, with "a clerkship or two," then feel free to consider Munger Tolles as a potential employer. If not, you can still consider Munger Tolles — but Munger Tolles probably won't consider you. In fact, according to one senior associate, "simply being in the top 10 percent at an Ivy League school is not enough; there must be something more," like "interesting work experience," a couple of those clerkships, or "publications." But don't expect to coast by on your superlative credentials either. "If you don't interview well," sniffs one insider, "you're toast." A tip on acing the interview: do your homework on the firm. To offer a dim ray of hope, several associates mention that the firm does hire a few associates from "non top-20" institutions.

A thorough job

Munger Tolles is very thorough in evaluating potential hires. "We generally check all of the employers an applicant lists on their resumes to see how their work was," comments one new associate. In-house screening is thorough as well. Explains one new hire: "Each candidate gets a recommendation from the recruiting committee and then the whole firm hears the candidate's reviews, views his or her resume and hears the committee's recommendation prior to a firm-wide discussion and a vote whether or not to extend an offer. There is no clear rule, but more than a few no votes will prevent an offer. Because it is a democratic process, strange things happen and some individuals who appear to be strong candidates will get dinged for idiosyncratic reasons." The interview process normally involves about six interviews with associates and partners, plus lunch and dinner.

Potential summer associates will find their time at Munger Tolles short but sweet; the firm "is free with splitting, so most people spend the second half of their summer at Munger." Even in that length of time, the firm "expects three written documents from each summer to ensure it gets sufficient info to assess each candidate for a full-time offer."

SURVEY SAYS

Munger Academy

The pressure to display smarts doesn't stop after you've been hired at Munger. Insiders say that "[Munger] places very high value on intellectual abilities and seeks people with outstanding academic achievement." One associate tweaks his peers' obsession with intelligence. "A lot of people here buy into the idea that we have the best and the brightest. While we do have people who went to the top law schools and got really good grades, it certainly does not necessarily mean we have the best lawyers, and I think people here miss that sometimes." The atmosphere amidst these geniuses is said to be "friendly" but "intense," especially in view of the firm's location on the laid-back West Coast. "For a law firm," comments one insider, "it is very non-hierarchical, but the atmosphere is nonetheless a little bit formal for California."

Surprisingly reasonable hours

Though hours "can be heavy" at Munger Tolles, associates express joy and satisfaction that "associates have a surprisingly amount of control over the hours they work." For those who need to work a more flexible schedule, the firm is said to be quite cooperative. "We do not have a written [policy regarding a] part-time program, but the firm has apparently been flexible regarding accommodating the need for part-time work," notes a happy insider. Although associates report increased focus on hours, the firm has not adopted any billable hour requirements and schedules are still said to be on the light side for a top firm. "So far I have had to work very few weekends or late evenings," raves one new associate. "Some firms might have better hours than Munger, but I seriously doubt that there are any firms that handle the size and quality of cases that Munger does without working substantially longer hours."

My trainer, my partner

Small firms often promote close working relationships between associates and partners. Munger Tolles is no exception. "I have often had trouble figuring out whether a lawyer was a partner or associate and it does not seem to matter too much in day-to-day work," comments an associate. Another insider concurs, raving that "most of the partners I have worked with always made me feel like a true colleague instead of an underling."

But while associates may be given the responsibility of partners, that's not necessarily an unmitigated good. "[Munger] isn't the firm to get detailed training," explains one wistful associate. "Everyone always thinks that is a good thing when they're choosing a firm. But a lot of times, when it's time to do the work, it's nice to have something more formal." For those seeking training, lawyers will "answer questions and provide guidance if you ask," though, according to one associate, "partners and senior associates vary widely in their willingness and ability to train." Munger is also willing to pay for associates to get training outside the firm, such as from NITA. One associate is particularly troubled at the lack of in-house training. "The lack of training or guidance makes some days really difficult to get through because the typical guidance one gets on a task one has never attempted before consists of the words, 'Do this.'"

Whether there are training opportunities or not, most associates agree that they enjoy good relationships with partners, despite the stray negative encounter. "I have heard a few negative comments about a few partners, but I have not witnessed any partner treat an associate with anything but respect, and that includes at least one partner who is reputedly difficult to work for," summarizes one new associate.

On the road

Munger Tolles seems to be a law firm with a historically low rate of associate turnover that has recently begun to experience a moderate rate of turnover. It's still low, but associates seem to be surprised that it's there at all. "[Munger] has a better rate of retention than most firms, but over the last year several associates have left for other LA-area firms, which was virtually unprecedented until recently," marvels a second-year. A senior associate concurs, observing that, "while historically the firm could proudly say no one leaves the firm for another firm, this recently has stopped being true and the firm has started to lose many good people." However, most attorneys still seem to leave for government positions, with the U.S. Attorney's office being an especially popular destination. "They go into government, and then often come back. So, any turnover may be lower than it appears," confirms an insider.

Ripe for a visit from *Trading Spaces*

If you're looking for gleaming mahogany desks, look elsewhere. "Frugal" Munger doesn't do much in the way of office decoration. The "views of the Hollywood hills" are said to be striking, as is the art, "thanks to Larry Barth." And that's about it. "The furniture is old and the wood is peeling off," carps one associate, while another indicates that "facilities and furnishings are a bit dated and rundown." No word on whether partners enjoy posher offices, though, according to one associate, "After two years you move to an office that is the same size as all the partners' offices. In fact, it is hard to tell who is a partner versus who is an associate."

Diversity: fair treatment, few special efforts

Munger Tolles seems to be paying renewed attention to the issue of recruiting and retaining women, minorities, and gays and lesbians. The firm has a separate committee focused on the recruiting of women and minorities and another committee addressing issues of retention. The firm, says one woman, "suffers from the same issues with regard to women as does the rest of the profession — how to balance the realities of being a working mother with the continuing and increasing pressure to bill more hours." Talking about the issue is a good way to start, and apparently two female associates "recently began convening monthly lunches for the women lawyers, which have been useful as a way to facilitate friendship between the women partners and women associates and to encourage discussion and debate about women's status at the firm." One woman, pleased so far, opines that Munger is "ahead of the pack" when it comes to women.

When it comes to minorities, on the other hand, Munger associates have little to say. While the firm is "receptive to hiring," one associate comments that Munger has a "problem retaining minorities." It's the same, sad old story. Take heart from one associate who volunteers, "I am a minority, yet I never felt as if I were treated differently, for better or worse." As for gays and lesbians, the firm has a number of "openly gay partners and associates." A gay man was elevated to partnership in 2001. Associates are pleased that the firm offers domestic partner insurance benefits and that "significant others are included" at firm social events.

Tunes and free lunches

Munger Tolles is a relatively frugal firm and hardly provides an overflowing fount of frills. By far the most cherished perk among the associates is a thrice-weekly CLE luncheon with free food. The food is "not quite restaurant quality but is far better than cafeteria food." The luncheons are also prized for the "CLE credit"; one insider enjoys the luncheons because "it's great to learn about what your colleagues are working on." The firm also has "nice Christmas dinners," with the occasional special guest. "Warren Buffett composed a song and sang to us at the firm's 40th anniversary party." (If that's not a perk, we don't know what is!)

Parking is free (not a small consideration in California). Associates who have been with the firm more than a year receive an annual contribution through the firm's 401(k) plan equal to 3 percent of the associate's annual compensation, up to the maximum amount permitted (currently $5,100 per year).

The work is the reward

For Munger's intellectual associates, the greatest reward is in working at a small, intense, collegial firm like Munger. One associate adores Munger's use of co-counsel, which permits the firm to avoid "the worst of the discovery process, allowing other firms to do lengthy document reviews and productions, which lets the lawyers here focus more on understanding the legal and factual issues." There's so much interesting work, half-complains an insider, that "working here is like eating at a Vegas buffet; everything looks so good that you wind up making yourself sick."

"Warren Buffet composed a song and sang to us at the firm's 40th anniversary party."

— *Munger Tolles associate*

Baker & McKenzie

One Prudential Plaza
130 E. Randolph Street
Suite 2500
Chicago, IL 60601
Phone: (312) 861-8000
www.bakernet.com

LOCATIONS

Chicago, IL (International Executive Offices)
Dallas, TX • Houston, TX • Miami, FL • New York, NY
• Palo Alto, CA • San Diego, CA • San Francisco, CA •
Washington, DC • 55 other offices worldwide

MAJOR DEPARTMENTS/PRACTICES

Banking & Finance • Corporate & Securities •
E-Commerce • Information Technology/Communications •
Intellectual Property • International Dispute Resolution •
International Trade • Labor, Employment & Employee
Benefits • Litigation • M&A • Major Projects/Project
Finance • Tax • Venture Capital

THE STATS

No. of attorneys: 3,100 +
No. of offices: 64 (as of July 1, 2002)
Summer associate offers: 21 out of 30 (2001)
Chairman of Executive Committee: Christine Lagarde
Hiring Attorneys: Miguel Noyola (Chicago); John Flaim
(Dallas); David Brakebill (Houston); James Barrett
(Miami); Grant Hannessian (NY); Ali Mojdehi (San
Diego); Peter Engstrom (San Francisco and Palo Alto);
Marc Paul (DC)

BASE SALARY

Chicago, 2002
1st year: $125,000
2nd year: $130,000
3rd year: $140,000
4th year: $150,000
5th year: $170,000
6th year: $180,000
7th year: $185,000
8th year: $190,000

New York, 2002
1st year: $125,000
2nd year: $135,000
3rd year: $150,000
4th year: $165,000
5th year: $170,000 — 185,000
6th year: $180,000 — 192,500

Washington, DC, 2002
1st year: $125,000
2nd year: $135,000
3rd year: $145,000
4th year: $165,000
5th year: $180,000
6th year: $190,000
7th year: $200,000
8th year: $215,000

San Francisco and Palo Alto, 2002
1st year: $120,000
2nd year: $120,000 — 135,000
3rd year: $130,000 — 145,000
4th year: $140,000 — 160,000
5th year: $150,000 — 180,000
6th year +: $160,000 — 200,000
Other first-year salaries include: Dallas ($110,000);
Houston ($110,000); Miami ($105,000); San Diego
($125,000).

THE BUZZ
WHAT ATTORNEYS AT OTHER FIRMS ARE SAYING ABOUT THIS FIRM

• "Awesome international practice"
• "Reputation better outside than inside the U.S."
• "The Jacoby & Meyers of corporate work"
• "Uneven quality, depending on office"
• "Size does matter"

NOTABLE PERKS

• Friday afternoon socials on the terrace
  overlooking the White House (DC)
• Annual regional conferences
• Airline and hotel discounts

UPPERS

- Opportunities to practice in foreign offices
- "Global colleagues and interesting client base"
- High-quality, sophisticated work

DOWNERS

- Intense pressure to bill, bill, bill
- Not enough work to go around
- Uninspiring commitment to pro bono work

EMPLOYMENT CONTACT

Chicago, Ms. Eleonora Nikol
Phone: (312) 861-2924
eleonora.nikol@bakernet.com

Dallas, Ms. Terry Deleon
Phone: (214) 978-3049
terry.a.deleon@bakernet.com

Houston, Ms. Nancy Rader
Phone: (713) 427-5009
nancy.a.rader@bakernet.com

Miami, Mr. Clement Noble
Phone: (305) 789-8908
clement.noble@bakernet.com

New York, Ms. Anne Zagorin
Phone: (212) 891-3573
anne.s.zagorin@bakernet.com

San Diego, Ms. Victoria Leach
Phone: (619) 235-7733
victoria.a.leach@bakernet.com

San Francisco/Palo Alto, Ms. Andrea Carr
Phone: (415) 984-3801
andrea.l.carr@bakernet.com

Washington, DC, Ms. Jane Lint
Phone: (202) 452-7024
jane.e.lint@bakernet.com

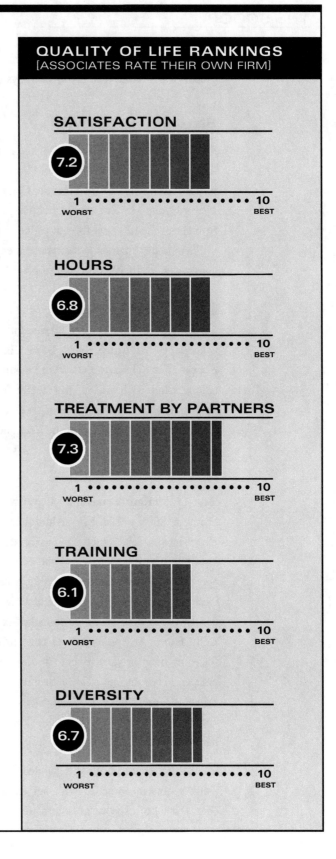

QUALITY OF LIFE RANKINGS
[ASSOCIATES RATE THEIR OWN FIRM]

SATISFACTION
7.2
1 WORST .... 10 BEST

HOURS
6.8
1 WORST .... 10 BEST

TREATMENT BY PARTNERS
7.3
1 WORST .... 10 BEST

TRAINING
6.1
1 WORST .... 10 BEST

DIVERSITY
6.7
1 WORST .... 10 BEST

THE SCOOP

What's it like to be the biggest law firm in the world? Just ask Baker & McKenzie. This truly global firm of more than 3,100 attorneys in 64 offices spans the globe in over 35 countries.

History: rapid growth

Russell Baker, a University of Chicago Law School grad who opened a firm in 1949, couldn't have known that his firm one day would become the largest in the world. This fact would most likely please Baker, who saw the potential for international law at that time and devoted his practice to it. Litigator John McKenzie's tax practice gave an added boost to the firm's overseas expansion. The firm established its first foreign office in Caracas, Venezuela, in 1955. (It was the first U.S. law office in Latin America.) Two years later, the firm opened shop in Washington, D.C., Amsterdam and Brussels. In 1958 it came to New York and Zurich; Manila and Tokyo were the first Asian offices in 1963. The firm's largest office, in London, opened in 1961. In April of 2002, the firm opened an office in Bologna, Italy, and is preparing for the July 2002 opening of its newest office in Antwerp, Belgium. About 80 percent of the firm's lawyers are based in foreign offices. "We're a single global partnership," Baker Executive Committee Chair Christine Lagarde told *The Economist* in February 2000. "We've built the infrastructure and we have a genuinely international culture." Indeed they have. In 1999 the firm received recognition at the Lawyer Awards in London for Best Global Law Firm, and in 2000, Baker won five awards at the Asian Law Awards in Hong Kong, including Law Firm of the Year and Best North American Law Firm.

New faces

Baker & McKenzie couldn't succeed without top people, and the firm reaped a bumper crop of talent in 2001. The Palo Alto office grew by nine in June with the addition of Robert Kirschenbaum and eight new associates. Kirschenbaum came from the Department of the Treasury, where his focus was the ever-engrossing Internal Revenue Service's advanced pricing agreement program. In August 2001, Stuart P. Seidel, former Assistant Commissioner of the U.S. Customs Service's Office of Regulations and Rulings, joined the Washington, D.C., office as a partner in the Firm's U.S. customs law practice group. In December 2001, the firm added Chris Kelly, Excite At Home's former chief privacy officer, as of counsel in the Palo Alto office. His focus is now privacy issues in the Information Technology/Communications E-Commerce practice. The Chicago office added Todd Golub to its internationally renowned tax practice group. Prior to joining the Firm, Golub was a partner at Katten Muchin Zavis where he focused on corporate and partnership taxation. The New York office grew as well; Willkie Farr & Gallagher partners Richard Rudder and David Wolin joined the Baker family in October.

In 2002 the Houston office expanded with the addition of Donette M. Dewer, strengthening the firm's global tax practice with her experience in advising multinational energy and high-tech clients on tax aspects of international mergers, acquisitions and restructurings. In April, international tax attorney and CPA Michael Lebovitz joined the Palo Alto office, focusing on business and tax planning. Lebovitz was formerly a partner at KPMG's International Tax Practice. Lee Stapleton Milford joined the Miami office in May and will focus on commercial litigation and white-collar criminal defense. Milford served as head of the Justice Department's Executive Office for Organized Crime Drug Enforcement Task Force in Washington prior to joining the firm.

Landmark in trademark

Baker & McKenzie's impressive client list includes an American institution, Levi Strauss & Co. In 2001, the firm hitched up their jeans and led the legendary company to an IP victory. In November of that year, a European Court of Justice ruled that the owner of a trademark has the right to control the import of trademarked goods into the European Economic Area (EEA). Three years prior to the ruling, two English department stores sold Levi's 501 jeans without the permission of Levi Strauss & Co. The two stores, Tesco Stores PLC and Costco Wholesale U.K. Ltd., imported and sold the jeans at prices lower than comparable stores in Europe. Levi Strauss demanded that the companies stop selling the jeans and sued for trademark infringement. Rejecting the argument that Levi Strauss & Co. had impliedly consented to importation of its products by failing to mark their goods to indicate they were not for sale in the EEA, the European Court of Justice fashioned a clear precedent that defines the rights of trademark holders. For their efforts, the Baker & McKenzie team was named the Intellectual Property Team of the Year by *Legal Business* magazine.

Gimme, gimme, gimme

With the global scope of Baker & McKenzie, it's no wonder the firm assists on countless acquisitions. In summer 2001, it advised OpenTV Corp., the world's largest interactive television and media solutions company, in its $51 million acquisition of Static 2358, an interactive media and entertainment company. Also that summer, the firm represented Calpine Corporation, a U.S. independent power company, in its acquisition of one of the United Kingdom's largest natural gas fired power plants, Saltend, from Entergy Corp. The transaction was valued at $800 million. In November 2001, France Telecom acquired a 12.5 percent share of Polish telecom operator Telekomunikacja Polska S.A. (TPSA) from the Polish Treasury, boosting its shares in the company to 47.5 percent. Baker & McKenzie advised France Telecom on the deal, which was valued at $900 million.

Making the news

How are stock options taxed in Singapore? What are the foundations of labor and management relations law in Germany? Attorneys at Baker & McKenzie want to make answering these questions an easy task for the many employment lawyers worldwide. That's why, in September 2001, the firm joined with CCH Incorporated, a leading provider of employment information, software and services, to produce *CCH Global Employment News Direct*, a monthly electronic newsletter delivered by e-mail. The newsletter contains current and relevant employment-related articles from around the world. To create the newsletter, the two made an agreement to license content from Baker & McKenzie's global labor, employment and employee benefits practice group's publications.

Getting things flowing

In July 2001, Baker & McKenzie aided in the financing of the Chad-Cameroon oil pipeline construction. Upon its completion in 2005, the 1,070-kilometer pipeline will run from the Doba Basin in the southwestern region of the Republic of Chad to the coast of the Republic of Cameroon, boosting the revenue of both countries. Baker & McKenzie advised the European Investment Bank in the $4 billion project.

Very taxing work

In some complex taxation work, Baker & McKenzie gained a victory for its client Compaq Computer Corp. in December 2001. In 1992 the IRS claimed that an arbitrage transaction Compaq undertook with Royal Dutch Shell was a "corporate tax shelter." The issue involved $3.4 million in foreign taxes withheld on $22.5 million in dividends that Royal Shell paid to Compaq and the question of whether $1.5 million in expenses relating to the arbitrage was deductible. The United States Court of Appeals for the Fifth Circuit found that the arbitrage transaction was indeed real and reversed the U.S. Tax Court holding in favor of the IRS.

GETTING HIRED

Random selectivity

Because Baker & McKenzie doesn't have a centralized hiring system — all hiring decisions are made by the individual practice groups at each office — associates say the selection process can be "selective, but random" and rather "haphazard." "I have no idea why we interview some candidates," says a fourth-year associate, while some applicants who "are better qualified do not even get through the front door." Regardless of the perceived unpredictability of the hiring process, associates say there are ways candidates can make themselves stand out from other applicants. "If you can show you have some unique skills in the practice area you are applying to you have a decent shot," suggests one insider. As for personal characteristics, the firm is looking for "mature, motivated, intelligent, hardworking individuals who understand that providing quality client service is paramount." Applicants should be "intelligent and competent," but also "friendly and down-to-earth." The process can be long because the "firm is generally slow to move on new hires, takes a conservative approach and only hires new associates when the work absolutely requires it."

It's not about the school

Although "some partners are more obsessed with prestige schools than others," the firm has a reputation for hiring top candidates regardless of what law school they attended. So relax. "Candidates who are a good fit but don't necessarily have Ivy League credentials have just as good a chance as anyone else." Associates who took part in the firm's summer associate program say the experience "accurately replicates life as a real associate."

OUR SURVEY SAYS

Great work, but little socializing

The office environment is "laid back and friendly, but not social. The firm possesses a 'close-your-door-and-do-your-own-thing' culture," reports an associate in one of the California offices. The firm as a whole is "somewhat formal," although "the associates are very friendly one-on-one," says an associate in Baker & McKenzie's D.C. office. "The culture in the Dallas office is very laid back and entrepreneurial. You have the freedom to build the kind of practice that you want to build," an intellectual property lawyer tell us. According to another attorney, the firm provides interesting work in the form of a "great range of clients and engagements."

"I find interaction with the associates uncommonly supportive, close-knit and respectful — none of the backstabbing or scheming I've found at other firms," says a San Diego attorney. A first-year lawyer who finds the office environment a little stiff attempts to look at the bright side: "The people I work with more than make up for any deficiencies in firm management and training."

Not enough hours in the month

Baker & McKenzie may be big, but it's no match for the effects of the weakening economy. Associates complain of an ever-increasing emphasis on billable hours and bonuses that seem unattainable. "The pressure to fulfill the [hours] requirements to obtain [the] bonuses can be overwhelming at times," remarks a Dallas associate. "The firm pays competitively," says a New Yorker, "but bonuses are hard to come by these days." Another associate objects, "I did not get my bonus because our section overhired and we did not have enough billable hours to pass around." Summarizes another associate, "I think they pay us well, but the bonus structure needs to be reworked."

Despite the grumbling, a number of associates don't see much reason to complain. Salaries at Baker & McKenzie "may not be the highest," but are "still very comparable and the hours worked more than make up for the lower level in compensation." "I think we are on par with other large D.C. firms," says an attorney from that office. A fourth-year associate says the firm "compensates for less money with a more humane lifestyle." And there are no reports of layoffs.

Hurry up and wait

A sagging economy does strange things to associates. Sometimes, as at Baker & McKenzie, it leaves them wishing for more hours instead of less. "I would actually prefer more hours," confess several survey respondents. Associates observe that work is sometimes slow these days but that pressure to bill is more intense than ever, thanks to compensation changes that force associates to take home less if they don't make their quarterly billable hours requirement. "Baker expects its associates to bill 2,100 hours to earn market pay," grumbles one associate, though another insider informs us, "The firm officially states that associates are to bill 2,000 hours." Not everyone thinks the firm is a monster when it comes to billable hours. Some associates admit the firm does not expect their lawyers "to be a slave to the clock." Though many report a bizarre longing for more work, that's not to say that things are always slow around the office. One associate says, "When things get ugly, they can get really ugly."

The jury's still out

"In our department, I don't think it helps to be a woman, [and it] probably hurts as you are not a 'golden boy' of the group," says a female attorney in a West Coast office. Surprisingly, a male attorney who works in the same department as the previous source says, the "department is definitely not an old boys' club. Women are treated the same as men."

While "the Dallas office has been extraordinary in tailoring flex-time programs for women desiring to spend more time with their children," an associate in that office believes "mentoring and promotion of women" needs improvement. An associate in the San Diego office says, "The female partners and associates here are incredibly supportive of other women in the firm and take extra efforts to mentor and guide more junior attorneys." Sources are disturbed by the perceived lack of women role models at the firm who have families and children. "This is a big issue for me," says one associate, who goes on to say, "Apparently you can't have kids and expect a balanced work and family life." This associate says the firm has made improvements with regard to promoting women, but that there is still more to be done. A labor attorney concurs: "The firm makes definite efforts to hire women, but it would seem that they have some difficulty retaining them."

Diversity with respect to minorities "appears to be really good," according to an intellectual property attorney. "This is a global law firm, so I see all colors, religions, races, cultures and so forth from all over the world." An environmental attorney remarks that the "international nature of firm and associate exchange program with other offices results in [a] diverse culture." "While we don't have a large number of minorities, it doesn't appear to be an issue," says an attorney in the Dallas office. The firm notes that in April 2002, it announced the appointment of Nam H. Paik as its Equal Employment Opportunity Program (EEOP) Partner, who will lead the firm's North American Diversity Initiative with the goal to increase minority hiring, recruiting, retention and advancement.

Little or no pro bono

When it comes to pro bono, Baker & McKenzie associates are, well, perplexed. Many associates expressed confusion or ignorance about Baker & McKenzie's pro bono policies, giving varying figures as to the number of pro bono hours that count toward billable hours. Some say 50 pro bono hours are accepted, while others say it's closer to 100. A Chicagoan says that even though "pro bono doesn't count for billable hours, it does count toward a non-billable bonus."

"The firm seems not to have made up its mind how much" pro bono work "it wants to do," comment some insiders. Many associates say the firm could use improvement in this area. "We have a pro bono coordinator who posts pro bono training and other opportunities, but a young associate is on her own to go after pro bono work," says a New York associate. "Our office really would prefer if you don't do pro bono since that might take away from billable hours," according to an associate in the Dallas office. Several other Dallas attorneys echoed that sentiment. "The pro bono partner and associate encourage us to take cases and to participate in the monthly legal aid staffing, but I have no idea whether my pro bono work will be considered in my reviews of my performance," a D.C. attorney tells us.

Cadwalader, Wickersham & Taft

100 Maiden Lane
New York, NY 10038
Phone: (212) 504-6000
cwtinfo@cwt.com
www.cadwalader.com

LOCATIONS

New York, NY (HQ) (Two locations)
Charlotte, NC
Washington, DC
London

MAJOR DEPARTMENTS/PRACTICES

Banking & Finance
Capital Markets
Corporate/Mergers & Acquisitions
Financial Restructuring
Global Public Affairs
Health Care/Not-for-Profit
Insurance & Reinsurance
Litigation
Private Client
Project Finance
Real Estate
Tax

THE STATS

No. of attorneys: 475
No. of offices: 4
Summer associate offers: 36 out of 36 (2001)
Managing Partner: Robert O. Link Jr.
Hiring Committee Chair: Paul W. Mourning

BASE SALARY

New York and Washington, DC, 2002
1st year: $125,000
2nd year: $135,000
3rd year: $150,000
4th year: $170,000
5th year: $190,000
6th year: $205,000
7th year: $220,000
8th year: $235,000
Summer associate: $2,400/week

NOTABLE PERKS

- Car service
- Laptop or desktop provided for home use and Blackberry e-mail pagers
- Free use of firm condo
- Month-long paid sabbatical after five years

THE BUZZ
WHAT ATTORNEYS AT OTHER FIRMS ARE SAYING ABOUT THIS FIRM

- "White shoe Wall Street classic"
- "Über sweatshop"
- "Excellent corporate firm"
- "They work on Christmas"
- "Old place with young partners"

UPPERS

- Reasonable billable hour policy that includes recruiting, mentoring, CLE and pro bono hours
- Growing global public affairs group
- Challenging and stimulating work

DOWNERS

- Grueling hours
- First-year associates have windowless offices
- Shaky partnership track

EMPLOYMENT CONTACT

Ms. Monica R. Brenner
Manager of Legal Recruitment
Phone: (212) 504-6044
Fax: (212) 504-6666
monica.brenner@cwt.com

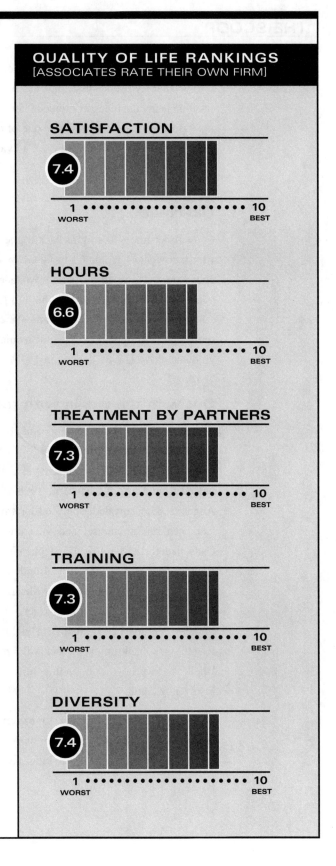

QUALITY OF LIFE RANKINGS
[ASSOCIATES RATE THEIR OWN FIRM]

SATISFACTION
7.4
1 WORST   10 BEST

HOURS
6.6
1 WORST   10 BEST

TREATMENT BY PARTNERS
7.3
1 WORST   10 BEST

TRAINING
7.3
1 WORST   10 BEST

DIVERSITY
7.4
1 WORST   10 BEST

THE SCOOP

With a name reminiscent of a cast of characters out of a Dickens novel, it's not hard to believe Cadwalader, Wickersham & Taft has been around for a while. Founded in 1792, the firm prides itself on being the oldest continuous law practice in the country. Though it's been around the block, it's hardly stodgy. In fact, it was one of the first Wall Street firms to institute a year-round casual dress code. At 475 attorneys, Cadwalader is the largest it has ever been, with plans for continued growth.

Old-timer

Cadwalader traces its origins back to the 18th century. John Wells in New York City founded the firm that would become Cadwalader, Wickersham & Taft in 1792. The firm thrived, adding the eponymous Cadwalader (John Cadwalader, a former Assistant Secretary of State) in 1878. A few years later, Cadwalader entered the '80s (the 1880s, that is) with technological innovations like the telephone and the typewriter. Cadwalader took on its current name in 1914. For those keeping score, the firm appointed the first woman partner of a major law firm, Catherine Noyes Lee, a graduate of NYU Law School, in 1941, and hired six more women lawyers during World War II.

Out with the old, in with the new

There have been lots of comings and goings in Cadwalader's London office, which has tripled in size since its doors opened in 1997. (In May 2002, the office relocated to new space affording it the possibility of doubling in size yet again.) Heading the office is Andrew Wilkinson, who was wooed from Clifford Chance in 1998 where he had headed that firm's bankruptcy practice. In August 2001, Cadwalader plucked Jeremy De Melo from Merrill Lynch's London office, where he had been senior counsel and vice president. De Melo is now a capital markets partner at Cadwalader. In March 2002, Stephen Mostyn-Williams joined as head of the firm's International Banking & Finance practice in London. Mostyn-Williams was formerly a partner and head of European Acquisition Finance at Shearman & Sterling, London. In 2000 Cadwalader's London office hired banking litigation partner Michelle Duncan from competitor law firm Weil, Gotshal & Manges. In June 2001, that firm yielded another partner to Cadwalader — Adam C. Rogoff. Rogoff is a bankruptcy partner who represents such clients as Casual Male and discounter Bradlees, somehow also finding time to edit and co-write the Collier International Business Insolvency Guide.

Indeed, 2001 was a banner year for bankruptcy lawyer poaching. (The teetering economy no doubt led to the enhanced desirability of bankruptcy lawyers.) While Cadwalader added Rogoff, it also lost five bankruptcy partners to other law firms that same year.

Gaining ground

Other departments at Cadwalader gained ground in 2001, and the firm increased by more than 60 attorneys over all. The firm's financial restructuring department stands at its largest ever with 44 attorneys. Richard Nevins, formerly based in Cadwalader's New York office, has brought his expertise in complex corporate transactions to the London financial restructuring team. Cadwalader's financial restructuring department represented the Unsecured Creditors Committee of Winstar Communications Inc. in one of the top 10 public filings in 2001. The firm also represented Lodgian Inc. and numerous subsidiaries in their Chapter 11 reorganization, as well as the Official Committee of Unsecured Creditors of Dictaphone Corporation and the Official Committee of Unsecured Creditors of RSL Communications.

In June 2001, the D.C. office, which was created as a "convenience office" in 1963 and converted to a full-service branch in 1967, added former Democratic National Committee chair and chair of the 2004 Democratic National Convention, Joseph J. Andrew, as head of its global public affairs group. In a spirit of bipartisanship, Doug Richardson and Paul Hatch, former heads of the Democratic and Republican Governor's Associations, respectively, joined Andrew in Cadwalader's Washington office. James K. Robinson, former Assistant Attorney General in charge of the Criminal Division of the U.S. Department of Justice, also joined the D.C. office in 2002. With the addition of Kenneth A. Freeling to the firm's New York office in April 2001, Cadwalader expanded its practice into the area of intellectual property.

Major money exchanging hands

In June 2001, the 169-year-old Houghton Mifflin, the fourth-largest publisher of educational materials in the United States, was acquired by Vivendi Universal, the second-largest publisher of educational materials in the world. Cadwalader represented Houghton Mifflin in the $2.2 billion deal. Dennis Block, who worked on the deal, joined the firm in 1998 after being courted by many other firms and now chairs the firm's corporate and litigation groups. Tops in M&A deals, he's one of the firm's star attorneys.

Cadwalader played a starring role in what Mergerstat, a leading provider of U.S. and international M&A information, named as one of the top five M&A transactions of the year in its M&A News and Trends for 2001. Cadwalader's corporate team represented Bear Stearns in its capacity as financial advisor to Hughs Electronics Corp. when EchoStar Communications acquired Hughes Electronics from General Motors. Cadwalader also represented GMAC Commercial Mortgage Corp., first in connection with the securitization of a mortgage on the World Trade Center Towers and Buildings Four and Five, and then in connection with insurance litigation against One World Trade Center.

In other acquisition news, Cadwalader advised TeleCorp PCS, a wireless services provider for 14 states and Puerto Rico, when it was acquired by AT&T Wireless Services Inc. in October 2001. The $4.7 billion transaction was all stock.

So long to summer program

Sorry, savvy London law students! Cadwalader announced in October 2001 that it has bid adieu to its popular London summer program, in which U.K.-trained law students spend a month working at the firm, including one week working in the firm's New York office. The program was a sweet deal for U.K. lawyers-to-be, who received gratis flights to the Big Apple, as well as free accommodations and a weekly stipend. In 2000 six lucky law students participated in the program. Despite the popularity of the program, the firm has nixed the New York trip in favor of an enhanced trainee program that consists of four six-month rotations.

Proactive preparation

After the devastation caused by the September 11 terrorist attacks, law firms and other companies realized they needed dependable backup of their work and the ability to access that work from places other than their offices. The ever-proactive Cadwalader is currently moving applications to the Internet to safeguard its files, in the event the unthinkable occurs again. The firm purchased the Web-based versions of Interface Software Inc.'s InterAction contract management and Elite Information System's time and billing software. In case remote access is a problem, Cadwalader IT favors attorneys downloading their InterAction contacts to their Palm Pilots daily. There must be a few former boy scouts among the Cadwalader troops.

GETTING HIRED

Keep your fingers crossed

Cadwalader follows the standard recruitment procedure: recruiting on campus and then inviting the cream of the crop to full-round interviews at the firm's offices. The firm recruits at a number of schools across the country, including NYU, Yale, Penn, Chicago, Northwestern, Harvard, Columbia, Boston College, Boston University, Howard, Berkeley and Fordham.

According to associates, "the interview process is fair but competitive," and candidates should expect to meet with two partners and two associates during the office interview. One corporate associate says the criteria for getting hired is "harder than it used to be." However, according to this same associate, because the firm is "actively trying to expand," getting an offer shouldn't be too difficult for those with the right credentials. An associate in the banking & finance department muses on the subjective nature of the interviews: "Once your foot is in the door, it is 100 percent luck as to whether you are hired. It all depends on whether you hit it off with each of your interviewers. If you want an offer from Cadwalader, I would advise keeping your fingers crossed and hope for the best."

The summer associate program gets a thumbs up from associates, and "if you make it into the summer program, it's pretty hard not to get hired," an attorney reveals. As for lateral candidates, "the ease or difficulty of being hired is simply a function of the market and how great the firm's need is."

OUR SURVEY SAYS

It's all relative

A third-year associate has this to say about the firm culture: "The firm claims to be relaxed and collegial, and some people have social relationships with their colleagues. But overall, this is a rather divisive workplace with a lot of secrets. The young associates are generally good people, but there are very few mid-levels, and there is a definite disconnect with the partnership." A real estate associate concurs: "Your major commitment in life has to be to the firm. They expect you to cancel plans upon little or no notice on a daily basis, even on weekends." Others are more forgiving, saying one's experience at the firm depends on the work one is doing and personal interactions with partners and colleagues. "The firm's culture is overall friendly, but personal interactions and level of formality vary significantly depending on who you are working with." Says an attorney in the capital markets department, "Generally, the people are fairly friendly, and as long as your performance is satisfactory, [Cadwalader] can be a pretty flexible place to work."

"Generally, the atmosphere at the firm is laid back with respect to the interaction between partners and associates and [among] associates. There is a very social atmosphere both in the office and out of the office," says an associate in the Charlotte office. Attorneys in the London office work with "a great group of colleagues" where the environment is "friendly and the lawyers tend to socialize together."

Associates' levels of satisfaction at the firm often differ because of "the nature of the industry as opposed to the specific atmosphere" at Cadwalader. An associate in the banking and finance department elaborates: "Being a corporate lawyer is generally boring work. I do not think it is the fault of the firm." A second-year lawyer in search of more challenging assignments comments: "My job mostly consists of research and writing. When I am given the opportunity to do something beyond that, then I find the job satisfying."

Money, power, respect

For the most part, Cadwalader associates are pretty pleased with their pay — even if some of them don't sound like it. While "no firm pays more," a number of associates note that Cadwalader is no salary leader. "Cadwalader seems to be a firmly committed follower" in the salary wars, states one associate. "We get paid well. In return, the expectations are high, but I don't feel that they are unreasonable," says a Charlotte-based attorney. A corporate associate expresses similar good feelings about the pay at Cadwalader. "I do not work very much, and I get paid a lot."

But you can't please everyone. A New York associate who acknowledges that the Cadwalader compensation "is competitive with the high end of the market," still sighs, "Regardless of the amount, it never seems like enough." A like-minded colleague opines, "I know my firm pays at least the same, if not more, than the other firms, but we deserve more." While most complaints about salaries are of the greed-is-good variety, some associates seem genuinely upset about how the firm handled bonuses in 2001. "The bonuses left us disappointed," says a litigation associate. "They try to act like they match market, but they really don't. They looked for reasons to not give people full bonuses this year," confides a third-year. The firm, however, notes that it paid bonuses to the vast majority of its associates in 2001. "Many associates billed high hours last year, partially based on promises of an additional bonus. The failure to pay that bonus created much resentment among the higher billing associates," a New York associate grumbles. Despite such grumbling, the firm points out that its associates enjoy top-of-the market compensation across all offices.

Time waits for some

The number of hours attorneys work is said to run "hot and cold. Some months you can bill 300 hours, and some you may bill only 140." As one capital markets attorney notes, "Sometimes I leave at 6 p.m. for a week, sometimes I work 15-hour days." Some associates report that their work hours have eased due to the slowing economy. While working fewer hours provides more time to spend those fat paychecks, it also makes some associates "just a bit nervous due to the lack of corporate work."

Others seem to be working just as much as ever. "This job might be satisfying in smaller doses, but 60 hours a week is too much," says a banking associate. A real estate associate expresses similar frustration over hours. "I'm not afraid of hard work or long hours, but hardly having a day off in 10 weeks, including Saturday or Sunday, during the summer is a bit much." While the hours tend to be long, associates say there's no "Big Brother is watching" mentality that keeps them in the office beyond the time they need to complete their work.

Pro bono limbo

As a group, associates say the firm is above average in its commitment to pro bono work. New pro bono matters are circulated to attorneys via weekly e-mails, and attorneys may view lists of all available pro bono assignments. However, a number of individual associates complain that there are fewer opportunities to participate in pro bono cases than they would like. "The firm does provide the pro bono opportunities, and such work does count toward hour totals, but the actual commitment to cases at the partnership level is somewhat lacking." A fifth-year associate reveals, "I have never done any pro bono work. The paying clients' work comes first, and there is too much of it." Remarks one Cadwaladerite, "They are trying to push pro bono work, but I have no idea who is doing it."

On the other end of the spectrum, a litigation associate praises that department's ability to coordinate pro bono activities. "We are always given updates on pro bono projects, and it is mandatory for each associate in our department to take on a pro bono project within the first two years of admittance to the bar." Improvements are being made to increase pro bono opportunities, associates say. Cadwalader has taken an active role in helping those who were affected by the September 11 tragedy. The firm is a founding member of the not-for-profit organization "Wall Street Rising" and has committed substantial funds and volunteer assistance to help restore, rebuild and revive downtown Manhattan. In addition, Cadwalader attorneys compiled the Handbook of Public and Private Assistance Resources for the Victims and Families of the World Trade Center Attacks. Several associates report being impressed with the firm's quick response following the September 11 crisis.

Trial by fire

While the formal training may not be all that associates hope for, they admit they are gaining invaluable skills on the job. The "steep learning curve" sometimes feels like "trial by fire." But associates say "the firm encourages people to attend conferences and seminars" to keep up with new developments in various practice areas. A few associates note a laissez-faire attitude toward training. "My partner tells me he will not train me," a New York attorney shares. "Either I read it on my own time, learn it by myself, or else I drown." More commonly, Cadwalader associates say that, while the training program is relatively good for first-year associates, the frequency of the formal training diminishes thereafter. "First-year introductory training is extensive and mostly useful. Later training is less frequent but well-thought-out," a first year reports.

Strides are being taken by management to improve training across the firm. "We have been poor at keeping to a regular training program. A full-time training organizer has recently been recruited, so this may well change," says an associate in the London office. Another new training initiative is the First-Year Fundamentals program for all newly hired attorneys, which kicks off with a comprehensive one-week orientation program in September and continues through the first year of practice. This program covers "substantive areas of law to give associates the background necessary to work in their respective departments." The firm also offers an extensive number of CLE trainings and in-house seminars. "They are actively trying to improve the training programs for junior associates, though it's too late for me," sighs a fifth-year associate. The firm notes that it has plans to expand the First-Year Fundamentals with a Business Skills Curriculum geared towards all associates, including mid-level and senior associates.

Hot and cold

Most Cadwalader associates had kind words for partners — though some note that when push comes to shove, some partners push associates. An associate in the real estate practice encapsulates this assessment. "Socially, the partners are great, but they have a sweatshop mentality" that some associates may view as overly demanding. A corporate attorney elaborates on the sweatshop culture: "Partners generally treat associates with respect, but when deadlines approach and clients put pressure on partners, partners do not treat associates as well as they normally do."

A litigation associate reports an entirely different experience with the partnership. "The partners are eager to teach new skills and provide feedback on a task-by-task basis. Although they expect a lot in terms of hours and quality of work, the partners are easily approached and generally conscious of the workload and stress levels of the associates." A different litigation associate has witnessed many "informal, and often downright friendly relationships" between partners and associates. Likewise, a health care associate finds the partners "very respectful and kind. They take the time to train me and provide feedback on daily basis."

"Your major commitment
in life has to be to the firm.
They expect you to cancel
plans upon little or no notice
on a daily basis, even
on weekends."

— *Cadwalader associate*

Orrick, Herrington & Sutcliffe LLP

Old Federal Reserve Bank Building
400 Sansome Street
San Francisco, CA 94111-3143
Phone: (415) 392-1122

666 Fifth Avenue
New York, NY 10103-0001
Phone: (212) 506-5000
www.orrick.com

LOCATIONS

Los Angeles, CA • Menlo Park, CA • New York, NY •
Sacramento, CA • San Francisco, CA • Seattle, WA •
Washington, DC • London • Singapore • Tokyo

MAJOR DEPARTMENTS/PRACTICES

Advocacy • Compensation & Benefits • Corporate •
Corporate & Technology • Employment Law • Global
Energy, Communications & Infrastructure • Intellectual
Property • Litigation • Market Regulation Finance •
Mergers & Acquisitions • Private Finance • Public
Finance • Real Estate • Structured Finance • Tax

THE STATS

No. of attorneys: 575
No. of offices: 10
Summer associate offers: 48 out of 56 (2001)
Chairman: Ralph H. Baxter Jr.
Hiring Attorneys: William W. Oxley (Los Angeles); Peter
A. Bicks (New York); Thomas J. Welsh (Sacramento);
Stephen M. Graham (Seattle); Dolph M. Hellman (San
Francisco); Melissa A. Finocchio (Silicon Valley); Kyle
W. Drefke (Washington, DC)

BASE SALARY

San Francisco, 2002
1st year: $125,000
2nd year: $135,000
3rd year: $150,000
4th year: $165,000
5th year: $185,000
6th year: $195,000
7th year: $205,000
8th year: $215,000
Summer associate: $10,400/month

NOTABLE PERKS

• Free breakfast and lunch (aka "The Trough")
• Concierge service
• Monthly cocktail parties
• On-site bar called "Whiskeytown" (Menlo Park)

THE BUZZ
WHAT ATTORNEYS AT OTHER FIRMS ARE SAYING ABOUT THIS FIRM

• "Very respected bond firm"
• "Good lawyers"
• "Still chugging along"
• "Stuffy for a West Coast firm"
• "Balkanized"

UPPERS

- Face time not required
- All associates get own office
- Supportive and reasonable partners

DOWNERS

- Shabby office furniture
- Emphasis on billable hours
- "Increasing administration headaches" with increasing size

EMPLOYMENT CONTACT

San Francisco
Ms. Karen E. Massa
Recruiting Administrator
Phone: (415) 773-5588
Fax: (415) 773-5759
kmassa@orrick.com

New York
Ms. Carrie Marker
Recruiting Administrator
Phone: (212) 506-5000
Fax: (212) 506-5151
cmarker@orrick.com
(See www.orrick.com for other employment contacts)

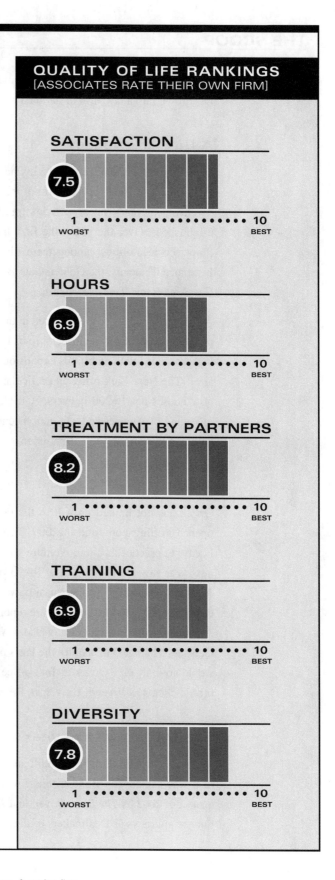

QUALITY OF LIFE RANKINGS
[ASSOCIATES RATE THEIR OWN FIRM]

SATISFACTION
7.5
1 WORST — 10 BEST

HOURS
6.9
1 WORST — 10 BEST

TREATMENT BY PARTNERS
8.2
1 WORST — 10 BEST

TRAINING
6.9
1 WORST — 10 BEST

DIVERSITY
7.8
1 WORST — 10 BEST

THE SCOOP

A recognized leader in the world of finance, San Francisco-based Orrick, Herrington & Sutcliffe has grown into a law firm of national repute, with offices on both coasts, as well as overseas.

A Bay Area legacy

Orrick's roots stretch back to 1863, when the German Savings and Loan Society (later part of the First Interstate Bank of California) was organized, with John R. Jarboe as its general counsel. Twenty-two years later, Orrick's predecessor firm, Jarboe, Harrison & Goodfellow, was established. Over the years, the firm has had a hand in the establishment of several other San Francisco institutions: among them, the Pacific Gas & Electric Company, the Fireman Fund's Insurance Company, the Golden Gate Bridge, Candlestick Park (now 3Com Park) and BART (the Bay Area Rapid Transit System).

Although the firm's profits suffered in the 1980s as a result of changes in bond tax law, Orrick soon recovered and, under the leadership of Ralph Baxter who took over the firm as chairman in 1990, has proceeded with ambitious expansion goals. During the 1990s, the firm more than doubled in size. The New York office in particular has mushroomed; opened in 1984 with six attorneys, it now houses nearly 200 lawyers. Orrick has expanded operations within California, opening an office in Los Angeles and a litigation center in Menlo Park. The Los Angeles office, which started with just two attorneys in 1985, is now home to more than 45 lawyers.

Ahoy!

Orrick has not limited growth to the domestic front. In 1995 Orrick's first overseas base was opened in Singapore; and in 2000 Orrick was one of only two American law firms awarded a license to practice as a joint venture with a Singapore law firm (Orrick HelenYeo Pte. Ltd.). The next year saw the opening of a Tokyo office (which in 1999 formed a joint enterprise with the Japanese bengoshi of Sho Kokusai Law Offices), and in the summer of 1998 a London branch was established. London's *The Lawyer* reported in February 2002 that Orrick beat out several major American firms (including Cadwalader, Wickersham & Taft, Simpson Thacher & Bartlett and Weil Gotshal & Manges) to acquire the Paris office of London's Watson Farley & Williams. The move would not only give Orrick its first office in Continental Europe but also furnish it with such high-profile clients as Vivendi Universal, Renault, France Telecom and BNP Paribas.

Finance firm of the year

Since its inception, Orrick has built an outstanding reputation in the realm of public finance. The firm was named Top Bond Counsel and Top Underwriters counsel for 2000, 2001 and the first quarter of 2002 by *The Bond Buyer*, and *The American Lawyer* has repeatedly named Orrick public finance attorneys as Dealmakers of the Year. Department head Roger Davis was honored in 1999, partner Tom Myers the following year, and partner Eileen Heitzler in 2002. Orrick's expertise covers a broad range of matters including general obligation bonds, education, redevelopment, public power, waste management, industrial development, pollution control, transportation, health care and housing.

In November 2001, Orrick made headlines when it acted as Note Counsel to complete the largest single municipal finance offering to date, with $5.7 billion in California 2001-02 revenue anticipation notes. Orrick has worked with state and local governments to securitize the future payments they are entitled to under the Master Settlement Agreement with the tobacco manufacturing companies. These governments include Wisconsin, South Carolina and California, as well as the City of New York and a number of counties in both New York and California. Named Structured Finance Law Firm of the Year in 1999 by the *International Financial Law Review*, the firm's impressive list of clients in the area of project finance and structured finance include Credit Suisse First Boston, J.P. Morgan Chase, Merrill Lynch, Goldman Sachs and Bear Stearns.

Bicoastal balance

Orrick's New York office has relationships with some of the city's transportation giants and most beloved cultural institutions, including the Port Authority of New York and New Jersey, all three New York area airports, the Museum of Modern Art, the American Museum of Natural History and Carnegie Hall.

Orrick's California roots show in its involvement with the high-tech world. Orrick has formed a strategic partnership with the Venture Law Group, a boutique technology firm in Silicon Valley. In July 2001, Orrick helped San Jose company PDF Solutions Inc. open on the Nasdaq with a $54 million initial public offering. Orrick names AOL Time Warner and New Jersey-based Lucent Technologies among its clients. From its young Seattle office, Orrick has already completed the largest public offering for an issuer based in the state of Washington and the largest biotechnology stock offering to date.

The firm takes technology in its offices seriously, too. This year, Orrick, with the goal of simplifying attorneys' computer desktops, introduced an ambitious Intranet portal. In the summer of 2001, the firm launched a video game on the recruitment pages of its web site.

Wins, losses and a couple of stings

Although Orrick experienced a few notable losses in the courtroom in 2001, the firm's litigators also enjoyed satisfying wins. In June 2001, Orrick client MP3.com suffered a disappointment when Judge Jed Rakoff of the Southern District of New York ordered a new trial on damages for copyright infringement by MP3.com after jurors informed the judge that they had intended to award the plaintiffs some $2.6 million more than the verdict originally announced. In an employment discrimination ruling issued in November, the Second Circuit Court of Appeals ruled against Orrick's client Adchem Corp. to find that compensatory damages are not a prerequisite to an award of punitive damages.

The firm ended the year on a more positive note, winning a First Amendment victory for the *Tahoe Daily Tribune* and a $775,000 jury verdict for clients Varian Medical Systems Inc. and Varian Semiconductor Equipment Associates in an Internet libel case. In March Orrick client CalWest Industrial Properties acquired Boston's Cabot Industrial Trust, in a $2.1 billion transaction that was named The Best Industrial Real Estate Deal of the Year by *The San Francisco Times*.

While vacationing in Paris last fall, corporate partner and managing director Mark Levie helped the French police catch an international hotel thief. Perhaps this small success helped console the firm for the crime committed against it by one of its temp paralegals. In October former Orrick paralegal Said Farraj pleaded guilty to stealing a tobacco plaintiff's litigation plan from the firm's computer system and attempting to sell it for $2 million. Unhappily for Farraj, the would-be buyer of the plan was an undercover officer, and Farraj was promptly arrested.

Orrick has been doing a lot more than just fighting crime. The firm won a landmark 2001 case in the U.S. Supreme Court resolving a critical issue of administrative law on behalf of an international leader in packaging and paper products. Orrick also defended successfully a major pharmaceutical firm in two trials and two appeals in one of the leading Delaware corporate disclosure cases.

Cost-cutting and staff-shifting

Like many firms, Orrick has taken some steps to cut costs in the last year. In January 2002, the firm closed its on-site childcare facility at the San Francisco office. (It now offers back-up care, with 20 days free-of-charge.) A few months earlier, the firm took the unusual step of moving a portion of its financial and technological support staff from its 10 offices to a global operations center in Wheeling, W. Va. *The Recorder* reported that the move would save the firm $1 million a year. While some consultants tout the move as the wave of the future, critics called it a de facto layoff and expressed concern over the quality of the new staff.

Though often controversial, cost cutting can have its upside. In February 2002, the firm announced that associates would get a lock step salary increase retroactive to January 1. "We feel associates and of counsel helped us pull through difficult times," Thomas Coleman, chair of Orrick's professional development committee, told *The Recorder*, "and we want to treat them accordingly."

Musical chairs

In the last year, Orrick lost a couple of top litigators when Terrence McMahon, who chaired Orrick's intellectual property practice group, defected to McDermott, Will & Emery and Barbara Caulfield, one of the Bay Area's most renowned litigators, moved in-house to the Santa Clara biotech company and Orrick client Affymetrix Inc. But Orrick has also brought in some potent new blood. Two attorneys from Howrey Simon Arnold & White, including leading copyright attorney William Coats and partner Vickie Feeman, joined Orrick last summer. And the firm managed to snag tax guru Peter Connors from Baker & McKenzie's New York office.

GETTING HIRED

Bring something to the table

What does it take to get hired at Orrick? The firm's looking for team players, say insiders. "We are clearly looking for the associate who is intelligent and hardworking, but also interested in quality of life and able to bring more to the table than just billable hours — i.e., a personality," ventures one associate. Candidates should "try to be friendly and normal, not a super geek, even if you are." One insider claims that there exists a "sliding scale" of hires. "The less prestigious your school, the better your grades need to be. For laterals, the grade thing is not as rigorous if you have the right experience." Still, while Orrick "elevated standards" in the buyer's market recruiting year of 2001, insiders say you've got a great shot if "you come from a top 10-15 school, your grades are respectable and you present reasonably well."

To suss out great personalities, says one recent hire, Orrick asks slightly non-traditional questions. "They didn't ask me questions relating to law school or my legal work experiences," says a first-year associate. They asked "questions about past non law-related jobs. I would say the questions seemed more designed to get to know me as a person, rather than just asking me to reiterate my resume in conversation."

A generally fun summer

If you're looking at Orrick's summer program, associates call it "relaxed, not too intimidating and generally fun." Dinners at homes of partners seem to be a staple of the Orrick summer, along with other amusing events such as "kayaking and The Donkey Show [a musical set to 1970s disco tunes]." One D.C. associate says, "The office tends not to schedule a summer function every single week because it believes that keeps the summer associate from enjoying his summer, but at the same time, by the end of the summer, the summer associate should have a good feeling of the office, the people and their work."

OUR SURVEY SAYS

In search of the hour

While Orrick associates enjoy relatively moderate hours, many associates describe unwritten billable-hours guidelines, which have left many associates vexed and perplexed. "Although the stated minimum is 1,950," confides one associate, "2,100 is the unwritten minimum acceptable, and they like more. The people who have made partner on the first round have billed 2,400-plus, year-in year-out." The reason for the hourly obsession? Hours are "by far the most significant factor considered in the assessment of lawyers, both with respect to short-term issues like compensation and bonuses, and longer-term ones like advancement and partnership prospects." Another associate confesses to vague unease about hours. "Although I maintain a satisfactory balance of work hours with life outside the office, I am consistently just below the firm's nominal minimum. This shortcoming is mentioned extremely rarely in reviews and informal feedback, however, resulting in uncomfortable uncertainty."

Most Orrickers describe relatively moderate workweeks. "I have only come in on a weekend two or three times in the last two and a half years," crows one insider. "As long as you get your job done, there is no need to stick around into the late evening." In the San Francisco headquarters, "almost everyone is out by 7 p.m." Orrick peers are flexible as well, say associates. "Hours are long, but they tend to balance out. If you work a lot one week, you'll end up working less the next. People try to work around your schedule if you have an event planned, like a weekend away or theater tickets."

Pleasant and indulgent partners

Orrick partners seem to be pleasant to a fault. One corporate associate "frequently" has "drinks, lunch or other interaction with" several partners. The partners at Orrick's New York office are said to be "quite young," with associates enjoying an "exceptional" working relationship. Says another associate, "If you're mature, bright and competent, you're well respected, and good relationships generally prevail. Indeed, a few associates who don't fit the bill are indulged too long." But while partners are inevitably "good lawyers," one insider contends that partners "could improve team work by involving associates in projects to a greater degree." That associate does allow that "some of the partners are great at communicating to associates."

Litigators in luck (for training)

Training at Orrick, according to survey respondents, varies from department to department. Litigators love their training, for the most part. "The advocacy training course is superb. You get the nuts and bolts needed for litigating but also the thoughts of experienced practitioners," burbles one junior associate. Raves another insider, "Training for new and mid-level litigation associates is also pretty good, including an intensive NITA trial advocacy training experience. Many senior associates spend time in one of the local DA's offices for a three-month stint trying misdemeanor cases."

Associates in other departments, however, say that most of their training is the good ol' "on the job" variety. One labor associate remarks that, while training is provided from time to time, "the most valuable training I receive is informal responses from our IT people and other support staff when I have a specific question, as opposed to formal, scheduled training, which is generally not very effective." A corporate associate shrugs, "My practice area does not provide much training."

Staying put at Orrick

Orrick associates enjoy working at the firm, for the most part, and they're certainly sticking around. "Associate attrition is very modest. Those who leave do so for reasons unrelated to Orrick," says an associate. A Californian is especially happy that Orrick hasn't undergone any "layoffs, stealth or otherwise, or 'performance-based terminations.'" Not everyone sees a clump of immovable Orrickers. Retention, contends an insider, is "no better or worse than other big firms; a small core from each class tends to be in it for the long term, and others trickle away within the first three to four years."

Unexceptional pay — and that's good

Orrick's compensation is unexceptional — which is to say that it's on par with most major law firms. One New Yorker says that the "pay structure is competitive with nearly all New York firms," while a Sacramento associate raves that Orrick offers "the best salary in Sacramento." But the Orrick compensation scheme is not without its eccentricities. Bonuses, for instance, are "linked entirely to hours." And the firm pays associates with other related degrees, such as an MBA, at a rate one year above their actual level. Some associates with long memories still complain about the fact that Orrick gave no boom-year bonuses back when economic times were flush. "It was a source of much tension," remembers one insider. On the whole, summarizes a mid-level, "the pleasant work environment makes up for any shortfall" in the compensation system.

Mixed report on offices

Orrick offices are by no means uniform, and opinions on office space vary considerably by location. In the San Francisco headquarters, the building itself, the "landmark Old Federal Reserve building," is much-admired. It's "a great building," one San Franciscan comments warmly. "Although there are no views" out of the building, "the individual associate offices are very large. On the other hand, the furniture is really crappy."

The scourge of crappy furniture plagues other offices as well. Silicon Valley associates especially lament the state of office furnishings. As in San Francisco, "the office space is amazing, with large offices, high ceilings and huge windows." On the other hand, the "office furniture is old and mismatched." One insider claims that the furnishings "haven't been replaced in a decade and show more wear and tear with each passing year." Bellows one Silicon Valley associate, "Time to move or refurnish!"

Orrick's New York associates seem to have come out ahead. The "interior is modern, bright, spacious and conducive to a comfortable atmosphere." The office is "located in a great spot" and all associates enjoy Aeron chairs, the *ne plus ultra* of back comfort. Any drawbacks? The "cigar club on the top floor is stinky."

The old college try

Orrick, like most top firms, is making a game effort to increase diversity amongst its ranks, with a mixed record of success. "Orrick tries harder than most firms," comments one contact, "but truthfully, we're pretty much white bread around here." A new associate confirms Orrick efforts, saying, "I am on the diversity committee, and the firm tries hard to recruit minorities of all kinds." A senior-level minority associate discusses the situation of minorities at Orrick: "I don't think being a minority will hold anyone back from making partner in this firm — it's about talent, ambition and making relationships." That associate continues, "For those minorities who believe that hiring in corporate America is systemically biased against them, you probably won't find this place is any different. For those who don't subscribe to that school of thought, you'll have no problems with the hiring here." And while "formal mentoring for all new associates is required," associates of color shouldn't "expect a minority mentor — there aren't enough minority partners to go around."

On the woman front, Orrick has made strides in recent years. "As of a couple of years ago, you could count the number of women partners on two hands and maybe a foot. The number has probably doubled since then," says an associate. Women "take an active role in the management of the firm." Entering classes boast a majority of women. "We still seem to have mostly male partners, but with more than 50 percent female associates, the next few years will be interesting to watch," says another contact. A mid-level female associate comments, "My summer class was almost entirely female. We had a women summer associate/women partner dinner at which we discussed issues relating to women at Orrick." One associate points out that the bulk of women partners at Orrick are in the litigation department, particularly in New York. The firm ntoes that in January, Orrick, for the second time since its inception, named a woman to its Executive Committee.

Orrick is welcoming to gays and lesbians, say insiders. "I'm openly gay," says one associate, " and have never encountered any negative comments or attitudes." In addition, "the firm sponsors GLBT events."

Good intentions on pro bono

Orrick seems not to mind pro bono, though it is apparently concentrated in the realm of the litigators. In New York, one litigation associate raves, "We have a great associate who is in charge of the firm's pro bono assignments. He's extremely committed and has won awards for his public service." Another litigator tells Vault, "I have had lots of opportunity to do pro bono [work] and have never been asked to scale back." Associates in other departments and offices say that the pro bono program is "a bit disorganized," but "to the extent anyone has time to find and bring in a pro bono project, the firm is supportive of such projects and we do get billable credit for our work on approved pro bono work."

Paul, Hastings, Janofsky & Walker LLP

515 South Flower Street, 25th Floor
Los Angeles, CA 90071-2228
Phone: (213) 683-6000
Fax: (213) 627-0705
www.paulhastings.com

LOCATIONS

Los Angeles, CA (HQ)
Atlanta, GA
Costa Mesa, CA
New York, NY
Orange County, CA
San Francisco, CA
Stamford, CT
Washington, DC
Beijing
London
Tokyo

MAJOR DEPARTMENTS/PRACTICES

Corporate
Employment
Litigation
Real Estate
Tax

THE STATS

No. of attorneys: 830+
No. of offices: 11
Summer associate offers: 80 out of 94 (2001)
Chair: Seth M. Zachary
Hiring Partner: Mary C. Dollarhide

BASE SALARY

All California offices, New York and DC, 2002
1st year: $125,000

Stamford, 2002
1st year: $112,500

Atlanta, 2002
1st year: $100,000

Summer associate: $1,750 - $2,400/week

NOTABLE PERKS

• Health club subsidy
• Blackberry pagers
• Reduced prices for theater and sports events
• Breakfast on Friday
• Backup child care

THE BUZZ
WHAT ATTORNEYS AT OTHER FIRMS ARE SAYING ABOUT THIS FIRM

• "Does anyone make partner here?"
• "Sweatshop"
• "The best in labor"
• "Anti-associate"
• "Bicoastal presence"

UPPERS

- Prestigious labor and employment practice
- No face-time requirement
- Corporate practice gaining in stature

DOWNERS

- Bonuses "way below market"
- Diversity needs improvement
- "Pro bono work is not encouraged at the firm"

EMPLOYMENT CONTACT

Ms. Joy McCarthy
Director of Attorney Recruiting Administration
Phone: (213) 683-6000
www.paulhastings.com

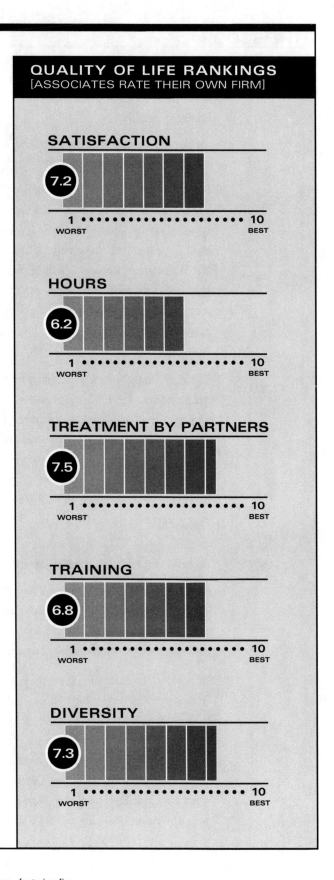

QUALITY OF LIFE RANKINGS
[ASSOCIATES RATE THEIR OWN FIRM]

SATISFACTION
7.2
1 WORST ·············· 10 BEST

HOURS
6.2
1 WORST ·············· 10 BEST

TREATMENT BY PARTNERS
7.5
1 WORST ·············· 10 BEST

TRAINING
6.8
1 WORST ·············· 10 BEST

DIVERSITY
7.3
1 WORST ·············· 10 BEST

THE SCOOP

In the past decade, Paul, Hastings, Janofsky & Walker's corporate practice has grown in repute. Known for its labor and employment practice, the reputation of this Los Angeles-based firm is climbing steadily.

History: staying west

Paul Hastings & Edmonds was founded in LA in 1946 by three friends, Robert Hastings, Lee Paul and Warner Edmonds. Four years later, Edmonds left to found his own firm. The year after that, Leonard Janofsky joined Paul and Hastings in their firm, and in 1962, partner Charles Walker came aboard, giving the firm its current name. Janofsky, who later served as president of the American Bar Association, initially led the firm's well-known employment department. In the 1970s, the firm began working with Japanese clients, helping them set up U.S. operations, distribution and joint ventures. A decade later, Paul Hastings opened its Tokyo office. The 1980s saw the firm branching out in its own borders, heading east to Atlanta, Washington, D.C., Stamford, Conn. and New York City.

The early 1990s brought some inner turmoil to Los Angeles-based firms, and Paul Hastings was no exception. In May 1993, the managing partner Robert DeWitt left his post because he was unhappy with the firm's management structure. Three other key partners followed suit, including litigation head William Campbell. After working through this tough time, the firm continued to grow. In June 2000, the firm combined with the New York real estate firm Battle Fowler, gaining 120 attorneys and boosting its East Coast presence. In January 2002, Lawrence Gornick jumped the Brobeck ship to set sail with Paul Hastings. He had worked in the complex litigation department of Brobeck, Phleger & Harrison for 13 years before leaving for Paul Hastings's San Francisco office.

A tower to call their own

In December 2001, Paul Hastings bought more space in their downtown Los Angeles office located in the widely-known ARCO Plaza. The "ARCO" sign on the building has been replaced, and the the 52-story building is now called the "Paul Hastings Tower." The Tower will be the only such building in the entire country to be named after a law firm.

To develop its international practice, the firm snatched partner Thomas Shoesmith from Cooley Godward in September 2001. Shoesmith had coordinated Cooley's international practice group. A former Baker & McKenzie partner, Shoesmith headed that firm's Southern California international and Latin American practice groups. Paul Hastings is also making an appearance on the New York stage. It is one of the many firms working on the scheduled 2003 opening of the AOL-Time Warner Center. When completed, the Center will house the headquarters and studios for AOL-Time Warner, a music hall, retail shops and restaurants, residential apartments and a hotel. Paul Hastings is assisting with financing and tax issues for the developer of the project, The Related Companies, a subsidiary of Columbus Centre Developer LLC. The Related Companies is developing the site with Apollo Real Estate Advisors.

Paul Hastings seals the bond

In September 2001, ValuBond Inc., a discount bond trading platform, acquired Bond Express, the largest online fixed income database. ValuBond is what is known as an alternate trading system (ATS), which is similar to a small stock exchange. Unique rules apply to changes in ATS corporate structure. No one knows that better than attorneys at Paul Hastings, who represented ValuBond in the deal. This isn't the first time Paul Hastings came to ValuBond's rescue. In March 2001, the firm arranged $15 million in Series B financing for the startup.

Olympic gold and a hole in one

Paul Hastings played a small role in the 2002 Winter Olympic Games. Partner Judith Richards Hope of the D.C. office is a board member of the Union Pacific Corp., a sponsor of the Olympics. As such, Hope was chosen to carry the Olympic torch on part of its pre-Salt Lake City Winter Olympics cross-country journey. Her jog took place on December 21, 2001. The firm was also one of the sponsors for the 9th Annual Crean Classic Golf Tournament in 2001. The proceeds of the golf tournament, which raised $90,000, benefited the Alzheimer's Association of Orange County, Calif.

Video interviewing

Forget the firm interview. No more sweaty palms. No more anxiety, anticipating what the interviewer will ask. According to an August 2001 report in the *New York Law Journal*, a new method of interviewing has been instituted by some New York area law firms. Students are asked a series of questions, and their responses are recorded on video, which is then sent to the interviewing firm along with a separate online application describing the student in more detail. Paul Hastings and a handful of New York firms are using this method for initial campus interviews. But don't stop practicing your firm handshake just yet. Successful candidates identified through the video interview process are then invited to the firm for face-to-face call back interviews.

A troll of a copyright

In December 2001, Dam Things from Denmark moved for a preliminary injunction against Russ Berrie & Company for infringing its copyright on troll dolls. The copyright of the troll dolls, which have delighted young and old alike for decades with their wild hair and cherubic faces, fell into the public domain in the early 1960s because Dam Things failed to comply with copyright regulations at the time. Instead of the copyright notice, the word "Denmark" was printed on the foot of some of the dolls. In 1996, pursuant to the Uruguay Round Agreements Act, Congress enacted 17 U.S.C. § 104A, which restores these copyrights lost to the U.S. public domain because of failure to comply with a formality. Robert L. Sherman and Romy Berk of Paul Hastings are representing Dam Things in the complex intellectual property case.

GETTING HIRED

All's fair in interviews

According to associates, the hiring process at Paul Hastings is "pretty typical." A New Yorker notes, "This firm is less obsessed than many big firms about where you went to law school. If you did extremely well at a mid-tiered school, it seems like you have a good chance here. Other places would rather have a mediocre Ivy Leaguer." In LA, "You also need to demonstrate that you are a personable and social individual who meshes with the firm culture in order to get hired." The interview process varies somewhat. In the small Connecticut office, an associate explains that she "interviewed once with everyone in the department," a process that took two days. Another associate had "three rounds of interviews." An LA associate adds, "I had a screening interview with the co-chairs of the corporate department, a second round with six attorneys in the corporate department and an offer the next day. The entire process from beginning to end was accomplished in one week."

Good summer mix

Associates at Paul Hastings agree that overall the summer program is a good fusion of fun and work that at least resembles real lawyering. An associate in the Connecticut office says, "While there were several social events, I also received real work, similar to the work I do currently." An LA associate gives percentages: "It's about 65 percent social, 35 percent work." Another LA associate explains, "The social activities were all good, but the best part was that I got to try every area of law that I was interested in. I also was able to do a lot of 'spectator' assignments, where I basically just observed meetings, depositions, arguments and mediations. All of that really helped me to figure out what kind of law I wanted to practice."

OUR SURVEY SAYS

Something's rotten in the state of New York

And it's not an apple. While most Paul Hastings associates are happy with the firm's laid-back culture, those in New York describe an office in the midst of a serious morale crisis.

One New Yorker sighs, "The atmosphere, attitude and general working environment is awful." Another associate from the Big Apple insists, "Institutional communications are abysmal, the result being that there are no clear ... messages given on policies, firm practices and procedures and associates' standing within the firm. This is all most disheartening because the people themselves are generally quite nice." Another New Yorker mentions that the quality of work affords associates a lot of opportunities "to work on a range of transactions from M&A, to securities deals, to corporate finance and so on," but "there seems to be a disconnect between management and the associates and in a recessionary economy, this makes it difficult for associates to truly feel at ease."

In contrast, the Connecticut office is a "close-knit" bunch with a "collegial environment." An associate there says, "We work together as a unit and get to know each other very well. It's a pleasant place to go to work each day — a rarity in today's law firms." The Atlanta office is described as "eclectic" and "professional," yet "relaxed." An associate there notes that there are "some conservative folks, some more outgoing, but there seems to be room for everyone."

Nothing beats the California offices. An LA associate remarks, "The partners and senior associates are extremely approachable, and the work atmosphere is friendly." Another lawyer agrees, "I love working here mainly because of the people. From staff to attorneys, everyone is extremely friendly and genuinely concerned about your comfort level at work. The associates (and sometimes even the partners) frequently hang out together outside the office, after work and on the weekends. There is a special camaraderie here that I believe is rare in large law firms." In San Francisco, the culture allows associates "to do their own thing." A San Franciscan says, "People aren't closely monitoring your movements. People can work extra hours from home rather than having to be in the office." Another notes, "I get to run my own show, with appropriate oversight and guidance from the partners."

Compensation woes

While many associates agree the compensation is "good" and "market," there are some regional complaints and others related to bonuses. In New York, an associate asks, "Since we're basically billing New York City rates, why not bring us fully in line with New York City salaries?" Another Big Apple associate clarifies: "Most associates are not paid market, but those who work market hours (for example, 2,200-2,400 hours) are." In Atlanta, an associate complains, "Atlanta is seriously behind the curve on associate compensation. We work every bit as hard, but our compensation is [less than the compensation of] our colleagues in other offices." The compensation in Stamford is "simply the best in Connecticut."

When it comes to bonuses, most associates agree they are "way below market." One associate sighs, "Most associates received nothing this year." A New Yorker notes, "I was disappointed not to receive any bonus whatsoever despite billing more than 2,000 hours, which requires lots of non-billable work as well." An LA associate says, "The bonuses are all hours-based, so they may not be all that feasible depending on your year and department." Another LA associate adds, "I would like to see more emphasis placed on merit. Right now compensation is tied almost exclusively to hours. There does not seem to be anything in place to reward efficiency."

Long hours

While the hours at Paul Hastings are long, associates at most offices seem OK with how long hours are handled. "The hours are long, it's true. But there is definitely down time. I can go weeks where I leave at a decent hour and don't have to come in on the weekends. There are of course those times when I have to work around the clock," says an LA associate. One associate in the Connecticut office notes, "There is no pressure for face time. If you could bill your time 9 to 5, no one would care." Another Los Angeleno applauds the firm's efforts on making good use of time. He says, "I am able to spend more of my time out of the office because of the advances in technology the firm has introduced." Another insider adds, "Sometimes there are long hours, but because the work is so interesting, it does not feel like a burden."

In New York and Atlanta, satisfaction with hours is quite different. Remarks one New Yorker, "We are expected to be available during all hours. It is assumed that you will be in the office late at night and on weekends. There is little understanding about any personal obligations you may have." An Atlanta associate adds, "Our billable hour requirement and expectation have increased since the salary adjustment several years ago. The requirement is not compatible with having a family and being able to participate in outside activities." As far as part-time work goes, one part-time worker notes, "The firm has been supportive of my career, while allowing me tremendous flexibility to be very involved with my children and their activities."

Right attitude, wrong approach

"People here don't judge based on religion, race or gender. As long as you are intelligent and treat people with respect you will fit in," notes one associate. In all, associates at Paul Hastings agree the firm embraces diversity; however, they say the firm is not proactive in its approach. "The management goes through the motions," says an Asian associate. A New Yorker notes, "Improvement is required as we lack diversity, as can be seen by looking at the numbers." However, one minority associate at the firm mentions, "I am actively involved in recruiting and the firm makes an incredible effort to attract people of color." As for gays and lesbians, the firm has a welcoming approach. A member of the Connecticut office says, "Gay and lesbian members of our office are treated not only with respect but with equal friendship." A gay associate is happy the firm offers domestic partner benefits. A lesbian notes, "There are several openly gay partners, male and female."

Female associates have concerns about promotion and retention as well as family considerations. One woman says, "There are not a whole lot of women partners here, and as a result, not a lot of mentoring of female associates. However, women are not necessarily treated any differently from men, which is both good and bad. On the one hand, women have different needs and concerns, which may not necessarily get acknowledged. However, they are certainly not precluded from any opportunities open to their male colleagues, which is a good thing." An Atlanta associate explains, "It is hard to make partner here, but I don't think it has anything to do with gender. In fact, our local office has recently instituted a women attorney network to address these issues." Some women see the firm as making strides for women attorneys. One associate notices, "Hiring of women seems on par with men, and the firm has part-time options for women and men." An LA associate notes, "In employment, the entire first- and second-year associate classes are female." Adds another lawyer, "I am a woman, I work in a predominantly male department and I don't feel like it is an issue. I am treated like everyone else."

Cahill Gordon & Reindel

80 Pine Street
New York, NY 10005
Phone: (212) 701-3000
www.cahill.com

LOCATIONS

New York, NY (HQ)
Washington, DC
London

MAJOR DEPARTMENTS/PRACTICES

Antitrust
Corporate
Litigation
Real Estate
Securities
Tax
Trusts & Estates

THE STATS

No. of attorneys: 220
No. of offices: 3
Summer associate offers: 49 out of 49 (2001)
Chairman: Immanuel Kohn
Hiring Partner: Roger Meltzer

BASE SALARY

New York, 2002
1st year: $125,000
2nd year: $135,000
3rd year: $150,000
4th year: $170,000
5th year: $190,000
6th year: $210,000
7th year: $220,000
8th year: $230,000
Summer associate: $2,400/week

NOTABLE PERKS

- Cars home after 8 p.m.
- Monthly happy hours
- Cookie trays twice a day
- Generous associate departure parties

THE BUZZ
WHAT ATTORNEYS AT OTHER FIRMS ARE SAYING ABOUT THIS FIRM

- "Corporate sweatshop with premier litigators"
- "High-yield geniuses"
- "All Floyd, all the time"
- "These guys made their last partner, what, 10 years ago?"

UPPERS

- No pressure to put in face time
- Associates can work in multiple departments
- Flexibility to choose with whom you work and what kind of work you do

DOWNERS

- Little formal training
- Assignment system leaves many associates overburdened and others underworked
- "Greed controls all"

EMPLOYMENT CONTACT

Ms. Joyce A. Hilly
Hiring Coordinator
Phone: (212) 701-3901
jhilly@cahill.com

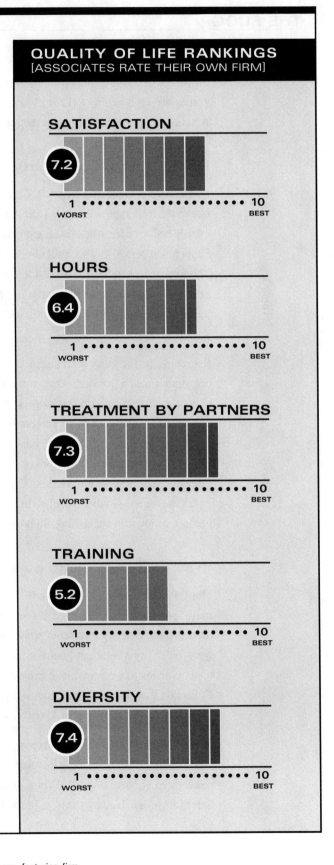

QUALITY OF LIFE RANKINGS
[ASSOCIATES RATE THEIR OWN FIRM]

SATISFACTION
7.2
1 WORST — 10 BEST

HOURS
6.4
1 WORST — 10 BEST

TREATMENT BY PARTNERS
7.3
1 WORST — 10 BEST

TRAINING
5.2
1 WORST — 10 BEST

DIVERSITY
7.4
1 WORST — 10 BEST

THE SCOOP

It's not the size of the dog; it's the size of its bite. Cahill Gordon & Reindel may be the little guy on the block in size (about 220 attorneys in three offices) but not in success. The firm earns noticeably high profits ($1.6 million per partner in 2000) and also attracts notice for its First Amendment practice, headed by the renowned Floyd Abrams.

History: small but mighty

Founded as a small firm in 1919, Cahill Gordon & Reindel is known for its litigation expertise. Under the leadership of former U.S. Attorney John Cahill, the firm grew rapidly. In 1935 the firm established an office in Washington, D.C. When *The New York Times* decided to publish the Pentagon Papers in 1971, Cahill Gordon was tapped as special litigation counsel for the newspaper. The firm had a hand in one of the most significant cases ever decided regarding the authority of the Federal Communications Commission, National Broadcasting Co. v. United States. In addition the firm is highly regarded in antitrust litigation, having played a role in cases like Times Picayune v. United States.

Beginning in the early 1980s, the firm represented many top investment banks, bolstering its corporate finance practice. Due to the erratic state of Wall Street in the late 1980s, the firm lost two of its top clients to bankruptcy, E.F. Hutton and Drexel Burnham Lambert. (The latter accounted for about 25 to 30 percent of firm billings in 1988 and 1989.) As the economy of the 1990s improved, Cahill Gordon's business did too. Many of the most prestigious investment banks in New York rely on Cahill Gordon, including J.P. Morgan Chase, Merrill Lynch, Credit Suisse First Boston, CIBC World Markets Corp., UBS Warburg, Salomon Smith Barney, Deutsche Banc Alex. Brown and Goldman Sachs. In 2000 Cahill moved its European office from Paris to London because its investment banking clients wanted it to have more of a presence in the United Kingdom.

"Too cool for a comb-over"

The Cahill crusader, Floyd Abrams, is known for his high-profile First Amendment cases. In a much publicized 1999 case, Abrams and fellow Cahill lawyer Susan Buckley successfully defended the Brooklyn Museum when the City of New York served it an eviction notice. Former New York City Mayor (and current national hero) Rudolph Giuliani had the notice delivered due to his aversion to a controversial exhibit entitled "Sensation: Young British Artists from the Saatchi Collection." Guiliani's wrath focused primarily on a portrait of the Virgin Mary by artist Chris Ofili called "The Holy Virgin Mary" that is splattered with elephant dung.

In 2000, Abrams unsuccessfully represented CNN in its desire to televise oral arguments before the U.S. Supreme Court regarding the disputed 2000 presidential election. Early the next year, Abrams represented Richard Behar, a *Time* magazine writer, in a libel case brought by the Church of Scientology. In January 2001, a federal appeals court ruled for Behar, finding his story on the church not libelous. In January 2002, Abrams defended *Sports Illustrated* in a libel case involving boxer Randall "Tex" Cobb. Cobb argued that his career had been ruined by an *SI* article that contended Cobb had "fixed" a fight and used cocaine. A federal appeals court found that *Sports Illustrated* had not acted with "actual malice" when it published the article.

Abrams' fame as a lawyer and a New York personality is considerable. Case in point: Abrams recently appeared in a spread for *GQ* entitled "How to Dress Your Job," in which he posed for the camera in his own natty Nautica suit, Brooks Brothers tie and shoes from Allen-Edmonds. In reference to Abrams' bald pate, a caption read "Too cool for a comb-over."

A-OK M&A

In January 2002, Accredo Health Inc., a pharmacy services provider, acquired the specialty pharmacy division of Gentiva Health Services Inc. for $415 million. In June 2001, the firm counseled General Electric Company in the $5 billion sale of its satellite unit to Société Européenne des Satellites S.A., a Luxembourg-based satellite broadcaster with hopes of making it into the U.S. market. The firm has advised GE on tax issues since the early 1990s. Cahill represented the buyer in an August 2001 sale in which Collins & Aikman Corp., a maker of floor and acoustic products for vehicles, bought TAC-Trim, the automobile trim business owned by Textron Auto Company.

Pro bono keeps up step

When it comes to contemporary dance, Cahill gets down. In August 2001, the sole heir of dance great Martha Graham and his assignees sued the Martha Graham Center of Contemporary Dance and the Martha Graham School of Contemporary Dance for trademark infringement. Graham's heir, Ronald Protas, sought to stop the defendants from using the names they were incorporated under since 1948 and to stop them from teaching what they call the "Martha Graham technique." In 1993 Protas applied to register trademarks for "Martha Graham" and "Martha Graham technique." Four of the plaintiffs' claims were dismissed, including the ones for injunction. Other claims were heard at a separate trial. Cahill represented the defendants in the pro bono case.

GETTING HIRED

Selective, not snobby

Insiders describe Cahill's hiring as selective rather than elitist. One alum claims that "if you went to Harvard, you get an offer," but many contacts maintain that the firm "will not overlook a qualified candidate that attends a school outside the top 25." Students from New York schools stand a particularly good chance: "I think they would rather take the top of the class at local New

York schools than middle or bottom at the Ivies." Cahill will also look further afield. A Florida recruit reflects, "Generally, they hire from the Ivies [and] the New York schools. It is a near miracle I got this job."

Although one associate calls the hiring process "a complete crapshoot" and another suggests that "there are some oddballs here — [it] can't be all that hard," most sources agree on the personal qualities essential to a successful applicant. The firm "seeks intelligent, assertive, independent candidates who will be able to produce quality work without a lot of hand-holding." Contacts emphasize motivation and "self-sufficiency" because "the lack of structure demands an eager willingness to seek out work." "Informal" interviews are reportedly "more about personality and whether you would fit in at the firm [than] about grades and what school you go to." Many associates speak highly, and longingly, about the fantastic summer program, but warn that the experience is "nothing like what your life will be like" later on.

OUR SURVEY SAYS

No shrinking violets

Cahill "culture is laid back and friendly." "Live and let live," intones one contact. "Call it an oxymoron, but this could be one of the most laid-back, hard-working places ever." The "informal and unstructured" environment, which includes "lots of 'Type-A' personalities," favors those who value flexibility and a "strong expectation that you'll perform as a non-whining grown up." Cahill "is not a good firm for a shrinking violet," notes one lawyer, "or a person who wants to just sit back and have work assigned to them." Qualities that some associates love — focus on function over appearance, "a lot of autonomy" and an "extraordinary amount of responsibility" — are the same factors that frustrate others, who decry the "shabby" offices, "sink-or-swim environment" and a "free market" assignment system that causes "glaring inequities in the distribution of work."

The firm is "very sociable," associates report. "Most people seem to like each other" and "lawyers go out for drinks together frequently." Cahill also hosts monthly happy hours "which are all well attended."

A Darwinian experiment

Cahill cares about "performance," not "personal idiosyncrasies." "You could pretty much come in with your hair on fire and no one would say anything to you as long as you did your work," claims one insider. The disdain for hand-holding thrills some lawyers; one associate believes the atmosphere "fosters the development of good judgment and sound skills. It is amazing how much being treated like a lawyer has to do with developing as a lawyer." "The work is interesting," writes another, "the people are smart, the pay is great and the hours aren't too bad. What more could an associate ask for?"

Quite a bit, it seems. "Laid back is all relative," one attorney dryly remarks. "When you're here at 4 a.m. on a Sunday, it's little comfort that you can call a partner by his first name." No home for the meek, many junior associates find it "intimidating to have to call around to partners that you don't know, asking for work." With its "lack of centralized management" and "do-it-yourself" assignment system, Cahill is "like a Darwinian experiment." Partners' "minimal communication with the associates" comes in for criticism, as does the absence of formal training.

Sink or swim, baby

According to one associate, "the training at Cahill, like everything else, is informal and unstructured. Training is on the job." Some associates thrive on the "real world exposure," while others express frustration with the "trial by fire" method. "We are often thrown into shark-infested waters without a visible means of rescue," says an insider. Life preservers are within reach, rejoins a lawyer. "No one is going to hold your hand but they'll field any questions if you ask them." Cahill also offers regular in-house CLE programs. One attorney advises, "For those who can thrive in this environment, the training and experience is excellent. For those who need more formal, classroom-type training, the training is inadequate."

Insiders find most partners "respectful" and "friendly." Several suggest that the assignment system forces partners "to be nice to associates or nobody would ever work for them." One common criticism is that "the firm as an institution does not communicate well with associates," a concern exacerbated by the recent firing of two first-year associates without explanation.

Top dollar

Cahill associsates are more than happy with their compensation package. "The only better place for money is probably Wachtell," sources say. Salaries are "comparable to other top firms in New York without being tied to billable hours." "Cahill will pay what other top firms pay — they won't like it, but they will pay it." This follow-the-leader approach has its detractors. Despite partners' pronouncement that "Cahill had its best year ever, while most other firms had reduced profits," last year's "bonuses were in keeping with what other law firms did … not in keeping with how Cahill overall performed in 2001." One disappointed lawyer grumbles, "It sucked to get a pay cut just because other firms cut bonuses." "We get paid a lot and can't really complain," most associates believe, but "what we don't get at Cahill are some of the smaller perks, like a technology stipend. We also don't have any dental insurance."

Feast or famine

Not surprisingly, Cahillites work long hours. "The hours are about what you would expect from a big New York City law firm," although some lament the "inconsistency." "My big complaint is that it is absolute feast or famine from month to month." Associates appreciate the absence of face time requirements, but find the free-market system of assignments a mixed blessing. "You can be as busy as you want to be, or you can get away with quite a lot," suggests one lawyer. Without an assigning partner, "associates are responsible for scouting out their own assignments," which "often makes for a very inefficient use of time." Invisible rules frustrate some; despite "increasing pressure to put in more hours," there are "no clear guidelines." "The firm has not historically had a part-time or flex-time program," one associate writes, "but has provided it to me on a limited basis for a limited time period." Despite the mutterings, many associates are resigned to long hours. "Hey, I'd love to get paid this much for doing less, but that doesn't make much sense, does it?"

Pro who?

Given the firm's "loosey-goosey" structure, most insiders profess ignorance of Cahill's pro bono policy. "Pro who?" quips one lawyer. One associate claims that "pro bono work does not count as billable per se, but it is recorded and is taken into consideration in evaluating the overall quality/quantity of associates' work." Few respondents feel it is actively encouraged. "Like most things at Cahill, if you want to do pro bono work you need to seek it out and pursue it on your own." Several associates suggest that it is "actively discouraged." Projects must be "approved by a partner who is not very pro-bono friendly," explains one attorney. This area is "the one true black eye for the firm. The partners in charge of pro bono would appear to have been selected for the very reason that they disapprove of pro bono." A few sources see "signs of improvement." One first-year associate's experience on "three pro bono matters" leads him to conclude that the "firm is very committed to pro bono."

Color blind and egalitarian

If Cahill's emphasis on the bottom line results in a "true meritocracy" in which "no one cares about your gender, race or sex life," it involves little active effort to promote diversity. Associates generally agree that "gender is just not an issue" but note that "the ratio of female partners is rather low" and there are "no mushy woman-to-woman programs like they have at other firms." Despite a couple of references to an "old-boy network," most women find the workplace "egalitarian."

The same approach extends to race and sexual orientation. One minority associate claims that "Cahill really does not care what you are. I don't think there's special outreach, but if 'color blind' is a good goal to reach, Cahill is definitely there." He adds, however, "The fact remains that the firm does not have a high percentage of minority lawyers." Respondents were happy to see the firm "promote their first black partner" this year, even if it was a bit late. Sources cite the presence of "one gay partner [and] several openly gay associates" and note that Cahill offers full domestic partner benefits. An associate remarks that "while this firm is a great place to work if you are openly gay, there is no mentoring or direction from older gay and lesbian lawyers."

The charm of Stalinesque offices

Cahill's "horrendous offices are legendary." "Poor lighting, stained carpets, dinged desks, dreary halls. Is this a law firm?" asks one New Yorker. "Sometimes it is depressing," sighs another, and sources claim that the "Stalinesque" space is so "embarrassing" that "even the partners always try to schedule client meetings outside the office." Yet even grumblers concede that offices are "spacious" and "comfortable" and that "all associates get window offices." The fact that "associates get their own office within their first year" is appreciated as well.

"Offices are not plush," agrees one lawyer, "but I'm a slob so I don't care." Indeed, the space's very ugliness casts a certain attraction. "It might sound odd, but there are those of us who love its threadworn charm," asserts a litigator. Another calls the offices "ridiculous, but endearing." Perhaps dinginess comforts the clumsy and careless. "Cahill's office space may not be pretty, but at least I'm not afraid of breaking anything" or "overly concerned about spilling my coffee on the carpet." Several associates scold colleagues for misplaced priorities. "It's the quality of the people and the work that matters — not the color of the carpet." Others find the Spartan setting an asset: "This firm attracts the kind of person who is not so caught up in appearances." In contrast to his colleagues across the Atlantic, a London respondent reports that his offices are "modern, comfortable, functional and extremely attractive."

Brobeck, Phleger & Harrison LLP

One Market
Spear Street Tower
San Francisco, CA 94105
Phone: (415) 442-0900
www.brobeck.com

LOCATIONS

San Francisco, CA (HQ)

Austin, TX • Dallas, TX • Denver, CO • East Palo Alto,
CA • Irvine, CA • Los Angeles, CA • New York, NY •
Reston, VA • San Diego, CA • Washington, DC • (plus
three joint venture Brobeck/Hale and Dorr offices in
London, Oxford and Munich)

MAJOR DEPARTMENTS/PRACTICES

Antitrust • Appellate • Bankruptcy • Business &
Technology • Business Litigation • E-Commerce •
Employee Benefits • Environmental Litigation •
Executive Compensation • Financing Transactions •
Insurance Coverage • Intellectual Property • Labor &
Employment Litigation • Mergers & Acquisitions •
Outsourcing • Products Liability • Public Offerings •
Real Estate & Land Use • Securities Litigation •
Strategic Partnering • Tax • Trade Secrets • Venture
Capital Financings

THE STATS

No. of attorneys: 700
No. of offices: 14
Summer associate offers: 108 out of 126 (2001)
Chairman: Richard S. Odom
Hiring Partner: Christopher H. McGrath

BASE SALARY

All domestic offices, 2002
1st year: $125,000
2nd year: $135,000
3rd year: $150,000
4th year: $165,000
5th year: $185,000
6th year: $195,000
7th year: $205,000
Summer associate: $2,400/week

NOTABLE PERKS

- In-house gym (some locations)
- "The technology available at our firm
  is unbeatable"
- On-site automotive repair (some locations)
- Matching funds for charities of your choice

THE BUZZ
WHAT ATTORNEYS AT OTHER FIRMS ARE SAYING ABOUT THIS FIRM

- "A good firm with a bad client base"
- "Tech-friendly"
- "Cutting edge and now cutting jobs"
- "Hip but tries too hard"
- "Man the lifeboats!"

UPPERS

- Commitment to improving associate life
- Early responsibility
- Friendly and collegial environment

DOWNERS

- Uncertainty about new firm management and firm direction
- Some beloved perks have been eliminated, such as mortgage assistance program
- "The layoffs were a real drag on morale"

EMPLOYMENT CONTACT

Ms. Ellen Zuckerman
Firm-wide Attorney Recruiting Manager
Phone: (213) 745-3562
Fax: (213) 745-3345
ezuckerman@brobeck.com

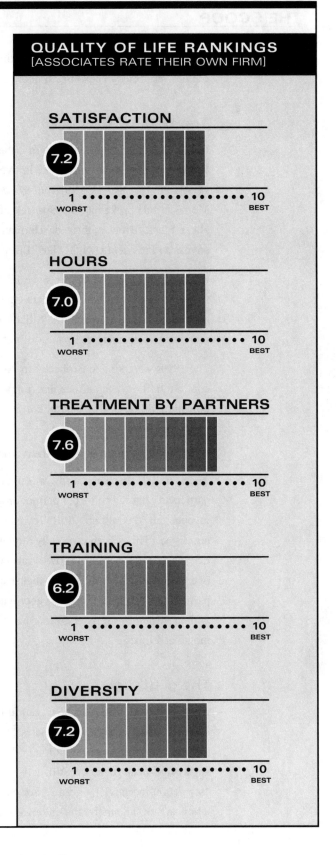

QUALITY OF LIFE RANKINGS
[ASSOCIATES RATE THEIR OWN FIRM]

SATISFACTION
7.2
1 WORST — 10 BEST

HOURS
7.0
1 WORST — 10 BEST

TREATMENT BY PARTNERS
7.6
1 WORST — 10 BEST

TRAINING
6.2
1 WORST — 10 BEST

DIVERSITY
7.2
1 WORST — 10 BEST

THE SCOOP

The 1990s were kind to tech wunderkind Brobeck, Phleger & Harrison. Now, Brobeck's sorting out new priorities in a post-tech boom future — and laying off associates and staff.

The birth of Brobeck

In the early part of the last century, there was a San Francisco firm named Morrison Dunne & Brobeck. In 1924 the firm broke in two, with some partners forming Brobeck and some forming what's now known as Morrison & Foerster. The story has it that some scoundrels from the Morrison side broke into the Brobeck office with an ax, absconding with client files. Despite the alleged theft, Brobeck thrived. Herman Phleger led the firm in the early days, also serving as an adviser to President Dwight "Ike" Eisenhower.

Brobeck has expanded rapidly since 1976, when it opened its Los Angeles office. Four years later, it opened in Silicon Valley, then an emerging tech center. In 1990 the firm opened its New York office, just in time to catch the Silicon Alley boom. Today, the New York office still represents most of the remaining companies of note in Silicon Alley.

The 1990s were kind to Brobeck. In 2000 the firm was flying high with record profits, taking in a cool $1 million per partner and topping all California firms. But with the recent economic downturn, things at Brobeck took a sharp turn as well.

When life gives you lemons ...

The year 2001, needless to say, was not a record year for the firm. The tech downturn hit Brobeck particularly hard. Profits per partner dropped from $1 million in 2000 to $660,000 in 2001. Gross revenue fell $29 million. Still, Tower Snow Jr., then chairman of Brobeck, vowed not to lay off attorneys. (This was an especially impressive goal, since the firm had hired 330 attorneys in 2000.) Cutting corners became Snow's raison d'etre. Meals, travel, messengers, entertainment and overtime were all slashed. In August of that year, he announced a voluntary program allowing partners and associates, with the approval of their practice group head, to take an unpaid sabbatical without losing benefits. Lawyers had the option of working a few days a week or taking off a month at a time.

The good fight

In efforts to keep its attorneys gainfully employed, the firm had lawyers play musical chairs. Brobeck moved about 30 associates from its corporate department to different areas with more demand, like securities litigation. Ten attorneys also moved to administrative areas, such as knowledge management. Still, it wasn't enough. In November 2001, the firm announced its "separation incentive program." Associates in the business and technology group who had billed less than 1,300 hours by the end of 2001 were deemed eligible to take a lump sum equal to their base pay through April 15 in exchange for leaving the firm. Out of the 130 associates eligible for the program, 82 accepted.

In January 2002, the firm initiated an associate salary freeze; managing partner Richard Parker admitted Brobeck had mis-timed the market by boosting first-year salaries to $135,000. Ultimately, however, these measures were not enough to save the firm from the inevitable. In February 2002, Brobeck laid off 54 associates and 85 staff members. Some partners were demoted as part of the cost-cutting move. (The layoffs were announced the day after Tower Snow Jr.'s departure as chair.) Then, just when you thought it was safe to go back to work, 35 more associates and 24 staff members were laid off in May 2002.

Puff

While Brobeck rarely represents plaintiffs in litigation cases, in 2001 it chose to represent a lone smoker in a battle against R. J. Reynolds Tobacco Co. and Philip Morris Inc. The move was odd, as Brobeck is better known for its product liability defense practice. (In fact, the move represented the first time a large, defense-oriented firm had represented an individual smoker.) But in October 2001, Brobeck's plans went up in smoke. The firm was disqualified from representing the smoker because the firm had served as R. J. Reynolds' chief counsel from 1954 to 1981 for smoking-related cases in California.

Snow long

After he stepped down as Brobeck's chairman in November 2001, the charismatic Snow announced that he would not seek re-election to a third term heading the firm. The year was a controversial one for Snow, and might have been his most difficult year since stepping up to the chairman plate in 1998. And the controversy didn't end there. In May 2002, Clifford Chance Rogers & Wells LLP finalized a deal with Snow and 21 other Brobeck partners to jump ship and open a new Clifford Chance office in San Francisco. Talks between Clifford Chance and the Brobeck group came to light a couple of weeks before the deal was finalized. When the news leaked out, Brobeck partners ousted Snow from the firm for his role in the Clifford Chance negotiations. Snow's successor is Richard S. Odom, who started his legal career at Brobeck in 1969. Most recently, he headed the firm's complex litigation group. Richard L. Parker was elected the new firm-wide managing partner. Parker got his start at Brobeck in 1981. His focus was business and taxation.

Dealing well with diversity

Brobeck has a history of sensitivity to diversity issues. Fifteen years ago, Brobeck hired a lawyer with physical disabilities who used a wheelchair. The firm had custom office furniture made and allowed him to fly first class. Brobeck's accommodating nature toward persons with disabilities has not changed. Today one of the firm's San Francisco associates is deaf. Associate Kirstin Wolf joined Brobeck in 1999, specializing in product liability litigation. Because her job involves heavy client contact, frequent travel and short-notice court appearances, the firm hired an interpreter to serve as Wolf's interpreter. As per the Americans With Disabilities Act of 1990, Wolf was given a teletypewriter, or TTY, and a pager upon her hiring. The firm made a twist in the role of interpreter: Wolf's interpreter was also trained as a paralegal to help on Wolf's cases. Brobeck also offered sign language classes to all Brobeck employees; about 50 took Brobeck up on the offer.

Big deals

Like many firms, Brobeck had a slow year in 2001, but it did work on some noteworthy deals. One was the acquisition of Brobeck client Platys Communications Inc. in July by Adaptec Inc. for $150 million. Also in July, Cisco Corp., the firm's biggest client, bought AuroraNetics Inc. for $150 million. It was a happy day for Brobeck; Cisco is one of the firm's largest clients, but rough economic times had meant a dearth of M&A transactions from Cisco.

GETTING HIRED

Whatever Brobeck wants, Brobeck gets

While a summer spent in the Brobeck world is still considered fun, several associates mention that things have slowed down in recent years. Summer associates do "some simple assignments" with "good exposure" to the firm without an "overwhelming social calendar." But don't get cocky if you spend a summer with Brobeck. Warns one San Francisco associate, "Working a summer here does not guarantee your spot." The firm looks for "high academic achievers who fit into the outgoing firm culture." According to an Austin associate, it's all about personality. "It's important to be someone who people want to work long hours with." With the economic slowdown, the firm's hiring is "very selective," and in New York the firm is "not hiring except for IP litigation." A San Diego associate says certain practice groups are hiring while others are not.

The interview

Interviews at Brobeck can be rigorous. "I had three rounds of interviews," notes a New York associate. In Austin one associate "interviewed with several attorneys and received a call offering me the job." Networking works in D.C., where one associate remarks, "I was hired through contacts within the office." A member of the firm's hiring committee shares insight. "With a two-tiered interview process, candidates need to have good grades — top 30 percent — from a good school in order to get a call back. In a callback interview, interviewers focus on personality, conversational skills, intellect and other non-resume factors. The input of every interviewer is taken into account. Often the judgment of a junior associate is weighed more heavily than that of a senior partner who rarely interviews."

OUR SURVEY SAYS

Shaky ground

While most associates agree Brobeck is "laid back" and "friendly," they acknowledge that economic adversity has affected the environment. It's especially evident in the New York office, say insiders, where one associate notes, "Job satisfaction has decreased dramatically this year, in part because the economic downturn has left corporate associates listless and without much substantive work, and in part because of perceived management problems, as well as recent layoffs and the less-than-straightforward way in which the firm handled them. The past year has seen the emergence of a closed-door culture and a decline in the open and non-hierarchal partner-associate relationships that used to set Brobeck apart. In the face of impending layoffs, the typically friendly, sociable relationships between associates have also suffered."

In Washington, D.C., things aren't much prettier: "The firm culture as a whole has changed for the worse since the old management stepped down in November. The firm feels at times like a burning building because it is being managed in a 'crisis mode,' and management does not seem to care about communicating with associates." The Austin office is said to have become a "pure money-is-everything firm."

Pushing the clouds aside?

Though Brobeck is having a tough year, all is not lost. Associates in San Francisco, while noticing a new gap between associates and partners, still say people "go out of their way to be friendly." San Diego is seeing sunny days. An associate there remarks, "Partners and senior associates are very approachable." Things in Dallas are just as rosy. "Very inclusive culture. No associate/partner divide so prevalent in other firms," comments one terse associate. Partners in San Diego are said to "respect the judgment of associates in the completion of assignments, allowing the associates to maintain their own schedules." Even in New York, associates still think Brobeck is a "truly great place to work." A happy associate sings, "I work on interesting, quality cases, and there is a good mix of subject matters." A litigation associate maintains, "I have lots of great work, variety and significant control over the type of work I do. There is not a lot of hand-holding here, but if you are willing to take on responsibility, you'll get it."

New York salary sourness

Brobeck associates in the Empire State are the only ones kvetching about salary. New York associates agree that their pay is below that of other comparable New York firms. An associate explains: "They prefer to pay the same in all offices. Austin and Colorado make out big time, while New York and San Francisco suffer." But the associates in San Francisco don't seem to agree: "Brobeck pays very well. It will continue to pay top-notch salaries for the Silicon Valley." No one is complaining in D.C. "Definitely the best paycheck around!" How about bonuses? Associates explain that the firm gave discretionary bonuses later than many other firms — in March 2002. Those New Yorkers can't be satisfied. "We do not receive the bonuses that other New York firms receive," sighs one.

Excellent hours

Most associates at Brobeck are happy with the hours they work. In New York, one insider says, "My hours are very reasonable. Although there have been spurts of putting in long hours on the weekend and at nights, it has not been the norm." Even when they do put in long hours, associates don't feel pressured. "I billed over 2,400 hours last year but never felt that I was tied to my desk. I maintained a large workload and was able to work at my own schedule," notes a San Diego associate. Also in San Diego, "There is plenty of great work, making the long hours more enjoyable because we are learning great skills." In D.C., the associates are glad they don't have a "face-time requirement," remarking that it helps when trying to balance work and family. "People regularly work from home and never have a problem taking vacation," chirps a lawyer in San Francisco.

Brobeck's New York corporate associates are worried about too little hours, rather than too many. The firm's corporate associates are happy to have manageable hours, but say work in their practice group "has declined so much, hours are far under what one would expect." In New York, an insider laments, "Hours right now are terrible. There is so little work coming in, it is ridiculous." A San Diego associate hopes that the lull in corporate work is temporary, while another New York associate complains that her mind is "atrophying."

Do you like basketball?

A female associate claims the firm is in a "rut" when it comes to women. "To succeed here," she clarifies, "you definitely have to be comfortable being the only woman in the room a lot of the time." This associate says there are many firm-sponsored events that are inclusive, though women aren't in on the "weekend boys' golf outings." A male associate shares his perspective on this issue: "My practice group is consistently labeled as a boys' club. Many of the attorneys enjoy playing basketball, and those attorneys tend to be male. If a female wished to play I could almost guarantee she'd be welcome." Another female associate thinks there are plenty of junior women around but not many women partners to emulate. In addition, she says, partners don't have a "particular interest in mentoring women," and the firm doesn't have a formal program for considering women's issues.

One female associate notes: "I don't see any women with children who aren't at least senior associate level. Most people seem to wait until they've made partner." One woman associate sees the position of women at the firm differently. "Women aren't treated differently here," she counters. Another agrees: "The firm is very proactive about hiring and promoting women without discrimination."

Diversity disagreement

Brobeck associates are in search of more racial diversity. "Racial diversity has not been mentioned at all in the six months that I have been here. There is no diversity committee or forum to discuss hiring, promotion or mentoring. There are no minority partners in my group," says one Asian associate. Another Asian lawyer reveals, "The firm makes an effort to recruit minorities, particularly with respect to the summer program. However, they are not making the same efforts with respect to elevating minorities to partner." A female associate says there are "not enough African-American and Hispanic attorneys, though the ratio is good for the staff."

Things at the firm seem to be better for gays and lesbians. "There are several gay and lesbian staff and attorneys," says one heterosexual associate. A transgendered associate who came out to the firm (and agreed to be quoted in this guide) maintains, "My reception by the firm was better than I could have dreamed of. Everyone I talked to was very supportive. I know several other attorneys at the firm who are gay or lesbian and they also appear to be doing fine. From my perception, the firm is happy to have good lawyers, whether gay or straight or transgendered."

The aftermath of the buyouts

According to a San Francisco associate, turnover at Brobeck has been "shocking." "No one I interviewed with one year ago is here any more." The firm did offer associates a generous incentive to leave, and more than a few associates took the offer and split. A New York associate says, "Almost a third of the associates that were in our office a year ago are gone." He blames layoffs. A San Francisco associate gets more specific: "People involuntarily leave because of layoffs and voluntarily leave the first chance they get." A San Diego associate says retention depends on temperament. "If you are motivated and hardworking, you can't find a better place to work. If you want to take it easy, you probably won't be happy here. Great work and high salaries aren't just handed out to those who get good grades in law school; you've got to keep working for it." Through the storm of layoffs and many associates fleeing the firm as fast as they can, those San Diego associates remain calm. "Most people," maintains a lawyer in the San Diego office, "seem very contented with their positions."

Proskauer Rose LLP

1585 Broadway
New York, NY 10036
Phone: (212) 969-3000
www.proskauer.com

LOCATIONS

New York, NY (HQ)
Boca Raton, FL
Los Angeles, CA
Newark, NJ
Washington, DC
Paris

MAJOR DEPARTMENTS/PRACTICES

Bankruptcy & Creditors' Rights
Corporate & Securities
Employee Benefits & ERISA
Entertainment, Sports & Intellectual Property
Estates, Wills, Trusts & Probate
Health
Labor & Employment
Litigation
Real Estate, Environmental & Zoning
Tax

THE STATS

No. of attorneys: 550
No. of offices: 6
Summer associate offers: 52 out of 52 (2001)
Chairman: Alan S. Jaffe
Hiring Attorney: Michael E. Foreman

BASE SALARY

New York, 2002
1st year: $125,000
2nd year: $135,000
3rd year: $150,000
4th year: $165,000
5th year: $185,000
6th year: $195,000
7th year: $205,000
8th year: $210,000
Summer associate: $2,403/week

NOTABLE PERKS

- Firm gala
- 15-minute massages every other week for litigation associates
- "The cookies are great!"
- Great access to sports and entertainment tickets

THE BUZZ
WHAT ATTORNEYS AT OTHER FIRMS ARE SAYING ABOUT THIS FIRM

- "Sports law powerhouse"
- "Quality firm with burnt-out associates"
- "Best labor and employment firm in the country"
- "They have the NBA. What else counts?"
- "Very New York-centric"

UPPERS

- Glamorous, high-profile sports clients
- Stellar labor and employment practice
- Emphasis on training

DOWNERS

- Hit by layoffs
- Few women and minorities in leadership positions
- First-years shut out of 2001 bonuses

EMPLOYMENT CONTACT

Ms. Diane M. Kolnik
Manager of Legal Recruiting
Phone: (212) 969-5060
dkolnik@proskauer.com

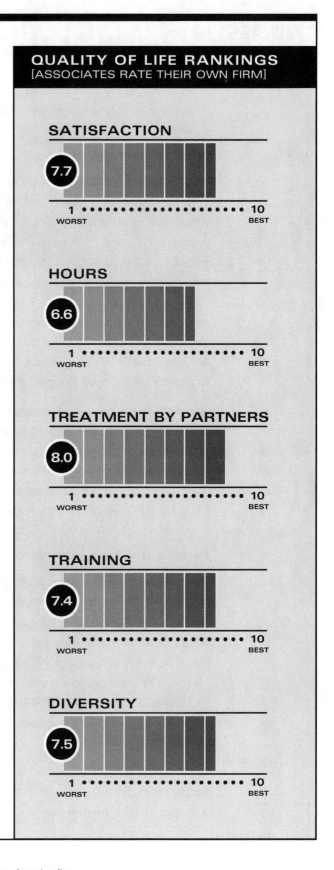

QUALITY OF LIFE RANKINGS
[ASSOCIATES RATE THEIR OWN FIRM]

SATISFACTION

7.7

1 WORST .... 10 BEST

HOURS

6.6

1 WORST .... 10 BEST

TREATMENT BY PARTNERS

8.0

1 WORST .... 10 BEST

TRAINING

7.4

1 WORST .... 10 BEST

DIVERSITY

7.5

1 WORST .... 10 BEST

THE SCOOP

While Proskauer Rose has a leading labor and employment practice, it can't be beat in sports. It shoots hoops for high-profile sports clients like the National Basketball Association, the National Hockey League, Major League Baseball, Major League Soccer and the ATP tour.

History: rosy beginnings

William R. Rose founded the firm Rose & Paskus in 1875, initially representing family businesses in real estate, retailing, tobacco and textiles. Before joining his father's firm in 1911, Rose's son, Alfred, clerked at the firm of James, Schell & Elkus where Judge Joseph Proskauer was a senior partner. The junior Rose served in the U.S. Navy during World War I as the firm began an international and tax practice, and after the war, he became partner. The firm took flight in 1930 when Judge Joseph M. Proskauer joined up. As a New York State Court of Appeals judge, Proskauer got to know New York Governor Alfred E. Smith, serving as his campaign adviser, speechwriter, golf partner and friend. Governor Smith had appointed Proskauer to the New York State Supreme Court in 1923. Upon his joining the firm, the name was changed to Proskauer, Rose & Paskus. In 1942 the firm became known as Proskauer Rose Goetz & Mendelsohn. In 1997 the name was changed again to the short and sweet Proskauer Rose.

Not everything at Proskauer Rose is coming up roses. The firm was infected with the layoff bug, and in November 2001, it laid off six of the 265 associates in the New York office. In January 2002, the firm's web site was criticized by Web consultant Larry Bodine in *Law Technology News*. Bodine cited the firm's use of Roman numerals on the site as looking like an "internal attorney manual." He said the site did not market the firm in the best way. Apparently the firm agrees. A new site had already been under development at the time of Bodine's article and has since been launched.

Proskauer Rose got game

Along with rival Weil, Gotshal & Manges, Proskauer Rose has dominated the arena of sports law since the mid-1970s. Then the firm was on the losing side of what may be its most famous case, the Oscar Robertson antitrust suit that established free agency in basketball. Lead litigator David Stern may have lost the battle, but he didn't lose the war. He so impressed the NBA that it hired him as its in-house counsel in 1978 and later promoted him to commissioner. Gary Bettman got his start at Proskauer Rose and went on to serve as commissioner of the National Hockey League. The firm held center court in 1998 when its New York headquarters served as the site of grueling negotiations surrounding the six-month lockout of the NBA players who threatened to shut down the pro basketball season.

In May 2001, the firm assisted in the formation of a new professional motorsports league, Team Racing Auto Circuit (TRAC). With the growing popularity of stock car racing, TRAC is set to be a success. It will consist of eight to 12 multiple car teams, which will represent various U.S. cities.

Proskauer partners Bradley Ruskin and Joseph Leccese are helping TRAC with management and economic issues. TRAC is set to start its engines in 2003. In the beginning of 2002, Proskauer Rose was chosen over Morgan, Lewis & Bockius to handle one of the most important sports negotiations in years. The high-stakes labor talks with the Major League Baseball Players Association could make or break the baseball season if a strike or lockout were to occur.

Labor and employment can't be beat

While in awe of Proskauer's sports practice, one may forget the firm's stellar labor and employment law department. Proskauer successfully defended Ivy League Yale University in a noteworthy labor and employment case back in 1997. The suit was filed by graduate student teaching assistants and argued before the National Labor Relations Board. The charges against Yale were dismissed. In a similar suit filed by New York University grad students in 2000, the NLRB ruled against Proskauer client New York University, giving the students the right to organize as a union.

Two of today's critical workplace issues are discrimination and harassment. No one knows that better than the experts at Proskauer Rose. That's why the firm teamed up with WeComply, Inc. to offer the first and only online training program for corporate managers on these topics. The program helps managers understand workplace discrimination and harassment and has the ability to be customized for individual firms. It consists of a 45-minute tutorial with interactive games and tests. The program debuted at the Corporate Legal Times Super-Conference in Chicago in June 2001.

Not all sports and labor either

Proskauer Rose wants to beef up its white-collar criminal defense practice. To do that, it snatched two top-notch litigators from Manatt, Phelps & Phillips LLP in May 2001. Jack DiCanio and Anthony Pacheco are former federal prosecutors. Their areas of expertise include white-collar criminal defense, special investigations, litigation before securities regulatory bodies and commercial litigation. Pacheco specialized in investor and financial institution fraud in the major fraud's section of the U.S. Attorney's Office Criminal Division beginning in 1994. DiCanio specialized in RICO and violent crime prosecutions as deputy chief of the General Crimes Section for the Central District of the U.S. Attorney's Office Criminal Division. Both attorneys will work with partner Richard Marmaro, the head of the West Coast white collar criminal defense practice. Currently Marmaro represents Credit Suisse First Boston broker John Schmidt.

Napster affects Hollywood

A major triumph for copyright owners came in December 2001 when the U.S. Circuit Court of Appeals for the Second Circuit upheld an order banning the publishing of or linking to computer codes used to decipher the copyright protections on DVD movies. The litigation came about because the web site known as Web Site 2600 and its publisher, Eric Corley, posted links to the computer code, DeCSS, which can crack the code that prevents DVDs from being copied in digital form. Proskauer partner Charles Sims represented the Motion Picture Association of America in the suit.

GETTING HIRED

Good schools, good grades

These hiring criteria may not be original, but they are what Proskauer looks for in a new associate, though Proskauer "will hire associates from the top of their classes at regional law schools." In addition, associates say that an applicant's personality "definitely counts." According to a senior associate, "Teamwork and controlled, professional energy are encouraged and appreciated." The firm wants "smart, confident self-starters who like a good challenge." One lawyer suggests that Proskauer "likes hiring an atypical bunch — the kind of people who pride themselves on being outsiders."

A litigator complains that "quality candidates with offers of employment often turn the firm down." Perhaps to counter this problem, the firm "often extends on-the-spot offers to students from the top-tier schools, without waiting for comments from all interviewers." But keep in mind, even though "we're no Wachtell … slackers and those who didn't make the grades in law school would be well advised to seek employment elsewhere." The firm's "reputation as the top labor and employment firm in the country" is a magnet for many experienced lawyers, although one lateral states that the firm "rarely" hires first- or second-year associates, preferring "to hire laterals who don't need much grooming or training."

OUR SURVEY SAYS

A culture of teamwork

Associates at Proskauer Rose seem to enjoy their work and respect their colleagues. "Nice partners, good assignments, top-name clients." A senior associate claims to "almost never have a dull day. Sometimes nerve-wracking, often long, but always interesting." One labor lawyer explains what makes him happy: "Assignments are handed out on an equitable basis, feedback and constructive criticism are good and senior attorneys are easy to work with." Many insiders feel the firm fosters a culture of "teamwork" and "helping out." According to a New York associate, "The firm's culture is a product of friendly, confident and hardworking lawyers."

Sources describe Proskauer's atmosphere as "laid back, friendly, and professional." Dress is business casual. The attitude in New York is "definitely not stuffy. You can say what you want to partners, because they do the same to you." Associates value that sense of teamwork: "You do not feel a dramatic difference between partner and associate in terms of attitudes. We are all simply lawyers who work together without all the silly hierarchy formalism of other places." These sentiments are not universally shared. A senior associate finds that the firm gets "less and less friendly as the years go by." Another lawyer complains that the people she works with are "not very nice at all. They hate their lives and take it out on the junior attorneys." A third-year associate gripes, "Mentoring is thus far non-existent."

While some attorneys point out that many of their work friendships have transcended the office and the workweek, others find that lawyers "do not tend to socialize together," although "everyone is extremely friendly and helpful during work hours." One associate warns candidates against taking that laid-back attitude too far: "While casual dress and attitudes are the norm, client work is taken very seriously and those with cavalier work ethics don't tend to make it in the long run."

Partners as mentors

Proskauer partners win praise from most insiders. Although they are demanding, partners are "very fair and patient" and, on the whole, "approachable and easy to work with." One labor lawyer describes relationships between associates and partners as "idyllic." Another considers his department to be "like a small family — sometimes dysfunctional, but nonetheless, a family." Of course, associates do run into the "occasional bad apples or simply loose bulbs, but partners generally treat associates as equals." A few attorneys complain that people are often "so busy" that "not enough partners take the time to have a relationship with the associates — it's only 'what have you done lately.'" Some lawyers suggest that the "emphasis on training" helps foster good working relationships in which partners "seem to take their mentoring responsibilities to heart."

Excellent training

Many associates believe Proskauer offers "one of the best training programs in New York City." Respondents praise the firm's innovative programs, such as shadowing, in which junior associates observe their more senior colleagues in action and receive billable time credit, and The Proskauer Institute, a one-week course, run by the firm's professional development group, that teaches new associates the foundation of their practice area before they start billable work. In addition, associates can attend "CLE programs and Proskauer-sponsored workshops and seminars that are very helpful and informative." According to some sources, the "best training is actually watching and doing — associates can get a lot of responsibility here." Still, other lawyers insist that the training "could be better." A few claim simply that training is "virtually non-existent" and really "depends on the partner."

Fairly reasonable hours

Proskauer insiders may not give their firm a high score on hours, but they don't voice very strenuous complaints. Many associates agree that the hours "are completely rational, considering the profession." "You have to work hard," acknowledges a lawyer, "but you have to work hard at any firm." A few respondents find that the hours are better than expected. "This is a dream job," reports a first-year. Associates appreciate that "face time around here means very little," working from home is a viable option and "people are respectful of your social commitments and your life in general."

This isn't to say that some lawyers don't experience "too much pressure to make hours." One attorney complains that "case mismanagement" results in "too many hours spent in the office by associates" — too frequently at night or on weekends. Another source claims that "long hours can often be a result of lean staffing that is sometimes too lean." According to a few New York lawyers, while they work fewer hours than colleagues at other big firms, "the partnership tends to stress the issue quite a bit." Long hours in the New York office may be more palatable — or at least comfortable — thanks to "great views" and very popular Herman Miller Aeron chairs. "New Aeron chairs rock," raves an enthusiastic associate.

Middle of the pack

Most Proskauer insiders feel they are fairly compensated, even if their firm "always lags just behind the other large firms." "Proskauer is not an industry leader when it comes to compensation," acknowledges an associate, "but it falls squarely in the middle of the big-firm pack." At least one lawyer believes an improved quality of life balances the less-than-leading pay: "I'll gladly take what they give me in exchange for the amount of hours I work and the quality of life I have."

Lawyers say their base salary is generally "competitive with all LA and New York big firm salaries." Several New Yorkers complain, however, that the firm "is below market when it comes to bonuses." First-year associates, in particular, feel they were "stiffed" on bonuses last year, noting that Proskauer was "one of few top firms that did not give bonuses to first-years in New York." A more senior attorney offers her perspective: "Cost of living increases, but salaries stay flat. Then again," she adds, "no one was complaining a few years ago when our salaries expanded quicker than Oprah's post-diet waistline."

No apparent discrimination

Associates praise Proskauer as "very progressive" with respect to gay and lesbian attorneys. Lawyers note that there are "several openly gay partners and associates" in the firm's offices and openly gay respondents report feeling very comfortable. "Very, very few firms do this better," asserts a New York lawyer.

The firm is generally considered "supportive" of women, and a female attorney declares she has "never felt uncomfortable, singled out or discriminated against in terms of either my work assignments or the evaluation of my work based on sex." On the other hand, many sources note that there are still "far too few women partners, especially women of color," and a male associate believes Proskauer "needs a better commitment to increasing its numbers of women in leadership positions." There is "only one woman partner in" the Los Angeles office, and "there is not, and there never has been, a woman partner in the D.C. office." Insiders would also "like to see more minority hiring." Most lawyers do not believe the firm intentionally discriminates against minority lawyers. However, Proskauer is still "overwhelmingly white."

Proactive pro bono program for first-years

Proskauer's requirement that all first-year associates "take on a pro bono assignment" is evidence of the firm's "proactive" commitment to pro bono, say insiders. Up to 125 pro bono hours count toward billable hours each year and the firm "distributes weekly e-mails about a variety of available pro bono projects." According to a New York associate, "Three different partners in three different departments — labor and employment, litigation and corporate — oversee pro bono assignments to the firm as a whole, and they are very good at what they do." However, some sources regard the 125-hour cap together with the firm's billable hours expectations as a practical limitation on the ability of associates to take on pro bono projects. In contrast to the lawyers in New York and Los Angeles who feel encouraged to do pro bono work, two Florida-based associates claim that pro bono has "never been mentioned" or at least "never been encouraged."

Cooley Godward LLP

5 Palo Alto Square
3000 El Camino Real
Palo Alto, CA 94306-2155
Phone: (650) 843-5000
www.cooley.com

LOCATIONS

Palo Alto, CA (HQ)
Broomfield, CO • Kirkland, WA • Menlo Park, CA •
Reston, VA • San Diego, CA • San Francisco, CA

MAJOR DEPARTMENTS/PRACTICES

Antitrust/Trade Regulation
Complex Commercial Litigation
Corporate
Credit Finance
Employee Compensation & Benefits
Employment & Labor Litigation
Immigration
Intellectual Property Litigation/Patent/Trademark
Life Sciences
Mergers & Acquisitions
Real Estate
Securities Litigation
Tax
Technology Transactions
Venture Capital

THE STATS

No. of attorneys: 600
No. of offices: 7
Summer associate offers: 71 out of 87 (2001)
Chairman: Stephen C. Neal
Hiring Partner: John C. Dwyer

THE BUZZ
WHAT ATTORNEYS AT OTHER FIRMS ARE SAYING ABOUT THIS FIRM

- "Great firm, bad time to be there"
- "California blue chip"
- "Layoffs hurt their image"
- "They stumble who run fast"
- "Lean now, but they will be back"

BASE SALARY

All Offices, 2002
1st year: $125,000
2nd year: $130,000
3rd year: $135,000
4th year: $150,000
5th year: $165,000
6th year: $185,000
7th year: $195,000
Summer associate: $2,400/week

NOTABLE PERKS

- Investment fund for associates
- Gym membership subsidy
- Regular attorney lunches
- Mortgage assistance program

UPPERS

• Virtually no dress code
• Fast-paced youthful environment
• No face time required

DOWNERS

• Can you say 'low morale'?
• Disappearing perks
• "Layoffs were difficult"

EMPLOYMENT CONTACT

Ms. Jo Anne Larson
Director of Attorney Recruiting
Phone: (650) 843-5050
Fax: (650) 857-0663
jalarson@cooley.com

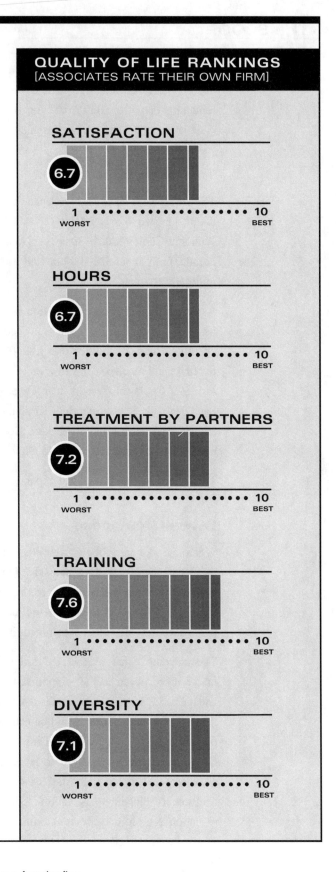

QUALITY OF LIFE RANKINGS
[ASSOCIATES RATE THEIR OWN FIRM]

SATISFACTION
6.7
1 WORST   10 BEST

HOURS
6.7
1 WORST   10 BEST

TREATMENT BY PARTNERS
7.2
1 WORST   10 BEST

TRAINING
7.6
1 WORST   10 BEST

DIVERSITY
7.1
1 WORST   10 BEST

THE SCOOP

Cooley Godward, known for happy associates and strong corporate and litigation departments, has had a notably difficult year in the wake of Silicon Valley's sharp economic decline. Despite remaining one of the Bay Area's top 10 grossing firms, the firm turned many heads after its firm-wide layoff of 86 lawyers last summer.

Too much too soon?

The 1990s were an expansive decade for Cooley — between 1990 and 2000, the firm more than doubled in size to over 700 lawyers. In 2000, in order to meet the needs of the booming high-tech economy, Cooley added 180 lawyers to its staff. Profits per partner more than quadrupled over that decade, from about $220,000 in 1990 to $904,000 in 2000. In 2000 the firm's profits hit $119.7 million, up 53 percent from 1999.

As part of the firm's rapid expansion and in keeping with its tech-focused practice, Cooley moved its base of operations from San Francisco to Silicon Valley, where its Palo Alto office expanded its operations with the addition of a 130,000-square foot building in early 2000. (Cooley was one of the first San Francisco firms to open an office in Silicon Valley when it opened its Palo Alto office in 1980.) Cooley also established offices in other high-tech corridors around the country, including San Diego, the Seattle suburb of Kirkland, Wash., and Reston, Va. Cooley consolidated its Denver and Boulder offices in Interlocken, Colo.'s hottest technology center, and announced plans to expand its San Francisco office to allow the firm to add another 50 employees.

The firm's glowing profits and expansion, however, belied the crises to come.

Lawyers cut loose

When the dot-com boom went bust in 2001, Cooley scrambled to recover. The virtual disappearance of the IPO, a mainstay of the corporate practice at Silicon Valley firms, together with a drop in mergers and acquisitions, hurt a number of prominent California law firms, including Cooley Godward. By the middle of 2001, the firm's high-speed growth had reversed itself, with perks like firm-wide retreats trimmed first.

Then, in a move that reverberated throughout the legal community, Cooley announced a firm-wide layoff of 86 lawyers and 50 support staff in late August 2001. The layoff targeted junior attorneys and the newly hired and resulted in a loss of approximately 17 percent of the firm's total associates. Anxiety that the measure would be echoed by other firms proved well-founded when at least six other Bay Area firms, including Fenwick & West, Brobeck, Phleger & Harrison and Venture Law Group, followed with their own layoffs. In June 2002, the firm laid off an additional three associates and five support staffers at its Kirkland, Wash., office. Despite the difficulty of the decision to implement the layoff, Cooley handled its layoffs honestly, without disguising its reduction as performance-based terminations.

Salaries stuck

Since then, consistent with the trend experienced by most tech-focused Silicon Valley firms, Cooley's per-partner-profits fell 21 percent last year. In January 2002, the firm decided to freeze most associate salaries at 2001 levels, only raising salaries for second-year associates $5,000 so that first- and second-years wouldn't start at the same base salary. Cooley's chief operating officer, partner Mark Pitchford, explained to *The Recorder* that the measure would provide "a competitive start against other firms' base compensation" and allow room for discretionary bonuses at the end of the year.

Despite layoffs and salary freezes, the firm continues to bring in new blood. In 2001 Cooley offered jobs to 80 percent of its 89 summer associates.

Still wheeling and dealing

On a more positive note, Cooley Godward continues to play a leading role in a number of high-profile cases and deals. In the historic and highly publicized Hewlett-Packard/Compaq proxy fight, Cooley represented Walter Hewlett, HP director and son of company co-founder William Hewlett, in his effort to prevent the merger. Although a Delaware judge ultimately ruled in favor of HP leadership, the Cooley team (led by litigator and CEO Steve Neal) received widespread kudos for its performance. The firm's securities litigation expertise was likewise reflected in a series of recent successes. Cooley obtained a complete dismissal with prejudice for its client PacifiCare Health Systems in a securities class action involving a significant drop in the company's stock. The firm also won a dismissal for its client Gateway in one of the largest securities litigations in the United States with alleged damages exceeding $6 billion.

In the massive IPO "laddering" litigation now pending in the New York federal court, Cooley represents 17 issuer companies — one of the largest concentrations of issuer clients of any law firm in the nation. The firm's diverse litigation practice also includes intellectual property disputes, complex public utility matters and cutting-edge cases concerning Internet use, including privacy-related disputes and cases involving the First Amendment. Among Cooley's litigation clients are eBay, Applied Materials, NVIDIA Corporation and Pacific Gas and Electric.

Cooley corporate

On the corporate front, Cooley completed more than 70 mergers and acquisitions, with a total transaction value exceeding $6 billion in 2001, and raised more than $1.5 billion in its handling of 15 public offerings. Cooley's venture capital team formed 58 venture capital and leveraged buyout funds with a capitalization totaling more than $8.4 billion. Cooley was counsel for the Mountain View company, Aspect Development Inc., in i2 Technologies Inc.'s acquisition of Aspect — a deal valued at approximately $8 billion and recognized as the largest M&A deal ever completed in the software sector. In November 2001, Cooley partner Rick Climan advised Bay Area biotech company Gilead Sciences, Inc. in the sale of its oncology operations to Massachusetts-based OSI

Pharmaceuticals, Inc. in a deal valued at approximately $200 million. And in one of the largest deals between two biotechnology companies, Cooley partner Keith Flaum represented Cor Therapeutics Inc in Millenium Pharmaceuticals Inc.'s acquisition of Cor for $2 billion worth of stock, a deal that closed in February 2002.

Tort trouble for tech firm

Cooley faces legal battles in addition to its financial struggles. After a Cooley associate struck and killed a teenager in March 2000 while allegedly making business calls for the firm from her cell phone, Cooley was hit with a $30 million wrongful-death suit in June 2001. In reaction to the lawsuit, which undoubtedly will be watched closely by other employers, several of the largest firms in Washington, D.C., ordered their attorneys not to use hand-held cell phones while driving. Although a Virginia judge later threw out the direct negligence claims against the law firm, including the allegation that the firm should have had a policy prohibiting the use of hand-held cell phones while driving, Judge McCahill of Loudoun Circuit Court let stand a claim for $25 million that the associate was acting within the scope of her employment when she hit the girl. The trial is scheduled for December 2002.

More recently, in what may be the largest legal malpractice case ever filed in California, Cooley's former client MP3.com Inc. has sued the firm for more than $175 million, attributing the company's decision to launch its My.MP3.com Internet music service — and the subsequent copyright infringement suits — to Cooley's bad legal advice. Since the January 2000 launch of My.Mp3.com, MP3.com has paid out millions of dollars in settlements, judgments and legal fees relating to copyright infringement claims. Cooley's former client now seeks to recover these amounts plus several hundred million dollars more based on loss of value and good will. Mark Pitchford, Cooley's chief operating officer, has called the claims "frivolous." In fact, MP3.com faces a steep uphill course in putting the blame on Cooley for the results of its actions, according to an article by Susan Beck in *The American Lawyer*.

GETTING HIRED

Cooley's ice age

Associates at Cooley agree that landing a job at their firm is far from easy. The firm is recruiting for its litigation and life sciences practices, but hiring in some other areas, along with pay, is frozen. And then there are those pesky layoffs. "Getting hired right now would be some trick," remarks one associate. When the firm is hiring, it looks for "good schools, good grades." Those who need not apply: "ivory tower types," "the bottom-line oriented" and those with big egos. An associate in the San Francisco office notes: "Cooley is concerned with its culture. They look for personality." The "rigorous" interview process consists of two or three rounds of interviews with attorneys from various practice areas. Even the firm's managing partner does his share of interviews. One lateral associate remarks, "I was asked substantive questions about the law during my interviews."

Oh, those summer nights

"Wining and dining" isn't how most summer associates at Cooley Godward spend their summer. Summer associates see their share of lavish events, but there is also lots of "hands-on learning." An associate who helped with a venture capital financing during his summer says, "I drafted all the documents, and saw it through to closing. It gave me a really good appreciation of what my practice would eventually be like. I'm doing exactly the same thing right now." A corporate associate agrees, "The work that I did as a summer associate was at the level of a first-year associate. Our projects ended up in the clients' hands."

OUR SURVEY SAYS

Honesty and uncertainty

The face of Cooley Godward, once known to be "laid back," "fairly informal" and "congenial," seems to have changed a great deal due to the firm's summer 2001 layoffs and the general poor state of the economy. One associate notes, "Morale is at an all-time low." A Reston associate sums it up: "Gone are the smiling faces, open doors and overall sense of working in a great place with great people and great opportunity. Replace that with terrible morale, overall distrust of the partnership and many closed doors, of both associate and partner offices." One associate applauds the firm for handling itself well in the sour economy. "The firm is honest and forthcoming on almost all fronts, and I don't believe I could find this type of open environment in any other law firm." Associates in the San Francisco office are in disagreement about the state of their office. An associate there says, "The culture here is very friendly. Lawyers definitely socialize together on a regular basis — happy hours, long lunches and so on." But a Golden Gater disagrees: "There is currently a lot of tension between associates and partners — especially compared to a few years back."

Working hard for the money?

While many associates express resentment regarding the salary freeze instigated in early 2002, others think associates get a "boatload" of cash for what they do. One associate says, "Considering how slow things are, I'm getting very well compensated for my work." Despite the fact that the firm didn't increase pay this past year, it raised associates' billing rates, leaving a "bad taste" in the mouths of many associates. One litigator comments, "We're working harder than ever but we didn't get our lockstep raises." Cooley says bonuses make up the difference. A sixth-year associate agrees: "My bonus partially made up for the lack of a lockstep class raise." However most associates disagree. "The high bonuses that Cooley says it gives are reserved for only the select few teachers' pets," complains one junior associate.

Counting the hours

These days, some Cooley offices are busier than others. A San Francisco associate says, "While it's great to not have to bill 200 hours a month, billing about 100-120 hours is cause for concern. We need more work here." Sources in San Diego insist that they're as busy as ever. In Northern Virginia, an associate doesn't see the low hours as a problem, remarking, "In general the hours are great, but the down economy means that there have been weeks where I haven't had much to do during the weekdays, but then I have to work all weekend." Litigation associates seem divided on whether there is enough work for them to do. One litigator enjoys low hours. "I'm satisfied with my personal time but dissatisfied in terms of professional development." Another disagrees: "There is too much work in litigation and not enough associates to do it all." A corporate associate criticizes partners in this practice group, saying they "have consistently demonstrated their inability to bring in business." While things may not be all roses for full-time attorneys, part-time associates seem pretty happy with their hours. One notes, "I work a significantly reduced schedule but still have significant responsibility and, I think, respect within the office."

Coasting through Cooley College

Notwithstanding the "slow times" and ensuing "budget cutbacks," most associates agree that the training at Cooley Godward remains "top-notch." "Best training in the country," declares a Silicon Valley lawyer. According to a senior associate, "The level of training provided by Cooley, both to new attorneys and on an ongoing basis to attorneys at all levels, is impressive." Another lawyer calls the firm's commitment "unparalleled."

Singled out for special praise is "Cooley College," an "extensive training program for first-year associates" touted as a "fantastic" head start for new attorneys. All first-year associates and lateral hires attend a 10 to 15 day training program in Palo Alto that "walks through every area of the firm's practice and gives both a macro and micro treatment of many subjects." Beyond this initial structured orientation, the firm offers "good practice group meetings" on a weekly or monthly basis. Several sources complain, however, that training for mid-level associates is "minimal." Moreover, since "most training" after the first year "comes through doing different types of deals," the slowdown in corporate work has "dramatically" impacted the opportunities for on-the-job training.

Quest for partnership

Women at Cooley are divided as to how women fare in their quest for partnership. One female associate notes, "They are trying, but promotion, mentoring and flexible schedules all need help." Another source agrees: "Mentoring is wholly lacking." A San Francisco associate notes, "There is no interest in mentoring women associates." While some associates praised the firm's weekly female attorney lunches, others were unimpressed, calling the firm "all talk." One male associate cites the case of a female co-worker on maternity leave who did not receive a bonus because she did not meet the minimum hourly requirement. In the San Francisco office, the policy for working mothers is "somewhere between reluctant tolerance and absolute refusal."

Cooley is said to lack a large minority presence. A Colorado associate says, "There is very little, if any, diversity with respect to minorities in our local office." A white associate thinks the atmosphere for minorities needs improvement. "Very few minorities are still with the firm," he says. Most respondents think things are much better for gay and lesbian attorneys. One associate notes, "Attorneys don't seem to be afraid or nervous of being out at the office." Members of the San Francisco and Colorado offices say the many openly gay employees in the firm are "treated like everyone else."

Pro bono encouraged

Depending on department, that is. Most sources agree that "there is a sincere firm-wide commitment to pro bono work" but acknowledge that the commitment is "more so on the litigation side than on the corporate side." A litigation associate backs this up. "So far, about 30 percent of my time has been committed to pro bono matters, and management seems encouraging of this." However, a few litigation attorneys disagree. "I have rarely heard anyone from Cooley management encourage pro bono work," maintains an insider. Another agrees. "No one will come to you and tell you to do this pro bono project, but if you go out and find an opportunity, they'll let you do it." Another associate quips, "It's easy to be committed now when there's not enough work."

Moreover, associates seem to disagree about how pro bono hours are counted. "Last year," one lawyer says, "pro bono hours comprised a significant portion of my billable hours, and they counted 100 percent." A tax associate remarks, "At Cooley it's been a refreshing change, where you get billable hour credit for pro bono, no associate is saddled with too much of it, and the associate is free to accept or reject such projects, entirely changing my view of doing pro bono. Cooley truly supports it." A few other associates claim that pro bono hours do not count towards billable hours at all. One lawyer claims, "Pro bono hours are technically counted but in reality are taken out." The firm notes that pro bono hours are given equal weight and credit as compared with other work, including billable matters.

A room with a view

That's how one San Francisco associate describes his office. Another cracks that his office "has not been remodeled since the 1970s." And while it has a "beautiful view of the peninsula and Bay Bridge," there is "no sound privacy." A San Francisco associate pontificates, "My office is bright, comfortable, close to my secretary and big enough for my files. Anyone who needs more than that should go devote their life to the New York partnership track." The San Diego office had a major facelift in 2001. Most associates like their new San Diego digs. "We have a four-story building occupied entirely by Cooley. It is clear that a lot of thought went into the design of the space, particularly common areas." Yet there is some criticism of the San Diego office. "The new offices are small. The firm did not do a very good job in laying out the new facilities." In Colorado, the office seems to be a study in contradictions: "Posh and luxurious, but sterile and entirely uninteresting." Colorado associates admire their offices for being "very technologically advanced," but the décor is considered "awful." In our nation's capital, associates praise the "cool modern offices and furniture."

"Gone are the smiling faces, open doors and overall sense of working in a great place with great people and great opportunity. Replace that with terrible morale, overall distrust of the partnership and many closed doors."

— *Cooley Godward associate*

Baker Botts L.L.P.

One Shell Plaza
910 Louisiana Street
Houston, TX 77002-4995
Phone: (713) 229-1234
www.bakerbotts.com

LOCATIONS

Houston, TX (HQ)
Austin, TX • Dallas, TX • New York, NY • Washington,
DC • Baku, Azerbaijan • London • Riyadh, Saudi Arabia

MAJOR DEPARTMENTS/PRACTICES

Antitrust • Bankruptcy & Insolvency • Corporate •
Energy, Oil & Gas • Entertainment, Media & Sports •
Environmental • Finance • Government Contracts •
Intellectual Property • International • Labor &
Employment • Legislation & Policy • Litigation • Real
Estate • Tax • Technology • Telecommunications •
White-Collar Crime

THE STATS

No. of attorneys: 650
No. of offices: 8
Summer associate offers: 96 out of 104 (2001)
Managing Partner: Richard C. Johnson
Hiring Partner: David Sterling (Houston)

BASE SALARY

Texas offices, 2002
1st year: $110,000
2nd year: $114,000
3rd year: $121,000
4th year: $130,000
5th year: $140,000
6th year: $145,000
7th year: $155,000
Summer associate: $2,100/week

NOTABLE PERKS

• Relocation expenses and broker's fees
• Option of desktop or laptop computer
• Blackberry wireless e-mail devices
• Subsidized health club memberships

THE BUZZ
WHAT ATTORNEYS AT OTHER FIRMS ARE SAYING ABOUT THIS FIRM

• "One of Houston's big three"
• "Strong transactional practice"
• "Good old boys from Texas"
• "Oil and gas mergers"
• "Stuffed shirts"

UPPERS

• Welcoming attitude towards gays and lesbians
• No face time required
• Respectful culture

DOWNERS

• Bonuses tied to billable hours
• "Sink or swim" attitude toward training in some offices
• Diversity needs improvement

EMPLOYMENT CONTACT

Ms. Melissa Moss
Director of Attorney Employment
Phone: (713) 229-2056
Fax: (713) 229-7856
melissa.moss@bakerbotts.com

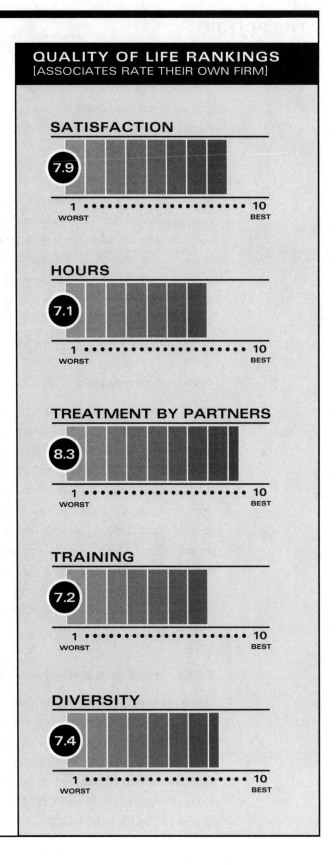

QUALITY OF LIFE RANKINGS
[ASSOCIATES RATE THEIR OWN FIRM]

SATISFACTION
7.9
1 WORST — 10 BEST

HOURS
7.1
1 WORST — 10 BEST

TREATMENT BY PARTNERS
8.3
1 WORST — 10 BEST

TRAINING
7.2
1 WORST — 10 BEST

DIVERSITY
7.4
1 WORST — 10 BEST

THE SCOOP

A part of Texas history for over 150 years, Baker Botts is the oldest law firm in the state and is among the largest firms in the country. With more than 650 attorneys in offices across Texas, the East Coast and the oil-rich regions of the Caspian Sea and the Middle East, Baker Botts has the natural resources to pursue a wide-ranging general practice.

Headline firm

Not surprisingly, a substantial portion of the Houston firm's business comes from the oil and energy industries. Technology and intellectual property law are also growing areas of expertise. In 2001 the firm recorded the largest technology M&A deal when it represented Schlumberger Limited in the acquisition of Sema plc in a deal valued at an impressive $5.3 billion. Currently, partners Joseph D. Garon and Doreen L. Costa represent the New York Stock Exchange in its appeal of a 1999 decision allowing a Las Vegas casino to use its registered logo. Attorneys in the firm's Houston office represented Dynegy, Inc. when it announced its acquisition of Enron Corp. for about $10 billion in November 2001.

Political prowess

The high-energy firm also boasts some high-profile partners and political connections. James A. Baker III, secretary of state to George Bush père and treasury secretary under Ronald Reagan, is currently a partner in the firm — as is his son, James A. Baker IV. On June 18, 2001, Stuart A. Levey, a partner in the D.C. office, was appointed associate deputy attorney general at the Department of Justice for Deputy Attorney General Larry Thompson. John P. Elwood, with the firm since January 2001, was appointed counselor to the assistant attorney general for the Department of Justice's Criminal Division, Michael Chertoff, on July 23, 2001, by United States Attorney General John Ashcroft. In September 2001, Baker Botts attorney Kirk K. Van Tine of the firm's D.C. office was sworn in as the U.S. Department of Transportation (DOT)'s general counsel. And in October 2001, President George W. Bush awarded another Baker Botts lawyer with a plum appointment when he named Robert Jordan, a founding partner of the Dallas office, ambassador to Saudi Arabia.

Baker gets gas and gives oil

Due to the natural gas shortage in California in the 1980s, Exxon Mobil Corporation sold natural gas to Pacific Offshore Pipeline Company (POPCO), a Southern California Gas Company (SoCalGas) affiliate at the time, under a gas sales contract. POPCO resold the gas to SoCalGas under a resale agreement. When gas prices were no longer high, SoCalGas tried to terminate the agreements unsuccessfully. After SoCalGas brought a federal suit, the companies settled, giving Exxon the option to purchase POPCO, which it did in 1998, and the right to terminate any previous agreements, which it did in 2000. Exxon terminated the resale agreement between POPCO and

SoCalGas, so SoCalGas sued. In March 2002, Judge Thomas P. Anderle found that Exxon had the right to terminate the resale agreement. Attorneys from Baker Botts in Houston represented Exxon in the case.

In March 2002, Shell Oil Company of Houston, a wholly owned unit of Royal Dutch/Shell Group of Hague agreed to acquire Pennzoil-Quaker State Company for $1.8 billion. Shell says this transaction will create the largest lubricant company in the world. Lawyers from the Houston office of Baker Botts represented Pennzoil-Quaker State. Also in March, Enterprise Products Partners, a Houston-based, publicly traded energy partnership, acquired a propylene fractionation business from D-K Diamond-Koch, L.L.C., Diamond-Koch, L.P., and Diamond-Koch III, L.P., jointly owned affiliates of Valero Energy Corp. and Koch Industries, for $231.5 million. Baker Botts represented Enterprise.

In May 2001, Pride International, Inc. merged with Marine Drilling Companies, Inc., producing the third-largest offshore drilling contractor, worth $6.2 billion. Baker Botts represented Pride International in the stock-for-stock transaction.

Yes to Yankees and no to entertainment

Attorneys at Baker Botts helped YankeeNets LLC create the Yankee Entertainment and Sports (YES) Network. The 24-hour, seven-day-a-week station, which launched in March 2002, features the 26-time World Champion Major League Baseball New York Yankees, the National Basketball Association New Jersey Nets and the 2000 Stanley Cup Champion New Jersey Devils National Hockey League teams. Lawyers from the firm's New York and Austin offices advised client YankeeNets.

Also in March 2002, Baker Botts represented USA Network majority shareholder, Liberty Media Corporation, in the former's sale of its entertainment division to Paris-based Vivendi Universal S.A. for approximately $10.3 billion. Lawyers from the firm's New York and D.C. offices represented Liberty Media Corporation.

Helping young inventors

Since 1991, Baker Botts has sponsored and judged the Richardson Independent School District's Invention Convention's "Most Patentable Invention Award." Attorneys at the firm volunteer their services to participants and the firm pays all fees and expenses regarding the patent application. In June 2001, Katie Ball, a third-grader at Moss Haven Elementary School in Dallas, won for her Automatic Closet System invention. The Automatic Closet System is a light in your closet that reflects the day's temperature, making it easy for you to decide what to wear.

GETTING HIRED

Happy summer associates

A Baker Botts summer is apparently a good summer. A Dallas associate remarks, "The summer here was almost more fun than work, although I believe that this may have changed some." Notes one New Yorker, "My summer experience was a good mix between realistic work that would be done as an associate and events for summer associates to get to know each other and the attorneys." Associates note that summer associates generally are expected to complete at least one major assignment during the summer, such as a 25-page memorandum, and several small assignments.

The summer program is the main source for new hires. Baker Botts candidates should expect an initial on-campus interview conducted by two lawyers, followed by a half-day of callback interviews at the firm. Warns one associate, "Not all interviewees who receive a callback are offered a summer associate position."

Looking to lateral

If you're looking to make a lateral move to Baker Botts, insiders say those with connections have it made. "I talked with an attorney that worked at my prior firm concerning opportunities," explains a lateral hire, "met with the partners in the practice group over dinner and, subject to conflicts, had an offer in a week without having any office visit." Associates also maintain that it is not unusual for in-house counsel of the firm's clients to join the Baker Botts team. One associate explains, "As an in-house attorney, I previously had worked with some of the attorneys at the firm. As a client, I respected their judgment and considered them to be some of the best attorneys with whom I had ever worked. When I decided to return to private practice, I wanted to work with those types of individuals."

SURVEY SAYS

It's not stuffy!

It's no secret that Baker Botts has a reputation for being a tad stuffy. A Houston associate refutes that image: "If being treated with respect is stuffy and uptight, I'll take it any day. Here, everyone is expected to treat others with respect, regardless of rank! That expectation results in an environment where everyone is appreciated for their contribution toward excellence. As an associate, I have found the staff, other associates and partners to be accepting and friendly." While Baker Botts attorneys may not be the happy hour type, they get along just fine. One insider in Austin remarks, "The firm is pretty laid back. The lawyers don't socialize all the time, but they do a lot more now than when I started here. Most people are married with kids so that cuts down on the partying opportunities, but group lunches are pretty popular." Most D.C. associates describe a similarly friendly vibe, though one lawyer says it's "pretty uptight and old fashioned." The New York office is considered "friendly" and "laid back."

Paychecks that please

Most associates at Baker Botts are quite pleased with their paychecks, saying their salary is "higher or comparable to other firms of our size and prestige." "Given the cooling of the Houston legal market, we are well compensated," remarks a senior associate. A fifth-year associate admits, "An associate and I recently discussed that somebody would have to offer us a lot more money to leave." Even part-timers are beaming. One part-timer says, "I was pleasantly shocked at how much I am being paid." One associate insists that "our pay is obscene in relation to what others in the workforce make." Explaining that his wife earns 25 percent of her husband's salary working as a teacher while logging in almost comparable hours, he remarks, "Young lawyers at large firms really have no basis to complain about their salaries. If they do, they should try working in the real world for a while."

To receive a bonus at Baker Botts, associates had better bill. A Dallas associate explains the bonus structure: "Bill 2,000 hours and you get your bonus with no questions asked. Bill less than 2,000 hours and you will have to explain what happened before you get your bonus. To date, no one that I know of hasn't received a bonus, even if they logged in less than 2,000 hours." While most associates agree that "our compensation levels are standard among top firms," some are less than thrilled with the firm's benefits package. "They are exceedingly stingy with cab and dinner reimbursements, they do not match your 401(k), and what you pay in health insurance is double what similarly situated attorneys pay," complains one frustrated associate.

Hours are good

Every lawyer realizes that long hours are part of the deal. At Baker Botts, folks seem happy despite the often-grueling hours. A Dallas associate notes, "We are blessed with an embarrassment of riches — read: too much work. That being said, I'd surely rather complain about hours than hear the crickets chirp and wonder if my pay check will bounce." An associate in D.C. says, "I consider myself lucky compared to most of my friends at large firms. Working late means past 7 p.m. I have only worked until midnight once." An associate in the New York office says there is a "high degree of autonomy," which makes longer hours "easier to tolerate." Insiders report that the firm doesn't require face time, so attorneys can do their work at the office or at home. A New Yorker adds that "all have time for other activities and family life." In the same vein, a Houston associate says, "As long as I come in early, I can be home for dinner every night."

Still a ways to go

When it comes to diversity, Baker Botts needs improvement. A female associate remarks, "This place has a somewhat deserved poor reputation when it comes to women. The recent implementation of part-time partners has improved the situation somewhat, but there is still a ways to go." Another woman agrees that the firm is making strides in the right direction but suggests that some partners presume women will jump ship after having children: "The training and mentoring of women is adversely affected by this attitude." Another insider makes clear that "women are treated entirely with respect." However, she points out that "there is no kind of mentoring program among women attorneys." Over in D.C., one woman cries, "I can count the number of female partners on one hand, in an office with 100 attorneys!" One insider addresses some common concerns of working parents: "Women associates with infants and young children work the same hours as their male counterparts, but do not have a stay-at-home wife to pick up the slack. The toll on mothers is very high, and we've lost some wonderful lawyers who felt they had to find less demanding jobs."

Associates state that diversity with respect to minorities needs improvement. A black associate insists that "firm-wide, the numbers are very disappointing. More aggressive works needs to be done." Minorities are "few and far between, and not particularly mentored. I have not, however, ever heard even a whisper of bad treatment," indicates an insider in the D.C. office. "We only have one minority partner," says a lawyer in Houston. "Mentoring could definitely improve." (The firm reports that the Houston office actually has four minority partners.) Still, not everyone agrees that diversity at Baker Botts needs fine tuning. "In large part, the firm is a meritocracy," explains a Houston litigator. "It tolerates people of all ethnicities and, for that matter, all dispositions who show an aptitude and ability to do the work the way it is expected to be done."

Things fare better for gays and lesbians. A lesbian associate notes that the firm is "very good with hiring. We have two openly gay senior associates who appear headed for partnership." Another lesbian says, "I am one of three openly gay associates. I bring my life partner to all firm functions and recruiting events, and we have always been warmly received. Nor have I ever felt any discrimination in terms of work assignments or evaluations." If there's one aspect about life at Baker Botts that has gay associates grumbling, it's the fact that the firm does not offer domestic partner benefits.

An average commitment

Associates give Baker Botts average marks for its commitment to pro bono work. A Dallas associate says, "The managing partner issued a statement several years ago that pro bono was strongly encouraged and that up to 40 hours per year would be counted toward your billable requirement. However, I do not think it is taken too seriously as far as counting toward your hours. On the other hand, the firm is willing to devote substantial resources toward helping those undertaking pro bono projects." "To some partners [pro bono] is very important," explains a D.C. associate, "but to most it is a pain they would rather young associates not deal with when we could be billing a paying client instead." Some associates express confusion and frustration over their firm's pro bono policies. "Although the firm really supports pro bono work and involvement in the community," explains an associate located in Austin, "I wish they would give us a definite policy regarding how many hours of pro bono work count towards billables and how much is too much." "I don't know if it counts or not, quite frankly," sighs one associate. That said, some associates are taking advantage of the pro bono system. Says one associate in Houston, "I spent over 200 hours on a family law case that went to trial. I worked it up and tried it and no one batted an eye about the amount of my time. In fact, I got an award!"

Sink or swim

Most associates at Baker Botts agree there is "absolutely no formal training" at their firm. "You are pretty much thrown into the water and you have to learn how to swim on your own," remarks a D.C. associate. "Some senior associates and partners are very helpful about helping you learn and some are too self-absorbed to explain what should be done and why." An associate in the Houston office says, "There is an expectation that you figure things out on your own, but there are also good teachers here if you can find them."

In New York, associates suggest that "all training is hands-on and of the highest caliber," while in Dallas, associates describe the training they receive in glowing terms. An associate there says, "Baker Botts has structured mentor programs, lots of feedback and an emphasis on developing attorneys. Associates will receive as much responsibility as they demonstrate they can successfully handle." Another Dallas associate brags, "We have an incredible mentoring program. One partner or senior associate is responsible for my workload, assignments and training. Any work I do must come through her. That sounds a little stifling, but in practice it works out great. She is evaluated, in part, on how well I am progressing. She is encouraged to get me a wide variety of work, to keep me busy but not swamped and generally to mentor me until I am prepared to take off the training wheels. It's a wonderful system."

Morgan, Lewis & Bockius LLP

1701 Market Street
Philadelphia, PA 19103-2921
Phone: (215) 963-5000

101 Park Avenue
New York, NY 10178-0060
Phone: (212) 309-6000

1111 Pennsylvania Avenue, N.W.
Washington, DC 20004
Phone: (202) 739-3001
www.morganlewis.com

LOCATIONS

Harrisburg, PA • Los Angeles, CA • Miami, FL • New
York, NY • McLean, VA • Philadelphia, PA • Pittsburgh,
PA • Princeton, NJ • Washington, DC • Brussels •
Frankfurt • London • Tokyo

MAJOR DEPARTMENTS/PRACTICES

Antitrust • Bankruptcy • Business & Finance •
Employee Benefits • Energy • Environmental •
FDA/Healthcare Regulation • Intellectual Property •
Investment Management • Labor & Employment • Life
Sciences • Litigation • Media • Mergers & Acquisitions
• Real Estate • Securities • Tax • Technology

THE STATS

No. of attorneys: 1,100
No. of offices: 13
Summer associate offers: 95 out of 125 (2001)
Firm Chair: Francis M. Milone
Hiring Partners: Coleen M. Meehan (Philadelphia);
Gregory L. Needles (Washington, DC); Christopher T.
Jensen (New York); Mark E. Zelek (Miami); John G.
Ferreira (Pittsburgh); Randolph Visser (Los Angeles)

THE BUZZ
WHAT ATTORNEYS AT OTHER FIRMS ARE SAYING ABOUT THIS FIRM

- "No employee loyalty"
- "Good minority recruitment efforts"
- "The big boys"
- "Philly office is fun and friendly"
- "Can you say pink slip?"

BASE SALARY

Philadelphia and Pittsburgh, 2002
1st year: $105,000
2nd year: $110,000
3rd year: $112,500
4th year: $120,000
5th year: $122,500
6th year: $130,000
7th year: $132,500
8th year: $132,500
Summer associate: $22,000/summer

Washington, 2002
1st year: $115,000 - $125,000
2nd year: $125,000 - $135,000
3rd year: $135,000 - $140,000
4th year: $150,000
5th year: $150,000 - $165,000
6th year: $170,000 - $180,000
7th year: $195,000
8th year: $205,000
Summer associate: $25,000/summer

New York, 2002
1st year: $125,000
2nd year: $$135,000
3rd year: $150,000 +
4th year: $167,000 +
5th year: $187,000 +
6th year: $200,000 +
7th year: $210,000 +
8th year: $220,000 +
Summer associate: $27,000/summer

NOTABLE PERKS*

- Monthly cocktail parties
- 24/7 snacks and beverages
- Backup child care
- In-house gym in Philadelphia and DC

*Not all perks available in all offices

UPPERS

- Collegial working environment
- Reasonable hours
- Sophistication and diversity of work

DOWNERS

- Bureaucratic hurdles
- Tight office space in New York
- Endless partnership track

EMPLOYMENT CONTACT

See www.morganlewis.com recruitment section for contacts in various offices

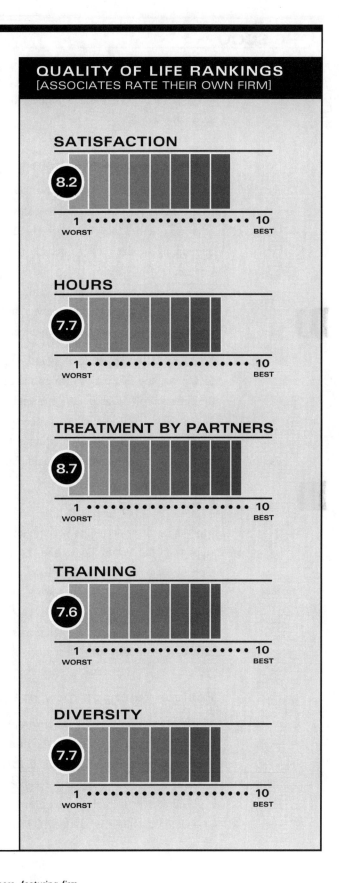

QUALITY OF LIFE RANKINGS
[ASSOCIATES RATE THEIR OWN FIRM]

SATISFACTION

8.2

1 WORST •••••••••••••••• 10 BEST

HOURS

7.7

1 WORST •••••••••••••••• 10 BEST

TREATMENT BY PARTNERS

8.7

1 WORST •••••••••••••••• 10 BEST

TRAINING

7.6

1 WORST •••••••••••••••• 10 BEST

DIVERSITY

7.7

1 WORST •••••••••••••••• 10 BEST

THE SCOOP

Big, bad and seriously well-respected, Morgan, Lewis & Bockius LLP employs more than 1,100 lawyers. Founded in Philadelphia, the firm may not have a headquarters, but it does have 13 offices across the world.

History: a patently rising star

Founded in Philadelphia 1873 by Civil War veterans Charles Eldridge Morgan Jr. and Francis Draper Lewis, the firm got off to a slow start. It wasn't until it was a century old that it moved to other major cities like New York (1972) and Los Angeles (1976). Once there, it grew fast, nearly quintupling in size. In the decade following, it branched out internationally, adding offices in London (1981), Tokyo (1988) and Brussels and Frankfurt (1989). In 1999 the firm underwent major management changes to centralize the decision-making process. These changes included giving the firm chair more power and creating managing partner positions for three areas: operations, practice and legal personnel.

Like many firms in 2001, Morgan Lewis experienced the effects of the economic downturn. In fact, it was the first major firm on the East Coast to announce sizeable layoffs. In October 2001, the firm laid off 50 associates from its U.S. offices. Two months later, the firm acquired the 35-lawyer New York intellectual property firm Hopgood Calimafde Judlowe & Mondolino. This acquisition should help boost Morgan Lewis' patent litigation practice. Both firms had a heavy hand in pharmaceutical and biotechnology industries, making the move a good fit.

Firm facelift

Morgan Lewis relocated its Washington, D.C. office in January 2002 to Pennsylvania Avenue, just steps from the White House and the Capitol. What's unusual about the new office is its new technological capability. The 14-floor, approximately 350,000-square-foot office has a conference and business center with a two-story conference room with seating for up to 135 people, a circular moot court room and a dining center with a rooftop terrace overlooking the Washington Monument. An interesting feature is a solar light pipe that spans 12 floors of the building, providing natural light to every floor by reflections made from prismatic glass.

Fashion faux pas may make business casual policy fizzle

Morgan Lewis managing partner of operations Tom Sharbaugh is glad the grunge look went the way of the dinosaur long before the firm instituted its business casual policy in 2000. In July 2001, Sharbaugh sent a firm-wide memo that the dress code is at risk of returning to formal business attire because of "a few bad apples." Fashion no-nos at the firm include capri pants; cargo pants; army-type attire; oversized clothes; exposed midriffs; low-cut necklines; see-through tops; halter, tube, or tank tops; miniskirts; shirts with team logos; sandals; men not wearing socks; floppy footwear;

and exposed tattoos and piercings other than in the ear. Sharbaugh also advised against wearing a white T-shirt with a V-neck sweater.

Mucho M&A and more

In the last three years alone, Morgan Lewis attorneys have overseen in excess of $157 billion in M&A transactions and $7.4 billion in public offerings. The firm represented New York Times Co., an investor in New England Sport Ventures, LLC, in its acquisition of the Boston Red Sox and New England Sports Network for $700 million. Morgan Lewis has also represented BNP Paribas SA in its $438.2 million acquisition of Consors Discount Broker AG, which created the largest discount broker in Europe. The firm served as special transaction counsel to Arnold Industries in a cash merger of Roadway Corporation for $550 million and lent a helping hand to Adolor Coporation in closing a significant global drug development and commercialization agreement with GlaxoSmithKline.

But Morgan Lewis isn't only about M&A. The firm boasts a top-notch litigation practice as well, with nearly 500 litigators (close to 200 of which focus on labor and employment matters) and several new litigation partners (including a former federal judge) to boot. The firm's IP practice is nothing to sneeze at either. Over 160 lawyers, patent agents, PhDs, scientists and others make up the IP group, which seved as special IP counsel to Diageo in its $8.15 billion acquisition of Seagram's wine and spirits business.

Morgan Lewis cares about kids

In January 2002, the firm announced it would make a $50,000 contribution to the Support Center for Child Advocates in Philadelphia. Individual Morgan attorneys matched the firm's donation by contributing personal funds, guiding the total donation to $100,000. The Support Center for Child Advocates provides legal representation and social work support to more than 600 abused and neglected children each year.

Morgan Lewis is committed to pro bono projects. In spring 2001, 124 summer associates were offered the option of spending only half their summer working at the firm. The other half would be spent taking part in the firm's new Public Interest and Community Service (PICS) program at a public interest organization of their choice. The associates would still be paid their normal summer associate salaries throughout the summer. Twenty-nine summer associates took the firm up on the offer.

GETTING HIRED

Casting a wide net for the best and brightest

While "a strong academic background" is a must for those candidates looking to work at Morgan Lewis, insiders emphasize the importance of character over law school name or class rank. According to a senior associate in New York, "The firm looks to hire the best and the brightest, but casts a wide net. That is, the firm does not limit itself to only certain schools or pools of candidates." It seeks "intelligent, diligent and independent candidates" who must "have some personality, exhibit confidence and an ability to interact effectively with clients, not be overly stiff or formal and demonstrate a commitment to teamwork and fostering a collegial environment." Several sources repeat that on top of being "bright" and "motivated," candidates should also be "friendly" or "personable" to "fit in with the collegial atmosphere Morgan Lewis tries to maintain."

Lateral associates describe the hiring process as both "rigorous" and "straightforward." It generally includes "an initial screening interview with one partner, followed by a second-round interview" with other partners and some associates in the group. One attorney reports that the process is "democratic," in that the decision to extend an offer is made "with the input of partners and associates." Several laterals appreciate the speed with which Morgan acts, having had to wait "only a week between initial interview and offer."

OUR SURVEY SAYS

Great job, great people

Most insiders at Morgan Lewis have nice things to say about their firm. They are "very happy with the level and quality of the work" and enjoy the "collegial" atmosphere. An associate in the labor & employment group declares, "Throughout my tenure as an associate I have received, and continue to receive, challenging and interesting work across a diverse range of industries. In addition, the collegiality and camaraderie of the attorneys with whom I work enhances the day-to-day practice of law." Many colleagues share his enthusiasm. "The work is stimulating; the people are enjoyable to work with. I am happy coming to the office each day," concludes one attorney. Associates appreciate "sophisticated and challenging" work, a "broad range of experience and immediate client contact."

More than one insider believes the "culture at Morgan Lewis is certainly one of the firm's strengths" and "have found the associates and partners to be friendly and team-oriented." The D.C. office "is a fun place to work." The firm's overall atmosphere is "generally relaxed" and "less formal than most would think." The amount of after-hours socializing "varies from practice group to practice group." One lawyer shrugs, "If you want to socialize, you can. If you don't, there is no pressure to do so." For those who like organized events, the New York office sponsors monthly cocktail parties and there are Friday happy hours in Philadelphia.

Despite all the cheerleading, some attorneys do voice complaints. These include the "bureaucracy" of a very large firm, which "makes getting simple tasks completed difficult" and an "emphasis on billable hours and the pressures that go with that." Some associates express nervousness over the layoffs of almost 50 associates in 2001. (The firm points out that this figure represents less than 5 percent of its lawyers.) But the following response better captures the opinion of many Morganites: "Great job, great people."

Positive experiences with partners

As several insiders point out, relations between partners and associates are always "a mixed bag," particularly in a firm of this size. That said, most Morgan Lewis associates believe that "relations between partners and associates here are about as good on a day-to-day basis as they can be in a large active firm." Sources appreciate respectful treatment by partners, some of whom "have developed close relationships with associates." The firm's open-door policy encourages direct contact between partners and associates. Many partners "are great mentors and teachers who take care and pride in your professional development." Others are respectful but maintain an "'us' versus 'you' mentality." Screaming and other demeaning tactics are apparently rare, since "poor treatment of associates is taboo here at Morgan Lewis." "If there is one common fault," suggests a Philadelphia lawyer, "it is that praise is impossible to find, no matter how hard the job."

Professional and elegant, without posturing

Associates are mostly content with, if not ecstatic about, their firm's office space. Insiders term the firm's Los Angeles offices "nice." Miami lawyers have "a great view of South Beach and Biscayne Bay." The new building in Washington, D.C. is "very nice with a lot of amenities," but associates complain of poor furniture that "is not ergonomically correct in any sense of the word." Junior associates in Philadelphia appreciate not having to share offices, and even if "the building is dowdy, it is conveniently located." New Yorkers voice the most complaints, mainly on the subject of a "space crunch that has resulted in associates sharing offices until their fourth year." The firm, however, is reportedly "adding two new floors that should hopefully relieve this problem." The building itself is beautiful, "with knockout views of Manhattan." While associates do not consider the space "luxurious," at least one lawyer believes the firm has the right approach, striving for a "nice balance between professional and elegant, without ridiculous posturing."

Few complaints about compensation

Some Morgan Lewis associates believe their firm's "compensation is above average, competitive" and "very generous with bonuses." Other associates claim that the firm is "known for not quite matching market," particularly when it comes to bonuses. Yet, even many of those who believe

Morgan "stays a bit behind the compensation leaders" find that "the favorable working conditions may make up for this." "There may be firms in New York that pay more, but in turn they require more billable hours," says one associate. According to another New Yorker, "the pay is especially attractive relative to the workload." Respondents in the Philadelphia and Princeton offices "believe [that] in the Philadelphia region, Morgan Lewis is one of the highest paying law firms."

On top of a "competitive" base salary, associates who meet the 2,000-hour threshold are eligible for bonuses which are "based upon a variety of criteria including hours, quality of work, citizenship and market factors." Some lawyers find the method of awarding bonuses "very unpredictable." But at least one source feels the system is "fair" and "gives the firm the opportunity to reward those who deserve it."

Livable hours — for a large law firm

Morgan Lewis lawyers expect to — and do — work hard, but on balance insiders seem to find their hours "very livable." According to several associates, the firm's hours requirements are "fair and manageable." "With a target of 2,000 hours, it is not very demanding as compared to other large New York City firms." Associates don't feel "the typical pressure of face time that most lawyers in firms feel" and work as necessary only to deliver quality product to their clients. The work often "goes in cycles" and many sources claim that "rarely are you required to work weekends." Nevertheless, some attorneys complain that there is in fact "pressure to bill over 2,000 hours a year," particularly for those who want to make partner.

Several associates praise the firm's part-time options. A part-timer believes "the firm is deeply committed to making the part-time program work. I continue to get great assignments, and large cases, even though I am part-time. The firm also will, and has, made part-time partners, and does not consider part-time status to be a hindrance or a barrier to partnership."

A serious commitment to pro bono

Although many Morgan associates say their firm actively encourages pro bono work, few seem convinced that "there are many takers." A fourth-year associate insists, "The firm actively supports pro bono activities. Such support includes counting such hours as billable and having an annual award ceremony for individuals committed to pro bono." He adds, however, "That being said, many associates do not participate in pro bono activities." One lawyer proudly notes that he "did a federal prisoners' rights jury trial that required hundreds of hours," for which he received billable credit. Other insiders report that each office has a partner in charge of pro bono, that attorneys receive regular e-mails "listing all the pro bono projects" and that time spent on pro bono counts "as regular billable hours for all purposes, including bonuses." Morgan Lewis also offers summer associates the opportunity to spend half of their summer "at a public interest organization of their choice." And this, says one source, "is our best commitment to pro bono."

"Miles to go" on diversity

Despite genuine efforts "to address the concerns of working women, particularly the work/family balance," some associates express distress that their firm still has "miles to go before we level the playing field at the top." Morgan Lewis' "unusual" practice of making part-time partners wins praise, as does its hiring of female attorneys in numbers equal to that of men, but a few sources sigh that it is still "a decidedly male culture." Many insiders are concerned "with the low number of minority senior associates, of counsel and partners," although they believe that minorities at Morgan are otherwise treated well. The firm gets credit for offering domestic partner benefits. While some associates assert that the firm "provides an environment that is open, tolerant, and respectful of gays and lesbians," another lawyer claims that "almost everyone is closeted."

The Minority Law Journal listed Morgan Lewis as 54th in the publication's Diversity Scorecard's top 100 national law firms. It was also noted that the firm had a higher percentage (11.3 percent) of minority lawyers than the national average.

Fulbright & Jaworski L.L.P.

1301 McKinney, Suite 5100
Houston, TX 77010-3095
Phone: (713) 651-5151
www.fulbright.com

LOCATIONS

Houston, TX (HQ)
Austin, TX • Dallas, TX • Los Angeles, CA •
Minneapolis, MN • New York, NY • San Antonio, TX •
Washington, DC • Hong Kong • London • Munich

MAJOR DEPARTMENTS/PRACTICES

Admiralty
Corporate
Energy & Real Property
Environmental
Health Law Administration & Litigation
Intellectual Property & Technology
Labor & Employment Law
Litigation
Public Law
Tax, Trusts, Estates & Employee Benefits

THE STATS

No. of attorneys: 770
No. of offices: 11
Summer associate offers: 102 out of 128 (2001)
Executive Committee Chairman: A.T. Blackshear Jr.
Hiring Committee Chairs: John Sullivan (Global); Edward
Patterson and Jerry Lowry (Houston)

BASE SALARY

Houston, 2002
1st year: $110,000
2nd year: $110,000
3rd year: $110,000
4th year: $115,000
5th year: $125,000
6th year: $135,000
7th year: $140,000
Summer associate: $2,100/week

NOTABLE PERKS

• Free Friday morning breakfast (by department)
• Subsidized parking (Houston)

THE BUZZ
WHAT ATTORNEYS AT OTHER FIRMS ARE SAYING ABOUT THIS FIRM

• "Grand old litigation firm"
• "Glorified lobbyists"
• "Arrogant"
• "Wonderful place to work"
• "Full of good ol' boys"

UPPERS

• Highly prestigious litigation and energy practices
• Reasonable hours

DOWNERS

• Relatively few minority and women partners
• Mind-numbing bureaucracy

EMPLOYMENT CONTACT

Ms. Cynthia A. Graser
Manager of Attorney Employment
Phone: (713) 651-3686
Fax: (713) 651-5246
CGraser@fulbright.com

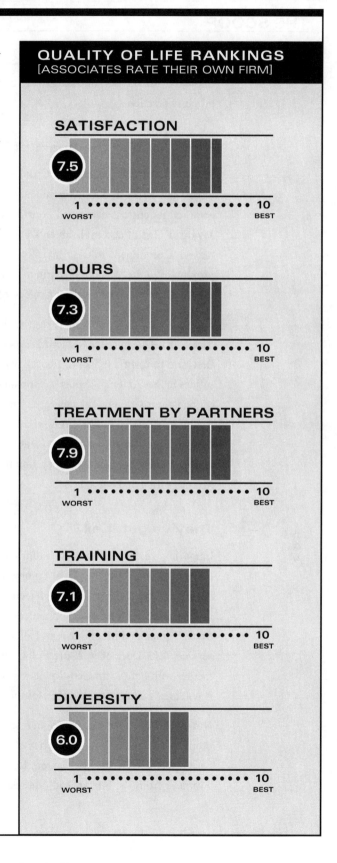

QUALITY OF LIFE RANKINGS
[ASSOCIATES RATE THEIR OWN FIRM]

SATISFACTION
7.5
1 WORST — 10 BEST

HOURS
7.3
1 WORST — 10 BEST

TREATMENT BY PARTNERS
7.9
1 WORST — 10 BEST

TRAINING
7.1
1 WORST — 10 BEST

DIVERSITY
6.0
1 WORST — 10 BEST

THE SCOOP

Big firm, big practice and big cases — Texas-grown Fulbright & Jaworski, L.L.P. continues to impress with its first-rate litigators, experienced corporate attorneys and growing intellectual property practice.

From deep in the heart of Texas

In 1919 R.C. Fulbright and J.H. Crooker launched Fulbright & Jaworski, which is today one of the largest law firms in both its home state of Texas and the nation. Fulbright, Crooker & Freeman acquired its current name and considerable talent after Leon Jaworski joined the firm in 1932. Jaworski's list of accomplishments is impressive; he helped build Fulbright's oil and gas practice, played a prominent role as investigator in the Nuremberg war crimes trials, acted as special prosecutor in the Watergate hearings and served as president of the State Bar of Texas, American Bar Association and American College of Trial Lawyers.

Fulbright may have roots in Texas, but its reach extends far beyond the borders of the Lone Star State. In 1927, in order to facilitate its work in the transportation industry, Fulbright became the first firm to open a branch office in Washington, D.C. In the 1970s and 1980s, the firm opened offices in San Antonio, Dallas, Austin and London. The 1989 merger with Reavis & McGrath, one of the largest U.S. law firm mergers ever, not only increased the firm's numbers but also provided it with new offices in New York and Los Angeles. In 1990 Fulbright once again took the lead as the first Texas-based law firm to establish an office in Hong Kong. The addition of a Minneapolis office in 2000 brought the firm's number of offices to a perfect 10 (with the later addition of a Munich office making it 11).

They've got it all

Large in size, broad in scope, Fulbright bills itself as an international full-service firm. It has earned the respect of the legal community for its expertise in the areas of litigation, corporate, securities, venture capital and high technology. Not surprisingly for a Houston-headquartered firm, Fulbright has built a bustling practice around the energy and oil industry. Oil giants like Exxon, Shell, Texaco and Mobil have all called on the firm for transactional, regulatory and development services. In December 2001, Fulbright represented Houston's Veritas DGS Inc. in a pending merger with Petroleum Geo-Services ASA of Norway; if the deal closes in mid-2002 as expected, it will create a company valued close to $1 billion.

Not one to be left behind, Fulbright responded to the technology boom by expanding its intellectual property practice. Through a series of moves beginning with the 1997 merger with Los Angeles-based Robbins, Berliner & Carson, LLP and featuring the February 2000 import of more than 30 attorneys from the Austin and Minneapolis offices of Arnold White & Durkee, an intellectual property boutique, Fulbright has greatly expanded its resources in this area. With 145 IP attorneys firm-wide, the Texas firm now has one of largest IP practices in the country.

Lone Star litigators

Fulbright's litigators are legion and legendary. Over 250 trial lawyers make up the firm's litigation team, among them stars like Linda L. Addison, recently named one of America's Top 50 Women Litigators by *The National Law Journal*. Addison currently serves as one of the lead counsel for The Northern Trust Company in litigation over Enron employee benefit plans. Also, Tom Godbold was recently elected president of the Houston Bar Association. High-profile litigation clients in recent years include 3M in silicone breast implant litigation, Toshiba of America in the $2.1 billion settlement of a class-action suit in which the company was accused of selling faulty floppy disk drives, and death row inmate Jose Santellan Sr. in the successful overturn of his capital murder conviction.

Fulbright's cases are frequently on the cutting edge. In January 2002, Fulbright won a major victory for client InfoRocket.com, Inc., sponsor of the LiveAdviceTM web site. In what may be the first ruling on the application of the trade dress doctrine to the appearance of a web site, Judge Loretta Preska of the Southern District of New York refused to grant a preliminary injunction to the client's competitor, Keen, Inc., on the claim that similarities in the appearances of the two web sites constituted patent and trade dress infringement. In February 2002, the firm helped German inventor Dr. Harry Gaus win a decade-long patent infringement battle against hair-dryer manufacturer Conair Corp. The jury awarded $28.5 million to the inventor and, should the New York City judge award treble damages for Conair's willful infringement, the final judgment could well top $100 million.

M&A monsters

It's not only in the oil industry that Fulbright deals have hit the headlines. The firm has handled a number of acquisitions topping the $100 million mark. Last July, when TMP Worldwide Inc., the parent company of Internet job site Monster.com, announced that it planned to swallow rival HotJobs.com Ltd., Fulbright represented TMP in the $460 million stock deal. The firm also lent a hand over the holidays to The Right Start, a manufacturer of upscale child and baby items, in its $55 million acquisition of certain assets of toy retailer FAO Schwarz.

Rewards of excellence

Fulbright's reputation extends both to the firm itself and the individuals who work there. Leon Jaworski represents but one illustrious star in the Fulbright galaxy. Many of Fulbright's attorneys are active in professional organizations, and several have served as president of the Texas State Bar as well as president of the American Bar Association. Fulbright has sent more members to the ABA's House of Delegates than any other firm in the nation. In August 2001, Texas Governor Rick

Perry appointed Xavier Rodriguez, a San Antonio labor lawyer and Fulbright partner, to the Texas Supreme Court. More recently, Governor Perry named partner Pike Powers to the newly formed Governor's Council on Science and Biotechnology Development.

Apart from the satisfaction of working for a respected employer, Fulbright offers more material compensation in the way of high profits, competitive salaries and a low attrition rate. Fulbright landed in the top third of *The American Lawyer*'s list of America's Highest-Grossing Law Firms for both 1999 and 2000. The Texas firm also hit the *New York Law Journal*'s 2001 "NYLJ 100" list of top law firms. Fulbright has continued to expand its practice even as other firms have been tightening belts, and new attorneys joined each of its U.S. offices in the last several months. In January 2002, the firm named eight new partners.

Lending a Texas hand

Six weeks after the terrorist attacks on the World Trade Center and the Pentagon, the firm pledged up to $250,000 to provide relief to families of victims. Attorneys from Fulbright's New York office also represented TransitCenter in obtaining a 10-year lease at 1065 Avenue of the Americas after the nonprofit issuer of Transit/Cheks lost its home in Two World Trade Center.

GETTING HIRED

If you've got personality ...

Then Fulbright is the place for you. A Houston associate notes, "Personality counts for a lot on all levels of the interview. Fulbright attorneys want people who they are going to enjoy hanging out with in and out of the office." So interviewees need to dazzle through "two rounds of interviews with seven or eight partners in total," says a New York associate. But it takes more than a winning smile to impress this firm. "Ranking of the law school attended and grades do matter in getting a callback." While the firm employs its share of candidates from top-tier law schools, those who excel at second-tier schools are given equal evaluation. A Houston associate adds, "If you get an offer for the summer, then you definitely have a foot in the door."

An endless party

A Fulbright summer may be fun, but it's also work. A New Yorker explains, "The summer program is designed to be fun but also to give you some realistic work." A Houston associate says, "I got substantial assignments that were not busy work and that actually required thought. Fulbright does a good job of giving the summer associate a fairly accurate picture of the type of work they would be doing." A Dallas associate happily adds, "I had the opportunity to work in a variety of areas and was given the choice to choose what department I wanted to be hired in." Another Houston associate maintains, "The quality of work assigned to me was very good and I had the opportunity to attend depositions and hearings."

OUR SURVEY SAYS

Culture varies from office to office

Each Fulbright office seems to have its own unique culture. The Houston office is said to be "conservative" and "wholesome." An associate there maintains, "I would describe the culture as professional but not uptight — people are relaxed but business-oriented." Another Houston associate suggests that partners in the Houston office "know and care how I'm doing and what I'm doing and whether I'm happy. Associates socialize with each other during and after work a great deal, as do some partners. Associates and partners tend to have informal but professional and not overly personal relationships with each other." In Dallas, "Overall, the atmosphere is relatively relaxed and informal, especially considering the size of the firm. My impression is that the majority of my co-workers take most, if not all, of their vacation time."

The New York office is "secretive" yet "friendly." Says a New Yorker, "It's quite informal but very segregated in terms of partners and associates." But another New Yorker disagrees: "Everyone's door is open, and people frequently stop in to talk and see how you are doing." That open-door policy is prevalent in San Antonio as well. "I am very satisfied with the quality of life in San Antonio and the work/life balance of the firm. Everyone is on a first-name basis and there is an open-door policy that creates a sense of openness." The LA office is reportedly "wonderful" and "laid back." An associate there says, "The quality of work is excellent, hours are very reasonable and the people are generally easygoing. I haven't seen any backstabbing during my tenure."

Happy campers

Most Fulbright associates seem happy with their salaries. One associate based in our nation's capitol notes, "My compensation is pretty much standard for big D.C. firms." Another D.C. associate remarks, "We are technically below market, but we get paid a lot of money for what we do. To complain would be sort of like walking down the street with a ham under each arm but being angry that you don't have any bread." While some in Houston think their salaries are below market, others feel they are making "gobs" of money. An attorney in San Antonio maintains, "I am very pleased with the compensation package." The only office where insiders express great dissatisfaction is New York. An associate there says, "The firm keeps changing bonus compensation structure and reduced associate salary without satisfactory explanation; further reduction in salary was not clearly announced, rather underhandedly slipped in a memo shown (and then taken back) to the associate at his/her year-end review."

Best hours in the biz

Associates at Fulbright seem pleased with their hours. An Austin associate says, "I work a lot of hours, but at the same time I'm grateful to have the opportunity to work a lot of hours." In D.C., another insider notes, "My hours are fair. No one working in a big law firm works 40 hours a week, especially as a young associate when it takes you three times as long to complete an assignment as it should. Usually when I work serious overtime, it's because I put the pressure on myself to go the extra mile. This is certainly not a sweatshop." In Houston, an associate remarks, "I work as much as I need to get the job done. There is no need to put in face time." A first-year associate mentions, "The firm is serious about its emphasis on quality work product and on letting the first-year attorney worry more about developing as a professional rather than billable hours. Some departments work harder than others, but the attorneys in them know what they're getting into when they sign up for it. As time goes on, of course, hours become important."

An LA associate adds, "Compared with our peers, the hours are pretty good. The office is deserted by 6:30 p.m. and on weekends, generally, only a few people come in." A Houston associate explains, "Typically, I come in about 8:00 a.m., and I leave about 6:00 p.m. Those times can vary by about a half hour to an hour either way, but usually do not. I cannot and do not complain about my hours. For the pay I receive and the job security I have, I could not ask for better. Our bonuses begin and end at a relatively low number of hours, and I have not been pressured to bill more hours beyond those very reasonable levels. I also have not seen or heard of any such pressure on anyone else. There is no pressure to come in on weekends, to come in early or to stay late. More than once I have been 'ordered' to leave early, either to go home and see my family or to head out for a drink."

Needs work on diversity

Women at Fulbright say the firm needs to take a second glance at women's issues. At Fulbright, it's the same problem endemic in the industry — women are hired in sufficient numbers but few are represented at the partnership level. "The firm has very few women partners, and although there is a diversity committee, no concrete steps have been taken yet to address the issues of promotion and mentoring among women." In D.C., a female attorney remarks, "We just had our first married and pregnant woman make partner. The other two female partners in D.C. are not married and do not have children. I think the firm is making a conscious effort to be more female-friendly, and more senior associates are now having babies and taking maternity leave." Another woman mentions, "As far as I can tell, little is done to mentor women or focus on women's issues at the firm. Any alternative working programs or schedules that have been created for women who wish to go off partner track or agree to a longer track, for whatever reason, are very hush-hush at the firm."

Minorities have similar concerns. An Hispanic associate notes, "I have not seen any focus on or special interest in retention of minorities." A black associate says, "Fulbright has no black or Asian partners, and a handful of Hispanic partners worldwide. There is a high attrition rate among the minority attorneys. The firm has started a minority diversity committee, but no concrete steps have been taken as yet to address the retention, mentoring and promotion issues. The minorities who are at Fulbright are a tight-knit group, and in general I don't think there is any difference in treatment based on race." An Asian associate mentions, "The firm could use some help here. On the plus side, the firm doesn't soften its standards for the sake of tokenism. On the minus side, it is not known for aggressively seeking the top minority candidates."

Great teachers

Most associates are happy with the training provided by Fulbright. While the amount and style of training differ at each office, for the most part, associates are learning well. "It's not uncommon for the partner I work for to spend 30 minutes to an hour explaining an assignment. Not only what he needs, but why he needs it, what sources he thinks I should look at and sometimes a 50-year historical retrospective of the problem I'm researching. I feel that I am always given the tools I need to perform well," says a D.C. associate. In Houston, litigation associates seem pleased as well. One Fulbrighter notes, "The firm has excellent training programs. The litigation training was an unparalleled experience — the equivalent if not better than my law school trial advocacy class. Mentoring also occurs both formally and informally." Another Houston associate agrees, "The firm makes sure you receive instruction in every aspect of your practice, from discovery to trial techniques and client development."

Associates in New York have mixed feelings about the training offered. One associate agrees with peers at other branches, saying, "Within my department I have received very good on the job training. Firm-wide, I am very appreciative of the CLEs offered in-house, particularly with respect to practice development." However, others feel differently. One associate asks, "What training?" while another contends that the firm offers "very little formal training, mostly on the job which can be like trial by fire." Yet another insider explains, "There are almost no internal lectures and presentations, for example, unless they are intended as business development events. Because of this, it is important to get quality work and to learn by doing it."

McDermott, Will & Emery

227 West Monroe Street
Chicago, IL 60606-5096
Phone: (312) 372-2000
www.mwe.com

LOCATIONS

Chicago, IL (HQ)
Boston, MA
Irvine, CA
Los Angeles, CA
Miami, FL
New York, NY
Palo Alto, CA
Washington, DC
London
Munich

MAJOR DEPARTMENTS/PRACTICES

Antitrust
Communications & Technology
Corporate
Employee Benefits
Estate Planning
Health Law
Intellectual Property
International
Regulatory & Government Affairs
Tax
Trial

THE STATS

No. of attorneys: 909
No. of offices: 10
Summer associate offers: 58 out of 66 (2001)
Chairman and Managing Partner: Lawrence Gerber
Hiring Attorney: Lydia R.B. Kelley

THE BUZZ
WHAT ATTORNEYS AT OTHER FIRMS ARE SAYING ABOUT THIS FIRM

- "Great tax firm"
- "Growing too fast"
- "Excellent health care practice"
- "Low associate morale"
- "Trying to make a comeback"

BASE SALARY

Chicago, Boston and Washington, DC, 2002
1st year: $125,000
2nd year: $135,000
3rd year: $150,000
4th year: $165,000
5th year: $175,000
6th year: $180,000
7th year: $185,000
Summer associate: $2,400/week

New York, Irvine, Los Angeles and Palo Alto, 2002
1st year: $125,000
2nd year: $135,000
3rd year: $150,000
4th year: $165,000
5th year: $185,000
6th year: $195,000
7th year: $205,000
Summer associate: $2,400/week

Miami, 2002:
1st year: $105,000
2nd year and beyond: Not on lockstep system
Summer associate: $2,000/week

NOTABLE PERKS

- Bagels weekly
- Paternity leave (as well as maternity leave)
- Subsidized gym membership
- Health plan includes laser eye surgery

UPPERS

- Esteemed tax practice
- Lean staffing allows direct contact with partners and clients
- Winning combination of market pay and reasonable hours

DOWNERS

- Emphasis on billable hours
- Lack of training and mentoring
- Penny-pinching approach to perks, bonuses and office support

EMPLOYMENT CONTACT

Ms. Karen K. Mortell
Legal Recruiting Manager
Phone: (312) 984-7784
Fax: (312) 984-7700
kmortell@mwe.com

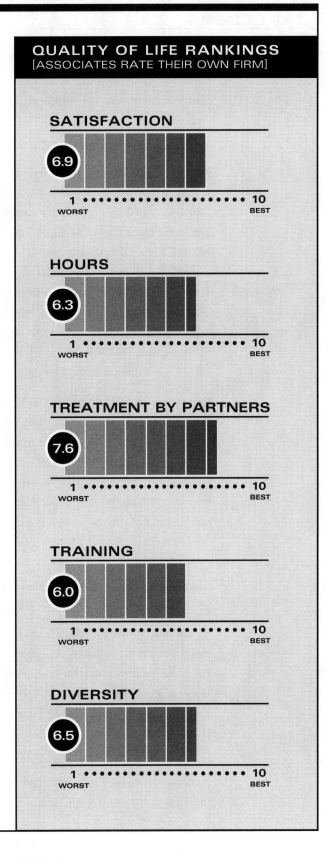

QUALITY OF LIFE RANKINGS
[ASSOCIATES RATE THEIR OWN FIRM]

SATISFACTION
6.9
1 WORST .... 10 BEST

HOURS
6.3
1 WORST .... 10 BEST

TREATMENT BY PARTNERS
7.6
1 WORST .... 10 BEST

TRAINING
6.0
1 WORST .... 10 BEST

DIVERSITY
6.5
1 WORST .... 10 BEST

THE SCOOP

McDermott, Will & Emery is one of the largest and most profitable law firms in the world. Originally established in Chicago as a tax practice, McDermott has expanded into a full-service firm with burgeoning departments in employee benefits, health care and intellectual property.

History — from the Midwest to Munich

McDermott, Will & Emery was founded in 1934 in Chicago as a tax firm. It has since evolved into a general practice firm with an international clientele. More than 900 lawyers work out of McDermott's 10 offices located across the United States and in Europe. The firm's tax department, among the largest in the world, is considered one of the most prestigious practices in this country. MW&E has also worked hard to develop its intellectual property practice, which has more than tripled in size in the last three years. The IP department is clearly doing something right; *Washington Business Forward* recently called McDermott one of the "hottest IP firms in town." The firm's work in the field of health law and employee benefits has also garnered national recognition. For the last two years, legal recruiters in *The American Lawyer*'s annual Associate Survey ranked MW&E the most prestigious firm in the United States for health law and ERISA/employee benefits. The same survey rated the firm's tax practice second in the nation.

Early this year, McDermott, Will & Emery opened the doors to one European office and closed the doors on another. The firm acquired five partners from the German firm Beiten Burkhardt Mittl & Wegener to launch a new office in Munich in January 2002. That same month, MW&E transferred control of its office in Vilnius, Lithuania to its Lithuanian lawyers. The firm maintains a substantial presence in London with more than 60 attorneys and is reportedly considering a merger with a Paris boutique. In another move calculated to expand the firm's international business and political connections, McDermott recently entered into "a strategic alliance" with The Cohen Group, a consulting firm started by former Secretary of Defense William S. Cohen.

Catching the West Coast wave

McDermott's aggressive efforts to develop its intellectual property practice are paying off. In March 2001, the firm made the top 10 in *IP Today*'s annual survey of top patent firms based on the number of patents issued by the U.S. Patent & Trademark Office in 2000. McDermott's reputation has lured a number of other high-profile attorneys into the firm's fold. In 2001, more than 35 lawyers, including several top IP attorneys, joined the firm's three California offices in Silicon Valley, Los Angeles and Orange County. The Menlo Park office alone gained seven lateral partners last year.

One of those partners is Terrence McMahon, former head of the IP group at Orrick, Herrington & Sutcliffe, who now leads McDermott's West Coast IP practice. When McMahon climbed aboard in January 2001, his luggage included premier clients Advanced Micro Devices, Logitech, Seagate, and Ericsson Inc., as well as Orrick associate Robert Blanch Jr., who became a partner at McDermott. Other recent immigrants include three former Wilson Sonsini Goodrich & Rosati attorneys, four Oppenheimer Wolff & Donnelly partners and four tax attorneys from Fenwick & West. The influx of legal talent so overwhelmed the firm's Menlo Park offices that in March 2002 McDermott moved to larger space in Palo Alto, Calif.

Love that dirty water

McDermott flexes that intellectual muscle in the courtroom. The firm won a victory for Broadcom Corp. against rival chipmaker Intel Corp. when a federal jury in Delaware found Broadcom had not infringed two Intel patents. Broadcom undoubtedly hopes this win is a harbinger of things to come, since seven other patents remain in dispute and the company is pursuing its own patent infringement suit against Intel in a Texas federal court. Fellow client Aptix Corporation likely breathed a sigh of relief last fall when MW&E lawyers helped persuade the Federal Circuit Court of Appeals to reverse a district court judgment declaring one of the company's existing patents unenforceable because of discovery misconduct by Aptix during an infringement suit.

On the environmental front, early this year the firm represented Exxon Mobil Corporation in one of the largest hazardous waste settlements ever negotiated. Just days before the case was scheduled to go to trial, Exxon reached an agreement with the Justice Department to pay $11.2 million for allegedly mishandling benzene-contaminated waste at a storage and distribution terminal in Staten Island, N.Y. Peter Sacripanti, one of the attorneys on that case and longtime counsel for Mobil, also acts as liaison counsel for the defendants in a pending, massive, multi-district litigation over alleged contamination of groundwater by the major oil companies (In re Methyl Tertiary Butyl Ether Products Liability Litigation).

Making connections

McDermott's team of transactional attorneys has also been hitting the headlines. In February 2002, the firm represented IDT Corporation in its $42.5 million purchase of the assets of bankrupt wireless company Winstar Communications. In late 2001, the London office advised the international engineering and construction group Kvaerner in the $100 million sale of its Hydrocarbons and Process Technology Divisions to the Russian-based Yukos Oil Company. The U.K. office also tendered its legal expertise to the European Investment Bank on the 1.2 billion financing of a high-speed rail link project in the Netherlands. Back in the States, lawyers from the firm's D.C. office helped the Monarch Beverage Company swallow PepsiCo's All Sport isotonic beverage when they acted as antitrust counsel to Monarch in connection with PepsiCo's buyout of Quaker Oats Co.

In the spring, MW&E attorneys in Chicago, Washington and New York worked together to complete a hospital mega-merger by counseling client Quorum Health Group in its union with

Triad Hospitals Inc. The transaction valued Quorum at $2.45 billion and creates the third-largest investor-owned hospital company in the United States.

Get 'em while they're young

Just in time for the school year, last September McDermott launched a firm-wide volunteer tutoring program. The pro bono program provides attorneys and staff in the firm's U.S. offices with the opportunity to coach elementary school children in basic reading and grammar skills. But schoolchildren aren't the only folks for whom MW&E will work for free. Thanks to the efforts of a pro bono team of McDermott lawyers from the firm's New York office, a Brooklyn man saw his 10-year old murder conviction overturned last summer. On July 12, 2001, the Second Circuit Court of Appeals reversed the denial of defendant Sami Leka's petition for a writ of habeas corpus, ruling that the prosecution's failure to tell the defense about a police officer who witnessed the murder violated Leka's constitutional rights.

Soon afterward, MW&E Chicago stepped in on the prosecutorial side, serving pro bono as counsel for the Judicial Inquiry Board in support of the removal of Cook County Judge Oliver M. Spurlock from the bench for sexual harassment and misconduct. Now, one of McDermott's own Chicago lawyers hopes to find a seat on the bench. Neil F. Hartigan, a partner at MW&E and former Illinois attorney general, is currently running unopposed for a vacancy on the First District Appellate Court. In addition, Robert Cordy, former head of the firm's Boston office, was appointed as associate justice of the Supreme Judicial Court of the Commonwealth of Massachusetts.

GETTING HIRED

A preference for prestigious schools

"A top-tier law school" is a must if you want to work for McDermott, according to many insiders. Those from lower-tier schools need to have impressive resumes — i.e., "you'd better be in the top 5 percent of your class, be on journal, have majored in rocket science and have resolved the Mideast conflict, or you don't have a realistic shot." Some lawyers are critical of their firm's "knee-jerk reactions to school prestige." "If you went to Harvard, Stanford, Michigan, Chicago, Northwestern or Virginia, you can be a soon-to-be-bad attorney and still get a job." A New Yorker suggests the emphasis on school name is misplaced and "ironic since some of the largest rainmakers in the office did not attend top schools."

If academic credentials motivate the initial cut, then "once candidates hit the interview stage ... personality and teamwork are very important characteristics." McDermott appreciates "good interpersonal skills." "With such small incoming classes," explains an attorney, "there's no room for someone you wouldn't want to sit next to at Thursday night attorney dinner." Several sources note that as "the economy has made a turn for the worse," hiring has become much more competitive.

OUR SURVEY SAYS

A commuter culture

McDermott as a whole "has no real defining culture." It is "highly office-specific, and even department-specific within individual offices." Insiders' levels of satisfaction accordingly run the gamut — from associates who find the firm "a terrific place to work" to attorneys who are decidedly "unsatisfied and in the process of looking for a new firm." Many lawyers praise the quality of work and opportunities for career development. A Boston-based associate enjoys a "dynamic working environment" with "lots of responsibility and client contact early on." And an attorney in Chicago responds simply: "Great work, great people and great culture." But other lawyers complain about a "lack of interesting work" and an increasing emphasis on the bottom line. One associate laments, "While McDermott is thriving financially, its associates and their quality of life unfortunately are falling prey to the idea that money (rather than humanity) is the bottom line."

The firm has a business casual dress policy and is frequently described as "friendly" but "not excessively social." One associate suggests that McDermott has the "culture of a commuter school: lawyers work hard, are friendly to each other in the office and go home as soon as they can." Many lawyers agree: "This is a place [where] you can shut your door, get your work done and go home." Some people appreciate this separation between professional and personal lives: "McDermott is a firm that takes pride in working hard and maintaining a life outside of the office." Others find the "lack of socialization" a drawback. An associate in the firm's Chicago headquarters declares, "McDermott is not a warm, cuddly place." Nevertheless, certain offices and practice groups are close knit, and a few attorneys say colleagues are among their "closest friends." Lawyers may find this "mammoth" firm's smaller offices, like Miami and Silicon Valley, more sociable, since "everyone knows everyone."

Reasonable hours but increasing pressure to bill

Like many in the law community, McDermott associates would prefer to work fewer hours. "We would all love to spend less time at the office," acknowledges an insider. But the "people I work with don't seem to care what your schedule is as long as you make your hours and get your job done, which is how it should be." This attorney's schedule — "I'm usually there 12 hours a day on weekdays and not at all on weekends" — is similar to those reported by several respondents who agree that "McDermott is not a 'face time' firm."

However, one complaint shared by many respondents is that "too much emphasis is placed on billable hours. If you do not hit at least 2,100 hours, it is unlikely that you will get a significant bonus, no matter how good your work is." And if you don't bill at least "2,000, the consequences can be serious," according to one lawyer. This pressure "creates stress during the low-billing months." A Boston attorney describes this anxiety as a "hangman's dilemma." He says, "My department has been slow, so I'm not spending too much time at the office; on the other hand, I (and other associates facing similar slowdowns) live with the stress of knowing the firm is constantly monitoring your billables — most recently, I am informed, on a day-to-day basis."

Still, many McDermott lawyers refuse to complain about their hours. "Yes, we work more than 9 to 5," one associate says, "but the attorneys are reasonable, and I will never complain about a job where I sit in a nice office, read and write and get paid very, very well."

Middle of the market

McDermott lawyers' compensation is "in line with other firms," but some insiders mutter that it is "not the highest in town." Even associates who argue that the firm is "very generous" note that "it lags ever so slightly behind those firms with which we purport to compete — seemingly by design." Most sources are satisfied with their "competitive" base salaries, but many feel that McDermott "is very tight with bonuses and benefits." "Clarifying the [bonus] policy and criteria to associates," one lawyer believes, might help stem the "widespread associate dissatisfaction with the bonus process." A few less diplomatic sources call McDermott "stingy" and "cheap" because it ties bonuses so closely to billable hours, has "no technology allowances, no [paid] sabbaticals," and "nickels and dimes you for phone calls." (The firm does not pay for long-distance personal phone calls.) Still, many associates feel "extremely grateful" to be paid such "a ridiculous amount of money."

Adequate office space

When you work for a "financially conservative, Chicago-based firm" like McDermott, you probably shouldn't expect posh office space, which "would be inappropriate and a waste of money." Instead, you're more likely to find offices that "are nice, comfortable and sufficient for [your] needs." Associates praise the "great views" from "one of the most beautiful buildings in Chicago." There's no "Starbucks in the break room, but all associates have their own offices with windows." Some attorneys complain that the "furniture is pathetic" and "everything is brown," but one lawyer concludes, "The space is more than adequate." Colleagues in Boston also enjoy "spectacular" views, "nice, not too flashy" offices that associates needn't share. New Yorkers like working in Rockefeller Center, although the offices themselves are little better than "average." The Washington, D.C. office "is conveniently located near a Metro stop." One savvy road-tripper rates the site as a "Marriott or Hilton — not a Four Seasons or Ritz-Carlton. But certainly above a Red Roof Inn or Super 8."

The work is the training

Associates continue to be critical of the training opportunities at McDermott. Despite recent efforts to expand in-house training, many respondents still feel they "have not received as much training as [they] would like." There are "very few" formal programs in-house and the firm "is picky about approving outside training sessions." In addition, "Training hours do not count towards billable [hours], which in effect discourages associates from receiving training." For the most part, associates agree, "the work is the training." Some lawyers love the "'real work' training" and value the informal mentoring from "terrific" partners. Others complain, "The training and guidance from the partnership is deplorable." "This is generally where the firm needs to improve," says a New York associate, who also acknowledges McDermott's efforts in this regard. "The firm in the recent past has been working on this and has now hired someone who is in charge of making sure this happens."

Not a big push for pro bono

Most McDermott insiders don't see a big push for pro bono participation — in part because the firm's policy on whether pro bono work counts towards billables is a "complicated matter." According to an associate, "The firm's policy is that 60 hours a year count toward billables. To receive credit for more than that, you must write to the pro bono committee seeking approval." But sources do not agree whether associates must first meet the 2,000 billable requirement before the 60 hours are credited or whether the 60 hours actually count toward that requirement. (The firm notes that the first 60 hours count towards the 2,000 billable hours.) Moreover, a litigator points out that 60 hours "is several hundred hours shorter than the typical case that gets disposed of in motion practice." "The firm voices support for pro bono," many associates believe, "but makes it difficult to be involved." Other lawyers insist McDermott "is committed to pro bono work" and is "taking great strides to involve associates in useful pro bono opportunities."

Stuck in the same rut

"There is a serious lack of minorities in all private firms in general," and McDermott is no exception. "Our firm wants to increase its minority attorneys but seems to be stuck in the same rut as most other large firms," reports one insider. While some associates of color say they "have never encountered any problems," most sources agree that there are still "far too few minorities" and the firm should "work on minority recruiting, retention and mentoring." The limited number of "women in management or leadership positions" troubles many associates, although they say that the firm "hires and promotes a good number of women." Some women complain that there is no "gender-specific mentoring," but individual "women in the firm try to provide a lot of mentoring opportunities." Several attorneys suggest that McDermott "needs improvement in dealing with our competing desires of career and family," noting that "the firm's less than fully supportive attitude towards part-time positions may make equity partnership more difficult for women." One bright spot is that the firm has approved domestic partnership benefits.

V/\ULT

THE VAULT 100:
FIRMS 51-100

Steptoe & Johnson LLP

1330 Connecticut Avenue, NW
Washington, DC 20036-1795
Phone: (202) 429-3000
www.steptoe.com

LOCATIONS

Washington, DC (HQ)
Los Angeles, CA
Phoenix, AZ
Brussels
London

MAJOR DEPARTMENTS/PRACTICES

Antitrust
Energy & Natural Resources
ERISA/Employment
International
Litigation
Tax
Technology
Transactions

THE STATS

No. of attorneys: 350
No. of offices: 5
Summer associate offers: 20 out of 20 (2001)
Chairman: J.A. (Lon) Bouknight Jr.
Hiring Partner: Stephen A. Fennell

NOTABLE PERKS

- In-house gym
- Lunch with new associates on the house for six months
- Luxury box at Washington's MCI Center
- Work effort, discretionary and tenure bonuses

EMPLOYMENT CONTACT

Ms. Rosemary Kelly Morgan
Director of Attorney Services and Recruiting
Phone: (202) 429-8036
Fax: (202) 828-3661
legal_recruiting@steptoe.com

Washington, DC, 2002
1st year: $125,000
2nd year: $131,000
3rd year: $138,000
4th year: $145,000
5th year: $155,000
6th year: $165,000
7th year: $172,000
8th year: $180,000
Summer associate: $2,400/week

THE BUZZ
WHAT ATTORNEYS AT OTHER FIRMS ARE SAYING ABOUT THIS FIRM

- "Past its prime"
- "Their associates love the place"
- "Think too highly of themselves"
- "Some excellent white-collar work"

THE SCOOP

Steptoe & Johnson, born in a West Virginia law office, was founded by Philip Steptoe and Louis Johnson in 1913. The firm moved to Washington, D.C., in 1945 when Johnson rejoined the practice after having held numerous government positions, including secretary of defense, for Franklin Roosevelt and Harry Truman. In 1980, the Washington, D.C., and West Virginia offices separated amicably. The firm has continued its tradition of government service; several current Steptoe attorneys have served in various government roles, including Susan Esserman, former Deputy U.S. Trade Representative, and Kevin Gover, former head of the Bureau of Indian Affairs. The firm's government connections have also helped it establish a prestigious lobbying practice. Steptoe also has a respected corporate practice, as well as prestigious energy and international practices.

GETTING HIRED

If you want to get your foot in the door at Steptoe & Johnson, study up. "While there does not seem to be a bias toward particular schools, the firm does tend to look for people who did very well in law school," reports one insider. "Of course the firm is looking to hire the cream of the crop," brags another contact. But don't expect eggheads only. "Grades mean everything at first," agrees another associate. "After that initial screening, you need to be friendly."

OUR SURVEY SAYS

Associates at Steptoe praise the firm's culture. Explains one associate, "The working relationships and general rapport between partners and associates, and among associates, can't be beat." One consistent gripe is the occasional breakdown in communication. "The firm administration is somewhat rigid and difficult to navigate," warns one attorney. "There is a tendency to leave policies unclear so as to leave room for discretion."

Steptoe associates appreciate hours that are a bit better than average, sources say. "For the most part, the number of hours one spends at the firm is up to the individual associate," says one contact. "Everybody's expected to make the target of 1,950 billable [hours] — which is not especially taxing — but there is only limited pressure to exceed that by any significant amount."

Associates acknowledge that they are "not at the top of the market" when it comes to pay, but some "think the good lifestyle makes up for the slightly sub-par salaries." The firm's deferred compensation system is another source of complaint. "We have this contrived compensation structure consisting of a base salary and then something called an 'additional base' salary that is earned only if the minimum 1,950 hours are billed," reports one associate. The firm says mid-level associates are eligible to have the additional base compensation included in their annual salary.

Chadbourne & Parke LLP

30 Rockefeller Plaza
New York, NY 10112
Phone: (212) 408-5100
www.chadbourne.com

LOCATIONS

New York, NY (HQ)
Los Angeles, CA
Washington, DC
Hong Kong
London
Moscow

MAJOR DEPARTMENTS/PRACTICES

Bankruptcy
Corporate
Employment
Environmental
Insurance/Reinsurance
Intellectual Property
Litigation
Product Liability
Project Finance
Real Estate
Tax
Trusts & Estates

THE STATS

No. of attorneys: 350+
No. of offices: 6
Summer associate offers: 35 out of 35 (2001)
Managing Partner: Charles K. O'Neill
Hiring Partner: Vincent Dunn

THE BUZZ
WHAT ATTORNEYS AT OTHER FIRMS ARE SAYING ABOUT THIS FIRM

- "Solid work"
- "Where booze and tobacco come together"
- "Very good in project finance"
- "Stuffy atmosphere"

NOTABLE PERKS

- Cashless online meal delivery system
- Gift from Tiffany's for passing the bar
- Blackberry pagers
- Significant gym subsidy

EMPLOYMENT CONTACT

Ms. Bernadette L. Miles
Director of Legal Recruiting
Phone: (212) 408-5338
Fax: (212) 541-5369
bernadette.miles@chadbourne.com

BASE SALARY

New York, 2002
1st year: $125,000
2nd year: $135,000
3rd year: $150,000
4th year: $170,000
5th year: $190,000
6th year: $205,000
7th year: $210,000
8th year: $215,000
Summer associate: $2,403/week

THE SCOOP

Happy birthday! The year 2002 marks the centennial of Chadbourne & Parke's birth. The solo practice begun by Thomas Chadbourne has evolved into an international law firm with more than 300 attorneys. Chadbourne & Parke is known for its project finance group, as well as its corporate and litigation practices. Chadbourne was among the first foreign law firms to open an office in Moscow and has established a network of offices and affiliations across Central Asia. One of the firm's most prominent practice areas is product liability. The firm secured a defense verdict for Jim Beam Brands in the first fetal alcohol syndrome case brought to trial and has represented Brown & Williamson Tobacco and other cigarette manufacturers. Currently, Chadbourne is helping defend the makers of the analgesic OxyContin against individual and class actions in 23 states.

GETTING HIRED

Chadbourne's hiring process, which past interviewees describe as "quite reasonable" with "no messing about," involves multiple rounds of interviews. In most cases, "you need good — but not stellar — credentials, and an exhibited background and desire to be part of [a given] practice group," says an insider. On the other hand, "in some practice groups, if you have a JD and a pulse, you're in." As for laterals, they usually endure "a screening interview with two to three people, and then they come back to meet a bunch more people," reports one associate.

OUR SURVEY SAYS

What is the best description of the Chadbourne corporate culture? Several associates describe the firm as "uptight but trying to project a laid-back image." Others disagree. "In my experience," explains an insider, "things are laid back and informal in terms of the way in which we interact with each other and with paralegals and staff. There is nothing laid back or informal, however, in terms of expectations regarding work product and the accuracy and professionalism thereof." Lauds one insider, "Many of the partners here are outstanding lawyers, and I've learned from observing, from asking questions and from feedback and criticism from them."

Insiders believe that at Chadbourne, the vibe is "probably far more life-friendly than at other firms of commensurate size and pay scale." As is common among its peer firms, "it's hot or cold at Chadbourne. You're either falling asleep or falling apart." While "partners are very cognizant of when people might be overworked," they are also very aware of who's spending adequate time in the office. "If asked, everyone will say that face time is not important — but it is," says an associate. "You can get burned in evaluations at bonus time if you haven't shown your enthusiasm for the work by showing your face at night or on weekends." The firm sets a 2,100-hour minimum for bonuses, which "includes pro bono hours and other internal-related hours and is easy to make if you are not totally lazy."

LeBoeuf, Lamb, Greene & MacRae, L.L.P.

125 West 55th Street
New York, NY 10019-5389
Phone: (212) 424-8000
www.llgm.com

LOCATIONS

New York, NY (HQ)

Albany, NY • Boston, MA • Denver, CO • Harrisburg, PA • Hartford, CT • Houston, TX • Jacksonville, FL • Los Angeles, CA • Newark, NJ • Pittsburgh, PA • Salt Lake City, UT • San Francisco, CA • Washington, DC • Almaty, Kazakhstan • Beijing • Bishkek, Kyrgyzstan • Brussels • Johannesburg • London • Moscow • Paris • Riyadh, Saudi Arabia • Tashkent, Uzbekistan

MAJOR DEPARTMENTS/PRACTICES

Bankruptcy & Restructuring
Corporate
Energy
Environmental, Health & Safety
Executive Compensation, Employee Benefits & ERISA
Financial Services/Insurance
Litigation
Real Estate
Tax
Technology & Intellectual Property

THE STATS

No. of attorneys: 750
No. of offices: 24
Summer associate offers: 36 out of 39 (2001)
Chairmen: Steven H. Davis and Peter R. O'Flinn
Hiring Partner: William G. Primps

THE BUZZ
WHAT ATTORNEYS AT OTHER FIRMS ARE SAYING ABOUT THIS FIRM

- "Strong insurance practice"
- "Not a bad place to be, briefly"
- "Nice people, friendly environment"
- "Who wants to do utilities work all the time?"

NOTABLE PERKS

- Tickets to sporting and cultural events
- Ability to work overseas
- Firm pays for NITA
- Regional retreats

EMPLOYMENT CONTACT

Ms. Jennifer Mathews
Manager of Legal Recruiting & Retention
Phone: (212) 424-8849
Fax: (212) 424-8500
jmathews@llgm.com

BASE SALARY

New York, 2002
1st year: $125,000
2nd year: $135,000
3rd year: $150,000
4th year: $170,000
5th year: $190,000
6th year: $200,000
7th year: $205,000
8th year: $210,000
Summer associate: $2,404/week

THE SCOOP

With 10 offices overseas and 14 locations across the United States, LeBoeuf, Lamb, Greene & MacRae is a truly international firm. Since its founding in 1929, the New York-based firm has built a multinational practice around its traditional client base in the insurance, financial and energy industries. In fact, over the last three years, LeBoeuf has been involved in more M&A transactions in the energy and the insurance industries than any other law firm. The firm serves as national litigation counsel for Alcoa Inc., and handles all nationwide litigation for the United States Filter Corp, the eastern U.S. litigation for Adelphia Cable and the U.S. litigation for Lloyd's of London. Additionally, LeBoeuf's bankruptcy work for fallen energy leviathan Enron is proving lucrative; the firm's services in the first month alone generated a $706,000 tab.

GETTING HIRED

At LeBoeuf, "credentials matter." "The firm is always eager to hire grads from top schools," notes one associate. While some former summer associates describe the summer program as "bare bones," others remark that "the social component of the summer was well-thought out and had diverse offerings." Sources praise the program for providing "a realistic approximation of life as an associate." "As a summer associate, I was given a good amount of substantive work and developed relationships that paid off when I came back full time," says an insider.

OUR SURVEY SAYS

Attorneys at LeBoeuf give the firm culture mixed reviews. It's "a curious mix of laid back and formal," reports a New Yorker. "The lawyers are very friendly and screamers are rare, but socialization outside the firm is minimal." Another lawyer remarks that he has "never even had lunch with a colleague, never mind socializing." Still, the lack of a wild social life doesn't faze everyone. An associate in Utah notes, "It is a very congenial and pleasant place to work."

When it comes to hours, most associates agree the firm has "reasonable expectations." Billable hours are seen as "humane," but "in order to be a star, you really have to exceed the expectations." Some associates complain that the work is uneven. "There is either no work or 100-hour weeks. No happy medium," sighs an insider.

The "financially conservative" but "fair" firm gains points for base compensation, which associates describe as "competitive" and "market." Bonuses, however, are another matter. Sources suggest that "bonuses are hardly [ever] given, and if they are, you have to be superhuman to receive one." (According to the firm, bonuses were paid to every associate who worked 2,000 hours and ranged from $5,000 to $50,000, based on seniority and hours.)

Irell & Manella LLP

1800 Avenue of the Stars
Suite 900
Los Angeles, CA 90067-4276
Phone: (310) 277-1010
www.irell.com

LOCATIONS

Los Angeles, CA (HQ)
Newport Beach, CA

MAJOR DEPARTMENTS/PRACTICES

Alternative Dispute Resolution • Antitrust • Appellate •
Art • Aviation • Corporate Securities • Creditors' Rights
& Insolvency • Employee Benefits & Executive
Compensation • Entertainment • Environmental •
High-Tech, Entertainment & IP Transactions • Insurance •
IP Litigation • Labor & Employment • Land Use •
Litigation • Personal Planning/Trust & Finance •
Real Estate & Finance • Taxation • White Collar
Criminal Defense

THE STATS

No. of attorneys: 225
No. of offices: 2
Summer associate offers: 36 out of 38 (2001)
Co-Managing Partners: Morgan Chu and
Kenneth R. Heitz
Hiring Chair: Daniel P. Lefler

NOTABLE PERKS

• Annual associate lunch
• "Gourmet" happy hours every other week
• In-house gym
• Profit-sharing for mid-level and senior associates

EMPLOYMENT CONTACT

Ms. Robyn Steele
Recruiting Administrator
Phone: (310) 277-1010
Fax: (310) 203-7199
rsteele@irell.com

BASE SALARY

Los Angeles, 2002
1st year: $130,000
2nd year: $135,000
3rd year: $150,000
Summer associate: $2,400/week

THE BUZZ
WHAT ATTORNEYS AT OTHER FIRMS ARE SAYING ABOUT THIS FIRM

• "Dream job for entertainment law"
• "Rough on associates"
• "High quality, odd people"
• "Inflated sense of self-worth"

THE SCOOP

If you're drawn to sunshine, a sophisticated practice and a glamorous clientele, then Southern California's Irell & Manella might just be the law firm for you. The 60-year-old firm with offices in Los Angeles and Newport Beach is known for its laid-back culture and cutting-edge IP practice. Originally founded as a tax boutique in Century City, Irell's tax department continues to enjoy a national reputation, and the firm now offers a full range of legal services from antitrust to environmental law to white-collar criminal defense. But it is in the areas of high-tech, entertainment and intellectual property law that Irell really shines. The firm serves major media players like Disney, LucasFilm Ltd. and *The National Enquirer*.

GETTING HIRED

"The firm is very strict about GPA requirements — if you don't meet the minimum, don't bother to apply," warns one associate. Indeed, grades and pedigree are very important. Says one source: "Being ranked toward the top of the class is an absolute must. Furthermore, those who have either clerked or participated in law review are favored." Even laterals are not immune. "Irell is one of the few firms that pays attention to law school grades when evaluating lateral candidates," says one insider. Some feel the stringent standards sometimes put the firm at a disadvantage. "If you have good grades, they will overlook personality faults," reports one lawyer.

OUR SURVEY SAYS

Irell associates enjoy a relaxed culture and an unusual amount of responsibility, say insiders. "The firm's culture is informal and comfortable," says one contact. "Although the attorneys are serious about their work, there is a lot of humor on a day-to-day basis. This is a place where you can be yourself." "Irell is the antithesis of hierarchical, which is nice because as long as you get your work done, no one pays too much attention to what you're doing," remarks another lawyer. You will, however, find your way onto interesting cases. "The firm's bread and butter is entertainment litigation and soft IP, areas of law that tend to lead to interesting cases," says one associate.

"Irell has a bonus structure that should keep billables down," says one source. "All associates in the same class receive the same bonus, regardless of hours. So there is little incentive to bill extreme hours for the sake of billing." Associates tell us that the target billable hours amount is 2,000 and that Irell's lockstep salary and bonus structure is A-OK. "The partnership has been extremely generous with both base salary and bonuses," gushes one lawyer. When the firm does well, senior associates share in the wealth. "Beginning as fourth-years, associates share in the firm's profits," states one associate.

Pillsbury Winthrop LLP

One Battery Park Plaza
New York, NY 10004
Phone: (212) 858-1000

50 Fremont Street
San Francisco, CA 94105
Phone: (415) 983-1000
www.pillsburywinthrop.com

LOCATIONS

Century City, CA • Costa Mesa, CA • Los Angeles, CA •
New York, NY • Palo Alto, CA • Sacramento, CA • San
Diego, CA • San Francisco, CA • Stamford, CT •
Tysons Corner, VA • Washington, DC • London •
Singapore • Sydney • Tokyo •

MAJOR DEPARTMENTS/PRACTICES

Antitrust • Bankruptcy & Creditors' Rights • Corporate,
Securities & Finance • Class Actions • E-Commerce &
Internet Law • Emerging Companies • Employment &
Labor • Executive Compensation & Benefits • Energy •
Environmental & Land Use • Intellectual Property •
International Transactions • Licensing, Technology &
Trade • Life Sciences & Technology • Litigation •
Media & Content • Real Estate, Project Development &
Construction • Tax • Telecommunications • Trusts &
Estates

THE STATS

No. of attorneys: 800
No. of offices: 15
Summer associate offers: Over 90% (2001)
Chair: Mary B. Cranston
Vice Chair: John Pritchard
Managing Partner: Marina H. Park
Hiring Partners: David Crichlow and Courtney Lynch

THE BUZZ
WHAT ATTORNEYS AT OTHER FIRMS ARE SAYING ABOUT THIS FIRM

- "Great merger of East and West"
- "Layoffs a-plenty"
- "Diluted by merger"
- "You go, girl!"

NOTABLE PERKS

- Emergency child care assistance
- Participation in firm VC fund
- Concierge service for car tune-ups, theater/movie tickets, restaurant reservations, etc.
- On-site chair massage sessions

EMPLOYMENT CONTACT

Ms. Denice Barnes
Silicon Valley Recruiting
recruit_SV@pillsburywinthrop.com

Ms. Dorrie Ciavatta
NY, CT and Foreign Office Recruiting
dciavatta@pillsburywinthrop.com

Ms. Vernona M. Colbert
DC and Northern VA Recruiting
recruit_DC@pillsburywinthrop.com

Ms. Mary Ellen Hatch
Los Angeles Recruiting
recruit_LA@pillsburywinthrop.com

Ms. Sela Seleska
San Francisco Recruiting
recruit_SF@pillsburywinthrop.com

(See www.pillsburywinthrop.com for other
employment contacts.)

BASE SALARY

All offices, 2002
1st year: $125,000
2nd year: $135,000
3rd year: $150,000
4th year: $170,000
5th year: $190,000
6th year: $195,000 + profit points
7th year: $195,000 + profit points
8th year: $195,000 + profit points
Summer associate: $2,400/week

THE SCOOP

Strategic mergers with firms in Los Angeles, New York and Washington, D.C., have turned the San Francisco-based Pillsbury Madison & Sutro into the bi-coastal Pillsbury Winthrop. Now numbering nearly 800 attorneys, Pillsbury Winthrop boasts a top IP practice, as well as strong litigation and corporate departments. Clients range from emerging high-tech firms to corporate giants like AOL Time Warner and Bristol-Myers. For Pillsbury associates, 2001 ended on a less optimistic note than it began. The $10,000 raise (to $135,000) for first-years announced in early 2001 vanished a year later, and in November 2001 the firm responded to the post-September 11 downturn in business by letting go 10 percent of its New York associates. On the brighter side, the firm remained one of the top-grossing Bay Area firms in 2001, and boasts one of the few female chairs in a major law firm, the influential Mary Cranston.

GETTING HIRED

"This firm looks for exactly the same things most others do — a combination of academic achievement, people skills, common sense and work ethic," says a second-year associate. Still, some things differ by office. For one thing, while "the New York office is very 'name brand' conscious, it does hire people from second- and third-tier schools" and also "drools over Columbia grads." One insider advises that "for the San Francisco office, a strong local connection helps enormously."

OUR SURVEY SAYS

Associates reveal that Pillsbury Winthrop's corporate culture is in a state of flux. The firm seems to be "confused at the moment." Post-merger, say associates, "the omnipresent specter of the San Francisco office looms and darkens the horizon." Others lament that "following successive rounds of layoffs, pay cuts and salary freezes, I'm not sure what remains of" the old Winthrop culture "beyond the bottom line." Associates in California seem happier, with many describing the firm as "collegial," "laid back and friendly." Opinions are more positive when it comes to training. "We do a good deal of training, and our training is almost always helpful," remarks an insider.

Associates are divided again when it comes to compensation. "I have no complaints," insist several attorneys, while one associate shrugs, "We get a lot of money for what we do." But some voice suspicion that "merit bonuses are only available to attorneys who bill over 2,600 hours," while one source complains, "Everything is hours now." (The firm says it just rolled out a new bonus program developed with associate input.) Associates applaud the fact that "the top two positions at this firm are held by women, and the leader of the corporate securities group is a woman." Because of "Mary [Cranston], we're the poster child for women's advancement."

Jenner & Block, LLC

One IBM Plaza
Chicago, IL 60611-7603
Phone: (312) 222-9350
www.jenner.com

LOCATIONS

Chicago, IL (HQ)
Dallas, TX
Washington, DC

MAJOR DEPARTMENTS/PRACTICES

Antitrust & Trade Regulation • Appellate & Supreme
Court Practice • Arbitration: Domestic & International •
Association Practice • Bankruptcy/Corporate Restructuring •
Class Action Litigation • Commercial Law & Uniform
Commercial Code • Complex Business Litigation •
Construction Law • Corporate • Employee Benefits &
Executive Compensation • Environmental, Energy &
Natural Resources Law • Estate Planning & Probate •
Family Law • Government Contracts • Health Care Law •
Insurance Litigation & Counseling • Intellectual Property
& Technology Law • Labor & Employment • Litigation
Practice • Media & First Amendment Practice •
Products Liability & Mass Tort Defense • Professional
Liability Litigation • Real Estate • Reinsurance Practice •
Securities Litigation • Tax Controversy Practice • Tax
Practice • Telecommunications • White Collar Criminal
Defense & Counseling

THE STATS

No. of attorneys: Approximately 400
No. of offices: 3
Summer associate offers: 66 out of 68 (2001)
Chairman: Jerold S. Solovy
Managing Partner: Robert L. Graham
Hiring Attorney: Craig C. Martin

THE BUZZ
WHAT ATTORNEYS AT OTHER FIRMS ARE SAYING ABOUT THIS FIRM

• "Sweatshop, but great litigation firm"
• "Laid back and friendly"
• "Great pro bono"
• "Corporate? Yep, and it's growing"

NOTABLE PERKS

• Firm assistance for house closings
• Tickets to sporting events
• Laptops
• Weekly happy hours

EMPLOYMENT CONTACT

Mr. James Flynn
Manager of Legal Recruiting
Phone: (312) 923-7881
Fax: (312) 527-0484
jflynn@jenner.com

BASE SALARY

Chicago, 2002
1st year: $125,000
7th year: Up to $205,000
Summer associate: $2,403/week

THE SCOOP

For nearly 90 years, Chicago-based Jenner & Block has boasted one of the nation's leading trial and appellate practices. The firm has become a champion of the First Amendment, challenging the constitutionality of the Communications Decency Act and the Children's Internet Protection Act. Jenner's commitment to public service (among the top five pro bono firms in the country for several years running, according to *The American Lawyer*) provides associates with significant hands-on experience in matters ranging from asylum proceedings to death penalty work to not-for-profit incorporation. Defending class-action lawsuits is another Jenner forte, on high profile matters ranging from employment to securities law to toxic torts. The firm's antitrust attorneys represented independent booksellers in the recent price discrimination suit against chain stores Barnes & Nobles and Borders and helped negotiate the parties' settlement in 2001.

GETTING HIRED

What's in a name? At Jenner & Block, the answer is plenty. Explains one source, "A recent shift has tended more to the big-name schools, making it more difficult for individuals from other schools to get a callback." Jenner also places a stronger-than-average emphasis on grades and law review experience. However, other insiders say that "the firm is looking to hire well-rounded people, not just the law school academic top performers," and that "people who are engaging, committed to client service and truly interested still have a strong likelihood of an offer."

OUR SURVEY SAYS

Jenner associates report that "the culture here is fairly laid back and friendly." The atmosphere is generally quite collegial but turns "extremely serious when it's time to focus" on the work at hand. Jenner lawyers are proud to admit they "love the law."

Most agree that "the hours are reasonable" and that face time isn't required. Most associates feel their compensation is similarly reasonable. Jenner has "a very fair system that rewards hard work and dedication," comments one attorney. But not everyone is satisfied. "The firm has a poor bonus structure," complains a first-year. "They claim that this is offset by the chance of becoming a partner, but truth be told, your chances of becoming a partner here are pretty slim." Other sources report that bonuses at Jenner are tied to billable hours.

Most partners are known to be "very approachable," and are described as "demanding, but reasonable in their expectations and criticisms." Several associates say that the opportunity they've had to work closely with — and to learn from — nationally respected practitioners is a plus at Jenner not found at many other firms.

Kaye Scholer LLP

425 Park Avenue
New York, NY 10022-3598
Phone: (212) 836-8000
www.kayescholer.com

LOCATIONS

New York, NY (HQ)
Chicago, IL • Los Angeles, CA • Washington, DC •
West Palm Beach, FL • Frankfurt • Hong Kong • London
Shanghai

MAJOR DEPARTMENTS/PRACTICES

Antitrust
Business Reorganization
Corporate & Finance
Employment & Labor
Entertainment, Media & Communications
Intellectual Property
International
Legislative & Regulatory
Litigation
Product Liability
Real Estate
Tax
Technology & E-Commerce
Trust & Estates
White Collar Crime
Wills & Estates

THE STATS

No. of attorneys: 438
No. of offices: 9
Summer associate offers: 45 out of 45 (2001)
Chairman: David Klingsberg
Managing Partner: Barry Willner
Hiring Attorney: James Herschlein

THE BUZZ
WHAT ATTORNEYS AT OTHER FIRMS ARE SAYING ABOUT THIS FIRM

- "Good, practical attorneys"
- "Could be worse, a bit intense"
- "Very nice guys"
- "Used to be better regarded"

NOTABLE PERKS

- Friday night cocktail parties
- Partially subsidized laptops
- Annual party at the Central Park Zoo

EMPLOYMENT CONTACT

Ms. Wendy Evans
Director of Legal Personnel
Phone: (212) 836-8000
Fax: (212) 836-8689
wevans@kayescholer.com

New York, 2002
1st year: $125,000
2nd year: $135,000
3rd year: $150,000
4th year: $165,000
5th year: $186,000
6th year: $196,000
7th year: $205,000
8th year: $210,000
Summer associate: $2,410/week

THE SCOOP

Believe it or not, 2001 was a good year for New York's Kaye Scholer, with revenues up 15 percent. A distinguished antitrust department has been the hallmark of Kaye Scholer's practice for over 50 years, and a noted white-collar defense team is led by former U.S. Attorney for the Southern District of New York Paul Curran. With one of the largest products liability defense practices in the nation, the firm most recently successfully defended Pfizer, Inc. against claims that the anti-impotence drug Viagra causes heart attacks. The firm is home to a large bankruptcy practice as well and recently opened an office in Chicago staffed with only bankruptcy lawyers. The firm's pro bono program has won honors for its attorneys' work on behalf of death row inmates.

GETTING HIRED

Kaye Scholer "is really looking for well-rounded individuals," explains one associate. "The people who really thrive here are able to keep perspective and, while recognizing that working hard is important, also know that maintaining a personal life provides important balance and makes for happier attorneys." The hiring process is also standard. Callback candidates usually meet "with four attorneys and often will be taken to lunch." Sources suggest that "the firm looks at [candidates' law] school and grades. But once the candidate receives an invitation for a callback interview, often the offer is his or hers to lose."

OUR SURVEY SAYS

One of the biggest concerns among Kaye Scholer associates is the firm's deferred compensation plan, which sources describe as "very frustrating" and which leaves many associates puzzled. "I don't understand why the firm doesn't just get rid of it," rants one contact, while another sighs, "I hate this system." But not everyone agrees. The firm "offers salaries and year-end bonuses that are very competitive with the most brutal top-tier New York firms," says one happy associate.

Most insiders agree that the firm "is fairly laid back." "Associates certainly socialize together, not only at the famed Friday night cocktail party but also outside the office." Reviews are mixed when it comes to the Kaye Scholer partners. Some sources claim that "incidents of disrespect at this firm are rare," though several associates insist that "there are some partners who are notorious for being screamers and are rude to associates."

When it comes to hours, associates must contend with a billable hours target of 2,000 hours. "Considering this firm bills itself as a lifestyle firm, the hours should be a lot better," gripes one associate. The work assignment system is also on associates' minds. "Some people's hours are through the roof every month because they get pounded with assignments," says one contact, "while others seem to fly under the radar and are never terribly busy."

Goodwin Procter LLP

Exchange Place
53 State Street
Boston, MA 02109
Phone: (617) 570-1000
www.goodwinprocter.com

LOCATIONS

Boston, MA (HQ)
New York, NY
Roseland, NJ
Washington, DC

MAJOR DEPARTMENTS/PRACTICES

Corporate
Environmental
ERISA & Employee Benefits
Estate Planning & Administration
Labor & Employment
Litigation
Real Estate
Tax

THE STATS

No. of attorneys: 514
No. of offices: 4
Summer associate offers: 29 out of 32 (2001)
Chairman and Managing Partner: Regina M. Pisa
Hiring Partner: Lawrence R. Cahill

NOTABLE PERKS

• Firm-wide Friday lunches
• Tickets to Red Sox, Bruins and Celtics games
• Annual weekend outings for each department

EMPLOYMENT CONTACT

Ms. Maureen A. Shea
Director of Legal Recruitment
Phone: (617) 570-1288
Fax: (617) 523-1231
mshea@goodwinprocter.com

BASE SALARY

Boston, 2002

Class of 2002: $125,000
Class of 2001: $135,000
Class of 2000: $135,000
Class of 1999: $145,000
Class of 1998: $155,000
Class of 1997: $165,000
Class of 1996: $180,000
Class of 1995: $190,000
Summer associate: $2,400/week

THE BUZZ
WHAT ATTORNEYS AT OTHER FIRMS ARE SAYING ABOUT THIS FIRM

• "Excellent all-around firm"
• "Great training"
• "Large, impersonal"
• "Lots of turnover"

THE SCOOP

Goodwin Procter has been a big name in Boston for 90 years. In 1998 the old New England firm made history when Regina Pisa became the first woman named both chairman and managing partner of a top American law firm. Goodwin Procter has also expanded its New York office, especially in litigation. Last spring's acquisition of Schneck Weltman & Hashmall boosted the firm's product liability and mass tort practice. The firm is national counsel for Philip Morris and recently represented the cigarette maker in an unsuccessful challenge to a Massachusetts statute requiring tobacco companies to disclose all added ingredients in their products.

GETTING HIRED

Want to work at Goodwin Procter? Expect to jump through some hoops. Candidates face an initial screening interview lasting about 20–30 minutes and a series of callback interviews including lunch. The firm seeks "students in the top 10–25 percent of their class" who have law review experience and "other outstanding academic or work experience," explains one source. "For summer associates, we look first at the top 10 percent of top-tier schools and try to hire as many qualified candidates from their ranks as we need," clarifies another insider. "The office usually determines first how many people it wants to hire. If our first choices don't choose us, we go down the list until we have the desired number of people."

OUR SURVEY SAYS

Associates at Goodwin Procter describe a culture that is generally collegial but does have its blemishes. "As far as law firms go, I don't think you can beat working here," enthuses one source. "The firm promotes a lot of interaction among its attorneys," says another associate. But sources report frustration with the firm's work assignment system. Insists a corporate attorney, "Everything is supposed to run through a central assignment system and be evenly distributed for the first three years. The reality is that in slow economic times most of the work is given directly to associates, leaving some extremely busy while others are struggling to find work."

Hours at the firm are about on par with the industry. "Anyone who goes to a 500-lawyer firm is kidding themselves if they don't think they're going to work hard," states an associate. The firm has a target of approximately 1,850–1,900 billable hours per year. "I have been told billing over 1,900 hours per year will only affect my bonus and not my partnership chances," says one source. "I have put in some real late nights and some weekends, but for the most part, I can leave by early evening," says one insider. The firm's compensation structure needs improvement, say insiders. "The firm is always the last [firm] in the market to raise salaries," sighs a mid-level, "but the first to roll them back when times get tough."

Sonnenschein Nath & Rosenthal

8000 Sears Tower
Chicago, IL 60606
Phone: (312) 876-8000
www.sonnenschein.com

LOCATIONS

Chicago, IL (HQ)
Kansas City, MO • Los Angeles, CA • New York, NY •
San Francisco, CA • St. Louis, MO • Washington, DC •
West Palm Beach, FL

MAJOR DEPARTMENTS/PRACTICES

Antitrust, Franchising & Distribution • Corporate &
Securities • E-Business • Employee Benefits & Executive
Compensation • Energy • Environmental • Government
Contracts • Growth Companies • Health Care •
Insolvency, Bankruptcy & Re-organization • Insurance •
Intellectual Property & Technology • International •
Labor & Employment • Litigation & Business Regulation •
Media, Libel & First Amendment • Products Liability •
Real Estate • Taxation • Telecommunications • Trusts &
Estates • White Collar Criminal/Federal Regulatory

THE STATS

No. of attorneys: 500
No. of offices: 8
Chairman: Duane C. Quaini
Hiring Partners: John C. Koski, Chair of Recruiting
Committee; Brett J. Hart, Co-Chair of Recruiting
Committee

NOTABLE PERKS

• "Way comfy office furniture"
• Free Scott Turow books
• Free dinner during the weeks
• Firm-wide mock trial program

EMPLOYMENT CONTACT

Chicago
Ms. Lori L. Nowak
Recruitment Coordinator
Phone: (312) 876-8112
Fax: (312) 876-7934
lnowak@sonnenschein.com
(See web site for employment contacts in other
cities)

BASE SALARY

Chicago, 2002
1st year: $125,000
Summer associate: $2,400/week

THE BUZZ
WHAT ATTORNEYS AT OTHER FIRMS ARE SAYING ABOUT THIS FIRM

• "Another one of these bogus lifestyle firms"
• "Chicago elite"
• "Women and diversity friendly"
• "Napoleon complex"

THE SCOOP

With eight offices and 500 attorneys nationwide, Chicago's Sonnenschein Nath & Rosenthal is among the 100 largest law firms in the country. (Until 1985 the firm was the largest single-office law firm in the United States.) Prestigious corporate, securities and real estate clients include Abbott Labs, Goldman Sachs, McDonald's, Prudential Insurance and Sun Microsystems. The rising IP and technology practice, with more than 75 lawyers, recently celebrated a win for defendant *The Chicago Tribune* in a trademark infringement suit over use of the phrase "the joy of six." Publishing fame is not limited to Sonnenschein's clients; best-selling novelist Scott Turow is a partner in the firm's Chicago office.

GETTING HIRED

Most sources at Sonnenschein say the firm seeks top-notch candidates from brand name law schools. "Several partners only want to hire the top students from the top law schools," comments one source. "If you didn't go to Harvard or Yale, you best be at the very top of your class and on a journal." Sniffs another, "We pretty much only hire candidates from top-tier schools with top-tier grades," though she admits that "for the top five law schools, we're a bit more lax about the grades. [We take the] top 50 percent instead of the top 15 or 30 percent."

OUR SURVEY SAYS

Insiders are resigned to the fact that most of their co-workers "are accepting and friendly but not particularly outgoing." As the firm is "definitely running a business," there is "not much socializing aside from going to lunch and coffee." Sums up one source, "It is friendly but you don't make friends here, unless maybe you were a summer associate." On the upside, "Sonnenschein has a 'no jerks allowed' policy that is strictly enforced," says one (presumably nice) associate.

Sonnenschein associates have a rather Zen attitude about the hours they work. "Given the nature of the practice, [billable hours] expectations are not out of whack," says a senior associate. Adds a colleague, "While I would like to work less, compared to friends at other New York firms, I have it rather easy." One woman offers a humorous spin on her busy schedule: "Compared to a lottery-financed early retirement, it is bad. In reality, I have a life, as do apparently most people here."

Hitting the magic number is a great concern, as one associate explains: "The salaries are done in holdbacks, so the base salary is low, but I am guaranteed a $20,000 bonus if I bill 1,950." While some call the holdback policy "bizarre," insiders overall say their pay is "not bad in the current market." For those making the bonus requirement, "the firm's compensation structure seems very favorable."

Heller Ehrman White & McAuliffe LLP

333 Bush Street
San Francisco, CA 94104-2878
Phone: (415) 772-6000
www.hewm.com

LOCATIONS

Anchorage, AK • Gaithersburg, MD • Los Angeles, CA •
Madison, WI • Menlo Park, CA • New York, NY •
Portland, OR • San Diego, CA • San Francisco, CA •
Seattle, WA • Washington, DC • Hong Kong •
Singapore

MAJOR DEPARTMENTS/PRACTICES

Antitrust & Trade Regulation • Corporate Securities,
M&A • Energy • Environmental Regulation & Litigation •
Financial Services • Information Technology • Insurance
Coverage • Intellectual Property Litigation • International
Labor & Employment • Life Sciences • Patents &
Trademarks • Product Liability • Real Estate • Securities
Litigation • Tax

THE STATS

No. of attorneys: 583
No. of offices: 13
Summer associate offers: 28 out of 37 (2001)
Chairman: Barry S. Levin
Hiring Shareholders: Barbara Gregoratos and Michael
Rugen (San Francisco) (Each office has its own Hiring
Shareholder[s].)

NOTABLE PERKS

• Liberal parental leave policy
• Annual trip to Yosemite for summer associates
• 401(k)-based retention bonus of up to $30,000
• $35 + /month transit checks (amount varies by
  office)

EMPLOYMENT CONTACT

San Francisco
Craig Blumin, Esq.
Professional Recruitment Manager
Phone: (415) 772-6000
Fax: (415) 772-6268
cblumin@hewm.com
(See firm web site for employment contacts in
other offices)

BASE SALARY

San Francisco, 2002
1st level: $125,000*
2nd level: $130,000
3rd level: $140,000
4th level: $150,000
5th level: $165,000
6th level: $175,000
7th level: $185,000
Summer associate: $2,400/week
* "Level" does not always correspond to the
number of years an associate has been practicing.
Levels above VII are individually determined and not
formalized.

THE BUZZ
WHAT ATTORNEYS AT OTHER FIRMS ARE SAYING ABOUT THIS FIRM

• "Best lawyers in the Bay Area"
• "Humane place to work"
• "A bit snooty"
• "Not nearly the 'lifestyle' firm they profess to be"

THE SCOOP

Heller Ehrman White & McAuliffe has one of the hottest practices in the country, with a cutting-edge concentration in the field of biotechnology and one of the largest life sciences groups in the country. The firm represents both Visa and Microsoft in antitrust litigation and serves as special counsel to Pacific Gas and Electric Co. in one of the largest bankruptcies in U.S. history. Heller Ehrman was one of the Bay Area's top 10 grossing firms in 2001, according to San Francisco's *Recorder,* and reported the greatest increase in per-partner profits. Also, *The American Lawyer* ranked Heller Ehrman's litigation department as one of the top 17 litigation departments in the country, and the firm continues to rank at the top of the AmLaw 100 annual pro bono survey.

GETTING HIRED

Associates insist that Heller Ehrman's hiring standards "are getting tougher every year." Of the well-pedigreed candidates interviewing on campus, "maybe 10 percent [get] offers." In addition to a name-brand law school, Heller Ehrman seeks applicants who are "excellent writers" and "who are funny, engaging and interesting." Those whose credentials do not meet the usual standards may still get an offer if they "have a certain specialty the firm is looking for — for example, a PhD in science for a patent associate [position]." Candidates interviewing on-site "see four to five people for 30-minute interviews and two more people during lunch or dinner."

OUR SURVEY SAYS

Sources describe a "relaxed, informal culture" at their firm, one that is "far less hierarchical than most big firms." But several associates suggest that Heller Ehrman's culture "has become increasingly uptight thanks to its ambitions to become a truly national firm."

The training at Heller Ehrman receives mixed reviews. "It's uneven," says one attorney. However, "all practice groups run ongoing training programs in each office," and "there is an effort to provide more advanced training." Partners garner mostly favorable reviews; the firm "does not generally suffer screamers."

Heller Ehrman didn't slash salaries, as many other firms did this year, but it did alter its compensation structure by "denying step increases to some associates." Another cause for concern: "Heller Ehrman back-ends our pay by requiring 2,000 hours billed to get the bonus that brings our salary up to what our counterparts at other firms make regardless of what they bill," complains one attorney. Otherwise, insiders seem content with their compensation; most just wish they didn't have to work quite so much for their pay. Laments one, "Why can't we bill 1,800 hours and take home less money? None of us is in danger of missing a mortgage payment."

Coudert Brothers LLP

1114 Avenue of the Americas
New York, NY 10036
Phone: (212) 626-4400
www.coudert.com

LOCATIONS

New York, NY (HQ)

Los Angeles, CA • Palo Alto, CA • San Francisco, CA •
San Jose, CA • Washington, DC • Almaty, Kazakhstan •
Antwerp • Bangkok • Beijing • Berlin • Brussels •
Budapest • Frankfurt • Ghent, Belgium • Hong Kong •
Jakarta • London • Mexico City • Milan • Moscow •
Munich • Paris • Prague • Rome • St. Petersburg •
Shanghai • Singapore • Stockholm • Sydney • Tokyo

MAJOR DEPARTMENTS/PRACTICES

Corporate/Commercial (Finance, Investment Funds &
Managers, Mergers & Acquisitions, Securities)
Energy & Natural Resources
Entertainment & Media
Financial Restructuring & Insolvency
Intellectual Property
International Trade & Customs
Litigation & Arbitration
Real Estate/Property
Tax
Telecommunications, Media & Technology

THE STATS

No. of attorneys: 700
No. of offices: 31
Summer associate offers: 22 out of 25 (2001)
Chairman: Steven R. Beharrell
Hiring Attorney: Edward H. Tillinghast III

THE BUZZ
WHAT ATTORNEYS AT OTHER FIRMS ARE SAYING ABOUT THIS FIRM

- "Sexy international practice"
- "Smooth and savvy"
- "Difficult work environment"
- "Best years are behind them"

NOTABLE PERKS

- Good catering
- Weekly wine and cheese happy hours
- Annual fall retreat

EMPLOYMENT CONTACT

Ms. Mary L. Simpson
Director of Legal Personnel
Phone: (212) 626-4400
Fax: (212) 626-4120
simpsonm@coudert.com

BASE SALARY

New York, 2002
1st year: $125,000
2nd year: $135,000
3rd year: $150,000
4th year: $170,000
5th year: $190,000
6th year: $200,000
7th year: $205,000
Summer associate: $2,400/week

THE SCOOP

Antwerp, Bangkok, Frankfurt, Hong Kong, Moscow, New York, Rome, Sydney, Tokyo.... Coudert Brothers calls 31 cities home. From the 1879 opening of the firm's first overseas office in Paris to the establishment of a Stockholm outpost in 2002, Coudert Brothers has built a global practice encompassing 18 countries on four continents. Coudert was the first American law firm to open a European office, the first to set up shop in the Soviet Union and the first to settle in Beijing after the Communist takeover. In October 2001, the firm achieved another first when it elected London partner Steven Beharrell as Coudert's first non-U.S. national chairman. Coudert's practice concentrates on corporate and commercial law for multinational clients, and areas of expertise include project finance, telecommunications and trade regulation.

GETTING HIRED

Due to its global nature, "Coudert prefers candidates with an international background and an interest in cross-border work." One insider asserts that "multiple languages are a must" for those hoping to get hired; the firm notes that it has no such requirement. The summer program is the best way to get ahead, as "the firm likes to give offers to every summer associate." Opines one attorney, "The firm seems to be interested, first and foremost, in bright, accomplished people rather than in the reputation of the law school attended." Adds another insider, "The key here is personality and outside interests. Go somewhere else if the law is your life."

OUR SURVEY SAYS

Coudert Brothers associates express conflicting views about their "very Euro-centric" firm. Some lawyers are bothered by the "weird culture of cliques that hang out together." Others insist that Coudert "associates socialize frequently and well." Sources agree that "yelling is not tolerated" at the firm. Most "partners are great and treat us as equals," says an associate. A newly formed associates' committee is considered "a very positive development."

After a recent bout of associate firings, many Coudert Brothers associates "would like to work more hours." Says a tax associate, "I do not have enough to keep me busy, and I am constantly worried about another round of firings because no one in my department has enough to do." A few sources report "wild fluctuations" in hours. But another attorney more happily reports, "While I am putting in the hours at work, I find the work I do almost entirely substantive and challenging, not mindless in any way."

While in general "base salary is competitive with other firms," bonuses are hours-based and, according to insiders, difficult to attain. Associates agree that "they really need to make the bonus program reachable. It is currently not even approachable for most associates."

Dechert

4000 Bell Atlantic Tower
1717 Arch Street
Philadelphia, PA 19103-2793
Phone: (215) 994-4000
www.dechert.com

LOCATIONS

Philadelphia, PA (HQ)
Boston, MA • Harrisburg, PA • Hartford, CT •
Newport Beach, CA • New York, NY • Princeton, NJ •
Washington, DC • Brussels • London • Luxembourg •
Paris

MAJOR DEPARTMENTS/PRACTICES

Business
Finance & Real Estate
Financial Services
Litigation
Tax

THE STATS

No. of attorneys: 700+
No. of offices: 12
Summer associate offers: 72 out of 76 (2001,
U.S. offices)
Chairman: Barton J. Winokur
Hiring Partners: Adrienne M. Baker and
John V. O'Hanlon (Boston); David R. Kraus (Harrisburg);
Timothy J. Boyce (Hartford); Sheldon A. Jones
(Newport Beach); Abbe G. Shapiro (NY); Geraldine A.
Sinatra and Frederick G. Herold (Philadelphia); Todd D.
Johnston (Princeton); David J. Harris and Karen L.
Anderberg (Vice Chair) (DC)

THE BUZZ
WHAT ATTORNEYS AT OTHER FIRMS ARE SAYING ABOUT THIS FIRM

• "Philadelphia's finest"
• "Ho-hum"
• "Intellectual, classy place"
• "I think I can, I think I can"

NOTABLE PERKS

• Free dinner and drinks on Thursday
• Laptops and Blackberries
• Starbucks coffee in the cafeteria

EMPLOYMENT CONTACT

Laterals
Ms. Carol S. Miller
Director of Associate Administration
Phone: (215) 994-2147
Fax: (215) 994-2222
carol.miller@dechert.com

Summer Associates–Entry Level
Ms. Alberta Bertolino
Director of Associate Recruitment
Phone: (215) 994-2296
Fax: (215) 994-2222
alberta.bertolino@dechert.com

BASE SALARY

Philadelphia and Princeton, 2002
1st year: $105,000
Summer associate: $2,000/week

Harrisburg, 2002
1st year: $92,000
Summer associate: N/A

Hartford, 2002
1st year: $95,000
Summer associate: $1,825/week

**Boston, Newport Beach, New York and
Washington, DC, 2002**
1st year: $125,000
Summer associate: $2,400/week (Boston, Newport
Beach, New York)
Summer associate: $2,250/week (Washington, DC)

THE SCOOP

What cheese steak is to Philly food, Dechert is to Philly law firms. But the firm's practice extends far beyond the Northeast. Dechert acts as national counsel for several major clients, including Philip Morris and GlaxoSmithKline, in mass tort litigation. The firm's prestigious mutual fund practice has expanded to the United Kingdom and Luxembourg. While most law firms suffered an economic crunch in 2001, Dechert's revenues were up 20 percent from the previous year, according to *The American Lawyer*. These days, Dechert makes the news as part of the Enron defense team.

GETTING HIRED

Dechert looks for "gifted, intelligent, hard-working individuals," and sources agree that there is an "extreme emphasis on grades and law school attended," while some feel the firm is too focused on pedigree. "The firm tends to focus on top-ranked schools such as Harvard to a fault." When the top students at those schools choose firms in New York, D.C. and San Francisco, Dechert is "stuck with the bottom of the barrel," complains one associate. But some associates see welcome changes ahead. "The firm is slowly shifting its focus to the top students at the next level, such as Boston College, Boston University, George Washington, Fordham, and so on."

OUR SURVEY SAYS

"Professional" is the name of the game at Dechert. "Everyone is treated as a professional," says one insider. While sources describe the firm culture as "friendly," others point out that "senior attorneys do not socialize with more junior attorneys." Complains one insider, "Partners respect the abilities of the associates, yet communication between partners and the associates is lacking" and leads to "an air of secrecy." Quips one associate, "I know more about the location of Dick Cheney than I do about the issues affecting the firm and the management's strategies for dealing with them."

When it comes to their hours, Dechert associates give the firm mixed reviews. Although there is "no formal minimum hours requirement," explains one associate, "since the institution of the automatic bonus at 1,950 hours, 1,950 has become the unofficial minimum." Another associate notes that this benchmark, which includes pro bono work, "is an increase over the previous requirement of 1,800 hours." Associates appreciate that "weekend work is rare, and often it may be brought home."

Of course, the flip side of fewer hours is less pay. The firm gets high marks for base salary, but associates consider bonuses "low or nonexistent." While associates in the headquarter office think Dechert "has, and does, set the upper limit for compensation in the Philadelphia market," many maintain that "Philadelphia salaries, at least before cost of living adjustments, are too low."

63

Fish & Neave

1251 Avenue of the Americas
New York, NY 10020
Phone: (212) 596-9000
www.fishneave.com

LOCATIONS

New York, NY (HQ)
Palo Alto, CA

MAJOR DEPARTMENTS/PRACTICES

Counseling & Risk Management • Intellectual Property
Asset Management • Intellectual Property Litigation
(Patent Infringement; Trademark, Unfair Competition &
Copyright; Trade Secrets, Licensing Disputes, Patent
Misuse & Antitrust) • Licensing • Transactions

THE STATS

No. of attorneys: 166
No. of offices: 2
Summer associate offers: 45 out of 45 (2001)
Managing Partner: Jesse J. Jenner
Hiring Attorneys: John M. Hintz, Frances M. Lynch and
Avi S. Lele

NOTABLE PERKS

• Firm keggers and outings
• Frequent lunches on the partners' dime
• Sky box at Madison Square Garden (New York)

EMPLOYMENT CONTACT

New York
Ms. Heather C. Fennell
Legal Recruitment Manager
Phone: (212) 596-9121
Fax: (212) 596-9090
hfennell@fishneave.com

Palo Alto
Rajeev Patel
Recruitment Administrator
Phone: (650) 617-4000
Fax: (650) 617-4090
rpatel@fishneave.com

BASE SALARY

All offices, 2002
1st year: $125,000
2nd year: $135,000
3rd year: $150,000
4th year: $165,000
5th year: $185,000
6th year: $200,000
7th year: $215,000
8th year: $230,000
Summer associate: $2,400/week

THE BUZZ
WHAT ATTORNEYS AT OTHER FIRMS ARE SAYING ABOUT THIS FIRM

• "Brilliant IP practice"
• "Eggheads"
• "Premier patent sweatshop"
• "Known as Bitch & Leave"

THE SCOOP

One of the leading IP firms in the country, Fish & Neave's client list presents a virtual who's who in invention and manufacturing over the last 100 years — from Alexander Graham Bell, Thomas Edison, Henry Ford and the Wright Brothers to AT&T, General Electric, Ford Motors and Boeing. Named Patent Litigation Team of the Year by *Managing Intellectual Property* in both 1999 and 2000, Fish & Neave also captured *IP Worldwide*'s title of No. 1 IP Counseling Firm in America. According to *IP Worldwide*, Fish & Neave is the second-most popular IP firm among Fortune 250 companies. In late 2001, Fish & Neave quietly laid off approximately 15 percent of its associates, blaming the post-September 11 economy. Following the annual review process, a small number of associates left the firm.

GETTING HIRED

Like every IP firm, Fish & Neave places an emphasis on technical knowledge. "If you have any technical background, you can get a job without stellar grades and without having attended a top 10 law school," reports one source. Fish & Neave "is willing to consider candidates from less prestigious schools with strong academic or engineering/science experience," notes another lawyer. But there is some room for aspiring lawyers without technical backgrounds. "The firm typically hires several associates that do not have technical degrees, a rarity among patent firms," says one contact.

OUR SURVEY SAYS

Fish & Neave associates point to a recent change in the firm's culture. "Historically, the firm has emphasized creating a civil environment," reports one insider. "More recently, the firm has begun placing a much heavier emphasis on reaching financial objectives in the form of billable hours. The firm has begun laying people off and that has created a ripple of tension regarding when the next series of layoffs may occur."

Many associates insist that F&N lawyers learn "via the sink or swim method." But some are delighted by signs that the firm has a newfound commitment to training. "Recently," notes a Californian, "the firm instituted a good series of in-house training from top partners in the firm."

Insiders remark that the firm's billable hours target is 1,950 hours for full-time associates. And when it comes to compensation, some associates think there's something fishy going on. "In 2000, we were told that our bonuses were lower than average because the firm is not affected by economic booms," reports one associate. "However, in 2001, the bonuses were cut in half, even though the firm had [an] increase in revenues." F&N responds that the firm's income was higher than projected, so supplemental bonuses were rewarded to the entire firm at the end of 2001.

1201 Third Avenue
Suite 4800
Seattle, WA 98101-3099
Phone: (206) 583-8888
www.perkinscoie.com

LOCATIONS

Seattle, WA (HQ)

Anchorage, AK • Bellevue, WA • Boise, ID • Chicago, IL
Denver, CO • Los Angeles, CA • Menlo Park, CA •
Olympia, WA • Portland, OR • San Francisco, CA •
Spokane, WA • Washington, DC • Beijing • Hong Kong

MAJOR DEPARTMENTS/PRACTICES

Antitrust & Trade Regulation • Business & Technology •
China Practice • Commercial Lending • Corporate
Finance • Creditor/Debtor • Energy • Environmental &
Natural Resources • Government Contracts •
Government Relations & Political Law • Immigration •
Internet & E-Commerce • Labor & Employment •
Litigation • Patent Prosecution • Personal Planning •
Product Liability • Real Estate & Land Use • Tax &
Employee Benefits • Technology & Licensing •
Trademark & Intellectual Property

THE STATS

No. of attorneys: 558
No. of offices: 14
Summer associate offers: 36 out of 40 (2001,
Seattle/Bellevue)
Chairman: Robert E. Giles
Hiring Partner: Steven Y. Koh

THE BUZZ
WHAT ATTORNEYS AT OTHER FIRMS ARE SAYING ABOUT THIS FIRM

- "Seattle's best"
- "Stuffy"
- "Not well-diversified"
- "Great Asia practice"

NOTABLE PERKS

- "Take a new associate to lunch" program
- PDA and home computer subsidy
- Paid parking in some locations
- Foosball and pool tables

EMPLOYMENT CONTACT

Ms. Laura MacDougall Kader
Lawyer Personnel Recruiter
Phone: (206) 583-8888
Fax: (206) 583-8500
LKader@perkinscoie.com

BASE SALARY

Seattle, 2002 (1,850 legal hours)
1st year: $100,000
2nd year: $102,000–$110,000
3rd year: $105,000–$118,000
4th year: $108,000–$128,000
5th year: $111,000–$140,000
6th year: $115,000–$150,000
7th year: $120,000–$160,000
Summer associate: $2,000/week

Bay Area, 2002 (1,950 legal hours)
1st year: $125,000
2nd year: $135,000
3rd year: $145,000
4th year: $160,000
5th year: $175,000
6th year: $195,000
7th year: $205,000
Summer associate: $2,400/week

THE SCOOP

Founded in 1912 by two lawyers in Seattle, Perkins Coie now has more than 500 attorneys in 14 offices in the United States and Asia. Perkins' client list includes high-tech and biotech giants like Adobe Systems, Amazon.com, Immunex Corporation and Yahoo!. Still a major player in its home state, Perkins serves as Boeing's principal outside counsel and represents the Seattle Mariners and Starbucks Coffee. In July 2001, Perkins acquired Menlo Park boutique Iota Pi Law Group. In October 2001, following the sudden collapse in IPO business, the firm laid off seven associates from its Bay Area offices.

GETTING HIRED

"Due to the economy, it is much harder to get a job here than it was two years ago," says a Perkins attorney. Perkins Coie expects the usual excellent academic performance, but "clearly has a preference for local schools over top-tier national schools." However, Perkins still only accepts candidates in "the top 10 percent at local law schools." It follows that "once you get past the first screening interview the real emphasis is on whether or not you are the kind of person with whom other associates would want to work." Perkins looks for "a certain laid-back, fun personality type, which isn't often found at law school."

OUR SURVEY SAYS

It's not easy to put your finger on the Perkins Coie vibe. According to one associate, it is "laid back on the surface, intense in reality." While "the dress is very casual and everyone is on a first-name or nickname basis," the firm is also described as "very conservative [with] little room for flamboyant characters." Lawyers "tend not to socialize outside the office, since even junior associates tend to be married," and it is "common for many people to eat lunch at their desks and go home at 5 or 6 p.m. without much interaction with others." Still, says one insider, "everyone is friendly, helpful and loose enough to joke around."

Many associates feel Perkins offers a "more reasonable lifestyle" than other large firms. The "Seattle office requires only 1,800 billable hours — plus 50 hours of 'legal' time such as pro bono [work] — which means that the firm is pretty cleared out by 6 or 7 each night." Even better, "The work hours are flexible... some associates come in early, others late, some go home early and work on the weekends, others never work weekends." A few associates lament that "this past year there has been not enough work."

As a result of that slowdown in business, "bonuses are, in reality, impossible to get," say associates. Many lawyers insist that "our salary is at market," but others complain that only the "bonus component of" salaries "really brings us up to 'market.'"

Howrey Simon Arnold & White, LLP

1299 Pennsylvania Ave., NW
Washington, DC 20004
Phone: (202) 783-0800
www.howrey.com

LOCATIONS

Houston, TX • Chicago, IL • Irvine, CA • Los Angeles,
CA • Century City, CA • Menlo Park, CA • San
Francisco, CA • Washington, DC • London • Brussels

MAJOR DEPARTMENTS/PRACTICES

Antitrust & Competition
Intellectual Property (Patent, Trademark, Copyright)
Global Litigation
Commercial Trial
Environmental
Government Contracts
Insurance Recovery
International Commercial Arbitration & Litigation
Securities
Supreme Court & Appellate
White Collar Criminal Defense

THE STATS

No. of attorneys: 521
No. of offices: 10
Summer associate offers: 44 out of 48 (2001)
Managing Partner: Robert F. Ruyak, Esq.
Hiring Partner: Richard A. Ripley, Esq.

THE BUZZ

WHAT ATTORNEYS AT OTHER FIRMS ARE SAYING ABOUT THIS FIRM

- "Excellent litigators"
- "Good IP shop, but enough with the magazine ads"
- "The proverbial salt mines"
- "Boot camp for associates? Be serious."

NOTABLE PERKS

- Dry cleaning service
- Free parking
- Free on-site gym (DC)
- Firm-wide retreats by practice area

EMPLOYMENT CONTACT

Ms. Janet Brown
Manager, Attorney Recruitment
Phone: (202) 783-0800
brownjanet@howrey.com

BASE SALARY

Washington, DC, 2002
1st year: $125,000
2nd year: $135,000
3rd year: $145,000
4th year: $155,000
5th year: $165,000
6th year: $175,000
7th year: $185,000

Houston, 2002
1st year: $115,000
2nd year: $123,000
3rd year: $132,000
4th year: $142,000
5th year: $152,000
6th year: $163,000
7th year: $175,000

California, 2002
1st year: $125,000
2nd year: $135,000
3rd year: $150,000
4th year: $165,000
5th year: $185,000
6th year: $195,000
7th year: $205,000
Summer associate: $12,000 for 5-week bootcamp
program

THE SCOOP

Washington, D.C.'s Howrey & Simon was an impressive firm even before its January 2000 merger with Houston's Arnold White & Durkee. But the merger pushed the now Howrey Simon Arnold & White over the top. Howrey is proud to be one of the world's largest antitrust practices with about 160 attorneys, and the firm's IP practice ain't too shabby either, as one of the world's largest with 230 IP professionals. Clients include Intel, Shell Oil, Johnson & Johnson and Procter & Gamble. In December 2001, the firm represented Nestlé on antitrust matters regarding the chocolate czar's $10.3 billion acquisition of Ralston Purina Co. The year before, Howrey led Anheuser-Busch to victory in an antitrust case brought against the beer brewer by Maris Distributing. Stellar at antitrust and IP, the firm also has a top-notch litigation practice.

GETTING HIRED

While Howrey "reviews grades carefully and does not make offers based on personality," insiders say that the firm has recently begun to expand its focus beyond the traditional top-tier law schools. Sources say "the firm loves judicial clerks and people interested in antitrust work." Prospective Howreyites should be aware that the firm has drastically changed its summer program recently, instituting the famed Howrey Bootcamp program, which emphasizes the teaching of lawyer skills rather than the typical wining and dining.

OUR SURVEY SAYS

Howrey's culture is an odd mix, say associates. "Supportive and friendly but intense," is one description. Agrees another source, "It's pretty laid back and friendly, although when the pressure is turned up things can get wound pretty tight." Historically, social interaction at the firm has been limited, but "the administration is making great efforts to provide social opportunities for the lawyers outside of the office."

When it comes to work hours, insiders appreciate that "associates are left to come and go as they please, so long as they keep on top of their assignments." The firm "seems particularly supportive of a part-time lifestyle. It allows part-time attorneys to make partner and allows individuals to work 60 or 80 percent [schedules]."

Complaints about base salary are few and far between, but the topic of bonuses elicits grumbling. "While my bonus was generous, the methodology used is completely opaque," complains one source. "Consequently, those who got less than what they thought they deserved had no idea why." The bonuses "are pretty much insulting," says one associate. But, says one contented associate, "Compensation is at market. No complaints here." Simply put, "We are being paid a ridiculous sum of money."

66 Alston & Bird LLP

One Atlantic Center
1201 West Peachtree Street
Atlanta, GA 30309-3424
Phone: (404) 881-7000
www.alston.com

LOCATIONS

Atlanta, GA (HQ)
Charlotte, NC • New York, NY • Raleigh, NC •
Washington, DC

MAJOR DEPARTMENTS/PRACTICES

Antitrust & Investigations • Bankruptcy, Workouts &
Reorganization • Capital Markets/Securities •
Compliance • Employee Benefits & Executive
Compensation • Entertainment & New Media •
Environmental & Land Use • Financial Services •
Government Investigations • Health Care • Intellectual
Property • Internet & E-Business • International • Labor
& Employment • Legislative & Public Policy • Life
Sciences • Litigation • Leveraged Capital • Privacy &
Data Management • Products Liability • Real Estate •
Securities Litigation • Tax • Technology •
Telecommunications • Wealth Planning

THE STATS

No. of attorneys: 605
No. of offices: 5
Summer associate offers: 91 out of 97 (2001)
Managing Partner: Ben F. Johnson III
Hiring Partner: Jonathan W. Lowe

THE BUZZ
WHAT ATTORNEYS AT OTHER FIRMS ARE SAYING ABOUT THIS FIRM

- "Big player in the South"
- "Sweatshop in sheep's clothing"
- "Happiest associates in the city"
- "Everybody not cool in high school is there"

NOTABLE PERKS

- Corporate discounts at Dell, Callaway Golf, Nissan, BMW and Tiffany's
- Free Blackberry pagers
- "Incredible" child care facility (Atlanta)

EMPLOYMENT CONTACT

Ms. Emily Leeson
Director of Attorney Hiring & Development
Phone: (404) 881-7014
Fax: (404) 881-7777
eleeson@alston.com

BASE SALARY

Atlanta, Charlotte and Raleigh, 2002
1st year: $100,000
2nd year: $105,000
3rd year: $110,000
4th year: $115,000
5th year: $122,000
6th year: $130,000
7th year: $137,000
8th year: $145,000
Summer associate $1,800/week

New York and Washington, DC, 2002
1st year: $125,000
2nd year: $135,000
3rd year: $145,000
4th year: $155,000
5th year: $165,000
6th year: $175,000
7th year: $185,000
8th year: $195,000
Summer associate $2,400/week

Patent Bar Members, 2002
1st year: $125,000
2nd year: $130,000
3rd year: $135,000
4th year: $140,000
5th year: $147,000
6th year: $155,000
7th year: $162,000
8th year: $170,000

THE SCOOP

One of the oldest and largest Southeastern law firms, Alston & Bird is a firm on the rise. Three years in a row, *Fortune* has included the firm in its ranking of the 100 Best Companies to Work for in America, and Alston has managed a steady climb up the list. The firm was placed at No. 36 in 2000, No. 24 in 2001 and jumped to a very impressive No. 9 in 2002. In January 2001, Alston & Bird merged with Walter, Conston, Alexander & Green, expanding the firm into New York and expanding its reach in Germany, Austria and Switzerland.

GETTING HIRED

Thanks to its high profile, Alston & Bird can afford to be selective when hiring. "Our firm is very popular and receives a lot of applicants," says one lawyer. But the firm looks beyond resumes. "Personality is the No. 1 trait that the firm looks for," reports one source. "We've passed by a lot of straight-A type candidates who just don't fit the firm's mold." The process is typical of the big-firm recruiting grind. After on-campus interviews, "the candidate will usually meet with several attorneys in half-hour sessions and will also enjoy a nice lunch interview with a few of the younger associates."

OUR SURVEY SAYS

According to Alston & Bird associates, *Fortune* was right — it really is a great firm to work for. "The firm puts a premium on culture above virtually all else," reports one insider. "Associate happiness actually does matter to partners." According to associates, Alston "is very accommodating to different lifestyles and different work habits." The Friday cocktail hour does wonders to foster close relationships among partners, associates and staff. And those relationships extend outside the office. "Taking vacations together with other lawyers at the firm is not unusual."

Like most firms, the hours at Alston & Bird can get onerous. "Don't be fooled — law is a business first," warns one no-nonsense lawyer. "Associates are expected to bill 2,000 hours. That means eight billable hours a day, five days a week, 50 weeks a year." But 2,000 is just the beginning. "I try to bill 2,100 hours per year," reports one insider. "If we hit this number, we are guaranteed a substantial bonus." On the upside, the firm is fairly flexible in how you reach the 2,000–2,100 hour plateaus. "When I feel I have been working hard, I feel like I can take an afternoon off and no one will bat an eye," says one contact.

Some associates are less than impressed with the firm's pay scale. Though most concede "the full-time pay is competitive with the Atlanta market," gripes remain. For one thing, first-year associates aren't eligible for bonuses. But that's not all. "We are below market value for large non-New York firms with a New York office," says one Big Apple lawyer.

Testa, Hurwitz & Thibeault, LLP

125 High Street
Boston, MA 02110
Phone: (617) 248-7000
www.tht.com

LOCATIONS

Boston, MA (HQ)

MAJOR DEPARTMENTS/PRACTICES

Business & Securities
Community & Industry Commitment
Creditors' Rights, Business Restructurings & Bankruptcy
Employee Benefits & ERISA
Environmental
Immigration
Labor & Employment
Litigation
Patent & Intellectual Property
Real Estate
Tax
Trusts & Estates

THE STATS

No. of attorneys: 370
No. of offices: 1
Summer associate offers: 61 out of 65 (2001)
Managing Partner: William B. Asher Jr.
Hiring Partner: Kenneth J. Gordon

NOTABLE PERKS

• $200 office decorating budget
• Concierge service
• Firm-sponsored venture capital fund

EMPLOYMENT CONTACT

Ms. Judith A. St. John
Recruiting Administrator
Phone: (617) 248-7401
Fax: (617) 248-7100
stjohn@tht.com

BASE SALARY

Boston, 2002
1st year: $135,000
2nd year: $150,000
3rd year: $165,000
4th year: $177,500
5th year: $190,000
6th year: $202,500
7th year: $215,000
Summer associate: $2,400/week

THE BUZZ
WHAT ATTORNEYS AT OTHER FIRMS ARE SAYING ABOUT THIS FIRM

• "East Coast firm with a West Coast edge"
• "Weren't they an '80s hair band?"
• "Fired paralegals and replaced with first-years"
• "Best in Beantown"

THE SCOOP

Boston's Testa, Hurwitz & Thibeault is nationally recognized for a practice specializing in venture capital and private equity. This tech-centric firm attracts a clientele of venture capitalists, investment banks and emerging companies in the computer and biotech industries. In the last two years, Testa Hurwitz helped raise more than $40 billion in capital funds. A range of other practice areas such as litigation, intellectual property, tax and employment supplement the primary practice group, business and securities. In pending litigation news, Testa Hurwitz is defending Chicago-based tech company Apropos in a class action suit alleging that the company defrauded investors by misrepresenting the role of key technology experts in its prospectus. Attorneys in the IP group are providing pro bono services to a patients' rights group for the detection of a rare genetic disease.

GETTING HIRED

Testa Hurwitz features a fairly relaxed hiring process. "The firm is looking to hire competent people that are easy to get along with," says one source. "Like most large firms, the door is easier to open if you come from a top-tier law school," reports one associate. "But the door is definitely open to all good candidates, and we have many associates hired from so-called lower-tiered schools who were toward the top of their classes." Another lawyer observes, "I believe the firm is very careful in who they hire. They are looking for mature, intelligent candidates who will make an honest commitment to providing quality service to our clients."

OUR SURVEY SAYS

Most associates express satisfaction with the atmosphere at Testa Hurwitz, though they admit it has its glitches. "For a big firm, I think Testa is fairly friendly and laid back," says one insider. "[The] culture is friendly, but has some quirks," continues another source. "People don't speak to each other in the elevators and sometimes don't say 'hi' in the halls, but there's a general vibe of camaraderie, and people work with their doors open." Some feel that the quirks go beyond that. "It's a 'drink the Kool-Aid' environment," warns one lawyer. "I think they should just go ahead and impose a 15-pieces-of-flair rule," he continues, referring to the cult comedy *Office Space*.

"The firm asks each associate to bill 1,850 per year," reports one associate. Not only is that a reasonable hours target, Testa Hurwitz has a policy of easing young lawyers into the mix. "There is no demand as a first-year associate to immediately begin billing ridiculous hours," says one contact. The firm has an unusual compensation structure that goes over well with associates. Unlike the vast majority of firms, Testa Hurwitz pays no bonuses. Instead the firm guarantees a substantially higher base salary. "I think we have one of the highest base salaries in the country," brags one associate. Sums up another insider, "This firm has been the highest paying firm in Boston for several years and apparently wishes to stay in that position."

Piper Rudnick LLP

6225 Smith Avenue
Baltimore, MD 21209-3600
Phone: (410) 580-3000

203 North LaSalle Street
Suite 1800
Chicago, IL 60601-1293
Phone: (312) 368-4000
www.piperrudnick.com

LOCATIONS

Baltimore, MD • Chicago, IL • Dallas, TX • Easton, MD
Edison, NJ • Los Angeles, CA • New York, NY •
Philadelphia, PA • Reston, VA • Tampa, FL •
Washington, DC

MAJOR DEPARTMENTS/PRACTICES

Corporate & Securities
Creditor Rights & Bankruptcy
Environmental
High Technology
Intellectual Property
Labor & Employment
Litigation
Private Client Services
Real Estate
Tax
Venture Capital & Emerging Growth Companies

THE STATS

No. of attorneys: 822
No. of offices: 11
Summer associate offers: 46 out of 56 (2001)
Chairpersons: Frank Burch and Lee Miller
Co-National Hiring Partners: Sally McDonald and
Jim Mathias

THE BUZZ
WHAT ATTORNEYS AT OTHER FIRMS ARE SAYING ABOUT THIS FIRM

- "Very prestigious firm"
- "Working hard at a national reputation"
- "Way too much infighting"
- "All real estate, all the time"

NOTABLE PERKS

- Firm-sponsored MBA for a few associates
- Thorough training at the Marbury Institute
- Tickets to sporting and cultural events

EMPLOYMENT CONTACT

Baltimore
Ms. Lindy Hilliard
Legal Recruiting Manager
Phone: (410) 580-4664
Fax: (410) 580-3669
lindy.hilliard@piperrudnick.com

Chicago
Ms. Marguerite Strubing
Legal Recruiting Manager
Phone: (312) 368-8928
Fax: (312) 236-7516
marguerite.strubing@piperrudnick.com

BASE SALARY

Baltimore, 2002
1st year: $115,000
2nd year: $117,500–$130,500
3rd year: $120,000–$128,000
4th year: $125,000–$150,000
5th year: $130,000–$160,000
6th year: $138,000–$148,000
7th year: $140,000–$165,000
8th year: $155,000–$180,000
Summer associate: $2,200/week

Chicago, 2002
1st year: $125,000
2nd year: $127,500–$130,500
3rd year: $130,000–$140,000
4th year: $140,000–$150,000
5th year: $150,000–$170,000
6th year: $160,000–$180,000
7th year: $170,000–$195,000
8th year: $175,000–$200,000
Summer associate: $2,400/week

THE SCOOP

One of the nation's 15 largest law firms, Piper Rudnick was formed in 1999 by a merger of Baltimore's 98-year-old Piper & Marbury with Chicago's 65-year-old Rudnick & Wolfe. The union combined each firm's strengths in litigation, venture capital, high technology, IP and real estate. (In April 2002, the merged firm changed its name from Piper Marbury Rudnick & Wolfe to Piper Rudnick.) Despite making some associate performance-based cuts in early 2001 (cuts that associates are describing as layoffs), the firm is going strong. In fact, seven attorneys who had voluntarily left the firm have since returned to the fold.

GETTING HIRED

Like many big firms, Piper Rudnick focuses on top students at top schools. "The interview and callback process zeroes in on the top students at a given law school, but does not overlook qualified candidates from law schools outside the top 10," reports one associate. "Grades and law review or other journal credentials are important." "I think the firm is looking for individuals who are academically strong with great writing and analytical skills, who have had valuable experiences that will be beneficial as an attorney, leaders, people who are involved in activities and have something to talk about beyond the law," agrees another source.

OUR SURVEY SAYS

Not surprisingly, the merger and recent associate cuts have changed Piper Rudnick's culture. While many still describe the firm as "laid back," it's clear that most feel the firm has lost something of late. "The culture used to be great, but after the merger, and especially after the recent cutbacks, the culture is downright awful," says one insider. Some feel the firm "lacks overall direction."

At Piper Rudnick, "2,000 hours are the minimum billables for receiving a raise and bonus," which is a little on the high side but "not unreasonable," say associates. However, that number is the "absolute minimum," according to firm sources.

Piper Rudnick gets an "E" for effort when it comes to its women attorneys. Piper "tries very hard to be accommodating to women and to look for ways to retain women. However, like most law firms, they have yet to really figure it out," says a senior associate. Women say a mentoring program would be appreciated but give the firm points for supporting flexible schedules.

When it comes to the Piper bigwigs, associates generally have nice things to say. "There are some characters, but generally partners treat associates as colleagues," says one Chicagoan. Others appreciate that "partners are very good at giving associates the chance to perform meaningful work."

Holland & Knight LLP

Suite 100
2099 Pennsylvania Avenue
Washington, DC 20006
Phone: (202) 955-3000
www.hklaw.com

LOCATIONS

Atlanta, GA • Annapolis, MD • Bethesda, MD • Boston,
MA • Bradenton, FL • Chicago, IL • Fort Lauderdale, FL •
Jacksonville, FL • Lakeland, FL • Los Angeles, CA •
McLean, VA • Melbourne, FL • Miami, FL • New York,
NY • Orlando, FL • Portland, OR • Providence, RI •
San Antonio, TX • San Francisco, CA • Seattle, WA •
St. Petersburg, FL • Tallahassee, FL • Tampa, FL •
Washington, DC • West Palm Beach, FL • Caracas* •
Helsinki • Mexico City • Rio de Janeiro • São Paulo •
Tel Aviv* • Tokyo

*Representative offices

MAJOR DEPARTMENTS/PRACTICES

Corporate, Tax & Securities
Finance
Litigation
Public Law
Real Estate, Environmental & Land Use
Trusts & Estates

THE STATS

No. of attorneys: 1,200
No. of offices: 32
Summer associate offers: 42 out of 61 (2001)
Managing Partner: Robert Feagin
Hiring Attorneys: Richard Dunnells and Janet Studley

THE BUZZ
WHAT ATTORNEYS AT OTHER FIRMS ARE SAYING ABOUT THIS FIRM

• "Good firm, but provincial reputation"
• "Bigger does not mean better"
• "Progressive, friendly"
• "Pac-Man firm with serious economic concerns"

NOTABLE PERKS

• 401(k) matching plan
• Domestic partner benefits
• Emergency day care (in most offices)

EMPLOYMENT CONTACT

Ms. Alida Coo-Kendall
Recruitment Coordinator (national)
Phone: (617) 573-5837
Fax: (617) 523-6850
acoo-kendall@hklaw.com

BASE SALARY

Washington, DC and McLean, 2002
1st year: $110,000
Summer associate: $2,200/week (2L);
$1,900/week (1L)

Boston and Chicago, 2002
1st year: $105,000
Summer associate: $2,000/week

Ft. Lauderdale, Miami and West Palm Beach, 2002
1st year: $80,000
Summer associate: $1,600/week

New York, 2002
1st year: $125,000
Summer associate: $2,400/week (2L);
$2,200/week (1L)

Los Angeles, 2002
1st year: $110,000
Summer associate: $2,115/week

Atlanta, 2002
1st year: $100,000
Summer associate: $1,750/week (2L)

THE SCOOP

Around the world in 10 years. That's the time it's taken Holland & Knight to span the globe, creating new offices as it goes. The firm has more than 30 of them worldwide. In the past four years, the firm has merged with firms in Chicago, Boston, Portland and even Finland. In February 2001, the D.C. office took on several attorneys to make the firm's real estate practice the largest in the nation. Responding to the economic slowdown of 2001, Holland & Knight froze associate pay in March 2002 (the freeze has since been lifted). The firm made headlines in summer 2001 when it rescinded summer associate offers to eight law students, though it made a comeback in public opinion in February 2002 when it cut partner, rather than associate, bonuses. In May 2002, the recession got the better of the firm once again, and H&K axed 27 associates and senior counsel, as well as 33 partners and 170 staff members, though it continues to hire lateral partners and associates.

GETTING HIRED

Holland & Knight reportedly looks for "individuals who have significant extracurricular interests" coupled with strong academics. "The firm is strongly enforcing a criteria based upon ranking of law schools and class ranking that excludes, except for extraordinary circumstances, any student not in the top quarter of the class, or even higher for schools outside the top 10 percent," comments a source. Though far from easy, the hiring process for lateral hires is usually quick. Relates one lateral, "By chance, through friends, I found out about an opening [at Holland & Knight]. I interviewed and liked my group. I was offered a job on the spot."

OUR SURVEY SAYS

Though Holland & Knight "is not a hugely social firm," its attorneys do enjoy each other's company. The firm's "'no jerks' policy isn't always followed, but generally lives up to expectations." These days, say associates, the culture is becoming more formal, and "recent financial problems will probably cause all offices to become more work-oriented."

It's no surprise that compensation is the No. 1 issue concerning associates at the firm, with the recently lifted salary freeze causing the most anxiety. There are not nearly as many worries when it comes to hours. "Holland & Knight's billable hours requirements are very reasonable," comments one insider. Adds another, "There is no such thing as face time here." In fact, even in the Big Law culture of New York City, "by 7 p.m., certain areas are completely clear and quiet."

Partners "are both accessible and helpful. They value the opinions of associates." And though "the reportedly low pay for partners combined with market rate pay for associates has caused a bit of tension lately," in general "the input of associates is given substantial weight when rendering both legal analysis and advice to clients."

Hunton & Williams

Riverfront Plaza, East Tower
951 East Byrd Street
Richmond, VA 23219
Phone: (804) 788-8200
www.hunton.com

LOCATIONS

Richmond, VA (HQ)
Atlanta, GA • Austin, TX • Charlotte, NC • Dallas, TX •
Knoxville, TN • McLean, VA • Miami, FL • New York,
NY • Norfolk, VA • Raleigh, NC • Washington, DC •
Bangkok • Brussels • Hong Kong • London • Warsaw

MAJOR DEPARTMENTS/PRACTICES

Administrative Law • Antitrust • Commercial litigation •
Corporate & Finance • Energy • Environmental •
Intellectual Property • Labor • Litigation • Project
Development Finance & Leasing • Public Finance •
Real Estate & Land Use • Regulated Industries &
Governmental Relations • Tax & ERISA • Technology

THE STATS

No. of attorneys: 850+
No. of offices: 17
Summer associate offers: 67 out of 106 (2001)
Chairman: Thurston Moore
Hiring Partner: David C. Landin

THE BUZZ
WHAT ATTORNEYS AT OTHER FIRMS ARE SAYING ABOUT THIS FIRM

• "Top-notch environmental"
• "Great in the Old South"
• "Tobacco-dependent"
• "Bow Ties 'R Us"

NOTABLE PERKS

• Emergency child care in Atlanta, DC and
  NY offices
• On-site gym (DC and Miami)
• Box seats at various sports venues
• Pre-tax transportation accounts

EMPLOYMENT CONTACT

Ms. Christine Tracey
Legal Recruiting Manager
Phone: (212) 309-1217
Fax: (212) 309-1100
ctracey@hunton.com

BASE SALARY

**Richmond, Charlotte, Knoxville, Norfolk
and Raleigh, 2002**
1st year: $100,000
Summer associate: $1,800/week

Atlanta, 2002
1st year: $100,000
Summer associate: $1,800/week

Austin and Dallas, 2002
1st year: $110,000
Summer associate: $2,100/week

Miami, 2002
1st year: $105,000
Summer associate: $1,800/week

McLean, New York and Washington, DC, 2002
1st year: $125,000
Summer associate: $2,400/week

THE SCOOP

More than a century old, Virginia's Hunton & Williams is one of the Southeast's leading law firms. Hunton's stellar reputation rests on more than its top-notch intellectual property practice. According to Thomson Financial, Hunton & Williams was the No.1 issuer's counsel for worldwide equity issuance by U.S. issuers in 2001. In 2001 alone, the firm handled six equity issuances worth $10 billion, including Kraft Foods' $8.7 billion IPO, the second largest in the nation's history. In January 2002, Hunton & Williams branched out west, merging with Texas-based Worsham Forsythe Wooldridge to beef up its energy, finance and regulatory practices. The firm opened an office in Miami in 1999 and hopes to migrate even farther south to Latin America.

GETTING HIRED

According to inisders, the firm is "trying to become more exclusive and increase its recruiting from the top schools." "Generally," suggests an associate, the firm is "looking for graduates of well-regarded national schools, or graduates near the top of their class from local schools." But Hunton knows that academic credentials aren't everything. A positive attitude, "friendly" demeanor and "good social skills" make a difference, too. Accordingly, interviews are less about grilling a candidate on the law than "getting to know [her] as a person."

OUR SURVEY SAYS

Associates value their firm's leading reputation in the community and enjoy producing "high-level work for high-level clients." Says a Richmond lawyer, "We have the best of all possible worlds — we get to work for a large international law firm with sophisticated clients and high-profile work, but we get to live in a city with a low cost of living, very little traffic and wonderful culture and history." Although "partners are generally respectful and approachable on a personal level," some suggest that associates are "certainly valued first and foremost as billing machines and only secondarily as human beings."

Last year, the firm changed its compensation system "from lockstep to a merit-based range system" and increased the minimum billable requirement to 2,000 hours. Neither change is very popular. Associates complain that there is "no formal bonus structure," that while base salary "is very competitive" bonuses "continue to be under market," and that "as a result of the new compensation system, many second- and third-year associates make less than first-year associates." The firm maintains that it is competitive in all of its markets at all associate levels.

Most everyone is in agreement about the firm's "strong commitment to pro bono work." Sources praise the "extremely organized" pro bono program and maintain that the firm seeks to meet or exceed the ABA's pro bono standard of giving 3 percent of billable hours to pro bono work.

Foley & Lardner

Firstar Center
777 East Wisconsin Avenue
Milwaukee, WI 53202-5367
Phone: (414) 271-2400
www.foleylaw.com

LOCATIONS

Milwaukee, WI (HQ)
Chicago, IL • Denver, CO • Detroit, MI • Jacksonville,
FL • Los Angeles, CA • Madison, WI • Orlando, FL •
Sacramento, CA • San Diego, CA • San Francisco, CA •
Tallahassee, FL • Tampa, FL • Washington, DC • West
Palm Beach, FL • Brussels

MAJOR DEPARTMENTS/PRACTICES

Copyright & Trademark
Finance/Public Finance
General Corporate
Health
Insurance
Intellectual Property/E-Business & Information
Technology
Labor/Employment
Litigation
Real Estate
Regulatory/Environmental Energy
Securities
Tax, Estates & Trusts, Benefits

THE STATS

No. of attorneys: 951
No. of offices: 16
Summer associate offers: 72 out of 87 (2001)
Chairman: Ralf-Reinhard Boer
Hiring Attorney: E. Robert Meek, Chair of Recruiting

THE BUZZ
WHAT ATTORNEYS AT OTHER FIRMS ARE SAYING ABOUT THIS FIRM

- "Excellent health care practice"
- "Boring, old school"
- "Terrific working environment"
- "Wants so badly to play with the big boys"

NOTABLE PERKS

- Free lunches at firm meetings
- Subsidized parking
- Reimbursement for cabs on late nights
- Annual firm retreat

EMPLOYMENT CONTACT

Ms. Patti Dixon
Director of Legal Recruitment & Development
Phone: (561) 650-5050
Fax: (561) 655-6925
pdixon@foleylaw.com

BASE SALARY

Milwaukee and Detroit, 2002
1st year: $115,000
2nd year: $120,000
3rd year: $125,000
4th year: $130,000
5th year: $140,000
6th year: $150,000
7th year: $185,000
8th year: $190,000
Summer associate: $2,100/week

THE SCOOP

Born in the nation's heartland, Foley & Lardner has one of the largest IP practices around, filing approximately 1,200 patents a year and employing about 125 attorneys. The firm itself is one of the largest in the country, with 951 attorneys. Located so close to the Motor City, it's no surprise the firm serves automotive clients. In May 2002, the firm announced the creation of an automotive industry team based in the Detroit office and consisting of more than 50 professionals from different practice areas around the country. In February 2001, the firm acquired Washington-based Freedman, Levy, Kroll & Simonds and Chicago-based Hopkins & Sutter. Later that year, it netted Washington-based Sullivan & Mitchell into its public affairs practice group.

GETTING HIRED

The hiring process at Foley "includes submission of an application, transcripts and numerous interviews." What is the firm looking for? "Hard-working team players" and "academic individuals who learn quickly and will add value to the firm." Sources appreciate the firm's summer associate program for offering a realistic view of life at the firm. One insider remarks, "During my summer I worked very hard, which gave me a truer experience than most programs of what to expect as an associate. There were also lots of planned events and opportunities to get to know people."

OUR SURVEY SAYS

"Friendly and laid back" are the two words that come to most associates' minds when describing F&L. "Foley & Lardner lawyers work hard and adhere to the highest ethical standards, but we have time for fun," says one associate. The firm has a highly "collegial" atmosphere where teamwork is emphasized. Regarding hours, one insider insists, "The firm is very serious about wanting its associates to have a life outside the office and has made a conscious effort to make this clear to associates."

Compensation at Foley & Lardner is "the highest in the Milwaukee market," say insiders. "You can live like a king in Milwaukee!" boast several pleased associates in the headquarter office. But some grumble that first-years receive nary a bonus. Others are displeased that "salaries get compressed as associates move up the ranks." However, "given the low hours requirement, the compensation package is very reasonable."

Insiders report that "the firm does well in recruiting women, but not as well retaining them and lacks women in management and upper-level positions." "Part-time/flex-time programs do not meet most women's needs," says one lawyer. The firm does have a minority scholarship but, as one minority explains, Foley needs to do more to foster minorities' professional growth.

VAULT TOP 100

72

PRESTIGE RANKING

Crowell & Moring LLP

1001 Pennsylvania Avenue, NW
Washington, DC 20004
Phone: (202) 624-2500
www.crowell.com

LOCATIONS

Washington, DC (HQ)
Irvine, CA
Brussels
London

MAJOR DEPARTMENTS/PRACTICES

Antitrust
Biotechnology
Business Crimes & Investigations
Energy
Government Contracts
Health Care
Intellectual Property
Labor & Employment
Litigation
Securities
Technology, Media & Telecommunications

THE STATS

No. of attorneys: 280
No. of offices: 4
Summer associate offers: 18 out of 20 (2001)
Chairman: John A. Macleod
Hiring Partner: Kent R. Morrison

NOTABLE PERKS

• Domestic partnership benefits
• Laptops at attorney request
• Weekly practice group lunches

EMPLOYMENT CONTACT

Ms. Michelle Blackwell Ray
Recruiting Coordinator
Phone: (202) 624-2779
Fax: (202) 628-5116
mblackwell@crowell.com

BASE SALARY

Washington, DC, 2002
1st year: $125,000
2nd year: $135,000
Summer associate: $2,400/week

THE BUZZ
WHAT ATTORNEYS AT OTHER FIRMS ARE SAYING ABOUT THIS FIRM

• "The most underrated firm in DC"
• "Can't get past Cruel & Boring"
• "A kinder, gentler firm"
• "Good SEC practice"

THE SCOOP

Founded in 1979, the Washington, D.C.-based Crowell & Moring is well known for its political lobbying, litigation, high-tech and government contract work. In May 2001, the D.C.-based IP boutique Evenson, McKeown, Edwards & Lenahan joined Crowell. In January 2002, two more securities partners joined the Crowell family, including Kathryn McGrath, the former head of the SEC's Division of Investment Management. The firm isn't afraid to take on high-profile, high-stakes litigation. In 2000 partner Stuart Newberger won $341 million in damages from Iran for ex-hostage Terry Anderson's 1979 torture and captivity.

GETTING HIRED

When it comes to hiring, Crowell has grades requirements, but after passing that hurdle, ability to fit in at the firm is key. Sources insist that "people with the right personality mix will often get offers over others with more impressive credentials on paper." Crowell recruits "generally from the top 20 to 25 law schools with a focus on the top 10 to 15 and D.C.-area schools." And the firm "looks for candidates who did very well in law school and who have journal" or "moot court experience." Sources praise the summer program for allowing participants to "work in many different [practice] areas."

OUR SURVEY SAYS

Attorneys describe Crowell as a firm that has a "friendly, comfortable atmosphere" staffed with "interesting people." "We work hard not to be uptight or formal," says one attorney. While many associates insist that "the lawyers are very friendly and nice people," some maintain that "this firm is not very social outside of the office." Other sources beg to differ: "The junior lawyers tend to socialize together," says a third year. Regardless, Crowell associates can have a life outside the firm if they want one. "Most attorneys leave [the office at] 6:30 to 7:00." In addition, "If you meet the 1,800 yearly requirement, you can count up to an additional 200 pro bono hours toward billable credit."

When it comes to compensation, Crowell associates are generally satisfied. "My compensation is appropriate for the amount I work. Other firms may pay more but expect associates to work more hours," says a senior associate. Some sources see evidence of changes ahead. "Generally, the [ratio of] salary to billable hours expected has been good," states a litigator, "but this appears to be changing. There is a greater demand on hours now."

Crowell is known for being "open-minded and liberal" and "is a comfortable place for women, minorities and gays/lesbians." The recruiting committee also "actively recruits top minorities."

Fenwick & West LLP

Two Palo Alto Square
Palo Alto, CA 94306
Phone: (650) 494-0600
www.fenwick.com

LOCATIONS

Palo Alto, CA (HQ)
San Francisco, CA
Washington, DC

MAJOR DEPARTMENTS/PRACTICES

Corporate
Employment & Labor
Intellectual Property
Licensing & Technology
Litigation
Mergers & Acquisitions
Patent
Tax
Trademark

THE STATS

No. of attorneys: 280
No. of offices: 3
Summer associate offers: 43 out of 56 (2001)
Chairman: Gordon Davidson
Hiring Attorneys: John Steele and Jeff Vetter

NOTABLE PERKS

- Use of firm's Hawaii condominiums
- Weekends getaways for associates who bill over 2,100 hours
- Pet insurance

EMPLOYMENT CONTACT

Ms. Karen Amatangelo-Block
Attorney Recruiting Manager
Phone: (650) 494-0600
Fax: (650) 494-1417
recruit@fenwick.com

BASE SALARY

All offices, 2002
1st year: $125,000
2nd year: $135,000
3rd year: $145,000
4th year: $160,000
5th year: $180,000
6th year: $195,000
7th year: $205,000
Summer associate: $2,400/week

THE BUZZ
WHAT ATTORNEYS AT OTHER FIRMS ARE SAYING ABOUT THIS FIRM

- "Great place to work"
- "Tops for tech"
- "Poorly managed"
- "Internet crash? Ouch!"

THE SCOOP

Situated in Silicon Valley, Fenwick & West is a high-tech firm with a global reach, serving this tech hotbed since its founding in 1972. In the past five years, Fenwick has doubled in size and now employs over 280 attorneys. Fenwick's M&A practice is nothing to sneeze at. A billion-dollar deal came in September 2001 when client VeriSign, Inc., the leading digital trust service provider, acquired Illuminet Holdings, Inc., an independent provider of telecommunications network and signaling services. When it comes to treating its employees well, Fenwick is known as the place to be. The firm is the only law firm to make *Fortune*'s list of the 100 Best Companies to Work For four years in a row. Some recently laid-off associates, however, may disagree with *Fortune*'s assessment of the firm; in 2001, Fenwick bid adieu to 32 associates and 15 paralegals.

GETTING HIRED

Because the firm has had a hiring freeze "for over a year," some insiders say it's "hard to tell" what it takes to score a job at Fenwick & West. "During the boom," claim associates, "it wasn't that hard to get a job." But now, they aren't sure "anyone is really getting hired." A third-year associate says the firm "looks to top national schools, plus some local schools. Top of class required."

OUR SURVEY SAYS

The pokey economy and 2001's layoffs have darkened the mood of many Fenwick insiders. Several associates claim that their firm's famously friendly and laid-back atmosphere is "becoming more uptight and backstabbing" as "people hoard work, steal work and desperately beg for work." Other attorneys, presumably those who remain busy, are more sanguine. They continue to enjoy working "with hot clients on their most interesting issues" in a "very collegial and friendly atmosphere."

While the decrease in business has reduced associates' workloads, it has not necessarily improved their quality of life. "Because of the slowdown in Silicon Valley, corporate attorneys are enjoying lighter work hours. However, this same slow-down has created considerable anxiety with respect to job security, which makes it difficult to completely enjoy the better schedules that we have." "Too many hours spent with nothing to do" is the lament of many a Fenwick lawyer.

Concern over hours is exacerbated by the firm's compensation scheme. Fenwick has a two-tiered salary structure — one for associates who bill a minimum of 1,800 hours and another for those billing at least 1,950 hours. But because work has dried up, "a majority of the associates are at the 1,800 rate when they would prefer to be billing 1,950." Notwithstanding the litany of complaints, insiders really value their colleagues, casual environment and "cool" partners, as well as "the cutting-edge work" — "when you can get it."

Kirkpatrick & Lockhart LLP

Henry W. Oliver Building
535 Smithfield Street
Pittsburgh, PA 15222
Phone: (412) 355-6500
www.kl.com

LOCATIONS

Boston, MA • Dallas, TX • Harrisburg, PA • Los
Angeles, CA • Miami, FL • Newark, NJ • New York, NY
Pittsburgh, PA • San Francisco, CA • Washington, DC

MAJOR DEPARTMENTS/PRACTICES

Antitrust • Bankruptcy • Construction • Corporate •
E-Commerce • Environmental • ESOP Transactions •
Franchise • Health Care • Insurance Coverage •
Intellectual Property/Technology • Investment
Management • Labor & Employee Benefits • Litigation •
Mergers & Acquisitions • Mortgage Banking •
Professional Liability • Product Liability • Securities
Enforcement • Tax/Trusts & Estates/Real Estate • Toxic
Tort • Transactional/Securities • White Collar Criminal

THE STATS

No. of attorneys: 642
No. of offices: 10
Summer associate offers: 45 out of 51 (2001)
Chair: Peter J. Kalis, Esq.

THE BUZZ
WHAT ATTORNEYS AT OTHER FIRMS ARE SAYING ABOUT THIS FIRM

- "I like what I've seen from them"
- "Lackluster litigation practice"
- "Extremely family friendly"
- "Seen better days"

NOTABLE PERKS

- Wednesday breakfasts
- Free lunches during the week
- In-house gym with cable TV

EMPLOYMENT CONTACT

Each office hires separately. See www.kl.com for
contacts in each office.

BASE SALARY

Boston, 2002
1st year: $115,000
Summer associate: $2,000/week

Harrisburg, 2002
1st year: $90,000
Summer associate: $1,600/week

Los Angeles, Dallas and Washington, DC, 2002
1st year: $110,000
Summer associate: $2,115/week (LA and DC),
$2,000/week (Dallas)

Miami, 2002
1st year: $93,000
Summer associate: $1,800/week

Newark, 2002
1st year: $102,000
Summer associate: $1,900/week

New York, 2002
1st year: $120,000
Summer associate: $2,307/week

Pittsburgh, 2002
1st year: $100,000
Summer associate: $1,920/week

San Francisco, 2002
1st year: $125,000
Summer associate: N/A

THE SCOOP

Born in Pittsburgh, Pa., Kirkpatrick & Lockhart remains Steeltown's largest law office. But, with approximately 650 lawyers and ten offices across the country, K&L has also raised its national profile. The firm has achieved prominence in several practice areas, notably investment management and insurance coverage. In 2000 K&L made the journey westward by opening offices in San Francisco and Los Angeles. (The LA office was the result of a merger with 17-lawyer securities boutique Freshman, Marantz, Orlanski, Cooper & Klein.) The Washington, D.C., office, which is the home of former U.S. Attorney General and Pennsylvania Governor Dick Thornburgh, recently added a new food & drug practice and now houses 127 attorneys. The firm also boasts sizable offices in Boston and New York.

GETTING HIRED

Looking to join Kirkpatrick & Lockhart as a summer associate? Plan to be at "the top of [your] class with journal and moot court experience." Don't despair if you're not at a top-tier school, as K&L recruits "at many schools that may be overlooked by some firms," says one associate. Sources agree that a summer at K&L is a great experience. An associate remembers, "We were allowed to indicate our preference in a particular area of law, and we received work assignments that were geared towards those preferences." Looking for another way in the door? Just ask. One associate remarks, "This firm hired me from a letter and resume sent independently to them."

OUR SURVEY SAYS

"K&L is a very friendly, laid-back place to work that fosters a casual and social environment among the attorneys," says one satisfied K&L-er. Many associates concur with the assessment. "The firm undertakes to make the transition from law student to associate as smooth as possible." Some sources complain about the firm's work assignment system. Explains a Pittsburgh associate, "It is principally the associate's responsibility to get work from upper level associates and partners. Because people tend to continue working with others they already have a working relationship with, it is sometimes hard to get work."

"Partners and associates typically have great working relationships. As a whole, the partnership at K&L places a higher priority than many firms on life outside the firm," says an associate. Which isn't to say that the occasional bad apple doesn't crop up in the mix — you just have to know the system: "Everyone knows the partners to avoid, and most people do." Associates must reach a reasonable billable hours target of 1,850 or 1,950 hours to receive a bonus. However, some say that just reaching the minimum target doesn't impress anyone: "To make it long-term at K&L, you are realistically expected to get to roughly 2,100 hours."

Bingham Dana LLP

150 Federal Street
Boston, MA 02110
Phone: (617) 951-8000
www.bingham.com

LOCATIONS

Boston, MA (HQ)
Hartford, CT
Los Angeles, CA
New York, NY
Washington, DC
London
Singapore

MAJOR DEPARTMENTS/PRACTICES

Corporate
Banking
Finance
Estate Planning
Investment Management
Project Finance
Real Estate
Litigation
Mergers & Acquisitions
Tax

THE STATS

No. of attorneys: 500
No. of offices: 7
Summer associate offers: 42 out of 43 (2001)
Managing Partner: Jay S. Zimmerman
Hiring Partner: Marijane Benner Browne

NOTABLE PERKS

• Red Sox tickets
• Subsidized gym membership
• Emergency day care
• Domestic partner benefits

EMPLOYMENT CONTACT

Ms. Maris L. Abbene
Director of Legal Recruitment
Phone: (617) 951-8556
Fax: (617) 951-8736
mlabbene@bingham.com

BASE SALARY

Boston, 2002
1st year: $125,000
2nd year: $130,000
3rd year: $135,000
4th year: $160,000
5th year: $180,000
6th year: $190,000
7th year: $200,000
Summer associate: $2,400/week

THE BUZZ
WHAT ATTORNEYS AT OTHER FIRMS ARE SAYING ABOUT THIS FIRM

• "A top firm in Boston"
• "Great advertising — so what?"
• "Well respected in a small market"
• "Larger doesn't mean better"

THE SCOOP

Boston's Bingham Dana will soon join the ranks of the nation's 25 largest law firms. In May 2002, the firm announced plans to merge with San Francisco-based McCutchen, Doyle, Brown & Enersen, effective July 1, 2002. The combined firm, Bingham McCutchen LLP, will have more than 800 attorneys. Bingham Dana had earlier expanded its New York presence by merging with Manhattan's Richards & O'Neil in May 2001. The firm's practice draws big names in almost every industry — like Aetna, Deutsche Bank, Kawasaki U.S.A., Inc. and Palm, Inc. Bingham also handles work for hometown favorites like *The Boston Globe*, Harvard University and the Boston Red Sox.

GETTING HIRED

This firm "definitely looks beyond the numbers," but "if you're not from a top 30 school," advises one associate, you should be "very close to the top of the class." According to one attorney, "law review will boost chances for an interview if [a] candidate is not from one of the preferred law schools," as will "a business background" and "ties to the area." Bingham Dana "likes people who are well-rounded — involved in athletics, community service, the arts, and so on." You should also have "outstanding writing and verbal skills."

OUR SURVEY SAYS

Bingham Dana lawyers enjoy a "sophisticated practice" in "a very non-competitive atmosphere." The firm offers "a nice balance between being social and being professional." "While many of the lawyers socialize together," says one source, "neither is the firm expected to be your primary social outlet." Associates appreciate the "tremendous respect" with which everyone — "whether partner, secretary, paralegal or associate" — is treated. There are "no real screamers or psychopaths among the partner ranks," and "people definitely have a good sense of humor."

Attorneys receive "a high degree of responsibility" early in their careers. A litigator considers "the formal and informal training I receive on a daily basis to be one of the most valuable aspects of my position." Another values "the freedom and flexibility to pursue [his] pro bono interests." The firm does expect "2,000 billable hours for each associate," which one respondent declares is "not unreasonable considering the pay."

Most sources are "very satisfied" with their compensation. One associate's "only complaint is how bonuses are determined." Another lawyer in a branch office claims that "as compared to other firms in the area we have the same starting rate, but after our second year our salary increases do not increase as much as other local firms." Indeed, several associates complain of "disparate treatment between the Boston office and all of the other offices."

Stroock & Stroock & Lavan LLP

180 Maiden Lane
New York, NY 10038-4982
Phone: (212) 806-5400
www.stroock.com

LOCATIONS

New York, NY (HQ)
Los Angeles, CA
Miami, FL

MAJOR DEPARTMENTS/PRACTICES

Commodities & Derivatives
Employment Law & Benefits
Energy & Project Finance
Entertainment
Financial Services Litigation
Insolvency & Restructuring
Insurance
Intellectual Property
Investment Management
Litigation
Mergers, Acquisitions & Joint Ventures
Personal Client Services
Real Estate
Securities
Structured Finance
Tax

THE STATS

No. of attorneys: 319
No. of offices: 3
Summer associate offers: 23 out of 24 (2001)
Managing Partner: Thomas E. Heftler
Hiring Attorney: James R. Tanenbaum

 ## THE BUZZ
WHAT ATTORNEYS AT OTHER FIRMS ARE SAYING ABOUT THIS FIRM

- "Screamers everywhere"
- "Sweatshop with a great view"
- "Smart, hardworking firm"
- "Very nice people"

NOTABLE PERKS

- $1,500 technology allowance every three years
- Subsidized gym membership
- Meals and car service after hours

EMPLOYMENT CONTACT

Ms. Diane Cohen
Director of Legal Personnel and Recruiting
Phone: (212) 806-5406
Fax: (212) 806-6006
dcohen@stroock.com

BASE SALARY

New York, 2002
1st year: $125,000
2nd year: $135,000
3rd year: $150,000
4th year: $170,000
5th year: $190,000
6th year: $205,000
7th year: $210,000
8th year: $215,000
Summer associate: $2,400/week

THE SCOOP

Stroock & Stroock & Lavan is one of the most active firms for companies issuing stock and filing for Chapter 11 protection. In each of the past five years, the firm has represented underwriters and issuers of securities totaling more than $30 billion a year. Attorneys in Stroock's renowned insolvency & restructuring practice have a reputation for representing large, high-profile bankruptcies. The firm also enjoys prominent real estate and capital markets work. When it comes to pro bono, Stroock is top-notch. At present the firm is representing Holocaust victims seeking reparations. And in 2001, it appointed sixth-year associate Kevin Curnin as the first attorney director of the firm's new Public Service Project. The position will be a rotating one in which the attorney serves full time on pro bono matters.

GETTING HIRED

Stroock & Stroock "is looking to hire candidates who are ambitious and bright, as well as personable." As far as academic credentials, the firm "generally culls mid-range students from top schools or higher-range students from mid-range schools." Some insiders believe the "firm spends way too much effort on recruiting at certain top-tier schools (like Harvard and Chicago) where we almost never land associates."

OUR SURVEY SAYS

The people at Stroock & Stroock are "fantastic," according to many insiders. "By far the best part of this place is the people." Associates admire colleagues' friendliness and "camaraderie." "Some of my fellow associates and others here are my best friends inside and out of work," declares a litigator. In fact, the litigation department seems to be particularly "laid back" and "sponsors periodic outings to jazz clubs or karaoke nights" as well as "the occasional happy hour."

Associates' feelings about partners are more mixed. Associate-partner relations are "very variable." Several insiders report that "with a few exceptions, the partners are very nice to associates." However, "there is little social interaction," and, while some partners are "very good teachers," others have a tendency to "dump and run," leaving associates to figure things out on their own. A few sources complain about uneven work distribution. Less busy associates lament, "Partners tend to funnel work to the same associates, without giving others a chance to prove themselves." The issue of compensation evokes varied reactions. "We are paid very well," maintains a senior associate. "Stroock follows its neighbors," shrugs another lawyer. "We are never the leader in bonuses or compensation, but we are in line with the average." Others disagree. Even if the "base salary is market, and high," many claim their "bonuses are very much below market and perceived by associates as arbitrary."

Patton Boggs LLP

2550 M Street, NW
Washington, DC 20037
Phone: (202) 457-6000
www.pattonboggs.com

LOCATIONS

Washington, DC (HQ)
Anchorage, AK
Boulder, CO
Dallas, TX
Denver, CO
McLean, VA

MAJOR DEPARTMENTS/PRACTICES

Administrative & Regulatory
Communications & Technology
Litigation & Dispute Resolution
Public Policy
Securities, Corporate Finance & Tax

THE STATS

No. of attorneys: 369
No. of offices: 6
Summer associate offers: 11 out of 12 (2001)
Chairman: Thomas Hale Boggs Jr.
Managing Partner: Stuart Pape
Hiring Partner: Darryl Nirenberg

NOTABLE PERKS

• In-house café (DC)
• Firm happy hour every third Thursday
• Subsidized health club membership

EMPLOYMENT CONTACT

Ms. Kara Reidy
Director of Professional Recruitment
Phone: (202) 457-6000
Fax: (202) 457-6315
kreidy@pattonboggs.com

BASE SALARY

Washington, DC, 2002
The firm has a two-tier system — 1,900 billable track and 1,650 billable track. First- and second-year associates are automatically compensated at the 1,900-hour level.
1st year: $120,000
2nd year: $125,000
3rd year: $135,000; $113,000
4th year: $145,000; $119,000
5th year: $155,000; $125,000
6th year: $165,000; $132,000
7th year: $175,000; $139,000
8th year: $185,000; $147,000
Summer associate: $2,200/week

THE BUZZ
WHAT ATTORNEYS AT OTHER FIRMS ARE SAYING ABOUT THIS FIRM

• "The lobbying mothership"
• "Internally competitive"
• "Well-connected"
• "Stodgy"

THE SCOOP

The year 2002 marks the 40th anniversary of Patton Boggs. Well known for its political connections, Patton Boggs has developed into a Washington lobbying powerhouse. In February 2002, the firm snatched five former Piper Marbury Rudnick & Wolfe attorneys to beef up its own biotech practice. October 2001 brought a big win when the firm, along with the Center for Justice & Accountability and the Center for Constitutional Rights, represented six plaintiffs in a suit alleging human rights violations by an Indonesian general in East Timor. General Lumintang was ordered to pay $66 million in damages for his role in the 1999 post-election massacres.

GETTING HIRED

"It takes a lot to get your foot in the door here," says one associate. Sources say the firm is "less concerned with law school pedigree and more with the overall quality of the person." Prospective laterals should expect a rigorous hiring process, including two half-day interview sessions with several associates and partners. "Firm committees make the process quite selective," says one insider.

OUR SURVEY SAYS

For the most part, Patton Boggs associates are a very satisfied bunch of attorneys. They get to work on "top-level" cases with "high-profile international and public policy" implications. The atmosphere around the office is described as laid back and friendly. Colleagues are "considerate," "thoughtful" and "very social." Says one insider, "We celebrate birthdays together" and "meet for drinks or all go out together after official functions." But don't worry if hanging out after hours isn't your thing: "More senior associates usually go home to their families."

Associates seem to take the firm's 1,900 billable hours target in stride. "At any law firm, associates work hard, and we do too. But the hours here allow us to still have an outside life. And we're not too exhausted to enjoy it." For some, the problem isn't too many hours, it's too few. "Work lately has been slow," admits a D.C. associate. "The annual expectation has not changed, but it's harder to get the hours necessary to meet that expectation." By all accounts, the firm is committed to pro bono work, requiring that all associates bill 100 hours of pro bono annually.

Compensation garners mixed reviews. D.C. associates feel the "firm's compensation for associates has traditionally been among the lowest of large D.C.-based firms." Some, though, see the salary as a blessing in disguise. "I think the firm is a little below market based on our peer firms in this area, but I think our billable hours expectations are also lower than comparable firms," explains an insider. No one likes the fact that "the firm has made big cuts in benefits," such as the reduction in 401(k) contributions.

Gray Cary Ware & Freidenrich, LLP

400 Hamilton Avenue
Palo Alto, CA 94301
Phone: (650) 833-2000
www.graycary.com

LOCATIONS

Palo Alto, CA (HQ) (3 offices)
Austin, TX
Sacramento, CA
San Diego, CA (2 offices)
San Francisco, CA
Seattle, WA
Washington, DC

MAJOR DEPARTMENTS/PRACTICES

Communications & Network Infrastructure
Corporate & Securities
Employment Services
Intellectual Property & Technology
Life Sciences
Litigation
Real Estate Services
Tax & Trusts

THE STATS

No. of attorneys: 460
No. of offices: 10
Summer associate offers: 47 out of 53 (2001)
Chairman: J. Terence O'Malley
Hiring Partner: Richard I. Yankwich

NOTABLE PERKS

- Blackberry wireless devices, laptops and cell phones
- Home office setup (copier, fax, printer, scanner)
- Free parking
- Firm contributions to child care expenses

EMPLOYMENT CONTACT

Ms. Leslie Colvin
Professional Recruiting Director
Phone: (650) 833-2133
Fax: (650) 833-1530
lcolvin@graycary.com

BASE SALARY

All offices, 2002
1st year: $125,000
2nd year: $135,000
3rd year: $150,000
4th year: $165,000
5th year: $180,000
6th year: $195,000
7th year: $205,000
8th year: $215,000
Summer associate: $2,400/week

THE BUZZ
WHAT ATTORNEYS AT OTHER FIRMS ARE SAYING ABOUT THIS FIRM

- "Good tech firm, solid client base"
- "Fenwick light"
- "Top-notch, but fearing the axe"
- "My dog ate your bonus"

THE SCOOP

Gray Cary Ware & Freidenrich was born as the result of a 1994 merger of a Palo Alto technology firm and a San Diego litigation star. In January 2002, the firm took the plunge again, this time merging with D.C.'s nine-attorney Blumenfeld & Cohen, giving the firm a presence on the East Coast and an edge in public policy law. Still, Gray Cary suffered along with other firms in 2001. August 2001 saw the institution of a pay freeze, and the firm laid off 46 associates and 68 support staff members just five months later. Though the number of IPOs plummeted in 2001, the firm's M&A business remained strong, with the firm orchestrating 90 M&A deals that year.

GETTING HIRED

Most contacts agree that Gray Cary "tends to look for something more than just grades or pedigree." Gray Cary "likes a diverse work force," and toward that end "tends to look at a candidate's entire life experience." One source notes that "many colleagues had interesting careers before making a switch to law." "Class rank is probably more important now given the economic downturn," asserts a lawyer, who says that the firm also prefers candidates from the top 25 law schools who "demonstrate a commitment to the Bay Area."

OUR SURVEY SAYS

"One of the great things about the firm," say associates, "is the lack of hierarchy." At Gray Cary, "partners generally treat associates at every level with respect" and "are genuinely interested in the professional growth of the associates." Sources describe a culture "both friendly and professional" where "IP litigators get together to drink a fine scotch and discuss the week" on "scotch Friday."

Strangely, many associates insist that the money, not the scotch, is the "best part of the job." Gray Cary pays "top-notch" salaries and bonuses that are both discretionary and tied to billable hours. Some first-year associates complain that their start dates were delayed last fall and their salaries were slashed by $10,000. But, one first-year acknowledges, "we still get a great paycheck." Several attorneys grumble that, hefty as the paychecks are, they aren't "sufficient to compete in the ridiculous housing market" of Silicon Valley.

"High pay equals high hours," reflects an insider. But many find Gray Cary's billable hours requirement of 1,950 hours reasonable "comparable to many other firms." Several associates appreciate that the "firm seems to actively promote a balance between work and free time." A few attorneys worry that the firm "culture is changing" and "becoming more formal." An associate cites the "first indication: no jeans on Friday anymore." People are still friendly, claims one attorney, but the "firm is transitioning from a 'lifestyle firm' to a top 50 firm, with all that entails."

Baker & Hostetler LLP

3200 National City Center
1900 East 9th Street
Cleveland, OH 44114-3485
Phone: (216) 621-0200
www.bakerlaw.com

LOCATIONS

Cincinnati, OH
Cleveland, OH
Columbus, OH
Costa Mesa, CA
Denver, CO
Houston, TX
Los Angeles, CA
New York, NY
Orlando, FL
Washington, DC

International Affliliates:
Juarez, Mexico
Sao Paulo, Brazil

MAJOR DEPARTMENTS/PRACTICES

Business
Employment & Labor
Litigation
Tax, Personal Planning & Employee Benefits

THE STATS

No. of attorneys: 526
No. of offices: 10
Summer associate offers: 30 out of 40 (2001)
Executive Partner: Gary L. Bryenton
Hiring Partner: Ronald G. Linville

NOTABLE PERKS

• Tickets to sporting events and concerts
• Summer retreat at a resort every other year

EMPLOYMENT CONTACT

Ms. Kathleen Ferdico
Attorney Recruitment and Development Manager
Phone: (216) 861-7092
Fax: (216) 861-6618
kferdico@bakerlaw.com

THE BUZZ
WHAT ATTORNEYS AT OTHER FIRMS ARE SAYING ABOUT THIS FIRM

• "Good regional firm"
• "Still waiting to play with the big boys"
• "Telecom is great"
• "Cleveland doesn't rock"

THE SCOOP

Baker & Hostetler has made a name for itself counseling clients on major and middle-market transactions as well as in labor, intellectual property and media and First Amendment law. In February 2002, the firm launched BakerER to provide employee relations consulting regarding important workplace issues such as reorganizations, mergers, acquisitions, IPO activities and cost-cutting efforts. This service follows the firm's spring 2001 kick-off of its private equity industry team, a firm-wide interdisciplinary group. In April 2001 the firm welcomed former Chairman of the House Judiciary Subcommittee on Crime Bill McCollum to the firm's Orlando office.

GETTING HIRED

To get a summer position at B&H, you have to be in the top of your class. The firm seeks "motivated" and "extroverted" people who are "personable." B&H interviews on campus and follows up with a full day of interviews at the firm. Being a summer associate at Baker & Hostetler is like being on a "honeymoon." "It is not a realistic portrayal of life as a first-year associate," says one associate. It may not be realistic, but it sure is fun. "My summer was incredible," raves an insider. She adds, "The workload is kept minimal so time can be spent getting to know the attorneys and firm atmosphere."

OUR SURVEY SAYS

"Few associates leave [Baker & Hostetler] for greener pastures" at other firms. An associate notes, "While there seems to be turnover every year, there are many people who have been here for years." Why do so many people stay? It could be the friendly vibe. "The environment is collegial and friendly. Attorneys often engage in social activities outside of the office together and are friendly while working. The best description of the majority of the attorneys is a firm of extremely bright, hardworking people who also know how to enjoy life and have fun," explains one associate.

Pro bono work is plentiful. "We can do as much as we want, so long as we still meet our billable requirements," notes an associate. Compensation is "more than fair." The hours are liveable. Regarding training, an associate notes, "This firm provides training for everything. Some is mandatory and some optional. There is actually an 'Associates Academy' each year that includes training in practical and procedural aspects of being a lawyer, as well as training in substantive areas." Another associate points out that mid-level associates receive training "via modules on drafting pleadings, taking and defending fact and expert depositions, and so on." It's also good to know partners are open to questions and "take time to explain things to associates." In fact, partner and associate relations seem to be good overall. Says one insider, "I have not yet been yelled at by any partner for anything."

McCutchen, Doyle, Brown & Enersen, LLP

Three Embarcadero Center
San Francisco, CA 94111
Phone: (415) 393-2000
www.mccutchen.com

LOCATIONS

San Francisco, CA (HQ)
Los Angeles, CA
Palo Alto, CA
Walnut Creek, CA

MAJOR DEPARTMENTS/PRACTICES

Bankruptcy
Biotechnology
Corporate
Energy
Environmental
Intellectual Property
Litigation

THE STATS

No. of attorneys: 334
No. of offices: 4
Summer associate offers: 34 out of 43 (2001)
Chairman: Donn P. Pickett
Firm-wide Recruiting Partner: Michael I. Begert

NOTABLE PERKS

- Ping-pong on Fridays
- Annual Oscar party
- Monthly birthday/anniversary parties
- Market-leading parental leave policies

EMPLOYMENT CONTACT

San Francisco/Walnut Creek
Ms. Beth M. Harris
Attorney Recruitment Manager
Phone: (415) 393-2302
Fax: (415) 393-2286
bharris@mdbe.com

Palo Alto
Ms. Darren M. Carmassi
Attorney Recruitment Manager
Phone: (650) 849-4871
Fax: (650) 849-4800
dcarmassi@mdbe.com

Los Angeles
Ms. Meyosha Spencer
Attorney Recruitment Manager
Phone: (213) 680-6456
Fax: (213) 680-6499
mspencer@mdbe.com

BASE SALARY

All offices, 2002
1st year: $125,000
2nd year: $135,000
3rd year: $150,000
4th year: $160,000
5th year: $180,000
6th year: $190,000
7th year: $200,000
8th year: $215,000
Summer associate: $2,400/week

THE BUZZ
WHAT ATTORNEYS AT OTHER FIRMS ARE SAYING ABOUT THIS FIRM

- "Strong West Coast firm"
- "Corporate practice is nonexistent"
- "Laid-back, good atmosphere"
- "Too needy for a merger partner"

THE SCOOP

McCutchen Doyle is one of the Golden State's largest and oldest firms. In 2002 it will join with Boston Brahmin Bingham Dana to form Bingham McCutchen LLP. In May 2002 the two firms announced plans to merge effective July 1, 2002. Among the assets McCutchen brings to the table is its excellent reputation in litigation. Other top McCutchen practices include environmental law, securities, IP and technology. The firm also shines at pro bono work and for the past 10 years has consistently ranked in the top 10 on the AmLaw Pro Bono Honor Roll. In 2002, for the second year in a row, McCutchen ranked among *Fortune* magazine's 100 Best Companies to Work For.

GETTING HIRED

Students seeking a McCutchen summer better study hard. "For new associates, top grades at a top school is a must. There's a little more slack for laterals with needed skills, such as patent lawyers with electrical engineering degrees." According to a lateral, "a positive and friendly personality goes a long way in our interview process, and communication skills are absolutely critical."

OUR SURVEY SAYS

"Here, I never feel as if I am just a fungible money-making unit, but an integral part of the firm's business and culture — and a future owner of the business," enthuses a fifth-year associate. Many insiders say McCutchen is a place where "partners treat associates as colleagues, not lackeys," young attorneys are respected and the "quality of work and clientele is outstanding." Some insiders, however, feel this way of life is slipping away because of the firm's focus on finding a merger partner and increasing profits: "Many of its unique features are being swept under the rug as McCutchen tries to primp itself up for merger candidates." Another source says, "The atmosphere is starting to change due to increased pressure to bill and partners' efforts to cut costs."

Those cuts have included associate salaries — and associates are peeved. "The firm is moving away from lockstep salaries," notes one attorney. Another grumbles, "The firm now says salary level is purely discretionary if minimum hours are not met, even if the reason they were not met is that the firm does not have enough work for everyone." Still, at least one attorney appreciates that "when changes in compensation structure are made, associate committees are involved from the very beginning and associate opinion is solicited before the firm makes any decisions."

McCutchen's associates applaud the firm's dedication to pro bono work. "From the most senior partners to the most junior associates, it is something the firm prides itself on," a third-year boasts. They just wish more than 50 pro bono hours counted towards the billable hours target. "One hundred might be better," suggests an environmental attorney. "I think the firm felt it used to be too encouraging of pro bono and has started to de-emphasize it."

Schulte Roth & Zabel LLP

919 Third Avenue
New York, NY 10022
Phone: (212) 756-2000
www.srz.com

LOCATIONS

New York, NY (HQ)

MAJOR DEPARTMENTS/PRACTICES

Business Reorganization
Capital Markets
Employment & Employee Benefits
Environmental Law
Financial Services
Individual Client Services
Intellectual Property
Investment Management
Litigation
Mergers & Acquisitions
Real Estate
Structured Finance
Tax

THE STATS

No. of attorneys: 315
No. of offices: 1
Summer associate offers: 26 out of 27 (2001)
Executive Committee: Martin Perschetz, Paul Roth,
Alan Waldenberg, Paul Weber and Marc Weingarten
Hiring Partners: Stephanie R. Breslow and
Kurt F. Rosell

NOTABLE PERKS

- Blackberries and Palm Pilots or laptops with DVD
- Decent cafeteria (with kosher food options!)
- Sabbatical opportunities

EMPLOYMENT CONTACT

Ms. Lisa Drew
Director of Recruiting
Phone: (212) 756-2093
Fax: (2112) 593-5955
lisa.drew@srz.com

BASE SALARY

New York, 2002
1st year: $125,000
2nd year: $135,000
3rd year: $150,000
4th year: $170,000
5th year: $190,000
6th year: $205,000
7th year: $220,000
8th year: $225,000
Summer associate: $2,403/week

THE BUZZ
WHAT ATTORNEYS AT OTHER FIRMS ARE SAYING ABOUT THIS FIRM

- "Cutthroat partners"
- "Good for hedge funds"
- "Very unhappy associates"
- "Good place for aspiring Asst. U.S. Attorneys"

THE SCOOP

With a single office located at the core of the Big Apple, Schulte Roth & Zabel has been steadily climbing its way into the upper echelons of the New York law firm community since its birth in 1969. Well known for its work in trusts and estates, Schulte Roth has several noteworthy clients, including the Rockefellers, the Lehmans and Toys 'R Us founder Charles Lazarus. In 2001 Schulte, along with several other law firms, played a role in one of New York's major new construction projects, the AOL Time Warner Center. The Center is expected to revitalize the Columbus Circle area of upper Manhattan upon its completion in 2003.

GETTING HIRED

For candidates seeking a spot in the Schulte Roth family, the most important factor is "the right personality." "We like to hire people we like, not just people with good grades or work experience," explains an associate. "We are a very tight group here, and there is a lot of 'will this person fit in?' emphasis." Others agree that "the firm is looking for people that have both good credentials and a good personality."

OUR SURVEY SAYS

Friendly, social and cooperative is how most respondents describe the culture at Schulte Roth & Zabel. "Everyone is on a first-name basis, there is very little incivility and we work as a team, with everyone getting credit for their work. I think the culture here is as good as it gets," concludes one happy associate. "Attorneys seem to genuinely like each other," with "none of that sugary fakeness that exists in other firms." Another lawyer affectionately likens the firm to "a [loud] family dinner."

But what is a friendly vibe without a nice paycheck to go with it? Not only do salaries at Schulte meet the going rate of other large firms, but last year the firm paid out bonuses "three times as high as the bonuses of most other New York City firms." Moreover, the "guaranteed bonuses, even for first-year associates, was truly unique." The firm pays a guaranteed minimum bonus for meeting target billable hours and an additional bonus for going above and beyond the billable hours goal. A few lawyers gripe that the "hours needed to qualify for the bonus structure totally are not worth it" and that bonuses are awarded unequally among senior associates. But overall, insiders seem to think their compensation is "pretty doggone good." And don't believe all those horror stories about partners-as-ogres. Schulte Roth partners "completely contradict the scary stereotype," according to associates. Lawyers acknowledge the presence of "a few bad apples." Yet junior associates generally feel respected and appreciate the opportunity to interact closely with partners, some emphasizing that they work "with the partners, not for the partners."

82

Bryan Cave LLP

One Metropolitan Square
211 North Broadway
Suite 3600
St. Louis, MO 63102
Phone: (314) 259-2000
www.bryancave.com

LOCATIONS

Chicago, IL • Irvine, CA • Jefferson City, MO • Kansas City, MO • Los Angeles, CA • New York, NY • Overland Park, KS • Phoenix, AZ • St. Louis, MO • Washington, DC • Abu Dhabi, U.A.E. • Beijing • Dubai, U.A.E. • Hong Kong • Kuwait City • London • Riyadh, Saudi Arabia • Shanghai

MAJOR DEPARTMENTS/PRACTICES

Business & Transactional Counseling
Litigation & Dispute Resolution

THE STATS

No. of attorneys: 635
No. of offices: 18
Summer associate offers: 38 out of 39 (2001)
Chairman: Walter L. Metcalfe Jr.
Hiring Partners: Robert T. Ebert (St. Louis); Robert M. Thompson (Kansas City); Jeffrey W. Morof (Los Angeles); John R. Wilner (DC); Elizabeth A. Bousquette (NY); Carla A. Consoli (Phoenix); Steven H. Sunshine (Irvine)

NOTABLE PERKS

• Free cell phone
• Paid out-of-town CLEs
• "Take a Lawyer to Lunch" program
• Three months paid maternity leave

EMPLOYMENT CONTACT

Ms. Jennifer J. Sloop
Recruiting Coordinator
Phone: (314) 259-2617
Fax: (314) 259-2020
jjsloop@bryancave.com

BASE SALARY

Irvine, 2002
1st year: $125,000
Summer associate: TBD

Kansas City, 2002
1st year: $85,000
Summer associate: $1,500/week

Los Angeles and New York, 2002
1st year: $125,000
Summer associate: $2,400/week

Phoenix, 2002
1st year: $95,000
Summer associate: $1,700/week

St. Louis, 2002
1st year: $90,000
Summer associate $1,500/week

Washington, DC, 2002
1st year: $120,000
Summer associate: $2,000/week

THE BUZZ
WHAT ATTORNEYS AT OTHER FIRMS ARE SAYING ABOUT THIS FIRM

• "Regionally respected"
• "Midwestern — and it shows"
• "Politically well-connected"
• "Old-fashioned, stodgy"

THE SCOOP

St. Louis' Bryan Cave has a unique operating structure: 30 client service groups are divided by area of law (e.g., international, environmental) or aimed at specific industry groups (e.g., health care, real estate). Big-name clients include The Boeing Company, Anheuser-Busch, Bank of America and Ralston Purina. The firm has four offices in the Middle East and even represented the Kuwaiti government regarding damages from the Gulf War. In 2001 Bryan Cave merged with Jewkes, Chan & Partners, a Hong Kong firm known for its corporate and commercial work. In July 2002, it merged with New York's Robinson Silverman Pearce Aronsoh & Berman LLP. The combined firm, with 800 lawyers firm-wide, ranks among the 25 largest in the world.

GETTING HIRED

A "great academic record" is key for landing a summer associate position, while "great prior experience" wouldn't hurt laterals. Law students are screened on campus followed by interviews at the firm. Associates praise the summer program's blend of "substance" and "wining and dining." "I had a fantastic summer experience, including the opportunity to play a major part in a significant pro bono case involving the entire St. Louis region," says a satisfied associate.

OUR SURVEY SAYS

Associates "who prove themselves are generally given significant responsibility on transactions for major firm clients." Overall, attorneys find the culture pleasing. "Many of the lawyers, including partners, are actually quite personable, the kind of people you might enjoy having a beer with." An attorney tells us, "There is no pressure to put in any face time or work weekends unless it is absolutely necessary." Hours-based bonuses give associates control over how much they work.

"'Respect' is a veritable byword at Bryan Cave," says one associate. "Many partners realize that overworked associates will burn out and move on. Considerable effort is made to ensure that associates have some balance in their lives." One associate is happy the firm "recently reinstituted their out-of-town CLE program, but the in-house training could use some work." Attorneys in some offices feel salary is slightly below market, but many say they are still well-compensated.

"The firm is good about hiring women and encouraging them to stay through the flex-time program," reveals a female attorney. Another insider says, "One of the women who was promoted to partnership last year was and is a part-time lawyer." An Hispanic lawyer reports "minority representation at all levels — associate, counsel and partner. My impression is that everyone has equal access to hiring, promotion and mentoring." Another source says, "The firm provides benefits to domestic partners and was recognized by a gay/lesbian publication for being hospitable to gays and lesbians."

Pennie & Edmonds LLP

1155 Avenue of the Americas
New York, NY 10036
Phone: (212) 790-9090
www.pennie.com

LOCATIONS

New York, NY (HQ)
Palo Alto, CA
Washington, DC

MAJOR DEPARTMENTS/PRACTICES

Intellectual Property and Industrial Property (divided into
three legal groups — Procurement, Litigation &
Consulting) with expertise in Biotechnology,
Pharmaceuticals, Chemistry, Materials Technologies,
Electrical Engineering, Computer Science, Internet, E-
Commerce, Mechanical Technologies and Trademark,
Copyright and Competition

THE STATS

No. of attorneys: 220
No. of offices: 3
Co-Managing Partners: John J. Normile and
Peter D. Vogl
Hiring Partner: Peter D. Vogl

NOTABLE PERKS

- Tickets to sporting and cultural events
- Annual firm dinner
- In-house gym & proximity to hiking/biking trails
  (Palo Alto)
- Continental breakfast on Fridays (DC) and annual
  golf outing (NY)

EMPLOYMENT CONTACT

Mr. Peter D. Vogl
Hiring Partner
Phone: (212) 790-6340
Fax: (212) 869-8864
voglp@pennie.com

BASE SALARY

New York, 2002
1st year: $125,000
2nd year: $135,000
3rd year: $150,000
4th year: $165,000
5th year: $185,000
6th year: $200,000
7th year: $210,000
8th year: $220,000
Summer associate: $2,400/week

THE BUZZ
WHAT ATTORNEYS AT OTHER FIRMS ARE SAYING ABOUT THIS FIRM

- "Killer IP boutique"
- "Endangered species"
- "Losing power"
- "Top in their field"

THE SCOOP

Founded in 1884, Pennie & Edmonds is one of the nation's largest intellectual property firms. Besides thriving litigation and procurement practices, the firm distinguishes itself with an IP consulting group that assists inventors and companies in patenting and marketing their products. The firm also helps venture capitalists target worthy patents for investment. Pennie & Edmonds has an impressive client list, including BN.com, Microsoft's Expedia, Hewlett-Packard and Bic Corporation. In a high-profile deal in August 2001, the firm represented Bristol-Myers Squibb in its $7.8 billion acquisition of E. I. du Pont de Nemours and Co.'s pharmaceutical line.

GETTING HIRED

Pennie just "loves PhDs," say insiders. "A doctorate is a valuable commodity for interviewing at Pennie & Edmonds" since "technical competence is valued as highly as one's potential as a lawyer." An attorney notes that "the firm is full of people for whom law is a second career." A PhD is not the only plus — a winning personality helps, too. The firm seeks "smart people who are easy to get along with." Even if the firm is not obsessed with grades and brand name schools, competition for a spot in this IP boutique is bound to be "a little stiff."

OUR SURVEY SAYS

Pennie & Edmonds "is a great place to work," rave associates. "The work is interesting and challenging," the "attire is 'business casual'" and colleagues "are approachable and friendly." Moreover, "base compensation is the same as other large firms in the area," associates say, "and the bonus system is especially generous." The "firm's bonus plan rewards associates not only for their intangible contributions to the firm, but also for hours worked beyond the minimum billables." What attorneys appreciate most is the autonomy: "The work is available if you want extra hours and a higher bonus; if you want more leisure time, you are free to make that decision." At Pennie & Edmonds, exclaims one lawyer, "you can get paid as if it's still the heyday of the Gunderson era!"

Most partners are "very good people with real lives, and they treat you like equals and give you a lot of responsibility." But some lawyers would like better communication with management. "The rumor mill tends to be the way that associates learn information about the firm," complains one source. He adds, however, "Communication between the partners and associates has vastly improved since Pennie appointed two co-managing partners." The firm would also benefit from more formal training, say several associates. Pennie & Edmonds is "a very hands-off place." This "works well for self-starters, as you get a lot of responsibility, provided you can handle it; however, if you need any handholding or a lot of guidance, this is not the place for you."

Shaw Pittman LLP

2300 N Street, NW
Washington, DC 20037
Phone: (202) 663-8000
www.shawpittman.com

LOCATIONS

Washington, DC (HQ)
Los Angeles, CA
McLean, VA
New York, NY
London

MAJOR DEPARTMENTS/PRACTICES

Corporate, Securities & Tax
Employee Benefits & Health
Energy & Environment
Financial Institutions
Government Contracts
Government Relations & Transportation
Litigation
Real Estate & Bankruptcy
Technology

THE STATS

No. of attorneys: 440
No. of offices: 5
Managing Partner: Paul Mickey
Hiring Partner: D. Craig Wolff, Esq.

NOTABLE PERKS

• Gym on premises
• Subaru VIP program
• In-office massage once a week
• Firm-sponsored monthly happy hours

EMPLOYMENT CONTACT

Ms. Kathleen A. Kelly
Chief Recruiting Officer and Director of Professional
Programs
Phone: (202) 663-8394
kathy.kelly@shawpittman.com

BASE SALARY

Washington, DC, 2002
1st year: $125,000
2nd year: $135,000
3rd year: $145,000
4th year: $155,000
5th year: $175,000
6th year: $185,000
7th year: $195,000
8th year: $200,000
Summer associate: $2,400/week

THE BUZZ
WHAT ATTORNEYS AT OTHER FIRMS ARE SAYING ABOUT THIS FIRM

• "Great IP and corporate in DC"
• "Definitely slipping"
• "Bad work environment"
• "Family friendly"

THE SCOOP

One of D.C.'s largest law firms, Shaw Pittman attracts considerable business in the tech market and the lobbying arena. As things in the technology sector have cooled off since the heady hey-day of years past, so has Shaw's run in that area. In 2001, 19 associates and several staff members were laid off, and the firm promoted fewer associates to the partner level than in years past. Though the economy continues to stagger along, the firm is thinking fast. It hired former Florida Senator Connie Mack as senior political advisor and merged with D.C.'s Fisher Wayland Cooper Leader & Zaragosa. In March it opened shop in Los Angeles, and four months later, it merged with 15-attorney Los Angeles-based Klein & Martin LLP.

GETTING HIRED

Shaw Pittman attorneys are looking for co-workers with "outstanding academic credentials." "Brand name schools" help, but the firm hires from local law schools as well. Summer associates are in for a "great summer experience." One insider remarks that "there is a huge diversity of projects to choose from. And there are many social events and opportunities to get to know the firm. One of the best summers I've had!" Associates caution that the firm isn't hiring many lateral hires these days. But those lawyers lucky enough to snag an interview can expect an initial hour-long interview with a partner, followed by approximately four callback interviews and lunch with two associates.

OUR SURVEY SAYS

According to Shaw Pittman associates, their firm is in the midst of an identity crisis. One insider notes, "This firm has no idea what its culture is. It is stuck between a desire to grow and build a brand name and having been burned for being too aggressive with the acquisition of new groups." Is Shaw Pittman a lifestyle firm? Associates just don't know anymore. One conflicted insider points out that "pressure to bill more hours has been increasing over the last four to five years, often at the expense of lawyer training and business development efforts," but that generally, partners and associates are "friendly and approachable." Others appreciate that "every employee treats every other employee, whether partner, associate or staff, with a great deal of respect."

Most everyone seems to agree that the firm excels in its pro bono commitment. Associates are impressed that the firm counts 100 percent of associate pro bono work as billable hours. When it comes to training, sources acknowledge the plentiful CLE seminars offered, though most say that the bulk of the training is the ever-popular "trial by fire" method. Insiders express frustration with the state of diversity at their firm. "This firm does not have a commitment to diversity," laments a black attorney. Another insider notes, "This firm says it treats women fairly, but women who take time off to have children are put at a disadvantage."

Dorsey & Whitney LLP

50 South Sixth Street, Suite 1500
Minneapolis, MN 55402
Phone: (612) 340-2600
www.dorseylaw.com

LOCATIONS

Anchorage, AK • Denver, CO • Des Moines, IA • Fargo,
ND • Great Falls, MT • Minneapolis, MN • Missoula, MT •
New York, NY • Orange County, CA • Palo Alto, CA •
Rochester, MN • Salt Lake City, UT • San Francisco,
CA • Seattle, WA • Reston, VA • Washington, DC •
Brussels • Hong Kong • London • Shanghai • Tokyo •
Toronto • Vancouver

MAJOR DEPARTMENTS/PRACTICES

Trial/Litigation Groups: Antitrust • Commercial/Contract •
E-Commerce • Environmental, Natural Resources &
Energy • ERISA • Estate & Trust • Franchise • Indian &
Gaming • Intellectual Property • International • Labor &
Employment • Legislative • Patents • Securities •
Technology • Telecommunications • Trademark • White
Collar Crime

Business Groups: • Bankruptcy • Broker-Dealer •
Capital Markets • Commercial & Banking • Emerging
Companies • Employee Benefits • Funds • Health •
Individual Estate & Trust • Institutional & Corporate
Trust • International • M&A • Private Companies •
Project Finance • Public Companies • Public Finance •
Real Estate • Securitizations • Tax

THE STATS

No. of attorneys: 700+
No. of offices: 23
Summer associate offers: 72 out of 85 (2001)
Chairman: Peter S. Hendrixson
Hiring Partner: David R. Melloh

THE BUZZ
WHAT ATTORNEYS AT OTHER FIRMS ARE SAYING ABOUT THIS FIRM

- "M&A power in MN? — You bet!"
- "Expanded too fast"
- "Good professional development of associates"
- "Unknown outside Midwest"

NOTABLE PERKS

- In-house gyms (Denver and Minneapolis)
- Six weeks paid parental leave
- Emergency childcare
- Nap room (Minneapolis)

EMPLOYMENT CONTACT

Ms. Nancy J. Gendler
Director of Lawyer Recruiting
Fax: (612) 340-2868
gendler.nancy@dorseylaw.com

BASE SALARY

Minneapolis, 2002
1st year: $90,000
2nd year: $95,000
3rd year: $100,000
4th year: $105,000
Summer associate: $1,750/week

New York, 2002
1st year: $125,000
2nd year: $130,000
3rd year: $140,000
4th year: $150,000
Summer associate: $2,400/week

Seattle, 2002
1st year: $95,000
2nd year: $110,000
3rd year: $115,000
4th year: $125,000
Summer associate: $1,750/week

Washington, DC, 2002
1st year: $105,000
2nd year: $110,000
3rd year: $120,000
4th year: $130,000
Summer associate: $1,750/week

THE SCOOP

Founded in Minneapolis in 1912, Dorsey & Whitney has 23 worldwide offices. In 2001 the firm added a Toronto office and expanded its Japanese office by merging with Tokyo-based Kyo Sogo Law Offices. (Walter Mondale serves as chair of the Asian practice group.) In May 2002, the firm augmented its intellectual property practice by joining forces with IP boutique Flehr Hohbach Test Albritton & Herbert LLP. Despite this expansion, the firm fell victim to the chilly economic climate, freezing associate pay in December 2001 and announcing that associates will not receive the usual raises on promotion to the next associate class. In June 2002, the salary freeze was lifted.

GETTING HIRED

Insiders say Dorsey & Whitney is the "most competitive firm in [the] Twin Cities market. Most associates are from top 20 schools or were in the top 5 percent of other local schools." Associates believe the firm seeks "well-rounded people" as well as "top-notch academic performers." Suggests one associate, "Good communication skills and a good fit with respect to personality are very important."

OUR SURVEY SAYS

"Dorsey's culture bears a Midwestern stamp," say insiders. The "atmosphere is friendly and people have lives outside the firm." The firm offers "great work and experience," yet manages to remain "quality-of-life-oriented," with "very humane hours" and "no cutthroat competition." One eager associate raves, "I've never met a group of more relaxed, friendly lawyers who truly look out for each other." Associates also appreciate the "tremendous amount of responsibility" they receive in their first years of practice. "I've been given opportunities here I know I would not have been afforded at most large firms," asserts an insider.

Attorneys are less than ecstatic about the "terrible" salary freeze. "No other firm in town" froze salaries, sighs a Minnesotan. But even many of these complaints are tempered by the acknowledgement that the "hours are humane" — a fact that "balances out the pay issue."

Most Dorsey associates find the billable requirement of 1,850 hours "comparatively reasonable." (The firm notes that 1,850 is the requirement for most offices outside D.C., New York and Orange County.) Lawyers say the firm is "very flexible" about "setting people up to work from home" and making part-time arrangements. Some attorneys express concern that there is "not enough work to go around," which causes "more stress over billable hours." Though the firm has recently reduced the number of pro bono hours that count toward billables, insiders still rave about Dorsey's commitment to pro bono work. Lawyers who take on "big cases" can get a waiver to credit more hours.

Vinson & Elkins L.L.P.

2300 First City Tower
1001 Fannin Street
Houston, TX 77002-6760
Phone: (713) 758-2222
www.velaw.com

LOCATIONS

Houston, TX (HQ)
Austin, TX
Dallas, TX
New York, NY
Washington, DC
Beijing
London
Moscow
Singapore

MAJOR DEPARTMENTS/PRACTICES

Business & International
Corporate & Securities & Tax
Energy
Litigation
Public Finance

THE STATS

No. of attorneys: 844 (as of May 1, 2002)
No. of offices: 9
Summer associate offers: 128 out of 164 (2001)
Managing Partner: Joseph C. Dilg
Hiring Partner: Thomas S. Leathurbury

NOTABLE PERKS

- Subsidized gym membership
- Lavish annual "prom" for lawyers and significant others
- Women's initiative program
- Blackberry wireless pagers

EMPLOYMENT CONTACT

Ms. Patty Harris Calabrese
Director of Attorney Employment
Phone: (713) 758-4544
Fax: (713) 758-2346
pcalabrese@velaw.com

BASE SALARY

Houston, 2002
1st year: $110,000
2nd year: $114,000
3rd year: $121,000
4th year: $130,000
5th year: $140,000
6th year: $145,000
7th year: $155,000
8th year: $160,000
Summer associate: $2,100/week

THE BUZZ
WHAT ATTORNEYS AT OTHER FIRMS ARE SAYING ABOUT THIS FIRM

- "Enronitis"
- "Good ol' boy"
- "Cream of the crop"
- "Good Texas firm"

THE SCOOP

Vinson & Elkins, one of the world's leading energy law firms, is the largest firm in Houston. Another 400 attorneys work in eight offices around the globe. The Texas firm that basked in the oil and energy boom now finds itself embroiled in the collapse of long-time client Enron. V&E's ties to the energy giant include former partner James V. Derrick Jr., the company's general counsel. Enron's bankruptcy would have been bad enough had it just meant the loss of V&E's largest revenue stream, but the firm also faces accusations by Enron officials that it drafted disclosure documents contributing to the company's collapse. V&E attorneys deny any wrongdoing.

GETTING HIRED

"Basically," says one associate, "the lower-tiered your law school is, the higher grades you need to have" to be hired by Vinson & Elkins. Some see "a preference for Texas law graduates" and one lawyer suggests that "good political connections" help. According to an associate, the firm seeks "smart, motivated but pleasant and cheerful people who are assertive without being aggressive." The good news, according to a first-year: "If you clerk here in the summer, you have an 85 percent chance of being hired and a 100 percent chance if you're not an idiot."

OUR SURVEY SAYS

"If you have to work for a living," declares a V&E associate, "this is the place to do it!" Many of her colleagues seem to agree. V&E offers "good work, smart lawyers and a friendly atmosphere." Most insiders describe a "sense of collegiality among Vinson & Elkins lawyers." The firm encourages mingling through many social events — including the annual "prom," for which all attorneys and their significant others are flown to Houston and put up at the Four Seasons for a weekend whose highlight is "a swanky black-tie party at the art museum."

Partners earn praise for being "respectful, helpful and encouraging." Although associates mention "a few very bad apples," the majority "are nice, hardworking people." Associates are also happy with their salaries. V&E's "pay scale is among the highest in Houston," boasts one lawyer. "Are you kidding?" asks another. "I'm 28 and making over $100,000 a year!" Several sources gripe that "bonuses are low," but at least "we aren't tied to billing a certain number of hours."

Speaking of hours…. "They aren't so bad here," says a third-year associate. Many say they work "very few weekends," and although one lawyer would "rather be on a beach," he acknowledges that he's not necessarily "working much harder than any of [his] friends who work in the legal, financial or business worlds." V&E also wins kudos for its "unparalleled" commitment to pro bono work, for its women's initiative program and for being "the first big firm in Houston to provide same-sex benefits."

Choate, Hall & Stewart

Exchange Place
53 State Street
Boston, MA 02109
Phone: (617) 248-5000
www.choate.com

LOCATIONS

Boston, MA (HQ)

MAJOR DEPARTMENTS/PRACTICES

Bankruptcy
Corporate
Environmental & Land Use
Health
Labor
Litigation
Patent
Real Estate
Tax
Trusts & Estate

THE STATS

No. of attorneys: 190
No. of offices: 1
Summer associate offers: 18 out of 20 (2001)
Managing Partners: William P. Gelnaw Jr.
and John A. Nadas
Hiring Partner: Mark O. Cahill

NOTABLE PERKS

• The "Firm Bite" (in-house cafeteria)
• Free tickets to Fleet Center corporate box
• TGIF parties quarterly

EMPLOYMENT CONTACT

Ms. Robin Carbone
Director of Recruiting
Phone: (617) 248-5000
rcarbone@choate.com

BASE SALARY

Boston, 2002
1st year: $125,000
Summer associate: $2,400/week

THE BUZZ
WHAT ATTORNEYS AT OTHER FIRMS ARE SAYING ABOUT THIS FIRM

• "Everybody's heard of them"
• "Bluest of the blue bloods"
• "Declining client base"
• "If you want to be in Boston, the place to be"

THE SCOOP

Founded in the late 19th century, Choate, Hall & Stewart has battled to stay small and local, to the disappointment of some partners. In 1999 and 2000, a number of partners defected despite the firm's impressive revenue and profit growth. Consistently eyed by larger firms for possible mergers, Choate is a litigation leader. And lately the firm's health care, real estate and labor and employment practices have taken flight. The firm is no stranger to big deals, either. In October 2001, the firm represented NMS Communications, a call processing systems developer, in its $60 million acquisition of telecommunications manufacturer Lucent Technologies' voice-enhancement business. Over the years, Choate has demonstrated a commitment to pro bono work. In July 2001, associate Thomas M. Griffin was named Pro Bono Attorney of the Year by the Political Asylum/Immigration Representation Project.

GETTING HIRED

"Only extremely well-qualified candidates need apply" to Choate, Hall & Stewart, asserts one insider, adding, "It helps if you went to a top 20 law school or a school in Boston." Another lawyer describes the "ideal candidate" as "someone who demonstrates a high level of intelligence, has strong communication skills and an interesting personality." Interviewers try to evaluate whether the applicant is someone they "would want to work with" and "someone who can deal directly with clients." For lateral hires, experience and expertise are more important than transcripts.

OUR SURVEY SAYS

Choate Hall offers a "collegial work environment" in which the "open-door policy is not just a gimmick, it's reality." Insiders describe the firm culture as "somewhat laid back" and "friendly" and insist that associates "certainly do socialize together." However, a number of respondents report increased tension since the firm, like several other Boston firms, slashed salaries in 2001 and implemented more severe cost-cutting measures. One insider insists that "the work is piling up and there are less people to do it."

Insiders' views on training run the gamut: from the attorney who considers the firm "weak when it comes to training" to the lawyer who enjoys "lots of feedback and training 'on the job' between partners and associates." One litigator complains that there is "very little ongoing help from partners and senior associates after" the first year. By contrast, a colleague praises partners who "really seem to care that [associates are] getting the kinds of opportunities" that will make them better lawyers. Opinions on compensation vary as well. "Choate is on the low side of average among the big firms in Boston," according to one lawyer. One Choatian believes "the big paycheck is nice but ultimately wacky!"

Arent Fox Kintner Plotkin & Kahn, PLLC

1050 Connecticut Avenue, NW
Washington, DC 20036-5339
Phone: (202) 857-6000
www.arentfox.com

LOCATIONS

Washington, DC (HQ)
New York, NY

MAJOR DEPARTMENTS/PRACTICES

General Business
International
Litigation & Dispute Resolution
Regulatory & Public Policy
Technology

THE STATS

No. of attorneys: 286
No. of offices: 2
Summer associate offers: 17 out of 20 (2001)
Managing Partner: Marc L. Fleischaker
Hiring Attorney: Quana Jew

NOTABLE PERKS

- Seats at Yankee Stadium (NY) and MCI
  Skybox (DC)
- Annual retreat for all attorneys
- Domestic partner benefits
- Emergency childcare
- Free gym in building

EMPLOYMENT CONTACT

Washington, DC
Ms. Amber Handman
Attorney Recruitment & Development Manager
Phone: (202) 857-6146
Fax: (202) 857-6395
DCAttorneyRecruit@arentfox.com

New York
Ms. Kay Carson
Director of Administration
Phone: (212) 484-3900
Fax: (212) 484-3990
NYAttorneyRecruit@arentfox.com

BASE SALARY

Washington, DC, 2002
1st year: $125,000
Summer associate: $2,300/week

THE BUZZ
WHAT ATTORNEYS AT OTHER FIRMS ARE SAYING ABOUT THIS FIRM

- "Better than most realize"
- "A firm in turmoil"
- "Nice second-tier firm"
- "Great place to work, but star may be fading"

THE SCOOP

With headquarters in the nation's capital and an outpost in New York, Arent Fox Kintner Plotkin & Kahn is well known for its government relations and regulatory practices as well as its work in the areas of health care, intellectual property and real estate. Many attorneys have backgrounds in federal, state and municipal government. The firm also has a practice group devoted solely to advertising law issues. The 300-attorney firm just missed a chance to become the nation's 29th-largest law firm, with 725 lawyers in 10 offices, when merger talks fell apart — for the second time — with Philadelphia's Pepper Hamilton. The on-again, off-again love affair between the Philly firm and the Washington, D.C.-based Arent Fox had dragged on for nearly a year before breaking off for good in March 2002.

GETTING HIRED

Arent Fox "prides itself on its unique culture and works at preserving that culture." That means the "firm is just as interested in a person's background, if not more so, than whether that person was on law review." We hear "the firm appreciates candidates who bear some unique characteristic and add something to the firm culturally." In determining "great lawyering potential" the firm looks beyond "the most impressive resumes." The firm certainly wants "academically credentialed and accomplished associates," but the candidates must also be "personable and outgoing."

OUR SURVEY SAYS

Arent Fox associates may not be making the biggest bucks in town, but many are happy to give up that little bit extra in order to enjoy a "better-than-usual quality of life." "Arent Fox provides the best of both worlds," declares one lawyer, "interesting and challenging work for significant clients with a collegial environment." Attorneys work hard but the atmosphere is "definitely not a pressure cooker."

Sources acknowledge that "most lawyers here, including partners, make somewhat less than lawyers make at some of the other big law firms." However, "for most of us, this was and is a deliberate lifestyle choice — we are willing to trade money for a great place to work and more time off." A few associates complain about the firm's new policy of deferring payment of a portion of salaries until billable hours are met. "I think it should be called what it is — a bonus if you meet your hours."

Arent Fox partners get high marks from associates. Excepting the obligatory "few bad apples," the "majority of partners treat associates with respect and encouragement." They "take an active role in mentoring and training associates." Moreover, there is a sense that "associates have a real chance to become partner here."

Greenberg Traurig, LLP

1221 Brickell Avenue
Miami, FL 33131
Phone: (305) 579-0500
www.gtlaw.com

LOCATIONS

Atlanta, GA • Boca Raton, FL • Boston, MA • Chicago,
IL • Denver, CO • Ft. Lauderdale, FL • Los Angeles, CA •
Miami, FL • New York, NY • Orlando, FL • Philadelphia,
PA • Phoenix, AZ • Tallahassee, FL • Tysons Corner,
VA • Washington, DC • West Palm Beach, FL •
Wilmington, DE

MAJOR DEPARTMENTS/PRACTICES

Americans with Disabilities Act • Antitrust • Appellate •
Corporate & Securities • Employment Law •
Entertainment • Environmental • Executive
Compensation & Employee Benefits • Financial
Institutions • Government Affairs • Health Business
Group • Immigration • Information Technology & E-
Commerce • Intellectual Property • International • Land
Use • Litigation • Public Finance • Real Estate •
Reorganization, Bankruptcy & Restructuring • Tax •
Trusts & Estates

THE STATS

No. of attorneys: 830
No. of offices: 17
Summer associate offers: 29 out of 32 (2001)
President and CEO: Cesar L. Alvarez
Chairman: Larry J. Hoffman
Hiring Attorneys: Richard J. Giusto and
Stephen L. Rabinowitz

THE BUZZ
WHAT ATTORNEYS AT OTHER FIRMS ARE SAYING ABOUT THIS FIRM

- "Miami up-and-comer"
- "Ruthless second-tier firm"
- "They do great work"
- "Sweatshop in paradise"

NOTABLE PERKS*

- Gym membership discount
- In-house CLE programs
- Free lunches and social events
- Firm-subsidized laptop

*Perks vary by office.

EMPLOYMENT CONTACT

Ms. Janet McKeegan
Director of Recruitment
Phone: (305) 579-0855
mckeeganj@gtlaw.com

BASE SALARY

All offices, 2002
1st year: $85,000-$125,000

THE SCOOP

Be aggressive! That seems to be Greenberg Traurig's motto these days. In the past five years, this firm from the Sunshine State has come on the scene like a tiger, merging and expanding its practice at every turn. The firm's reputation for voracity came in handy during the 2000 presidential election; litigation partner Barry Richard was chosen as one of President George W. Bush's chief lawyers in the infamous voting controversy. But Greenberg Traurig has faced criticism, too. In a July 2001 *American Lawyer* article, an ex-partner took a stab at the firm, saying Greenberg isn't vigilant enough in its hiring practices. Apparently, this setback hasn't discouraged the mighty warrior, as the firm opened an office in Albany in January 2002. Former New York City Deputy Mayor Robert M. Harding heads the new office.

GETTING HIRED

"Strong academics" should be a top concern for candidates who want to work at Greenberg Traurig. "Personality and fit are equally important," adds an associate. As for hiring, "there is an initial interview (either on campus or at a job fair), then a callback at the firm where you interview with at least two partners and two associates," explains an associate. A long resume is a plus. "The firm would be more likely to hire someone who worked before law school than someone who went straight from undergrad into law school," notes an associate.

OUR SURVEY SAYS

If the early bird catches the worm, Greenberg associates have more worms than they can handle. Greenberg associates are a bunch of "early-risers" and tend to arrive at work between 7:30 and 8:00 a.m. Partying late into the night isn't practical when you're up so early. "Because most associates are in the same age group and many have young families, there is very little in the way of Friday happy hour socials or similar socializing outside of the office," explains one associate. At Greenberg Traurig, associates are given lots of responsibility from the get-go. "The level of responsibility given to me from day one is extraordinary," a second-year associate remarks. "I manage many of the cases I work on and attend or take depositions and go to court frequently."

Many Greenberg Traurig associates express disappointment with their compensation. "Our bonus and salary structure are hinged on our billable hours," explains one New Yorker. "They are currently changing this and allowing for more discretion. But we don't know if this will work for us or against us yet. [The year] 2001 was just a bad year, and our salaries this year reflect that." However, as one associate notes, "ours may not be the highest [salaries], but we have never been denied our bonuses or had a freeze on salaries or raises." Miamians seem to be the most content of all the Greenberg associates, saying, "This is one of the higher paying firms in the area."

90

Gunderson Dettmer Stough Villeneuve Franklin & Hachigian, LLP

155 Constitution Drive
Menlo Park, CA 94025
Phone: (650) 321-2400
www.gunder.com

LOCATIONS

Menlo Park, CA (HQ)
Austin, TX
Boston, MA
New York, NY

MAJOR DEPARTMENTS/PRACTICES

Corporate & Securities
Executive Compensation
Labor
Mergers & Acquisitions
Tax
Technology, Intellectual Property & Corporate Partnering

THE STATS

No. of attorneys: 95
No. of offices: 4
Summer associate offers: 26 out of 31 (2001)
Managing Partner: Steve Franklin
Hiring Attorneys: Daniel E. O'Connor, Gregory Lemmer and Anthony McCusker

NOTABLE PERKS

- Relocation expenses
- Investment profit sharing plan

EMPLOYMENT CONTACT

Ms. Corinne Dritsas
Director of Legal Recruiting
Phone: (650) 463-5248
Fax: (650) 321-2800
cdritsas@gunder.com

BASE SALARY

Menlo Park, 2002
1st year: $125,000
2nd year: $135,000
3rd year: $145,000
4th year: $160,000
5th year: $175,000
6th year: $190,000
7th year: $195,000
Summer associate: $2,400/week

THE BUZZ
WHAT ATTORNEYS AT OTHER FIRMS ARE SAYING ABOUT THIS FIRM

- "Very good in venture capital"
- "Classic story of hubris"
- "Innovative and fun"
- "Hit hard by tech recession"

THE SCOOP

In less than a decade, the California firm of Gunderson Dettmer Stough Villeneuve Franklin & Hachigian, LLP has put its long name on the map as an ambitious corporate boutique in the heart of Silicon Valley. With its practice closely tied to the region's fortunes (and misfortunes), however, the popular employer and one-time salary leader has, like its competitors, felt the impact of the dipping economy. Gunderson has established an impressive practice focusing on the growing technology industry.

A Bay Area boutique

Along with new companies in the computer and medical technology fields, the firm has worked with such financial giants as CS First Boston; Goldman Sachs & Co.; Bear Stearns; Lehman Brothers and Morgan Stanley.

In the late 1990s, Gunderson experienced the heady flush of IPO fever. In 1999 the firm worked on 24 initial public offerings, revenues estimated at $70 million and profits-per-partner reached $900,000. In 2000 IPO work thinned to a trickle, and Gunderson only completed two IPOs. But deal-making continues to keep Gunderson busy. The firm's M&A activity was livelier in 2001 than it had been in 1999, even if it did not reach the dizzying heights of 2000 when the firm's aggregate deals were valued at some $20 billion.

Layoffs for laid-back lawyers

The combination of a relaxed working atmosphere (including a year-round casual dress policy and a fashionable Menlo Park office housed in a converted warehouse) and a league of high-tech clients have made the young firm a box office draw for many lawyers. Little more than a year ago, Gunderson flaunted its success and caused a rippling wave of salary hikes when it raised associate base salaries from the area's standard of $96,000 to an unprecedented $125,000 and guaranteed its most junior associates a $20,000 bonus. But by the middle of 2001, the wave had crested and Silicon Valley firms, including Gunderson, began tightening their belts.

As the region's economic climate became bleaker, the firm introduced more drastic measures. First Gunderson failed to match rival Brobeck Phleger's $10,000 across-the-board salary hike (from which Brobeck recently retreated). In June 2001, the firm cancelled its program of guaranteed bonuses and offered a $10,000 incentive to incoming associates who postponed their start dates from September to January. Then, last October, Gunderson let go 16 of its 138 associates and 28 members of its staff. (The firm provided associates with three months severance and outplacement assistance.)

The layoffs, which Gunderson attributed to a shortage of work rather than to a loss in profits, targeted the Menlo Park and Austin offices and represented almost 12 percent of the firm's associates.

Finnegan, Henderson, Farabow, Garrett & Dunner, L.L.P.

1300 I Street, NW
Suite 700
Washington, DC 20005-3315
Phone: (202) 408-4000
www.finnegan.com

LOCATIONS

Washington, DC (HQ)
Atlanta, GA
Cambridge, MA
Palo Alto, CA
Reston, VA
Brussels
Tokyo

MAJOR DEPARTMENTS/PRACTICES

Biotech/Pharmaceutical
Chemical/Metallurgical
Electrical & Computer Technology
IP Specialties
Mechanical
Trademark & Copyright

THE STATS

No. of attorneys: 302
No. of offices: 7
Summer associate offers: 36 out of 41 (2001)
Managing Partner: Christopher Foley
Hiring Partner: James Monroe

NOTABLE PERKS

• Free cell phone plan
• Health club on premises
• Stipend for dinner and cab rides for late nights
• Summer outing

EMPLOYMENT CONTACT

Mr. Paul Sevanich
Attorney Recruitment Manager
Phone: (202) 408-4000
Fax: (202) 408-4400
attyrecruit@finnegan.com
(See firm web site for employment contacts in other cities)

BASE SALARY

Washington, DC, 2002
1st year: $125,000
Summer associate: $2,400/week

THE BUZZ
WHAT ATTORNEYS AT OTHER FIRMS ARE SAYING ABOUT THIS FIRM

• "IP geeks"
• "Premiere patent shop"
• "Family atmosphere"
• "Spread too thin"

THE SCOOP

"Boutique" hardly captures the scope of IP powerhouse Finnegan, Henderson, Farabow, Garrett & Dunner. With seven offices housing more than 300 attorneys and a full complement of technical specialists and legal assistants, Finnegan is the largest intellectual property firm in the country and one of the most widely respected. Finnegan lawyers have appeared before the U.S. Court of Appeals for the Federal Circuit more than any other law firm in the country. November 2001 brought a surprising defeat when the Supreme Court refused to review a damage award against Finnegan client Biomet, a maker of orthopedic devices — even though the $20 million in punitive damages exceeded the $520 compensatory award by a ratio of 38,000-to-1. Despite this setback, 2001 was a successful year for the young firm; revenue climbed by 20 percent and Finnegan celebrated the opening of two new offices in Cambridge, Mass., and Reston, Va.

GETTING HIRED

At Finnegan, one must have "exceptional academic and/or technical credentials to get in the door." An associate there notes, "Finnegan looks for the very best minds who want to practice intellectual property." Most attorneys at the firm have had prior experience in a technical field or at the U.S. Patent and Trademark Office. The interview process is standard — a screening interview followed by a callback round where the candidate meets with six partners and four associates. "The [10] people then provide their comments to the hiring committee," says an associate.

OUR SURVEY SAYS

Associates dig the laid-back Finnegan vibe, which they call "collegial," "friendly," "balanced," and filled with "lots of socializing." An associate explains that "everyone — partners, associates and staff — works as a team for each client." Says one associate, "Management goes out of its way to match associates to the type of work they prefer and to help them in building whatever practice and skill base they desire."

Associates at Finnegan are expected to hit a billable hours target of 2,000 hours, a number most associates find "reasonable." Many sources report billing considerably more than the minimum, but most are quick to point out the hard work is "self-inflicted." Those who do put in the extra hours are rewarded with a 20 percent bonus if they reach 2,400 hours. Says one hardworking insider, "I work a lot of hours — over 2,400 per year — but the firm's new bonus schedule provides compensation for these increased hours."

Finnegan associates are thrilled with the training they receive. Reports one Finnegan-er, "This firm provides outstanding in-house legal and technical training and fully supports any desired outside training."

Fish & Richardson P.C.

225 Franklin Street
Boston, MA 02110-2804
Phone: (617) 542-5070
www.fr.com

LOCATIONS

Boston, MA
Dallas, TX
Minneapolis, MN
New York, NY
Redwood City, CA
San Diego, CA
Washington, DC
Wilmington, DE

MAJOR DEPARTMENTS/PRACTICES

Appellate
Complex Litigation
Corporate & Securities
International Regulatory Group
Patents
Trademarks & Copyrights
U.S. International Trade Commission Proceedings

THE STATS

No. of attorneys: 250 +
No. of offices: 8
Summer associate offers: 30 out of 38 (2001)
President: Peter J. Devlin

NOTABLE PERKS

• $500 annually for attorney development
• Free sodas, juice and beer in some offices
• Huge discounts on client products
• Gourmet coffee machines on every floor

EMPLOYMENT CONTACT

Ms. Jill McDonald
Director of Attorney Hiring
Phone: (858) 678-5070
Fax: (858) 678-5099
work@fr.com

BASE SALARY

All offices, 2002
1st year: $135,000
2nd year: $145,000
3rd year: $150,000
4th year: $160,000
5th year: $175,000
6th year: $180,000
7th year: $190,000
8th year: $195,000
Summer associate: $2,400/week (2L);
$2,200/week (1L)

THE BUZZ
WHAT ATTORNEYS AT OTHER FIRMS ARE SAYING ABOUT THIS FIRM

• "Great patent litigation work"
• "Losing its spark"
• "Brainy"
• "Struggling to find their market niche"

THE SCOOP

Originally founded in 1878 as Wadleigh & Fish, Fish & Richardson is one of the country's oldest and largest firms specializing in patent and technology law. Early in its history, the firm represented technological luminaries such as Thomas Edison, Alexander Graham Bell and the Wright brothers. Today, its roster of clients includes Microsoft, audio equipment maker Bose Corporation, Marconi Communications, Intel, 3M, Millennium Pharmaceuticals, Nokia, Alcatel and Clariant LSM. The firm counts 54 PhD's among its attorneys and technology specialists and obtains over 1,400 patents each year for its clients, ranking F&R among the top 15 patent firms in the country. The firm is also among the top firms obtaining trademarks. According to a survey published by *IP Worldwide* in May 2002, Fish & Richardson is the leading patent litigation firm in the United States.

GETTING HIRED

"Only the top-notch need apply," say Fish & Richardson associates. One attorney offers the following capsule summary for would-be candidates: "Top science background: you're hired. No science background: don't get your hopes up." "The firm will look at any qualified candidate," reveals an intellectual property attorney, "but a technical or scientific background is preferred — more so in certain offices and practice groups than in others." An insider at the Boston office says the summer program was fun but warns that its calm vibe is "unrepresentative of life at the firm."

OUR SURVEY SAYS

Fish & Richardson is a "collaborative, informal, hardworking, intellectually challenging" firm filled with "friendly, cooperative, casual" attorneys in an environment where "competitiveness is not a virtue." While most wouldn't mind working fewer hours, the majority of Fish & Richardson associates say their hours are reasonable and they don't feel any pressure to spend extra time in the office just to impress the firm's principle attorneys. "Pay is at the forefront of the market," say associates. They love the hours-based bonus system, which rewards attorneys for every 100 hours they bill above the target. Surprisingly, the base salary, which is "slightly lower than at other firms," is considered "one of the best aspects of Fish & Richardson." Sources explain that the billable goal is lower as well, and that "those who work killer hours receive bonuses. Those who want to work less can meet their billable goal and enjoy more free time."

F&R isn't big on pro bono, Vault hears. "Some associates have organized an informal pro bono program, but they did this with little or no assistance from the firm," explains a Bostonian. Under the firm's new policy, announced after associates took our survey, associates who reach their minimum billable hour requirement will receive billable credit of 50 percent of the time that they spend in pro bono matters, up to 50 hours credit.

Hughes Hubbard & Reed LLP

One Battery Park Plaza
New York, NY 10004-1482
Phone: (212) 837-6000
www.hugheshubbard.com

LOCATIONS

New York, NY (HQ)
Los Angeles, CA
Miami, FL
Washington, DC
Paris

MAJOR DEPARTMENTS/PRACTICES

Banking
Corporate
Corporate Reorganization
Employee Benefits
Environmental
Financial Services
Intellectual Property & Technology
Labor and Employment
Litigation
Pacific Basin
Personal Affairs
Real Estate
Tax

THE STATS

No. of attorneys: 300
No. of offices: 5
Summer associate offers: 28 out of 28 (2001)
Chairman: Candace K. Beinecke
Hiring Partners: George A. Tsougarakis and
Carolyn B. Levine

THE BUZZ
WHAT ATTORNEYS AT OTHER FIRMS ARE SAYING ABOUT THIS FIRM

- "It's an all-around amazing place"
- "Used to be better"
- "Great litigators"
- "Burnt-out associates"

NOTABLE PERKS

- Free yoga sessions
- Subsidized health club
- Pizza on Thursday and breakfast on Tuesday

EMPLOYMENT CONTACT

Mr. Adrian Cockerill
Director of Legal Employment
Phone: (212) 837-6131
Fax: (212): 422-4726
cockeril@hugheshubbard.com

BASE SALARY

New York, 2002
1st year: $125,000
2nd year: $135,000
3rd year: $150,000
4th year: $165,000
5th year: $175,000
6th year: $180,000-$185,000
7th year: $170,000-$200,000
8th year: $190,000-$200,000
Summer associate: $2,403/week

THE SCOOP

Did somebody say there's a recession? Attorneys at Hughes Hubbard & Reed wouldn't know. In 2001 they made it to the "600 Club," meaning partners there had billing rates reaching $600 per hour. The firm owes much of its success to its high-profile and diverse client base, including PricewaterhouseCoopers, the Los Angeles Dodgers, and MTV and its parent company, Viacom. The firm defended the Boy Scouts of America in a prominent discrimination case stemming from the Scouts' quest to exclude gay scoutmasters. The firm is also committed to international work, as demonstrated by its successful office in Paris and a robust presence throughout Europe, the Pacific Basin and Latin America. The firm also has demonstrated a commitment to diversity. It offers domestic partnership benefits, was the first major New York firm to name a woman as managing partner and boasts that women comprise 21 percent of the firm's partnership.

GETTING HIRED

Hughes Hubbard seeks attorneys who are "smart," "sociable" and "hardworking." The firm goes weak in the knees for candidates from top-tier law schools or top students from second-tier schools. "The emphasis is on grades," says an associate, "although personality is a key factor." When you do get through the door, you'll get a good idea of what associate life looks like through the firm's summer associate program. "You can get any kind of work that you are interested in trying, the events are varied and fun, and just about everyone — including the partners — makes an effort to make you comfortable."

OUR SURVEY SAYS

While attorneys at Hughes Hubbard find their co-workers "friendly" and "amicable," we heard conflicting reviews of the firm itself. "Hughes Hubbard is not a lifestyle firm, as it has been touted to be," says one associate. Another agrees, "They seem to be moving away from the lifestyle image that was one of the main reasons I came here." Still, some sources insist that "the firm's culture is extremely friendly." The topic of hours elicits the typical groans, though some associates insist that the hours "aren't too bad."

Associates articulate gripe after gripe regarding compensation. Junior associates complain that first-year associates were left out of the bonus party entirely. And more seasoned insiders grumble that "senior associates make a lot less [at Hughes Hubbard] than their counterparts at other firms." Associates are pleased, however, with the level of training they receive, including the "really helpful" training seminars for first-years. In addition, junior associates often get the opportunity to take depositions and have client contact very early. Says one Hughesian, "We are very fortunate that most of the partners take pride in teaching, and virtually none of them believe in yelling or unfairly criticizing associates."

Wiley Rein & Fielding LLP

1776 K Street, NW
Washington, DC 20006
Phone: (202) 719-7000
www.wrf.com

LOCATIONS

Washington, DC (HQ)
McLean, VA

MAJOR DEPARTMENTS/PRACTICES

Advertising • Antitrust • Appellate • Aviation &
Aerospace • Bankruptcy • Business & Finance •
Communications • Election Law • Employment & Labor
• ERISA • Food & Drug • Franchise • Government
Affairs • Government Contracts • Health Care •
Insurance • Intellectual Property • International Trade •
Litigation • Postal • Privacy • White Collar Defense

THE STATS

No. of attorneys: 215
No. of offices: 2
Summer associate offers: 20 out of 23 (2001)
Managing Partner: Richard E. Wiley
Hiring Partner: Scott McCaleb

NOTABLE PERKS

• All the Tang and peanut butter you can eat
• Subsidized home computers
• Gym in the building

EMPLOYMENT CONTACT

Ms. Irena McGrath
Director of Professional Development
Phone: (202) 719-7000
Fax: (202) 719-7049
wrfrecruit@wrf.com

BASE SALARY

Washington, DC, 2002
1st year: $110,000 (1,800); $125,000 (1,950)*
2nd year: $120,000; $135,000
3rd year: $130,000; $145,000
4th year: $140,000; $155,000
5th year: $150,000; $165,000
6th year: $160,000; $175,000
7th year: $170,000; $185,000
Summer associate: $2,400/week

*Wiley has a two-tier salary structure based on
1,800 and 1,950 billable hour benchmarks.

THE BUZZ
WHAT ATTORNEYS AT OTHER FIRMS ARE SAYING ABOUT THIS FIRM

• "A kindler, gentler sweatshop"
• "Telecom leader"
• "Excellent regulatory practice"
• "Almost there"

THE SCOOP

Wiley Rein & Fielding's leadership in communications law is built on extensive Beltway experience. The 19-year-old firm is home to several veterans of the FCC, including managing partner Richard Wiley. Connections to government undoubtedly benefit the firm's other major practice areas — insurance, government contracts and international trade. Wiley Rein has advised more than one U.S. president on governmental appointments. In the fall of 2001, the firm led a coalition of Internet speech advocates to victory in their challenge to a Virginia statute limiting online display of sexually-oriented materials.

GETTING HIRED

Want a job at Wiley? Sources say it is "helpful if a candidate has an interest in one of Wiley's specialty practices," such as insurance or communications law. An IP attorney says the firm seeks students "preferably from a top-10 school or at the very top of their class at a lesser known school," though a colleague sneers, "Wiley is looking to hire associates who went to good law schools, regardless of whether they will be good lawyers or not." The "firm is well respected in town, and therefore, especially in this market, getting hired is not a sure thing," warns a D.C. associate.

OUR SURVEY SAYS

Most sources suggest that Wiley Rein's culture "is very friendly, with a strong emphasis on a separation between work and personal time." "In the litigation and insurance practice groups, the cases are leanly staffed, which promotes professional as well as personal interaction between partners and associates," reports one associate. But not everyone feels the camaraderie. One lawyer claims that "when it comes right down to it, this firm is all about every man for himself."

Associates like the firm's two-tiered salary structure, which they say "provides flexibility and relieves some pressure, especially for first-year associates." While some consider the compensation "slightly below market," many think "the overall package is very favorable," considering the reasonable hours. "What good is making a ton of money if you don't have time to spend it?" Only associates on the higher-hours track earn hours bonuses (all associates are eligible for merit bonuses), and not everyone is cheering about those figures, which one associate calls "pitiful."

Most sources agree that the "D.C. office needs a lot of help." Complaints include "elevators that get stuck" and décor that "is way too Howard Johnson." But help may be on the way. The firm notes that its ongoing multi-million dollar renovation will upgrade common areas as well as associate offices. A good thing, since "significant renovation is needed to raise the quality of the office space to match the level of prestige the firm is gaining."

Kelley Drye & Warren LLP

101 Park Avenue
New York, NY 10178
Phone: (212) 808-7800
www.kelleydrye.com

LOCATIONS

New York, NY (HQ)
Chicago, IL
Los Angeles, CA
Parsippany, NJ
Stamford, CT
Tysons Corner, VA
Washington, DC
Brussels
Hong Kong

MAJOR DEPARTMENTS/PRACTICES

Bankruptcy
Corporate
Employee Benefits
Environmental
Labor
Litigation
Private Clients
Real Estate
Tax
Telecommunications

THE STATS

No. of attorneys: 351
No. of offices: 9
Summer associate offers: 24 out of 26 (2001)
Chairman: John M. Callagy
Hiring Partner: Jonathan K. Cooperman

THE BUZZ
WHAT ATTORNEYS AT OTHER FIRMS ARE SAYING ABOUT THIS FIRM

- "Old standby"
- "Past its prime"
- "Struggling"
- "Well-liked in the profession"

NOTABLE PERKS

- Blackberries
- Car service after 8 p.m.
- Free real-estate attorney to handle your house closing
- $25 for dinner

EMPLOYMENT CONTACT

Ms. Megan C. Clouden
Recruiting Coordinator
Phone: (212) 808-7510
Fax: (212) 808-7897
recruiting@kelleydrye.com

BASE SALARY

All offices, 2002
1st year: $125,000
2nd year: $135,000
3rd year: $150,000
4th year: $165,000
5th year: $180,000
6th year: $195,000
7th year: $205,000
Summer associate: $2,403.85/week

THE SCOOP

Founded way back in 1836 and having once represented then-President Abraham Lincoln, Kelley Drye & Warren has a firm foothold in history. Today Kelley Drye may not represent presidents, but it does have an impressive client list that includes J.P. Morgan Chase (the firm represented pre-merger Chase Manhattan Bank for over 100 years), Union Carbide (for over 75 years), DaimlerChrysler, Bacardi, Pitney Bowes, Cigna and Equitable Life. In 2002 Kelley Drye joined the Enron litigation party taking over where Davis Polk & Wardwell left off. When a conflict of interest caused DPW to be disqualified from representing J.P. Morgan Chase, which is seeking to collect on $183 million in Enron-related surety bonds, J.P. Morgan Chase selected Kelley Drye to take over the high-profile (and highly lucrative) litigation.

GETTING HIRED

At Kelley Drye, "bookworms and geeks" need not apply. "I think they want people who are skilled and good at thinking on their feet," says an associate. A New Yorker says, "Summer associates get involved in real transactions and perform substantive work. This is balanced with plenty of free time to explore the city and enjoy firm events." The lateral hiring process is "relaxed," with candidates often enduring only one day of interviews.

OUR SURVEY SAYS

"Our firm is one of the oldest in New York, but definitely one of the friendliest and least stuffy," boasts an insider. Associates appear pleased with the level of responsibility they are given but insist that the "feast or famine cliché" is alive and well at their firm, "and it sucks." A first-year associate laments, "Either I have no work but am tied to my desk surfing the Web for eight hours a day just to pass the time before I can leave at 5:30 p.m., or I am billing 100-plus hours per week." Despite the grumbling, some sources point out that "no one will call you at odd hours or make you come in on weekends or work late hours unless there is a genuine deadline."

Despite the contention of some associates that the firm is accommodating of new parents and part-timers, many insiders suggest that Kelley Drye is less than sensitive to women's issues. "Forget about partnership," sighs one insider. Women and minority associates also complain about the lack of a mentoring program.

Although most everyone is pleased with their base salary, many associates consider bonuses "low and unsatisfactory." Summarizes a New Yorker, "Discussing the bonus structure at this firm causes me distress. Need I say more?"

Mintz Levin Cohn Ferris Glovsky and Popeo, P.C.

One Financial Center
Boston, MA 02111
Phone: (617) 542-6000
www.mintz.com

LOCATIONS

Boston, MA (HQ)
New Haven, CT
New York, NY
Reston, VA
Washington, DC

MAJOR DEPARTMENTS/PRACTICES

Bankruptcy & Commercial
Biotechnology
Business & Public Finance
Communications
Employment, Labor & Benefits Immigration
Environmental
Health Care
High Technology
Immigration
Intellectual Property & Patent
Litigation
Real Estate
Tax & Trusts & Estates
Telecommunications

THE STATS

No. of attorneys: 502
No. of offices: 5
Summer associate offers: 51 out of 62 (2001)
Chairman: R. Robert Popeo
Hiring Partners: Timothy J. Langella and
Charles E. Carey

THE BUZZ
WHAT ATTORNEYS AT OTHER FIRMS ARE SAYING ABOUT THIS FIRM

- "Growing practice"
- "Should stop laying off its associates"
- "Sinking ship"
- "Great on diversity"

NOTABLE PERKS

- Paid paternity leave
- On-site emergency child care
- Free tickets to sporting events
- Free Blackberries for all associates

EMPLOYMENT CONTACT

Ms. Julie E. Zammuto
HR Manager, Attorney Recruitment
Phone: (617) 348-4929
Fax: (617) 542-2241
jzammuto@mintz.com

BASE SALARY

Boston, 2002
1st year: $125,000
2nd year: $135,000
3rd year: $145,000
4th year: $155,000
5th year: $170,000
6th year: $175,000
7th year: $180,000
8th year: $190,000
Summer associate: $2,400/week

THE SCOOP

Well known for its tech savvy, Mintz Levin Cohn Ferris Glovsky and Popeo has had a surprisingly good year despite the withering economy. The firm jumped up 22 spots in *The American Lawyer*'s 2000 annual revenue survey of the top 100 law firms. In 2001 *Of Counsel* magazine named Mintz Levin one of the Best U.S. Law Firms to Work At. In February 2002, the firm hired Jeff Snider, former senior vice president and general counsel of Lycos, Inc., as of counsel in its business and finance group. But Mintz Levin has not been entirely immune to the effects of the recession. In March and July of 2001, Mintz Levin fired a number of associates in what the firm called performance-based cuts, and in June 2002 it axed 17 associates due to the poor economy.

GETTING HIRED

If you're interested in joining Mintz Levin, it might be easier than ever to do so. As a result of the layoffs, some insiders say, "The firm is having difficulty recruiting first-year associates and summer associates." Still, it would behoove candidates to have "top-level academic credentials" and a winning personality. Laterals may have to wait a while. "During the boom," says one associate, "there was a hiring frenzy. Now lateral hiring has come to a dead stop."

OUR SURVEY SAYS

Though some associates describe the Mintz Levin culture as "friendly," "personable" and "laid back," several insist that these days morale is way down. "Since the beginning of the recession, the firm has changed dramatically. Management's handling of the economic downturn has been very disappointing," says a fifth-year associate. "The firm's decision not to give annual step-up raises to associates is very shortsighted and has made associate morale very bad," says another attorney.

Several associates complain that there is not enough work to go around, though "associates are [still] expected to be on call 24/7 and to be in the office for long hours even when there is nothing to do," says a frustrated fifth-year. But not everyone finds the hours so difficult. "We work hard, but compared to the sweatshop large firms in town, it's manageable," says one attorney. A colleague in New York agrees, saying management's expectations are "reasonable compared with top New York firms." Because "certain pro bono projects and certain CLE training count toward the target," associates say the 1,950 billable hour target isn't impossible to achieve.

Attitudes regarding partners vary, but the general consensus among associates is that "80 to 90 percent of them are very respectful and treat associates well." There is an "open-door policy for every partner in the real estate department," says one attorney, "and, with very few exceptions, I understand that this is common throughout the firm."

Katten Muchin Zavis Rosenman

525 West Monroe Street
Suite 1600
Chicago, IL 60661-3693
Phone: (312) 902-5200
www.kmzr.com

LOCATIONS

Charlotte, NC • Chicago, IL • Los Angeles, CA •
Newark, NJ • New York, NY • Palo Alto, CA •
Washington, DC

MAJOR DEPARTMENTS/PRACTICES

Corporate • Customs & International Trade • Employee
Benefits/Executive Compensation • Entertainment •
Environmental Services • Financial Services • Health
Care • Intellectual Property • International Trade • Labor
& Employment • Litigation • Music Law • Private Client
Services • Public Finance • Real Estate • Sports Law &
Sports Facilities • Tax • White Collar Criminal & Civil
Litigation

THE STATS

No. of attorneys: Over 600
No. of offices: 7
Summer associate offers: 98 percent of class (2001)
National Managing Partner: Vincent A.F. Sergi
Hiring Partners: Andrew Small, Brian Richards and
Wayne Wald

THE BUZZ
WHAT ATTORNEYS AT OTHER FIRMS ARE SAYING ABOUT THIS FIRM

- "Young, hip"
- "Good firm trying to play on the national scene"
- "Chicago sweatshop — and it's hard to sweat in
  Chicago"

NOTABLE PERKS

- Free soda, Starbucks coffee and bagels
- Health insurance for same sex domestic partners
- One-month paid sabbatical after five years of
  service
- Tickets to events in all offices

EMPLOYMENT CONTACT

Chicago
Ms. Kelley Lynch
Director of Legal Recruiting
Phone: (312) 902-5526
Fax: (312) 577-8937
kelley.lynch@kmzr.com

New York
Ms. Kim McHugh
Legal Recruiting Manager
Phone: (212) 940-6386
Fax: (212) 940-8776

Los Angeles
Ms. Donna Francis
Legal Recruiting Manager
Phone: (310) 788-4766
Fax: (310) 712-8253

Washington, DC
Ms. Judy Brown
Legal Recruiting Manager
Phone: (202) 625-3652
Fax: (202) 625-7570

BASE SALARY

Chicago and Los Angeles, 2002
1st year: $125,000
2nd year: $130,000
3rd year: $142,500
4th year: $157,500
5th year: $170,000
6th year: $180,000
7th year: $190,000
Summer associate: $2,403/week

THE SCOOP

After several years of courting, Chicago's Katten Muchin and New York's Rosenman & Colin announced a merger in March 2002. Katten Muchin Zavis Rosenman is the official name of the newly merged firm. While the pre-merger KMZ had a reputation for high-quality corporate, high-tech, sports and entertainment law, it didn't have much of a presence in the Big Apple — until now. Clients include Jerry Reinsdorf, chairman of the Chicago Bulls. KMZR has advised Reinsdorf in the construction of Comiskey Park and stadium projects in Portland, Seattle and Greenville, South Carolina. Other big name clients include Universal Studios.

GETTING HIRED

Getting a job at Katten Muchin can be "very tough." Although the firm "is more likely than other large Chicago-based firms to consider law students enrolled in lower-tier law schools," say associates, "those students need to be in the top of their class." According to a senior associate, "The best candidate would be hardworking, personable, independent and would have already decided upon an area of specialization." Others say the firm seeks a "Katten dynamic personality" — e.g., "people who are likely to thrive in our less structured, more laissez-faire atmosphere."

OUR SURVEY SAYS

One of the few points on which KMZR associates agree is the "dismal" décor of their Chicago offices. Individual offices may be "surprisingly spacious," but the "office furniture appears to be an odd collection of hand-me-downs." However, more than one lawyer believes "it would be stupid to make a decision about your career based on what the office looks like."

More significant factors presumably would be the "excellent variety of assignments," the "high degree of responsibility" accorded to associates and the level of compensation. Lawyers' dress is "business casual," but insiders disagree on how casual the atmosphere is. Where one lawyer feels "a general sense of togetherness and helpfulness," another finds that "many co-workers will walk right by you in the halls without saying hello or even making eye contact."

Associates also give mixed reviews to partner-associate relations. Many contacts report that they have "always been treated well by the partners" who are "fair" and "respectful." Other attorneys believe that "formal communications between partners and associates regarding the firm, its policies, practices and health are not as forthcoming as they would like." A few complaints about a "boys' club subculture" mirror last year's description of a "fraternity" atmosphere.

Contacts are generally pleased with compensation near "the top of the Chicago market," though the firm's "decision to withhold one half of all associates' raises this year — to be repaid at [the] end of 2002 if they make minimum [billable] hours — did not go over particularly well."

Foley Hoag LLP

155 Seaport Boulevard
Boston, MA 02210
Phone: (617) 832-1000
www.foleyhoag.com

LOCATIONS

Boston, MA (HQ)
Washington, DC

MAJOR DEPARTMENTS/PRACTICES

Administrative
Business
Environmental
Intellectual Property
Labor
Litigation
Real Estate
Tax

THE STATS

No. of attorneys: 236
No. of offices: 2
Summer associate offers: 29 out of 32 (2001)
Managing Partners: Peter M. Rosenblum and Michele A. Whitham
Hiring Attorney: Anthony D. Mirenda

NOTABLE PERKS

• Free cab rides home after late work nights
• Home technology subsidy
• Emergency day care center

EMPLOYMENT CONTACT

Ms. Dina M. Wreede
Director of Legal Recruiting & Professional Development
Phone: (617) 832-7060
dwreede@foleyhoag.com

BASE SALARY

All offices, 2002
1st year: $125,000
2nd year: $135,000
3rd year: $140,000
4th year: $145,000
5th year: $155,000
Summer associate: $2,400/week

THE BUZZ
WHAT ATTORNEYS AT OTHER FIRMS ARE SAYING ABOUT THIS FIRM

• "Premier Boston firm"
• "Ivory tower intellectuals"
• "Excellent working atmosphere"
• "Thinks mighty highly of itself"

THE SCOOP

Founded in 1943, Foley Hoag LLP is considered one of Beantown's most esteemed firms for corporate and securities law, and its litigation and IP departments deserve stars as well. One of the leading litigators in the city is partner Michael Keating, whose representation of W.R. Grace in a toxic tort suit was made into the book and movie, *A Civil Action*. The firm is proud of its membership in the international organization of law firms, Lex Mundi, and in December 2001, Foley Hoag attorneys were chosen to chair four of the organization's 26 committees. The firm is also committed to diversity. In 1979 it made Charles Beard the first African-American to be awarded the status of equity partner at a Boston law firm. Today a woman, Beth E. Arnold, heads its life sciences practice, and another woman, Michele A. Whitham, serves as co-managing partner.

GETTING HIRED

Like most firms, Foley Hoag seeks associates with excellent academic credentials from top law schools. Associates explain that Foley also appreciates a candidate who is "personable, who takes initiative, who's hardworking, mature and responsible." Candidates who have what it takes can expect to pass through a round of interviews with partners and associates at various levels of seniority. But prospective lateral hires may be disappointed, as "not a lot of lateral hiring is done." The summer associate program provides law students with "real client work."

OUR SURVEY SAYS

While Foley Hoag has an "informal," "friendly" and "laid-back" culture, there isn't much socializing outside of the office. Be prepared to project confidence: "If you require lots of hand-holding, you will likely be unhappy. Initiative is rewarded and expected." But "help is always available should you need it, and nearly everyone is willing to assist." Regardless, the firm is "not big" on formal training, though partners are supportive and respectful. When it comes to hours, sources are pleased as punch. The billing requirement of 1,850 hours is considered "reasonable." Most associates are equally pleased with their compensation, which they say is "on par" with peer firms in Boston. Though "other firms pay bigger bonuses," they also "make you work harder, so it is a trade off."

Associates swoon over their firm's pro bono program. "Work on as much as you want, the hours are counted as though they were billable and nobody asks you any questions." Diversity is another issue. Like many firms, women and minorities are hired in impressive numbers but don't stay long. An associate notices, "The firm seems to try hard but few women stick around to make partner. The firm tries hard to recruit minority candidates, [but there are] only a handful of minority partners." The firm is doing something right when it comes to diversity for gays and lesbians, as there are "many gay and lesbian attorneys at the firm."

McGuireWoods LLP

One James Center
901 East Cary Street
Richmond, VA 23219-4030
Phone: (804) 775-1000
www.mcguirewoods.com

LOCATIONS

Richmond, VA (HQ)
Atlanta, GA • Baltimore, MD • Charlotte, NC •
Charlottesville, VA • Chicago, IL • Jacksonville, FL •
New York, NY • Norfolk, VA • Pittsburgh, PA • Tysons
Corner, VA • Washington, DC • Almaty, Kazakhstan •
Brussels • Moscow (of counsel)

MAJOR DEPARTMENTS/PRACTICES

Commercial Litigation
Corporate Services
Financial Services
International
Labor & Employment
Product Liability & Litigation Management
Real Estate & Environmental
Taxation & Employee Benefits

THE STATS

No. of attorneys: 572
No. of offices: 15
Chairman: Robert L. Burrus Jr.
Managing Partner: William J. Strickland
Hiring Attorney: Jacquelyn E. Stone

THE BUZZ
WHAT ATTORNEYS AT OTHER FIRMS ARE SAYING ABOUT THIS FIRM

- "Up and coming"
- "High turnover"
- "Good Virginia firm"
- "Internal conflict"

NOTABLE PERKS

- Cell phone reimbursement
- "State of the art" laptop computers
- Free continental breakfast on Fridays (in some offices)

EMPLOYMENT CONTACT

Ms. Pamela S. Malone
Director of Lawyer Recruitment and Development
Phone: (202) 857-1732
Fax: (202) 857-1737
pmalone@mcguirewoods.com

BASE SALARY

Richmond, 2002
1st year: $95,000
Summer associate: $1,800/week

THE SCOOP

McGuireWoods traces its roots back to 1834 with the opening of Egbert Watson's solo practice in Charlottesville, Va. Since then the firm has added 11 U.S. offices and three locations overseas and evolved through several mergers and name changes into its current identity, McGuireWoods LLP. Through client and industry focused teams, the firm serves public, private, government and nonprofit clients for such industries as energy resources, technology and transportation. Two years ago, the firm launched an expansive extranet service, McGuireWoods Connect, through which the firm shares information and documents with clients around the world. The firm recently expanded into public affairs and business consulting with the creation of two subsidiaries, McGuireWoods Consulting LLC and the McGuireWoods Capital Group.

GETTING HIRED

McGuireWoods "looks for smart people who will fit in well with the group." The firm likes "the kind of person who is civil and courteous with everyone." Although the hiring process may not be "as competitive as it is in bigger cities," several insiders believe "the firm has become much more discriminating." According to a senior associate, "The firm used to fill its summer classes with 80 percent of only the top students from the top 20 schools, and the other 20 percent were much more well-rounded. Today, I think the figures are closer to 95 percent to 5 percent."

OUR SURVEY SAYS

Most insiders find their experience at McGuireWoods "quite fulfilling." They enjoy the civility and friendliness of a "traditional Southern firm," together "with national practice offerings and objectives." The atmosphere is described as "friendly and somewhat formal," although some say the "satellite offices are more relaxed and laid back" than the firm's Richmond headquarters. They are also apparently better appointed than the home office, which is widely described as "run-down" and "in drastic need of renovations." "The '70s reign," laments one associate.

Lawyers praise the quality of work and friendliness of colleagues as among the best things the firm has to offer. "Some lawyers do socialize together," according to sources, but McGuireWoods is also a "good place if you are married." A few associates express concern about an increasing emphasis on billable hours.

Associates would also feel more encouraged to take on pro bono projects if the hours counted toward bonuses. As it is, pro bono hours are credited toward the "billable hours target for purposes of meeting the firm's expectations for annual raises" but not toward the higher target used for bonuses. "Until pro bono hours are counted toward bonuses," lawyers believe, "it won't take a high priority for most lawyers at the firm."

Thelen Reid & Priest LLP

New York [Until November 30, 2002]
40 West 57th Street
New York, NY 10019
Phone: (212) 603-2000

New York [As of December 1, 2002]
875 Third Avenue
New York, NY 10022
Phone: (212) 603-2000

San Francisco
101 Second Street, Suite 1800
San Francisco, CA 94105
Phone: (415) 371-1200
www.thelenreid.com

LOCATIONS

Los Angeles, CA • Morristown, NJ • New York, NY • San Francisco, CA • Silicon Valley, CA • Washington, DC

MAJOR DEPARTMENTS/PRACTICES

Business & Finance • Commercial Litigation • Construction & Government Contracts • Government Affairs • Labor & Employment • Project & Asset Finance • Real Estate • Tax, Benefits, Trusts & Estates

THE STATS

No. of attorneys: 421
No. of offices: 6
Summer associate offers accepted: 26 out of 31 (2001)
Chairman: Richard N. Gary
Hiring Attorneys: Richard Lapping (San Francisco); Sharon Carlstedt and Michael Fitzpatrick (NY); Charles English (DC); Keith Slenkovich (Silicon Valley); Timothy Pierce (LA)

THE BUZZ
WHAT ATTORNEYS AT OTHER FIRMS ARE SAYING ABOUT THIS FIRM

- "Rising star"
- "Small player"
- "Solid reputation"
- "Merger problems"

NOTABLE PERKS

- New offices in New York, Los Angeles and Silicon Valley in 2002
- Paternity leave
- Bonus for new business
- $10,000 referral bonus

EMPLOYMENT CONTACT

East Coast
Diane Taranto
Attorney Recruiting Manager
Phone: (212) 603-2000
Fax: (212) 541-1518
dtaranto@thelenreid.com

West Coast
Holly Saydah
Attorney Recruiting Manager
Phone: (415) 371-1200
Fax: (415) 369-8794
hsaydah@thelenreid.com

BASE SALARY

All offices, 2002
1st year: $125,000
2nd year: $125,000–$135,000
3rd year: $130,000–$150,000
4th year: $135,000–$165,000
5th year: $140,000–$185,000
6th year: $145,000–$195,000
7th year: $150,000–$205,000
8th year: $155,000–$210,000
9th year: $160,000–$215,000
Summer associate: $2,400/week

THE SCOOP

While many Bay Area firms were wounded in 2001's economic recession, Thelen Reid & Priest rose from the ashes of the tech boom due in part to its top litigation and energy practices. Granted, the firm did lay off about five associates from the San Francisco office in July 2001, but today it's going strong, with over 420 attorneys in six offices. Since January 2002, the firm has welcomed 10 new partners to the D.C. office. In late 2001, former D.C.-based managing partner Stephan Minikes was appointed to serve in the Bush Administration.

GETTING HIRED

Snagging a position at Thelen Reid is no walk in the park. One associate notes, "The firm does not hire unless there is a long-term need for a permanent associate." Another explains, "We are currently only looking at candidates who have passed the patent bar and intend to pursue or have experience in prosecuting patents. Candidates with interest and experience in intellectual property litigation are also being considered." The firm looks for lawyers who are "capable, motivated and easy to get along with." Summer associates can expect a realistic view of life at the firm, though frivolity plays a role as well. "The social aspect was very rewarding," an associate notes.

OUR SURVEY SAYS

Sources disagree about the corporate vibe at Thelen Reid. Some describe a "generally relaxed and friendly atmosphere" made up of "team players" who are "friendly and laid back." "If you're going to practice law in a big firm, this is a damned fine place to do it," says one happy associate. Associates appreciate the high-caliber and sophisticated work. But other sources describe an atmosphere that is downright unpleasant. Laments one San Franciscan, "While individuals are friendly, there is absolutely no socializing. Attorneys spend all day in their office working, eating lunch at their desk."

However, most associates agree that the hours at Thelen Reid are reasonable. "People rarely stay at the office past 6:30 or 7:00," says one associate. An LA insider mentions, "The hours requirement here is not as high as many other LA firms." A part-timer has it made: "I am happy with the part-time program. The partners generally respect my schedule. I feel no hostility about my working part-time, and I feel the pay and bonus framework is fair." Associates are also happy with their salary, describing it as "generous."

Thelen Reid earns mixed reviews when it comes to diversity. While some sources point out that there are "significantly more female associates at this point, which certainly bodes well for the hiring attitudes," sources regret that "very few [women] seem to have made it to the partner ranks." Yet in the beginning of 2002, five of eight attorneys promoted to partnership status were women.

BEST OF
THE REST

Andrews & Kurth L.L.P.

600 Travis, Suite 4200
Houston, TX 77002
Phone: (713) 220-4200
www.andrews-kurth.com

LOCATIONS

Houston, TX (HQ) (2 offices)
Austin, TX (2 offices) • Dallas, TX • Los Angeles, CA
New York, NY • The Woodlands, TX
Washington, DC • London

MAJOR DEPARTMENTS/PRACTICES

Antitrust • Banking & Finance • Bankruptcy •
Biotechnology • Corporate & Securities • Energy •
Environmental • ERISA • Intellectual Property •
Internet/E-Commerce • Labor & Employment • Litigation
Mergers & Acquisitions • Project Finance • Public Law •
Real Estate • Tax • Trusts & Estates

THE STATS

No. of attorneys: 365
No. of offices: 10
Managing Partner: Howard Ayers
Hiring Partners: Jeffrey E. Spiers and
Chanse McLeod (Houston)
(See firm web site for hiring partners in other offices)

NOTABLE PERKS

• Free parking
• Out-of-state moving expenses

EMPLOYMENT CONTACT

Houston
Ms. Kimberly Klevenhagen
Recruiting Manager
Phone: (713) 220-4140
Fax: (713) 238-7327
kimberlyklevenhagen@akllp.com
(See firm web site for employment contacts in
other offices)

BASE SALARY

Houston, 2002
1st year: $110,000

THE BUZZ
WHAT ATTORNEYS AT OTHER FIRMS ARE SAYING ABOUT THIS FIRM

• "Friendly Texas firm"
• "Good ol' boys' club"
• "Fast-moving, but too fast?"

Ballard Spahr Andrews & Ingersoll, LLP

1735 Market Street
51st Floor
Philadelphia, PA 19103-7599
Phone: (215) 665-8500
www.ballardspahr.com

LOCATIONS

Philadelphia, PA (HQ)
Baltimore, MD
Denver, CO
Salt Lake City, UT
Voorhees, NJ
Washington, DC

MAJOR DEPARTMENTS/PRACTICES

Business & Finance
Financial Planning & Management
Litigation
Public Finance
Real Estate

THE STATS

No. of attorneys: 416
No. of offices: 6
Summer associate offers: 27 out of 28 (2001)
Chairman: Arthur Makadon
Hiring Partner: Mark S. Stewart

NOTABLE PERKS

• Monthly firm lunches
• Twice-monthly happy hours
• Stipend of $5,000 for first-year associates
• D.C. office conveniently located at Metro Center

EMPLOYMENT CONTACT

Philadelphia
Ms. Kimberly Gilbert
Recruitment Coordinator
Phone: (215) 864-8167
Fax: (215) 864-9184
gilbertk@ballardspahr.com
(See firm web site for other offices)

BASE SALARY

Philadelphia, 2002
1st year: $107,000
Summer associate: $2,000/week

THE BUZZ
WHAT ATTORNEYS AT OTHER FIRMS ARE SAYING ABOUT THIS FIRM

• "A solid regional firm"
• "Well-connected in Philadelphia"
• "Small market presence"

Blank Rome Comisky & McCauley LLP

One Logan Square
Philadelphia, PA 19103-6998
Phone: (215) 569-5500
www.blankrome.com

LOCATIONS

Philadelphia, PA (HQ)
Allentown, PA
Baltimore, MD
Boca Raton, FL
Cherry Hill, NJ
Cincinnati, OH
Media, PA
New York, NY
Trenton, NJ
Washington, DC
Wilmington, DE

MAJOR DEPARTMENTS/PRACTICES

Corporate • Financial Services • Government Relations •
Health Law • Intellectual Property • Labor • Litigation •
Matrimonial Law • Public Finance • Real Estate • Tax &
Fiduciary

THE STATS

No. of attorneys: 400
No. of offices: 11
Summer associate offers: 23 out of 28 (2001)
Chairman: David F. Girard-diCarlo
Hiring Committee Chair: Grant S. Palmer (Philadelphia)

NOTABLE PERKS

• Four weeks vacation
• Dependent care spending account

EMPLOYMENT CONTACT

Ms. Donna M. Branca
Director of Attorney Relations
Phone: (215) 569-5751
Fax: (215) 569-5555
branca@blankrome.com

BASE SALARY

Philadelphia, 2002
1st year: $105,000

THE BUZZ
WHAT ATTORNEYS AT OTHER FIRMS ARE SAYING ABOUT THIS FIRM

• "Thoughtful litigators"
• "The 'happy go lucky' Philly firm"
• "Very political"

Bracewell & Patterson, L.L.P.

711 Louisiana Street, Suite 2900
South Tower Pennzoil Place
Houston, Texas 77002-2781
Phone: (713) 223-2900
www.bracepatt.com

LOCATIONS

Houston, TX (HQ)
Austin, TX • Corpus Christi, TX • Dallas, TX • Fort
Worth, TX • Reston, VA • San Antonio, TX •
Washington, DC • Almaty, Kazakhstan • Astana,
Kazakhstan • London

MAJOR DEPARTMENTS/PRACTICES

Appellate • Bankruptcy/Creditors' Rights • Corporate &
Securities • Construction • Counter-Terrorism, Public &
Corporate Security • Election Law • Emerging
Companies • Employee Benefits • Energy •
Environmental • Finance • Government Relations,
Advocacy & Strategy • Health Care • Hospitality •
Insurance • Intellectual Property • International •
Internet, Telecom & E-Commerce • Labor &
Employment • Latin American Business • Litigation •
Manufacturing • Not-for-Profit • Public Law • Real
Estate • Regulated Industries • School Law • Tax •
Trusts & Estates • Water Law • Wealth Management

THE STATS

No. of attorneys: 350
No. of offices: 11
Managing Partner: Patrick C. Oxford
Hiring Partner: Jennifer W. Jacobs

THE BUZZ
WHAT ATTORNEYS AT OTHER FIRMS ARE SAYING ABOUT THIS FIRM

- "Relaxed, friendly atmosphere"
- "Second-tier Houston firm"
- "Cordial, but small-time"

NOTABLE PERKS

- Sabbaticals for partners
- Subsidized parking
- Blackberry wireless e-mail devices
- Alternative work arrangements

EMPLOYMENT CONTACT

Ms. Jean P. Lenzner
Director of Attorney Employment
Phone: (713) 221-1296
Fax: (713) 221-2145
jlenzner@bracepatt.com

BASE SALARY

Austin, Dallas, Fort Worth and Houston, 2002
1st year: $105,000

San Antonio and Corpus Christi, 2002
1st year: $95,000

Washington, D.C., 2002
1st year: $110,000

Reston, 2002
1st year: $105,000

Brown Rudnick Berlack Israels, LLP

One Financial Center
Boston, MA 02111
Phone: (617) 856-8200
www.brownrudnick.com

LOCATIONS

Boston, MA (HQ)
Hartford, CT
New York, NY
Providence, RI
Dublin
London

MAJOR DEPARTMENTS/PRACTICES

Banking & Finance
BRF&G Consulting Group
Business
Government Relations
Health Care
Intellectual Property
International
Litigation
Real Estate

THE STATS

No. of attorneys: 218
No. of offices: 6
Summer associate offers: 12 out of 14 (2001)
Chairman: André C. Jasse
Hiring Partner: William R. Baldiga

NOTABLE PERKS

• Emergency child care
• Paid bar membership
• Flexible spending account

EMPLOYMENT CONTACT

Ms. Linda Manning
Hiring Coordinator
Phone: (617) 856-8316
Fax: (617) 856-8201
lmanning@brbilaw.com

BASE SALARY

Boston, 2002
1st year: $125,000
Summer associate: $2,404/week

THE BUZZ
WHAT ATTORNEYS AT OTHER FIRMS ARE SAYING ABOUT THIS FIRM

• "Innovative family-friendly policies"
• "Good firm, but second tier"
• "After big tobacco success, pretty average"

Davis Wright Tremaine LLP

2600 Century Square
1501 Fourth Avenue
Seattle, WA 98101-1688
Phone: (206) 622-3150
www.dwt.com

LOCATIONS

Seattle, WA (HQ)

Anchorage, AK • Bellevue, WA • Honolulu, HI • Los Angeles, CA • New York, NY • Portland, OR • San Francisco, CA • Washington, DC • Shanghai

MAJOR DEPARTMENTS/PRACTICES

Admiralty & Maritime • Aircraft Industry • Antitrust • Business & Corporate • China Practice • Communications, Media & Information Technologies • Construction & Government Contracts • Corporate Finance & Securities • Credit Recovery & Bankruptcy • Education • Emerging Business & Technology • Employment/Employee Benefits • Energy • Environmental & Natural Resources • Financial Institutions • Food & Agriculture • Health Care • Hospitality • Immigration • Intellectual Property • International Law • Internet & eCommerce • Legislation • Litigation • Municipal Finance • Real Estate & Land Use • Sports • Tax • Tax Exempt Organizations • Telecommunications • Trusts & Estates

THE STATS

No. of attorneys: 400
No. of offices: 10
Summer associate offers: 16 out of 17 (2001)
Managing Partner: Richard D. Ellingsen
Hiring Partner: Bergitta K. Trelstad (Seattle)

THE BUZZ
WHAT ATTORNEYS AT OTHER FIRMS ARE SAYING ABOUT THIS FIRM

- "Sexy media practice"
- "Cares about quality of life"
- "Where the lazy guy you knew from law school works"

NOTABLE PERKS

- Firm-wide retreat every 18 months
- Paid bar review/exam expenses
- Bar stipend

EMPLOYMENT CONTACT

Seattle
Ms. Carol Yuly
Recruiting Administrator
Phone: (206) 628-3529
Fax: (206) 628-7699
carolyuly@dwt.com
(See firm web site for other employment contacts)

BASE SALARY

Seattle and Bellevue, 2002
1st year: $90,000

Anchorage, 2002
1st year: $80,000

Los Angeles, 2002
1st year: $102,500

Portland, 2002
1st year: $80,000

San Francisco, 2002
1st year: $110,000

Drinker Biddle & Reath LLP

One Logan Square
18th & Cherry Streets
Philadelphia, PA 19103-6996
Phone: (215) 988-2700
www.drinkerbiddle.com

LOCATIONS

Philadelphia, PA (HQ)
Berwyn, PA
Florham Park, NJ
Los Angeles, CA
New York, NY
Princeton, NJ
San Francisco, CA
Washington, DC

MAJOR DEPARTMENTS/PRACTICES

Business and Finance: Antitrust • Banking &
Commercial Law • Communications Law •
Communications • Corporate & Securities • Education •
Employee Benefits • Government Affairs • Health Law •
Intellectual Property • Investment Management • Public
Finance • Real Estate • Tax • Workout & Bankruptcy •
Litigation: Environmental • General Civil • Insurance •
Labor & Employment • Products Liability • Professional
Liability • White Collar/Corporate Investigations
Personal Law

THE STATS

No. of attorneys: 455
No. of offices: 8
Summer associate offers: 28 out of 32 (2001)
Chairman: James M. Sweet
Hiring Partner: William H. Clark Jr.
Florham Park Hiring Partner: Michael R. Clark

THE BUZZ
WHAT ATTORNEYS AT OTHER FIRMS ARE SAYING ABOUT THIS FIRM

- "Good lawyers in small market"
- "Sleepy, old-school Philly firm"
- "Very impressed with themselves"

NOTABLE PERKS

- $7,500 stipend for all first-year associates and judicial clerks
- $10,000 Federal judicial clerk bonus
- Complimentary fitness center
- Bi-weekly happy hours
- 12 weeks paid leave for birth or adoption

EMPLOYMENT CONTACT

Ms. Maryellen Wyville Altieri
Director of Professional Recruitment
Phone: (215) 988-2663
Fax: (215) 988-2757
Maryellen.Altieri@dbr.com

BASE SALARY

Philadelphia, 2002
1st year: $105,000
Summer associate: $2,019/week

Washington, DC, 2002
1st year: $110,000
Summer associate: $2,115/week

San Francisco, 2002
1st year: $105,000
Summer associate: $2,019/week

Florham Park, 2002
1st year: $95,000
Summer associate: $2,000/week

Duane Morris LLP

One Liberty Place
Philadelphia, PA 19103-7396
Phone: (215) 979-1000
Fax: (215) 979-1020
www.duanemorris.com

LOCATIONS

Philadelphia, PA (HQ)
Allentown, PA • Atlanta, GA • Bangor, ME • Boston,
MA • Cherry Hill, NJ • Chicago, IL • Harrisburg, PA •
Houston, TX • Miami, FL • Newark, NJ • New York, NY •
Palm Beach, FL • Philadelphia, PA • Princeton, NJ • San
Francisco, CA • Washington, DC • Westchester, NY •
Wilmington, DE • London

MAJOR DEPARTMENTS/PRACTICES

Commercial, Municipal and Affordable Housing Finance
Group • Corporate • Employment, Benefits &
Immigration • Energy, Environment & Resources •
Estates & Asset Planning • Financial Products • Health
Law • Intellectual Property • Real Estate •
Reorganization & Finance • Tax • Trial

THE STATS

No. of attorneys: 481
No. of offices: 19
Summer associate offers: 12 out of 14 (2001)
Chairman: Sheldon M. Bonovitz
Hiring Partner: James J. Holman

NOTABLE PERKS

• 4 weeks vacation
• Weekly wine and cheese receptions
• Domestic partner benefits
• Flexible benefits/spending accounts

EMPLOYMENT CONTACT

Ms. Patricia M. Stacey
Director of Legal Recruitment & Retention
Phone: (215) 979-1279
pmstacey@Duanemorris.com

Ms. Peggy Simoncini Pasquay
Law Student and Lateral Associate Hiring
Coordinator
Phone: (215) 979-1161
simoncini@duanemorris.com
(See web site for additional recruiting information)

BASE SALARY

Philadelphia, 2002
1st year: $105,000
Summer associate: $2,109/week

THE BUZZ
WHAT ATTORNEYS AT OTHER FIRMS ARE SAYING ABOUT THIS FIRM

• "Friendly, well-regarded Philly firm"
• "Expansion problems"
• "Baker & McKenzie lite"

Foster Pepper & Shefelman PLLC

1111 Third Avenue, Suite 3400
Seattle, WA 98101-3299
Phone: (206) 447-4400
www.foster.com

LOCATIONS

Seattle, WA (HQ)
Anchorage, AK
Portland, OR
Spokane, WA

MAJOR DEPARTMENTS/PRACTICES

Antitrust & Trade Regulation • Business • Construction •
Creditors' Rights & Bankruptcy • Emerging Company &
Venture Capital • Employee Benefits & Executive
Compensation • Employment & Labor • Environmental
& Land Use • Estate Planning • Family Law • Financial
Institutions • Franchise • Health Care • Institutional
Pensions Investing & Operations • Insurance •
Intellectual Property • International • Litigation & ADR •
Mergers, Acquisitions & Reorganizations • Municipal &
Public Finance • Real Estate • SEC • Sports • Tax

THE STATS

No. of attorneys: 127
No. of offices: 4
Summer associate offers: 3 out of 4 (2001)
Executive Committee Chair: J. Tayloe Washburn
Hiring Committee Chair: Jeffrey S. Miller

NOTABLE PERKS

• Flexible salary structure based on billables
• Firm condo
• Pro Se Café (in-house cafeteria)

EMPLOYMENT CONTACT

Ms. Tyra Reolandt
Manager, Recruiting & Benefits
Phone: (206) 447-4700
Fax: (206) 447- 9700
tyra@foster.com

BASE SALARY

Seattle, 2002
Base salary at 1,800 billable hours:*
1st year: $100,000
2nd year: $105,000
Summer associate: $1,550/week

*Base salaries are determined by the number of
hours billed by associates. Associates are also paid
annually for all hours billed over 1,800 according to
a "per additional hour" formula. There is, therefore,
no maximum annual salary.

THE BUZZ
WHAT ATTORNEYS AT OTHER FIRMS ARE SAYING ABOUT THIS FIRM

• "Good Northwest firm"
• "Average"
• "Kinder, gentler firm"

Haynes and Boone, LLP

901 Main Street, Suite 3100
Dallas, TX 75202-3789
Phone: (214) 651-5000
www.haynesboone.com

LOCATIONS

Dallas, TX (HQ)
Austin, TX
Fort Worth, TX
Houston, TX
Richardson, TX
San Antonio, TX
Washington, DC
Mexico City

MAJOR DEPARTMENTS/PRACTICES

Antitrust • Appellate • Business Litigation • Business
Reorganization/Bankruptcy • Corporate/Securities •
Employee Benefits/Executive Compensation •
Energy/Power • Environmental • Finance • Government
Contracts • Health Care • Immigration • Insurance •
Intellectual Property • International • Investment Funds •
Labor & Employment • Media Law • Mergers &
Acquisitions • Real Estate • Securities Litigation • Tax,
Business & Estate Planning • Venture Capital • White
Collar Criminal Defense

THE STATS

No. of attorneys: 415
No. of offices: 8
Summer associate offers: 87 out of 123 (2001)
Managing Partner: Robert E. Wilson
Recruiting Partner: Taylor H. Wilson

THE BUZZ
WHAT ATTORNEYS AT OTHER FIRMS ARE SAYING ABOUT THIS FIRM

- "Great place to work"
- "Friendly, but second tier"
- "Unabashedly cowboyesque"

NOTABLE PERKS

- Palm Pilots
- Extensive training program for first-years
- Quarterly attorney pizza lunches

EMPLOYMENT CONTACT

Ms. Marina O'Con
Manager of Attorney Recruitment
Phone: (214) 651-5720
Fax: (214) 200-0694
oconm@haynesboone.com

BASE SALARY

Dallas, 2002
1st year: $110,000
Summer associate: $2,100/week

Kilpatrick Stockton LLP

1100 Peachtree Street, Suite 2800
Atlanta, GA 30309-4530
Phone: (404) 815-6500
www.KilpatrickStockton.com

LOCATIONS

Atlanta, GA • Augusta, GA • Charlotte, NC • Miami, FL • Raleigh, NC • Reston, VA • Washington, DC • Winston-Salem, NC • London • Stockholm

MAJOR DEPARTMENTS/PRACTICES

Anti-Terrorism • Antitrust & Trade Regulation • Banking & Finance • Biotechnology & Life Sciences • Business Transactions • Construction Law & Public Contracts • Corporate Finance & Securities • Customs • E-Commerce & Internet • Employment & ERISA • Environmental • Financial Restructuring • Franchising • Government • Government Contracts • Health Care • Infrastructure & Land Use • Insurance Coverage • Intellectual Property • International • Investment Management • Labor & Employment • Litigation • Real Estate • Tax • Technology • Telecommunications • Trusts & Estates • Utilities • White Collar Criminal Law

THE STATS

No. of attorneys: 533
No. of offices: 10
Summer associate offers: 50 out of 52 (2001)
Managing Partner: William H. Brewster
Hiring Partner: Paul V. Lalli

THE BUZZ
WHAT ATTORNEYS AT OTHER FIRMS ARE SAYING ABOUT THIS FIRM

- "Growing regional power in Southeast"
- "Technology train left town last year"
- "Struggling with its image"

NOTABLE PERKS

- Annual weekend retreat
- Subsidized attorney dining room
- $5,000 reimbursement for startup costs for entry-level associates and excellent benefits package

EMPLOYMENT CONTACT

Atlanta
Ms. Michelle Reed
Phone: (404) 815-6500
Fax: (404) 815-6555
MiReed@KilpatrickStockton.com

(See firm web site for employment contacts in other offices)

BASE SALARY

Atlanta, 2002
1st year: $100,000
7th year: $160,000
Summer associate: $1,800/week

Washington, DC, 2002
1st year: $125,000
7th year: $210,000
Summer associate: $2,200/week

Littler Mendelson, P.C.

650 California Street, 20th Floor
San Francisco, CA 94108-2693
Phone: (415) 433-1940
www.littler.com

LOCATIONS

Atlanta, GA • Bakersfield, CA • Baltimore, MD •
Chicago, IL • Columbus, OH • Dallas, TX • Denver, CO •
Fresno, CA • Houston, TX • Las Vegas, NV •
Los Angeles, CA • Minneapolis, MN • Newark, NJ •
New York, NY • Oakland, CA • Palm Desert, CA •
Philadelphia, PA • Phoenix, AZ • Pittsburgh, PA •
Reno, NV • Sacramento, CA • San Diego, CA • San
Francisco, CA • San Jose, CA • Santa Maria, CA •
Santa Rosa, CA • Seattle, WA • Stockton, CA •
Walnut Creek, CA • Washington, DC • Yakima, WA

MAJOR DEPARTMENTS/PRACTICES

Employment & Labor Law

THE STATS

No. of attorneys: 380
No. of offices: 31
Summer associate offers: 3 out of 6 (San Francisco only, 2001)
Managing Director: Wendy L. Tice-Wallner
Hiring Partner: Robert G. Hulteng (San Francisco)

NOTABLE PERKS

• Free parking after first year
• Reimbursement of cell phone bills
• Laptop computers

EMPLOYMENT CONTACT

Ms. Karen Herz
Recruiting Department
Phone: (415) 433-1940
Fax: (415) 399-8447
lawrecruit@littler.com

BASE SALARY

San Francisco, 2002
1st year: $110,000
Summer associate: $2,000/week

THE BUZZ
WHAT ATTORNEYS AT OTHER FIRMS ARE SAYING ABOUT THIS FIRM

• "Great at what they do"
• "Union busters"
• "Kmart of labor and employment"

Lord, Bissell & Brook

115 South LaSalle Street
Chicago, IL 60603
Phone: (312) 443-0700
www.lordbissell.com

LOCATIONS

Chicago, IL (HQ)
Atlanta, GA
Los Angeles, CA
New York, NY
London

MAJOR DEPARTMENTS/PRACTICES

Appellate • Bankruptcy, Insolvency & Reorganization •
Banks & Financial Institutions • Business Litigation &
Arbitration • Construction • Corporate • Employee
Benefits & Executive Compensation • Environmental •
Health Care • Insurance • Intellectual Property &
Technology • Labor & Employment • Product Liability •
Real Estate • Tax • Transportation • Wealth
Preservation & Estate Planning

THE STATS

No. of attorneys: 321
No. of offices: 5
Summer associate offers: 21 out of 25 (2001)
Managing Partner: Daniel I. Schlessinger
Hiring Chair: Lawrence A. Gray

NOTABLE PERKS

• Referral bonus
• Full-time business casual
• 401(k) and defined benefit plan

EMPLOYMENT CONTACT

Chicago and New York
Ms. Kerry Jahnsen
Recruiting Coordinator
Phone: (312) 443-0455
Fax: (312) 443-0336
kjahnsen@lordbissell.com

Atlanta
Ms. Erin Corbin
Recruiting Coordinator
Phone: (404) 870-4600
Fax: (404) 872-5547
ecorbin@lordbissell.com

Los Angeles
Ms. Marilyn Yruegaz
Recruiting Coordinator
Phone: (213) 485-1500
Fax: (213) 485-1200
myruegaz@lordbissell.com

BASE SALARY

Chicago, 2002
1st year: $125,000
Summer associate: $2,403/week

Atlanta, 2002
1st year: $100,000
Summer associate: $1,923/week

New York, 2002
1st year: N/A
Summer associate: $2,403/week

THE BUZZ
WHAT ATTORNEYS AT OTHER FIRMS ARE SAYING ABOUT THIS FIRM

• "Decent but quiet Chicago firm"
• "Well-known insurance law firm"
• "Incredibly stuffy"

Miller Nash LLP

3500 U.S. Bancorp Tower
111 SW Fifth Avenue
Portland, OR 97204-3699
Phone: (503) 224-5858
www.millernash.com

LOCATIONS

Portland, OR (HQ)
Seattle, WA
Vancouver, WA

MAJOR DEPARTMENTS/PRACTICES

Admiralty & Maritime • Agriculture • Aviation & Aircraft
Finance • Banking & Financial Institutions • Business &
Corporate • Construction • Education & Public
Institutions • Emerging Business, Technology & E-
Commerce • Employee Benefits • Environmental &
Natural Resources • Health Care • Insolvency,
Reorganization & Bankruptcy • Intellectual Property •
International • Labor & Employment • Land Use •
Litigation, Arbitration & Mediation • Products Liability •
Public Finance • Public Policy & Government • Real
Estate • Securities • Tax • Telecommunications &
Regulated Utilities • Trusts, Estates & Charitable
Organizations

THE STATS

No. of attorneys: 146
No. of offices: 3
Summer associate offers: 11 out of 16 (2001)
Managing Partner: Thomas C. Sand
Hiring Attorney: Bruce L. Campbell

NOTABLE PERKS

• Flexible health care
• Profit sharing plan
• 401(k)

EMPLOYMENT CONTACT

Ms. JoJo Hall
Director of Legal Recruitment
Phone: (503) 224-5858
Fax: (503) 224-0155
jhall@millernash.com

BASE SALARY

Portland and Seattle, 2002
1st year: $85,000
Summer associate: $1,400/week

THE BUZZ
WHAT ATTORNEYS AT OTHER FIRMS ARE SAYING ABOUT THIS FIRM

• "Very family-oriented"
• "Short hours, very nice people, traditional firm"
• "Losing ground"

Palmer & Dodge LLP

111 Huntington Avenue at Prudential Center
Boston, MA 02199
Phone: (617) 239-0100
www.palmerdodge.com

LOCATIONS

Boston, MA (HQ)

MAJOR DEPARTMENTS/PRACTICES

Affordable Housing Finance • Antitrust • Bankruptcy,
Reorganization & Workout • Biomedical • Business Law •
Construction • Employee Benefits & Executive
Compensation • Energy • Environmental & Land Use •
Finance • Hospitality • Insurance • Intellectual Property •
International • Internet/E-Commerce • Investment
Management • Labor & Employment • Litigation •
Patent • Private Client • Product Liability & Negligence
Defense • Public Law • Public Offerings & Public
Companies • Publishing & Entertainment • Real Estate •
Schools & Colleges • Tax • Technology •
Telecommunications • Transportation • Venture Capital
& Private Equity

THE STATS

No. of attorneys: 196
No. of offices: 1
Summer associate offers: 14 out of 17 (2001)
Managing Partner: Jeffrey F. Jones
Hiring Partner: Daryl J. Lapp

NOTABLE PERKS

• Dependent care program
• Emergency day care
• Subsidized health club membership
• Bar dues and exam fees paid

EMPLOYMENT CONTACT

Ms. Katy von Mehren
Director of Associate Recruitment
Phone: (617) 239-0172
Fax: (617) 227-4420
kvonmehren@palmerdodge.com

BASE SALARY

Boston, 2002
1st year: $110,000
2nd year: $120,000
3rd year: $130,000
4th year: $140,000
5th year: $150,000
6th year: $160,000
7th year: $170,000
8th year: $180,000
Summer associate: $2,115/week

THE BUZZ
WHAT ATTORNEYS AT OTHER FIRMS ARE SAYING ABOUT THIS FIRM

• "Good work environment"
• "Nice old firm, but fading in prestige"
• "Bold move with new office building location"

Preston Gates & Ellis LLP

5000 Columbia Center
701 Fifth Avenue
Seattle, WA 98104-7078
Phone: (206) 623-7580
www.prestongates.com

LOCATIONS

Seattle, WA (HQ)
Anchorage, AK
Coeur d'Alene, ID
Los Angeles, CA
Orange County, CA
Portland, OR
San Francisco, CA
Spokane, WA
Washington, DC (Preston Gates Ellis & Rouvelas Meeds LLP)
Hong Kong

MAJOR DEPARTMENTS/PRACTICES

Corporate/Business • Employment & Labor • Environmental/Land Use • Litigation • Municipal • Public Policy • Real Estate/Bankruptcy • Technology & Intellectual Property

THE STATS

No. of attorneys: 393
No. of offices: 10
Summer associate offers: 24 out of 28 (2001)
Chairman: Richard Ford
Managing Partner: B. Gerald Johnson
Hiring Partner: Paul J. Lawrence

NOTABLE PERKS

• $1,200 technology allowance every two years
• Free parking after three years
• Sabbatical after 10 years

EMPLOYMENT CONTACT

Ms. Kristine Immordino
Director, Attorney Recruiting
Phone: (206) 623-7580
Fax: (206) 623-7022
krisi@prestongates.com

BASE SALARY

Seattle, 2002
1st year: $100,000
2nd year: $104,000
Summer associate $1,900/week

THE BUZZ
WHAT ATTORNEYS AT OTHER FIRMS ARE SAYING ABOUT THIS FIRM

• "Good Seattle firm for Microsoft"
• "Enjoyable place to work"
• "Do they have more than one client?"

Schiff Hardin & Waite

6600 Sears Tower
233 South Wacker Drive
Chicago, IL 60606
Phone: (312) 258-5500
www.schiffhardin.com

LOCATIONS

Chicago, IL (HQ)
Lake Forest, IL
Merrillville, IN
New York, NY
Teaneck, NJ
Washington, DC
Wilmette, IL
Dublin

MAJOR DEPARTMENTS/PRACTICES

Bankruptcy • Construction • Corporate &
Securities/Finance/Municipal • Employee Benefits •
Energy • Environmental • Estate Planning/Tax •
Intellectual Property/Patent Prosecution • Labor &
Employment • Litigation/Antitrust/Class Action/
Reinsurance • Market Regulation • Product Liability •
Real Estate

THE STATS

No. of attorneys: 285
No. of offices: 8
Summer associate offers: 19 out of 20 (2001)
Chairman: Peter V. Fazio Jr.
Managing Partner: Scott E. Pickens
Hiring Attorney: Carol R. Prygrosky

NOTABLE PERKS

• Domestic partner benefits
• Two paid bar memberships
• Bar exam stipend
• Moving expenses

EMPLOYMENT CONTACT

Ms. Lilly Beltran
Law Student Recruitment Coordinator
Phone: (312) 258-4832
Fax: (312) 258-5600
lbeltran@schiffhardin.com

BASE SALARY

All offices, 2002
1st year: $125,000
Summer associate: $2,400/week

THE BUZZ
WHAT ATTORNEYS AT OTHER FIRMS ARE SAYING ABOUT THIS FIRM

• "Great for family/work balance"
• "Slipping"
• "Securities regulation specialty"

Stoel Rives LLP

900 SW Fifth Avenue
Suite 2600
Portland, OR 97204
Phone: (503) 224-3380
www.stoel.com

LOCATIONS

Portland, OR (HQ)
Boise, ID
Sacramento, CA
Salt Lake City, UT
San Francisco, CA
Seattle, WA
Tahoe City, CA
Vancouver, WA

MAJOR DEPARTMENTS/PRACTICES

Commercial Law, Bankruptcy
Construction & Design
Corporate Securities & Finance
Environment, Natural Resources, Land Use
Intellectual Property, Trademark, Patent
Labor & Employment, Employee Benefits
Public Law & Finance, Utilities
Real Estate
Tax, Trusts & Estates
Trial, Appellate

THE STATS

No. of attorneys: 375
No. of offices: 8
Summer associate offers: 12 out of 12 (2001)
Chair of the Firm: Henry H. Hewitt
Managing Partner: Stephen O. Kenyon
Hiring Attorney: Stephen L. Griffith (Portland)

THE BUZZ
WHAT ATTORNEYS AT OTHER FIRMS ARE SAYING ABOUT THIS FIRM

- "Very prestigious in the Pacific Northwest"
- "Stiff"
- "Welcoming to women, good part-time work policies"

NOTABLE PERKS

- Moving expenses up to $4,500
- Sabbatical
- Pre-tax flexible spending account
- Domestic partner benefits

EMPLOYMENT CONTACT

Portland
Ms. Michelle Baird-Johnson
Lawyer Recruiting Manager
Phone: (503) 294-9539
Fax: (503) 220-2480
mbjohnson@stoel.com

BASE SALARY

Portland, 2002
1st year: $80,000

Boise, 2002
1st year: $70,000

Salt Lake City and Seattle, 2002
1st year: $85,000

San Francisco, 2002
1st year: $110,000

Sutherland Asbill & Brennan LLP

999 Peachtree Street, NE
Atlanta, GA 30309-3996
Phone: (404) 853-8000

1275 Pennsylvania Avenue, NW
Washington, DC 20004-2415
Phone: (202) 383-0100
www.sablaw.com

LOCATIONS

Atlanta, GA
Austin, TX
New York, NY
Tallahassee, FL
Washington, DC

MAJOR DEPARTMENTS/PRACTICES

Antitrust & Trade Regulation • Biotechnology & Life
Sciences • Business Restructuring & Bankruptcy •
Corporate • Dealer & Franchise Litigation • Employment
Litigation • Energy & Commodities • Environmental •
Financial Services • Health Care • Hospitality •
Intellectual Property • International • Litigation •
Professional Liability Litigation •
Real Estate • Securities Enforcement & Litigation •
Structured Finance • Tax • Technology •
Telecommunications • Timber & Forest Products

THE STATS

No. of attorneys: 338
No. of offices: 5
Summer associate offers: 23 out of 28 (2001)
Managing Partner: James L. Henderson III
Hiring Partners: William G. Rothschild (Atlanta) and
James M. Cain (Washington)

THE BUZZ
WHAT ATTORNEYS AT OTHER FIRMS ARE SAYING ABOUT THIS FIRM

- "Losing nerdy image"
- "Nice Atlanta firm with good DC tax practice"
- "Concerned about quality of life"

NOTABLE PERKS

- Bagels and doughnuts every Friday
- Twelve weeks paid maternity leave
- Twice-monthly on-site massages

EMPLOYMENT CONTACT

Atlanta, Austin and Tallahassee
Ms. Victoria D. Tate
Manager of Attorney Recruitment
Phone: (404) 853-8000
Fax: (404) 853-8806
vdtate@sablaw.com

Washington, D.C. and New York
Ms. Melissa C. Wilson
Manager of Attorney Recruitment
Phone: (202) 383-0100
Fax: (202) 637-3593
mwilson@sablaw.com

BASE SALARY

Atlanta, 2002
1st year: $100,000
2nd year: $106,000
3rd year: $111,000
4th year: $116,000
Summer associate: 2Ls $1,750/week and 1Ls
$1,500/week

Washington, DC, 2002
1st year: $110,000
2nd year: $116,000
3rd year: $124,000
4th year: $132,000
Summer associate: 2Ls and 1Ls $2,100/week

Swidler Berlin Shereff Friedman, LLP

3000 K Street, NW
Suite 300
Washington, DC 20007-5116
Phone: (202) 424-7500

405 Lexington Avenue
New York, NY 10174
Phone: (212) 973-0111
www.swidlaw.com

LOCATIONS

Washington, DC (HQ)
New York, NY

MAJOR DEPARTMENTS/PRACTICES

Antitrust & Trade Regulation • Bankruptcy & Creditors'
Rights • Corporate • E-Commerce • Employment Law •
Energy • Environmental • Government Affairs •
Franchising • Housing • Insurance Coverage •
Intellectual Property • Litigation • Mergers &
Acquisitions • Public & Private Offerings •
Real Estate & Structured Finance • Tax/ERISA •
Telecommunications • Venture Capital

THE STATS

No. of attorneys: 300
No. of offices: 2
Summer associate offers: 23 out of 23 (2001)
Managing Partner: Barry B. Direnfeld
Hiring Attorneys: Brian Fitzgerald (Washington) and
Scott Zimmerman (New York)

NOTABLE PERKS

• Professional development program
• Summer associate pro bono fellowship program
• 4-week parental leave, 12-week maternity policy
• Free sodas (DC)

EMPLOYMENT CONTACT

Washington
Ms. Amy Fredenburg
Recruiting Coordinator
Phone: (202) 424-7658
Fax: (202) 424-7664
afredenburg@swidlaw.com

New York
Ms. Judith Abraham
Recruiting Manager
(212) 891-9325
Fax: (212) 891-9598
jmabraham@swidlaw.com

BASE SALARY

Washington, DC, 2002
1st year: $125,000
Summer associate: $2,400/week

New York, 2002
1st year: $130,000
Summer associate: $2,500/week

THE BUZZ
WHAT ATTORNEYS AT OTHER FIRMS ARE SAYING ABOUT THIS FIRM

• "No shot at making partner"
• "Up and coming lobbyists"
• "Good regulatory practice"

Troutman Sanders LLP

Bank of America Plaza
Suite 5200
600 Peachtree Street, NE
Atlanta, GA 30308-2216
Phone: (404) 885-3000
www.troutmansanders.com

LOCATIONS

Atlanta, GA (HQ)
Norfolk, VA
Richmond, VA
Tysons Corner, VA
Virginia Beach, VA
Washington, DC
Hong Kong
London

MAJOR DEPARTMENTS/PRACTICES

Corporate
Finance
Litigation
Public Law (Regulatory)
Real Estate

THE STATS

No. of attorneys: 497
No. of offices: 8
Summer associate offers: 38 out of 42 (2001)
Managing Partner: Robert W. Webb Jr.
Hiring Attorney: Stephen E. Lewis

NOTABLE PERKS

• Tickets to sporting events
• Health club membership
• Associate retreat

EMPLOYMENT CONTACT

Summer Associates
Ms. Clare Roath
Recruiting Manager
Phone: (404) 885-3000
Fax: (404) 962-6572
clare.roath@troutmansanders.com

Laterals/Entry Level
Ms. Betsy Glass
Director of Recruiting
Phone: (404) 885-3000
Fax: (404) 962-6927
betsy.glass@troutmansanders.com

BASE SALARY

Atlanta, 2002
1st year: $100,000
Summer associate: $1,750/week

Norfolk and Virginia Beach, 2002
1st year: $85,000
Summer associate: $1,750/week

Richmond, 2002
1st year: $90,000
Summer associate: $1,750/week

Tysons Corner and Washington, DC, 2002
1st year: $120,000
Summer associate: $2,300/week

 **THE BUZZ**
WHAT ATTORNEYS AT OTHER FIRMS ARE SAYING ABOUT THIS FIRM

• "Family friendly"
• "Highly sophisticated"
• "Good ol' boys"

Venture Law Group

2775 Sand Hill Road
Menlo Park, CA 94025
Phone: (650) 854-4488
www.vlg.com

LOCATIONS

Menlo Park, CA (HQ)
Kirkland, WA
Reston, VA
San Francisco, CA

MAJOR DEPARTMENTS/PRACTICES

Corporate & Securities
Intellectual Property
Tax, Compensation & Employee Benefits

THE STATS

No. of attorneys: 78
No. of offices: 4
Summer associate offers: 9 out of 16 (2001)
Managing Partner: Craig W. Johnson
Hiring Partner: Michael A. Morrissey

NOTABLE PERKS

• Profit-sharing
• Associate equity programs

EMPLOYMENT CONTACT

Ms. Coryn Lake
Human Resources Manager
Phone: (650) 854-4488
Fax: (650) 233-8386
jobs@vlg.com

BASE SALARY

Menlo Park, 2002
1st year: $100,000
2nd year: $105,000
3rd year: $115,000
4th year: $130,000
Summer associate: $2,400/week

THE BUZZ
WHAT ATTORNEYS AT OTHER FIRMS ARE SAYING ABOUT THIS FIRM

• "Dot-bomb"
• "They did not hire their summer class"
• "Don't count them out yet"

Wolf, Block, Schorr and Solis-Cohen LLP

1650 Arch Street
Philadelphia, PA 19103-2097
Phone: (215) 977-2362
www.wolfblock.com

LOCATIONS

Philadelphia, PA (HQ)
Cherry Hill, NJ
Harrisburg, PA
Newark, NJ
New York, NY
Norristown, PA
Wilmington, DE

MAJOR DEPARTMENTS/PRACTICES

Business Litigation • Communication • Complex
Liability/Surety/Fidelity • Corporate/Securities •
Employee Benefits • Employee Services • Environmental
Law • Estates & Trusts • Family Law • Financial
Services • Government Assisted & Affordable Housing •
Health Law • Intellectual Property & Information
Technology • Real Estate • Tax • Utility Regulation

THE STATS

No. of attorneys: 257
No. of offices: 7
Summer associate offers: 16 out of 19 (2001)
Chairman: Mark Alderman
Hiring Attorney: Jodi T. Plavner

NOTABLE PERKS

• Emergency child care
• Four weeks paid vacation
• Domestic partner benefits
• Parental leave

EMPLOYMENT CONTACT

Ms. Eileen M. McMahon
Director, Legal Personnel & Recruitment
Phone: (215) 977-2362
emcmahon@wolfblock.com

BASE SALARY

Philadelphia, 2002
1st year: $107,000
Summer associate: $2,050/week

New York, 2002
1st year: $110,000
Summer associate: $2,100/week

THE BUZZ
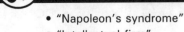
WHAT ATTORNEYS AT OTHER FIRMS ARE SAYING ABOUT THIS FIRM

• "Napoleon's syndrome"
• "Intellectual firm"
• "Shrewd"

LEGAL EMPLOYER DIRECTORY

VAULT CAREER LIBRARY

Akin, Gump, Strauss, Hauer & Feld, L.L.P.
Robert S. Strauss Building
1333 New Hampshire Avenue, NW
Washington, DC 20036
Phone: (202) 887-4000
www.akingump.com
Ms. Mary G. Beal
Director of Recruitment
Phone: (202) 887-4181
Fax: (202) 887-4288
mbeal@akingump.com

Akin, Gump, Strauss, Hauer & Feld, L.L.P.
2029 Century Park East
Suite 2400
Los Angeles, CA 90067
Phone: (310) 229-1000
Fax: (310) 229-1001
www.akingump.com
Ms. Julie A. Burnett
Recruiting Manager
Phone: (310) 229-3804
Fax: (310) 229-3892
jburnett@akingump.com

Akin, Gump, Strauss, Hauer & Feld L.L.P
590 Madison Avenue
New York, NY10022
Phone: (212) 872-1000
Fax: (212) 872-1002
www.akingump.com
Ms. Jean Marie Campbell
Manager of Legal Recruitment and
Professional Development
Phone: (212) 872-8099
Fax: (212) 872-1002
jmcampbell@akingump.com

Akin, Gump, Strauss, Hauer & Feld, L.L.P.
One Commerce Square
2005 Market Street, Suite 2200
Philadelphia, PA 19103
Phone: (215) 965-1200
Fax: (215) 965-1210
www.akingump.com
Ms. Kathleen Casey-Shannon
Director of Business Development and
Recruiting
Phone: (215) 965-1352
Fax: (215) 965-1210
kcaseyshannon@akingump.com

Akin, Gump, Strauss, Hauer & Feld, L.L.P.
300 West 6th Street
Austin, TX 78701
Phone: (512) 499-6200
Fax: (512) 499-6290
www.akingump.com
Ms. Emily Galatzan
Recruiting Coordinator
Phone: (512) 505-5434
Fax: (512) 499-6290
egalatzan@akingump.com

Akin, Gump, Strauss, Hauer & Feld, L.L.P.
1700 Pacific Avenue
Suite 4100
Dallas, TX 75201
Phone: (214) 969-2800
Fax: (214) 969-4343
www.akingump.com
Ms. Whitney Adams
Recruiting Manager
Phone: (214) 969-4647
Phone: (214) 969-2766
wadams@akingump.com

Akin, Gump, Strauss, Hauer & Feld, L.L.P.
1900 Pennzoil Place - South Tower
711 Louisiana Street
Houston, TX 77002
Phone: (713) 220-5800
Fax: (713) 236-0822
www.akingump.com
Ms. Stacey Nelson
Recruiting Coordinator
Phone: (713) 220-5800
Fax: (713) 236-0822
snelson@akingump.com

Akin, Gump, Strauss, Hauer & Feld, L.L.P.
300 Convent Street
Suite 1500
San Antonio, TX 78205
Phone: (210) 281-7000
Fax: (210) 224-2035
www.akingump.com
Ms. Christy Meador
Recruiting and Business Development
Manager
Phone: (210) 281-7181
Fax: (210) 224-2035
cmeador@akingump.com

Alston & Bird LLP
One Atlantic Center
1201 West Peachtree Street
Atlanta, GA 30309-3424
Phone: (404) 881-7000
www.alston.com
Ms. Emily Leeson
Director of Attorney Hiring &
Development
Phone: (404) 881-7014
Fax: (404) 881-7777
eleeson@alston.com

Arent Fox Kintner Plotkin &
Kahn, PLLC
1050 Connecticut Avenue, NW
Washington, DC 20036-5339
Phone: (202) 857-6000
www.arentfox.com
Ms. Amber Handman
Attorney Recruitment & Development
Manager
Phone: (202) 857-6146
Fax: (202) 857-6395
DCAttorneyRecruit@arentfox.com

Arnold & Porter
555 12th Street, NW
Washington, DC 20004
Phone: (202) 942-5000
www.arnoldporter.com
Ms. Lisa Pavia
Manager of Attorney Recruitment
Phone: (202) 942-5059
Fax: (202) 450-4500
Lisa_Pavia@aporter.com

Baker & Hostetler LLP
3200 National City Center
1900 East 9th Street
Cleveland, OH 44114-3485
Phone: (216) 621-0200
www.bakerlaw.com
Ms. Kathleen Ferdico
Attorney Recruitment and
Development Manager
Phone: (216) 861-7092
Fax: (216) 861-6618
kferdico@bakerlaw.com

Baker & McKenzie
One Prudential Plaza
130 E. Randolph Street
Suite 2500
Chicago, IL 60601
Phone: (312) 861-8000
www.bakernet.com
Ms. Eleonora Nikol
Phone: (312) 861-2924
eleonora.nikol@bakernet.com

Baker Botts L.L.P.
One Shell Plaza
910 Louisiana Street
Houston, TX 77002-4995
Phone: (713) 229-1234
www.bakerbotts.com
Ms. Melissa Moss
Director of Attorney Employment
Phone: (713) 229-2056
Fax: (713) 229-7856
melissa.moss@bakerbotts.com

Bingham Dana LLP
150 Federal Street
Boston, MA 02110
Phone: (617) 951-8000
www.bingham.com
Ms. Maris L. Abbene
Director of Legal Recruitment
Phone: (617) 951-8556
Fax: (617) 951-8736
mlabbene@bingham.com

Boies, Schiller & Flexner LLP
80 Business Park Drive
Suite 110
Armonk, NY 10504-1710
Phone: (914) 273-9800
www.bsfllp.com
Ms. Christine Schopen
Legal Recruiting Coordinator
Phone: (914) 273-9800
Fax: (914) 273-9810
cschopen@bsfllp.com

Brobeck, Phleger & Harrison LLP
One Market
Spear Street Tower
San Francisco, CA 94105
Phone: (415) 442-0900
Fax: (415) 442-1010
www.brobeck.com
Ms. Laurie Meyer
Recruiting Manager
Phone: (415) 979-2554
Fax: (415) 442-1010
lmeyer@brobeck.com

Brobeck, Phleger & Harrison LLP
38 Technology Drive
Irvine, CA 92618
Phone: (949) 790-6300
Fax: (949) 790-6301
www.joinbrobeck.com
Ms. Jeanne CaBell
Recruiting Manager
Phone: (949) 790-6425
Fax: (949) 790-6301
jcabell@brobeck.com

Brobeck, Phleger & Harrison LLP
550 S. Hope Street
Suite 2300
Los Angeles, CA 90071
Phone: (213) 489-4060
Fax: (213) 745-3345
www.joinbrobeck.com
Ms. Ellen Zuckerman
Firmwide Recruiting Manager
Phone: (213) 745-3562
Fax: (213) 239-1323
ezuckerman@brobeck.com

Brobeck, Phleger & Harrison LLP
2000 University Avenue
Palo Alto, CA 94303
Phone: (650) 331-8000
Fax: (650) 331-8100
www.joinbrobeck.com
Ms. Jennifer Sabbe
Recruiting Manager
Phone: (650) 812-2399
Fax: (650) 496-2600
jsabbe@brobeck.com

Brobeck, Phleger & Harrison LLP
12390 El Camino Real
San Diego, CA 92130
Phone: (858) 720-2500
Fax: (858) 720-2555
www.joinbrobeck.com and
www.brobeck.com
Ms. Caryn S. Schreiber
Attorney Recruiting Manager
Phone: (858) 720-2500
Fax: (858) 720-2555
cschreiber@brobeck.com

Brobeck, Phleger & Harrison LLP
370 Interlocken Boulevard
Suite 500
Broomfield, CO 80021
Phone: (303) 410-2000
Fax: (303) 410-2199
www.joinbrobeck.com
Mr. Martin Edwards
Office Administrator
Phone: (303) 410-2000
Fax: (303) 410-2199
medwards@brobeck.com

Brobeck, Phleger & Harrison LLP
1333 H Street, NW
Suite 800
Washington, DC 20005
Phone: (202) 220-6000
Fax: (202) 220-5200
www.joinbrobeck.com
Ms. Lisa Holland
Recruiting Manager
Phone: (202) 220-6000
Fax: (202) 220-5200
lholland@brobeck.com

Brobeck, Phleger & Harrison LLP
1633 Broadway
47th Floor
New York, NY 10019
Phone: (212) 581-1600
Fax: (212) 586-7878
www.joinbrobeck.com
Ms. Heather Rutner
Office Manager
Phone: (212) 237-2568
Fax: (212) 586-7878
hrunter@brobeck.com

Brobeck, Phleger & Harrison LLP
300 Crescent Court
Suite 1400
Dallas, TX 75201
Phone: (214) 468-3700
Fax: (214) 468-3704
www.joinbrobeck.com
Ms. Kathy Kimmel
Office Administrator
Phone: (214) 468-3760
Fax: (214) 468-3704
kkimmel@brobeck.com

Brobeck, Phleger & Harrison LLP
4801 Plaza On The Lake
Austin, TX 78746
Phone: (512) 330-4000
Fax: (512) 330-4001
www.joinbrobeck.com
Ms. Julie Lewis
Recruiting Manager
Phone: (512) 330-4055
Fax: (512) 330-4001
jklewis@brobeck.com

Brobeck, Phleger & Harrison LLP
2100 Reston Parkway
Suite 203
Reston, VA 20191
Phone: (703) 621-3000
Fax: (703) 621-3001
www.joinbrobeck.com
Ms. Lisa Holland
Recruiting Manager
Phone: (703) 621-3000
Fax: (703) 621-3001
lholland@brobeck.com

Bryan Cave LLP
One Metropolitan Square
211 North Broadway
Suite 3600
St. Louis, MO 63102
Phone: (314) 259-2000
www.bryancave.com
Ms. Jennifer J. Sloop
Recruiting Coordinator
Phone: (314) 259-2617
Fax: (314) 259-2020
jjsloop@bryancave.com

Bryan Cave LLP
1 Renaissance Square
Two North Central Avenue, Suite 2200
Phoenix, AZ 85004-4406
Phone: (602) 364-7000
Fax: (602) 364-7070
www.bryancave.com
Ms. Lynne Traverse
Recruiting Coordinator
Phone: (602) 364-7400
Fax: (602) 364-7070
ltraverse@bryancave.com

Bromberg & Sunstein LLP
125 Summer Street
11th Floor
Boston, MA 02110 -1618
Phone: (617) 443-9292
Fax: (617) 443-0004
www.bromsun.com
Ms. Christine A. Brennan
Recruitment Coordinator
Phone: (617) 443-9292
Fax: (617) 443-0004
employment@bromsun.com
Number of Attorneys: 36
Number of Offices: 1
Summer Offers (2001): 2 out of 3
Chairman: Lee Carl Bromberg
Hiring Attorney: Joel R. Leeman
Key Facts: All attorneys at Bromberg & Sunstein LLP are immersed in the challenging and fast-paced world of intellectual property law. We represent nationally prominent clients in a wide range of industries. Our attorneys are comfortable working in the most sophisticated and advanced areas of science and technology. Our work environment emphasizes collegiality and the sharing of specialized knowledge and expertise across disciplines both to deliver outstanding services to our clients and to foster professional growth of our attorneys.

Bryan Cave LLP
2020 Main Street
Suite 600
Irvine, CA 92614-8226
Phone: (949) 223-7000
Fax: (949) 223-7100
www.bryancave.com
Ms. Lynne Traverse
Recruiting Coordinator
Phone: (602) 364-7400
Fax: (602) 364-7070
ltraverse@bryancave.com

Bryan Cave LLP - Los Angeles
120 Broadway
Suite 300
Santa Monica, CA 90401-2386
Phone: (310) 576-2100
Fax: (310) 576-2200
www.bryancave.com
Ms. Sheryl Jones
Recruiting Coordinator
Phone: (310) 576-2303
Fax: (310) 576-2200
sajones@bryancave.com

Bryan Cave LLP
700 Thirteenth Street N.W.
Washington, DC 20005-3960
Phone: (202) 508-6000
Fax: (202) 508-6200
www.bryancave.com
Mr. Christopher Manning
Recruiting/Marketing Coordinator
Phone: (202) 508-6080
Fax: (202) 508-6200
csmanning@bryancave.com

Bryan Cave LLP
3500 One Kansas City Place
1200 Main Street, Suite 3500
Kansas City, MO 64105-2100
Phone: (816) 374-3200
Fax: (816) 374-3300
www.bryancave.com
Ms. Cristy Johnson
Recruiting/Marketing Coordinator
Phone: (816) 374-3362
Fax: (816) 374-3300
cmjohnson@bryancave.com

Bryan Cave Robinson Silverman
1290 Avenue of the Americas
New York, NY 10104
Phone: (212) 541-2000
Fax: (212) 541-4630
www.bryancave.com

245 Park Avenue (second NY office)
New York, NY 10167-0034
Phone: (212) 692-1800
Fax: (212) 692-1900

Ms. Elizabeth Breslow
Director Legal Personnel and Recruiting
Phone: (212) 541-1114
Fax: (212) 541-4630
efbreslow@bryancave.com

Cadwalader, Wickersham & Taft
100 Maiden Lane
New York, NY 10038
Phone: (212) 504-6000
cwtinfo@cwt.com
www.cadwalader.com
Ms. Monica R. Brenner
Manager of Legal Recruitment
Phone: (212) 504-6044
Fax: (212) 504-6666
monica.brenner@cwt.com

Cadwalader, Wickersham & Taft
1201 F Street, NW
Suite 1100
Washington, DC 20004
Phone: (202) 862-2200
Fax: (202) 862-2400
www.cadwalader.com
Ms. Amy Balbach
Manager of Associate Development and Recruitment
Phone: (202) 862-2356
Fax: (202) 862-2400
amy.balbach@cwt.com

Cadwalader, Wickersham & Taft
227 West Trade Street
24th Floor
Charlotte, NC 28202
Phone: (704) 348-5100
Fax: (704) 348-5200
www.cadwalader.com
Ms. Emily Morrison
Manager of Associate Development and Recruitment
Phone: (704) 348-5238
Fax: (704) 348-5200
emily.morrison@cwt.com

Cadwalader, Wickersham & Taft
265 Strand
London, WC2R 1BH, England
Phone: 44 (0) 20 7170 8700
Fax: 44 (0) 20 7170 8600
www.cadwalader.com
Mr. Matthew Crossland
Legal Recruitment Manager
Phone: 44 (0) 20 7170 8768
Fax: 44 (0) 20 7170 8600
matthew.crossland@cwt-uk.com

Cahill Gordon & Reindel
80 Pine Street
New York, NY 10005
Phone: (212) 701-3000
www.cahill.com
Ms. Joyce A. Hilly
Hiring Coordinator
Phone: (212) 701-3901
jhilly@cahill.com

Chadbourne & Parke LLP
30 Rockefeller Plaza
New York, NY 10112
Phone: (212) 408-5100
www.chadbourne.com
Ms. Bernadette L. Miles
Director of Legal Recruiting
Phone: (212) 408-5338
Fax: (212) 541-5369
bernadette.miles@chadbourne.com

Chadbourne & Parke LLP
350 South Grand Avenue
Suite 3300
Los Angeles, CA 90071
Phone: (213) 892-1000
Fax: (213) 622-9865
www.chadbourne.com
Mr. Jay Henneberry
Hiring Partner
Phone: (213) 892-2016
career@chadbourne.com

Chadbourne & Parke LLP
1200 New Hampshire Avenue, N.W.
Washington, D.C. 20036
Phone: (202) 974-5600
Fax:(202) 974-5602
www.chadbourne.com
Mr. Kenneth Hansen
Hiring Partner
Phone: (202) 974-5656
career@chadbourne.com

Choate, Hall & Stewart
Exchange Place
53 State Street
Boston, MA 02109
Phone: (617) 248-5000
www.choate.com
Ms. Robin Carbone
Director of Recruiting
Phone: (617) 248-5000
rcarbone@choate.com

Cleary, Gottlieb, Steen & Hamilton
One Liberty Plaza
New York, NY 10006
Phone: (212) 225-2000
www.cgsh.com
Ms. Norma F. Cirincione
Director of Legal Personnel
Phone: (212) 225-3150
Nyrecruit@cgsh.com

Clifford Chance Rogers & Wells LLP
200 Park Avenue
New York, NY 10166
Phone: (212) 878-8000
www.cliffordchance.com
Ms. Carolyn S. Older
Manager of Legal Recruiting
Phone: (212) 878-8252
Fax: (212) 878-8375
carolyn.older@cliffordchance.com

Cooley Godward LLP
5 Palo Alto Square
3000 El Camino Real
Palo Alto, CA 94306
Phone: (650) 843-5000
www.cooley.com
Ms. Jo Anne Larson
Director of Attorney Recruiting
Phone: (650) 843-5050
Fax: (650) 857-0663
jalarson@cooley.com

Coudert Brothers LLP
1114 Avenue of the Americas
New York, NY 10036
Phone: (212) 626-4400
www.coudert.com
Ms. Mary L. Simpson
Director of Legal Personnel
Phone: (212) 626-4400
Fax: (212) 626-4120
simpsonm@coudert.com

Covington & Burling
1201 Pennsylvania Avenue, NW
Washington, DC 20004-2401
Phone: (202) 662-6000
www.cov.com
Ms. Lorraine Brown
Director, Legal Personnel Recruiting
Phone: (202) 662-6200
legal.recruiting@cov.com

Cravath, Swaine & Moore
Worldwide Plaza
825 Eighth Avenue
New York, NY 10019-7475
Phone: (212) 474-1000
www.cravath.com
Ms. Lisa A. Kalen
Associate Director of Legal Personnel
and Recruiting
Phone: (212) 474-3216
Fax: (212) 474-3225
lkalen@cravath.com

Crowell & Moring LLP
1001 Pennsylvania Avenue, NW
Washington, DC 20004
Phone: (202) 624-2500
www.crowell.com
Ms. Michelle Blackwell Ray
Recruiting Coordinator
Phone: (202) 624-2779
Fax: (202) 628-5116
mblackwell@crowell.com

Davis Polk & Wardwell
450 Lexington Avenue
New York, NY 10017
Phone: (212) 450-4000
www.dpw.com
Ms. Bonnie Hurry
Director of Recruiting
Phone: (212) 450-4144
Fax: (212) 450-5548
bonnie.hurry@dpw.com

Debevoise & Plimpton
919 Third Avenue
New York, NY 10022
Phone: (212) 909-6000
www.debevoise.com
Ms. Ethel F. Leichti
Manager of Associate Recruitment
Phone: (212) 909-6657
Fax: (212) 909-6836
recruit@debevoise.com

Dickstein Shapiro Morin & Oshinsky LLP
1177 Avenue of the Americas
New York, NY 10036
Phone: (212) 835-1400
Fax: (212) 997-9880
www.legalinnovators.com
Ms. Dana M. DiCarlo, Esq.
Senior Manager of Recruiting and
Retention
Phone: (202) 955-6614
Fax: (202) 887-0689
DiCarloD@dsmo.com
Number of Attorneys: 51
Number of Offices: 2
Firm Revenues (2001):
$152,200,000
Chairman: Robin Cohen,
Managing Partner
Hiring Attorney: Peter J. Kadzik, Esq.
Key Facts: Dickstein Shapiro Morin &
Oshinsky LLP is a multi-service law
firm with offices in Washington, DC
and New York City dedicated to
innovative approaches to problem
solving. Attorneys at Dickstein
Shapiro value the kind of creative
thinking that converts obstacles into
opportunities. Dickstein Shapiro also
prides itself on its attorneys and
support staff who are client-oriented,
decisive, and innovative thinkers.
Dickstein Shapiro hosts one of the
most diverse practices around. The
Firm efficiently and effectively utilizes
the resources of its five core groups,
comprised of Complex Dispute
Resolution, Corporate and Finance,
Litigation, Legislative and Regulatory
Affairs, and Technology.

Dechert
4000 Bell Atlantic Tower
1717 Arch Street
Philadelphia, PA 19103-2793
Phone: (215) 994-4000
www.dechert.com
Ms. Alberta Bertolino
Director of Associate Recruitment
Phone: (215) 994-2296
Fax: (215) 994-2222
alberta.bertolino@dechert.com

Dickstein Shapiro Morin & Oshinsky LLP
2101 L Street, NW
Washington, DC 20037
Phone: (202) 785-9700
Fax: (202) 887-0689
www.legalinnovators.com
Ms. Dana DiCarlo
Senior Manager of Attorney Recruiting and Retention
Phone: (202) 955-6614
Fax: (202) 887-0689
DiCarloD@dsmo.com
Number of Attorneys: 275
Number of Offices: 2
Firm Revenues (2001):
$152,200,000
Summer Offers (2001): 26 of 30
Chairman: Angelo V. Arcadipane, Managing Partner
Hiring Attorney: Peter J. Kadzik, Esq.
Key Facts: Dickstein Shapiro Morin & Oshinsky LLP is a multi-service law firm with offices in Washington, DC and New York City dedicated to innovative approaches to problem solving. Attorneys at Dickstein Shapiro value the kind of creative thinking that converts obstacles into opportunities. Dickstein Shapiro also prides itself on its attorneys and support staff who are client-oriented, decisive, and innovative thinkers. Dickstein Shapiro hosts one of the most diverse practices around. The Firm efficiently and effectively utilizes the resources of its five core groups, comprised of Complex Dispute Resolution, Corporate and Finance, Litigation, Legislative and Regulatory Affairs, and Technology.

Dewey Ballantine LLP
1301 Avenue of the Americas
New York, NY 10019
Phone: (212) 259-8000
www.deweyballantine.com
Mr. William H. Davis
Legal Personnel & Recruiting Manager
Phone: (212) 259-7328
Fax: (212) 259-6333
nyrecruiting@deweyballantine.com

Dorsey & Whitney LLP
Suite 1500, 50 South Sixth Street
Minneapolis, MN 55402
Phone: (612) 340-2600
www.dorseylaw.com
Ms. Nancy J. Gendler
Director of Lawyer Recruiting
Fax: (612) 340-2868
gendler.nancy@dorseylaw.com

Downey, Brand, Seymour & Rohwer LLP
555 Capitol Mall
10th Floor
Sacramento, CA 95814
Phone: (916) 441-0131
Fax: (916) 441-4021
www.dbsr.com
Ms. Norma Paterson
Recruiting Director
Phone: (916) 441-0131 ext 6444
Fax: (916) 441-4021
npaterson@dbsr.com

Fenwick & West LLP
Two Palo Alto Square
Palo Alto, CA 94306
Phone: (650) 494-0600
www.fenwick.com
Ms. Karen Amatangelo-Block
Attorney Recruiting Manager
Phone: (650) 494-0600
Fax: (650) 494-1417
recruit@fenwick.com

Finnegan, Henderson, Farabow, Garrett & Dunner, L.L.P.
1300 I Street, NW
Suite 700
Washington, DC 20005-3315
Phone: (202) 408-4000
www.finnegan.com
Mr. Paul Sevanich
Attorney Recruitment Manager
Phone: (202) 408-4000
Fax: (202) 408-4400
attyrecruit@finnegan.com

Fish & Neave
1251 Avenue of the Americas
New York, NY 10020
Phone: (212) 596-9000
www.fishneave.com
Ms. Heather C. Fennell
Legal Recruitment Manager
Phone: (212) 596-9121
Fax: (212) 596-9090
hfennell@fishneave.com

Fish & Richardson P.C.
225 Franklin Street
Boston, MA 02110-2804
Phone: (617) 542-5070
www.fr.com
Ms. Jill McDonald
Director of Attorney Hiring
Phone: (858) 678-5070
Fax: (858) 678-5099
work@fr.com

Foley & Lardner
Firstar Center
777 East Wisconsin Avenue
Milwaukee, WI 53202
Phone: (414) 271-2400
www.foleylaw.com
Ms. Patti Dixon
Director of Legal Recruitment & Development
Phone: (561) 650-5050
Fax: (561) 655-6925
pdixon@foleylaw.com

Foley Hoag LLP
155 Seaport Boulevard
Boston, MA 02210
Phone: (617) 832-1000
www.foleyhoag.com
Ms. Dina M. Wreede
Director of Legal Recruiting and Professional Development
Phone: (617) 832-7060
dwreede@foleyhoag.com

Ford & Harrison LLP
1275 Peachtree St., NE
Suite 600
Atlanta, GA 30309
Phone: (404) 888-3800
Fax: (404) 888-3863
www.fordharrison.com
Wendi B. Fairchild
Director of Attorney Recruitment
Phone: (404) 888-3800
Fax: (404) 888-3863
apply@fordharrison.com
Number of Attorneys: 138
Number of Offices: 10
Chairman: C. Lash Harrison, Esq.,
Managing Partner
Key Facts: Founded in 1978 by 14 attorneys, Ford & Harrison LLP has grown to a national labor and employment firm with over 130 attorneys nationwide representing employers in connection with all phases of the employment relationship. Ford & Harrison seeks candidates who have excellent academic credentials, outgoing personalities, and strong work ethic. Please check out our website at www.fordharrison.com.

Fried, Frank, Harris, Shriver & Jacobson
One New York Plaza
New York, NY 10004
Phone: (212) 859-8000
www.friedfrank.com
Elizabeth M. McDonald, Esq.
Director of Recruiting
Phone: (212) 859-8621
Fax: (212) 859-4000
mcdonel@friedfrank.com

Fulbright & Jaworski L.L.P
1301 McKinney, Suite 5100
Houston, TX 77010
Phone: (713) 651-5151
www.fulbright.com
Ms. Cynthia A. Graser
Manager of Attorney Employment
Phone: (713) 651-3686
Fax: (713) 651-5246
CGraser@fulbright.com

Gibson, Dunn & Crutcher LLP
333 South Grand Avenue
Los Angeles, CA 90071-3197
Phone: (213) 229-7000
www.gibsondunn.com
Ms. Leslie Ripley
Director, Professional Development & Recruiting
Phone: (213) 229-7273
Fax: (213) 229-7520
lripley@gibsondunn.com

Goodwin Procter LLP
Exchange Place
53 State Street
Boston, MA 02109
Phone: (617) 570-1000
www.goodwinprocter.com
Ms. Maureen A. Shea
Director of Legal Recruitment
Phone: (617) 570-1288
Fax: (617) 523-1231
mshea@goodwinprocter.com

Gray Cary Ware & Freidenrich, LLP
400 Hamilton Avenue
Palo Alto, CA 94301
Phone: (650) 833-2000
www.graycary.com
Ms. Leslie Colvin
Professional Recruiting Director
Phone: (650) 833-2133
Fax: (650) 833-1530
lcolvin@graycary.com

Greenberg Traurig, LLP
200 Park Avenue
New York, NY 10166
Phone: (212) 801-9200
Fax: (212) 801-6400
www.gtlaw.com
Ms. Melissa Wally
Recruitment Coordinator
Phone: (212) 801-9237
Fax: (212) 805-9237
wallym@gtlaw.com
Number of Attorneys: 200 (NY)
Number of Offices: 17
Firm Revenues (2001):
$419,650,000 (firm gross revenues)
Summer Offers (2001): 6 of 6 (NY)
Chairman: Larry J. Hoffman
Hiring Attorney:
Stephen L. Rabinowitz
Key Facts: The New York office of Greenberg Traurig comprises seasoned practitioners who are nationally recognized leaders in their practice areas including banking, bankruptcy, corporate, entertainment, employment, governmental, information technology, intellectual property, international, litigation, real estate, tax, trusts & estates. Greenberg Traurig clients include Fortune 500 companies, established closely-held private and entrepreneurial companies, financial institutions, governments, new media and technology ventures, other law firms and charitable and civic organizations.

Greenberg Traurig, LLP
1221 Brickell Avenue
Miami, FL 33133
Phone: (305) 579-0500
www.gtlaw.com
Ms. Janet McKeegan
Director of Recruitment
Phone: (305) 579-0855
Fax: (305) 579-0717
mckeeganj@gtlaw.com

Gunderson Dettmer Stough Villeneuve Franklin & Hachigian, LLP
155 Constitution Drive
Menlo Park, CA 94025
Phone: (650) 321-2400
www.gunder.com
Ms. Corinne Dritsas
Director of Legal Recruiting
Phone: (650) 463-5248
Fax: (650) 321-2800
cdritsas@gunder.com

Hale and Dorr LLP
60 State Street
Boston, MA 02109-1816
Phone: (617) 526-6000
www.haledorr.com
Ms. Evelyn M. Scoville
Director of Legal Personnel
Phone: (617) 526-6590
Fax: (617) 526-5000
evelyn.scoville@haledorr.com

Harris Beach LLP
Albany, Buffalo, Ithaca, New York City,
Plattsburgh, Rochester and
Syracuse, New York, Newark, NJ and
Washington, DC
Phone: (585) 419-8800
Fax: (585) 419-8801
www.harrisbeach.com
Ms. Louise Spinelli
Manager of Legal Recruiting and
Training
Phone: (585) 419-8924
Fax: (585) 419-8817
lspinelli@harrisbeach.com

Heller Ehrman White & McAuliffe LLP
333 Bush Street
San Francisco, CA 94104-2878
Phone: (415) 772-6000
www.hewm.com
Craig Blumin, Esq.
Professional Recruitment Manager
Phone: (415) 772-6000
Fax: (415) 772-6268
cblumin@hewm.com

Hogan & Hartson L.L.P.
555 Thirteenth Street, NW
Washington, DC 20004
Phone: (202) 637-5600
www.hhlaw.com
Ms. Ellen M. Swank
Associate Recruitment and Professional
Development Director
Phone: (202) 637-8601
Fax: (202) 637-5910
emswank@hhlaw.com

Holland & Knight LLP
Suite 100
2099 Pennsylvania Avenue
Washington, DC 20006
Phone: (202) 955-3000
www.hklaw.com
Ms. Alida Coo-Kendall
Recruitment Coordinator (national)
Phone: (617) 573-5837
Fax: (617) 523-6850
acoo-kendall@hklaw.com

Howrey Simon Arnold & White, LLP
1299 Pennsylvania Ave., NW
Washington, DC 20004
Phone: (202) 783-0800
www.howrey.com
Ms. Janet Brown
Manager, Attorney Recruitment
Phone: (202) 783-0800
brownjanet@howrey.com

Hughes Hubbard & Reed LLP
One Battery Park Plaza
New York, NY 10004-1482
Phone: (212) 837-6000
www.hugheshubbard.com
Mr. Adrian Cockerill
Director of Legal Employment
Phone: (212) 837-6131
Fax: (212): 422-4726
cockeril@hugheshubbard.com

Hunton & Williams
Riverfront Plaza, East Tower
951 East Byrd Street
Richmond, VA 23219
Phone: (804) 788-8200
www.hunton.com
Ms. Christine Tracey
Legal Recruiting Manager
Phone: (212) 309-1217
Fax: (212) 309-1100
ctracey@hunton.com

Irell & Manella LLP
1800 Avenue of the Stars
Suite 900
Los Angeles, CA 90067-4276
Phone: (310) 277-1010
www.irell.com
Ms. Robyn Steele
Recruiting Administrator
Phone: (310) 277-1010
Fax: (310) 203-7199
rsteele@irell.com

Jenner & Block, LLC
One IBM Plaza
Chicago, IL 60611-7603
Phone: (312) 222-9350
www.jenner.com
Mr. James Flynn
Manager of Legal Recruiting
Phone: (312) 923-7881
Fax: (312) 527-0484
jflynn@jenner.com

Jones, Day, Reavis & Pogue
North Point - 901 Lakeside Avenue
Cleveland, OH 44114-1190
Phone: (216) 586-3939
www.jonesday.com
Ms. Jolie A. Blanchard
Firm Director of Recruiting
Phone: (202) 879-3939
Fax: (202) 626-1700
jablanchard@jonesday.com

Katten Muchin Zavis Rosenman
525 West Monroe Street
Suite 1600
Chicago, IL 60661-3693
Phone: (312) 902-5200
www.kmzr.com
Ms. Kelley Lynch
Director of Legal Recruiting
Phone: (312) 902-5526
Fax: (312) 577-8937
kelley.lynch@kmzr.com

Kaye Scholer LLP
425 Park Avenue
New York, NY 10022-3598
Phone: (212) 836-8000
www.kayescholer.com
Ms. Wendy Evans
Director of Legal Personnel
Phone: (212) 836-8000
Fax: (212) 836-8689
wevans@kayescholer.com

Kelley Drye & Warren LLP
101 Park Avenue
New York, NY 10178
Phone: (212) 808-7800
www.kelleydrye.com
Ms. Megan C. Clouden
Recruiting Coordinator
Phone: (212) 808-7510
Fax: (212) 808-7897
recruiting@kelleydrye.com

King & Spalding
191 Peachtree Street
Suite 4900
Atlanta, GA 30303-1763
Phone: (404) 572-4600
www.kslaw.com
Ms. Patty Blitch Harris
Recruiting Manager
Phone: (404) 572-4990
Fax: (404) 572-5100
pbharris@kslaw.com

King & Spalding
1730 Pennsylvania Avenue, N.W.
Washington, DC 20006-4706
Phone: (202) 626-2387
Fax: (202) 626-3737
www.kslaw.com
Ms. Kara K. O'Connor
Recruiting Manager
Phone: (202) 626-2387
Fax: (202) 626-3737
koconnor@kslaw.com

King & Spalding
1185 Avenue of the Americas
New York, NY 10036
Phone: (212) 556-2200
Fax: (212) 556-2222
www.kslaw.com
Ms. Abigail B. Golden
Recruiting Coordinator
Phone: (212) 556-2200
Fax: (212) 556-2222
agolden@kslaw.com

King & Spalding
1100 Louisiana
Suite 4000
Houston, TX 77002-5219
Phone: (713) 751-3200
Fax: (713) 751-3290
www.kslaw.com
Ms. Ann Harris
Recruiting Manager
Phone: (713) 751-3200
Fax: (713) 751-3290
aharris@kslaw.com

Kirkland & Ellis
Aon Center
200 East Randolph Drive
Chicago, IL 60601
Phone: (312) 861-2000
www.kirkland.com
Ms. Kimberley J. Klein
Attorney Recruiting Manager
Phone: (312) 861-8785
Fax: (312) 861-2200
kimberley_klein@chicago.kirkland.com

Kirkpatrick & Lockhart LLP
10100 Santa Monica Boulevard
Seventh Floor
Los Angeles, CA 90067
www.kl.com
Phone: (310) 552-5000
Fax: (310) 552-5001
Ms. Stephanie Kutrumbis
Recruiting Coordinator
Phone: (310) 552-5035
Fax: (310) 552-5001
skutrumbis@kl.com

Kirkpatrick & Lockhart LLP
Four Embarcadero Center
10th Floor
San Francisco, CA 94111
Phone: (415) 249-1000
Fax: (415) 249-1001
www.kl.com
Ms. Patsy R. Pressley
Office Administrator
Phone: (415) 249-1060
Fax: (415) 249-1001
ppressley@kl.com

Kirkpatrick & Lockhart LLP
1800 Massachusetts Avenue, N.W.
Second Floor
Washington, DC 20036-1221
Phone: (202) 778-9000
Fax: (202) 778-9100
www.kl.com
Ms. Halle S. Sabo
Legal Personnel Director
Phone: (202) 778-9190
Fax: (202) 778-9100
hssabo@kl.com

Kirkpatrick & Lockhart LLP
201 South Biscayne Boulevard
20th Floor
Miami, FL 33131-2399
Phone: (305) 539-3300
Fax: (305) 358-7095
www.kl.com
Mr. Scott S. Wilkenson
Office Administrator
Phone: (305) 539-3349
Fax: (305) 358-7095
swilkenson@kl.com

Kirkpatrick & Lockhart LLP
75 State Street
Boston, MA 02109
Phone: (617) 261-3100
Fax: (617) 261-3175
www.kl.com
Ms. Nancy F. Feldman
Legal Recruiting Coordinator
Phone: (617) 261-9257
Fax: (617) 261-3175
nfeldman@kl.com

Kirkpatrick & Lockhart LLP
One Riverfront Plaza
Seventh Floor
Newark, NJ 07102
Phone: (973) 848-4000
Fax (973) 848-4001
www.kl.com
Ms. Michele A. Bowens
Office Administrator
Phone: (973) 848-4015
Fax: (973) 848-4001
mbowens@kl.com

Kirkpatrick & Lockhart LLP
599 Lexington Avenue
New York City, NY 10022-6030
Phone: (212) 536-3900
Fax: (212) 536-3901
www.kl.com
Ms. Karen van Nouhuys
Office Administrator
Phone: (212) 536-3935
Fax: (212) 536-3901
vannouka@kl.com

Kirkpatrick & Lockhart LLP
240 North Third Street
Harrisburg, PA 17101-1507
Phone: (717) 231-4500
Fax: (717) 231-4501
www.kl.com
Ms. Wendy S. Neiss
Office Administrator
Phone: (717) 231-4511
Fax: (717) 231-4501
wneiss@kl.com

Kirkpatrick & Lockhart LLP
535 Smithfield Street
Pittsburgh, PA 15222-2312
Phone: (412) 355-6500
Fax: (412) 355-6501
www.kl.com
Roslyn M. Pitts, Esq.
Legal Personnel Director
Phone: (412) 355-8273
Fax: (412) 355-6501
rpitts@kl.com

Kirkpatrick & Lockhart LLP
2828 North Harwood Street
Suite 1800
Dallas, TX 75201-6966
Phone: (214) 939-4900
Fax: (214) 939-4949
www.kl.com
Ms. Mary Lou Weiss
Office Administrator
Phone: (214) 939-4912
Fax: (214) 939-4949
mweiss@kl.com

Latham & Watkins
633 West Fifth Street
Suite 4000
Los Angeles, CA 90071-2007
Phone: (213) 485-1234
www.lw.com
Ms. Debra Perry Clarkson
National Recruiting Administrator
Phone: (619) 236-1234
Fax: (619) 696-7419
debra.clarkson@lw.com

LeBoeuf, Lamb, Greene & MacRae, L.L.P.
125 West 55th Street
New York, NY 10019-5389
Phone: (212) 424-8000
www.llgm.com
Ms. Jennifer Mathews
Manager of Legal Recruiting & Retention
Phone: (212) 424-8849
Fax: (212) 424-8500
jmathews@llgm.com

Leonard, Street and Deinard
150 South Fifth Street
Minneapolis, MN 55402
Phone: (612) 335-1500
www.leonard.com
Ms. Mary Stenswick
Recruiting Coordinator
Phone: (612) 335-1528
Fax: (612) 335-1657

Mayer, Brown, Rowe & Maw
190 South LaSalle Street
Chicago, IL 60603-3441
Phone: (312) 701-7002
www.mayerbrownrowe.com
Ms. Laura L. Kanter
Legal Recruiting Coordinator
Phone: (312) 701-7003
Fax: (312) 701-7711
lkanter@mayerbrownrowe.com

McCutchen, Doyle, Brown & Enersen, LLP
Three Embarcadero Center
San Francisco, CA 94111
Phone: (415) 393-2000
www.mccutchen.com
Ms. Beth M. Harris
Attorney Recruitment Manager
Phone: (415) 393-2302
Fax: (415) 393-2286
bharris@mdbe.com

Manatt, Phelps & Phillips, LLP
11355 West Olympic Blvd.
Los Angeles, CA 90064
Phone: (310) 312-4000
Fax: (310) 312-4224
www.manatt.com
Ms. Kimberly A. Firment
Recruiting Manager
Phone: (310) 312-4187
Fax: (310) 312-4224
kfirment@manatt.com
Number of Professionals: 280
Number of Offices: 7
Firm Revenues (2001): $120 million
Summer Offers (2001): 12
Chief Executive: Paul H. Irving
Hiring Attorney: Keith Allen-Niesen
Key Facts: Founded in 1965, Manatt, Phelps & Phillips, LLP, is recognized as one of the nation's premier law and consulting firms providing strategic counsel and government advocacy to the financial services and entertainment industries. Over the years, the Firm developed a broad commercial practice and a powerhouse litigation capability, with more than half of its professionals involved in dispute resolution for major national and international clients. Manatt clients are among the world's most prestigious enterprises from a variety of industries including energy and natural resources, entertainment, financial services, real estate and land use, healthcare, telecommunications and technology. Manatt professionals serve client needs from offices in Los Angeles, Orange County, Palo Alto and Sacramento, California; Washington, D.C.; and Mexico City and Monterrey, Mexico.

McDermott, Will & Emery
227 West Monroe Street
Chicago, IL 60606-5096
Phone: (312) 372-2000
www.mwe.com
Ms. Karen K. Mortell
Legal Recruiting Manager
Phone: (312) 984-7784
Fax: (312) 984-7700
kmortell@mwe.com

McGuireWoods LLP
One James Center
901 East Cary Street
Richmond, VA 23219-4030
Phone: (804) 775-1000
www.mcguirewoods.com
Ms. Pamela S. Malone
Director of Lawyer Recruitment and Development
Phone: (202) 857-1732
Fax: (202) 857-1737
pmalone@mcguirewoods.com

Milbank, Tweed, Hadley & McCloy LLP
One Chase Manhattan Plaza
New York, NY 10005
Phone: (212) 530-5000
www.milbank.com
Ms. Joanne DeZego
Manager of Legal Recruiting
Phone: (212) 530-5966
Fax: (212) 530-5219
Jdezego@milbank.com

Mintz Levin Cohn Ferris Glovsky and Popeo, P.C.
One Financial Center
Boston, MA 02111
Phone: (617) 542-6000
www.mintz.com
Ms. Julie E. Zammuto
HR Manager, Attorney Recruitment
Phone: (617) 348-4929
Fax: (617) 542-2241
jzammuto@mintz.com

Miles & Stockbridge P.C.
10 Light Street
Baltimore, MD 21202
Phone: (4100 727-6464
Fax: (410) 385-3700
www.milesstockbridge.com
Randi S. Lewis, Esq.
Director of Recruitment & Professional Development
Phone: (410) 385-3563
Fax: (410) 385-3700
rlewis@milesstockbridge.com
Number of Attorneys: 160
Number of Offices: 8
Summer Offers (2001): 5
Chairman: Lowell R. Bowen, Esq.
Hiring Attorney: Jeffrey H. Seibert, Esq.
Key Facts: Ranked third nationally and first for both atmosphere and overall experience in the 2001 Summer Associates' Survey conducted by "The American Lawyer" and "L" Magazine, our summer associate program is a dynamic program designed to provide summer associates with a variety of work and experiences that mirror the experience of a first year associate with Miles & Stockbridge.

Morgan, Lewis & Bockius LLP
1701 Market Street
Philadelphia, PA 19103-2921
Phone: (215) 963-5000
www.morganlewis.com
See www.morganlewis.com recruitment section for contacts in various offices

Morrison & Foerster LLP
425 Market Street
San Francisco, CA 94105-2482
Phone: (415) 268-7000
www.mofo.com
Ms. Jane Cooperman
Senior Recruiting Manager (Firm-wide Information)
Phone: (415) 268-7665
Fax: (415) 268-7522
jcooperman@mofo.com

Mitchell Silberberg & Knupp
11377 West Olympic Boulevard
Los Angeles, CA 90064
Phone: (310) 312-2000
Fax: (310) 312-3100
www.msk.com
Mr. Charles L. Curtis
Director of Human Resources
Phone: (310) 312-2000
Fax: (310) 312-3100
clc@msk.com
Number of Attorneys: 125
Number of Offices: 2
Chairman: Thomas P. Lambert
Hiring Attorney: Jean P. Nogues
Key Facts: Our 125 attorneys practice business law with an emphasis on Complex and Class Action Litigation, Intellectual Property & Technology, Entertainment and New Media, Labor and Employment, Immigration and Benefits, Corporate Business Transactions & Tax, Bankruptcy and Family Wealth Planning. Quality is the basis for our reputation as the premier mid size firm in Southern California. We achieve quality by maintaining a size that allows us to enforce rigorous hiring and performance standards and by concentrating our services within certain legal disciplines and industries in order to excel in our selected practice areas. Our hallmark is achieving the rare blend of extraordinary professional challenge with satisfying personal lives. Our attorneys receive and accept challenges and responsibility early in their careers. Our staffing practices and team approach foster interaction among all team members. MS&K is a great fit for you if you combine high academic achievement, creativity, a genuine love of the law, a commitment to providing quality client service, take pride in doing the best job every time, good interpersonal skills, a sense of humor and take pleasure in contributing to a team that works together to achieve great outcomes for their clients. For additional information regarding the firm please visit us at www.msk.com.

O'Melveny & Myers LLP
400 South Hope Street
15th Floor
Los Angeles, CA 90071
Phone: (213) 430-6000
Fax: (213) 430-6407
www.omm.com
Ms. Michele Marinaro
Attorney Recruiting Manager
Phone: (213) 430-6677
Fax: (213) 430-8064
mmarinaro@omm.com
Number of Attorneys: 777
Number of Offices: 13
Summer Offers (2001): 89 of 92
Firm Revenues: $490 million (2001)
Chairman: Arthur B. Culvahouse
Hiring Attorney: David Enzminger
Key Facts: Visiting 40 campuses each year, O'Melveny & Myers LLP seeks over 100 of the nation's most promising law students to get to know us better through participation in our summer associate programs in: Century City (with approximately 90 attorneys); Los Angeles (280); New York (120); Newport Beach/Irvine Spectrum (70); San Francisco/Silicon Valley (80) and Washington D.C./Tysons Corner (130). All five of the firm's practice departments expect to enjoy continued growth and the need for talented new associates, experienced lateral attorneys and judicial clerks to join the O'Melveny team. We invite you to contact our Recruiting Administrators or visit www.omm.com to learn more about opportunities with our firm.

Munger, Tolles & Olson LLP
355 South Grand Avenue
35th Floor
Los Angeles, CA 90071-1560
Phone: (213) 683-9100
www.mto.com
Ms. Kevinn Villard
Director of Legal Recruiting
Phone: (213) 683-9242
Fax: (213) 687-3702
villardkc@mto.com

O'Melveny & Myers LLP - Century City
1999 Avenue of the Stars
Suite 700
Los Angeles, CA 90067
Phone: (310) 553-6700
Fax: (310) 246-6779
www.omm.com
Ms. Luly Del Pozo
Attorney Recruiting and Development Administrator
Phone: (310) 246-6821
Fax: (310) 246-6779
ldelpozo@omm.com

O'Melveny & Myers LLP - Newport Beach & Irvine Spectrum
610 Newport Center Drive
17th Floor
Newport Beach, CA 92660
Phone: (949) 760-9600
Fax: (949) 823-6994
www.omm.com
Ms. Kathy Fleming
Attorney Recruiting Administrator
Phone: (949) 823-6974
Fax: (949) 823-6994
kfleming@omm.com

O'Melveny & Myers LLP - San Francisco & Silicon Valley
275 Battery Street
26th Floor
San Francisco, CA 94111
Phone: (415) 984-8700
Fax: (415) 984-8701
www.omm.com
Ms. Paige Drewelow
Attorney Recruiting & Development Administrator
Phone:(415) 984-8937
Fax: (415) 984-8701
pdrewelow@omm.com

O'Melveny & Myers LLP - Washington, DC & Tysons Corner
555 13th Street, N.W.
Suite 500 West
Washington, DC 20004
Phone: (202) 383-5300
Fax: (202) 383-5414
www.omm.com
Ms. Jacqueline Wilson
Attorney Recruiting & Development
Administrator
Phone: (202) 383-5334
Fax: (202) 383-5414
jwilson@omm.com

O'Melveny & Myers LLP - New York
153 East 53rd Street
54th Floor
New York, NY 10022
Phone: (212) 326-2000
Fax: (212) 326-2061
www.omm.com
Ms. Cynthia Perrone
Attorney Recruiting and Development
Administrator
Phone: (212) 326-2877
Fax: (212) 326-2061
cperrone@omm.com

Orrick, Herrington & Sutcliffe LLP
Old Federal Reserve Bank Building
400 Sansome Street
San Francisco, CA 94111-3143
Phone: (415) 392-1122
www.orrick.com
Ms. Karen E. Massa
Recruiting Administrator
Phone: (415) 773-5588
Fax: (415) 773-5759
kmassa@orrick.com

Patton Boggs LLP
2550 M Street, NW
Washington, DC 20037
Phone: (202) 457-6000
www.pattonboggs.com
Ms. Kara Reidy
Director of Professional Recruitment
Phone: (202) 457-6000
Fax: (202) 457-6315
kreidy@pattonboggs.com

Paul Hastings, Janofsky & Walker LLP
555 South Flower Street
Los Angeles, CA 90071-2371
Phone: (213) 683-6000
Fax: (213) 627-0705
www.phjw.com
Ms. Joy McCarthy
Director of Attorney Programs
Phone: (213) 683-6000
recruit@phjw.com

Paul, Weiss, Rifkind, Wharton & Garrison
1285 Avenue of the Americas
New York, NY 10019
Phone: (212) 373-3000
www.paulweiss.com
Ms. Patty Morrissy
Legal Recruitment Director
Phone: (212) 373-2548
Fax: (212) 373-2205
pmorrissy@paulweiss.com

Pennie & Edmonds LLP
1155 Avenue of the Americas
New York, NY 10036
Phone: (212) 790-9090
www.pennie.com
Mr. Peter D. Vogl
Hiring Partner
Phone: (212) 790-6340
Fax: (212) 869-8864
voglp@pennie.com

Piper Rudnick LLP
6225 Smith Avenue
Baltimore, MD 21209-3600
Phone: (410) 580-3000
Fax: (410) 580-3001
www.piperrudnick.com
Ms. Lindy Hilliard
Legal Recruiting Manager
Phone: (410) 580-4664
Fax: (410) 580-3669
lindy.hilliard@piperrudnick.com
Number of Attorneys: 822
Number of Offices: 11
Summer Offers (2001): 46 out of 56
Chairpersons: Frank Burch and Lee Miller
Co-National Hiring Partners: Sally McDonald and Jim Mathias
Key Facts: Piper Rudnick has more than 800 lawyers working in Chicago, Washington, Baltimore, New York, Tampa, Philadelphia, Dallas, Reston, Los Angeles and New Jersey. The firm's practice is focused on: (1) Business and Technology: communications, intellectual property, information technology, e-commerce, life sciences and corporate IPO's, mergers and acquisitions; (2) Real Estate: industrial, commercial and residential property transactions, finance and securities; (3) Litigation: white collar, national products liability, securities litigation, and government regulatory practices. Other disciplines include: business tax, bankruptcy, labor, employee benefits, health care, insurance, public finance and estate planning. We like what we do, we like one another and we'd like you to consider joining us. Please take time to learn more about the firm at www.piperrudnick.com.

Perkins Coie LLP
1201 Third Avenue
Suite 4800
Seattle, WA 98101-3099
Phone: (206) 583-8888
www.perkinscoie.com
Ms. Laura MacDougall Kader
Lawyer Personnel Recruiter
Phone: (206) 583-8888
Fax: (206) 583-8500
LKader@perkinscoie.com

Pillsbury Winthrop LLP
One Battery Park Plaza
New York, NY 10004
Phone: (212) 858-1000
Ms. Dorrie Ciavatta
NY, CT and Foreign Office Recruiting
dciavatta@pillsburywinthrop.com

Proskauer Rose LLP
1585 Broadway
New York, NY 10036
Phone: (212) 969-3000
www.proskauer.com
Ms. Diane M. Kolnik
Manager of Legal Recruiting
Phone: (212) 969-5060
dkolnik@proskauer.com

Ropes & Gray
One International Plaza
Boston, MA 02110-2624
Phone: (617) 951-7000
www.ropesgray.com
Mr. Thomas A. Grewe
Director of Legal Recruiting
Phone: (617) 951-7239 (local)
(800) 951-4888 (long distance)
Fax: (617) 951-7050
legalhiring@ropesgray.com

Ross, Dixon & Bell
2001 K Street, N.W.
Washington, DC 20006
Phone: (202) 662-2000
Fax: (202) 662-2190
www.rdblaw.com
Ms. Rhonda Hill
Recruiting Coordinator
Phone: (202) 662-2933
Fax: (202) 662-2190
rhill@rdblaw.com

Schnader Harrison Segal & LLP
1600 Market Street
Suite 3600
Philadelphia, PA 19103
Phone: (215) 751-2000
Fax: (215) 751-2205
www.schnader.com
Jamie P. O'Brien
Manager of Legal Recruitment
Phone: (215) 751-2225
Fax: (215) 751-2205
jobrien@schnader.com

Schulte Roth & Zabel LLP
919 Third Avenue
New York, NY 10022
Phone: (212) 756-2000
www.srz.com
Ms. Lisa Drew
Director of Recruiting
Phone: (212) 756-2093
Fax: (212) 593-5955
lisa.drew@srz.com

Shaw Pittman LLP
2300 N Street, NW
Washington, DC 20037
Phone: (202) 663-8000
Fax: (202) 663-8007
www.shawpittman.com
Ms. Kathleen A. Kelly
Chief Recruiting Officer and Director of
Professional Programs
Phone: (202) 663-8394
Fax: (202) 663-9245
kathy.kelly@shawpittman.com

Shearman & Sterling
599 Lexington Avenue
New York, NY 10022
Phone: (212) 848-4000
www.shearman.com
Ms. Suzanne Ryan
Manager, Professional Recruiting
Phone: (212) 848-4592
Fax: (212) 848-7179
sryan@shearman.com

Sidley Austin Brown & Wood LLP
Bank One Plaza
10 South Dearborn Street
Chicago, IL 60603
Phone: (312) 853-7000
www.sidley.com
Ms. Jennifer C. Hernandez
Recruiting Manager
Phone: (312) 853-7495
Fax: (312) 853-7036
jherna01@sidley.com

Simpson Thacher & Bartlett
425 Lexington Avenue
New York, NY 10017
Phone: (212) 455-2000
www.simpsonthacher.com
Ms. Dee Pifer
Director of Legal Employment
Phone: (212) 455-2687
Fax: (212) 455-2502
dpifer@stblaw.com

Skadden, Arps, Slate, Meagher & Flom LLP and Affiliates
4 Times Square
New York, NY 10036
Phone: (212) 735-3000
www.skadden.com
Ms. Carol Lee H. Sprague
Director of Legal Hiring
Phone: (212) 735-3815
Fax: (212) 735-2000
csprague@skadden.com

Skadden, Arps, Slate, Meagher & Flom LLP
300 South Grand Avenue
34th Floor
Los Angeles, CA 90071
Phone: (213) 687-5000
Fax: (213) 687-5600
www.skadden.com
Ms. Kendall Nohre
Legal Hiring Coordinator
Phone: (213) 687-5598
Fax: (213) 687-5600
knohre@skadden.com

Skadden, Arps, Slate, Meagher & Flom LLP
525 University Avenue
Suite 1100
Palo Alto, CA 94301
Phone: (650) 470-4500
Fax: (650) 470-4570
www.skadden.com
Ms. Jazmin Cabrera
Legal Hiring Coordinator
Phone: (650) 470-4500
Fax: (650) 470-4570
jcabrera@skadden.com

Skadden, Arps, Slate, Meagher & Flom LLP
Four Embarcadero Center
Suite 3800
San Francisco, CA 94111
Phone: (415) 984-6400
Fax: (415) 984-2698
www.skadden.com
Ms. Roxanne Gabrielle Hall
Administrative Manager
Phone:(415) 984-6400
Fax: (415) 984-2698
ghall@skadden.com

Skadden, Arps, Slate, Meagher & Flom LLP
1440 New York Avenue, N.W.
Washington, DC 20005
Phone: (202) 371-7000
Fax: (202) 393-5760
www.skadden.com
Ms. Kimberly C. Barry
Professional Personnel Administrator
Phone: (202) 371-7730
Fax: (202) 393-5760
kibarry@skadden.com

Skadden, Arps, Slate, Meagher & Flom LLP
One Rodney Square
Box 636
Wilmington, DE 19899
Phone: (302) 651-3211
Fax: (302) 651-3001
www.skadden.com
Ms. Jean M. DiSabatino
Legal Hiring Administrator
Phone: (302) 651-3211
Fax: (302) 651-3001
jdisabat@skadden.com

Skadden, Arps, Slate, Meagher & Flom (Illinois)
333 West Wacker Drive
Chicago, IL 60606
Phone: (312) 407-0700
Fax: (312) 407-0411
www.skadden.com
Ms. Ann Cohen
Legal Hiring Administrator
Phone: (312) 407-0845
Fax: (312) 407-0411
acohen@skadden.com

Skadden, Arps, Slate, Meagher & Flom LLP
One Beacon Street
Boston, MA 02108
Phone: (617) 573-4800
Fax: (617) 573-4822
www.skadden.com
Ms. Michelle Benoit
Supervisor of Attorney Development & Hiring
Phone: (617) 573-4880
Fax: (617) 573-4822
mbenoit@skadden.com

Skadden, Arps, Slate, Meagher & Flom LLP
1600 Smith Street
Suite 4400
Houston, TX 77002
Phone: (713) 655-5100
Fax: (713) 655-5200
www.skadden.com
Ms. Paula Goodson
Administrative Coordinator
Phone: (713) 655-5100
Fax: (713) 655-5200
pgoodson@skadden.com

Skadden, Arps, Slate, Meagher & Flom LLP (London)
One Canada Square
Canary Wharf
London, E14 5DS, UK
Phone: 011-44-171-519-7000
Fax: 011-44-171-519-7070
www.skadden.com
Ms. Karen Pritchett,
Legal Hiring Coordinator
Contact for: Brussels, Frankfurt, London, Moscow, Paris & Vienna
Phone: 011-44-171-519-7000
Fax: 011-44-171-519-7070
kpritche@skadden.com

Skadden, Arps, Slate, Meagher & Flom LLP (International)
30/F Tower Two
Lippo Centre
89 Queensway
Central, Hong Kong
Phone: 011-852-2820-0700
Fax: 011-852-2820-0727
www.skadden.com

Skadden, Arps, Slate, Meagher & Flom LLP
Contact for Bejing, Hong Kong, Singapore, Sydney & Tokyo
Ms. Carol Sprague
4 Times Square
New York, NY 10036
Phone: (212) 735-2076
Fax: (212) 735 - 2000
csprague@skadden.com

Sonnenschein Nath & Rosenthal
8000 Sears Tower
Chicago, IL 60606
Phone: (312) 876-8000
www.sonnenschein.com
Ms. Lori L. Nowak
Recruitment Coordinator
Phone: (312) 876-8112
Fax: (312) 876-7934
lnowak@sonnenschein.com

Steptoe & Johnson LLP
1330 Connecticut Avenue, NW
Washington, DC 20036
Phone: (202) 429-3000
www.steptoe.com
Ms. Rosemary Kelly Morgan
Director of Attorney Services and
Recruiting
Phone: (202) 429-8036
Fax: (202) 828-3661
legal_recruiting@steptoe.com

Stroock & Stroock & Lavan LLP
180 Maiden Lane
New York, NY 10038
Phone: (212) 806-5400
www.stroock.com
Ms. Diane Cohen
Director of Legal Personnel and
Recruiting
Phone: (212) 806-5406
Fax: (212) 806-6006
dcohen@stroock.com

Sullivan & Cromwell
125 Broad Street
New York, NY 10004
Phone: (212) 558-4000
www.sullcrom.com
Ms. Sarah K. Cannady
Manager of Legal Recruiting
Phone: (212) 558-4847
cannadys@sullcrom.com

Testa, Hurwitz & Thibeault, LLP
125 High Street
Boston, MA 02110
Phone: (617) 248-7000
www.tht.com
Ms. Judith A. St. John
Recruiting Administrator
Phone: (617) 248-7401
Fax: (617) 248-7100
stjohn@tht.com

Thelen Reid & Priest LLP
New York (until November 30, 2002)
40 West 57th Street
New York, NY 10019
Phone: (212) 603-2000
New York (as of December 1, 2002)
875 Third Avenue
New York, NY 10022
Phone: (212) 603-2000
www.thelenreid.com
Ms. Diane Taranto (East Coast)
Attorney Recruiting Manager
Phone: (212) 603-2000
Fax: (212) 541-1518
dtaranto@thelenreid.com

Vinson & Elkins L.L.P.
2300 First City Tower
1001 Fannin Street
Houston, TX 77002-6760
Phone: (713) 758-2222
www.velaw.com
Ms. Patty Harris Calabrese
Director of Attorney Employment
Phone: (713) 758-4544
Fax: (713) 758-2346
pcalabrese@velaw.com

Wachtell, Lipton, Rosen & Katz
51 West 52nd Street
New York, NY 10019-6150
Phone: (212) 403-1000
www.wlrk.com
Ms. Ruth Ivey
Recruiting Director
Phone: (212) 403-1374
Fax: (212) 403-2374
recruiting@wlrk.com

Weil, Gotshal & Manges LLP
767 Fifth Avenue
New York, NY 10153
Phone: (212) 310-8000
www.weil.com
Ms. Donna J. Lang
Manager of Legal Recruiting
Fax: (212) 735-4502
donna.lang@weil.com

White & Case LLP
1155 Avenue of the Americas
New York, NY 10036-2787
Phone: (212) 819-8200
www.whitecase.com
Ms. Dana E. Stephenson
Director of Attorney Recruiting &
Employment
Phone: (212) 819-8200
recruit@whitecase.com

Wiley Rein & Fielding LLP
1776 K Street, NW
Washington, DC 20006
Phone: (202) 719-7000
www.wrf.com
Ms. Irena McGrath
Director of Professional Development
Phone: (202) 719-7000
Fax: (202) 719-7049
wrfrecruit@wrf.com

Williams & Connolly LLP
The Edward Bennett Williams Building
725 12th Street, NW
Washington, DC 20005
Phone: (202) 434-5000
Ms. Donna M. Downing
Recruiting Coordinator
Phone: (202) 434-5605
ddowning@wc.com

Willkie Farr & Gallagher
The Equitable Center
787 Seventh Avenue
New York, NY 10019-6099
Phone: (212) 728-8000
www.willkie.com
Ms. Patricia Langlade
Recruiting Coordinator
Phone: (212) 728-8469
Fax: (212) 728-8111
planglade@willkie.com

Wilmer, Cutler & Pickering
2445 M Street, NW
Washington, DC 20037-1420
Phone: (202) 663-6000
Fax: (202) 663-6363
www.wilmer.com
Ms. Mary W. Kiley
Lawyer Recruitment Administrator
JoinWCPLawyers@wilmer.com

Wilson Sonsini Goodrich & Rosati
650 Page Mill Road
Palo Alto, CA 94304
Phone: (650) 493-9300
www.wsgr.com
Attorney Recruiting Department
1 (888) GO2-WSGR
attorneyrecruiting@wsgr.com

Winston & Strawn
35 West Wacker Drive
Chicago, IL 60601-9703
Phone: (312) 558-5600
Fax: (312) 558-5700
www.winston.com
Ms. Paulette R. Kuttig
Senior Legal Recruiting Manager
Phone: (312) 558-5742
Fax: (312) 558-5700
pkuttig@winston.com

Winston & Strawn
333 South Grand Avenue
Los Angeles, CA 90071-1543
Phone: (213) 615-1700
Fax: (213) 615-1750
www.winston.com
Ms. Paulette R. Kuttig
Senior Legal Recruiting Manager
Phone: (312) 558-5742
Fax: (312) 558-5700
pkuttig@winston.com

Winston & Strawn
1400 L. Street, N.W.
Washington, DC 20005-3502
Phone: (202) 371-5700
Fax: (202) 371-5950
www.winston.com
Ms. Victoria Rozanski
Legal Recruiting Manager
Phone: (202) 371-5896
Fax: (202) 371-5950
vrozansk@winston.com

Winston & Strawn
200 Park Avenue
New York, NY 10166-4193
Phone: (212) 294-6700
Fax: (212) 294-4700
www.winston.com
Ms. Lisa Soderberg
Legal Recruiting Manager
Phone: (212) 294-6815
Fax: (212) 294-4700
lsoderbe@winston.com

Winston & Strawn
21 Avenue Victor Hugo
75116 Paris, France
Phone: (33-0) 1-53-64-82-82
Fax: (33-0) 1-53-64-82-20
www.winston.com
Ms. Paulette R. Kuttig
Senior Legal Recruiting Manager
Phone: (312) 558-5742
Fax: (312) 558-5700
pkuttig@winston.com

Winston & Strawn
43 Rue du Rhone
1204 Geneva, Switzerland
Phone: (41-22) 317-75-75
Fax: (41-22) 317-75-00
www.winston.com
Ms. Paulette R. Kuttig
Senior Legal Recruiting Manager
Phone: (312) 558-5742
Fax: (312) 558-5700
pkuttig@winston.com

LEGAL
SEARCH FIRM
DIRECTORY

Use the most **targeted** job search tools for lawyers on the Internet.

Vault's Law Job Board and VaultMatch™ Resume Database

▪ Law Job Board

The most comprehensive and convenient job board for legal professionals. Target your search by practice area, function, and experience level, and find the job openings that you want. No surfing required.

▪ VaultMatch™ Resume Database

Vault takes match-making to the next level: post your resume and customize your search by practice area, trial experience, level and more. We'll match job listings with your interests and criteria and e-mail them directly to your in-box.

Find out more at http://law.vault.com

Abelson Legal Search
1700 Market Street
Suite #2130
Philadelphia, PA 19103
Phone: (215) 561-3010
Fax: (215) 561-3001
www.abelsonlegalsearch.com
Cathy Abelson
President
Phone: (215) 561-3010
Fax: (215) 561-3001
abelson@abelsonlegalsearch.com

AMERICAN Legal Search
1425 21st Street South Suite 206
Birmingham, AL 35205
Phone: (205) 930-9128
Fax: (205) 930-9811
www.americanlegalsearch.com
Richard Brock, Esq.
President & General Counsel
Phone: (205) 930-9128
Fax: (205) 930-9811
Richard@americanlegalsearch.com

AMERICAN Legal Search
209 10th Ave South Suite 344
Nashville, TN
Phone: (615) 251-9600
Fax: (415) 532-1641
www.americanlegalsearch.com
Joe Freedman
CEO
Phone: (615) 251-9600
Fax: (415) 532-1641
joe@americanlegalsearch.com

Bickerton & Gordon, LLC
60 State Street
Suite 700
Boston, MA 02109
Phone: (617) 371-2929
Fax: (617) 371-2999
www.bickertongordon.com
Brion Bickerton; Richards Gordon
Principals
Phone: (617) 371-2929
Fax: (617) 371-2999
info@bickertongordon.com

E.P. Dine, Inc.
115 East 57th Street
Suite 1230
New York, NY 10022
Phone: (212) 355-6182
Fax: (212) 755-8486
www.epdine.com
Laurie Becker
President
Phone: (212) 355-6182
Fax: (212) 755-8486
Lbecker@epdine.com
Number of Recruiters/Consultants: 8
Domestic offices: 1
International offices: 0
Chairman: Laurie Becker, Esq.
Date founded: 1975
Percentage of business devoted to placing attorneys: 100%
2001 Placements (Law Firm vs. Corporate Legal Department): 30% of business is from placing partners, counsel and associates in law firms, 60% is from placing in-house counsel and 10% is from handling acquisitions and transfers of practice groups.
2001 Law Firm Placements (Associate vs. Partner): 80% of law firm placements were associates, 20% partners or counsel.
2001 Law Firm Placements (by Practice Area): 45% corporate, 20% litigation, 10% real estate, 10% tax, 10% bankruptcy, 3% intellectual property, 2% environmental.
Key Facts: The premier legal recruiting firm since 1975. Recruiters placing partners and associates in law firms, corporations and financial situations. Our in-house placements run the gamut from retained General Counsel searches to staff attorney searches. We also place attorneys in non-legal positions with top tier investment banks, consulting firms and other companies.

Carpenter Legal Search, Inc.
One Oxford Centre, Suite 3030
301 Grant Street
Pittsburgh, PA 15219-6401
Phone: (412) 255-3770
Fax: (412) 255-3780
www.carpenterlegalsearch.com
Lori J. Carpenter
President
Phone: (412) 255-3770
Fax: (412) 255-3780
lcarpenter@carpernterlegalsearch.com

Chicago Legal Search, Ltd.
180 North LaSalle Street
Suite 3350
Chicago, Illinois 60601
Phone: 312-251-2580
www.chicagolegalsearch.com
Gary A. D'Alessio, Esq.
President
Phone: 312-251-2580
Fax:312-251-0223
attorneys@chicagolegalsearch.com

Glasberg Olander Legal Search
269 South Beverly Drive, # 700
Beverly Hills, CA 90212
Phone: (310) 829-0191
Fax: (310) 829-0201
www.golegalsearch.com
M. Lauren Olander, Esq.
Partner
Phone: (310) 829-0191
Fax: (310) 829-0201
mlolander@golegalsearch.com

Interactive Legal Search Inc.
4900 Hopyard Rd. Suite# 240
Pleasanton, CA 94588
Phone: (800) 211-1513
Fax: (925) 468-0391
www.interactivelegalsearch.com
Gay Carter
President
Phone: (925) 468-0397
Fax: (925) 468-0391
GCILS@aol.com

Kaplan & Jass, Inc.
211 Congress Street
Boston, MA 02110
Phone: (617) 422-5678
Fax: (617) 422-5682
www.kaplanjass.com
Gail Kaplan
President
Phone: (617) 422-5678
Fax: (617) 422-5682
kaplanjass@kj1.com
Number of Recruiters/Consultants: 6
Domestic offices: 2
Chairman: Gail Kaplan
Date Founded: 1996
Percentage of business devoted to placing attorneys: 85%
2001 Law Firm Placements (Law Firim vs. Corporate Legal Department): 70% vs. 30%
2001 Law Firm Placements (Associates vs. Partner): 75% vs. 25%
Key Facts: Kaplan & Jass is a national legal recruiting firm servicing a client base of top law firms and corporations, with a special emphasis in intellectual property. IP positions at all levels in law firms and corporations nationwide include the areas of patent, trademark, licensing/transactional, and IP litigation. General corporate counsel positions are with major high technology, biotechnology, and pharmaceuticals clients. General legal openings are in the areas of corporate, litigation, tax, real estate, health care, trusts & estates, environmental and telecommunications.

Jane Sender Legal Search LLC
100 Boylston Street
Suite 1035
Boston, MA 02116
Phone: (617) 426-5300
Fax: (617) 426-0015
www.jslegalsearch.com
Sarah H. Minifie
Senior Recruiter
Phone: (617) 357-1642
Fax: (617) 426-0015
sminifie@jslegalsearch.com

Klausner Group, Ltd., The
45West 45th Street
New York, NY 10036
Phone: (212) 557-5800
Fax: (212) 557-3833
www.klausnergroup.com
Morley Klausner
President
Phone: (212) 557-5800
Fax: (212) 557-3833
mklausner@klausnergroup.com
Number of Recruiters/Consultants: 14
Domestic Offices: NYC
Chairman: Morley Klausner
Date founded: 1997
2001 Placements (Law firm vs. Corporate Legal Department): 60% Law Firm
2001 Law Firm Placements (Associates vs. Partner): 75% Associates
Key Facts: We are staffed with a top-notch team of attorneys and professional consultants whose goal is to be fully acquainted with the hiring requirements for our clients as well as the long-term personal and professional goals of the attorneys we represent. Each consultant focuses on the placement of attorneys who specialize in a particular area of the law. Additionally, each counselor concentrates on a defined geographic region. Thus, the counselors develop an expertise in their specific marketplace. This structure uniquely positions us to provide the intimate contacts of a local recruiter with the network of a national enterprise.

Klein Landau and Romm
1040 Avenue of the Americas
Suite 2400
New York, NY 10018
Phone: (212) 512-0523
Fax: (212) 512-0524
www.jurisjob.com
David Claypoole
Partner
Phone: (212) 512-0523
Fax: (212) 512-0524
dclaypoole@jurisjob.com

Klein Landau and Romm
1715 K Street NW
Suite 602
Washington, DC 20006
Phone: (202) 728-0100
Fax: (202) 728-0112
www.jurisjob.com
Gary Klein
President
Phone: (202) 728-0100
Fax: (202) 728-0112
gklein@jurisjob.com

Klein Landau and Romm
1500 Market Street
12th Floor, East Tower
Philadelphia, PA 19102
Phone: (215) 665-5729
Fax: (215) 665-5723
www.jurisjob.com
David Claypoole
Partner
Phone: (215) 665-5729
Fax: (215) 665-5723
dclaypoole@jurisjob.com

Major Legal Services, LLC
510 Park Plaza
1111 Chester Ave.
Cleveland, OH 44114
Phone: (216) 579-9782
Fax: (216) 579-1662
www.majorlegalservices.com
Dennis J. Foster
President
Phone: (216) 579-9782
Fax: (216) 579-1662
dennis@majorlegalservices.com

Northwest Legal Search, Inc.
P.O. Box 25186
Portland, OR 97298
Phone: (503) 296-9500
Fax: (503) 296-9555
www.nwlegalsearch.com
Linda Green Pierce
President
Phone: (503) 296-9500
Fax: (503) 296-9555
Linda@nwlegalsearch.com

New England Legal Search, LTD
280 Commonwealth Ave.
Suite 304
Boston, MA 02116
Phone: (617) 266-6068
Fax: (617) 266-8510
www.newenglandlegalsearch.com
Dee B. McMeekan & Linda J. Kline
Managing Directors
Phone: (617) 266-6068
Fax: (617) 266-8510
Number of Recruiters/Consultants: 3
Domestic Offices: Boston, Ma
International Offices: Affiliate
relationships worldwide
Chairman: Dee B. McMeekan,
Managing Director
Linda J. Kline, Managing Director
Date founded: 1982
Percentage of business devoted to
placing attorneys: 100%
2001 Placements (Law Firm vs.
Corporate Legal Department): 40%
vs. 60%
2001 Law Firm Placements
(Associates vs. Partner): 58% vs. 42%
2001 Law firm Placements (by
Practice Area): Corporate 75%
Litigation 10%
RE 10%
Tax 5%
Key Facts: New England Legal
Search, founded in 1982, is the
region's oldest attorney recruiting
firm. Comprised of three full-time
recruiters, all attorneys, we focus
exclusively on the permananet
placemnt of attorneys with law firms
and corporations. Our legal
experience, the depth of our
knowledge of legal careers, and our
commitment to and reputation for
exceptional client service have
enabled us to become the leading
legal recruiter in the region. NELS is a
Founding Member of the National
Association of Legal Search
Consultants and managing Director
McMeekan has served as its Vice
President and Board member.

Sivin Tobin Associates, LLC
516 Fifth Avenue, 14th Floor
New York, NY 10036
Phone: (212) 573-9800
Fax: (212) 573-6122
www.sivintobin.com
Eric Sivin or David Tobin
Principals
Phone: (212) 573-9800
Fax: (212) 573-6122
info@sivintobin.com
Number of Recruiters/Consultants: 10
Domestic Offices: 1
International Offices: 0
Chairman: Eric Sivin, David Tobin
Date Founded: 1994
Percentage of Business Devoted to
Placing Attorneys: 100%
2001 placements (Law Firm vs.
Corporate Legal Department): 75%
Law firm/25% Corporate Legal
Department
2001 Law Firm placements
(Associates vs. Partner): 40%
Associates/60% Partners
2001 Law Firm placements (by
Practice Area): All areas of business
related law
Key Facts: The two principals of Sivin
Tobin have an aggregate of over 35
years of legal recruiting experience.
Over that time frame, they have
placed a myriad of lawyers at firms
and companies throughout the US
and internationally. Many of those
attorneys have risen to senior
positions in their organizations,
providing Sivin Tobin with a range
and breadth of contacts throughout
the legal community which is second
to none. The firm's leading position in
partner and practice group movement
also enables it to work on associate
positions which other firms do not
have access to, enhancing its service
in that area. Finally, the firm is also
an industry leader in intellectual
property placement.

Swan Legal Search
11500 W. Olympic Blvd., Suite 370
Los Angeles, CA 90064
Phone: (310) 445-5010
Fax: (310) 445-0621
www.swanlegal.com
Delia K. Swan
Owner
Phone: (310) 445-5010
Fax: (310) 445-0621
info@swanlegal.com
Number of Recruiters/Consultants:
5 recruiters
Domestic Offices: Los Angeles
International Offices: None
Date Founded: November 3, 1997
Percentage of Business Devoted to
Placing Attorneys: 100%
2001 placements (Law Firm vs.
Corporate Legal Dept.): 90% law firm
vs.10% corporate legal Dept.
2001 Law Firm Placements (by
Practice Area): All Practice Areas
Key Facts: Swan Legal Search
conducts business in all of Northern
and Southern California. Comprised
of former practicing attorneys, SLS
understands what makes an attorney
successful, as well as what law firms
and in-house legal departments are
seeking. SLS was recently ranked by
the California Law Business section of
the Los Angeles and San Francisco
Daily Journal as one of the top 10
legal recruiting firms in California for
the placement of both partners and
associates. The success of SLS is a
direct reflection of the commitment,
accountability and integrity brought
into each search.

Phyllis Hawkins & Associates, Inc.
105 East Northern Avenue
Phoenix, AZ 85020
Phone: (602) 263-0248
Fax: (602) 678-1564
www.Azlawsearch.com
Phyllis Hawkins
President
Phone: (602) 263-0248
Fax: (602) 678-1564
phassoc@qwest.net

Zeldis & CO
300 Park Avenue. 17th floor
New York, NY 10022
Phone: (212) 691-5479
Fax: (212) 691-5582
www.zeldis.com
Nancy Zeldis
Phone: (212) 691-5479
Fax: (212) 691-5582
nzeldis@zeldis.com
Number of Recruiters/Consultants: 3
Domestic Offices: 1
International Offices: None
Date Founded: 1997
Percentage of Business Devoted to Placing Attorneys: 100%
2001 placements (Law Firm vs. Corporate Legal Dept.): 50/50
2001 Law Firm placements (Associates vs. Partner): 60/40
2001 Law Firm Placements (by Practice Area): All Practice Areas
Key Facts: We work closely with our clients and candidates to ensure the best possible fit. We work efficiently to bring the best candidates to market so as not to waste our clients' time. We present a candid and honest appraisal to best suit the needs of everyone.

Princeton Legal Staffing Group, LLC
116 Village Boulevard, Suite 200
Princeton, NJ 08540
Phone: (609) 730-8240
Fax: (609) 730-8363
www.princetonlegal.com
David S. Garber, Esq.
President
Phone: (609) 730-8240
Fax: (609) 730-8363
dgarber@princetonlegal.com

Sterling Careers, Inc.
777 S. Flagler Dr.
#800 - West Tower
Phillips Point, FL 33401
Phone: (561) 514-8001
Fax: (561) 814-8435
www.sterlingcareers.biz
Yvonne L. Ellis
President
Yvonne@sterlingcareers.biz

APPENDIX

Alphabetical Index of Law Firms

ALPHABETICAL INDEX OF LAW FIRMS (cont'd)

Firms by Main Offices

Armonk, NY

Boies, Schiller & Flexner LLP 348

Atlanta, GA

Alston & Bird LLP 538

Kilpatrick Stockton LLP .621

King & Spalding 340

Troutman Sanders LLP 631

Sutherland Asbill & Brennan LLP 629

Boston, MA

Bingham Dana LLP 556

Brown Rudnick Berlack Israels, LLP 615

Choate, Hall & Stewart 580

Fish & Richardson P.C. 590

Foley Hoag LLP 602

Goodwin Procter LLP 522

Hale and Dorr LLP 264

Mintz Levin Cohn Ferris Glovsky and Popeo, P.C. . . .598

Palmer & Dodge LLP 625

Ropes & Gray 306

Testa, Hurwitz & Thibeault, LLP 540

Chicago, IL

Baker & McKenzie 404

Jenner & Block, LLP 518

Katten Muchin Zavis Rosenman 600

Kirkland & Ellis 170

Lord, Bissell & Brook 623

Mayer, Brown, Rowe & Maw 358

McDermott, Will & Emery 498

Schiff Hardin & Waite 627

Sidley Austin Brown & Wood LLP 206

Sonnenschien Nath & Rosenthal 524

Winston & Strawn 384

Cleveland, OH

Baker & Hostetler LLP 564

Jones, Day, Reavis & Pogue 248

Dallas, TX

Haynes and Boone, LLP 620

Houston, TX

Andrews & Kurth L.L.P. 611

Baker Botts L.L.P. 474

Bracewell & Patterson, L.L.P. 614

Fulbright & Jaworski L.L.P. 490

Vinson & Elkins L.L.P. 578

Los Angeles, CA

Gibson, Dunn & Crutcher LLP 222

Irell & Manella LLP 514

Latham & Watkins 144

Munger, Tolles & Olson LLP 394

O'Melveny & Myers LLP .256

Paul, Hastings, Janofsky & Walker LLP 432

Menlo Park, CA

Gunderson Dettmer Stough Villeneuve Franklin &
Hachigian, LLP 586

Venture Law Group 632

Miami, FL

Greenberg Traurig, LLP 584

Milwaukee, WI

Foley & Lardner 548

Minneapolis, MN

Dorsey & Whitney LLP 576

New York, NY

Cadwalader, Wickersham & Taft 412

Cahill Gordon & Reindel .440

Chadbourne & Parke LLP 510

Cleary, Gottlieb, Steen & Hamilton 128

Clifford Chance Rogers & Wells LLP 280

FIRMS BY MAIN OFFICES (cont'd)

FIRMS BY MAIN OFFICES (cont'd)

About the Authors

Brook Moshan is the law editor at Vault. She holds a JD from the Fordham University School of Law and a BA in English from Vassar College. Before joining Vault, she was a prosecutor for the City of New York. This is her second Vault Guide.

Marcy Lerner is the Executive Editor at Vault. She holds a BA in history from the University of Virginia and an MA in history from Yale University. This is her fifth Law Guide.

Hussam Hamadeh is co-founder of Vault. He holds a BA in economics from ULCA and a JD/MBA from the Wharton School of Business and the University of Pennsylvania Law School, where he was an editor on Law Review. He is a member of the New York Bar and is a member of the Board of Managers of the University of Pennsylvania Law School.

Mark Oldman is co-founder of Vault. He graduated Phi Beta Kappa from Stanford University with a BA and MA in English and a JD from Stanford Law School. He designed and taught a course on the U.S. Supreme Court at Stanford University and has authored numerous books on career-related subjects. He is a member of the New York Bar.

Tyya N. Turner is a graduate of Howard University. She has worked at several publishing companies, including Pocket Books, McGraw-Hill and Miller Freeman, as both a writer and an editor.

Vera Djordjevich is a writer and editor in New York. She holds a JD from New York University and a BA in history from Stanford University. A former litigator, she has worked as an editor at American Lawyer Media and is currently the senior editor of On the Page magazine (www.onthepage.org).

Dina Di Maio is a freelance writer. She holds an MFA in writing from New York University and a BA in communications from Meredith College. Dina has written and edited for the American Bar Association. One of these days she will finish law school.

Cover Design and layout by Robert Schipano.

Use the most **targeted** job search tools for lawyers on the Internet.

Vault's Law Job Board and VaultMatch™ Resume Database

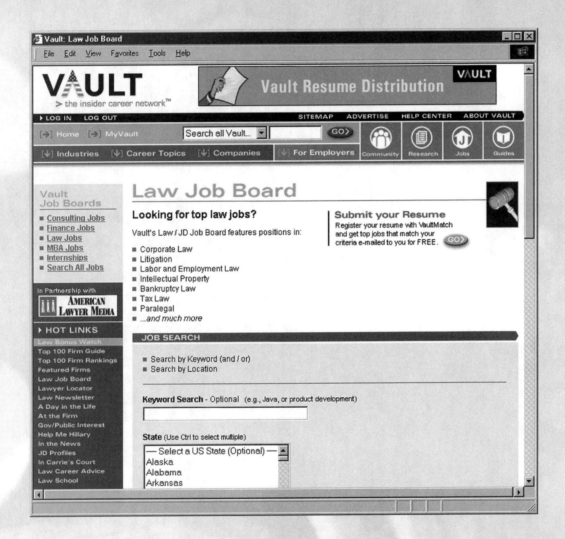

■ Law Job Board

The most comprehensive and convenient job board for legal professionals. Target your search by practice area, function, and experience level, and find the job openings that you want. No surfing required.

■ VaultMatch™ Resume Database

Vault takes match-making to the next level: post your resume and customize your search by practice area, trial experience, level and more. We'll match job listings with your interests and criteria and e-mail them directly to your in-box.

VAULT
> the insider career network™

Find out more at www.law.vault.com

Ready to hold yourself in contempt
for career stagnation?

Take control of your career with
Vault's Resume Review
and Career Coaching!

■ Resume Review

Make your first impression your
best impression. Have your
resume reviewed by our law
career experts.

■ Career Coach

An instant mentor for your career.
We coach professionals like you
on topics such as job-search
strategy, leaving the law industry,
and professional development.

> the insider career network™

Find out more at:
www.vault.com/careerservices/careerservices.jsp